The
Companion
to
20th-Century
Music

The Companion to 20th–Century Music

Norman Lebrecht

First published in Great Britain by
Simon & Schuster Ltd in 1992
A Paramount Communications Company

Simon & Schuster Ltd
West Garden Place
Kendal Street
London W2 2AQ

Simon & Schuster of Australia Pty Ltd
Sydney

A CIP catalogue record for this book is
available from the British Library
ISBN 0-671-71019-2

Typeset in Caxton and Garamond by
Florencetype Ltd, Kewstoke, Avon
Printed and bound in Great Britain by
Butler & Tanner Ltd, Frome

Contents

INTRODUCTION
The Reinvention of Music

The history of music both ended and began in a Milan hotel room at 3 a.m. on 27 January, 1901, when Giuseppe Verdi drew his final breath. Verdi was the last of the titans whom music had brought forth with miraculous fertility ever since the near-simultaneous birth in 1685 of Johann Sebastian Bach and Georg Frideric Handel. When one creative force expired another was ready and waiting to pick up the baton of progress. This illusion of inexorable continuity was shattered by Verdi's demise; four years earlier, it had been dashed symphonically in Vienna when Johannes Brahms died without leaving an obvious successor. Italian and German music, rulers of the art from time immemorial, found themselves bereft of leadership. The history of western 'classical' music was over and its eulogy was recited at great length and solemnity in the journals of the day.

Yet, even as Verdi's cortège trundled through Milan to the sound of his Slaves' Chorus from *Nabucco*, the history of music was being actively reinvented. There was widening recognition among composers that music could not proceed much further on its narrow gauge of textbook harmonies. Its tonality had been over-worked and its theatricality overblown in an excess of romantic grandiloquence. Faced with a crisis of resources, composers emulated Bach in retrieving whatever was usable and transmissible from the past. The search led them to pre-classical ideas and non-western tones. New relations were conceived between notes of the scale and new priorities emerged among the basic components of sound – theme, texture, rhythm, dynamics, duration.

As the century dawned, the consensus on how music was composed and how it should sound was breaking down, giving way to an unprecedented diversity that bewildered musicians and listeners alike. A new art was evolving painfully in circumstances of combustible uncertainty that mirrored the geo-political mood of pre-war continental Europe. Music, once the soother of savage breasts, suddenly inflamed uncontrollable passions. In concert halls and recital rooms, corseted ladies and top-hatted gentlemen traded punches and obscenities over unfamiliar, inexplicably disturbing sonorities. An Italian clique of self-designated Futurists proclaimed an epoch of unadulterated noise. Richard Strauss, the playful composer of *Till Eulenspiegel*, now plotted a 'terrible silence' in *Salome* amid the loudest clangour ever heard upon an opera stage. Composers seemed to be taking leave of their loyal audience, perhaps of their senses, to pursue an unwelcome future at all costs.

What sounded like anarchy was, in fact, the birth of a unique diversity that would, in retrospect, make this the most exciting of musical centuries. Music was gearing itself to reflect social and scientific revolutions, responding with a sensitivity envied and unequalled by other arts. Beethoven was able to describe Napoleon's battles with the orchestra at his command. His successors had to invent the means to react to Stalingrad and Hiroshima, Auschwitz and the Gulag Archipelago.

Their solution was a creative plurality that encompassed Polynesian village bands and mainframe computers, pre-medieval monody and compositional theorems of Einsteinian complexity. Never before had so many musical styles clashed, co-existed and crossfertilized; never had consumers of music been offered such stylistic choice and cerebral stimulus.

While Brahms was alive, everyone knew what to expect of a symphony. It had four movements and ended in spiritual uplift. In the opening year of the 20th century Gustav Mahler, director of the Vienna Court Opera, presented a symphony that had no recognizable finale but trailed off in an inconclusive song of childish naïvety. A symphony, in Mahler's view, had to embrace the entire human condition; it must be, he declared, 'like the world'. In the opposite corner of symphony debate, Jean Sibelius was aiming determined to refine textures towards an icy clarity and ineluctable structural logic. His fellow-Scandinavian, Carl Nielsen, was pushing towards an open-plan, stream-of-consciousness symphony. Arnold Schoenberg, Mahler's protégé, contemplated abolishing the symphony altogether. In January 1901 Schoenberg was writing cabaret songs for a living in Berlin while waiting for someone to perform *Verklärte Nacht*, a sextet that stretched the stressed tonality of Wagner's *Tristan* to its ultimate breaking point.

Opera was under equal pressure. In Paris, Debussy was about to achieve his refutation of Wagnerian bombast with the ethereality of *Pelléas et Mélisande*. In the provincial Moravian town of Brno, Leoš Janáček was distilling an operatic tragedy, *Jenůfa*, more realistic than the most gruesome of Italian verisimilitudes. Puccini, meanwhile, was exploring Asiatic exotica in *Madama Butterfly* while Richard Strauss consorted with dissonance and blasphemy in *Salome*.

The expatriate Italian, Ferruccio Busoni, talked of inventing 'a new language for music'. In Russia, Alexander Skryabin composed in colours and cosmic metaphors. In the corporate towers of Manhattan, an insurance millionaire called Charles Ives was retuning his piano to find the microtones between its keys and scrawling out scores of inscrutable difficulty.

These trends were in full flower before the century was a month old, but a dozen years elapsed before musical revolution spilled onto the streets. Schoenberg, abetted by his pupils Alban Berg and Anton von Webern, introduced Vienna to a free atonality that recognized no 'dominant' key and challenged the 'natural' order. It aroused violent hostility both within and beyond the world of music and produced a generic masterpiece in *Pierrot Lunaire*. In the Paris springtime of 1913, Igor Stravinsky released from the feral depths of Russian folklore a throb of terrifying rhythms that motorized his ballet, *The Rite of Spring*, and drove a Champs Elysées audience to riot. Neither *Pierrot* nor *The Rite of Spring* were definable as music by existing criteria of something that could be sung or tunefully played. They transformed the very nature of music in the first of its 20th-century upheavals.

No sooner had they taken root than the eruption of World War challenged the function of art. How could music presume to express the purposeless death of millions? Who dared sing when the world mourned an entire generation? The questions would be asked with redoubled emphasis a quarter of a century later, after Auschwitz and the atom bomb. Some composers, like Rachmaninov and, briefly, Elgar, took refuge in a nostalgic or morbid remembrance of things past. Younger bloods in the Parisian Les Six and republican Berlin blazed away in jazzy merriment as if there were no tomorrow.

It fell to Schoenberg and Stravinsky again to reconstitute the art, for neither felt able to compose as before. Schoenberg in 1921 rewrote the laws of music for a second time, reorganizing the 12 available notes in new 'rows' and disciplines. Stravinsky, cut off from Mother Russia, took the structures and sounds of the baroque era and remodelled them in a neo-classical style. They were joined in the foreground of musical thought by the Hungarian Béla Bartók, whose field-trips into remote cultures had equipped him with complex rhythms and microtones that he allied to a Mahlerian introspection and moral purpose.

While these three headed the inter-war intellectual agenda, they did not impose stylistic conformity. Jazz percolated concert music from the early 1920s in works by Darius Milhaud and Maurice Ravel. In Weimar Germany, it was harnessed by Kurt Weill and Paul Hindemith to an idealistic quest for a music that would be 'useful' in the lives of ordinary people. Alois Hába in liberal Czechoslovakia diced up microtones into unplayable dots. Edgard Varèse, a Frenchman in America, imagined a sound that would not require human intervention.

The advent of radio and electrical records in the 1920s altered the state of music from an art that had to be actively played or consciously attended to one that could be passively absorbed while reading a newspaper, making love or brushing teeth. Erik Satie invented 'furniture music' or aural wallpaper that existed but was not noticed. It was the forerunner of Muzak and the ambient sound that cannot be suppressed in hotel elevators and grounded aircraft. Knowing that they wrote for an increasingly supine public, composers responded with complexities that only professionals could perform. Chamber music, formerly a domestic pastime, acquired impassioned intricacy and profundity.

Arguments might rage over ideas and methods, but mutual respect and tolerance prevailed between the senior composers. Schoenberg was proud to shake Puccini's hand and Berg would not have missed a Gershwin concert. Stravinsky cultivated friendships with such antipodes as Debussy and Ravel, Pierre Boulez and Leonard Bernstein. Exiled in Los Angeles, however, Schoenberg and Stravinsky took care to avoid one another.

The sporadic violence that greeted their initial innovations now turned systematically repressive. Josef Stalin outlawed modernism in 1935, enforcing a doctrine of Socialist Realism that hamstrung Soviet composers for half a century. *The Rite of Spring* was almost 50 years old before it was passed fit for Russian ears. Adolf Hitler ended the centrality of German music by banishing its best minds and terrorizing most of those who remained into infantile submission. If German music was not heroic and national, said his cultural enforcer Joseph Goebbels, it would not exist at all. Setting aside the tragic personal cost for countless musicians and their families, these edicts testified to the power and maturity of modern music. Never before had politicians tried to alter the course of music. No-one muffled Mozart or hampered Haydn. In the 20th century, music troubled dictators to the point where they had to control it.

Even more heartening were the means that music found to confront tyranny and subvert it. In the Soviet Union, Dmitri Shostakovich encoded a secret history in 15 symphonies and string quartets that audiences understood and commissars could not prohibit. Luigi Dallapiccola composed 12-note prison songs against Mussolini's fascist laws. In Nazi Germany, Karl Amadeus Hartmann went into 'inner exile', pretending to be silent while composing furtively for the future. In the Terezin concentration camp, Viktor Ullmann wrote an opera about the day Death went on strike.

The devastation of 1945 prompted a fresh upheaval in musical thought. Young composers looked angrily back at the cultural traditions that bred two holocausts and rejected them in their entirety. War had developed the technology to make music by unmusical means. Pierre Schaeffer in Paris invented a musique concrète that was as grim as its name. Varèse lived to achieve an unearthly electronic sound. John Cage jammed household objects between the strings of grand pianos and urged performers to make independent decisions. With one electronic bang, said Karlheinz Stockhausen, 'I'll be able to blow the whole city [of Vienna] sky-high.' 'Schoenberg is dead!' proclaimed Pierre Boulez with ill-disguised relief. There was no place in their world for the principled morality that had failed in the past. Instead, the new generation took the ascetic, issue-less rigidity of Webern as their starting point and claimed the support of Stravinsky who experienced a late conversion to 12-note methodology.

With the implicit authority of the two main streams of 20th-century music, the post-war avant-garde imposed a political correctness on the art. Boulez, who described himself as '300 percent Leninist', denounced Shostakovich and Benjamin Britten as traitors to musical progress. Herbert Eimert, founder of the first electronic music studio in Cologne, echoed Goebbels with the statement that 'either music exists as it is in the vanguard, or it does not exist at all'.

This totalitarianism was reinforced by US composer-academics, European broadcasting chiefs and state-salaried intendants. Concert music was composed on a tight little grid of serialism that mattered mainly to its makers and sponsors, leaving musicians dismayed and audiences alienated. Mellifluous symphonists fell into disuse; Rachmaninov became almost a term of abuse. Andrzej Panufnik, Poland's foremost composer when he fled to Britain in 1954, went nine years without a broadcast on the dogmatic BBC. US composers who sought an orchestral commission learned to compute serial formulae like Milton Babbitt and Roger Sessions. Each summer at Darmstadt, Dartington and Donaueschingen, leaders of the revolution would plot its course and dictate policy to young acolytes. It was symptomatic of their quintessential elitism that the post-war avant garde formed new music 'ghettos', a term that implied selective enclosure and mutual support. New music became the province of the like-minded. Boulez, as conductor in New York and London, applied populist methods to make abstruse novelty more palatable but his impact on public taste was ephemeral.

Like the corruptions of communism, the abuses of modernist hegemonism would be exposed in its latter-day collapse. Much remains to be written on a conspiracy of charismatic composers and starstruck administrators, conducted with the complicity of critics who abrogated journalistic detachment to militate for a progressive cause. There was, of course, much good music being written in both cutting-edge and conventional styles but there is no denying that the third quarter of this century was comparatively barren in terms of lasting creativity, and the blame for this must lie with those who imposed a dictatorship of fashion. In no other art, either verbal or visual, was there a comparable *Kulturkampf* by modernism against traditionalism. Francis Bacon and Andy Warhol did not seek to exclude Constable and David Hockney from the Tate Gallery and the Guggenheim. The Nobel Prize for Literature might fall once in a decade to a French constructivist, but the regular and popular choices were story-tellers like Saul Bellow and Isaac Bashevis Singer.

Blessedly, music recovered its fertile pluralism in the final quarter of the century, flourishing in forms as diverse as Harrison Birtwistle's granitic mythologies and Philip Glass's hypnotic minimalism. The gravely introspective string quartets of Elliott Carter and Wolfgang Rihm were played by ensembles in spiky hair-dos and designer gear. Composers came out of the ruins of the workers states equipped with advanced techniques of irony and subversion. Alfred Schnittke defined his music as 'poly-stylist', incorporating a medley of sonorities that protested against any kind of conformity. Boulez in 1992 came close to conceding defeat. 'There is no single line of development,' he admitted. 'Evolution is like a tree; there are branches all over the place.' Stockhausen interred himself in a long-drawn-out cycle of seven operas. Lesser composers were bemused by the loss of certainty and outraged by the arrant simplicity of music by John Adams and Steve Reich, among others. It contradicted the secularist religion of 20th-century 'progress' and reverted to a Biedermeier state of affairs when art and popular music were virtually indistinguishable.

This phase, too, is bound to pass – though probably not before the century is out. At the moment of writing, one is able to view the century almost in its totality and assess its contents from a perspective of near-completion. Trends that had overwhelming importance for a decade or two can be safely assigned a place in history, from whence they may yet be retrieved and adapted in some future revolution. Atonality, neo-classicism, nationalism, serialism, jazz, computer music, minimalism, electronics, folklorism, 'happenings' and sheer chance – all went into the making of 20th-century music, but none dictated its style as romanticism did in the 19th century and classicism in the 18th. The triumph of music in the 20th century was its abundant pluralism. This *Companion* is, I believe, the first to define and applaud that diversity.

Every dictionary has a standpoint, no matter how strenuous its pretence at impartiality. Even multi-tomed encyclopedias assembled by international teams of scholars are founded on shared beliefs and common values. The selection of entries and the space given to each entry reflect the taste, outlook and prejudice of its compilers. This *Companion* makes no claim to neutrality and sticks its neck out on key issues. It makes no excuse for preferring democratic pluralism to cultural dictatorship; artistic inspiration to scientific slog; individualism to collectivism; and moral purpose to expedience. It treats musicians on artistic merit rather than ideological or institutional eminence.

This is not a matter of personal likes and dislikes but the application of a non-aligned critical-historical faculty to a field littered with misplaced commitment. Too much criticism has backed a single composer or group at the expense of others. Too many music critics stand on the side of the composer rather than the readers and listeners for whom they are supposedly writing. I have sought to redress the balance by providing an overview that places the listener's needs above the composer's aims. Works are judged on outcome rather than aspiration and composers are discussed in terms of proven achievement, not wishful theorizing.

By paying no dues to hierarchies and ideologies, I have been able to eliminate hundreds of meretricious academics and party hacks whose work-lists clog up other dictionaries. Their removal has made way for many composers who are retrieved from undeserved oblivion, among them several dozen who appear here for the first time. In each case, their inclusion signals my conviction that their work is of lasting value, although often unacknowledged at the time of writing.

Selection is a dangerous process, but I am confident that no significant composer is omitted. I have used ears, eyes and commonsense to arrive at my conclusions, having listened to thousands of hours of music and assimilated innumerable texts. Wherever a work is discussed, you may rest assured that I have heard it several times, often with score in hand. Other reference works employ consultants in different countries to advise on regional conditions. This results at best in the inclusion of composers of purely local renown at worst in undue recognition for the remote adviser's relatives and friends. I have chosen to do all my own legwork, travelling extensively to search for music and musicians that are of universal interest and durability.

This *Companion* differs from other reference works in another vital respect: it is designed to be read, rather than merely browsed. It has been written narratively and with a minimum of technical jargon and abbreviations. It aims, of course, to be as accurate in its facts, dates and work-lists as any other reference work. While its conclusions may occasionally be controversial, the data are, I hope, incontrovertible.

Instead of writing birth-to-death capsular biographies, I have highlighted the singularity of an artist's contribution and relegated his or her passport details to the foot of the entry. I have also broken with convention in refusing to categorize a subject as a 'Polish composer', or 'British-born conductor', or 'Russian-born US pianist'. Such definitions are pretty meaningless in the most international of arts and are frequently rendered obsolete by political change. The *New Grove Dictionary* lists hundreds of entries as 'Soviet composers', a term that is not only outdated but is positively misleading when applied to composers like Shostakovich and Schnittke whose works were often directed *against* the Soviet system. Similarly, to describe Britten as a 'British composer' is to distort his cosmopolitanism, the quintessential characteristic that raised him artistically above his countrymen. Even Bartók, as nationalist as any Magyar musician, can scarcely be described as a 'Hungarian composer' when he was born under Austrian rule, on Romanian soil, and raised in the capital city of Slovakia.

The process of selection did not end with deciding who and what to incorporate but involved singling out key works for discussion and consigning the rest to a summary below. Asterisks, used sparingly, indicate an interesting cross-reference. The life and works of composers are treated as inseparable. The main abbreviations used are: *b.* = born; *d.* = died; st = studied; orch. = orchestra/orchestral.

To understand the music of the 20th century, it is necessary to have some grasp of its principal techniques and technologies. I have tried to explain these in layman's language with very few technical terms. This *Companion* avoids definitions of the sort that explain how Webern 'discovered the aptness of serial methods to strict canon and symmetrically patterned variations'. That kind of shorthand may be meaningful to a musicologist on a Berlitz course but to a music lover trying to decide whether or not to buy a Webern recording it means about as much as a computer analysis of the dots on a compact disc. This kind of phraseology reinforces a myth of complexity that has been erected around Webern's music and much other 20th-century art. No-one says that Webern or Boulez is easy, but their music is more approachable than most analysts allow. My purpose in this book is to demythologize, to enlighten and to entertain – an objective not unlike the function of musical performance itself.

St John's Wood, London
May 1992

Claudio ABBADO Reformist head of La Scala (1972–86) and *Karajan's unexpected heir at the Berlin Philharmonic (1989–), the shy Milanese used his institutional authority to advance modern works by *Berio, *Nono, *Rihm and *Stockhausen, whose *Licht cycle he commissioned. Gesturally discreet, his conducting is notable for a surreptitious tightening of tension.

    b. Milan, Italy, 26.vi.33; st with Hans Swarowsky in Vienna; cond. LSO 1979–87, art. dir. Vienna State Opera 1987–91; founded European Community Youth Orch. and Gustav Mahler Youth Orch.

Abbey Road Record studios in St John's Wood, London, opened by *Elgar in 1931, celebrated on cover of seminal 1969 *Beatles album.

Hans ABRAHAMSEN Leader of a 1970 Copenhagen students rebellion with an anarchic orchestral piece called *Skum* (1970), he graduated with a Symphony in C whose puerile three-note theme heralded a *new simplicity and placed him among the early minimalists. He expanded his technique to included poetic fragments and sudden explosions in an elegiac *Nacht und Trompeten* (Night and trumpets) for the Berlin Philharmonic (25.iii.82, cond. *Henze) and a small-scale cello concerto *Lied in Fall* ('Song in autumn', 1988) for the *London Sinfonietta.

    b. Kongens Lyngby, Denmark, 23.xii.52; st with *Nøgard.

Jean ABSIL The Belgian polyphonist's 1st piano concerto was the set piece at the 1938 *Ysaÿe competition, won by Emil Gilels. His 1955 *Divertimento* for four saxophones is the only work much played abroad.

    b. Bon-Secours, Belgium, 23.x.1893; *d.* Brussels, 2.ii.74. *other works:* five symphonies, four string quartets, several ballets, *Rumanian Rhapsody* for violin and orch. (1943).

absolute music (1) The opposite to *programme music, a work of no obvious meaning. (2) The proposition that music exists in isolation from its composer, fiercely argued by the post-1945 *avant-garde. The notion that Beethoven would have sounded much the same if he were black, and Bach if he were Catholic, does not need much demolition. But the concept makes some sense when applied to didactic *serialism and emotionless *experimentalism, where the composer's individuality, environment and moment in time are immaterial to his ivory-tower occupation.

abstract music A derivation of post-1945 abstract art, random daubings practised by *Cage and his clique.

Abstrakte Oper Nr. 1 Emotion-laden opera by *Blacher to a nonsense text by *Egk, it was denounced as 'the worst opera ever written'. fp: Mannheim, 17.x.53

abuse of instruments Modernist attacks on expensive instruments prompted violent resistance from virtuosi. No classical pianist approved Cage's *prepared piano, in which household objects were stuck betwen the strings, and violinists regularly rejected demands to beat, bang or otherwise mangle their fiddles. A BBC cellist smashed up what remained of his instrument in a public protest at the end of Hans *Flammer's piano concerto in 1988. *Rock and *punk musicians commonly ended their concerts in this way.

academicism Mid-century dictatorship of compositional policy, particularly in the US, by professorial composers at East Coast colleges. *Babbitt and *Sessions aimed to impose a conformist complexity on US concert commissions.

Joseph ACHRON Russian-Jewish émigré who reworked bitter-sweet Chasidic melodies for concert consumption. Jascha *Heifetz popularized his virtuosic Hebrew Melody (1911) and Hebrew Lullaby (1912); Arnold *Schoenberg called Achron a 'profound and original composer'. He wrote three violin concertos depicting the Rabbi of Prague and his man-made Golem.
> *b.* Losdseje, Poland, 13.v.1886; st with *Auer in St Petersburg; served in Tsar's Army; worked at Petrograd Hebrew Theatre 1919–21; emigrated to Germany, Palestine and US 1922–25; settled in Hollywood 1934, playing fiddle in film studios; *d.* there, 29.iv.43. *other works*: Golem suite for chamber orch. (1932), Hazan ('Cantor') for cello and orch (1912), Sabbath Eve Service (1930), sextet (1938), piano concerto (1941).

acid house Amplified offshoot of *psychedelic rock, it became synonymous with exceptionally noisy all-night parties for impressionable adolescents in respectable middle-class suburbs.

acoustics The dispersion of sound interested many composers. *Mahler started a trend for stationing ensembles around the hall, *Boulez devised a 'salle modulable' for his IRCAM centre, where the acoustic could be altered from reverberant to terse at the flick of a switch.
  Concert-hall acoustics aroused controversy when architects abandoned traditional 'shoebox' designs and wood and brick materials. Many post-1945 halls have been acoustic disasters. The sound at London's Royal Festival Hall (1951) has been expensively improved by means of hidden microphones. The Sydney Opera House (1973) had a ramp that caused singers to arrive breathlessly on stage. The People's

Hall in Prague (1986) was boycotted by its intended residents, the Czech Philharmonic. Modern halls with acceptable acoustics include Berlin's octagonal Philharmonie (1963) and Birmingham's Symphony Hall (1991).

adagietto 'Little adagio' – *Mahler's title for the strings-and-harp 4th movement of his 5th symphony (1904), ostensibly a love song to his bride but introverted enough to arouse doubts about his intentions. As the theme music of Visconti's 1971 movie *Death in Venice*, it helped popularize Mahler.

Adagio for strings Samuel *Barber's transcription for string orch. of the slow movement from his string quartet. Played at Roosevelt's funeral, it became a quintessential US obsequy and was reused as the theme of a Vietnam War movie, *The Deer Hunter.* fp: NY, 5.xi.38, cond. *Toscanini.

Emil ADAMIC Composer of picturesque *Tartar Suite* and *Aquarelles from Ljubljana*.
> *b.* Dobrova, Austro-Hungary, 25.xii.1877; *d.* Ljubljana, 6.xii.36.

John ADAMS The shackles of arid *academicism were thrown off by American composers in the late 1970s. Some, like *Druckman and *Rochberg, turned the clock back to an imitative *new romanticism. Others, following *Glass and *Reich, took their cue from *rock music and invented a *minimalism that amounted to prolonged repetition of syncopated musical snippets. Adams belonged to its West Coast chapter. Instead of chopping up prerecorded tapes like Reich, he composed orch. pieces that signalled a way out of self-limiting minimalism. *Shaker Loops* (1978), a simple figure of varying length for each of seven string players, produced an ever-fluctuating harmonic pattern. *Grand Pianola Music* (San Francisco, 20.ii.1982) for small orch., percussion and three sopranos, was half-an-hour of soothing hypnotism. But *Eros Piano* (London, 24.xi.89), a quasi-concerto mourning the death of *Morton Feldman, worked its way out of minimalism into an elegant lugubriousness that recalled *Ravel and *Busoni. With the sax-y *Fearful Symmetries* (1988) and

Wound Dresser, a Walt Whitman setting, it took Adams in his early 40s to the front rank of concert composers, although such scores were more suitable as living-room *wallpaper music than as concentrated experiences.

Adams' priority was opera. 'Basically, I'm like *Strauss, writing the *Alpine Symphony* until the next libretto is ready,' he said. His operas, like *Glass's, were based on historic events and characters. The difference is that Adams chose recent headlines and composed freely and tunefully. *Nixon in China* (Houston, 22.x.87), written by Alice Goodman and staged by Peter Sellars, offered psychological insights into a US president at the summit of his diplomacy and the eve of his disgrace, and a communist patriarch reduced to impotence by a scheming wife. Less resourceful, because more exploitative, was *The Death of Klinghoffer* (Brussels, 19.iii.91), dealing with the Palestinian hijack of a cruise liner and the murder of a crippled passenger. While the TV-news aspect of both operas played perilously close to soap, it went over the edge of good taste in *Klinghoffer*.

b. Worcester, Massachusetts, 15.ii.47; st with *Kirchner; played clarinet in Boston SO; taught San Francisco Cons. 1971–81; *other orch. works: Harmonium* (1981), *Harmonielehre* (1987), *El Dorado* (San Francisco, 11.xi.91).

Richard ADDINSELL His film score for *Dangerous Moonlight* (1941) caught the tremor of wartime romance in a sub-Rachmaninov pastiche. Billed as the *Warsaw Concerto*, it enjoyed a brief concert vogue. Addinsell's other movie hits were *Goodbye Mr Chips* (1939) and Jean Anouilh's *Waltz of the Toreadors*.

b. London, 13.i.04; *d*. there, 14.xi.77.

Theodor Wiesengrund ADORNO The anti-existential Marxist writer, canonized by the academic left in West Germany, was part-social scientist, part-musicologist. In the first capacity he worked with Walter Benjamin and Max Horkheimer; in the other he studied with *Berg, edited at *Universal Edition, wrote hyperbolic treatises on Wagner and Mahler and advised Thomas Mann on his composer's novel *Doktor Faustus* while exiled in California.

He reviled all music written for commercial purposes and worshipped Schoenberg as messiah. At Darmstadt in 1951 he clashed head-on with *Stockhausen, who ridiculed his presumption to rationalize music and subsequently said that 'a creative person is always most excited when something happens that he cannot explain'. Adorno composed some sentimental Theodor Däubler Songs (1923–4) and six short orch. pieces which feebly emulated Schoenberg's newly codified 12-tone system.

b. Frankfurt-am-Main, Germany, 11.ix.03; taught at Oxford 1934–8, Princeton 1938–41, Frankfurt 1949–69; *d*. Visp, Switzerland, 6.viii.69. *writings include: Philosophy of modern music* (1949), *Einleitung in die Musiksoziologie* (1968), *In search of Wagner* (1952).

aesthetics What is music? No longer definable in harmonic, structural or social terms, composers like *Cage and *Paik argued that it could encompass *silence and public acts of *self-mutilation. The debate continues.

Africa Its rhythms excited *Reich and *Volans, who studied them intensively. Central African bands became popular in France, their music affecting young European musicians. The East German folklorist *Griesbach wrote a politically-inspired *African Symphony* (1963). No major composer has yet emerged from the continent. The music of north and west Africa bears the legacy of Arab dominance; southern music has a stronger ethnic integrity.

Age of Anxiety Bernstein's 2nd symphony, inspired by *Auden's poem. fp: Boston, 8.iv.49, cond. Koussevitsky.

Age of Gold Debut ballet by *Shostakovich on adventures of a touring Soviet soccer team. fp: Leningrad, 26.x.30.

... agm ... Work for 16 voices and three instrumental groups by *Birtwistle, based on fragments of Sapphic poetry. fp: Paris, 9.iv.79, cond. Boulez.

Agon Abstract ballet by *Stravinsky for 12 dancers and changing instrumental combinations, modelled on 17th-century French dances and composed in mixed *neo-classical and *serial episodes. Its timbre and technique were revelatory to *Boulez and *Birtwistle. fp: (as staged ballet) NY 1.xii.57.

Kalevi AHO Individualist Finn who abandoned *Sibelian refinement in favour of *Mahler's all-embracing outlook. His turning point was the 5th symphony (Helsinki, 19.iv.77), a welter of unrelated themes that required two conductors and abstained from drawing a neat conclusion. It resembled, he said, 'a bus terminal at rush hour', its components arriving from every direction and in varying states of health and happiness. The 7th symphony (Helsinki, 26.x.88), used music from his opera, *Insect Life*, a satire by the Czech playwright, Capek. It included disturbing fairground and military episodes, resembling Schnittke's *polystylism. Aho diverged from all other *Scandinavian symphonists, and many considered him the finest of his generation.
  b. Forssa, Finland, 9.iii.49; st with *Rautavaraa and *Blacher; lecturer at Helsinki U. 1974– ; *other works*: concertos for cello (1.ix.84) and piano (29.viii.90), three string quartets, orchestrated Mussorgsky's *Songs and Dances of Death*.

Joseph (Johannes Clemens) AHRENS Organist renowned in Germany for a *Toccata eroica* (1934) and *12-note Catholic Mass (1966).
  b. Sommersell, Westphalia, 17.iv.04; taught Berlin Hochschule 1936–69; organist at St Hedwig's Cathedral 1934–39.

Akhnaten Ancient-Egypt minimalist opera by Glass. fp: Stuttgart, 24.iii.84.

Yasushi AKUTAGAWA The son of *Rashōmon*'s author was drawn to Russian culture and reflected it in several symphonies. He wrote the film score for *Gate of Hell*.
  b. Tokyo, 12.vii.25; cond. Tokyo SO 1956–69; *d.* Tokyo, 31.i.89. *other works*: TV opera *Orpheus of Hiroshima* (1967).

Jehan ALAIN Dazzling young organist killed in the defence of France, Alain wrote with clarity, irony and not a little irreverence for an instrument that often sounds upholstered. Although he shared *Messiaen's interest in Asian and medieval musics, their works could scarcely be more different. Alain's 2 *Dances to Avni Yavishta* (1934) and Variations on a theme of Clément Jannequin (1936) contain memorable strains of melancholy and menace in an an incisive, unclouded sound. His *Litanies* (1937) are motorized by the rhythms of his daily commuter train. At his death, aged 29, he had written 127 works. Mobilized into the French army, he was evacuated from Dunkirk to England but insisted on sailing home to see his newborn third child. In a last rearguard action before France surrendered, he was shot by advancing German troops.
  b. St. Germain-en-Laye, nr. Paris, 3.ii.11; *d.* Petit-Puy, nr. Saumur, 20.vi,40.
  His sister, Marie-Claire Alain (*b.*1926), became his devoted interpreter. A brother, Olivier Alain (*b.*1918), composed a *Chant funèbre sur les morts en montagne* (Funeral song on the mountain dead, 1950).

Domenico ALALEONA Composer of a symphony, 12 *Canzoni* and an opera, *Mirra* (Rome, 31.iii.20) that was hailed as a modernist breakthrough but was never revived. He was Italy's foremost commentator on contemporary music.
  b. Montegiorgio, Italy, 16.xi.1881; *d.* there 28.xii.28.

Isaac (Manuel Francisco) ALBENIZ Busking his way across Europe to pianistic fame, he went to Bizet's teacher in Paris, to Grieg's in Leipzig and to Liszt himself before joining *Pedrell's revivalism and applying himself to hispanic musical *nationalism. Living in France, his ideas were refined by contact with Debussy and Ravel. He preferred to write harmonic intricacies for piano rather than guitar. Like Pedrell, Granados and Casals, he was Catalan. He spent three years in London, paid by a banker to compose his librettos, the worthless *Magic Opal* (1893) and *Henry Clifford* (1895), and the slightly worthier *Pepita Jimenez* (1896). Bohemianism and Bright's Disease cut short his career. He retired to Nice in 1903 to compose his national masterpiece, the four books of *Iberia*.
  b. Camprodón, Catalonia, 29.v.1860; st with Marmontel, Gevaert, Reinecke, Liszt, *Dukas; married his pupil, Rosanna Jordana, 1884; *d.* Cambô-les-Bains, French Pyrenees, 18.v.09.

Stephen (Joel) ALBERT The American neo-romantic has a seismographic sensitivity for atmosphere and mood. He won the 1985 Pulitzer Prize for *Riverrun*, a symphonic evocation of James Joyce's *Ulysses*. The same book inspired vocal settings, *A Flower of the Mountain* and *To Wake the Dead*. Although conversant with *serialism, Albert achieves a flowing confluence of words and music that harks back to the shifting tonalities of, say, Schoenberg's *Book of Hanging Gardens*, richly emotional and actually hummable.

> *b*. NY, 6.ii.41; st with *Milhaud, *Rochberg; *other works*: *Voices Within* for orch. and pit band (1975), *Into Eclipse* tenor and orch. (Seattle, 8.ix.86), violin concerto (1986).

Eugen d'ALBERT Scots-born pupil of Liszt, he wrote some 20 heavily decadent operas of which *Tiefland* (Prague, 15.xi.03), the lowland tale of a landowner's lust, retains a steamy popularity in Germany. His six marriages and stormy divorces won him as much celebrity as his musicianship.

> *b*. Glasgow, 10.iv.1864; *d*. Riga, Latvia, 3.iii. 32. *other operas*: *Die tote Augen* (Dresden, 5.iii.16), *Revolutionshochzeit* ('Revolutionary wedding'; Leipzig, 26.x.19), *Der Golem* (Frankfurt, 14.xi.26), *Mister Wu* (Dresden, 29.ix.32).

Albert Herring Village comedy by Britten. fp: Glyndebourne, 20.vi.47.

Aldeburgh Festival June event founded by *Britten in 1948, centred on his own music, Schubert, Holst, Mahler and Shostakovich. There were important premières by Birtwistle, Walton and Lutosławski. After Britten's death, *Knussen and the Russian cellist Rostropovich played key roles.

aleatory music Works in which players are given limited freedoms to change the score. The trend started in the US, where it is better known as *indeterminacy, with the libertarian ideals of *Cage who set the ball rolling with *Music of Changes* (1950). *Stockhausen followed with *Zeitmasze* (1956) and *Boulez with his 3rd piano sonata but, while most Westerners reverted to disciplinarian composition, the idea took root behind the Iron Curtain as a metphor for individual freedom. *Penderecki in his *Threnody for the Victims of Hiroshima* and *Lutosławski in *Venetian Games*, the string quartet and his 3rd symphony gave scope to their players to ad lib.

Cage in some works asked players to throw a dice or toss a coin at a particular point to determine how a performance should proceed. In others, he calculated his operations from the Chinese I Ching, thus relating the element of choice to the smooth running of the universe.

Alexander Nevsky Rousing cantata adapted by *Prokofiev from his Eisenstein film score. fp: Moscow, 17.v.39.

Alexander's Ragtime Band 1911 hit song and musical that made Irving Berlin's fortune.

Alexander ALEXANDROV Composer of the Soviet anthem, *Hymn of the Bolshevik Party* (1944).

> *b*. Plahino, near Riazan, Russia, 1.iv.1883; *d*. Berlin 8.vii.46.

Anatoli ALEXANDROV Follower of *Skryabin, he wrote 14 piano sonatas and two operas.

> *b*. Moscow, 25.v.1888; *d*. there, 16.iv.82.

Franco ALFANO The chance to complete *Puccini's deathbed opera should have made Alfano's name. Instead, it almost finished his career. *Toscanini first refused to perform his ending to *Turandot*, then cut it so savagely that it lost cohesion. Alfano was blamed for the abrupt ending until 1982 when Ricordi released his original score, a skilled musical development of the ice-princess into a credible lover.

He had been picked on the strength of his Asiatic opera *La leggenda di Sakuntala* (Bologna 10.xii.21), confirming a penchant for exotica and a gift for succulent orchestration. He had also written a comedy-ballet *Napoli* for the Folies Bergères (28.i.01) and a dramatic opera on Tolstoy's impenetrable tract, *Resurrection* (Turin, 4.xi.04). After the Turandot débâcle, he turned to instrumental music, writing three symphonies and string quartets. He kept clear of politics, ran the conservatories of

Turin and Palermo and lost his possessions in Allied bombing.

> *b.* Posilippo, near Naples, Italy, 8.iii.1875; *d.* San Remo, 27.x.54. *other works*: three settings of poems by Rabindranath *Tagore.

Hugo ALFVÉN The Swedish tone-poet painted his native landscape on souvenir postcards entitled *Midsummer Vigil* (Stockholm, 10.v.04) and a *Tale of the Skerries*, the latter giving rise to a programmatic Fourth Symphony (4.xi.19) with wordless tenor and soprano. Dedicated to his 14-year-old daughter, it was damned as immoral and dubbed 'sinfonia erotica'. More than 30 years passed before his next symphony (30.iv.52), which the composer disliked so much that he withdrew all but the opening movement. His remaining 220 works are mostly choral.

> *b.* Stockholm, 1.v.1872; music director at Uppsala U., 1910–39; *d.* Falun, Sweden, 8.v.60.

Frangis ALI-ZADE Azerbaijani composer of a piano sonata in memory of Alban *Berg and a modernist oratorio, *Songs from Home* (1978). She has premiered piano music by Messiaen, Cage and Webern before mystified Islamic audiences, and her static, fragile string quartet was the hit of the 1991 ISCM festival in Zurich.

> *b.* Baku, 1947;

allegro barbaro Brutal piano suite by *Bartók, composed 1911, fp: Budapest, 27.ii.21.

Humberto ALLENDE Chilean symphonist in folkloric style with hints of *Ravel.

> *b.* Santiago de Chile, 29.vi.1885; *d.* there, 16.viii.59. *works*: symphony (1910) cello concerto (1915), violin concerto (1942), piano concerto (1945).

Juan ALLENDE-BLIN Visually oriented Chilean refugee living in western Germany.

> *b.* Santiago, 1928; *works*: *My blue piano* for organ (1970), *Rapport sonore* (1983).

Alpine Symphony *Strauss's bombastic bid to outdo nature. fp: Berlin, 28.x.15.

William ALWYN Founder of the Composers Guild of Great Britain, he wrote five pastoral symphonies and a Strindberg opera, *Miss Julie* (1977), alongside many film scores.

> *b.* Northampton, 7.xi.05; *d.* Southwold, Suffolk, 11.ix.85.

Amahl and the Night Visitors First opera written for television, *Menotti's Christmas show takes its theme from Hieronymus Bosch's painting *The Adoration of the Magi*. fp: NBC TV, 24.xii.51.

Amarus Cantata by *Janáček. fp: Kroměříž, 2.xii.1900.

America Symphonic rhapsody by *Bloch that won *Musical America* magazine's contest for a concert work evoking US history. fp: NY, 20.xii.28.

American music Art music, a luxury in a pioneering society, rose on a wave of *fin-de-siècle* prosperity, when orchestras were founded and concert halls built by newly-rich industrialists. Indigenous compositions were rooted in hymns and European hero-worship. *Macdowell, the first composer of overseas stature, echoed his master Liszt. *Ives and *Ruggles composed for the drawer and avoided society concerts. *Gershwin pointed the way to a synthesis between mass culture and high art; his use of *jazz was refined by *Weill, *Copland and *Bernstein. The search for an American symphony was led by the conductors *Koussevitsky and *Stokowski, who promoted the late-romantic, overtly patriotic genre of Barber, Harris, Piston and Schuman, that led nowhere.

From 1945 the creative scene was dominated by the high minds of Babbitt and Sessions, who insisted on uniform serialism, a grip that was broken in the 1970s by imitative *neo-romanticism and the following decade by repetitive minimalism. Avant-garde iconoclasm centred on the quirky personalities of *Cage and *Feldman. America led the world in electronic technology and music though not, despite *Boulez's best efforts in New York, in progressively minded audiences.

An American in Paris Jaunty memoir by *Gershwin. fp: NY, 13.xii.28.

Amériques Huge orch. work by *Varèse portraying both halves of the American continent, it requires sleighbells, steamboat whistles and fire-sirens. fp: Philadelphia 9.iv.26, cond *Stokowski.

Fikret (Jamil) AMIROV Folk composer of Azerbaijan, he wrote suites to suit his Soviet masters – *To the Memory of the Heroes of the Great National War* (1944), *The Pledge of the Korean Guerilla Fighter* (1951), etc. His opera *Sevil* (Baku, 25.xii.53) has the status of a national monument. Three symphonic works are based on local modes called 'mugamas' and two of them were espoused by *Stokowski. Amirov headed the Azerbaijani composers association and the opera house in the state capital, Baku.
  b. Kirovabad, USSR, 22.xi.22; *d*. Baku, 20.ii. 84. *other work*: piano concerto on *Arab themes (1957).

David (Werner) AMRAM The New York Philharmonic's first composer-in-residence (1966–7) was a hornist who played jazz and travelled widely on State Department missions, absorbing exotic sounds in North Africa and Latin America. *Tompkins Square Park Consciousness Expander* (1966) adds an Arab 'ud and Pakistani flute to Western orch.; the triple concerto (1970) quotes Brazilian rhumba. As music director of New York's Shakespeare festival (1956–67), he wrote accompaniments to 18 Shakespeare plays.
  b. Philadelphia, 17.xi.30.

Gilbert AMY Boulez's successor as director of the Parisian *Domaine Musicale (1967–73) followed him closely in sound, style and cultural affinities. He wrote a dense piano sonata (1960), a Mallarmé soprano setting, *D'un espace déployé* (Paris 10.iii.73) and large orch. works with enigmatic titles – *Chant* (1968), *Réfrains* (1972), *Strophes* (1977).
  b. Paris, 29.viii.36; st with *Milhaud, *Messiaen and Boulez; founder-cond. Radio France New Philharmonic Orch. 1976–81, dir. Lyons Conservatoire 1984– ; *other work*: Missa cum jubilo (1983).

Barrie (Michael Gordon) ANDERSON New Zealand-born composer whose love-affair with live electronics derailed a mainstream pianist career and consigned him to an avant-garde fringe and early death. His Eureka moment was hearing *Stockhausen's *Kontakte*. He formed Electro-Acoustic Music Association of Great Britain (EMAS) in 1979 and helped *Birtwistle integrate electronics in his opera, *The Mask of Orpheus*. This occupied several years. He died hours after directing the première of *ARC* for string quartet, bass clarinet and sound tapes, a score of haunting musicality.
  b. Stratford, NZ, 22.ii.35; *d*. Paris, 27.v.87. *other works*: student opera *Maui* (1964), *En face de . . .* for soprano and double bass, with added version for electronic modulation (1977), *Domingus*, tape realization of Paul Hyland poem (1978).

Laurie ANDERSON Performance artist who played the violin while skating on ice and ran a two-night, six-hour mix of comedy, music, electronics and moving images called *United States* (1983). Working with rock musicians like Peter Gabriel, she was more pop phenomenon than straight musician and reached number two in the charts with a 1981 song, 'O Superman'.
  b. Chicago, 5.vi.47;

Leroy ANDERSON Bass player in the Boston Pops, he did many of its orchestrations and scored a monumental hit with swoony 'Blue Tango' (1951). His 'Penny Whistle Song' and 'The Typewriter' belong in the travel chest of every light orchestra.
  b. Cambridge, Massachusetts, 29.vi.08; st with *Hill, *Piston, *Enesco; *d*. Woodbury, Connecticut, 18.v.75.

Volkmar ANDREAE The Swiss conductor composed two late-romantic operas, *Ratcliff* (1914) and *Casanova's Adventures* (1924), and two symphonies.
  b. Berne, Switzerland, 5.vii.1879; cond. Zurich Tonhalle Orch. 1906–49; *d*. Zurich, 18.vi.62.

Hendrik (Franciscus) ANDRIESSEN Dutch-Catholic composer concerned with cadences of Gregorian chant.
  b. Haarlem, Netherlands, 17.ix.1892; succeeded father as organist at St Josephs, Haarlem (1916–34) and Utrecht Cathedral (1934–49); dir. Royal Conservatory, The Hague, 1949–57; *d*. Heemstede, 12.iv.81.

works: two operas, four symphonies, Couperin variations (1944).

Jurriaan ANDRIESSEN Hendrik's elder son. A centre-ground *eclectic with an affinity for jazz, worked as a theatre composer in The Hague. He wrote a Rotterdam Concerto for jazz combo and orch., as well as three operas and five symphonies.
b. Haarlem, 15.xi.25; st with father and *Copland.

Louis ANDRIESSEN Jurriaan's younger brother started out as a riotous experimentalist – *What it's like* for live electronics and 52 strings (Rotterdam, 14.ix.70) and *Beethoven's 9 symphonies* for promenade orchestra and ice cream bell (1970). He settled into an inspired early *minimalism, of which the high point was an operatic setting of selections from Plato's Republic (*De Staat*, 1976). In contrast to the soporific repetitions of *Glass, Andriessen gave his performers freedom of choice and cursed them if they failed to exercise it. *De Staat* protests against musical establishments in a breezy jazz ambience. The Symphony for open strings (1978) has an unvibrated plangency that could be Balinese or medieval Dutch.
b. Utrecht, 6.vi.39; st with father, van *Baaren and *Berio; founded Hoquetus ensemble of amplified instruments; *other works: 2 Anachronies* in memory of Charles *Ives (1968–9), *Reconstruction* (with de Leeuw and others, 1970).

George ANTHEIL Self-styled 'Bad Boy of Music' – the title of an angry autobiography – Antheil outraged Europe with cacophonies celebrating heavy industry and culminating in the *Ballet mécanique* for eight pianos, percussion and aeroplane engines (Paris, 19.vi.26). When audiences objected, he pulled a pistol from his pocket and laid it deliberately on top of his concert grand – inspiring the aphorism 'ne tirez pas sur le pianist' – 'don't shoot the pianist'. An *Airplane Sonata* and *sonata sauvage* (both 1922) for piano enjoyed a certain vogue. His music is not noisy by modern standards but heavily and often attractively rhythmic with syncopations that veer from pure jazz to Prokofiev-like sophistication. By the time he reached a 4th piano sonata

(1948) he was writing almost in the manner of the Russian master's celebrated sixth. His 4th symphony (NBC, 13.ii.44, cond. *Stokowski) feels like a war-movie soundtrack or a lesser work by Shostakovich. Antheil settled in Hollywood, where he syndicated a gossip column.
b. Trenton, New Jersey, 8.vii.1900; st with *Boulanger and befriended Ezra Pound and James Joyce; married niece of Arthur Schnitzler, 1930; returned to US 1935; *d*. NY, 12.ii.59. *other works*: four operas, notably *Transatlantic* (Frankfurt, 25.v.30), six symphonies of which the 5th is known as *Joyous* (Philadelphia 21.xii.48), three string quartets, four violin sonatas, five piano sonatas, trumpet sonata and ballets for George Balanchine (*Dreams*, 1935) and Martha Graham (*Course*, 1936).

anthems The crumbling of empires created an unprecedented demand for national anthems. None commanded the gut-loyalty of the British, French and German archetypes, nor did many new hymns claim artistic distinction. *Stenhammar's 'Sweden' (1905), Rabindranath Tagore's 'Jana-Gana-Mana' (India, 1950), *Eisler's 'Auferstanden aus Ruinen' for the German Democratic Republic and Israel's 'Hatikvah' (1948), using a folk-theme from Smetana's *Ma Vlast*, were among the better-crafted. The USA did not have an anthem until 3 March 1931 when Congress ratified 'The Star-Spangled Banner', written by Francis Scott Key in 1814.

Russia had four during the course of the century: 'God Save the Tsar' was replaced in 1917 by the Internationale, itself ousted in 1944 by *Alexandrov's 'Hymn of the USSR'; in 1991 Russia reverted to a chorus from Glinka's opera *A Life for the Tsar*.

In Austria, Haydn's Emperor's Hymn (1797), gave way in 1920 to Wilhelm Kienzl's republican 'Deutsch-Österreich du herrliches Land', was reinstated with new verses in 1929 but ousted by the homicidal *Horst Wessel Lied* of Nazism. Since 1946 Austrians salute 'Land der Berge, Land am Strome' with music supposedly by Mozart. Haydn's tune served Wilhelminian Germany and the Weimar Republic to the words 'Deutschland, Deutschland, über alles'; it united the Federal Republic under the title 'Einigkeit und Recht und Freiheit'.

In *Hymnen* (Cologne, 30.xi.67), *Stockhausen submitted most European anthems to electronic distortion.

John (Henry) ANTILL The first Australian to explore aboriginal sources, he produced a truly indigenous work in *Corroborree* (1947). He also wrote three operas, six ballets and a harmonica concerto.
b. Sydney, 8.iv.04; worked for ABC 1934–71; *d*. Sydney, 29.xii.86.

George APERGHIS Greek avant-gardist living in *Xenakis' shadow in Paris. Much of his music has a theatrical dimension. He made a remarkable television film, *Enumérations* (1989), in which six actor-musicians occupy a derelict house and create a wordless musical ambience from footsteps, dripping water, tearing paper and other everyday sounds.
b. Athens, 23.xii.45; st with Xenakis; *other works*: *Bis*, musical spectacle for ten actors and ten instruments (1968), *Symplexis* for 22 jazz soloists and orchestra (1970), *Pandemonium* (1973).

Apollon musagète (*Apollo, leader of the muses*) *Stravinsky's first ballet for George Balanchine, composed for string orch. He revised it in 1947 under the title *Apollo*. fp: Library of Congress, Washington, D.C., 27.iv.28.

Appalachian Spring Martha Graham ballet by *Copland depicting a Pennsylvania Shaker wedding with a nod to Stravinsky's *Les Noces*. Scored for 13 instruments, its textures are incisively appealing. fp: Library of Congress, 30.x.44.

Hans Erich APOSTEL Servant of the Second Vienna School as a *Universal editor, Apostel offered an atonal string quartet in 1935 to celebrate Alban Berg's 50th birthday, only to find himself mourning his death. Its 2nd movement quoted *Wozzeck, and the scherzo was woven around the notes of Berg's initials, A.B., and his own, H.E.A. He waited 20 years before writing another quartet, by which time he was ready to advance into Webern's total *serialism. This led to a Chamber Symphony (1967) and *Paralipomena dodekaphonica* (1969), or 12-note variations on a theme of Joseph Haydn (he had

previously written an atonal set of Haydn variations in 1949). Unlike most modernists, Apostel remained in Vienna through the Nazi era and helped revive new music in its aftermath.
b. Karlsruhe, Austria, 22.i.01; st with Schoenberg and Berg 1921; worked for UE 1930–8; *d*. Vienna, 30.xi.72. *other works*: piano concerto (1958), *Kubiniana* – ten pieces for solo piano (1950).

Arab music Except for quotations by Egyptian and Israeli composers and politically-motivated East Europeans, there is little trace of Arab sounds in modern Western music. The concert tradition had no place in Arab society. Music was rooted either in religion or in popular culture, both of which continued to hold the public imagination. Millions turned out on the streets of Cairo in 1973 for the funeral of a vocalist, Umm Kulthoum.

Arabella Strauss's last opera with Hofmannsthal, an attempt to recapture the light-headedness of *Rosenkavalier*. The music is almost as lush but the story lacks lustre. fp: Dresden, 1.vii.33.

Enrique Fernández ARBOS Orchestrator of Albéniz's *Iberia* and Spain's foremost conductor.
b. Madrid, 24.xii.1863; hon. prof. at RCM London 1894–1916; founder-cond. Madrid Symphony Orch. 1904; *d*. San Sebastian, 2.vi.39.

Arcana Vast orchestral work by *Varèse, proceeding in slow-moving blocks of sound. fp: Philadelphia, 8.iv.27, cond. *Stokowski.

Violet (Balestreri) ARCHER Canadian pupil of *Bartók and *Hindemith, she occupied a twilight zone between tonality and *atonality. Her orch. works include concertos for piano (1956) and violin (1959).
b. Montreal, Canada, 24.iv.13.

architecture As structure became more important than sound, composers talked about the 'architecture' of their works. In *Xenakis' case this was meant literally, as he applied ideas derived from the atelier of his teacher, Le Corbusier. A visual resemblance to building design was also evident in the *graphic notation of Morton *Feldman and Earle *Brown.

The institutions that musicians built often reflected the spirit of their music. *Boulez's underground IRCAM studios, intentionally deprived of natural air and light, symbolized the artificial music synthesized within. *Karajan's ochre-coloured, octagonal Philharmonie in Berlin suggested wealth and world power.

ARDITTI String quartet formed in London (1974), dedicated to abstruse modernisms and dedicatee of works by *Xenakis, *Ferneyhough, *Carter, *Ligeti. They gave around 150 premières and their high-minded asceticism was a counterfoil to *Kronos' populism. Named after founder and 1st violinist, Irvine Arditti, the group has a Swiss-based record series under its name.

Anton ARENSKY Retired on a state pension at the age of 40, a victim of tuberculosis, *Rimsky-Korsakov's star pupil composed an exotic ballet, *Egyptian Nights*, and a 2nd piano trio. In his prime, he taught *Rachmaninov and *Skryabin and wrote two delightful piano concertos.
  b. Novgorod, Russia, 12.vii.1861; *d.* Terijoki, Finland, 25.ii.06.

Dominick ARGENTO A lonely wanderer among the regimented *note-rows of American music, Argento and his soprano wife formed a company in Minneapolis in 1964 to produce his tuneful operas. *Postcard from Morocco* (Minnesota, 14.x. 71), his 7th stage work, caught European attention just as the serial hegemony was crumbling and Argento emerged from its reception at the head of a neo-traditional wave. In many respects, the lyrical tradition he continued was *Britten's. With a dozen operas in production, he penetrated Sweden and Germany with imaginative adaptations of US literature: *The Aspern Papers* (Dallas, 19.xi.88), after Henry James, and *The Voyage of Edgar Allan Poe* (Minnesota, 24.iv.76) – the latter an artist's anguished reflection on his life and work. Argento's operas are lyrical, narrative, easily paced and beautifully written for the voice. He is incapable of writing an ugly chord. Even when he attempts a 12-note series, in the opening of *Variations for Orchestra (The Mask of Night)* (Minnesota, 26.i.66), the effect is unconsciously Mozartian.
  b. York, Pennsylvania, 27.x.27; st with *Weisgall and *Nabokov at Baltimore and *Dallapiccola in Florence; taught at U. of Minnesota 1959–; married Carolyn Bailey 1954; *other operas: Sicilian Limes* (1954), *The Boor* (1957), *Christopher Sly* (1962), *The Shoemaker's Holiday* (1967), *Miss Havisham's Fire* (NY, 22.iii.79), *Casanova's Homecoming* (Minnesota, 12.iv.85). *nonstage works*: oratorio *Jonah and the Whale* (1974), *Ode to the West Wind* for soprano and orch. (1956), *From the Diary of Virginia Woolf* for voice and piano (1974 Pulitzer Prize).

Ariadne auf Naxos Intended as a companion piece to Molière's comedy *Le Bourgeois Gentilhomme* for which *Strauss wrote incidental music, it was expanded into a two-act opera whose static impracticibility is redeemed by its arias. fp: (1st version) Stuttgart 25.x.12, (2nd version) Vienna, 4.x.16.

Ariane et Barbe-bleu Dukas' only opera, after a Maeterlinck drama, it gave Bartók the idea for his masterpiece. fp: Paris, 10.v.07.

Louis ARMSTRONG The public face of trad(itional) *jazz, he was its first mass-audience star as a trumpeter, band-leader and gravelly vocalist. His cavernous maw earned him the nickname 'Satchmo', short for Satchelmouth. A wild kid, sent to a delinquents' home at 12 for playing with guns, he married at 17 and ousted King Oliver from his band, though they soon teamed up as twin cornets in Chicago. In 1924 he married the singer Lil Hardin and joined her band, cutting the first of numerous records.
  Armstrong's instrumental improvisations left the singer free to pursue her own riffs. His duo with Ella *Fitzgerald possessed the intimacy and intensity of *Callas and Gobbi. His own singing was invariably ahead or behind the beat, yet somehow supported it. He was adulated in Europe in 1933 and returned to start a movie career. When the big-band era ended after 1945, he led the way with small ensembles and scored his greatest hits with 'Blueberry Hill', 'Hello Dolly' and 'Mack the Knife'.

Radical blacks called him an 'uncle Tom' but Armstrong never bowed his head nor sang from anywhere but the heart. He was a figure of enormous dignity and a musical innovator of universal importance.

b. New Orleans, Louisiana, 4.vii.01; *d*. NY, 6.vii.71

Malcolm ARNOLD A 1957 Academy Award for David Lean's *Bridge on the River Kwai* did no good at all for Arnold's concert career. A sniffy British establishment, suspicious of a former London Philharmonic player who presumed to write symphonies, crossed him off its agenda. Arnold undaunted, continued composing in a distinctly Mahlerian mould, his tuneful music hinting at deeper, sadder things. The concerto for two violins (*Menuhin, Bath, 24.vi.62) has a nagging darkness beneath its pleasant pastorality. He challenged fellow-virtuosi with 15 concertos, of which the guitar concerto (1959) has a compelling blues movement and two horn concertos reflect the exuberance of Dennis Brain. He also wrote a Philharmonic Concerto for his former orchestra (1977).

His ambition, though, was always symphonic. The 1st symphony (Cheltenham, 6.vii.51) echoed Mahler's grim premonitions; the 3rd (Liverpool, 2.xii.57) reverted to classical counterpoint; the 5th (1961) played ironic games with popular tunes; the 6th (Sheffield, 28.vi.68) contained a frank homage to the jazzman Charlie Parker. The 7th (London, v.74) had much in common with Shostakovich's paramount Eighth – a thunderous shout against destructive social and political events. The 8th (NY, 5.v.79) returned to folksy mood with Shostakovich-like dissimulation, while the 9th addressed itself so bleakly to matters of life and death that its première was long postponed (Manchester, 15.i.92).

A descendant of the conductor William Hawes (1785–1846), Arnold took up playing the trumpet in homage to Louis *Armstrong. He made his mark with *English Dances* and *Beckus the Dandipratt* (1943), but even in these folkeries Arnold operated subversively from within a straitlaced convention. He wrote music that orchestral musicians liked to play, and this counted against him with intellectuals and managers. An enormous appetite for drinking and wenching prompted a collapse that was diagnosed as severe depression and led to a spell in a mental hospital.

b. Northampton, 21.x.21, st with *Jacob and George Dyson; 1st trumpet in LPO 1941–48; *other works*: toy symphony, 3 sinfoniettas, sets of English, Scottish, Irish and Cornish Dances, two string quartets, 20-minute opera, *The Open Window*, after a Saki story).

Bib: Hugo Cole, *Malcolm Arnold*, London 1989.

Girolamo ARRIGO Paris-based protest composer, elevating left-wing causes in 1970s 'epic' operas *Orden* and *Addio Garibaldi!*

b. Palermo, Sicily, 2.iv.30; st with *Boulez.

art music Term used to define concert music that could no longer be called 'classical'.

Arts Council of Great Britain (ACGB) Body formed in 1945 to dispense state funds to the arts, protecting their independence by means of an 'arms' length' principle that cut out politicial interference in the disbursement. Its budget exceeded £200 million in the 1990s but its autonomy was eroded by Conservative governments.

Vyacheslav ARTYOMOV Meditative Muscovite whose compelling interest in eastern philosophies led him to investigate, with *Gubaidulina, the potentialities of ethnic instruments. He was among the first in the USSR to write for percussion ensemble and to involve percussion prominently in symphonic works. *Lamentations* (1985) for strings, percussion, piano and organ combines the plangent summons to prayer of Western and eastern religions with a morose contemplation of a moral wasteland and a desolate, distant beauty that might portend salvation. The *Symphony of Elegies* (1977) is one of those very slow east-European expanses that owe their origins to *Pärt and *Gorecki. The *Sonata for Meditation* (1978) is purely rhythmic. *The Way to Olympus*, his largest orch. work, occupied him for six years (1978–84) until the Gorbachev liberalization provided an outlet for his art.

b. Moscow, 29.vi.40; *other works*: ballet *Sola Fide* 'By Faith Alone', after Tolstoy story, 1987), *In memoriam*, symphony with a violin solo (1968–84), *Capriccio for New Year's Eve* for saxophones and vibraphone (1975); double-chorus *Requiem* (1988).

Boris ASAFIEV The Soviet musicologist blew with the wind, eulogizing Stravinsky in an important 1929 study before denouncing him at Stalin's behest. He committed the same treachery to *Shostakovich at the time of *Lady Macbeth*. Much of his writing appeared under a pseudonym, Igor Glebov. In the 1930s he composed socially-useful ballets.
   b. St Petersburg, 29.vii.1884; *d*. Moscow, 27.i.49.

ASCAP American Society of Composers and Performers, founded in 1914 to pursue copyright protection in the United States and bring pirates to bay.

asceticism *Avant-gardist inclination to decry pleasurable textures and pursue sounds that are painful but good for you. Chief proponent was *Boulez, who refused to conduct a note of Tchaikovsky and condemned Britten as a renegade because he persisted with melody.

Robert (Reynolds) ASHLEY In the 1960s Ashley was a leading mover in an alliance of *avant-garde arts to form a *Gesamtkunstwerk*. From an *electronics background, he staged *happenings and festivals and ran a contemporary music centre at Mills College, California. In *The Wolfman* (1964), he bellowed his own amplified voice at stoned audiences. In *Purposeful Lady Slow Afternoon* (1971) a female reciter described being forced to perform oral sex. Such pieces were a prelude to his magnum opus, which emerged piecemeal as *Perfect Lives (Private Parts)* a 'video opera' mixing live and filmed events. By 1983, when it was finished, Ashley's innovations were commonplace in pop concerts and his fame waned, but he had set a trend for *Glass and Robert Wilson to extend.
   b. Ann Arbor, Michigan, 28.iii.30; ran electronic music centre at Ann Arbor with *Mumma 1958–66; formed ONCE festival 1961–68.

Asrael Momentous C-minor symphony by *Suk named after the Angel of Death and mourning the deaths of his father-in-law, Dvořák, and his own wife, Otylka. Rich in musical quotations, it ends in a Mahlerian movement of deep consolation. fp: Prague, 3.ii.07, cond. Kovařovic.

Association for Contemporary Music Modernist 1923 Russian group founded by *Roslavets, it ran concert series and published magazines that introduced the revolutionary generation to Hindemith, Mahler, Schoenberg and Berg – decisive influences on *Shostakovich and Miaskovsky. Banned by Stalin's henchmen in 1932, its name and spirit were revived in 1990 by *Denisov, *Smirnov and *Firsova with concerts conducted by *Boulez.

Atmosphères Large orchestral work by *Ligeti. fp: Donaueschingen, 22.x.61.

atonality The breach with tonal rules that governed music for half a millennium came in 1908 and lasted little more than a decade. In the middle of his second string quartet, Arnold *Schoenberg broke free of any discernible key and moved into new harmonic regions of intriguing dissonance. While *Nielsen and *Mahler switched keys in mid-symphony but preserved normal relations between notes, the atonality embraced by the Schoenberg circle was free of all previous strictures. It amounted, in his assessment, to 'the emancipation of dissonance'.
   Schoenberg preferred the term 'pantonality', believing atonality implied an antimusical process and confirmed the prejudices of his enemies. The term stuck, nonetheless, and was applied with varying degrees of accuracy to unrelated composers. Atonal episodes were found in Stravinsky's *Rite of Spring, *Prokofiev's first piano concerto and Skryabin's piano music – and back in Liszt's late piano works of the 1880s.
   Schoenberg was never entirely happy with liberalization, despite such masterpieces as *Pierrot Lunaire and Berg's *Wozzeck. In 1921 he announced a new departure, 'the method of composing music with all 12 tones of equal weight', otherwise known as *serialism or *twelve-

note music. Atonal, he wrote that year, 'could only mean something entirely out of keeping with the nature of tone.'

Kurt (Magnus) ATTERBERG Deeply conservative Swede who carried on writing symphonies as if Schumann were still alive. A Germanic 2nd symphony (Sonderhausen, 27.vii.13) was typical of what followed. The 6th (Cologne, 15.x.28) won a Schubert centennial prize before being exposed as a pastiche of the eminent composers who judged the contest. His music was admired in Nazi Germany.
   b. Gothenburg, 12.xii.1887; st with *Schillings; worked at Royal Patent Office, Stockholm 1912–68; *d.* Stockholm, 15.ii.74; *other works*: five operas, five concertos.

W(ystan) H(ugh) AUDEN The poet wielded a formative influence over Britten and scripted his first opera. He also collaborated with Stravinsky and Henze and defined the Age of Anxiety, on which Bernstein wrote a 2nd symphony.
   b. York, England, 21.ii.07; *d.* nr. Vienna, 29.ix.73.

audience Schoenberg and Stravinsky endured riots in 1913; half a century later, Cage vainly encouraged public participation. None altered the passive role of the music consumer. In contrast to the genuine outrage aroused by music before the First War, recent 'scandals' have been manufactured by publicists or politicians. *Nono's *Intolleranza 1960* in Venice and *Goehr's *Arden muss sterben* in Hamburg were targets of social rather than artistic unrest.

aural wallpaper Background music began in courts where nobility feasted while string players sawed. *Satie invented its modern counterpart, possibly as a joke, prescribing *musique d'ameublement* – *furniture music – to be played during the interval of a 1920 Paris concert and protesting violently when people stopped their conversations to listen. *Muzak is the commercial application of his invention, anonymous sounds seeped at low volume through offices, hotels, restaurants and airports. Designed to soothe and reassure, it avoids dissonance, sharp transitions and anything surprising or likely to attract attention – typical fare consists of Chopin

medleys rearranged for recessed piano and strings. At sales conferences and shareholders meetings, musicians are sometimes assigned to provide a subliminally optimistic score to offset a company's retrenchment plans after adverse results.

Georges AURIC Staid affiliate of radical Les *Six, he adored *Satie and *Stravinsky and wrote ballets for *Diaghilev but found his métier in the movies with a vivid score for René Clair's *A nous la liberté* (1931). He wrote the music for Jean Cocteau's films, for a UK Ealing comedy, *The Lavender Hill Mob* (1947) and for Hollywood's *Moulin Rouge* (1952). He ran the Paris opera houses for six years of *Boulez-led turbulence (1962–68) and was president of the French Union of Composers and Artists (1954–77).
   b. Lodève, nr. Montpelier, France, 15.ii.1899; st with d* 'Indy and *Roussel; *d.* Paris, 23.vii.83. *other works*: 12 ballets including Nijinska's *Les Fâcheux* (1925) and Massine's *Les Matelots* (1925); suite symphonique (1960), violin sonata (1937), flute sonata (1964).

Larry (Don) AUSTIN *Experimentalist who flourished in 1960s California, advocating freedoms of *improvisation that he called 'open style'. *Improvisations for Orchestra and Jazz Soloists* (1961) and *Open Style for Orchestra with Piano Soloist* (1965) attracted attention when telecast by *Bernstein.
   b. Duncan, Oklahoma, 12.ix.30; professor U. of California at Davis, 1958–72, U. of S. Florida, 1972–8; Texas 1978–; *other work*: *2nd Fantasy on *Ives' Universe Symphony* for clarinet, viola, keyboards, percussion and soprano.

Australasia A late developer in musical terms, the antipodes contributed sopranos – Nellie Melba, Florence Austral, Joan Sutherland, Kiri te Kanawa – and little else. The Australian Broadcasting Commission (ABC), with an educative bias, cultivated musical taste, created orchestras and imported performers. Local composers imitated Europe but, from *Antill onwards, took note of ethnic resources. *Sculthorpe won international respect for exploring polynesian sonorities. New Zealand provided its share of singing stars, Frances

Alda at their head, and electronics composer Barry *Anderson.

authenticity The ideal of an accurate performance was turned into a fetish by *Toscanini, who revered every slip of a composer's pen but privately made alterations to suit his personal style. His adage of literal meticulousness was taken up by the *early music movement, which proclaimed that all music should be performed not only as written but on the instruments and in the style of its particular period. The opposite to authenticity was demonstrated in the spontaneity of interpretation of such formative conductors as *Nikisch, *Mahler, *Furtwängler and *Bernstein.

autobiography The first titled memoir in music was probably Bedřich Smetana's 1876 string quartet *Aus meinem Leben* (From my life), written as he faced deafness. But it was *Strauss's symphonic poems describing his conjugal life and personal habits – *Ein Heldenleben, Sinfonia Domestica* – that removed inhibitions. *Mahler, in all his symphonies, tackled aspects of his life: infant mortality (1, 6, 9), love and betrayal (5, 6, 10), religious dilemmas (2, 3, 8) and the search for innocence (4 and 7).

In his art, however, the personal was inextricably woven with the universal, each issue possessing social and political connotations that were not immediately apparent. *Shostakovich wrote symphonies that were a chronicle of his personal life and a secret history of Soviet society. Janáček reported a secret love affair in two fiery string quartets.

Their individualism was rejected by the century's musical dogmatists. Stravinsky's *neo-classicism advocated stylized objectivity; Webern's *serialism vaunted abstract accuracy; fascism and communism relegated the composer to a feelingless cipher; and the post-1945 *avant garde was obsessed with technical experimentation above personal emotions. Nevertheless, the Strauss-Mahler autobiographical strain persisted to provide some of the century's most revealing music – Schoenberg's 2nd string quartet, composed as his wife walked out on him; Elgar's cello concerto reflecting on the war that had wrecked his world;

Strauss's four last songs; *Bartók's middle string quartets; *Reich's *Different Trains*.

avant-garde (French = vanguard) Artists who work in advance of public taste. In music, it meant composers who ignored audience needs – specifically the post-1945 *Darmstadt circle led by Boulez and Stockhausen who advocated *serialism, *experimentalism and *electronics. One Darmstadt eminence, *Eimert, echoed Goebbels by declaring that 'today, either music exists as it is in the vanguard, or it does not exist at all'. This group and its ideas dominated contemporary music until the 1980s.

Aventures/Nouvelles Aventures Animalist opera by *Ligeti in which three singers utter primeval sounds while chasing one another through undergrowth in optional stages of undress. The only distinct word is 'lux' – light. fp: Stuttgart, 19.x.66.

Aaron AVSHALOMOV Russo-Jewish composer who went to China in 1914 and wrote two operas on local subjects – *Kuan Yuin* (Peking, 24.iv.25) and *The Great Wall* (Shanghai, 26.xi.45). Concertos for piano and violin and a 1st symphony reflected native sounds; he emigrated to the US in 1947.
  b. Nikolayevsk, Siberia, 11.xi.1894; *d.* NY, 26.iv.65.

His son, **Jacob AVSHALOMOV**, gained a US foothold through *Stokowski, who gave his father's *Peiping Hutung* in 1935 and conducted Jacob's *Taking of T'ung Kuan* in 1952. It won him a New York Critics Circle award but, veering eclectically from one ethnic idiom to another, he failed to make a lasting impression. He conducted the US première of *Tippett's *Child of our Time*.
  b. Tsingtao, China, 28.iii.19; st with his father, *Toch and Copland; taught at Columbia Univ 1947–54 and other campuses.

Charles AZNAVOUR Paradigmatic French crooner, actually an Armenian refugee who graduated from hawking newspapers on Parisian street corners to topping world charts with 'The Old-fashioned Way' (1973) and 'She' (1975).
  b. Paris, 22.v.24, as Shahnour Aznavurjan.

Still the best initial for a major composer. If Bach, Beethoven and Brahms dominated musical thought in the 19th century, then Bartók, Busoni, Berg and Boulez were the 4 Bs of modernist ideology, joined by 3 Ss – Schoenberg, Stravinsky and Stockhausen.

Baal Opera by *Cerha after early *Brecht play. fp: Salzburg, 7.viii.81.

Baal Shem Three joyous dances by *Bloch for violin, and piano (1923) or orch. (1939), celebrating the founder of Hassidic Judaism.

Kees van BAAREN Transitional figure in Dutch music, he adapted the 'germ-*cell' theories of his teacher *Pijper to prevalent *12-note orthodoxies. As director of the Utrecht (1953–57) and Hague (1953–70) conservatories, he dominated Dutch music teaching. He was known abroad for a 1948 cantata setting of T. S. Eliot's *The Hollow Men*.
    b. Enschede, Netherlands, 22.x.06; *d.* Oestgeest, 2.ix.70. *other works*: *Variazioni* for orchestra (1959).

Milton (Byron) BABBITT More than anyone else, Babbitt established a hegemony of east-coast academicism over *American music in the mid-century. The son of a mathematician, he wrote pop songs while studying with *Sessions and produced a landmark analysis of the *Bartók quartets, but his heart belonged to *Schoenberg and he developed a theory of total *serialism in 3 *Compositions for piano* (1947) that encompassed more components than *Webern had ever imagined. It completely subjugated the composing process to a pre-ordained order of notes, rhythms and intervals and was said to amount 'virtually to a second 20th-century musical revolution'.

Babbitt joined the Princeton faculty in 1948 and from that vantage point ruled the ideology of American concert music. He co-founded the *Columbia-Princeton electronic studios, and led the *avant-garde into a synthesized sound that was organized on serial lines. He scorned audience taste and in 1958 published an article in *High Fidelity* entitled 'Who Cares if You Listen?' So long as a composer understood what he was doing, nothing else mattered.

His *combinatoriality and precise definitions of intrumental timbres and dynamic levels, assigned for serial purposes, were used by numerous composers in the US and abroad, and he was showered with academic and public honours. His music, however, was scarcely performed or recorded. It happens to be less forbidding than his reputation. Like *Boulez, Babbitt was blessed with charm. Amid the plinkings of his piano concerto (1985) lurks a discernible warmth. He adored the female voice and in *Philomel* (1964), perhaps his archetype composition, he brought to life a poem of a raped virgin who turns into a nightingale by metamorphosing the soprano's voice electronically into actual birdsong. *A Solo Requiem* is pure emotion and *The Head of the Bed* opera (1981) sounds like a toned-down *Pierrot Lunaire*. Whatever his protestations to the contrary,

Babbitt tried to seduce the ear. His star pupil was Stephen *Sondheim.

b. Philadelphia, 10.v.16; *other works: Relata I + II* (1965–8), *All Set* (1957) for jazz octet; 5 string quartets; *Composition for Synthesizer* (1961).

Babi-Yar Symphony 13th symphony by *Shostakovich with bass solo, attacking Kremlin antisemitism by quoting Yevgeni Yevtushenko's poem on official indifference to Nazi genocide. fp: Moscow 18.xii.62.

Grazyna BACEWICZ Gentle Pole who adhered to the *neo-classicism favoured by her teacher, Nadia *Boulanger until late in life, when she veered towards *Lutosławski. A concert violinist of high pedigree – she was once a pupil of Carl Flesch – she wrote seven concertos for her own instrument, two for cello and one for viola (1968) which is entirely atonal yet amiably lyrical. Her *Music for strings, 5 trumpets and percussion* (1958) reflects rising awareness of *Bartók in eastern Europe.

b. Lodz, Poland, 5.v.13; *d.* Warsaw, 17.i.69. *other works:* three ballets, six symphonies, Concerto for Orch. (1962), seven string quartets, five violin sonatas, two piano quintets.

B-A-C-H The hallowed name of Johann Sebastian Bach was *codified into compositions by Reger, Piston, Casella, Busoni, Schoenberg and many others.

Bachianas Brasilieiras Nine works by *Villa-Lobos supposedly reimagining Bach in Brazilian form but actually cashing in cannily on the *neo-classical fad.

Sven-Erik BÄCK Studies in medievalism at Basle enabled Bäck to produce a body of motets for the Church of Sweden. He used the religious modes for electronic modulation.

b. Stockholm, Sweden, 16.ix.19; st with *Rosenberg, *Petrassi; head of Swedish Radio music school 1959-; *other works:* solo flute sonata (1949, based on choral psalm setting), *Webernian *A Game around a Game* for strings and percussion (Donaueschingen, 17.x.59), three operas, ballets, theatre and film music.

Ernst BACON Winner of the 1932 Pulitzer Prize for his 1st symphony, which has a prominent piano part, Bacon studied with *Schmidt in Vienna and assisted *Goossens at the Rochester Opera Company. A published poet, he composed many vocal settings of Walt Whitman and Emily Dickinson.

b. Chicago, 26.v.1898; supervised Federal Music Project in San Francisco 1934–37; married four times; *d.* Orinda, Calif., 16.iii.90. *other work: Emily's Diary* for soprano, alto, women's chorus and orch.

Henk BADINGS The leading Dutch composer after 1945 arrived in Holland as a colonial orphan and was assigned to study mine engineering. He became a national figure at 23 when the Concertgebouw performed his first symphony, solid and unsmiling. His *polytonal agility aroused foreign interest, particularly the 3rd symphony (1934) and Symphonic Variations (1936). During the German occupation he ran The Hague conservatory but was acquitted of collaboration. He rebuilt his career as an *experimentalist, using engineering know-how to create *electronic operas for radio (*Orestes*, 1952) and TV (*Salto mortale*, 1969). He wrote the first all-electronic ballet, *Kain* (1956) and devised a 31-note scale of *microtones which he used in a 1969 concerto for two violins.

b. Bandung, Java, 17.i.07; st one year with *Pijper, otherwise self-taught; *d.* Maarheeze, Netherlands, 26.iv.87. *works include:* opera *The Night Watch* (after Rembrandt's famous painting, 1942); 14 symphonies, many concertos.

Simon BAINBRIDGE An eloquent viola concerto (1977) is the young Englishman's high-water mark to date.

b. London, 30.viii.52. *other works:* Fantasia for two orch. (1984), concerto for oboe and clarinet (1988).

Tadeusz BAIRD Polish composer of Scots ancestry, he was convenor of a 'Group 49' writing music for the masses in best Stalinist style. The winds of progress at the 1956 *Warsaw Autumn turned him into an avid *avant-gardist. His four orch. *Essays (1958) were fully *12-note, as were *4 novels* for chamber orch. (1967). His only opera, *Tomorrow* (1966), after a Joseph Conrad story of an old man awaiting his son's return, has a *Bergian texture, its dissonances considerably softened by Polish speech inflexions. An almost Chopinesque romanticism tinged his severest scores. A slow writer with a short lifespan, he produced his finest work after 40. The 3rd symphony (1969), *Elegia* for string orch. (1972) and *Concerto lugubre* (1975) for viola and orch. are individualistic and introspective.

  b. Grodzisk Mazowiecki, Poland, 26.vii.28; spent 1944–5 in labour camp; *d*. Warsaw, 2.ix.81. *other works*: Concerto for Orch. (1953), *Erotica* for soprano and orch. (1961), *Psychodrama* (1962).

Mily BALAKIREV The 'Mighty Five' loner wrote his 2nd symphony (Moscow 23.iv.09) and 2nd piano concerto in the 20th century, both rooted in romantic nationalism.

  b. Nizhny-Novgorod, Russia, 2.i.1837; *d*. St Petersburg, 29.x.10.

Sandor BALASSA A metalworker when he discovered music at 19 on seeing a film of *Il Trovatore*, he longed to invent modern opera. After intensive 12-note studies at the Budapest conservatory he produced *The Man Outside* (1978), an opera of militarist alienation somewhat on the lines of *Wozzeck*.

  b. Budapest, 20.i.35; *orch. works*: *Requiem for Lajos Kassák* (1969), symphonic poem *Iris* (1971), *Calls and Cries* (Boston, 21.x.82, BSO centenary commission).

ballad Eight-bar sentimental song, the staple of *pop charts.

ballet The more adventurous music became, the more it needed theatrical props to reach a general audience. Ballet played a vital role in making modern scores acceptable. *Diaghilev and his Ballets Russes brought *Stravinsky and the *Rite of Spring* to the Champs Elysées; in a concert hall the work would have occasioned less scandal. George Balanchine (1904–83) was responsible for making *Agon* a second cornerstone of modernism. Martha Graham (1894–1991) commissioned *Copland's outstanding *Appalachian Spring*. Merce

Cunningham (1904–83), who danced in it, took *Cage as music director of his company and brought the *prepared piano to public attention. Dancers, for the first time since antiquity, joined the vanguard of the arts, not only for their music but for scenery by Picasso and Matisse. None of this novelty greatly affected traditional ballet, which furnished such stars as Anna Pavlova, Vaslav Nijinsky, Isadora Duncan, Rudolf Nureyev, Margot Fonteyn and Mikhail Baryshnikov.

Don BANKS An Australian working in London, he turned *serialist under *Babbitt's aegis, though less solemnly than most. Flashes of jazz and occasional rude noises enliven his music, which became fluent in the 1960s with concertos for horn (1965) and violin (1968). He went home in 1972 to teach advanced composition at Canberra, but died young.

  b. Melbourne, 25.x.23; *d*. Sydney, 5.ix.80.

(Sir) Granville (Ransome) BANTOCK A choral serialization of the Rubaiyyat of Omar Khayyam at UK music festivals made Bantock's name in 1906. A surgeon's son, earmarked for imperial service, he read copiously in Persian and Arabic and submitted to oriental intoxication. *The Witch of Atlas* (Worcester, 10.ix.02), an orch. poem inspired by Shelley, has a prelude that predicts two of *Mahler's most original ideas – the Abschied of *Das Lied von der Erde* and the motionless end of his 9th symphony. Bantock was also a keen fan of *Sibelius and applied his landscape techniques to the British isles. The Hebridean Symphony (Glasgow, 14.ii.16) trudged into an Anglo-Wagnerian mire but the Celtic Symphony (1940), for strings and six harps, is plangent and haunting.

  b. London, 7.viii.1868; married Helen von Schweitzer 1898; prof. of music at Birmingham U. 1908–34; knighted 1930; *d*. London, 16.x.46. *other works*: operas *The Pearl of Iran* (1894), *The Seal Woman* (1924); 14 of an intended cycle of 24 symphonic poems on Robert Southey's Indian epic, *The Curse of Kehama*; incidental music to Electra (1908) and Salome (1918): *Hamabdil* for cello and orch. (after Jewish prayer, 1919); Pagan Symphony (1923–8), Four Chinese Landscapes (1936); many choral works; string quartet, 'A Chinese Mirror'; two cello sonatas.

Samuel BARBER At 25 Barber wrote America's greatest concert hit and heard the rest of his music damned by comparison. Why couldn't he write another Adagio? moaned the critics with each new piece. The *Adagio for Strings*, an orchestrated section of his 1936 quartet (NY 5.xi.38, cond. *Toscanini) voiced the spirit of the troubled age in its havering between the ominous and the optimistic. It played throughout the War and was broadcast on the announcement of President Roosevelt's death; in due course it was the theme of a Vietnam war movie, *The Deer Hunter*. Recalling the *Adagietto of Mahler's 5th symphony with a slight French accent, it sounds lugubrious with added strings, more disquieting in the quartet version.

Barber had a lyrical way with small forms, displayed in the delicious *Dover Beach* (NY, 5.iii.33) for baritone and string quartet, its soaring beauty overcoming a gloomy Victorian text. Of Pennsylvania stock, he was taught the finer points of European subtlety by Gian-Carlo *Menotti, with whom he formed a lifelong intimacy at college. The quality of refinement in Barber's scores was entirely new to American music.

After a decade of serenities, he applied a spikier mode in the helterskelter finale of the violin concerto (Philadelphia, 7.ii.41), initially pronounced unplayable but soon acknowledged as the finest US work of its kind, conveying throughtful introspection in a flurry of virtuosity. An irrepressible nostalgia for a simpler age was voiced in *Knoxville: Summer of 1915* (Boston 9.iv.48), a soprano snapshot of a quiet evening in a small town, as evocative as a Wyeth painting photographed in monochrome. For the female voice, it provides a fluid, luminous release of pent-up sentiment.

His single-movement First Symphony (Rome, 13.xii.36) was much-revised, differing from *Hanson's nationalist genre by an undeclamatory softness. The 2nd (Boston, 3.ix.44), honouring the Army Air Corps in which he served, was later withdrawn as Barber burned all but the 2nd

movement, entitled *Night Flight*. His symphonism found expression in three ten-minute *Essays (1938 –42–78). Lacking the textural clarity of *Copland, his orchestral music felt opulent without clotting up in anachronisms.

In his search for fresh means he attempted *12-note passages in an expressive piano sonata for Vladimir Horowitz (Havana, 9.xii.49). *Andromache's Farewell* (NY, 4.iv.63) for soprano and orch. has a passing resemblance to *Wozzeck*, but Barber did not function well without melody and returned to a tonal centre before the work was out. He was despised by *academics and remains the least appreciated of leading US composers.

Always attracted to the stage, he wrote a ballet for Martha Graham – *The Serpent Heart* (NY, 10.v.46), renamed *Medea* and turned into a dramatic orch. suite, rich in pseudo-oriental melismas. Menotti, who enjoyed operatic hits in the 1940s, helped him on the road to the Met, writing the libretto for the richly romantic *Vanessa* (NY Met, 15.i.58), an American *Rosenkavalier*, describing the rivalry between a fading baroness and her beautiful niece. He provided a weaker text for *A Hand of Bridge* (1959) and was involved again in rewriting *Antony and Cleopatra* after its disastrous première that opened the new Metropolitan Opera House (16.xi. 66). Shocked by its failure, Barber fled to Italy and produced little more of substance, apart from a curious choral version of the *Adagio* set to the text of the Agnus Dei; the string version was played at his funeral.

b. West Chester, Pennsylvania, 9.iii.10, a doctor's son and nephew of contralto Louise Homer; st with Isabelle Vengerova and Fritz Reiner; gave recitals as a baritone; won Pulitzer travelling scholarship to Rome, 1935; served USAAF and taught at Curtis Institute, 1942–5; bought house with Menotti at Mt Kisco, NY, 1943; won Pulitzer prizes, 1958, 1963; *d*. (of cancer) NY, 23.i.81. *other works*: *Serenade for strings* (1928), Overture to Sheridan's *School for Scandal* (Philadelphia, 30.viii.33), Capricorn concerto (for flute, oboe, trumpet and strings, NY, 8.x.44), cello concerto (Boston, 5.iv.46), piano concerto (NY, 24.ix.62), *Fadograph of a Yestern Scene* (after *Joyce; Pittsburgh, 10.ix.71), *The Lovers* (for baritone, chorus and orch, Philadelphia, 22.ix.71); cello sonata (1932); *Excursions* (piano solo, 1944), Souvenirs (piano four hands, 1953); many songs.

Vytautas BARKAUSKAS Lithuanian exposed to avant-gardism at the *Warsaw Autumn festivals; his 2nd symphony (1971) is enriched with note-*clusters and mechanical noises.

b. Kaunas, Lithuania, 25.iii.31; taught at Vilnius 1961–; *works*: five symphonies, concertos.

Wayne (Brewster) BARLOW A *Vaughan Williams sound-alike, his suite for oboe and strings *The Winter's Passed* (Rochester, 18.x.38) is a sinuous winding of two Appalachian songs in a concert rhapsody not unlike *The Lark Ascending*. Unable to repeat its sucess, he enlisted in the 1960s avant-garde and founded an electronic studio at the Eastman School, *Hanson's late-romantic stronghold.

b. Elyria, Ohio, 6.ix.12; taught Eastman School 1937–78; *other works*: Psalm XXIII for chorus and orch. (1944), *Soundscapes* for tape and orch. (1972).

Jean BARRAQUE Barraqué's was a dual tragedy. Three years younger than *Boulez, he could not compete for *avant-garde precedence in Paris; a devotee of Beethoven, he found his hero-worship unfashionable in an irreverential era. He died of alcoholism and loneliness at 45, leaving a dense 40-minute piano sonata (1952) that moved from aggravated atonal violence to extended stretches of *silence and which devotees describe as a modern Hammerklavier sonata.

The anchor of his work was Hermann Broch's novel *The Death of Virgil* which he discovered in 1955 and aimed to convert into a musical drama 'without actors or action' in a sequence of huge works for voices and orch. They were titled: *au delà du hazard* (Paris, cond. Boulez, 26.i.60), *Chant après chant* (Strasbourg, 23.vi.66) and *Le Temps restitué* (Royan, 4.iv.68), and cover Broch's evocations of night, loneliness, love, death and art. In the course of its composition he wrote a related concerto for clarinet, vibraphone and six instrumental ensembles (London, 20.xi.68).

After *musique concrète beginnings, Barraqué stuck with orthdox *serialism but would marry two small *note-rows to produce a third, a procedure known as 'proliferating series'. He eschewed all other techniques and stuck, like Beethoven, to a vision of artistic and human progress, haunted by the shadows of Auschwitz and Hiroshima and eternally preoccupied with death. 'To write music just for pleasure, as Rossini did, is no longer possible,' he declared.

b, Puteaux, nr. Paris, 17.i.28; st with Jean Langlais and *Messiaen; *d*. Paris, 17.viii.73. *other works*: electronic *Etude* for tape (1954); *Séquence*, after Nietzsche for soprano and ensemble (Paris, 10.iii.56).

Henry BARRAUD After gallantry in the resistance, Barraud was named head of music on French radio (1944–65), opening the narrow state-controlled wavebands to a diversity of musics from medievalism to Webern. The most moving of his conservative compositions is the orch. *Offrande à une ombre* (Offering to a shadow) (1942), in memory of his brother, murdered by the Gestapo.

b. Bordeaux 23.iv.1900; st with Louis Aubert and *Dukas; *works*: two operas, three symphonies (3rd fp by Boston SO, 7.iii.58), Rimbaud suite *Une saison en enfer* (A season in hell, 1969).

Lionel BART *Oliver!* (London, 10.vi.60), Bart's musical based on Dickens, was one of the longest-running shows in history and a fabulous movie to boot. *Twang!*, its Robin Hood-based followup in 1965, suffered frost-bite at the box-office and destroyed Bart's fortune and career.

b. London, 1.viii.30 (as Lionel Begleiter); played in a skiffle group; composed 'Living Doll' hit for Cliff Richard and *Fings Ain't Wot They Used To Be* show for Tommy Steele.

Béla BARTÓK In the trinity of modern masters, Bartók's contribution was the least specific. *Schoenberg twice rewrote the rules of composition; *Stravinsky discovered an intrinsic value in rhythm and revealed ways of utilizing music history.

Bartók did nothing so spectacular, yet his influence was no less than theirs. His

was a modest and passionate art, rooted in the love of nature and homeland. To composers floundering in a bewilderment of contemporary styles, he seemed a paragon of certainty and sincerity – a moral example to modern man and his music.

Hungarian by blood, he came from an area claimed by Romania and grew up in polyglot Pressburg-Poszonyi-Bratislava, a Magyarized city within earshot of Vienna. Early peregrinations, prompted by the death of his schoolmaster father, nurtured in the sickly Bartók an appetite for sampling different cultures. Almost invalided out of college, his vitality was restored by hearing Strauss's *Also sprach Zarathustra* and he responded with a highly-spiced symphonic poem, *Kossuth* (Budapest, 29.ii.04), performed in Manchester by Hans Richter before the year was out. Undecided about his future, in 1905 he entered a Paris competition as pianist and composer, failing in both categories. The experience familiarized him with a great metropolis and the subtleties of *Debussy.

He then set off with Zoltán *Kodály on expeditions to notate and record folklore that was threatened by the march of progress. Starting in Hungary, he visited Transylvania, Slovakia, Romania and, in 1913, North Africa, gaining a profound respect for simple societies and an enrichment of his musical resources. He transcribed ethnic *pentatonic songs and dances into piano suites, preserving their essence for lifelong use. He acquired a facility for primitive rhythm that equalled Stravinsky's, and a Schoenberg-like disdain for the limitations of concert tonality.

A passion for the violinist Steffi Geyer (1881–1956) drew out an intimacy in a violin concerto that was unplayed until her death (Basle, 30.v.58). Its *Tristan*-like heavings declared the misery of a youth who, denied conjugal bliss, sought solace in nature. Bartók had learned to tranform raw emotion into art. In 1909 he finished the first of six string quartets, telling his new 16-year-old bride, Marta Ziegler, that his music 'revealed more accurately than a biography' what he had experienced and felt in his life. The quartet opens dolorously, working into ever-faster and wilder rhythms and culminating in an echo of his 2nd Romanian Dance, op 8a. Performed at an all-Bartók concert (19.iii.10), it announced the arrival of a mature talent. With Kodály and *Dohnányi, he put Hungary on the musical map.

Finding the home audience apathetic, he moved to the suburbs to compose a uxoricidal opera dedicated, curiously, to his wife. *Duke Bluebeard's Castle*, inspired by *Dukas' triumph, was rejected by publishers and went back into the drawer while Bartók returned to ethnic researches, fearing rightly that war would destroy his sources. The 2nd string quartet (3.iii.18) contains strong leanings towards *Arab music.

Aware of Stravinsky's ballet success, he next ventured into dance, winning acclaim for *The Wooden Prince* (Budapest, 12.v.17) and using it as a foil for *Bluebeard* (24.v.18) in a double bill. The opera revealed a *Janáček-like synthesis of blood-stained humanity and nature, with a soaring soprano line and consolatory finale. It was his only opera, and he wrote no symphonies. Bartók created his own forms, leaving fewer large-scale works than virtually any other composer of comparable importance.

After the collapse of Austro-Hungarian rule he became a national emblem, until chauvinists turned on him for quoting music of detested Romania. A *Dance Suite* (19.xi.23) for Budapest's jubilee restored him to favour, but his status was never entirely secure. The early years of Hungarian independence were a troubled time in his life, yielding two violin-piano sonatas in which he strayed close to Schoenberg's atonal piano music and *Szymanowski's explorations. He divorced and remarried in 1923, writing for the sons of each marriage ingenious piano exercises with the titles *Out of Doors* (1926) and *Mikrokosmos* (1926–39).

During this hiatus he assumed full command of his means. The *Miraculous Mandarin* provoked ructions at its première (Cologne, 27.xi.26), its atonal episodes, *quarter-tones and prostitute heroine outraging the city's mayor, Konrad Adenauer. Schoenberg followers claimed him as a brother in *expressionism, but Bartok was unmoved. In the piano sonata (Budapest, 8.xii.26), his model was Liszt and his mode wilfully free of fashion. To dissonance and irregular rhythms, he proceeded to add note-*clusters, smacked together on the keyboard with the palm or forearm. His first piano concerto (Frankfurt, 1.vii.27, cond *Furtwängler) was alarmingly ferocious, crashing percussively into its theme and giving soloist and listeners little relief. The 2nd concerto (Frankfurt, 23.i.33, cond. Rosbaud) was less fatiguingly dense, its textures clearing to display wonders of a well-stocked mind.

The summit of his keyboard art was a sonata for two pianos and percussion (Basle, 16.i.38), later made into a concerto (London, 14.xi.42), which proved pentatonically melodious and refreshingly unaggressive, every note and crash having a purpose. Nothing was done for show or to shock.

The 3rd, 4th and 5th quartets were the central chapter of his personal story, achieving levels of intensity rare even in chamber music. The 3rd quartet (London, 19.ii.29) cannot suppress a gypsy wildness and seems incongruous when played by men in frock coats; the 4th (Budapest, 20.iii.29) invented a new method of string plucking, known as 'Bartók pizzicato'; the 5th (Washington, D.C., 8.iv.35) toned

down the excesses of its predecessors, as if to give audiences time to catch up.

Throughout the 1930s he spoke out against fascism, withdrawing his music from performance in Germany and Italy. He switched from *Universal to a British publisher in 1937 and bewailed the corrupt dictatorial state that Hungary had become. Yet he kept his feelings out of his music, which moved into a transcendent phase. Two chamber-orch. commissions from the Swiss maecenas, Paul *Sacher, softened his rebarbative manner into subtly penetrative sounds. *Music for strings, percussion and celesta* (Basle, 21.i.37) arched effortlessly from dark A-major to luminous E-flat and back again. The Divertimento for strings (Basle, 11.vi.40) was rather like a Baroque concerto grosso with a touch of Haydnesque charm. The magnificent 2nd violin concerto (Amsterdam, 23.iii.39, cond. *Mengelberg) was outwardly smiling, inwardly resolute.

So long as his beloved mother was alive, he could not leave Hungary. On her death in 1940, he left for the United States, bearing the unplayed score of a 6th string quartet (NY, 20.i.41), serene and cerebral. For two years, he was chronically homesick and unable to compose. Then he was stricken with leukaemia. *Koussevitsky, learning of his plight, gave him $1,000 to write a piece for Boston while *ASCAP paid his hospital bills. The *Concerto for Orch.* (Boston, 1.xii.44) was a metaphor for international relations, each instrument playing its productive part in the world order. Amid its warmth and fervour, there was also wit and malice in a 4th-movement parody of *Shostakovich's 7th symphony, whose wartime celebrity Bartók despised. The finale was a defiantly optimistic declaration from a dying man.

When they took him back to hospital in September 1945, Bartók begged in vain for a day in which to finish his 3rd piano concerto. He left it complete down to 17 last bars, which were orchestrated by his pupil Tibor *Serly (Philadelphia, 8.ii.46). This sweet and gentle work yearns for the flora and fauna of his native land, its 'adagio religioso' central movement making peace with creation in a quotation from the 'heiliger Dankgesang' of Beethoven's string quartet op. 132. Bartók went out not with a percussive bang, nor with a whimper, but with a message for humanity.

Hungary reclaimed him posthumously, body and soul, shrouding his music in a gaudy national flag. What was special about Bartók, however, was the universality of his vision, not the narrow nationality he struggled to transcend. He lived on as a model for composers in societies under stress. His rediscovery in 1950s Poland by *Lutosławski and *Penderecki launched a new dawn of musical freedom in eastern Europe.
    b. Nagyszentmiklos (Sinnicolau Mare), Austro-Hungary, 25.iii.1881; *d*. NY, 26.ix. 45. *other works*: *Cantata profana* (1930), viola concerto (1945), Rhapsodies for violin and piano (1928), *Contrasts* for piano, clarinet and violin (1940), solo violin sonata (1944), *Allegro barbaro* for piano (1911).
    Bib: Malcolm Gillies, *Bartók Remembered*, London (Faber), 1990.

Bruno BARTOLOZZI His 1967 textbook explaining how to play odd chords and *microtones on wind instruments led to his noises being collectively named as 'Bartolozzi sounds'. His compositions, including a concedrto for orchestra (1952) and bassoon concerto (1963) resemble *Dallapiccola's lyrical *serialism.
    b. Florence, 8.vi.11; *d*. Fiesole, 12.xii.80.

Jan Zdeněk BARTOŠ Czech composer of seven traditional, diatonic symphonies.
    b. Dvur Kralove nad Labem, 4.vi.08; *d*. Prague, 1.vi.81.

(William)   Count   BASIE Jazz-band leader who directed single-fingered from the keyboard; his sound erred on the side of blandness. His hits include 'April in Paris'.
    b. Red Bank, New Jersey, 21.viii.04; *d*. Hollywood, Florida, 26.iv.84.

The Bassarids Greek mythological opera by *Henze to libretto by *Auden and Chester Kallman. fp: Salzburg, 6.viii.66.

Bastille Opera Modernist edifice intended by the French socialist government as a people's palace on the site of the 1789 prison, it opened in the bicentennial year amid international ructions over the sacking of its inaugural music director,

Daniel Barenboim, whose programmes were deemed too highbrow and his fees too high. The house was boycotted by *Boulez and initially by most leading conductors, an intended hall with variable acoustics was left unbuilt and its populist mission never seemed destined for fulfilment.

Yves (Marie) BAUDRIER *Messiaen's partner in *Young France, he became and out-and-out romantic and expert film composer.
    b. Paris, 11.ii.06; *d*. there, 9.xi.88.

Marion (Eugenie) BAUER Author of romantic piano pieces with flowery titles – *A Garden is a Lovesome Thing, From the New Hampshire Woods, Sun Splendour* (orch. vers. fp by. *Stokowski, NY, 25.x.47) – and educational music books. She also composed an *American Youth* piano concerto (1943) and a cantata on *China* (1944).
    b. Walla Walla, Washington, US, 15.viii. 1897; st with *Boulanger; taught NY U. 1926–51; *d*. South Hadley, Massachusetts, 9.viii.55.

Alison (Margaret) BAULD A Shakespearian actress in Sydney, she studied composition with *Lutyens and started writing about women and Australia. *Nell* (London, 2.vi.88), heroine of her bicentennial opera, got raped in the outback; *One Pearl* (1973) is a stage piece about a tormented female; *Van Diemen's Land* (1976), a fidgety cantata, tells of shipwreck on the way to Tasmania. Bauld has written most of her own texts with *Tippett-ish whimsy.
    b, Sydney, 7.v.44; *other works*: *Dear Emily* for soprano and harp (1973), *Exiles*, music theatre (1974), *Once upon a time*, music theatre (1986).

(Sir) Arnold BAX The problem with Bax is patchiness. The first symphony (London, 4.xii.22) opens with bold invention, only to meander into mediocrity after a few pages. The third (London, 14.iii.30) and most sustained of seven symphonies has a central movement of shivering quietude and an epic climax; the fifth, dedicated to *Sibelius (London, 15.i.34), has heroic moments; the seventh is inscribed 'to the American people' (NY, 9.vi.39). The tone-poem *Garden of Fand* (1916) is a quasi-*Delian miniature that combines Straussian bombast with the delicacy of late Debussy. His best work was inspired by immoderate passions for Ireland, alcohol and women, lastly for the pianist Harriet Cohen (1895–1967) for whom he wrote a stormy concerto *Winter Legends* (1930) and much solo music. She, along with the Irish Rising, brought on his best period; whisky diluted the rest. Born rich, he did not compose to eat. His chamber music is underrated. The 1st symphony proves more effective in its original piano sonata form and, while his cello concerto (1934) contains only a nocturne of any merit – and that an *Elgar imitation – his 11-minute rhapsodic ballad for solo cello (1939) surges with ideas.

   b. Streatham, London, 8.xi.1883; knighted 37; *d.* Cork, Ireland, 3.x.53. *other orch. works*: Symphonic variations for piano and orch. (1917), *November Woods* (1917), *Tintagel* (1917), Russian Suite (for *Diaghilev, 1919) *Mediterranean* (1922), violin concerto (for *Heifetz, 1938), film score, *Oliver Twist* (1948).
   Bib: Arnold Bax, *Farewell my Youth*, London (Longman Green & Co.), 1943.

Francois BAYLE *Messiaen-bred musique concrète and electronic composer.
   b. Tamatave, Madagascar, 27.iv.32; *works include*: *Archipelago* for string quartet and tape (1963), *Colours of the Night* (1983), *Motion-Emotion* (1985).

Bayreuth Festivals Siegfried *Wagner ran his father's legacy faithfully until 1930; his widow Winifred converted it to Hitlerism. Their sons Wieland and Wolfgang used abstract stagings after 1945 to erase the political past.

BBC The British Broadcasting Corporation, pioneer of public service broadcasting, relayed the first radio opera from Covent Garden on 8.i.23. Funded by a household licence fee from 1927, the BBC flexed its financial muscle to take over London's Promenade Concerts and form its own orchestras and choruses. In September 1946, it added a Third Programme (later Radio 3), devoted primarily to serious music. Torn between modernism and vested interests, BBC music lagged behind German and Italian radio in the serialist and electronic eras. Attacked for waste in the 1970s and elitism in the 1980s, the BBC disbanded some of its orchestras and watered down its musical diet. BBC television addressed itself to mass tastes; a second channel, BBC2, reached a large public with the 1976 Bayreuth Ring cycle run as soap opera.

Mrs Amy BEACH Concert pianist who, in 25 years of marriage to a Boston physician, gave up her stage career and composed a Mass (Boston, 18.ii.1892), Gaelic Symphony (30.x.1896) and piano concerto (6.iv.1900) in *Stanford-like late-Victorian mode. Widowhood in 1910 brought her back to the stage and she was celebrated in Europe as an American reincarnation of Clara Schumann.
   b. Henniker, New Hampshire, 5.ix.1867, as Amy Marcy Cheney; married 1885–1910 to Dr H. H. A. Beach; *d.* NY, 27.xii.44. *other works*: piano quintet (1908), string quartet (1929).

the BEATLES Four lads from Liverpool who twice shattered the mould of *popular music – first, by shifting the emphasis from solo stars to ensembles, then by a melodic sophistication that others could merely envy. Their cockiness and rhythmic vitality aroused Beatlemania on both sides of the Atlantic. Leonard *Bernstein played 'Norwegian Wood' on TV to demonstrate sonata form; *The Times'* chief critic called them 'the greatest songwriters since Schubert'. They were summoned to Buckingham Palace to collect an award 'for services to export'. John Lennon said they were 'more famous than Jesus Christ'; his assassination cemented their immortality.
   Formed in 1959 as a guitar-toting trio with drum backing, they were spotted in a Liverpool club, The Cavern, by Brian Epstein who, as manager, cut their hair in a rounded fringe and kitted them out in identi-suits. The EMI record group mitigated their feral rhythm-and-blues with classical sounds added by producer George Martin. He gave string quartet backing to 'Yesterday', itself a Tchaikovsky derivation, hired an octet for 'Eleanor Rigby' and a french horn in 'For No One'. They were among the first to mix four tracks in studio; each Beatle would arrive at *Abbey

Road with a selection of pre-recorded sound effects. 'A Day in the Life' ended with 20,000 Hz noises that only dogs could hear. Indian mysticism and psychedelic substances led them to the sitar and transcendental meditation. The Beatles refused to stand still from one album to the next, though there was a decline after the 1967 high noon of *Sgt. Pepper's Lonely Hearts Club Band* and they reverted in the final lap to hymnal simplicities in 'Hey Jude' and 'Let it Be'. Chanting 'All You Need is Love', the Beatles were destroyed by interpersonal strife involving two spouses and commercial interests. They disbanded in 1970.

Argument rages as to whether Lennon or Paul McCartney was the presiding genius. Since neither attained the same heights of invention in their subsequent solo careers, it may safely be assumed that the spark resided in symbiotic friction. The Beatles' impact on popular music, lasting barely six years, was so explosive that no-one has approached it again, and immediate successors were obliged to respond with *punkish anarchy.

McCartney composed a semi-autobiographical *Liverpool Oratorio* that enjoyed a certain vogue. Inhibited in formal technique, he assigned its instrumentation to the film composer, Carl Davis, and took no part in its worldwide performances (fp: Liverpool, 28.vi.91).

The Beatles: 1959–70:
John (Winston) Lennon, *b*. Liverpool, 9.x.40; *d*. NY, 8.xii.80.
(James) Paul McCartney, *b*. Liverpool, 18.vi.42;
George Harrison, *b*. Liverpool, 25.ii.43;
Pete Best, replaced in August 1962 by **Ringo Starr** (Richard Starkey), *b*. Liverpool, 7.vii.40;

Beat Generation/Beat Poets/Beatniks
1950s youth for whom rock music was the meaning of life.

bebop Aggressive *jazz playing, current in 1940s New York. A short melody was variegated with fast, jagged rhythms and discordant counterpoints. Chief exponents were Charlie *Parker, Dizzy *Gillespie and Thelonious *Monk.

Conrad BECK The Swiss polyphonist found his voice in 1920s Paris, where he

wrote five promising symphonies and a concerto for string quartet and orch. (1929) that won the *Coolidge prize.
  b. Lohn, Schaffhausen canton, Switzerland, 16.vi.01; st with *Roussel, Honegger, Ibert, Boulanger; head of music at Basle Radio 1939–66; avid mountaineer; *d*. Basle, 31.x.89. *other works*: ballet *La Grande Ourse* (1936), oratorio *Death in Basle*, cello concerto (1968), five frugal string quartets.

John J(oseph) BECKER Associate of *Ives and *Cowell, he hitched up to modernism in 1929 with the dissonant 3rd of seven symphonies. He ventured into percussiveness with *Abongo* (1933) and produced a discordant flute concerto. He believed the composer's role was to express social issues and wrote *A Life of Man* ballet (1943).
  b. Henderson, Kentucky, 22.i.1886; *d*. Wilmette, Illinois, 21.i.61.

David (Vickerman) BEDFORD A sixties freewheeler, Bedford went from *Ligeti-like ethereality in settings of the American poet Kenneth Patchen to playing rock music with Mike Oldfield. Stylistically adrift in the 1980s, he converted his cellular style to outright *minimalism, underpinned by an almost *Holst-like orchestration in pieces like *Sun Paints Rainbows on Vast Waves*.
  b. London, 4.viii.37; st with *Berkeley and *Nono; *other works*: children's opera, *The Rime of the Ancient Mariner* (1978), *Star's End* for rock instruments and orch. (1974), *The Garden of Love* (1970) for five players and pop group, Variations on a rhythm by Mike Oldfield (1973) for 84 instruments, three players and cond.

(Sir) Thomas BEECHAM Dominant British conductor for half a century, he founded countless London orchestras and opera companies and was *Delius' foremost interpreter.
  b. St Helens, Lancs, England, 29.iv.1879; *d*. London, 8.iii.61.

Jack BEESON Composer of US realist operas, the most celebrated being *Lizzie Borden* (NY City Opera, 25.ii.65) about a *fin-de-siècle* serial killer.
  b. Muncie, Indiana, 15.vii.21; st with *Hanson and *Bartók; taught Columbia U. 1945– ; *other operas*: *My Heart's in the Highlands* (NET TV, 17.iii.70), *Dr Heidegger's Fountain of Youth* (NY, 17.xi.78).

David BEHRMAN The son of playwright S.N. Behrman and Jascha *Heifetz's sister, he was born amid the Salzburg Festival and seemed predestined for music. The music he made, however, rejected his antecedents. Working with *Pousseur and *Stockhausen turned him into an all-American *avant-gardist, centred on media and gadgetry. His new music series for CBS brought minimalism into the living room with a debut recording of *Riley's *In C*. Electronic instruments he built in the backyard sounded like domestic vacuum cleaners until harmonies and emotions broke through the racket. He composed with *Cage, *Tudor and *Mumma for the Merce Cunningham Dance Company, gradually replacing acoustic sounds with live instruments in potent electronic conceptions like *On the Other Ocean* (flute/bassoon) and *Figure in a Clearing*.
    b. Salzburg, Austria, 16.viii.37; st with *Rieger, Piston, Pousseur and Stockhausen.

Bix BEIDERBECKE Cornet player who inaugurated *Chicago-style jazz, he was exiled to New York in 1928 and died there of alcoholism at 28.
    b. Davenport, Iowa, 10.iii.03; *d*. NY, 6.viii.31.

Belgium Maurice Béjart's Ballet du XXme Siècle at the Théâtre de la Monnaie gave Brussels a taste for contemporary music that was reinforced by Gérard Mortier's visionary 1980s directorship at the opera. The creative quotient of Belgian composers, though, was negligible.

Sergei BELIMOV Soviet avant-gardist who, like *Pärt, adopted Baroque backgrounds but mixed them with orientalist ululations in an intriguingly listenable synthesis. *Concerning Water*, an oboe concerto (1988), quotes the prelude to *Die Walküre* among many collagist allusions.

Ján Levoslav BELLA The doyen of Slovak composers was a colliery priest who was seduced from his altar by the siren of nationalism. His symphonic poem *Fate and the Ideal* (Prague, 17.ii.1876) was conducted by Richard *Strauss in 1890, but his Wagnerian opera *Wieland the Blacksmith* awaited national liberation for performance (Bratislava, 28.iv.26, cond. *Nedbal).

After 36 years as director of music in Sibin (now Romania), Bella retired in 1921 to Vienna before returning to die in his homeland.
    b. Liptovský Svätý Mikuláš, 4.ix.1843; *d*. Bratislava, 25.v.36.

The Bells Russo-religious poem for orchestra, chorus and soloists by *Rachmaninov. fp: St Petersburg, 30.xi.13. Revised version: Sheffield, 21.x.36.

Belshazzar's Feast Exuberant cantata by the young *Walton. fp: Leeds, 8.x.31.

Ralph BENATZKY His reputation rests on a revue written with a great deal of help. *Im weissen Rössl – The White Horse Inn* (Berlin, 8.xi.30) is a colossal piece of kitsch that barely amounts to operetta. It smirkingly recounts the Hapsburg-era flirtation between a hotelier and her headwaiter at a well-known wayside inn on the Wolfgangsee. Six numbers were contributed by Robert *Stolz and others; Benatzky pulled the bits together and wrote an eponymous theme song. Czech born, he left Germany in 1933 and wound up in Hollywood. He was not, however, *verboten* and continued to compose UFA films, among them a star vehicle for Hitlerite heartthrob, Zarah Leander.
    b. Budweis, Moravia, 5.vi.1884; *d*. Zurich, Switzerland, 17.x.57. other operettas: *Casanova* (using Johann Strauss melodies, 1928), *The Three Musketeers* (1929), *Liebestraum* (borrowing Liszt themes, 1951).

Xavier BENGUEREL Catalonian who embraced *avant-gardism, then cast it aside.
    b. Barcelona, 9.ii.31; *works include*: *Arbor*, cantata to texts by Goethe, Dante, Shakespeare, Hitler, Mussolini, Ché Guevara, et al. (1972), cello concerto (1977), opera *Spleen* (1984).

Paul BEN HAIM Forced to leave Germany when the Nazis came to power, Paul Frankenburger migrated to Palestine, Hebraised his name and became national composer of the newborn state of Israel. Late-romantic by nature, he assembled Arabic chant, oriental folksong, Jewish liturgy and biblical tropes in Western symphonic casings. His violin concerto (1960) and Sonata for solo violin (1952) appealed to Jewish virtuosi from *Menuhin onwards. Two symphonies (1940, 45) are Sibelian in all but temperature; the Psalm adagio of the 1st symphony packs the propagandist uplift of wartime movies. *The Sweet Psalmist of Israel* (1953) is an engaging though slightly cloying orch. suite.

> *b.* Munich, 5.vii.1897; cond. in Augsburg 1924–31; 1st president, Israeli Composers Assoc. 1948; *d.* Tel Aviv, 25.i.84. *other works*: cello concerto (1962), *The Eternal Theme* (1965), much choral and vocal music.

Arthur BENJAMIN Emigré Australian, he turned his hand to everything from opera to TV. He wrote a rippling harmonica concerto (1953) for Larry Adler and started a fad for calypso music with *Jamaican Rumba* (1938), which became a summer concerts favourite. His Dickensian opera *A Tale of Two Cities* won a Festival of Britain prize in 1951. His brooding wartime symphony, composed in Canada, is starkly contemplative.

At the Royal College of Music, Benjamin was Britten's piano teacher and dedicatee of his *Holiday Diary* but not a lasting influence on him. He was soloist in the first British performance of *Rhapsody in Blue*, which coloured his own piano concertino of 1926.

> *b.* Sydney, 18.ix.1893; moved to London 1911, served infantry and air force 1914–18, cond. Vancouver Symphony 1941–6; *d.* London, 10.iv.60. *other orch. works*: *Red River Jig* (1945), *Caribbean Dance* (1946), Divertimento on themes by Gluck (1952).

George BENJAMIN At 20, the youngest composer ever to receive a première at the BBC Proms, he went unaccountably silent after a handful of scores. A *Messiaen pupil, he proved precociously adept at landscape art in *Ringed by the Flat Horizon* (London, 25.viii.80), evoking a Mexican desert thunderstorm. *A Mind of Winter* (Aldeburgh, 26.vi.81) for soprano and chamber orch. and *At First Light* (London, 23.xi.82, cond. Rattle) veered towards the bleakness of a *Birtwistle soundscape. In the next decade, he managed just 24 minutes of orchestral music in *Antara*, fitted with electronics at *IRCAM (Paris, 25.iv.87), while working on an opera. Deceleration was not unexpected after so rapid a lift-off and Benjamin probably

needed to put some distance between himself and Messiaen in order to assert his individuality.

> *b.* London, 31.i.1960;

Richard Rodney BENNETT English composer as much at home in *squeaky-wheel serialism as in *pop song. Writing *12-tone music when he was only 16, he won a French government grant to study with *Boulez, whom he imitated in ensemble works like *Calendar* (1960). He followed it with *Jazz Calendar*, changing to tunefulness. Two symphonies were succeeded by movie scores, of which *Billy Liar*, *Far from the Madding Crowd* and *Equus* were outstanding.

> *b.* Broadstairs, Kent, 29.iii.36; st with *Ferguson, *Berkeley and *Boulez; vice president Royal College of Music 1983– ; *other works*: operas *The Mines of Sulphur* (London, Sadler's Wells, 12.ix.61), *A Penny for a Song* (Sadler's Wells, 2.xi.67), *Victory* (Covent Garden, 13.iv.70); ballet *Isadora* (Covent Garden, 30.iv.81); orch. *Aubade* (1964); many songs, carols and piano pieces.

Robert Russell BENNETT Broadway's orchestrator in chief, Bennett arranged over 300 musicals from *Rose Marie* to *My Fair Lady*, working several into concert suites. A mature pupil of Nadia *Boulanger, he composed an opera on the diva *Maria Malibran* (NY, 8.iv.35) and an Abraham Lincoln symphony (Philadelphia, 24.x.31) which shared a $10,000 prize with works by Bloch, Copland and Gruenberg. The real money, however, was in media. He won an Oscar for *Oklahoma* and became head of music at Mutual Broadcasting.

> *b.* Kansas City, Missouri, 15.vi.1894; *d.* NY, 17.viii.81. *other works*: violin concerto (NBC, 26.xii.41), Hollywood Scherzo (NBC, 15.xi.36), Symphony in D for 'Dodgers' (NY, 3.viii.41).

Niels (Viggo) BENTZON The irrepressible Dane composed some 400 works, including 18 symphonies, eight piano concertos, 22 piano sonatas, seven ballets and a substantial opera, *Faust III*. Initially influenced by *Nielsen, he roamed energetically through Hindemith, Bartók, Schoenberg and jazz – offering a piano suite for Duke Ellington's 75th birthday.

He endorsed Gunter *Schuller's *Third Stream fusion between jazz and symphonic music and contributed an improvisatory *Third Stream Music*, op 179, for instrumental ensemble. He followed just about every fad from *prepared piano to 1960s *happenings (e.g. *European vitality*, op 198) and, despite copious recordings and sensational headlines, remained merely a local hero.

> *b.* Copenhagen, Denmark, 24.viii.19; prof. at Royal Danish conservatory 1949– ; *other works*: four violin concertos, three cello concertos, 11 string quartets, Paganini variations (1968).

Jørgen BENTZON Niels' cousin was a *Nielsen pupil and clerk to the Supreme Court. He wrote a 1941 symphony in D major describing Dickens characters.

> *b.* Copenhagen, 14.ii.1897; *d.* Hœrsholm, 9.vii.51.

Cathy BERBERIAN Improbably versatile US singer, she married *Berio in 1950 and set him on a fruitful path of vocal experiment. *Cage, *Pousseur, *Stravinsky *(Elegy for JFK)* and *Henze composed for her three-octave range, but Cathy sang what she pleased – anything from Monteverdi operas to quirky settings of the Communist Internationale and, hilariously, the *Beatles. She composed *Stripsody* (1966), a realization of newspaper comic strips, and *Morsicat(h)y* (1971) for solo piano. More than just a singer, she was an antecedent of 'performance artists' like Joan La Barbara and Meredith Monk. Berio enshrined her art in *Concert for Cathy* (1972) and mourned her death in a distraught *Requies* (1984).

> *b.* Attleboro, Massachusetts, 4.vii.25, of Armenian parents; married Berio 1950, divorced 1968; *d.* Rome, 6.iii.83.

Nicolai BEREZOWSKY A violinist at the Bolshoi Opera and the NY Philharmonic, he turned the children's classic *Babar the Elephant* into an opera, killing himself with a drug overdose soon after. Koussevitsky conducted two of his four symphonies as well as his *Concerto lirico* (1934), which the soloist, Piatigorsky, found inept.

> *b.* St Petersburg, 17.v.1900; *d.* NY, 27.viii.53.

Alban (Johannes Maria) BERG He may have lacked the intellect, the integrity or the industry of his partners-in-revolution, Arnold *Schoenberg and Anton *Webern; yet it was Berg's music that changed the culture and left its mark on the public at large. He alone of the *Second Viennese School fixed his name to a distinctive sound, known as 'Bergian', and he altered the nature of opera in ways that affected every subsequent composer.

Berg proved that post-tonal music could be rendered acceptable to a broad audience; but the means by which he made it acceptable contravened *atonal and *12-note orthodoxies. While Schoenberg predicted that milk-delivery boys would one day whistle his tunes, Berg insinuated into his scores melodies that were already whistled by tradesmen. His two operas and the ethereal violin concerto mingled among their dissonances familiar quotations from folk music and Bach.

He was, first and foremost, Viennese: ingratiating, morally flexible and wafting a whiff of sexual corruption. Of all the great composers none possessed so malleable or servile a character. From the day he took a sheaf of immature Lieder to Schoenberg in October 1904, he submitted totally to the prophet's will, currying his favour with menial services and thoughtful gifts. When Schoenberg moved to Berlin in 1911 Berg frantically raised money for him and, by way of thanks, was admonished: 'Wake up! . . . be a man!' He continued to address Schoenberg in obsequious tones long after his own works were universally successful. Schoenberg overwhelmed his existence, more than any intimate or family relationships. At the age of 50, a letter from Schoenberg could reduce him to helpless tears.

The son of a shopkeeper selling Catholic artefacts in the shadow of St Stephen's Cathedral, Berg tried to kill himself at 18 after a servant-girl in the household, Marie Scheuchl, became pregnant by him; he sent money for their daughter, Albine, but never saw her. In the dual morality of fin-de-siècle Vienna, he consorted with prostitutes and wallowed in self-disgust. His sister and confidante, Smaragda (1887–1953), lived openly, notoriously, as a lesbian. Outwardly bourgeois, Berg utilized these dangerous subjects in his operas which, together with the Lyric Suite, swayed from sensuality to shivering revulsion. His attitude to Vienna – 'this city of song, which one cannot hate too much' – was tinged with ambiguity.

Blocked by parental fiat from marrying the willowy Helene Nachowski, reputedly the natural child of the Emperor Franz Joseph, he vented his frustration in a single-movement 11-minute piano sonata (Vienna, 7.xi.07) to which, with Schoenberg's approval, he assigned his first opus number. No tonality was specified, although it conformed in general terms to the B-minor of Liszt's famous sonata and in mood to the sensual gloom of *Tristan, while softer in texture and dynamics. Spurned by a publisher, he expressed his feelings in a tonally-stressed string quartet op.3 (Vienna, 24.iv.11), coloured by Mahler and Debussy – the opening of *Pelléas, Act five is quoted in the third theme – more than by any desire to change the world. On 3.v.11, after a persistent four-year courtship, he married Helene in what, to all appearances, was a lifelong love-match. Both suffered chronic ill-health, he being a martyr to bronchial asthma, and their concern for one another was touching.

Marriage, Mahler's death and Schoenberg's departure accelerated Berg's liberation from tonal constraints, finally achieved in five sumptuous songs to brittle 'postcard texts' by the coffee-house poet Peter Altenberg (1859–1919). The première of two of them occasioned a riot at the 'scandal concert' of 31.iii.13 that launched the Second Vienna School in a flurry of arrests and vitriolic reviews. Berg was damned as a dangerous anarchist, irrespective of the luxuriantly seductive textures of his songs. The 3 pieces for orch. op.6 (Oldenburg, 14.iv.30) took their title and style from Schoenberg's 5 pieces for orch. but, in retrospect, can be heard moving clearly into the enriched, personally hallmarked atonality that Berg would devise for Wozzeck. Unwilling to emulate his teacher alone, Berg opened with the dying cadences of Mahler's 9th symphony and shifted its lonely fiddle solos and horrific marches into a functionally modernistic landscape, rather like the façade of a Bauhaus building, imposing to behold but resting on emotionally insecure foundations.

Two other works contributed to his operatic evolution. In 1913 he published an intensive study of Schoenberg's *Gurrelieder and assisted its conductor, Franz Schreker, by preparing a vocal score of his sexually-charged opera, Der *ferne Klang. In May 1914 he was transfixed by the belated Viennese première of Georg Büchner's (1813–37) play, Woyzeck, about the execution of a tormented soldier for the murder of his mistress. He went to see the play time after time and began sketching an opera, when war broke out and he was distracted by depression and military service at the War Ministry. A decade passed before Berg finished another work.

In Wozzeck he was the first composer to confront the problem of writing a full-length opera without a supportive tonal scaffold. His solution was to erect a symmetrical framework into which action and scenery were matched to specific musical patterns so that everything in the opera interlinked in cosmic unity. The soldier Wozzeck was portrayed with prescient modernity as a victim of society; his girlfriend Marie was the only rounded, sympathetic character in the opera. Berg gave musical emphasis to her uncomplicated sexuality while, true to Viennese character, bowdlerizing Büchner's vulgarities. His soldiers had violent sex on stage but were not allowed to say the word 'piss'. With a huge orchestra and difficult vocal passages, *Wozzeck* was finally staged, after 34 full rehearsals, by the redoubtable Erich Kleiber at the Berlin State Opera on 14.xii. 25, a date that entered history as the birth of modern opera. With its anti-militarism and its rejection of bourgeois domesticity, the opera aroused a first-night furore but reflected the inter-War *Zeitgeist* so acutely that it received 150 performances in a decade. Berg, the slowest and least assertive of the Vienna radicals, became their bashful spokesman.

Schoenberg meanwhile had forsaken atonality for his method of composing with 12 notes of equal value and Berg obediently changed techniques at the summit of his celebrity. He composed a Chamber Concerto for piano and violin with 13 wind instruments (Berlin, 27.iii.27, cond *Scherchen) that flattered Schoenberg's *chamber symphonies by imitation and his new system by elegant assimilation – though not yet by formal adoption for it was partly tonal, atonal and 12-tone. Dedicated to his teacher on his 50th birthday, it interwove the notes of his *initials, A and B, with Schoenberg's and Webern's and played clever games with the numerals of their respective ages, 50, 39 and 41. Berg's attraction to 12-note music was rooted in more than just fidelity. He was fascinated to the point of crankiness by the mysteries of numerology, astrology and the occult which, allied to a taste for conspiracy, pervaded his ensuing music.

In May 1925, while in Prague for a performance of *Wozzeck* fragments, he fell in love with his hostess, Hanna Fuchs-Robettin, married sister of the novelist Franz Werfel, himself the third husband of Alma *Mahler, the composer's widow and Helene Berg's close friend. For the last decade of his short life, Berg was passionately involved with Hanna (who told her daughter that there was no physical consummation). Berg, while assuring Helene

that 'faithfulness is one of my chief qualities', is known to have slept with other women. He was not highly sexed or physically appealing and obtained a perverse voyeuristic arousal from plotting sexual entanglements among his friends. What Hanna brought to his life was a constant, forbidden erotic stimulus, not unlike *Janáček's last love. Their connection remained secret until half a century after Berg was dead, when he appeared in a dream to the widow of the Prague composer and music director Alexander *Zemlinsky, nominal dedicatee of the *Lyric Suite*, and ordered her to disclose the truth.

The suite, initially a second string quartet (Vienna, 8.i.27) from which three movements were orchestrated for strings (Berlin, 31.i.29, cond. Horenstein), took its title and one Adagio passage from Zemlinsky's *Lyric Symphony, itself a mirror-image of Mahler's Das *Lied von der Erde. Its mortal premonitions are few, however, and the overpowering sensation is of an erotic intoxication. This was implied by a quotation of the opening bars of *Tristan and confirmed in a secret copy of the score, presented to Hanna and preserved by her daughter, in which the composer twined the notes of his initials with hers and pencilled in different colours the stretches of music that described themselves, her husband, Herbert, and her children.

As well as musical characterization, he made great play of the significance of two numerals, 10 and 23, which he deemed to be their 'fateful numbers'. Throughout the work, the tempi are given in metronome multiples of these figures and the themes change at fateful numbers. The opening allegro gioviale is 138 (23 x 6) bars long and has a metronome mark of 100 (10 x 10); the second subject enters at bar 23; and so on.

Berg had been harping on for years about the meaning of 23 in his life. It was, for example, the date on which he suffered his first asthma attack. He was convinced of its symbolism by the Berlin quack Wilhelm Fliess, who once misled the impressionable Sigmund Freud with nasal theories, and his beliefs were fortified further by the Viennese biologist, Paul Kammerer, whose fraud would be exposed in the case of the midwife toad. Berg was a sucker for pseudo-scientific cults and involved them in the creation of his music.

The *Lyric Suite*'s techniques of concealment, mysticism, dodecatonality and frank quotation combined again to form the violin concerto, palpably the most affecting work of the entire Vienna School. It was, in every respect except technique, a romantic masterpiece of almost religious self-absorption. Named 'in memory of an angel', a eulogy to Alma Mahler's teenaged daughter, Manon Gropius, who died of polio, it was written in an uncustomary rush of four months in a requiem mood that, like Mozart's, was intended for himself. It was composed in 12-note form with copious self-quotations from *Lulu* and constant play on his number, 23, and Hanna's, 10, as well as their initials. In addition, there is a Bach chorale, 'Es ist genug – It's enough', and a bawdy Carinthian folk ditty about a certain Mizzi – short for Marie, his adolescent servant love. All of Berg's life is here, except Helene, as she realized at its first, posthumous performance (Barcelona, 19.iv.36, cond. Scherchen).

Her exclusion prompted Helene, previously uninterested in his music, to take a hand in the fate of *Lulu*. Berg was 20 when he saw Frank Wedekind's (1864–1918) twin dramas of a modern woman who picks lovers of both sexes but is reduced to prostitution and meets Nemesis in the shape of Jack the Ripper. His music was as lurid as its theme, erotically explicit and stridently feminist. Begun in 1929, he got stuck in 1934, partly over a possible reluctance to lead Lulu-Hanna to her fate, partly in despair at the banning of his music in Nazi Germany and the exile of his teacher to distant California. He died with the 3rd act unfinished; a letter to Webern suggested that he meant to abandon the finale. The opera was premièred in two acts (Zurich, 2.vi.37) after Schoenberg refused to complete it, deterred by its inherent amorality and by a perceived anti-semitism in the characterization of a banker – as if Berg was seeking to ingratiate himself with the new masters of Germany.

Helene Berg, aware at last of her husband's murky secrets, imposed a ban on the completion of the third act but was outwitted by the publishers, *Universal Edition, who, with Viennese discretion, commissioned a completion from Friedrich *Cerha that was performed after the widow's demise (Paris, 24.ii.79, cond *Boulez). Although musically absorbing to the last bar, *Lulu* lacks the dramatic coherence and social intuition of *Wozzeck*. It flounders meaninglessly in the dim-lit society where Berg was formed.

In August 1935, on finishing the violin concerto in his Carinthian woodland retreat, Berg developed an abcess on his back that turned septic. He prepared a symphonic suite from *Lulu* for performance in Berlin (30.xi.34) – a concert that resulted in the emigration of its conductor Erich Kleiber and the tightening of Nazi controls on *decadent music. After hearing the work in Vienna, days later, he was admitted to hospital in great pain and died, like his boyhood hero Mahler, of an incurable infection in his 50th year. Notwithstanding the official date of death, relatives maintain that he stopped breathing in the 23rd hour of the 23rd of December, fateful to the last.

With fewer than 15 original works to his name, virtually everything he wrote was a milestone in modernism. His violin concerto is a triumph of art over expedience and his operas haunted Britten and Shostakovich, Henze and Zimmermann, Penderecki and Stockhausen, Gershwin and Bernstein – indeed, every western composer who sought to make his mark on the 20th-century dramatic stage.

b. Vienna, 9.ii.1885; *d.* there, 24.xii.35. *other works*: Early Songs (pub. 1928), four pieces for clarinet and piano (Vienna, 17.x.19), soprano concert aria *Der Wein* (Frankfurt, 4.vi.30), dedicated to Herbert Fuchs-Robettin who possessed a magnificent cellar; various Strauss arrangements for Schoenberg's *private concert society.
Bib: *The Berg-Schoenberg Correspondence*, ed. Brand, Hailey, Harris; NY (Norton), 1986; Mosco Carner, *Alban Berg*, London (Duckworth), 1983.

Arthur (Victor) BERGER A member of *Copland's Young Composers Group in 1930s NY, he was, like many of that time and place, a *Boulanger pupil torn between *Stravinsky and *Schoenberg. Until 1957 he composed *neo-classically, sharing an idiom with Irving *Fine. For the next five years he wrote *serially, then combined both modes. *Chamber Music for 13 Players* (1956), his transitional work, is an intriguing freeze-frame of a composer teetering on the brink of decision.

> *b.* NY, 15.v.12; music critic NY 1943–53; founded *Perspectives of New Music* journal 1962; prof. at Brandeis U. 1953–; *other works*: woodwind quartet (1941), Serenade concertante (1944), string quartet (1958), string trio (1980).

Jean BERGER German refugee in Latin America, he wrote a choral *Brazilian Psalm* (1941) and *Caribbean concerto* for harmonica, before moving to the US.

> *b.* Hamm, Westphalia, 27.ix.09; st with *Wellesz and Louis Aubert; fled to France, Poland and Brazil, settling in US 1943, taught Middlebury College and U. of Illinois and Colorado; *other works*: dramatic cantata *The Fiery Furnace* (1962).

Theodor BERGER Pupil of Franz *Schmidt, he had an urge to smash orchestras into fragments. *Malinconia* for 27-part string orch. sounds romantic nonetheless, portraying the landscape of lower Austria. His four symphonies have descriptive titles – 'chronic', 'homeric', 'parabolic' and 'seasonal' – and briefly excited the interest of *Furtwängler and *Stokowski.

> *b.* Traismauer, Lower Austria, 18.v.05;

Erik BERGMAN Father of Finnish modernism, Bergman (pronounced 'Beriman') learned serialism from *Vogel but was never a ragged-toned radical and wrote music of Sibelian clarity and bleakness. *Aubade* (Helsinki, 20.xi.59) was Finland's first fully-serial orchestral piece. He gradually abandoned *12-note composition in a quest for sounds that imitated nature. The flute concerto *Birds in the Morning* (Warsaw, 18.ix.79) is among his most fetching creations. *Lemminkäinen* (Helsinki, 5.viii.85) is his weightiest work. He strove for new vocal textures, the cleverest of which are buried in light-hearted offerings like *Bim Bam Bum* (Uppsala, 23.iv.77). In his 70s Bergman wrote an opera, *The Singing Tree*.

> *b.* Uusikaarlepyy, Finland, 24.xi.11; taught Sibelius Academy 1963–76; *other works*: piano concerto (Helsinki, 16.ix.81), violin concerto (Mainz, 11.v.84), *Bardo Thödol* (from Tibetan Book of the Dead, for chorus, soloists and orch., Helsinki, 19.v.75); *Fåglarna (The Birds*, chorus/percussion,

1963); string quartet (Kuhmo, 21.vii.82), *Borealis* for 2 pianos and percussion (Washington, D.C., 19.xi.83).

Luciano BERIO Lucky Luciano had the outstanding good fortune to meet and marry a formidable instrument that enabled him to extend vocal fantasy. During his years with Cathy *Berberian (1950–66), he veered from ear-prickling settings of 11 quasi-*Folksongs* (1964, for mezzo and seven insts.), two of them Berio originals, to the enthralling *Sequenza III* (1966), in which aspects of everyday life were melded into music less artificially than, say, by *Strauss in his domestic self-portraiture. Coughs, sobs, laughter and mouth-clicks, sounds never notated before, rolled wave-like into coloratura singing and out again. It expressed the integrity of music and life 44 varied emotions voiced in 7½ minutes. At one time it seemed only Mrs Berio could make these sounds; today the piece is routinely sung. Berio claimed to have taught Cathy certain techniques, such as the 'girl-bird' mimicry of Italian rural tradition, but it was her virtuosity that unleashed his creativity and he happily acknowledged his Italianate admiration for fiery showmanship. The vocal Sequenza was one of a running series (1958–) of ten works for various solo instruments. The 7th, for Heinz *Holliger's oboe (1969) was singularly dazzling. It was obvious from these pieces that Berio was a composer who, unlike certain fellow-avantgardists, actually liked musicians and their instruments.

A second seminal influence was friendship with the semiologist Umberto Eco, famed for his medieval thriller, *The Name of the Rose*, and the poet Eduardo Sanguinetti. Eco alerted Berio to the onomatopoeic nature of poetry – sounds imitating nature – and helped him discover the musical naturalism of the 11th chapter of *Ulysses*. *Ommagio a Joyce* (1958) was a breakthrough *electronic composition compiled on tape from Cathy's tri-lingual reading of passages from *Ulysses*; in *Visage* (1961), she gave a two-track onomatopaeic 20-minute depiction of a human life-cycle.

Sanguinetti underlined the importance of everyday words. *A-Ronne* (1974), a radio documentary for five actors, was not so much a recitation or dramatization of a Sanguinetti text, more an analysis of common words in several languages, a new kind of *sprechgesang. Cries of London (1974) was a harmonic realization for eight voices of the calls of street vendors. In these works and Circles (1960), a setting of e e cummings poems for female voices, harp and two percussion, Berio showed a Janáček-like fascination with speech modes and the lives of ordinary people. Berberian's voice was essential equipment and, nearly two decades after their divorce, he was distraught at her death. Movingly, the Requies (1984) he wrote in her memory, eliminates the human voice: a chamber orchestra plays quietly around and about a hidden tune, giving a nagging sense of something tragically missing.

He was ever stimulated by close relationships. Musically he was heir to a long line of village organists, the son of a piano player in cinemas and light orchestras. Immunized paternally against the operatic imperative, he was instructed by *Ghedini in the instrumental and vocal resources of the distant baroque era. An eight-week encounter with *Dallapiccola at Tanglewood in 1952, two Italians in America, was particularly formative. Berio composed five piano variations on a three-note cell from Dallapiccola's masterpiece, Il prigioniero, and adopted his lyrical soundworld for the transcendently beautiful Chamber Music (1953) for female voice, cello and harp, on Joyce texts.

Bruno *Maderna, the second don of Italian modernism, introduced him to *Darmstadt where Berio enlisted in the vanguard of electronic trials. In Différences (1959), he was among the first to combine unreliable prerecorded tapes with live musicians – flute, clarinet, viola, cello and harp. With Maderna in 1955 he set up an electronic studio at Italian Radio (RAI) in Milan and in 1974 joined *Boulez's inaugural team at *IRCAM. But he was never an ideologist of progress or a salesman of computer wonders and tapes account for about one-eighth of his 100-odd published works. Technology was simply a means to a sonic end, which usually clings to a tuneful source. He stood in relation to Boulez as Berg did to Webern: the acceptable face of modernist revolution.

Polyglot, witty and civilized, he spent a decade (1962–71) in the US teaching at Mills College, Harvard and Juilliard. It was in New York that he won celebrity with Sinfonia (10.x.1968), a collagist tapestry containing snippets from more than a dozen composers, including a chunk of *Mahler's Resurrection Symphony – peppered with cries of 'keep going' – and texts by Martin Luther King, Samuel Beckett and Parisian campus walls. It split conservative resistance to new music; one leading critic hailed it as 'one of the musics of the future', another wrote simply, 'it stinks'. At a distance of quarter of a century, it sounds charmingly naïve, a piece, unlike Mahler's, of its time.

Although his best-known and most-recorded work, Sinfonia is something of an aberration, for Berio was never so wildly eclectic again. In 1975, when he wrote Coro for 40 voices and instruments, he reverted to the manner of Folksongs. It marked also a return to concert conventionality, with concertos for two pianos (1973), cello (1977) and the misleading titled Voci (1984), perhaps the most engaging viola concerto since Bartók's. A web of orchestral sound twined around faintly-heard Sicilian folk-songs, it is rich in visual and aural stimuli as two small orchestras bounce sounds back and forth off each other and at one point the soloist strums his viola like a guitar.

His comments on opera were generally derogatory. In the satirical Opera (1970), he composed a tenor who cannot sing and a chorus of mothers singing their babies, and the audience, to sleep. Un rè in ascolto (A king in waiting, Salzburg, 7.viii.84) has more in common with circus and mixed-media events than traditional opera, though its instrumental base is uncommonly fine. In the 1980s Berio seemed as uncertain of the direction music was taking as any of his generation. Outraged by *minimalism, he condemned all *American music from Ives and Varèse onwards as uneventful. He continued to produce lyrical works of no outstanding novelty and opted to pursue financial security with unremarkable orchestrations of songs by Schubert, Mahler, Verdi and de Falla.

b. Oneglia, Italy, 24.x.25; st Milan Cons. 1946–51; gave up piano ambitions at 19 after hand accident; married (1) US-Armenian singer Cathy Berberian (2) Japanese psychologist Susan Oyama (3) Israeli musicologist Talia Packer; *other works*: concertino (1949), *Opus No. Zoo* for woodwind quintet (1951), *Mutazioni* (for tape, 1955), *Epifanie* for voice and orch. (1961), *Passagio* (1962, theatre piece after Sanguinetti), *Calmo* in memoriam Bruno Maderna (1974). *Formazioni* (1987), string quartet (Vienna, 21.x.91).

(Sir) Lennox (Randall Francis) BERKELEY The leading Francophile among British musicians, Berkeley was directed by Nadia *Boulanger to his timbre: a hint of *Ravel on a *neoclassical Stravinskian base. He befriended *Britten at the 1936 Barcelona *ISCM and jointly composed, the *Mont Juic* suite: he won attention in his own right with a pastoral *Serenade for strings* (1939) that reflected a Virginia Woolf landscape against darkening skies of war. His two piano concerto (1948) and Sinfonietta (1950) reflected close links with *Poulenc but a long-gestated opera on *Nelson* (14.ii.53) lacked dramatic thrust and caused Berkeley to be relegated into the ranks of also-rans. An amiable, private man, he included among his pupils *Maw, *Bedford and *Tavener.
    b. Boar's Hill, nr. Oxford, 12.v.03; st French and philosophy at Oxford, converted to R.C. faith 1928; st with *Boulanger 1927–32; BBC producer 1942–45; taught Royal Academy of Music (1946–68); *d.* London, 26.xii.89. *other works*: four symphonies, violin concerto (for *Menuhin, 1961), guitar concerto (for Julian Bream, 1974).

His son, **Michael BERKELEY**, has composed an anti-nuclear oratorio, *Or Shall We Die* (1982), with the novelist Ian McEwan and a fluent clarinet concerto (1991).
    b. London 29.v.48;

Berlin A cultural backwater during the 19th century, the capital of the Weimar Republic became from 1918 to 1933 a melting pot for new ideas and art forms, from collage to cinema. While political blood was shed on the streets, rival musical ideologies co-existed in relative peace. *Busoni and *Schoenberg respected one another; *Berg, whose *Wozzeck* première in 1925 marked the birth of modern opera, had no animosity for *Weill, whose *Threepenny Opera* took a radically different direction. Both employed *jazz rhythms that were all the rage.
    Otto *Klemperer at the Kroll Opera directed new music of all kinds from conservatism (Hindemith) to neo-classicism (Stravinsky), from naturalism (Janáček) to atonality (Schoenberg). Stage direction and design at the three major opera houses were adventurous and some concert societies operated on socialist principles. Modernism was banned by the Nazis and did not recover after the War. The communist sector had *Brecht, *Eisler and *Dessau and Walter Felsenstein (1901–75) at the Komische Oper raised a generation of inventive stage directors. In West Berlin, concert life under Herbert von *Karajan was sleek and conservative; the foremost composer was *Blacher. After reunification in 1989, attempts to restore Berlin as an artistic centre were dogged by financial restraints. Throughout the century, the Berlin Philharmonic was a showcase international orchestra.

Irving BERLIN America's greatest hits were written by a man who only played the black keys and was virtually unable to read music. A refugee from Russian pogroms, he became rich with 'Alexander's Ragtime Band' in 1911, sold over 100 million records of 'White Christmas' (1942) and produced the nation's unofficial anthem, 'God Bless America' (1918), while serving with the US forces in Europe; he donated its royalties to the Boy Scouts Association. Another hit, 'Always' (1925), was a wedding gift to his second wife. He had his piano fitted with a lever that enabled him to play any note on the black keys. In 1973 he gave his piano to the Smithsonian Institute but continued composing until his 100th birthday. His total output was 1500 songs. Jerome Kern once said: 'Irving Berlin has no place in American music. He is American music.'
    b. Tyumen, Russia, 11.v.1888; emigrated 1893; *d.* NY, 22.ix.89.

Lord BERNERS A sometime British diplomat, Berners fitted his Rolls-Royce with a piano and dyed the pigeons on his estate to match the day's dinner menu. His music was frothy, eclectic and elegant. *Diaghilev commissioned *The Triumph of Neptune* (London, 3.xii.26), and Balanchine choreographed his *Luna Park* (1930). Addicted to self-parody, he wrote *Trois petites marches funèbres* (1914) for a statesman, a pet canary and a rich aunt, and prefaced the UK concert première of *Rite of Spring* (7.vi.21) with a *Fantaisie espagnole* that mocked other composers' pseudo-Iberianisms. He painted proficiently and was wholly unserious about anything.

b. Arley Park, Bridgnorth, UK, 18.ix.1883, as Gerald Hugh Tyrwhitt-Wilson; became 14th Baron Berners in 1918; *d.* Faringdon House, Berkshire, 19.iv.50. *other works*: comic opera *Le Carrosse du Saint Sacrement* (1923), *A Wedding Bouquet*, ballet with Gertrude Stein (London, 27.iv.36); film score for *Nicholas Nickleby* (1947); two autobiographies and six novels.

(Louis) Leonard BERNSTEIN One of the century's central personalities, it is difficult to assess where his contribution was greatest. As a composer, he left an enduring mark on both concert and popular music. He was also a highly-charged conductor and compelling teacher. He elucidated musical ideas with enviable ease and introduced to musical discourse ideas from disparate philosophies. No other musician of his time could explain Schoenberg and Schopenhauer to an enraptured audience of ten-year-olds, studding his presentations with examples from the Bible, the Beatles and the Bhagavad-Gita. As a communicator, he was without equal. Several of his works seem destined for a contentious immortality, their merits argued afresh at each performance. One composition, *West Side Story*, is an unarguable masterpiece.

In terms of public persona, Bernstein was the first native-born American to lead the NY Philharmonic and the first US-reared musician to captivate Vienna. His 12 years with the Philharmonic were the most exciting in its history, winning young fans for *Mahler and performing Stravinsky and Nielsen, Sibelius and Shostakovich, with irresistible conviction. He bounded into the rostrum like a gnat-stung gymnast, a mannerism copied from his predecessor, *Mitropoulos. His interpretations veered according to momentary mood; a pianist might find his concerto taken at half the rehearsal tempo, or twice as fast, because Bernstein was on a high or low at the time. In Europe, he personified the romantic artist prey to tempestuous passions. He even got away in Berlin with changing the words of Beethoven's 9th symphony, to mark the fall of the Wall.

His 'joy of music' presentations and 1973 Harvard lectures, both internationally televised, were object lessons in conveying

Bernstein (r.) and Sondheim rehearsing the chorus from West Side Story

difficult concepts to an intelligent mass audience. He courted public attention obsessively and paid a high price when his lurid emotional life was exposed by prurient biographers. He slept little and radiated high energy. When Bernstein blew into a room, no-one left it untouched. This nuclear combustion stemmed from dichotomies in his restless character. His duality was revealed in celestial and earthy utterances within one and the same sentence in a life torn between public morality and private hedonism. His primary impulse was an instinctual urge to reach out, to touch, to teach.

Bernstein's serious music suffered from his gaudy celebrity and was maimed by Broadway success. Yet his music, so complex in its apparent simplicity, must be viewed as a creative whole. To pigeon-hole any work of Bernstein's is to lose sight of his renaissance-man quality.

The son of Russian-Jewish immigrants, he was nurtured by the conductors Fritz Reiner, Mitropoulos and, above all, *Koussevitsky. In 1943, aged 25, he emerged simultaneously as a symphonist, songwriter, ballet and Broadway composer, and neophyte conductor whose last-minute national début made the front page of the *New York Times*. That same November month, his cheeky song-cycle *I Hate Music* was heard at New York Town Hall. Then came his first symphony, titled *Jeremiah* (Pittsburgh, 28.i.44), mourning the destruction of Jerusalem in Jewish liturgical tropes woven into a 25-minute dissertation with lamentative mezzo finale. It won the music critics' award as best new work of the year. His ballet, *Fancy Free* was staged at the Metropolitan (18.iv.44) and moved to Broadway as *On The Town* (28.xii.44). It brandished a new anthem, 'New York, New York, it's a Wonderful Town' – a confident cry repeated in his second musical, *Wonderful Town* (NY, 25.ii.53).

While the fluency of his writing earned comparisons with *Gershwin, his sophisticated ideas had no precedent in popular music. He wrote best under deadline pressure. *Wonderful Town* was composed in a month; when he took time off to compose 'great' works, the results were feebler.

Success went to his head. He was the golden boy in a fertile generation, desirable to men and women alike. In tandem with intoxication ran an ineluctable sense of guilt. While he was toast of the town, his people in Europe were being carted to gas chambers. These reflections found echoes in *Auden's contemporary poem, *The Age of Anxiety*, the theme and title of his 2nd symphony for piano and orchestra (Boston, 4.iv.49, cond. *Koussevitsky). Its dolorous opening dialogue between two clarinets gives way to solo pianism of Ravellian clarity. It is the least Mahlerian, least autobiographical, of his music but manifests its author unmistakably in fearsome collaborations and collisions of piano and celesta and its awesome, lightly-scanned range of ideas. The symphony is somewhat skeletal, waiting to be fleshed out by a conclusive intellectual stance.

At *Tanglewood, he premiered Messiaen's *Turangalîla* and conducted the first US performance of Britten's *Peter Grimes*, both of which extended his compositional means. He hoped to succeed Koussevitsky at Boston but was ruled out by his homosexual and leftist inclinations. Under McCarthyite oppression, his passport withdrawn by a paranoid administration, he went into a shell with a half-baked opera, *Trouble in Tahiti* (Brandeis U., 12.vi.52) and a movie score for Elia Kazan's *On the Waterfront* that oddly quoted the gravitas of Mahler's 9th.

His *Serenade* for violin and orchestra (Venice, 12.ix.54), modelled on Plato's *Symposium* and vestigially on *Berg's concerto, contains some of his bitterest utterances in an introverted mood that Britten must have found familiar. He married and raised a family but, pushing 40, was in professional limbo. Then came a second annus mirabilis, 1956, with two Broadway hits and the leadership of the New York Philharmonic.

Candide (Boston, 29.x.56) was a comparative flop with only 229 performances. It was a high-risk gambit to mix comedy with Voltairean anti-optimism – 'all is *not* for the best in the best of all possible worlds' – the more so since Bernstein was subtly attacking McCarthyism in a hidden subtext. The show underwent numerous metamorphoses over the next quarter of a century. A 1973 version for Brooklyn's Chelsea Theater cut the philosophy and half the score; New York City Opera's 1982 revival restored the musical cuts but reshuffled the numbers; Scottish Opera (1988) replaced Lillian Hellman's dialogue with new narration by Bernstein and John Wells that led the way to a final, resounding version which was the last of his works that Bernstein lived to conduct. Despite its messy history, *Candide*'s energy is unmistakable and its eclecticism undisguised – everything from Randall *Thompson choruses to Gilbert and Sullivan patter arias. The overture could not have come from any other composer. Only Bernstein could switch seamlessly from swing to smooch, pathos to joy, and back again twice in four minutes. If ever he wrote a signature tune, it was the *Candide* overture.

Into *West Side Story* he put everything he technically knew – a 'Cool' fugue with a 12-note row, high-rise chords in 'Somewhere', jazzcopations in 'Jet Song', Latin rhythms in 'America', a grand operatic aria in 'Maria' – yet knowledge was worn throughout with fetching humility.

It may well be that Bernstein's emotional excesses were tempered structurally by his lyricist, Stephen *Sondheim, and his choreographer, Jerome Robbins, but the whole was his own and with it Bernstein effectively killed off the Broadway musical. No subsequent show could match the sublimity and sophistication of *West Side Story* which, in time, found its way into formal opera houses.

As hero of the Great White Way and Carnegie Hall, he was New York's equivalent to John F. Kennedy in the White House – young, brash, brimful of vigour. He identified with Kennedy's Camelot and was devastated when its figurehead fell, followed by his brother and the civil rights leader Martin Luther King. As America slumped into Vietnam war and rightwing Republicanism, Bernstein was bugged by the CIA.

While head of the orchestra, he lost his touch as a composer and, with one exception, never regained it. Conductor and composer could not, seemingly, co-exist. He wrote a 3rd symphony on the Jewish Kaddish prayer of mourning, but it missed the intended mark in both the original (Tel Aviv, 10.xii.73) and revised (Mainz, 25.viii.77) versions. His *Mass* for the Kennedys offended the Pope with puerile banalities – 'God loves all simple things' – and sexually heated rhythms. A *Songfest* for the US bicentennial (Washington, 11.x.77) mocked US hypocrisies. The reworking of his failed opera into *A Quiet Place* (1983) was poorly received.

The single work that retained his untamed effervescence was *Chichester Psalms* (NY, 15.vii.65), an orchestral setting of Hebrew texts for boy treble and mixed choir in an English cathedral which, between rhythmic outer movements reminiscent of *Rite of Spring*, achieved an oasis-like centre in which the Lord is shepherd. The Mahlerian irony so acidly underscored in his early works gave way to tender sentiment. *Chichester Psalms*, unaffectedly devout, is singable by any musical child.

In his last two decades, Bernstein wandered the world. He summered at Tanglewood and founded sister-festivals in Germany and Japan, revelling in the elixir of young admirers. Against the icy remoteness of *Karajan, he restored a pulsating warmth to musical performance. 'I am a musician who performs various musical functions from composing to teaching, among them what is known in the commercial world as conducting,' he said.

In his dying year, he returned to the mode he knew best, a little set of *Arias and Barcarolles* that sang out the poignant comedy of the human condition in a late-night dialogue between man and wife, and the coda of a Schubertian lullaby. When he died, men and women wept in the streets of New York.

b. Lawrence, Massachusetts, 25.viii.18; st with (inter alia) Piston, Edward Burlingame Hill, Isabelle Vengerova, Randall *Thompson; debut NY Philharmonic, 14.xi.43; music adviser Israel Philharmonic 1948–9; professor of music at Brandeis U. 1951–6; cond. NY Philharmonic 1957–69; *d.* New York, 14.x.90. *other orch. works*: Prelude, Fugue and Riffs (1949), *Dybbuk* ballet (1974), *Divertimento* (Boston, 25.ix.80), *Halil* (1981).

Bib: Joan Peyser, *Leonard Bernstein: A Biography*, New York, 1987.

Günther BIALAS Oblivious to the raging clash of doctrines and dogmas, Bialas took whatever technique he deemed suitable for a particular work and paid no dues to any school. He has written in romantic, atonal and serial styles for German audiences, his central works being three short operas and concertos for viola (1940), violin (1949) and cello (1962).
  b. Bilschowitz, Silesia, 19.vii.07; taught Munich 1959–72.

Antonio BIBALO Norwegian composer of Italian birth and Slovak origins, he studied in London with *Lutyens and applied himself to writing *12-tone dramatic works, frequently for television. His opera *Macbeth* was presented at the 1990 *ISCM in Oslo, its gritty score adding no extra dimension to Shakespeare's text, sung in English.
  b. Trieste, Italy, 18.i.22; Norwegian citizen 1968; *other works: The Smile at the Foot of the Ladder* (after Henry Miller story, Hamburg State Opera, 6.iv.65), *Miss Julie* (after Strindberg; Aarhus, Denmark, 8.ix.75); ballet *Pinocchio* (Hamburg, 17.i.69); three piano concertos and a sonata (1974).

Les Biches Ballet and concert suite by *Poulenc. fp: Monte Carlo, 6.i.24.

big band jazz Derogatory generic term for the ever-growing ensembles of *Ellington and *Whiteman that climaxed in the blaze of Glenn *Miller. By concert standards these were chamber ensembles but in jazz terms anything over a dozen players was an uncomfortable crowd.

Billy Budd *Britten's naval opera, centering on a captain torn over issues of guilt and innocence. fp: Covent Garden, 1.xii.51.

Billy the Kid Wild-west ballet, later suite, by Copland, adopting slightly revisionist stance on official version of the outlaw's death. fp: Chicago, 16.viii.38.

birds Birdsong penetrated the concert hall in *Respighi's *Pines of Rome* and was imitated in his *The Birds*. *Messiaen catalogued many species and borrowed their tunes. Cage invented a *Bird Cage* (1972) –

'12 tapes to be distributed by a single performer in a space in which people are free to move and birds to fly.'

(Sir) Harrison BIRTWISTLE At first hearing, the listener is hard pressed to place Birtwistle in any known category of composer. He is neither tonal nor serialist, romantic or ascetic, reactionary or avant-garde. He certainly does not sound like an English composer. His music is rhythmic, propulsive, often loud and angry; yet, at the same time, it has a shy, warm and humane quality.
  Birtwistle is a rarity in modern music, a composer whose sound is wholly distinctive – once heard, never forgotten. As a child wandering the rural fringe of an industrial town he 'heard a music that didn't exist' and set out to find it. Aged 11, he wrote a piece for clarinet and mime that was the archetype for all that followed, combining vivid theatricality with a personal sound. As a student in *Manchester, he joined a group of pro-*serialist rebels but did not submit anything for performance until he was long out of college, nor did he ever try to write like *Webern. He liked late *Stravinsky – *Agon* was a lasting influence – and unwittingly shared *Janáček's vision of nature in the raw. Yet, from the outset, the music Birtwistle wrote was uniquely his own.
  The division between opera and concert works is misleading in his case. His instrumental music is highly theatrical while his operas have a musical rather than a textual thrust. *Punch and Judy* (Aldeburgh 8.vi.68), his operatic debut, so outraged *Britten with its brutality that the senior composer walked out. Its evocation of childhood terrors rang demonstrably truer than Britten's tender nostalgia. A child of its time, this Clockwork Orange of an opera contains more killings than *Bluebeard* and *Lulu* put together as Punch carves his way through a baby, Judy, a doctor, a lawyer and other obstacles to his amorous ambition. The finale claims it was all a comedy, a commentary on the nature of opera, but *Punch* is an angry young man's opera and one that appeals to young audiences; its rhythms and sing-song chants lodge immovably in the memory.

Its successors, *Down by the Greenwood Side* (Brighton, 8.v.69) and *Bow Down* (London, 5.vii.77), were likewise founded on savage legend yet, at their loudest, remain listenable.

Birtwistle's first large-scale opera, *The Mask of Orpheus* (London, ENO, 21.v.86) burst like *Peter Grimes* on receptive terrain, to fertilize an English operatic renaissance. Birtwistle turned the myth into variations on a familiar tale, perceived from different angles and sung in the finale in an imaginary language. The score had electronic episodes devised at *IRCAM with the New Zealand composer Barry *Anderson and contained ethereal movements of timeless mourning. *Orpheus* was the first major opera house production to use computer sound technology, and the effect was dramatic and unforced. The curtain came down after six performances, ostensibly for financial reasons, and the opera was not seen again.

Another chamber opera, *Yan Tan Tethera* (London, 5.viii.86), accompanied by strings alone, was less gripping. The poet Tony Harrison had written a northern tale of two rival shepherds who shouted at one another in dialect; the rest of the cast was mainly sheep. Birtwistle spent the next five years writing what may be recognized as his masterpiece. *Gawain* (Covent Garden, 30.v.91), the travails of an innocent knight at King Arthur's moribund court, refined and enriched the Orpheus sound without technological embellishment. Orpheus's wail is echoed in Gawain's protestation, 'I am not that hero' and the percussive passages possess a ferality that Stravinsky would have been proud to acknowledge.

But the substance of the score is a sumptuous orchestral texture allied to ethereal soprano duets and mock-medieval chants that give the work a character and richness all its own. These monkish choruses are neither imitation nor pastiche but creative reinvention, Birtwistle's neo-mediaeval riposte to Stravinsky's *neo-classicism (his concert output contains previous reworkings of 14th–15th century motets by Ockeghem and Machaut). Gawain's journey is the moral quest of modern man and his epic resembles a *Parsifal* for our times.

The orchestral Birtwistle is harder to penetrate because less explicit. Easily the most immediate piece is *Endless Parade* (Basle, 1.v.87), a concerto for trumpet, string orchestra and vibraphone which its first soloist, Håkan Hardenberger, proclaimed as the finest trumpet concerto since Haydn's. Its title came from a carnival the composer saw passing at Lucca but the material is not fleeting and fragmentary, rather a multifarious portrait of the human condition held together by a memorable four-note motif. This technique, and its innate preoccupation with life passing by, was devised by Birtwistle in *The Triumph of Time* (London, 1.vi.72), a substantial symphonic work that unfolds slowly as if it were being created in public by Breughel – after whose engraving of the same name it is titled. Taking as its essence the purpose of life on earth, it stands in direct descent to Mahler's *Resurrection Symphony*.

Another derivation from the visual arts was *Melencolia 1*, for clarinet, harp and two string orchestras (Glasgow, 18.ix.76), recalling a copper engraving made by Dürer when he was 43 and profoundly depressed; Birtwistle was the same age and in a parallel frame of mind. Birtwistle has described his work as a corrective to the prevailing abuse of music: 'Because of the disposable nature of our society, music has lost its currency. It's something we switch on and don't listen to . . . You have to listen to my music or you have to switch it off.' At the same time, the stimulus for all his music is theatrical and ritualistic, meaning that the music is far from being abstract. Several works are connected by title and content to operas-in-progress. Others, like *Earth Dances* for Mahlerian-sized orchestra, explicitly reveal their natural imagery while retaining enough dramatic surprises to captivate an audience. His interest in the arts of ancient Greece attained an apotheosis in . . . *agm* . . . Paris, 9.iv.79, cond. Boulez), a half-hour vocal piece based on Sapphic verses, in which tiny fragments of text and sound are merged mysteriously into a coherent whole.

Another key work is *Carmen Arcadiae Mechanicae Perpetuum* (London, 24.i.78): a Stravinskian rhythmic drive is wound like clockwork around an almost-discernible nursery rhyme or fairground tune. It is an antidote to *minimalism and a statement of faith in musical tradition. Birtwistle, never succumbing to passing fashion, persisted in his lonely way with the eternal prerogative of the artist to take an individualist stance.

b. Accrington, Lancs, 15.vii.34; formed New Music Manchester Group with *Goehr, Maxwell *Davies, John Ogdon and Elgar Howarth 1953; worked in menial jobs and as music teacher in girls' school; married 1958, three sons; studied at Princeton and U. of Colorado 1966–67; formed Pierrot Players with Davies 1967; taught at US colleges 1973–75; music director of National Theatre, London, 1975–83, writing music for a dozen productions, including *Amadeus*; moved to remote French village of Lunegarde 1984; *other works*: *Tragoedia* (20.viii.65), *Chorales for Orchestra* (14.ii.67), *Nomos* (23.viii.68), *Verses for Ensembles* (12.ii.69), *An Imaginary Landscape* (2.vi.71, cond. Boulez), *Grimethorpe Aria* for brass band (Harrogate, 15.viii.73), *Silbury Air* (9.iii.77); *Nenia: the Death of Orpheus* (20.xi.70), *The Fields of Sorrow* (Dartington, 7.viii.71).

bitonality Using two keys at the same time, as Stravinsky did from Petrushka onwards.

Julius BITTNER Viennese judge who founded the music journal *Der Merker*, assessed Mahler's estate for probate, obtained Schoenberg's release from active service in the First War and composed some 20 fairytale operas and other stage works, mostly in Viennese dialect. His Great Mass and Te Deum (Vienna, 2.ii.26) was considered a cornerstone of Austrian art and is still performed.

b. Vienna, 9.iv.1874; *d.* there, 9.i.39. *other works*: two symphonies, two symphonic poems, two string quartets.

Boris BLACHER A central personality in post-Hitler Berlin, Blacher revelled so uninhibitedly in stylistic freedoms that his individuality got lost in the process. He wrote 21 operas and ballets and numerous concert works with a facility for rapid and ingenious orchestration that was showcased in his *Variations*, opus 26, on Paganini's hackneyed theme (Leipzig, 27.xi.47). In his version, the theme metamorphosed into march rhythms, *blues, bleak lamentations and blazing affirmations, amounting to a 15-minute concerto for orchestra. It led Blacher to his sole technical invention – *variable metres, in which the time signature (or rhythm) of a piece is varied according to a predetermined arithmetical formula. In effect, he applied Webern's total serialism to pulsation. The system was introduced in his piano *Ornamente* (1950) and *Orchester-Ornament* (Venice, 15.ix.53) and filtered into the thinking of *Boulez.

Born in China of part Russian and Jewish parentage, Blacher passed his adolescence in Siberia before studying architecture and mathematics in Berlin. Hot jazz permeated his opus 1, *Jazzkoloraturen* (1922, for soprano, altosax and bassoon), and recurred throughout his music, notably in Concertante Musik (Berlin 6.xii.37), two poems for jazz quartet (NY, 14.xi.58) and the opera *Rosamunde Floris* (Berlin, 21.ix.60). He lived untouched through the Nazi era, staging harmonically innocuous operas in Kassel, Krefeld and Wuppertal (*Fest im Süden*, 4.ii.35; *Harlekinade*, 14.ii.40; *Fürstin Tarakanowa*, 5.ii.41), a symphony in Berlin (5.ii.39) and a concerto for string orchestra in Hamburg (18.x.42). After the War he became professor of composition at Berlin's Hochschule für Musik and in 1953 its director. His pupils included von *Einem, whose early operas he co-scripted, Aribert Reimann and the Israeli Noam Sheriff. He set up a seminar in electronic music at the city's technical university.

Blacher enjoyed brief notoriety with two operas – *Die Nachtschwalbe* (The Night Swallow*, Leipzig, 22.ii.48) which dealt with prostitution, and *Abstrakte Oper Nr 1* (Mannheim, 17.x.53), a plotless allegory devised with Werner *Egk that was deemed 'the worst opera ever written'. He applied serial techniques strikingly in the Requiem (Vienna, 11.vi.59) but an attempt to repeat the Paganini hit with variations on a theme by Muzio Clementi (3rd piano concerto, Berlin, 4.x.61) was unsuccessful.

b. Niu-chang, China, 6.i.03; *d.* Berlin, 30.i. 75. *other works*: pacifist chamber opera *Romeo und Julia* (Berlin, 1947); incidental music and ballets to standard repertory plays; three piano concertos for his wife, Gerty Herzog, and an intriguingly complex cello concerto (1964).

David (Leonard) BLAKE *Eisler-ite British composer whose two works at English National Opera aroused extra-musical controversy. The first, *Toussaint l'ouverture* (28.ix.77), dealt with a slaves' revolution in Haiti and took as its theme Aimé Césaire's maxim: 'no race has a monopoly of beauty, of intelligence, of strength'. A related orchestral work, *Rise Dove* (1983), urgently supported the black consciousness movement. His second opera, *The Plumber's Gift* (23.v.89), was an assault on Thatcherite conservatism, set in a seaside boarding house with the television blaring cleverly parodied extracts from Mahler's abandoned opera, *Wilhelm Ratcliff*. Academic by profession and *serialist by confession, Blake derived a social conscience from Eisler and exotic sonorities from *Messiaen, developing a knack for direct communication with an audience – albeit one of above-average intelligence.

b. London, 2.ix.36; prof. at York U. 1976–; *other works*: Chamber symphony (in memoriam Hanns Eisler, 1966), *In Praise of Krishna* for soprano and ensemble (1973), violin concerto (1976), *Cantata in Homage Nelson Mandela* (1982).

Howard BLAKE A TV Christmas perennial, *The Snowman* (1982), generated untold wealth for its populist composer. Around the six-note theme of its hit-song 'Walking in the Air' was a score of derivative banality worthy of *Lloyd Webber, though better worked. At its best, it recalled Britten – the moodiness of *Peter Grimes* rather than his children's pieces.

Blake's simplicity attracted a commission to write a bland piano concerto with a pop-ballad theme for the Princess of Wales's 30th birthday (London, Royal Festival Hall, 19.v.91). An hour-long dramatic oratorio *Benedictus* (Worth Abbey, Sussex, 10.v.80) aspired somewhat higher in evoking the social life of a medieval monastery with tuneful and unsentimental music.

b. London, 1938; st with *Ferguson; *other works*: clarinet concerto (30.v.85), *Diversions for cello* and orch. (29.iii.89); *Shakespeare Songs* (1991).

Oskar Gottlieb BLARR Jerusalem sounds, church bells and Jewish shofar blasts decorated a poignant 1981 sonata by this German organist, who produced a small Lieder cycle for soprano, harp and organ on a similar theme. His music is unsophisticated but heartfelt, especially in the setting of an Else Lasker-Schüler poem, 'Ich suche aller Landen einer Stadt'.

b. Düsseldorf, 1934; organist at Neanderkirche 1961–81;

Leo BLECH The German opera conductor wrote six late-romantic epics, of which *Aschenbrödel* (1905) retains a following.

b. Aachen, 21.iv.1871; st with *Humperdinck; cond. Berlin Staatsoper 1926–37, Riga 1937–41, Stockholm 1941–49, Berlin City Opera 1949–53; *d.* Berlin, 25.viii.58.

(Sir) Arthur (Edward Drummond) BLISS Gassed in the First War, Bliss responded with tonal asperities that alarmed his musical countrymen. He was the first Englishman to adopt *Stravinsky's neo-classicism. The *Colour Symphony* (Gloucester, 7.ix.22) sounded moderately modern and *Morning Heroes* (Norwich, 22.x.30), a choral piece mourning his fallen brother and comrades, attained a static raptness in an eighth-century vigil by Li Tai-Po that forms the work's third section. His twenties style proved unprofitable, however, and Bliss discovered a native gift for *Elgar imitations and blowsy ballets – *Checkmate* (Paris, 15.vi.37), *Miracle in the Gorbals* (London, 26.x.44), made him the perfect Master of the Queen's Music (1953–75), ever ready with a facile piece for royal occasions. A piano concerto, written for the New York World Fair (NY, 10.vi.39), enjoyed a short-lived splashy popularity that enabled him to pose equally as a people's composer.

b. London, 2.viii.1891; st with *Stanford, *Vaughan Williams; lived in California 1923–5, 1939–41; *d.* London, 27.iii.75. *other works*: *Adam Zero* (ballet, 1946), *The Olympians* (opera, Covent Garden, 29.ix.49), cello concerto (for *Rostropovich, Aldeburgh, 24.vi.70) Metamorphic Variations (Lon, 21.iv.73, cond. *Stokowski), two string quartets, H. G. Wells film score *Things to Come* (1935).

Marc BLITZSTEIN East Coast, communist, Jewish and bisexual, he was everything America was taught to hate in the McCarthy era. Blitzstein never feared to voice his affinities and died in a brawl with French sailors in a Martinique bar. Born into a Philadelphia banking family, he studied with *Boulanger in Paris and *Schoenberg in Berlin but rejected neo-classical refinement and serial dissonance when he found America gripped by Depression. He joined the Communist Party, studied with *Eisler and worked with *Brecht. He aimed to write songs that workers could sing in their struggle for liberation. *The Cradle will Rock* (NY, 16.vi.37), his seventh stage work after a string of failures, was closed down by a coalition of management, federal government and theatre unions angered by its revolutionary depiction of trouble at a steel mill. Banned from the stage, the cast sang from stalls seats and the composer played a pit piano. Orson Welles directed.

In the Second War, Blitzstein served with the US Air Force in England, wrote a choral *Airborne* symphony (NY, 23.iii.46) to honour the corps and *Freedom Morning* (London, 28.ix.43), celebrating the unsung role of black soldiers. *Regina* (Boston 11.x.49), an opera of Lillian Hellman's Deep South stage hit *The Little Foxes*, contains little more than agitprop to link its few good songs. Against the spirit of the times, he disinterred Brecht and Weill's *Threepenny Opera* and made it bitingly relevant to complacent America. More than mere translation, it sharpened the Berlin score, revived Lotte Lenya's career and ran for years on Broadway.

At the time of his murder, Blitzstein was attemping for the second time to compose an opera for the Metropolitan Opera based on the Sacco and Vanzetti injustice and toying with two Bernard Malamud novels. His songs survive him, many of them long and strident; a late set of e e cummings poems, tender and funny, finds him at his best. Blitzstein's ballads of social conscience foreshadowed America's protest songs of the 1960s. He left an indelible mark on Leonard *Bernstein who borrowed a snippet of *Regina* in *West Side Story* and reverted to Blitzstein protest mode in *Mass*.

b. Philadelphia, 2.iii.05; *d.* Fort-de-France, Martinique, 22.i.64. *other works*: *The Condemned* (first Sacco and Vanzetti opera, 1932), *Reuben, Reuben* (musical, 1955), piano concerto (1931), string quartet (1930), piano sonata (1927).

Ernest BLOCH A composer in search of a country, Bloch was born Swiss, became famous for Jewish themes, spent a decade in Italy and longed to be recognized as an American. *Schelomo* (NY, 3.v.17), a 'Hebraic rhapsody' for cello and orch., avoided overtly Jewish tunes, conveying mystic yearnings through a solo instrument fighting through a *Straussian swamp. *Baal Shem* (1923) and *Abodah* (1929) for violin and piano were definedly Jewish, as was his choral setting of the Sabbath service, *Avodath Hakodesh* (Turin, 12.i.1934) and *Israel* symphony (NY, 3.v.17). The violin concerto (Cleveland, 15.xii.38) opens each movement with an authentic American Indian motif but lapses into Jewish wistfulness before the page is out.

In 1927 Bloch won a contest for a US-oriented work with a rhapsody for chorus and orch. entitled *America* (NY, 20.xii.28). He never gave up hope that its finale would be adopted as the national *anthem. In between national aspirations, Bloch composed a *neo-classical Concerto Grosso for his Cleveland students (1.vi.25). Substituting a modern piano for baroque harpsichord, it hovers agreeably in a musical no-man's-land between Brahms and Rachmaninov. A second, more abstract, Concerto Grosso (BBC London, 11.iv.53) reveals a reflective master of many styles, sometimes resorting to pastiche. His five late string quartets have a Bartók-like granite quality.

b. Geneva, 24.vii.1880; st with Jaques-Dalcroze, *Ysaÿe and Knorr; opera *Macbeth* staged at Paris Opéra-Comique, 30.xi.10; visited US 1916 as conductor for dancer Maud Allan, US citizen 1924; dir. Cleveland Inst. of Music 1920–25, San Francisco Conservatory 1925–30, taught at UCLA 1942–52; *d*. Portland, Oregon, 15.vii.59.
other works: *Three Jewish Poems* (Boston 23.iii.17), symphonic poem *Helvetia* (Chicago, 18.ii.32), *Voice in the Wilderness* (cello/orch, L.A., 21.i.37), *Concerto symphonique* (for piano and orch, Edinburgh, 3.ix.49), E-flat symphony (London, 15.ii.56).

Karl-Birger BLOMDAHL Mover and shaker of Swedish modernism, he formed a 1940s 'Monday Group' that rejected pastoralism and consorted with *Hindemith. A 3rd symphony called *Facetter* that won Blomdahl recognition (Frankfurt *ISCM 24.vi.51) had a *Bergian lyricism; he avoided Webern's radical serialism.

His main achievement was an opera *Aniara* (Stockholm, 31.v.59), hailed as the world's first space opera and staged soon after the initial Soviet sputnik missions. *Aniara*, with text by Sweden's Nobel Laureate, Harry Martinson, did the rounds of Europe's opera houses, but acquired permanence only in Sweden. It recounts a journey to Mars by the last surviving humans, accompanied by a singing computer. Blomdahl's part-*electronic score rose on a slow crescendo into enormous climaxes, which shattered under their accumulated weight and sent splinters of sound flying off into the abyss, only to form again and restart the process. He set up an electronic studio in Stockholm and was head of music at Swedish Radio. His music was published by Schott in Germany and performed more than any other Swede's, but his outlook on music and life remained pessimistic, and he died at 51 while writing an opera in which man is replaced by computers.
b. Växjö, Sweden, 19.x.16; st with *Rosenberg; *d*. Kungsängen, nr. Stockholm, 14.vi.68. *other works*: Comic opera *Herr von Hancken* (1965), ballets *Sisyphus* (1957), *Game* for 8 (1962), orch. suite *Forma Ferritonans* (1961).

blue notes A *blues trick of playing 3rd and 7th degrees of the scale slightly flat.

blues A moody type of *jazz that resists precise locational or notational definition, its shape and sound originating from Black experience on American plantations. Legend has it that the music began as a 'holler' given by a man at the start of a cotton-picking line and echoed all the way down. Its lyrics are morose and the notes are often slurred, giving a sense of gloom. Published as sheet music from 1912, blues assumed a structure of three lines with four bars each. Poor whites in the American south developed their own blues in obvious imitation; the *zydeco strain had French folk origins. Recent thinking suggests that blues did not contribute to jazz, but were a wholly separate music with a longer history and clearer identity. Bill Broonzy and Mamie Smith were first blues stars on record, followed by the unrelated, unequalled Bessie Smith, pianist Memphis Slim, guitarists John Lee Hooker and Lightnin' Hopkins and the electric combo of Muddy Waters in 1940s Chicago.

This urban variant, known as rhythm-and-blues, became the prime factor in *popular music, the starting point for every chart-topper from Elvis *Presley to the *Beatles, from the *Grateful Dead to *Madonna. In concert music, Ravel wrote a blues movement in his 1927 violin sonata, Gershwin mimicked a bluesy wail in *Rhapsody in Blue, *Milhaud picked up its harmonics in *La création du monde* and *Tippett discovered his second style in blues borrowings.

Philippe BOESMANS Belgian *Boulezite, he was a pillar of the Brussels opera under Gérard Mortier's progressive regime and composed *La Passion de Gilles* (28.x.83) to his commission. The opera, a conflict between good and evil, makes its points by subtle repetition rather than violent noise. Later he turned, in *Extases*, to electronic synthesizers.
b. Tongeren, Belgium, 17.v.36; st with *Pousseur; music producer at RTBF radio 1971-; *other works*: *Explosives* (1968) for harp and ten insts; *Multiples* for two pianos and orch., piano concerto (1978), violin concerto (1979).

Le boeuf sur le toit (*The ox on the roof*) Tango-samba ballet by *Milhaud that set the tone, named a café, and provided a catchphrase for jazz age Paris, fp: 21.ii.20.

William BOLCOM Crossover composer between jazz and classics, and between different classical periods and styles, his violin concerto (Saarbrücken, 3.vi.84) has the fence-sitting feel of Stravinsky's east-west Duo Concertant of 1931. His Fantasia Concertante (Salzburg, 26.i.86, cond. Levine) is a straight take-off of Mozart.

The third movement of the 5th symphony (1990) plays counterpoint games with the Wedding March from *Lohengrin*, the Anglican hymn 'Abide with Me' and some snatches of *Tristan* to intimate an ironic *Bergian elegy for dead friends in the concert world. Technical assurance and the desire to impress overshadows any genuine emotion, though the work is far from negligible – of the same type and time as *Corigliano's AIDS symphony. His music theatre piece on monetary greed, *Casino Paradise* (1990), occupies a fertile socio-musical terrain between *Weill and *Bernstein and can be staged with as much relish as *Street Scene*.
> *b*. Seattle, US, 26.v.38; st with *Milhaud; played, duets with jazz legend Eubie Blake (1883–1983) and set William Blake's *Songs of Innocence and Experience*; taught U. of Michigan 1973–; *other works*: Adaptation of The Beggar's Opera (1978), *Ragomania* for orch. (1982), *Commedia for almost-18th century orch*. (1991).

Boléro Remorseless piece by *Ravel in which melody, harmony and tempo are repeated unchanged as the volume increases. 'I have written only one masterpiece – Boléro,' said Ravel. 'Unfortunately, there's no music in it.' fp: Paris, 22.xi.28.

Willem Friderik BON Expressive Dutch composer of sombre, *Bartók-like Concerto for string orch. (1970) and a first symphony based on Edgar Allan Poe's *Fall of the House of Usher* (1970).
> *b*. Amersfoort, Netherlands, 15.vi.40; *d*. Niejeholtpade, 14.iv.83. *other work*: *Passacaglia in Blue* (1972) for 12 wind and double-bass.

The Book of the Hanging Gardens 15 decadent poems by Stefan George set by Schoenberg in 1908 in his new atonal

mode, the acme of *expressionism. fp: Vienna, 14.i.10.

Daniel BÖRTZ Ingmar Bergman's partner in an opera on Euripides' *The Bacchantes* (Stockholm, 2.xi.91) is an austere symphonist with a tendency to long instrumental lines. His nine symphonies (1974–) achieve a saga-like progress toward warmth and light.
> *b*. Hässenholm, Sweden, 8.viii.43; st with Rosenberg, Blomdahl, Lidholm.

Hans-Jürgen von BOSE German cosmopolite whose imported themes satisfied locals but looked ersatz to foreign eyes. *63: Dream Palace* (Munich, vi.90), after a James Purdy novel about brotherly hate in 1950s Chicago, used atmospheric blues and brass without evoking any particular time or place. His orchestral pieces flourished enviable colours but scant substance.
> *b*. Munich, 24.xii.1953; *works*: operas after Pirandello, Ramon del Valle-Inclan, Goethe and Lorca; ballet *Die Nacht aus Blei* (Berlin, 1.xi.81); 1st symphony (Munich, 10.iii.78, cond. *Halffter), *Idyllen* for Berlin Philharmonic centenary (Berlin, 28.iv.83), *Sappho songs* (mezzo and chamber orch., Donaueschingen, 15.x.83, cond. *Eötvös), *. . . other echoes inhabit the garden* (oboe and orch., Donaueschingen, 16.x.87, cond. *Gielen).

Bossa nova 'New bump' Brazilian dance that enjoyed a 1960s vogue.

(Marco) Enrico BOSSI World-famous organist, he wrote an agreeable concerto for his instrument (1908) and died after an exhausting US concert tour.
> *b*. Salò, Italy, 25.iv.1861; *d*. at sea, 20.ii.25.

His son, **Renzo BOSSI,** composed four operas, one on Shakespeare's *Taming of the Shrew* (1925) and another after Oscar Wilde, *Rosa Rossa* (1940).
> *b*. Como, Italy, 9.iv.1883; *d*. Milan, 2.iv.65.

Boston Francophile powerhouse of American music while *Koussevitsky was in charge of the orchestra (1924–49), cultivating confident nationalism and a summer nursery at Tanglewood. While the orchestra lost its taste for adventure, Sarah Caldwell's opera company staged US premières of such cornerstone modernisms as

Zimmermann's *Soldiers* and *Moses and Aron*

André BOUCOURECHLIEV Franco-Bulgarian experimentalist, he wrote a key study of *Stravinsky and composed a series of *Archipels* for varied ensembles, inviting performers to dip in and out of pieces which may be played in different versions at the same concert.

> *b*. Sofia, 28.vii.25; French citizen 1956; prof. at Aix-en-Provence; *other works*: piano concerto (Lisbon, 7.v.75), *Orion* series (1979–83), *Lit de neige* (Paris, 12.xi.84); *Ombres* for 11 strings, based on clips from Beethoven quartets (1970).

Rutland BOUGHTON Would-be English Wagner, he composed a cycle of five grandiose operas on the Arthurian legend and planned to build a Festspielhaus at the shrine of Glastonbury. A pagan opera, *The Immortal Hour* (Glastonbury, 26.viii.14), ran 500 nights in post-War London. When his Arthurian dreams foundered, he retired to a Gloucestershire farm and wrote folkish symphonies and concertos. In 1924 he joined the British Communist Party.

> *b*. Aylesbury, 23.i.1878; *d*. London, 25.i.60. *other works*: *Pioneers*, Walt Whitman cantata for tenor, chorus and orch. (1925), *Deidre* symphony (1927), B-minor symphony (1937), cello sonata (1948).

Lili (Marie-Juliette Olga) BOULANGER Dead at 24, she was preserved as an ideal by a worshipful sister who taught most of America's young composers. Of her chamber music, two violin-piano duos, Nocturne (1911) and Cortège (1914), add a vinegary tinge to *Fauréan lyricism. The real substance lies in her religious works for chorus and orchestra. The 1917 psalm-setting *Du fond de l'abîme* (*From the depths I have called thee*) sustains a breath-catching tension; a *Buddhist prayer* of the same year amounts to a heartfelt plea for peace. The *Pie Jesu* she dictated for her own funeral has a coolly distant, almost other-worldly sonority. She longed to emulate Debussy with a Maeterlinck opera but left two acts incomplete. Devoutly Catholic, deeply depressed – 'at the mercy of an indescribable melancholy' – she was consumed before her talent could mature.

> *b*. Paris, 21.viii.1893, st with Paul Vidal, won Prix de Rome 1913 with *Faust et Hélène*, first woman to do so, but lasted only weeks in Italy before War and ill-health intervened; *d*. Mézy, 15.iii.18.
> *Bib*: L. Rosenstiel, *The Life and Works of Lilli Boulanger*, NY, 1978.

Nadia (Juliette) BOULANGER Her elder sister, was the century's outstanding teacher, also a pioneering conductor and fine pianist. She premiered *Stravinsky's *Dumbarton Oaks* in Washington (1938), was the first to record Monteverdi and the first woman to direct the Boston Symphony and New York Philharmonic. At the keyboard, she gave the first performance of an organ symphony that *Copland wrote for her.

Having abandoned composition on recognizing Lili's superior talent, she devoted herself to bringing out the best from young composers. In Copland's slip-stream came *Piston, *Harris, *Carter and *Glass; her guidance, said *Thomson, helped 'overcome American timidity about self-expression'. British pupils included *Berkeley, *Musgrave and *Maw; *Françaix and *Markevitch were her French alumni. While she taught many styles of composition, including 12-note methods which she deplored, her models were Debussy, Ravel and, above all, her friend Stravinsky. A rigid disciplinarian and Roman Catholic – she once sacked a pupil who divorced – she spent the Second War in the US, returning to find her pre-eminence usurped by *Messiaen.

> *b*. Paris, 16.ix.1887, st with Fauré, taught at Conservatoire and the American Conservatory at Fontainebleu; *d*. Paris, 22.x.79.
> *Bib*: Alan Kendall, *The Tender Tyrant*, London (Macdonald and Janes), 1976.

Boulevard Solitude *Henze's updated version of *Manon Lescaut*. fp: Hanover 17.ii.52.

Pierre BOULEZ Every artist wants to change the world. Most aim to do so by means of what they create. A few, frustrated by the limitations of an individual voice, pursue the power to effect change on a wider scale. *Wagner was their paragon. He wrote polemics, formed alliances, attacked social institutions and used his artistic charisma in impure political ways to achieve a supra-musical platform from which to affect the currents of German art and nationalism. *Schoenberg, concerned for the future of music, devised systems to regulate creativity – or, as he saw it, to liberate composers from obsolescent contraints. *Stravinsky was surrounded by propagandists who promoted the 'correctness' of his current style. All three composed fluently while engaged in revolution.

Pierre Boulez did not. He was an activist before he was an artist and, nearing the end of his creative road, must be judged on his activism more than on his small, self-admittedly uncertain musical output. As a youth in post-War Paris, he led an anti-Stravinsky demonstration during a concert to advance the rival cause of Schoenberg. Soon after, he alienated loyal serialists with a banner headline, SCHOENBERG IS DEAD. The new god was *Webern, who applied *12-note strictures not only to notes but to durations, intervals, rhythms and every other component of a musical piece. Unless a composer submitted to these disciplines, said Boulez, he had no right to call himself a composer. Anyone who had not felt 'the necessity of the 12-tone language' was, in his view, 'superfluous'.

In statements such as this Boulez indicated that he was more determined to control a culture than to increase its resources. The venom of his utterances was not diluted by the smiles with which he shrugged them off. This was a musician who called for the burning down of opera houses, undeterred by parallels of the Nazis' *auto-da-fé*. A conductor who banned Tchaikovsky and Verdi from his concerts as 'inferior' and Britten and Shostakovich as 'conservative'. A composer who dismissed almost everything written before 1900 as 'nostalgia'.

In the 1970s he applied his writ as chief conductor in New York and London, at the Philharmonic (1971–77) and BBC (1971–75). 'In politics you call this "entryism",' he confessed. 'You cannot forever bark outside like a dog . . . so I progressively accepted positions of responsibility to change, not the whole world, but part of it.' By performing ascetic modernism in place of timeworn favourites he believed he could transform public taste. Contemporary composers of varying merit enjoyed a heyday and a younger audience was attracted to his concerts, but Lincoln Center subscriptions fell away and Boulez was replaced at both orchestras by traditionalists, Zubin Mehta and Gennady Rozhdestvensky. The effects of his experiment proved ephemeral.

In France, he announced a voluntary self-exile in 1966 over the government's decision 'to entrust the administration of music to a composer' (*Landowski). What irked him was the elevation of a non-radical composer. He was reconciled in 1970 by a lavish artistic bribe, a decision by President Pompidou to invest 90 million francs in a subterranean Paris studio, the Institut de Recherche et Coordination Acoustique/Musique, *IRCAM for short, where scientists, technologists and musicians might jointly investigate the musical future. No composer since Wagner had squeezed so much state money to pursue a personal dream. Computers, declared Boulez, were 'as necessary to a composer as a knowledge of counterpoint and fugue'. Twenty years later, IRCAM had yielded a handful of worthwhile musical works and some minor contributions to submarine warfare but seemed to have drawn no closer to the promised land. Boulez, for his part, was virtually silenced as a composer, as politics, administration and conducting consumed his available time.

Unlike Wagner, he had no passionate relationships beyond the coterie of loyal acolytes. He never married nor admitted to having a close friend. His advent to New York was headlined 'The Iceman Cometh',

Nono, Boulez and Stockhausen in 1959

though this, too, was a misnomer. When working with musicians and arguing his case, conducting complex modernities and issues without baton or score, Boulez generated tremendous warmth and affection.

His music was cerebrally, rather than emotionally, stimulated. The one work that reacted immediately to an emotional event was his orchestral masterpiece *Rituel*, in memoriam Bruno *Maderna, (London, 2.iv.75), mourning the early death of a fellow-revolutionary in tones as primitive, for all their complicated array, as a polynesian funeral chant. The ensemble in *Rituel* is divided into eight groups and the work into 15 parts but the music is a seamless, timeless dirge of unarguable beauty.

It was one of few works that Boulez left as finished, rather than nagging away, as he did at most scores, with endless revisions, extensions and excisions. This indeterminacy in a man so certain of his ideas suggests that a lack of confidence in his creative originality propelled him into politics, on the side of artistic radicalism and, in France, leftist socialism.

The sources of his music are audible to the untutored ear even when technology dictates their production. Late *Debussy, the composer of *Jeux*, was an inescapable forebear. The massive chords and oriental tinkles of his teacher *Messiaen pervaded many of his scores, alongside the neoclassic clarity of *Stravinsky and the fanatical orderliness of Webern. His musical handwriting was the smallest and neatest of any composer. Boulez was as much a product of a wider culture, absorbing the abstract paintings of Wassily Kandinsky (1866–1944) and Piet Mondrian (1872–1944), the violent, necromantic theatre of Antonin Artaud (1896–1948), the breathless immobility of Samuel Beckett (1906–89) and the aphoristic verses of René Char (1908–88) whose poetry he set in a landmark trilogy: *Le Soleil des eaux* (three versions, 1948–65), *Le Visage nuptial* (1946–51–89) and *Le Marteau sans maitre* (*The masterless hammer*, Baden-Baden, 18.vi.55, cond. Rosbaud). This last work, which marked his international breakthrough, was devoutly modelled on Schoenberg's *Pierrot Lunaire*, scored for

contralto and six players with an array of percussion and the stipulation of significant *silences, which he may have derived from friendly exchanges with *Cage. All told, the effect is softer, suaver and more sensual than its predecessor.

Boulez, contrary to his protestations, was not a follower of orthodox serialism for very long. *Ligeti analysed his piano piece *Structure 1a* (1951) as a model of 'old serialism', but the 2nd book of Structures took on board *Messiaen's serial reorganization and everything after that was unreadable by 12-note rules. Another early piano piece, *Notations* (1945) gained fresh impetus as a shimmering, somewhat *Bergian orchestral suite (Paris, 18.vi.82), as did a 1949 string quartet, revised as *Livres* for string orch. (Brighton, 8.xii.68).

The exposure he won with *Le Marteau* established Boulez with *Stockhausen as leader of the international *avant-garde. He taught at Darmstadt and Basle and was in great demand as a conductor of contemporary works. His ideas were clearly enunciated and he lost no chance to expound and enforce them on musicians whose intellect and personality were weaker than his own. He defined his mission in 1954 in the following terms: 'Get rid of a number of prejudices about a Natural Order; rethink our ideas about acoustics in light of recent experiments; face the problems arising from electro-acoustic and electronic techniques.' These goals were his unwavering beacon through to the end of the millennium.

His venture into *musique concrète with two études (1951) proved unsatisfying and with *Poésie pour pouvoir* (1958–) for tape and two orchestras he began exploring the gentler aspects of *electronic sound. For the most part, though, his larger works were purely instrumental, interdependent and oddly unfinished. *Eclat* (Los Angeles, 26.iii.65), introducing some *improvisatory freedoms and an asiatic ambience, was reworked as *Eclat Multiples* (London, 21.x.70) and remains a work in progress. His susceptibility to extra-musical ideas was manifested at the time of *cummings ist der dichter* (Stuttgart, 25.ix.70) for 16 voices and 24 instruments, when Boulez wrote a series of eulogies in the French press in the unpunctuated uncapitalized manner of the American poet e e cummings. His poetic pinnacle for voice and orch. was *Pli selon pli (Fold over fold,* Donaueschingen, 20.x.62), subtitled 'a portrait of Mallarmé'.

Once IRCAM was built, it was up to Boulez to prove its worth. He came up with *Répons* (Donaueschingen, 18.x.81) in which the mainframe 4X computer and technicians played live electronics with and against a chamber orchestra that he conducted. As pure music it was enchanting, as sensual and stimulating as his Mallarmé settings and the *Rituel*. But it was not the great leap forward that Wagner demonstrated at Bayreuth and performances were limited by the enormity of the mainframe computer, which soon became obsolescent. Boulez continued to revise *Répons* through the next decade, and composed very little else. In 1992 he resigned from IRCAM and accepted a commission from the German National Opera in Berlin.

IRCAM's concert hall had acoustics that could be adjusted to the scale of a work or a composer's whim. Boulez proposed a similar small hall for the *Bastille Opera but its construction was delayed by the expense and by mounting public criticism of IRCAM and its unachieved dreams. Boulez continued to conduct internationally, promote the music of his generation and propound his theories convincingly but, as the century drew to an end, he began to look forlornly like a god that failed.

b. Montbrison, France, 26.iii.25; st with *Messiaen and *Leibowitz; dir. of music for Renaud Barrault theatre 1946–52 and *Domaine Musical seasons 1953–4; cond. centenary Bayreuth Ring 1976; founder-dir. IRCAM, 1970-; *other orch. works: Figures-Doubles-Prismes* (Strasbourg, 10.i.64), *Domaines* (Brussels, 20.xii.68), *explosante-fixe* (NY, 5.i.73); also three piano sonatas (1946–57) and a sonatine for flute and piano (1946).
Bib: Dominique Jameux, *Boulez,* London (Faber), 1990.

(Sir) Adrian (Cedric) BOULT In founding the first radio orchestra, Boult gave a high-minded modernistic bias to music broadcasting. He introduced *Wozzeck and *Doctor Faust* to UK audiences. His con-

cert premières included Holst's *Planets* (29.ix.18), Delius's violin concerto (30.i.19) and Vaughan Williams's *Pastoral* (26.i.22), 4th (10.iv.35) and 6th (21.iv.48) symphonies. He learned from *Nikisch that a conductor need not be showy, and stood almost immobile on the concert platform.
b. Chester, UK, 8.iv.1889; cond. City of Birmingham Symphony Orch. 1924–30, BBC SO 1930–50, London Philharmonic Orch. 1950–57, Birmingham (again), 1957–59; *d.* London, 22.ii.83.
Bib: Michael Kennedy, *Adrian Boult,* London (Hamish Hamilton), 1988.

La boutique fantasque Ballet by *Respighi on reworked Rossini. fp: London, 5.vi.19.

Paul (Frederic) BOWLES The American novelist started out as a composer under the aegis of *Copland and *Thomson. His 1930s piano music was francophone and tinged with *Satie-an hollowness; some pieces with Spanish titles were picked up in trips to Mexico. He composed a ballet, *Yankee Clipper* (Philadelphia, 19.vii.37), before retreating to the warmth and privacy of Morocco, where he wrote his major novel, *The Sheltering Sky* (1949).
b. Jamaica, NY, 30.xii.10; *other works:* operas *Denmark Vesey* (1938), *Yerma* (after Lorca, 1958); flute sonata (1932), *Scènes d'anabase* for voice, oboe and piano (1932).

Attila BOZAY The contrasting pulls of *Bartók rhythms and strict serialism enrich Bozay's chamber music with intriguing tensions; *Mirrors* (1977) for zither and cembalom is both indigenous and serially complex. Large-scale works like *Pezzo sinfonico* no. 2 (1976) tend to be overblown.
b. Balatonfüzfö, Hungary, 11.viii.39; st with Farkas; *other works:* viola concerto (1965), two string quartets.

Darijan BOZIC Slovene opera composer with tendencies to *jazz, *collage and necrology. He has composed an Anne Frank scenario for narrators and synthetic sound (1963) and a *Requiem – to the memory of a murdered soldier – my father* (1969).
b. Slavonski Brod, Yugoslavia, 29.iv.33;

Eugène BOZZA French composer of test-pieces for wind and woodwind instruments.
b. Nice, 4.iv.05;

Francisco Ernani BRAGA *Villa-Lobos' teacher was an unabashed late-romantic who wrote sweet songs for Rio drawing rooms and conducted the city's orch. (1908–33). His tone poems, one titled *Insomnia*, can be heard in Latin America.

b. Rio de Janeiro, 15.iv.1868; d. there 14.iii.45.

Glenn   BRANCA Incredibly   noisy downtown New York experimentalist, pushing *minimalism to the limits of aural tolerance in five overamplified, overlong symphonies for massed electric guitars, bass and drums (1981–84). In terms of volume, style and audience, he belonged principally to the post-punk rock arena.

b. Harrisburg, Pennsylvania, 48;

Max BRAND The last sensation of the Weimar Republic, he invented industrial realism – soon expropriated by Stalin – in *Maschinist Hopkins* (Duisburg, 13.iv.29), an award-winning opera that swept Europe like wildfire until the Nazis doused it (it had a 1986 BBC revival in London). Brand fled to Vienna, Rio and in 1940 to the US, where he lived until 1975 when a modest revival restored him to Europe. After 1958, he wrote nothing but *electronic music.

b. Lvov, Poland, 26.iv.1896; d. Langenzersdorf, Austria, 5.iv.80. *other works*: *Nachtmusik* for chamber orch. (1923), ballet *Die Wippe* (1925), 12-tone *Kyrie Eleison* (1940, cond. *Villa-Lobos), tone poem *Night on the Bayous of Louisiana* (1953), *The Astronauts, an epic in electronics* (1962).

Jan (Willem Frans) BRANDTS BUYS Dutchman who settled in *Salzburg as a noted bibliophile and teacher of, among others,   the   future   festival   director Bernhard Paumgartner. One of his eight operas, *The Tailors of Schonau* (Dresden, 1.iv.16), received more than 1500 European performances. His early-century piano music has the rural pleasantness of Grieg with an undercoating of urban grime.

b. Zutphen, Netherlands, 12.ix.1868; d. Salzburg, Austria, 7.xii.33. *other works*: two piano concertos, two concert pieces for cello and orch.

Henry (Dreyfus) BRANT One of *Copland's Young Composers Group, Brant frightened the horses with *Whoopee in D* for full orch. (1938). *In Music for a*

Five-and-dime Store (1931), he composed for kitchenware; *Angels and devils* (1931), his most performed piece, is written for flutes, piccolos and alto flutes. He talked of mixing a Dixie band with gamelan to break down stylistic barriers. Ahead of *Stockhausen, he scattered instrumental groups around and outside the hall in *Antiphony 1* (1953), the start of many *spatial music experiments. *Millennium 2* (1954) surrounds the audience with brass and percussion; *Voyage 4* (1963) has musicians playing above and below the hall; in *Windjammer* (1969), the players mingle with the public. Alongside his avant-gardism, he orchestrated for the bands of Benny Goodman and André Kostelantetz, and taught composition at Columbia, Juilliard   and   Bennington   College, Vermont.

b. Montreal, Canada, 15.ix.13, son of a US violinist; st with Rubin *Goldmark, *Riegger, *Antheil and *Copland; *other works*: violin concerto with lights (1961), *Fire in Cities* (1961) for chorus, orch., two pianos, three groups, three conductors; *Kingdom Come* (1970) for two orch. and organ; *Orbits* for voice, organ and 80 trombones; *Prisons of the Mind* 'Spatial Symphony' (1990).

Georges BRASSENS The caustic anti-clerical humour and political jibes of Georges Brassens made him a best-selling troubadour in France and a model for musical   satirists   in   other   European countries. Unlike *Brel's, his songs were virtually untranslatable.

b. Sète, 22.x.21; d. there, 30.x.81.

Walter BRAUNFELS Neo-Wagnerian of Roman Catholic faith, his five operas were suppressed by the Nazis and never regained the stage, with the exception of *Die Vögel* (after Aristophanes, Munich, 4.xii.1920). He wrote a variety of orch. works,   including   a   set   of   Scottish variations.

b. Frankfurt-am-Main, 19.xii.1882; head of Cologne conservatory 1925–33 and 1945–54; d. Cologne, 19.iii.54.

Bertolt BRECHT Such was the magnitude of the German playwright's personality that scholars have falsely suggested he wrote much of the music for *Threepenny Opera* and later shows. There may be a certain similarity in the scores composed by *Eisler and *Dessau but the idiom stems primarily from *Weill. Brecht's plays furnished operas for Cerha and Wagner-Régeny. He was among the century's foremost theatrical innovators.

b. Augsburg, 10.ii.1898; *d.* Berlin, 14.ii.56.

Jacques BREL Cabaret singer who balanced biting social satire with a fundamentally sunny outlook; his songs were widely swiped by Anglo-US popsters.

b. Brussels, 8.iv.29; *d.* Bobigny, Paris, 9.x.78.

(William) Havergal BRIAN Just after the First World War, a British composer of modest repute began writing a symphony of unprecedented dimensions. It was modelled on a Gothic cathedral and was scored for an orchestra of 200, a children's choir, two massed choruses and three soloists. By the time he finished in 1927, Brian had become a nonentity and could not get a note of his music performed for three decades. The BBC finally played his 8th symphony in 1954, encouraging Brian to write another 24 symphonies in the 18 years until his death at the age of 96. The *Gothic* – originally his second symphony but renumbered first – was premiered on 24.vi.61, and repeated on his 90th birthday. The composer Robert *Simpson declared it superior to Mahler's Eighth, with which it shares a basis in Goethe's *Faust*. The two-hour edifice contains a mass of interesting themes, some of which flit by never to be repeated. Mood and tonality shift imperceptibly and the chord-*clusters produced by overlapping choral lines possess an intriguingly modern aura within a romantic setting. This inherent tension produces, strangely, greater coherence than exists between the disparate halves of Mahler's Eighth. The *Gothic* is more than the sum of its parts and certainly more than an English eccentricity – indeed, no Englishman before *Tippett wrote anything as ambitious and open-minded. It was recorded in 1990 on the Marco Polo label.

Of Brian's other symphonies, only the 4th has comparable dimensions and its quality cannot be judged from the score alone. The 3rd symphony in C# minor (comp. 1931, fp Birmingham, 17.v.87) is the longest and largest of the rest – 55 minutes of Brucknerian atmospherics, disrupted by the intrusion of two pianos. The 7th has Gothic and Goethean connotations, echoing the great bell of Strasbourg Cathedral (comp. 1948; fp 19.iii.68). The remainder are mostly in single movements and become progressively shorter, petering out at around 13 minutes per symphony by the time he reached the 32nd. Brian stands or falls by the fate of the *Gothic* – and its stature is growing all the time.

b. Dresden, Staffordshire, 29.i.1876; *d.* Shoreham-on-Sea, Sussex, 28.xi.72. *other works:* operas – *The Tigers* (1929), *Turandot* (1950), *The Cenci* (1952), *Faust* (1956), *Agamemnon* (1957).

Frank BRIDGE His immortality was long vested in Benjamin *Britten, who borrowed the second of his *3 Idylls for string quartet* (London, 8.iii.07) to create *Variations on a Theme of Frank Bridge* for string orchestra, a tribute and secret portrait of his formative teacher. Founder-violist of the English String Quartet (1906–15), Bridge was adept at using chamber music to subvert English convention. The *Idylls* show a relish for French *impressionism and decaying tonality; texturally, they stand between *Verklärte Nacht* and *La Mer*.

He opened Britten's ears at 14 to what the world had to offer. Bridge was the first British composer to abandon key signatures, following the example of *Berg in his third (1926) and fourth (1937) string quartets. He was accused by the *Times* critic of seeking 'to uglify his music to keep it up to date', but won the financial support of Elizabeth Sprague *Coolidge who brought him three times to the US to conduct his works.

Like many of his generation, Bridge's life was shadowed by loss of friends and security in the First War. A D-minor sonata for cello and piano, begun with serene lyricism in 1913, subsided into morbid frustration before he finished (13.vii.17). At this time he wrote a *Lament* (15.ix.15) for string orchestra dedicated 'to Catherine, aged 9', who drowned with her family on the Lusitania; his rugged piano sonata (1925) was inscribed to the composer Ernest *Farrar, killed in the trenches.

The *bitonal 2nd piano trio (31.i.29) is mournfully lucid, its bright keyboard cascades emphasizing the irresolvable sorrow of the strings. He was unable to find in tonality the means to express overwhelming despair. Two quasi-concertos confirm the pervasiveness of his grief. *Phantasm* (10.i.34) for piano and orchestra twinkles falsely like the trio, to a depressive backdrop. *Oration* (17.i.36), for cello and orchestra, is expressive, bitter and very slow. Bridge had forgotten how to smile. Even the pastoral suite, *There Is a Willow Grows Aslant a Brook* (20.vii.27) is flecked with shadows, bearing scant resemblance to the pastel landscapes of Butterworth and Vaughan Williams.

In dimpled youth, Bridge had written jolly songs – 'Go Not Happy Day' and 'Love Went A-riding' – and silly portraits, *The Two Hunchbacks* (17.xi.10). His pre-War peak was a magniloquent four-piece orchestral suite, *The Sea*, (24.ix.12), wilder and saltier than Debussy's and giving a vivid foretaste of the Sea Interludes from *Peter Grimes*. Like Britten, Bridge was born and died within sound of the sea; he was a loner, a pacifist and an explorer. Neither composer can be understood without the other; Britten devotedly preserved Bridge's music at *Aldeburgh.

> b. Brighton, 26.ii.1879; d. Eastbourne, 10.i.41. *other works*: children's opera *The Christmas Rose* (8.xii.32); *A Prayer*, chorus, orch. (1916), *Enter Spring* for orch. (Norwich, 27.x.27).

Britain 'The Land Without Music' broke its prolonged isolation with *Elgar's Enigma Variations on the very eve of the new century, instantly penetrating the international repertoire. Elgar was a conservative and backward-looking figurehead, but his success encouraged a fertile generation, extending from the folk-revivalists Holst and Vaughan Williams to the abstract music of Frank *Bridge who, in turn, nurtured Benjamin *Britten.

National progress was Anglocentric and spasmodic. Scots, Welsh and Irish composers made little headway and the health of English music hinged on a dominant personality. Vaughan Williams was anathema to Europeans and Britten became increasingly introverted. Of his successors, only *Birtwistle advanced in a straight and certain line. The generation of the 1980s and 1990s havered between *Messiaen and post-*minimalism.

Despite creative limitations, London became a world capital of music by dint of its efficient orchestras and eminent conductors – from Thomas Beecham to Simon Rattle – its busy record industry and 1930s influx of European refugees. The *BBC added a layer of musical infrastructure. State funding of music, started in 1945, sustained orchestras in Birmingham, Liverpool, Manchester and Glasgow, national opera companies in England, Scotland and Wales, and an international house of variable fortunes at Covent Garden. More music of international quality was played nightly in London than in any city on earth.

The quality of British music scholarship was widely respected. It was the bedrock of the Grove *dictionary industry and fostered, among other phenomena, the *early music revival.

British *popular music made a dual onslaught on world tastes. In the 1960s the *Beatles and *Rolling Stones topped US charts and created a cult for iconoclastic adaptations of Afro-American *rhythm-and-blues. The following generation witnessed *punk rejections of musical and social values, a wave that began in Britain in frustrated reaction to Beatles perfectionism. Individual singer-songwriters from Noël *Coward to Phil Collins have enjoyed immense success on the world stage.

(Edward) Benjamin BRITTEN Britain treated its most successful composer with icy reserve. Pacifist, socialist and homosexual, Britten was suspect to the establishment and a paradox to the middle classes; his essentially bourgeois, buttoned-up outlook on life and art denied him intellectual support. His music was deemed regressive by modernists and 'too clever by half' (*Grove V*) by traditionalists. He was an outsider, like *Mahler whom he admired from boyhood, prey to bouts of paranoia that coloured his music with biting ironies. He could also be as affecting as Mozart, able to touch the emotions with an original

His boyish cantata *A Boy was Born* was sung by the BBC on the day of Elgar's death (23.ii.34), a coincidence many found symbolic. Barely 20, he fell into the raffish company of W. H. Auden and Christopher Isherwood, who overwhelmed him with their lust and sophistication and steered him into writing music for their documentary films and an experimental play, *The Ascent of F6*. At 22 he was signed up by Boosey & Hawkes and the following year introduced at *Salzburg his *Variations on a Theme of Frank Bridge*, opus 10.

Written in the space of four weeks, it broke with the English string elegies of Elgar and Vaughan Williams, presenting a slightly astringent voice that was not afraid to parody, successively, the conventions of classical France, operatic Italy and waltzing Vienna. Each variation also represented a different facet of his teacher's character, though Bridge forbade Britten to list his traits in the published score. As well as the identified opening theme, the penultimate fugue contains quotations from five works by Bridge – most notably from *The Sea*.

A piano concerto, played at the Promenade Concerts (18.viii.38), was less coherent, exposing a weakness for devising ingenious solutions from weak material. Its latter movements showed affinities with *Shostakovich parody and rhythmic brutality. Depressed by the approach of war, Britten and Pears followed Auden and Isherwood to America in May 1939, staying until April 1942. The exile was unusually fruitful, yielding works of real maturity in the incisive violin concerto (NY, 28.iii.40) and *Sinfonia da Requiem* (NY, 30.iii.41, both cond. Barbirolli), a symphonic epitaph for his parents. The *Michelangelo Sonnets* and *Les Illuminations*, a cycle of Rimbaud poems for high voice and string orchestra, broke new ground in his vocal writing. Contacts with Serge *Koussevitsky produced a commission for his first fullscale opera.

He worked with Auden on a folkloristic songspiel, *Paul Bunyan* (Columbia U., NY, 5.v.41), intended for high-school concerts and containing some whistleable numbers, including a country-and-western pastiche. It parallels in many respects Kurt *Weill's folk opera, *Down in the Valley*. In

chord and twist them around its resolution. The sunniness of such music was difficult to reconcile with the tetchiness of the man.

His major operas focus on a lone man at odds with society. Beauty, both physical and spiritual, is insistently pursued. Amid his own solitude he found love and fulfilment in the person of Peter Pears, an energetic tenor who became his inseparable companion and interpreter in 1938. Key works, from the luxuriant *Michelangelo sonnets* (London, 23.ix.42) to the climatic *Death in Venice* (Aldeburgh, 16.vi.73), are inscribed simply 'To Peter'.

The North Sea that raged through *Peter Grimes* was in his ears the day he was born at Lowestoft, Suffolk, in 1913 on the nameday of the patron saint of music, St Cecilia. He was the fourth and youngest child of a dentist and his strong-willed wife, who believed Ben to be the fourth B in the concert constellation. He started composing at the age of five and his tuition was tended by Frank *Bridge, the most cosmopolitan and forward-looking of English composers. He instilled in Britten a hatred of war and a cognizance of Europe.

Los Angeles in 1941, Britten came across an article by E. M. Forster on the 18th-century Suffolk poet George Crabbe and 'suddenly realized where I belonged and what I lacked'. Pears found Crabbe's poems in a rare book shop and he began work on *Peter Grimes*, helped by reading *Rosenkavalier*, 'to see how the old magician makes his effects'.

The couple returned home in mid-War, marking their comeback with a phenomenal première of the *Serenade for tenor, horn and strings* (London, Wigmore Hall, 15.x.43), which carried English song into the realms of late-romantic Lieder. Pears joined the Sadler's Wells company while Britten persisted painfully with his projected opera.

On 7.vi.45, weeks after the end of war in Europe, British opera was reborn with *Peter Grimes*. Almost strangled at birth by a cabal of sexual-political adversaries, it was tonally rich in a most un-English way with lashings of Mahler, especially in the 3rd act (the shimmering Dawn interlude echoes the Eighth symphony's central Vorspiel). Grimes was through-composed as a symphony rather than strung together in a succession of arias and set-pieces. There are no big vocal numbers. As drama, it dealt with the hounding of a fisherman accused of the death of his apprentice-boys. The blend of persecution, East Anglian pettiness and hints of paedophilia was acutely personal to Britten, who saw himself as Grimes and wrote the role for his lover to sing. Yet, despite intense identification, the music is highly objective. Neither the sadistic protagonist nor the clamouring villagers are caricatured, and sympathy for the boy is aroused by allusion alone; he has nothing to sing. Everyone, implied Britten, shared blame for his death: 'the more vicious the society, the more vicious the individual', he told *Time* magazine.

Grimes was acclaimed as a masterpiece and received a dozen international productions in three years; *Bernstein led the 1946 US première at Tanglewood. Many would latterly regard it as the pinnacle of Britten's achievement, though he was still only 32 and had room to mature. *Billy Budd* (1.xii.51), a second summit six years later, dealt more starkly with the same theme of man's inhumanity to boys. It quotes the Serenade for tenor, horn and strings and provides a haunting Heave-ho chorus. Adapted by E. M. Forster and Eric Crozier from Herman Melville's novel of British naval mutiny, Budd portrays a captain's dilemma over the hanging of an innocent seaman – reworking Biblical metaphors of Abraham and Isaac, and the Crucifixion. It confronts man and fellow-man, man and his conscience.

None of the remaining nine operas except the last attained an equivalent balance. The village comedy *Albert Herring* (Glyndebourne, 20.vi.47) had a narrowly English humour while *The Rape of Lucretia* (Glyndebourne, 12.vii.46), despite a superb contralto role, was disappointingly fleshless. *Gloriana* (Covent Garden, 8.vi.53), for the coronation of Elizabeth II, was undermined by an overwrought score and imputations of a sexual relationship between the first Queen Elizabeth and her favourite, Essex. Its play on Morris dances and madrigals presaged a revival of Tudor music.

Britten was sufficiently irked by radical critics to attempt discreet *12-note rows in *The Turn of the Screw* (Venice, 14.ix.54) and *A Midsummer Night's Dream* (Aldeburgh, 11.vi.60), losing none of his richness but sacrificing something in spontaneity. The Shakespeare setting was a faithful bardic transference, using authentic period music to underpin an inventive score. The last two operas are retrospective but, whereas *Owen Wingrave* (TV, 16.v.71) adds little to its literary subject, *Death in Venice* (Aldeburgh, 16.vi.73) brought Thomas Mann's novella to new life by addressing personal preoccupations from a standpoint of mortality. Britten was suffering from a serious heart ailment and knew that his days were numbered. In the novella, he found essential elements of sea, forbidden beauty, sex and guilt. Years before, Mann had said, on hearing Pears sing the *Serenade*, that Britten was only man capable of composing his turbulent tale.

Rejected by established companies, Britten invented his own institutions. In 1946 he founded an English Opera Group and made new settings of John Gay's *The

Beggars' Opera and Purcell's *Dido and Aeneas*. The company also sponsored new work by other British composers, among them Berkeley, Walton, and Birtwistle. He set up home at Snape in East Anglia in 1938 and a decade later founded a spring festival at nearby Aldeburgh. His programmes were exploratory, not experimental. Aldeburgh was his refuge from enemies but its defensive character built another wall around the composer and his loyalists.

In 1955, while touring the Far East with Pears, he acquired two new elements. A visit to a Japanese Noh-play inspired *Curlew River* (Orford Church, 12.vi.64), the highly-stylized first of three 'parables' intended for church performance. Its companion works were *The Burning Fiery Furnace* (9.vi.66) and *The Prodigal Son* (10.vi.68). The gamelan orchestras of Bali and their delicate percussive instruments gave rise to his only ballet, *The Prince of the Pagodas* (1.i.57), and lastingly pervaded his music. The virtuosic Symphony for Cello and Orch. (Moscow, 12.iii.63) chimes with gongs and tamtams. After a surly opening, the Symphony warms into a soft-hearted adagio and a passacaglia that is worth all that preceded it. The work, along with three unusually playful suites for solo cello and one for cello and piano, arose from a blazing and improbable amity with *Rostropovich.

The *War Requiem* (30.v.62), written for the consecration of the new Coventry Cathedral, was an eclectic yet effective conception, combining the text of the Latin Mass and war poems by Wilfrid Owen in a format that recalled Verdi. It was his most popular choral piece and struck Shostakovich dumb with envy. The Russian, whose *Lady Macbeth of Mtsensk* foreshadowed *Peter Grimes*, now modelled his 14th symphony partly on Britten's *Nocturne* for tenor and small orchestra (Leeds, 16.x.58). That work, in turn, was dedicated to Alma Mahler, widow of a composer who strongly influenced both men, Shostakovich and Britten. In such cellular cycles did 20th-century music make progress. Britten's moving 2nd and 3rd string quartets (1945, 1973) pay overt homage to the great cycle by his Russian colleague.

It was above all as a vocal composer, however, with Pears as constant inspiration, that Britten's originality was stirred. Among many choral works, the *Spring Symphony* (Amsterdam, 9.vii.49) is rooted in primeval tradition: the welcoming in song of a new season. Harmonically and rhythmically unorthodox – the opening movement is in B, the climax in C major – it plucks lyrics eclectically from medieval and modern sources, and ends in a cross-rhythmic setting of the oldest English song 'Sumer is icumen in' belted out by tenor, two sopranos and boys' choir. Unless tightly conducted, it degenerates into a sloppy mess – amateurs beware.

The *Cantata Accademica* (Basle, 1.vii.60) for the 500th anniversary of Basle University, is a dusty in-joke, opening with a formal row of 12 notes in the despisedly 'academic' *Schoenberg mode, but proceeding with unblemished tonality and enormous vitality. The *Hymn to St Cecilia* (London, 22.xi.42) for unaccompanied adult voices is sublime and personal, written at sea on his return from American exile to verses by Auden, for the patron saint of music on whose name-day he was born.

His cycles for voice and piano led Britten to be regarded in Europe as 'the renewer of his country's art song'. The most intense are The Holy Sonnets of John Donne (London, 22.xi.45), written at high speed while sick in bed after returning from a tour of liberated concentration camps in Germany. The songs begin in the deep abyss of 'O my blacke Soule' and lighten very gradually to the brave defiance of 'Death, be not proud' – an extraordinary sentiment in the circumstances.

The William Blake songs and proverbs that he wrote for Dietrich Fischer-Dieskau (Aldeburgh, 24.iv.65) on the death of his wife are unremittingly grave, contrasting starkly with *Vaughan Williams' comparable settings.

Childless, yet nostalgic for childhood, Britten wrote numerous works with children in mind. Many sound frankly patronizing. *A Young Person's Guide to the Orchestra* (Liverpool, 15.x.46) uses a rondo by Henry Purcell to introduce the various instruments in variation form. With or without Eric Crozier's coy commentary, the piece now sounds outmoded. *Let's Make an Opera* (Aldeburgh, 14.vi. 49), also known as *The Little Sweep*, is more on the lines of Hindemith's *utility music, a simple piece that anyone can sing, act and play; it, too, is flawed by Crozier's pedantic text and Edwardian mannerisms. Other pieces that involve children's voices – *Spring Symphony, Noye's Fludde* (Aldeburgh, 18.vi.58) – leave a certain unease about their proclivities.

Confined to a wheelchair for his last three years, he was elevated to the House of Lords in his dying months but never enjoyed the nation's wholehearted gratitude. His final quartet departs with some bitterness but his legacy as a whole endures as a miracle of 20th-century culture.

b. Lowestoft, Suffolk, 22.xi.13; st with Bridge 1928–35; further studies at RCM with *Ireland and *Benjamin; Maltings concert hall opened 2.vi.67, burnt down 7.vi.69, reopened 7.vi.70; open-heart surgery 8.v.73; *d.* Aldeburgh, 4.xii.76. *other works*: Sinfonietta (Lon, 31.i.33) Simple Symphony (Norwich, 6.iii.34), Young Apollo (Toronto, 2.vii.39), Canadian Carnival (Bristol, 6.vi.40), Scottish Ballad (two pianos and orch., Cincinnati, 28.xi.41), Diversions (left hand piano and orch. Philadelphia, 16.i.42), Lachrymae (viola and string orch, Recklinghausen, 3.v.77), reorchestration of God Save the Queen (London, 1.iii.67); *Our Hunting Fathers* (text by Auden, Norwich, 25.ix.36), *Phaedra* (text by Robert Lowell, Snape, 16.vi.76), A Ceremony of Carols (Norwich, 5.xii.42), Songs from the Chinese (high voice and guitar, 1958); solo music for guitar, piano, organ and harp; more than 20 GPO film unit scores, notably *Night Mail* (1936).
Bib. Humphrey Carpenter, *Benjamin Britten, a biography*, London (Faber), 1992.

Broadway Home of an art formula rather than a form, it reached a zenith of commercial success c. 1950 with *South Pacific* and the derivative *Kismet*, only to be devastated by the unrepeatable brilliance of *Bernstein's *Candide* and *West Side Story*. The best efforts of *Sondheim & Co. could not arrest the subsequent decline.

Max BROD Prague polymath who achieved international exposure for *Janá-

ček through ecstatic reviews in the German press, excellent translations of his librettos and an inaugural biography. A respected novelist in his own right, Brod saved Franz Kafka's manuscripts from the bonfire and discovered the callow talent of Franz Werfel. Forced to escape the Nazis, he headed Tel Aviv's Habimah Theatre and composed a *Requiem Hebraicum* (1943), among various ethnicities.
b. Prague, 27.v.1884; *d.* Tel Aviv, 20.xii.68.

Sten BROMAN Long-serving Swedish rep at *ISCM (1933–62), he moved with the times in eight symphonies, from tonality to electronic experiments.
b. Uppsala, 25.iii.02; *d.* Lund, 29.x.83.

Leo BROUWER The leading composer in revolutionary Cuba, he kept in touch with the European avant-garde through visits by *Nono and *Henze and applied some of their less radical techniques to his music. He is best known for slightly morose guitaristic miniatures.
b. Havana, 1.iii.39; *works*: Sonograma for *prepared piano (1963), *Homage to Mingus* for jazzband and orch. (1965), *Hexahedron* for six players (1969), flute concerto (1972), guitar concerto (1972).

Earle BROWN *Cage's sidekick in the early 1950s, his scores became more familiar by sight than by sound – *eye music of graphic originality and numerical *indeterminacy. Sections of *Folio* (1952) can be played forwards, backwards, upside down or in any order by any number of players; but Brown blew up when, in the midst of the *aleatory *December 1952*, one disrespectful player chimed in with 'Old Macdonald had a Farm'. In 1965 he reduced players' freedoms and insisted that stretches of his string quartet be played 'straight through' without variation or improvisation.
b. Lunenburg, Massachusetts, 26.xii.26; worked with *Cage on tape project 1952–55; married (1) dancer Carolyn Rice, (2) art expert Susan Collins; composer in residence, Peabody Conservatory 1968–73, Rotterdam Philharmonic 1974, California Institute of Arts 1974–83; *other works*: New Piece Loops (1971), *Sounder Rounds* for orch. (1982).

Dave BRUBECK A pupil of *Schoenberg and *Milhaud, in 1951 he formed a jazz quartet that applied tempo strictures and fugal techniques in the successful albums *Time Out* and *Time Further Out* (1960–61).
   b. Concord, California, 6.xii.20;

His brother, **Howard BRUBECK** was a straight composer and head of the music faculty at a junior college in San Marcos. He composed, inter alia, *4 Dialogues* for jazz combo and orch. (1956), A *California Suite* (1945) and sundry variations on his kid brother's themes.
   b. Concord, 11.vii.16;

Max BRUCH The composer of the G minor violin concerto, *Kol Nidrei* and the *Scottish Fantasy* had little to contribute to the century beyond a concerto for two pianos, texturally massacred by its US dedicatees Otilie and Rose Sutro in 1916 and given up as lost until 1974 when it regained concert circulation in Bruch's original version. He taught at Berlin's Hochschule für Musik, where his pupils included *Vaughan Williams.
   b. Cologne, 6.i.1838; *d* Friedeneau near Berlin, 2.x.20.

Alfred (Louis Charles Bonaventure) BRUNEAU On reading the works of Emile Zola (1840–1902), Bruneau had a blinding revelation that he was to be the novelist's operatic incarnation. They collaborated successfully in *Le Rêve* (*The Dream*, Paris, 18.vi.1891), shared the opprobrium of Zola's defence of Captain Dreyfus and triumphed again with *L'Ouragan* (*The Hurricane*) (29.iv.01) and *L'Enfant-Roi* (*The Child-King*, 3.iii.05). Zola's death in 1902 left Bruneau rudderless. He wrote a requiem oratorio, *Lazare*, but did nothing to have it performed (it was finally broadcast by French Radio, on 15.iv.57) and carried on composing Zola adaptations with ever-diminishing returns. His operas, long defunct, broke new ground in France with Wagnerian orchestration and a dramatic verisimilitude that anticipated Puccini. *Lazare* is superior to most of *Saint-Saëns, and the *Chants de la vie* (1913) are eloquent and engaging.
   b. Paris, 3.ii.1857; st with Massenet; first

cond. at Opéra-Comique (1903–04); *d.* Paris, 15.vi.34.

Evgeni BRUSILOWSKY Leningrad graduate dispatched in 1933 to Kazakhstan to teach the locals how to make concert music out of folktunes; he showed the way with nine ethnic operas and eight symphonies.
   b. Rostov-on-the-Don, Russia, 12.xi.05; *d.* Moscow, 9.v.81.

Joanna BRUZDOWICZ Polish expatriate, living in Belgium, her 1987 opera on the children's crusade, *Gates of Paradise*, was widely televised.
   b. Warsaw, 17.v.43; st with *Boulanger, *Messiaen, *Schaeffer; *other works*: opera *Les Troyennes* (1973), piano concerto (1974), symphony (1975), two string quartets.

Gavin BRYARS Thoughtful collagist, he combined *minimalism and populist pedagoguery by enveloping complex ideas in simple music. *Effarene* (London, 3.iii.84) for soprano, mezzo, six percussionists and four pianists is a hypnotic 40-minute cantata on Marie Curie's definition of scientific research, a bull on photography by Pope Leo XIII, a passage from Jules Verne and a poem on the Queen of the Sea. Intended as a companion piece to George *Antheil's notorious *Ballet mécanique*, it walks a tightrope between kitsch and banality. *Jesus Blood Never Failed Me Yet* (1972) is a *Reichian composition around a revolving tape-loop of a London tramp singing an old hymn. A polytechnic lecturer in out-of-way Leicester, he contrived two stage spectacles with the director Robert Wilson – the opera *Medea* (Lyons, 23.x.84) and *Civil Wars*, an extravaganza intended for the 1984 Los Angeles Olympics but finally celebrated in Europe
   b. Goole, Yorks, 16.i.43; *other works: 3 Viennese Dances* (1983), string quartet (1985), Homage to *Vivier (1985).

Valentino BUCCHI *Malipiero-like traditionalist; composed four operas and various concertos.
   b. Florence, 29.xi.16; st with *Dallapiccola; *d.* Rome, 9.v.76.

Budapest The red-letter night of the Hungarian capital was its 50th anniversary concert on 19.xi.23 that heard premières of masterpieces by three resident composers –

Dohnányi's Festive Overture, Bartók's Dance Suite and Kodály's Psalmus Hungaricus. Creativity was subdued in the next generation but revived with the collapse of communism.

Buddhism Fatalist oriental philosophies, especially of the Zen variety, held fatal attractions to performing musicians, who are preconditioned to submit themselves passively to the superior will of a composer. *Karajan and *Bernstein propagated Buddhist ideas from the podium. *Cage understood Buddhism as a means of opting out from decision-making as a composer – go with the flow – and let chance make the choices in music.

John BULLER A late starter who graduated in music at 37, he won an English National Opera Commission in his 60s on the strength of a stilted orch. piece, *The Theatre of Memory* (1981), that he wrote for the BBC. The resultant *Bakxai* (London, 5.v.92) was embarrassingly uneventful. All the action took place off-stage and was sung about in ancient Greek, with the only soprano aria reserved for the end. This did not prevent some critics acclaiming the 100-minute bore as a paradigm for the operatic future.
   b. London 7.ii.27;

Anthony BURGESS (pen-name of John Burgess Wilson) The irrepressible British novelist had ambitions as a composer. His 3rd symphony and an operetta on James *Joyce were broadcast but not published. His D. H. Lawrence suite played in Nottingham during the author's 1985 centenary. Burgess updated Weber's opera *Oberon* unimposingly and rendered *Carmen* in modern English. His fiction was inflected by music, notably *Napoleon Symphony*, modelled on Beethoven's *Eroica* and the binary sonata-form *Abba, Abba*. His view of music was antediluvian. 'As an art dedicated to the plumbing of the depths of the human soul, or . . . the disclosing of heavenly visions, [music] ceased to exist at about the time of the death of Mozart,' he wrote. Can music teach anything to the novelist?' he once asked. 'Yes: the importance of structure.'
   b. Manchester, 25.ii.17; major novels: *Malaysian Trilogy, Earthly Powers.*

Bib: A. Burgess, *This Man and Music*, London (Hutchinson) 1982.

Geoffrey (Alan) BURGON Communicative British composer who added a quantifiable dimension to TV serials of John Le Carré's *Tinker, Tailor, Soldier, Spy* and Evelyn Waugh's *Brideshead Revisited* with deceptively simple, poignant scores. His concert music includes a visionary *Requiem* (1976).
   b. Hambledon, Hampshire, 16.vii.41; *other works*: opera *Hard Times* (after Dickens, 1991).

Emil (František) BURIAN Nephew of the celebrated tenor Karl Burian (1870–1924), a member of Mahler's New York ensemble, and son of a Prague operatic baritone, Burian grew up in the theatre and made his name as a composer, poet, singer, dramatist and administrator. In 1928 he stormed the *ISCM festival at Siena with an improvisatory 'voice band' that sang music of preset rhythms but without predetermined notes or words. He ran the Brno theatre for several years and founded a Dadaist company in Prague (1933–41, 45–9), for which the Nazis sent him to a concentration camp. His jazzy, folksy scores are reminiscent of Les *Six.
   b. Plzen, Czechoslovakia, 11.vi.04; *d.* Prague, 9.viii.59. *works*: six operas of which *Marysa* (1938) was successful; five ballets; songs with jazz band; eight string quartets; accordion concerto (1949).

Willy BURKHARD *Hindemith-like Swiss oratorio composer of extensive local influence.
   b. Leubringen, Switzerland, 17.iv.1900; *d.* Zurich, 18.vi.55; *works*: opera *Die schwarze Spinne (The Black Spider)* (1949), violin concerto (1943), one-movement symphony (1944), organ fantasy *Ein feste Burg ist unser Gott* (1939).

Francis BURT Emigré Englishman, living in Vienna since 1956. He was greatly taken with Ibo drumming, heard while serving with the British Army in Nigeria.
   b. London, 28.iv.26; st with *Ferguson and *Blacher; *works*: opera *Volpone* (on Ben Jonson, 1961), ballet *Der Golem* (1963).

Fritz BUSCH The Dresden conductor premièred three Strauss operas, Busoni's *Doktor Faust* and Hindemith's *Cardillac* before fleeing the Nazis and co-founding the *Glyndebourne Festival. His brothers Adolf and Hermann formed the nucleus of the Busch Quartet (1919–52).

> *b.* Siegen, Westphalia, 13.iii.1890; conductor in Riga, 1910–12, Aachen 1912–18, Stuttgart 1918–22; Dresden State Opera, 1922–33, Glyndebourne Festival Opera, 1934–39; *d.* London, 14.ix.51.

Alan (Dudley) BUSH An ardent communist, Bush recanted the astringencies of his *Dialectic* string quartet (1929) and wrote simple tunes and rousing anthems that Stalin liked to hear. His four agit-prop operas were staged in East Germany; *Boult suppressed the applause at one of his rare UK concerts by playing the National Anthem. In the 1947 violin concerto, soloist and orchestra are meant to represent the individual and society.

> *b.* London, 22.xi.1900; st with *Schnabel, *Ireland; joined CP 1935; formed Workers Music Association 1936; *operas*: *Wat Tyler* (Berlin, 3.iv.52), *The Men of Blackmoor* (Weimar, 18.xi.56), *Guayana Johnny* (Leipzig, 11.xii.66), *Joe Hill* (Berlin, 29.ix.70).

Geoffrey BUSH English pastel artist, resembling sanitized *Britten in his vocal cycle, *A Summer Serenade* (1948).

> *b.* London, 23.ii.20; chorister at Salisbury Cathedral; st with *Ireland; taught Oxford and London universities, 1947–80; *other works*: five operas, two symphonies.

business of music A contradiction in terms became reality in the 20th century as musicians pursued high rewards. The 1940s produced a *million-dollar trio, the 1980s a million-dollar conductor, Lorin Maazel, earning that salary for a dozen weeks' work. Corporate sponsors, rather than concertgoers, paid the price.

Ferruccio (Dante Michelangelo Benvenuto) BUSONI Ranked with *Schoenberg as a composer whose ideas sounded more compelling than his music, Busoni preached a doctrine of renewed classicism – not *neo-classicism – that would restore the instinctual qualities of Bach and Mozart. He pursued simplicity without simple-mindedness and wanted new music to correlate with current arts and ideas. An intellectual and bibliomane, he shared pupils with Schoenberg in Berlin and both respected the other's thinking.

Like Schoenberg, he lacked melodic

imagination but his Italian blood permeated his best music with passion and pathos. The *Berceuse Élégiaque*, (NY, 21.ii.11), provoked by his mother's death and premièred by *Mahler in his last mortal concert, was so admired by the Schoenberg circle that they rescored it for chamber ensemble for their *private concerts. It amounts to a ten-minute consolatory trance.

His mature works – in 1907 he disowned all previous scores – are classically structured with a modern intonation. The climax of his efforts was the opera *Doktor Faust*, a parable of unprincipled ambition based on medieval legend and Christopher Marlowe rather than the over-familiar Goethe. Its relevance was inescapable – Busoni wrote the entire libretto in six days during the first Christmas of World War I. His Faust demanded from the Devil unlimited genius, the dream of every creator. Lacking a finale when the composer died, it left audiences perplexed in the lame ending prepared by his loyal pupil Philipp Jarnach (Dresden, 21.v.25); Antony Beaumont's reconstruction of the composer's sketches (London, 26.iv.86) provides a more convincing conclusion.

He compensated with adult luxury for a miserable childhood. His pianistic genius was exploited from the age of seven by his clarinettist father and he was on the road continuously until settled by a sensible Swedish wife in a lavish Berlin apartment. His collection of books was world famous and his mind was well stocked with their contents. He was fluent in most west European languages. He was as much at home in St Petersburg as in New York and while crossing America opened his heart to the deprived Indians, composing a *Red Indian Diary* for solo piano (1915) and *Indian fantasy* for piano and orch. (12.iii. 14). His pupil Kurt *Weill called Busoni: 'the last Renaissance Man'.

He produced one of the notorieties of the new century – a gargantuan piano concerto with choral finale (10.xi.04), its monstrous dimensions concealing flashes of wit and an impressive 23-minute adagio. The rest of his concert music came from operas he was writing. The thoughtful divertimento for flute (13.i.21) found its way into the first tableau of *Doktor Faust*. Two of the operas were initially coupled as a double-bill: *Arlecchino*, a mid-War romp that turns memorably sour, and the pre-Puccini *Turandot* (Zurich, 11.v.17). The least polished of his stage works was *Die Brautwahl* (Hamburg, 13.iv.12), after an E.T.A. Hoffmann fable. All are sung in German.

Bach looms over his piano music; his six volumes of piano transcriptions of Bach chorales produced many virtuoso encores. He wrote cadenzas for nine Mozart concertos, variations on Chopin themes and an extrapolation of one of Schoenberg's Op. 11 piano pieces. His *Sonatina super Carmen* (London, 22.vi.20) is not a transcription, rather a flying-fingered riposte to Wagnerian pomposity based on Bizet themes. The seven Elegies (1908) bring together many of his preoccupations from opera to Bach chorales, Italian street songs to diabolical meditations. Among its oddities is the Elizabethan song 'Greensleeves' which Busoni mistook for a Chinese theme and was planning to use in *Turandot*. A tripartite Toccata for solo piano, written in 1920, contains elements of *Doktor Faust* against a Baroque format that creates formidable fingering difficulties. It was the most virtuosic piece of Busoni's last years and few pianists have the courage and intellect to confront its conundra.

> *b.* Empoli, Italy, 1.iv.1866; met Liszt 1877; married Gerda Sjöstrand, 1890; taught in US 1891–94; published *Outline of an Aesthetic of Music*, 1907; left Berlin 1915 to live in New York and Zurich, returning in 1920; *d.* Berlin, 27.vii.24; *other works*: Nocturne Symphonique (2nd elegy for orch. 12.iii.14); *Fantasia contrappuntistica* for piano (Basle, 30.ix.10).
> *Bib*: Antony Beaumont, *Busoni, the composer*, London (Faber), 1986.

Henri-Paul BÜSSER Debonair musician, he orchestrated a Debussy suite and conducted the 3rd performance of *Pélleas*, without showing great originality, though he composed assiduously and reached the age of 101.

> *b.* Toulouse, France, 16.i.1872; *d.* Paris, 30.xii.73. *works*: operas *Daphnis et Chloë* (1897), *Colomba* (Nice, 4.ii.21).

Sylvano BUSSOTTI Wild man of Italian opera, he attempted every avant-garde device from squeaks to electronics without losing a fundamental concern for beauty. The 'chamber mystery play' *La Passion selon Sade* (Palermo, 5.ix.65) contained abundantly sensual vocalities for the triple heroine, Juliette, Justine and O. In *Lorenzaccio* (Venice, 7.ix.72) he designed the stage set and 230 costumes. He habitually quoted undigested chunks of Rossini, Verdi and Puccini. Much of his opera and concert music verged on *happenings. In *L'ispirazione* (1988) he raised and lowered the orchestra on ropes as it played. He was appointed artistic director of the Teatro La Fenice in 1975.

> *b.* Florence, Italy, 1.x.31; st there with *Dallapiccola, in Paris with *Boulez and at *Darmstadt with *Cage; *other works*: *5 Pieces for David Tudor* (1960), *The Rara Requiem* (1970), *Opus cygne* for soprano and orch. (1979).

Nigel BUTTERLEY Australian who endeared himself to philatelists with *First Day Covers* for narrator and orch. (1972).

> *b.* Sydney, 13.v.35; st with *Rainier; music adviser to ABC 1955–72; *other orch. works*:

violin concerto (1970), *Fire in the Heavens* (1973).

George (Sainton Kaye) BUTTER-WORTH By the time he met a hero's death on the Somme, aged 31, Butterworth had done enough to qualify for posterity. His six-minute folkish rhapsody, *A Shropshire Lad*, was resoundingly premièred by Arthur *Nikisch at the Leeds Festival (2.x.13) – its perfection, said *Boult, eliminates every superfluous note – and *The Banks of Green Willow* was warmly received in London (20.iii.14). It was Butterworth who guided *Vaughan Williams towards symphonic composition and helped prepare his *London Symphony*.

A railway child, son of the general manager of the North-Eastern network, he studied at Eton and Oxford and was *Times* music critic. While out collecting folk songs, he became expert in country dancing and liked to displayed his agility on stage, once in wartime Paris. He was killed defending a sector renamed the 'Butterworth Trench'.

b. London, 12.vii.1885; killed in the battle of Pozières, 5.vii.16, and posthumously awarded the Military Cross. *other work*: *Love Blows as the Wind Blows* for baritone and string quartet (1914).

Max BUTTING Socialist German composer of ten late-romantic symphonies (1923–63) and an equivalent number of string quartets (1914–71).

b. Berlin, 6.x.1888; *d.* there, 13.vii.76.

cabaret Nightclub satire that thrived in societies under stress, particularly Paris before the First War, Berlin of the Weimar Republic and New York during the Vietnam War. The shows usually reeked of sexual decadence. *Satie, *Schoenberg, *Weill and *Sondheim wrote the best songs.

cadenza Space in a concerto where the soloist can improvise but usually resorts to a script provided by an eminent virtuoso or composer. Joseph Joachim (1831–1907) dictated standard cadenzas for the Beethoven and Brahms violin concertos, Leopold Auer (1845–1930) for Tchaikovsky and Glazunov. Fritz *Kreisler wrote a Beethoven alternative; *Busoni and *Schnabel left much-played cadenzas for Beethoven and Mozart piano concertos. The minimalist Philip *Glass wrote a repetitive interlude to a Mozart piano concerto for Rudolf Serkin (1903–91); the violinist Gidon Kremer weaved an unrelated sonata by *Reger into the Brahms concerto. *Schnittke caused a furore in 1979 with a cadenza for the Beethoven violin concerto that collated themes from every major concerto from Bach to Berg. In his 4th symphony, Schnittke wrote a satiric cadenza for conductor in which the orchestra sits silently while the maestro waves his arms about.

Charles Wakefield CADMAN   Explorer of Amerindian music.
  b. Johnstown, Pa., US, 24.xii.1881; *d.* Los Angeles, 30.xii.46. *works*: opera *Shanewis* (NY Met, 23.iii.18), symphonic poem, *Pennsylvania* (Los Angeles, 7.iii.40).

John CAGE   One day in 1938, John Cage began to destroy music. This is not editorial comment, but historical fact. In a series of actions and statements over the next two decades, Cage altered the nature and meaning of music as it had stood for two millennia. He demonstrated that music need not be humanly pre-determined; it could come about by *chance, or be generated by machines. A composer's duty, he said, was to *experiment; the presence and response of an audience was immaterial. Instruments were no longer sacrosanct: they could be tampered with and wrecked at will. Any object could make music, any noise constituted music. Even *silence was musical. Music had no intrinsic purpose. 'Nothing is accomplished by writing, hearing or playing a piece of music,' he wrote in 1961.

Such heresies were heaven-sent to the post-war *avant-garde, avid to detach themselves from corrupted European traditions. It belonged to an emergent West Coast culture that scorned buttoned-up East Coast academic strictures. Cage, from traditionless California, approached art with refreshing lack of clutter and regard for rules. At their most malignant his ideas occasioned an era of stage outrages and *happenings in which Cage played a leading role, firing pistols in mid-concert and encouraging performers to remove their clothes. On the constructive side his iconoclasm helped relieve composers of their stifling attachment to *Webern's serialism by indicating the freedoms they could accord to performers. *Ligeti exulted in his liberalism, *Lutosławski in his *Concert for*

Piano and Orchestra (NY, 15.v.58), 'to be played in whole or part, in any sequence'. *Boulez and *Stockhausen took cautious note. He took *Darmstadt by storm in 1958 and was published henceforth by the venerable Edition Peters of Frankfurt.

The son of a technical inventor, Cage studied (1933–34) with Henry *Cowell, who anticipated many of his ideas but lacked the personality to promote them. He moved on to *Schoenberg (1935–37), who told him he had no ear for music, that he was not a composer but an inventor. In 1938, while writing piano accompaniments for a ballet troupe, he became frustrated with the instrument's lack of percussiveness. 'In a flash, I saw what was wrong; it wasn't me but my piano. I began therefore to experiment with the interior. I inserted magazines, newspapers, ashtrays, baking pans. Every object seemed to change the sound as I hoped . . .' The *prepared piano was born. It gave a sound not dissimilar to that of the *gamelan, slightly comic and generally monotonous. *Satie, one of Cage's icons, would have appreciated both the wit and the boredom that ensued. The prepared piano entered circulation in 1942 when Cage moved to New York as Merce Cunningham's lifelong music director, composing countless tinkly pieces for the dance company.

His path to *aleatory music, or 'indeterminacy' as he preferred to call it, ran through exposure to the fatalistic passivism of Zen Buddhism as preached by Daisetz Suzuki, whose lectures were also attended by Allen Ginsberg and other Beat poets. Buddhism to Cage meant that if something was boring after two minutes, try it for four, eight or however long it took to become meaningful.

It was an outlook that communed with nature by taking minimal decisive action. The notorious *4'33"* called for a concert performer to sit motionless at any instrument while he and the public listened to ambient noises and meditated on sounds of silence. It was 'performed' by David Tudor in Woodstock, NY (29.viii.52), and has been recorded. A shorter version, *0'0"*, was prepared for a Japanese tour (Tokyo, 24.x.62). Absurdity aside, these pieces represented the ultimate in performer and audience freedom, ending the composer's right to dictate sounds.

He laid out *Music of Changes* for piano solo (1951) in charts of 64 elements, corresponding to the Chinese I Ching, which was consulted to pick the combination of sounds and dynamics for a performance. This process could be *computerized or decided by someone tossing a coin or drawing a straw to see how to proceed. He rendered rhythm nonsensical by demanding such unattainable durations as 4/7 of an 1/8th note. In due course, Cageian indeterminacy came to mean: anything goes. *Variations* (1958–78) 'for any number of players, any sound-producing means' had its few directions drawn on transparent plastic sheets that were hung around the stage. Cage staged the very first *happening with *Theater Piece* for Cunningham in 1952.

His involvement with *electronics went back to 1939 when, in *Imaginary Landscapes, he fooled around with record-players to manipulate strange noises from recordings of radio test-signals played at different speeds. He did not believe in the wonders of high technology but harnessed whatever he needed to fulfil his experimental urge. In the 1960s he pioneered live electronics in *HPSCHD* (Urbana, Illinois, 16.v.69), a coalescence of pre-recorded tapes, amplified instruments, photographic stills, films and lighting effects, all coordinated by computer. It was a landmark in *mixed-media events. Cage was progressing, it seemed, from music-without-music to music-about-music, a direction confirmed by his *Europera* series (1987–91). His comments on the nature of opera involved having a soprano enfolded in white bandages until she stopped singing an aria from *Figaro* and crowning a mezzo with rabbits' ears while she sang something out of *Pique Dame*. Too puerile for words but staged at the Frankfurt Opera and the Almeida Theatre, London, with utmost seriousness. His *notation ranged from the relatively explicit to the vaguest of wavy lines.

Cage's interests always ran beyond art. He was an expert mycologist – mushroom collector – and an early convert to macrobiotic health diets. *Child of Tree* (1975) 'for percussion solo, using amplified plant materials' illustrated his premature ecological concerns. His knowledge of English literature was profound and in 1989 he served as Norton professor of poetry at Harvard.

He denied being a *dadaist, although he was friendly with the anti-art pioneer Marcel Duchamp (1887–1968) and played public chess with him on a board organized by aleatory procedures. His music is commonly deemed inferior to his theories and critics predicted that it would not survive him. There are likely exceptions, however, to this sweeping extinction. In a recorded compilation of US piano music, Cage's fragments strike the ear with piercing luminosity, outshining the melodism of Copland and Bernstein. In *3 Dances for 2 Prepared Pianos* (1945) he switched virtuosically from simplicity to complexity and back, from eastern sounds to western. His creaky-door, excruciatingly slow *String Quartet in 4 Parts* (1950) is both an ancestor to monotonous *minimalism and a probable successor. Along with *Piano Concert* (1957), it is a modern classic.

Cage was accused by jealous traditionalists of unscrupulous self-promotion. With such extraordinary notions as his, he could hardly fail to command worldwide attention and his impact on music was probably more profound than any other American's.

b. Los Angeles, 15.ix.12; musical director American Dance Company 1944–68; *d*. NY, 12.viii.92. *other works*: clarinet sonata (1933), *The Wonderful Widow of 18 Springs* for voice and closed piano (1942), *Sonatas and Interludes* for prepared piano (1946–48); *Music for Marcel Duchamp* for prepared piano (1947), Suite for Toy Piano (1948), *Cartridge Music* (1960), *Lecture on the Weather* for 12 vocalists, tape and film (1975), *Freeman Etudes* for violin solo (1971), *Lecture on Anarchy* (1988), *Roaratorio* (1988).

Maria CALLAS It was not so much the soprano's sleekness or volume that captivated but the dramatic energy she invested in a harmless phrase. She resurrected *belcanto* heroines by Bellini and Donizetti and acted the Tosca of the century. She retired at 42, consorted with the Greek shipping magnate Aristotle Onassis and died after

he left her for Jacqueline Kennedy.

b. NY, 3.xii.23 of Greek parents and baptized Maria Anna Sophia Cecilia Kalegoropoulos; *d*. Paris, 16.ix.77.

Hector CAMPOS-PARSI A *Boulanger pupil from Puerto Rico, he has written in national and international styles. *Sonetos Sagrados* (*Sacred Sonnets*, 1986), composed for the 500th anniversary of Columbus's voyage to the New World, consists of five songs from the Spanish golden age set for soprano and wind quintet in an imaginative, un-nostalgic neo-classicism.

b. Ponce, Puerto Rico, 1.x.22; st with *Copland, *Fine, *Messiaen and four years with *Boulanger; dir. Institute of Puerto Rican Culture; *other works*: *Tissu* for accordion and small orch. (1984).

Edith CANAT de CHIZY *Ohana disciple, she won a state prize and feminist award for a 20-minute *Yell* for full orchestra (1986).

b. Lyon, France, 26.iii.50; *other works*: *Saxy* (1985) for saxophone and piano, *Llama* for a capella choir (1986), *Kyoran* (1987) for strings and percussion.

Candide Bernstein's thrice-failed Voltairean musical, a coded commentary on McCarthyism with the brightest overture anywhere. fp: Boston, 29.x.56.

Canon The medieval device of staggered repetition or imitation of a theme acquired intense relevance to the *12-tone method, which required a basic row of notes to be fully articulated before it could be altered. Almost all of *Webern's music is canonic; from opus 21 onwards he followed Bach as much as he did Schoenberg. *Berg's violin concerto is another classic example of canon.

Cantata Accademica *Britten's doffed cap to Basle U. in its 500th year. fp: Basle, 1.vii.60.

Cantata Profana *Bartók choral work, premièred on the *BBC, 25.v.34.

(Marie-) Joseph CANTELOUBE French folksong collector, alerted to national heritage by d'*Indy whose biography he wrote, his four orch. sets of *Songs of the Auvergne* were a godsend to sopranos of limited expressive range. His country operas, *Le Mas* (1913) and *Vercingetorix* (1932), were staged in Paris; his symphonic works, including a Poème for violin and orch., were not.

b. Annonay, nr. Touron, 21.x.1879; *d.* Gridny, 4.xi.57.

Canti di prigionia (*Songs of imprisonment*) *Dallapiccola's wartime resistance to fascism, the first Italian work to apply serialism. fp: Rome, 11.xii.41.

Des Canyons aux Etoiles *Messiaen's symphonic tribute to the great outdoors. fp: NY, 20.xi.74.

André CAPLET *Debussy aide who orchestrated *Le martyre de Saint Sébastian* and conducted its première. His compositions were imbued with Debussian transparency – notably the *Epiphanie* cello concerto (Paris 29.xii.23) and *Le miroir de Jésus* (1.v.24) for string quartet, harp and three voices. He died at 47 of the effects of wartime gas poisoning.

b. Le Havre, 23.xi.1878; won Prix de Rome 1901; cond. Boston Opera Co. 1910–14; *d.* Paris, 22.iv.25. *other works*: harp concerto *The Masque of the Red Death* (after Poe, 7.iii.09).

Capriccio Strauss's last opera discusses the principle *prima la musica, poi le parole* (first comes the music, then the words). fp: Munich, 28.x.42. Also title of left-handed piano concerto by *Janáček (1926) and two-handed piece for piano and orch. by *Stravinsky (1929).

Cornelius CARDEW Cardew started out as a *Stockhausen groupie, was drawn towards *Cage and was hailed by *Wolff of the *avant-garde as 'the most important British composer since Dunstable' (1390–1453). 'Any direction modern music will take in England will come about only through Cardew, because of him, by way of him,' affirmed Morton *Feldman in 1966. He became a part-time teacher at the Royal Academy of Music and worked with former jazz musicians in a band, AMM, that tried to bridge musical chasms. His 193-page score *Treatise* (1963–67) was a *graphic alternative to composed music – subjectively 'explained by the situation of a composer who is not in a position to make music'.

Around the end of the decade he experienced a blinding conversion to radical Maoism, joined the politburo of the Revolutionary Communist Party of Britain and denounced his former idol in a dazzling tract entitled 'Stockhausen Serves Imperialism' (1974). He formed a *Scratch Orchestra composed of musicians and non-musicians who hacked as best they could through simple classics and pieces Cardew wrote for them. His objective was democratization – music for mass involvement – but the band broke up after two years of wearisome Marxist-Leninist debates. Not, however, before it played his major polemical work, *The Great Learning*, a blend of formal composition, improvisation and political propaganda, at the 1972 Promenade Concerts, where the BBC banned the revolutionary banners demanded by the composer as part of the concert.

Cardew's politics were naïve and very much of his time – the Dutch film-maker Joris Ivens was another who depicted China's Cultural Revolution as a turning point for mankind. He refused to recognize that pianists were having their fingers broken by Mao's police for playing 'bourgeois' music. Cardew spent the Seventies composing insurrectionist songs and themes. One dark night in December 1981, while walking home in East London, he was knocked down and killed by a hit-and-run driver. Although his music is virtually unheard, his charisma and cultish ideas were perpetuated in the music of several sometime followers, Richard Barratt, Michael Finnissy and Howard Skempton.

b. Winchcombe, Gloucestershire, 7.v.36; *d.* London, 13.xii.81. *other piano works*: *Thälmann Variations* (1974), *Vietnam Sonata* (1976), *We Sing for the Future* (1981).

Cardillac Hindemith's first full-length opera, a Faustian account of a jeweller who murders his customers. fp: Dresden, 9.xi.26, cond. Busch.

Jan CARLSTEDT Swedish disciple of *Britten, founded Stockholm Contemporary Music Society (1960).

b. Orsa, Sweden, 15.vi.26; *works include*: two symphonies, the second in memory of Martin Luther King; four string quartets.

Carmen Bizet's opera (Paris, 3.iii.1875) became ever more popular. *Busoni and *Horowitz wrote brilliant piano fantasies on its themes, *Corigliano created a *Naked Carmen* with rock group and synthesizer, and an all-black *Carmen Jones* was staged by Oscar Hammerstein on Broadway (2.xii.43) and filmed in Hollywood.

Carmina Burana Student songs of the Middle Ages, lasciviously restored by Carl *Orff in a cantata for three soloists, chorus and large orch. Its comradely ethos echoed the Nazis' *Volksgemeinde* myth and its heavy beat later attracted pop-fanciers and deodorant advertisers. fp: Frankfurt 8.vi.37.

John Alden CARPENTER An *Elgar admirer, he was among the first composers to experiment with jazz in his ballet *Krazy Kat* (Chicago, 23.xii.21). *Skyscrapers* (NY, 19.ii.26), which *Diaghilev commissioned but did not stage, became a symphonic evocation of US city life. Virgil *Thomson burst his bubble of fame by dismissing the 2nd symphony (NY, 22.x.42) as 'rich man's music'.
    b. Park Ridge, Chicago, 28.ii.1876; st with *Paine and Elgar; worked in family shipping firm until 1936; *d.* Chicago, 26.iv.51. *other orch. works*: *Adventures in a Perambulator* (1914), *Sea Drift*, symphonic poem after Whitman (1933), violin concerto (1936), Carmel concerto (1948); songs to poems by Tagore (1913), four Chinese songs with chamber orch. (1918).

Julián CARRILLO Mexican of Indian blood and German tutelage, he played violin in the Leipzig Gewandhaus under Nikisch, returning home in 1905 to form orchestras of his own. His D-major symphony, performed in Leipzig in 1902, was unremarkably romantic. Dismayed by its decadence, Carrillo started writing atonally and sought what he called 'sonido 13', the 13th sound that lay beyond traditional tuning. From 1924 he began splitting notes into 1/4, 1/8 and 1/16 parts, writing a Concertino for Fractional Tones (Philadelphia, 4.iii.27) and training musicians to play between the notes. *Stokowski commissioned several more works and toured Mexico in the 1930s with Carrillo's *Sonido 13* for orch. The composer devised a range of instruments to play his new music, but performing difficulties on conventional instruments and the competitive lure of 12-tone music pushed Carrillo to the fringe. Nevertheless, his influence persists among Latin American composers, such as *Kagel and Davidowsky, and his music is ripe for rediscovery. Much of it was recorded by the composer.
    b. Ahualulco, San Luis Potosi, Mexico, 28.i.1875; directed National Conservatory in Mexico 1913, 1920–24; *d.* San Angél, Mexico, 9.ix.65. *works include*: four atonal string quartets (1917–20); *Sonido 13* for small orch. (Mexico City, 2.i.31, cond. *Stokowski), *Horizontes* (Pittsburgh, 30.xi.51), 12 more microtonal works for orch., among them two violin concertos in 1/4ths, 30 works for chamber ensemble, 32 solo pieces and a microtonal Mass for Pope John XXIII (1962).

Elliott (Cook) CARTER There are two strains of complexity in American music. The first was the rough-hewn frontiersmanship of *Ives and Cowell, piling notes and themes upon one another in an unbreachable wall of resourcefulness. The other, cultivated in East Coast *academies by *Babbitt and Sessions, invented mathematical brain-teasers for dedicated cerebralists. Carter, a quiet easterner of impeccable lineage, applied to the pioneering spirit the polish of intellectual suavity, without actively subscribing to either sector. His parents bought life-insurance policies from Ives and as a youth he edited the disabled composer's illegible manuscripts. He went to Harvard to study with *Piston and on, inescapably, to Nadia Boulanger's classes in Paris (1932–35), returning like most fellow-alumni a *neo-classic francophile. But he read Joyce and Proust as they were published and strove for a place in modern art.
    After a decade in ballet and the Office of War Information, he politely signalled a personal direction in the 23-minute piano sonata of 1946 (revised 1982) that changed its time signature with bewildering frequency and oddity to produce a static texture that suggested jazz without rhythms.

Coloured by his friend Copland's previous sonata, it disrupted the basic components of musical sound and was frustratingly hard to play with any degree of accuracy. Carter's music would ever after challenge its interpreters to get it right. Devotees who consider him 'the greatest living composer' (Andrew Porter, 1979) argue that those who dislike or fail to understand his music are not hearing it properly. That privilege will be reserved for future generations. *Boulez said his was 'one of the most original languages of our time'.

The first string quartet of 1951, composed during a year spent isolated in the Arizona desert, seemed impossibly dense and unnecessarily complex, charges that stuck to his music ever after. In fact, the quartet's novelty lay in its linear separation, each instrument entering on its own and pursuing a private agenda, like characters in a Beckett play. The incomprehension that greeted the work in 1953 has given way to profound admiration. The next two quartets (1959, 71) won Pulitzer Prizes for ingenuity; Carter likened the instruments in the 2nd to opera singers; the 4th (1986) sounded simpler, but that may be by comparison. If the chamber music was tough – and *Night Fantasies* (1980) is an unbroken nightmare for solo pianist – the orchestral works were wholly intractable and, until the 1980s, rarely performed. The Double Concerto for harpsichord, piano and two chamber orchs. (NY, 6.ix.61) won *Stravinsky's encomium, but the piano concerto (Boston, 6.i.67), Concerto for Orchestra (NY, 5.ii.70) and *Symphony of 3 Orchestras* (NY, 17.ii.77) strained the tolerance of players and conductors when so little aural reward was repaid for such intellectual and manual effort.

Steadily assimilating *12-note techniques, Carter loosened his tie in the 1980s with a flow of orchestral works that added a glow of human warmth to textural severities, albeit a dry, desert warmth like a close-shaven cheek. The turning point was *In Sleep, in Thunder*, a 1981 setting of Robert Lowell poems for tenor and 14 players, followed by *Triple Duo* (London, 23.iv.83) and an oboe concerto of confident serenity (Zurich, 17.vi.88). There was gentle humour in *A Celebration of Some 100 × 150 Notes* (1986), a three-minute concert-opening fanfare that replaced Copland's political populism with technical strictures of inherent moral force.

Carter has never touched a popular audience and is played more in the new music *ghettos of Europe than in his own country, although greatly cherished by the Anglo-American academic establishment and its critical satraps. The rock group *Grateful Dead have subsidized recordings of his concertos and composers as varied as *Knussen and *Donatoni admit their debt to the reticent Carter. He denied writing complexities for their own sake and was confident that time would vindicate his music. As a boy in Boston, he recalled, people would say the Emergency Exit in Symphony Hall meant 'this way, in case of Brahms'.

b. NY, 11.xii.08; married Helen Frost-Jones, 1939; *other orch. works*: ballets *Pocahontas* (1936), *The Minotaur* (1947); jazzy 1st symphony (Rochester, 27.iv.44); *Holiday Overture* (Baltimore, 7.i.48), *Variations for Orch.* (1955), *Penthode* for 5 instrumental quartets (1985), *Remembrance* (1988), *A Mirror on Which to Dwell* (1975) for soprano and chamber ensemble, *Elegy* (1943) for string orch. or quartet.

Enrico CARUSO The buttery, poignant tenor voice of a sometime Neapolitan street urchin bestowed credibility to the embryonic record industry on ten cylinders taken in Milan in March 1902. He had the warmth of a baritone and the penetration of a high tenor. As well as frequent appearances at La Scala and Covent Garden, he appeared at the Metropolitan Opera from 1903 to 1920, creating the role of Dick Johnson in Puccini's *Girl of the Golden West*.

b. Naples, 27.ii.1873; *d.* there of pneumonia, 2.viii.21.

Tristram CARY Son of the novelist Joyce Cary, he was probably the first Englishman to dabble in *musique concrète and built his own electronic studio in 1952. On top of many taped works, he composed a cantata, *Peccata Mundi* (1972), and various film and TV scores before emigrating to Australia in 1982.

b. Oxford, 14.v.25; taught Royal College of Music 1967–82, U. of Adelaide, 1982–.

Francois Louis CASADESUS Founder of Nadia *Boulanger's American Conservatory at Fontainebleau, he composed four operas and a *Scandinavian Symphony*.
   b. Paris, 2.xii.1870; *d*. there 27.vi.54.

His brother, **Marius CASADESUS,** a violinist and *early music pioneer, discovered Mozart's so-called *Adelaïde* concerto (Paris, 24.xii.31). Some 46 years later, he confessed to counterfeiting the work.
   b. Paris, 24.x.1892; *d*. there,13.x.81.

Their nephew **Robert CASADESUS** was a celebrated pianist, who composed a two-piano concerto for himself and his wife, Gaby (NY, 25.xi.50) and a three-piano concerto with a role for their son, Jean (NY, 24.vii.65). Based on Bach, they are seasoned with piquant sonorities and propulsive rhythms and immune from Gallicisms and the cloying intimacy that might be expected from a family circle. Robert Casadesus also composed seven symphonies and took over his uncle's conservatory from 1946. His son was tragically killed in a Canadian road accident in January 1972.
   b. Paris, 7.iv.1899; *d*. there, 19.ix.72.

Pau (Pablo) CASALS The Catalan cellist and humanist revived the public performance of Bach's six solo suites but sponsored few contemporary works apart from ephemeral concertos from *Tovey and *Moór. He prompted *Schoenberg to reconstruct G. M. Monn's 1746 harpsichord concerto, but never performed it. Wedded to Romantic ideals as player, composer and politician, Casals was a figurehead of Republican Spain and lifelong opponent of Franco's regime, refusing at first to play in any country that recognized it. He founded a festival at Prades, on the Franco-Spanish border, and another in Puerto Rico where, aged 80, he married a 20-year-old pupil. His works include *La Sardana* for cello ensemble (1926), a Christmas oratorio *El pessebre* (*The Manger*, Acapulco, Mexico, 17.xii.60) and choral settings of Catalan tunes, simple to the point of naïvety and delightful to sing.
   b. Vendrell, Catalan Spain, 29.xii.1876; début Barcelona 23.ii.1891; toured globally, played in the White House for Theodore Roosevelt (15.i.04) and John F. Kennedy (13.xi.61), cohabited 1906–12 with Portuguese cellist Guilhermina Suggia, married (1) Susan Metcalfe 1914–28 (2) Marta Montanez 1957–73, formed famed trio with French pianist Alfred Cortot and violinist Jacques Thibaud, headed Casals Orchestra in Barcelona, 1919–36; *d*. San Juan, Puerto Rico, 22.x.73.

André CASANOVA Neo-classical Frenchman with some cautious modernisms among three symphonies and much chamber music.
   b. Paris, 12.x.19; st with *Leibowitz;

Alfredo CASELLA *Mahler's Italian disciple continued to promote *modernism under fascist rule. His 2nd symphony in C minor (1909) was modelled on Mahler's, before reaping success with *neo-classical reworkings of Italian masters – *Scarlattiana* (1926) and *Paganiniana* (1942). When Mussolini marched to power, Casella envisaged a pan-European musical millennium in which all modernists, from Schoenberg to Stravinsky, worked together in supranational harmony. He protected dissonant young composers from fascist repression, while offering a celebratory opera, *Il deserto tenato*, when Italy invaded Abyssinia.
   b. Turin, 25.vii.1883; lived in Paris 1895–1915 as student of *Fauré and admirer of *Debussy;, taught Santa Cecilia Academy, Rome, 1915–47; founded Siena summer festival 1939; *d*. Rome, 5.iii.47. *other works*: *Elegia eroica* (Rome, 21.i.17), concerto for string quartet (1924), violin concerto (Moscow, 8.x.28), triple concerto (1933), 3rd symphony (Chicago, 27.iii.41).

John CASKEN Any modern attempt by a northern Englishman to reinterpret legend provokes unfavourable comparisons with *Birtwistle. Casken's maiden opera, *Golem* (London, Almeida Festival, 28.vi.89), resembles *The Mask of Orpheus* in electronic surges but lacks its musical invention. Casken's version of the clayman who grew independent of his rabbinic maker is remote from the Prague original and bloodless in conception. Its harmonic ingenuities won the first Britten award for composition. A gifted painter, Casken balances rough aural landscapes against an instinctive attraction for the Baroque.

There are hints of Scarlatti and madrigals in the opening act of *Golem*.

> *b.* Barnsley, Yorks., 15.vii.49; st with Joubert and Dickinson in Birmingham, and with *Lutosławski in Warsaw; lecturer at Durham University, 1981-; *other works*: piano concerto (1980), *Kagura* for 13 wind (1973), *Masque* for oboe and chamber orchestra (1982), *Vaganza* (1985), string quartet (1982), *Ia Orana* a life of Gauguin for soprano and piano (1978), *To Fields we do not Know* for unaccompanied chorus (1985), piano quartet (1990).

cassette   Miniature ⅛″ tape-reel invented by Philips for office use around 1960 but soon becoming principal carrier of *portable music.

Mario   CASTELNUOVO-TEDESCO Exiled from Italy in 1939 by official antisemitism, he sought inspiration in the Bible and Shakespeare and achieved success with concertos for *Heifetz and *Segovia. The 2nd violin concerto (NY, 12.iv.33, cond. Toscanini), entitled 'the Prophets', has movements named after Isaiah, Jeremiah and Elijah and sentimentally evokes a Sephardic-Jewish heritage. His many guitar works for Segovia are affectionately rhapsodic, as is the cello concerto for Piatigorsky (NY, 31.i.35). In Hollywood, his style was ideally suited to film scores, which he wrote anonymously; he gave lessons to Henry *Mancini and André *Previn. His ten operas include *The Merchant of Venice* and *All's Well That Ends Well* and he set 33 Shakespeare songs and sonnets. For the oratorios *Ruth* (1949) and *Jonah* (1951) and the piano suite King David's Dances (1925) he exploited ancient melodic sources.

> *b.* Florence, 3.iv.1895; st with Pizzetti; *d.* Los Angeles, 16.iii.68. *other works*: chamber opera, *The Importance of Being Earnest* (1962); two piano concertos, concerto for two guitars; various Shakespearian overtures; entire Sacred Service of Sephardic liturgy.

Niccolò CASTIGLIONI   After running a central 20th-century line from *Mahler (*Aprèslude*, 1959) to *Boulez (*A Solemn Music*, 1965), he arrived at an ironic pluralism that makes continuous nostalgic reference to romanticism. Settling in the US 1967–69, ill health enforced his return to Italy.

> *b.* Milan, 17.vii.32; st with *Blacher; *works include*: operas *Oberon* and *The Lord's Masque* (1980), radio opera *Through the Looking Glass* (after Lewis Carroll, 1961), two symphonies, *Canti* for orch. (1956), Psalm XIX for two sopranos, chorus and orch. (1980), *Romanze* for string quartet (London, 28.x.91).

Juan José CASTRO   Cornerstone of an Argentine musical dynasty, he studied with *d'Indy and composed uncomplicated musical *nationalisms that did not travel far. He conducted abroad in Melbourne (1952–53) and Puerto Rico (1959–64).

> *b.* Avellaneda, nr Buenos Aires, 7.iii.1895; *d.* Buenos Aires, 3.ix.68. *works include*: four operas, two of them to Lorca plays; *Sinfonia Argentina, Sinfonia de los compos* and three other symphonies.

His elder brother, **José Maria CASTRO,** conducted the Buenos Aires Philharmonic from 1930 and composed three ballets and many concert works.

> *b.* Avellaneda, 15.xii.1892; st with d'*Indy; *d.* Buenos Aires, 2.viii.64.

The younger brother, **Washington CASTRO,** wrote two symphonies and three string quartets.

> *b.* Buenos Aires, 13.vii.09;

Catalogue d'oiseaux   Seven piano books of birdsong by Messiaen. fp: Paris, 15.iv.59.

Cats   Andrew *Lloyd Webber's cleverest show, based on T. S. Eliot's *Old Possum's Book of Practical Cats* and containing the hit-song 'Memory'. fp: London, 11.v.81, and still running.

celesta   Piano-like instrument with metal plates instead of strings, it was introduced by Tchaikovsky in the *Nutcracker* ballet and won star billing in *Bartók's Music for Strings, Percussion and Celesta. It has been ever since an essential adjunct of modern orchestration.

cell   A short musical motif, sometimes just three or five notes, around which an entire work is constructed, usually by *serial methodology.

cello   The big instrument had only two popular concertos by Schumann and Dvořák until charismatic soloists like *Casals and *Rostropovich reactivated composers. Important concertos flowed from Elgar, Honegger, Shostakovich (2) and Lutosławski. Prokofiev composed a Sinfonia Concertante, Britten a Cello Symphony and Bloch the tone-poem, Schelomo. Sonatas flowed from Debussy, Kodály, Britten, Hindemith, Rachmaninov and Schnittke.

Central Park in the Dark Orch. impressions by *Ives, composed 1898–1907, fp: NY, 11.v.46.

Friedrich CERHA Co-founder of the Viennese die *Reihe modern concerts, Cerha was commissioned by *Universal to complete *Berg's unfinished *Lulu. He began secretly, without the widow's knowledge, and fulfilled the task with self-effacing competence, ever a master of understatement. Shaking off *12-note constraints, he next composed a dramatic opera on Brecht's play, Baal (Salzburg 7.viii.81), inserting enough familiar objects in his score to grip audience attention. His 3rd Langegger Nachtmusik for orchestra, offstage band and two conductors (Berlin 9.iv.91) depicted in very slow, Bergian and beautiful sounds the nocturnal landscape around his country home, while simultaneously recalling the elements in Dürer's famous etching, Melancholia. The work placed Cerha among the leading *expressionists. His natural observations alerted *Ligeti to cloud formations. Like *Cage, he was an expert on mushrooms.

Awarded the Austrian State Prize in 1986, he tossed up the $20,000 as a prize for anyone who promoted a concert series that would help modernize Viennese taste. He ironically dedicated a Requiem to the young musicians of his country.
> b. Vienna, 17.ii.26; st with *Uhl; head of electronics at Vienna Music Academy 1960; led die Reihe 1958–80; other works: opera Der Rattenfänger (after Zuckmayer, 1987); symphony (1975), double concerto for violin and cello (1976), Keintate 1 and 2 (1982–4); Curriculum for 13 wind instruments (1972); two string quartets (1989–90).

George Whitefield CHADWICK Leader of the 'Boston Classicists' who sought to fix American music anachronistically in early romantic mode, his lyric drama, Judith (Worcester Festival, 26.ix. 01), could have been written by any of Mendelssohn's staider pupils. He directed the New England Conservatory from 1897 until his death.
> b. Lowell, Mass., 13.xi.1854; st at Leipzig with *Reinecke and Jadassohn and at Munich with Rheinberger; headed music festivals at Springfield and Worcester; d. Boston 4.iv.31. works: three symphonies (1883–94), symphonic poems, five string quartets.

Cha-cha Cuban dance that was all the rage in 1958.

Francis CHAGRIN Cosmopolitan UK practitioner of Balkan *neo-classicism.
> b. Bucharest, Romania, 15.xi.05; st with *Dukas, *Boulanger, *Seiber; joined BBC World Service 1941; d. London, 10.xi.72. works include: two symphonies, piano concerto, Suite Romaine (1948).

Luciano CHAILLY Head of music on Italian radio (1950–67) and director of several opera houses including La Scala (1968–71), he composed 14 neo-classical operas with some modernisms. His son, Riccardo (b. Milan, 20.ii.53), became principal conductor of Amsterdam's Concertgebouw Orch. in 1988.
> b. Ferrara, Italy, 19.i.20; other works: 12 Sonate tritematiche for varied inst. combinations.

Feodor CHALIAPIN The mighty Russian bass introduced Boris Godunov to Covent Garden and the Met and created title roles in Rimsky-Korsakov's Mozart and Salieri and Massenet's Don Quichotte. His dramatic sensitivity was as finely tuned as his voice was deep. A friend of *Rachmaninov's, he was the ideal interpreter of morose Russian drawing-room ballads.
> b. Kazan, Russia, 13.ii.1873; emigrated 1922; d. Paris, 12.iv.38.

chamber music Although radio and records killed of domestic music making, chamber music enabled composers to convey personal intimacies and political secrets, as *Shostakovich did wordlessly with his 2nd piano trio and quintet. The string *quartet sustained its appeal and sonatas abounded. *Schoenberg found chamber music more receptive to post-tonal music than symphonic form; *Debussy discovered its power in his dying years; *Bartók found in its privacy an outlet for personal turmoil.

chamber opera Operas intended for cramped conditions and small halls, among them Stravinsky's *Soldier's Tale*, Britten's *Turn of the Screw* and Birtwistle's *Punch and Judy*.

chamber symphony A *Schoenberg invention (1906), it was picked up by *Berg and *Webern as well as by the traditionalists *Schreker and *Milhaud. *Hindemith called his small-ensemble compositions 'Kammermusik.' By keeping the number of players below 20, a composer could design a diaphanous soundscape.

Cécile (Louise Stephanie) CHAMINADE Pianist whose salon pieces faded with her playing career. She is survived by a creamy little concertino for flute and orchestra, composed in 1902 for end-of-term exams at the Paris Conservatoire. Her lyric symphony, *Les Amazones* (1888), might provide a feminist anthem.
  b. Paris, 8.viii.1857; *d.* Monte Carlo, 18.iv. 44. *other work*: Concertstück for piano and orch. (Philadelphia, 7.xi.08).

chance operations *Cage's term for giving performers freedom of choice within a piece of music by, for example, letting them throw dice to determine the next note or passage in *Music of Changes*.

Le Chant du Rossignol Nightingale's song – a symphonic suite taken by Stravinsky from his opera, *The *Nightingale*. fp: Geneva, 6.xii.19.

Charleston 1920s dance craze of American origin.

Gustave CHARPENTIER She was poor, but she was honest – and her story made him rich. Charpentier's opera *Louise*, a little seamstress who left home to live with an artist, blended social conscience, women's liberation and musical eroticism to such profit that the composer was able to found a singing school for abused dressmakers. Although its shock value was ephemeral, the opera is eternally evocative of *fin-de-siècle* Paris, its sounds, sights and ineluctable cruelty. Among those impressed by the plush score was *Mahler, who conducted the Vienna première. Charpentier attempted a follow-up with *Julien* (4.vi.13), the story of Louise's lover. Despite Caruso's impassioned portrayal, it never took off.
  b. Dieuze, Alsace-Lorraine, 25.vi.1860; worked in a factory after German invasion, won Prix de Rome 1887; *d.* Paris, 18.ii.56.

Jacques CHARPENTIER Recruited by André Malraux in 1966 as chief inspector of music for the whole of France, Charpentier found there were barely 50 music schools in a country which, in 1789, had 450. He expanded music education, with reactionary emphasis on plainchant, organ playing and folk music. He rose ever higher in political spheres, becoming national director of music, opera and dance in 1979 and titular head of the Paris opera houses and orchestras. He was forced out after three years and moved south to become head of music in Nice. There he composed an Acropolis Symphony, his 7th, for the opening of a municipal music complex.
  b. Paris, 18.x.33; st with Tony Aubin and *Messiaen; went to Calcutta 1953 to explore Indian music; organist of St-Nicolas-du-Chardonnet in Paris 1974-; *other works*: concerto for *ondes martenot (1959), *Shiva Natarya* – 3rd symphony (1968); ten concertos for string orchestra and solo instruments.

Abram CHASINS His three *Chinese Pieces* played happily in 1920s parlours and *Toscanini had one of them orchestrated for the NY Philharmonic (8.iv.31). He composed fantasies on *Carmen* and *Schwanda the Bagpiper* and two piano concertos, the second of which was premièred by Gabrilowitsch at the keyboard and *Stokowski on the rostrum (Philadelphia, 3.ii.33). Chasins pioneered music broadcasting on US radio and wrote several interesting books.
  b. NY, 17.viii.03; *d.* NY, 21.vi.87.

Carlos CHÁVEZ The most outward-looking of Latin American composers,

Chávez was friendly with *Cowell, *Varese, *Stokowski and, most influentially, *Copland whom he propelled into populism with *El salón México*, written while visiting Chávez and conducted by him. He formed a Mexican Symphony Orch. and ran it for 20 years (1928–48), introducing music by Stravinsky, Schoenberg and other titans. He also headed the national conservatory, won generous state funding for the arts and raised generations of Mexican composers. His own output was substantial, adventurous and individual, rooted in Mexican and Amerindian sonorities while absorbing the language of modernism. Of six completed symphonies, the first, *Sinfonia de Antigonia* (Mexico City, 15.xii.33), is least ethnic. It was drawn from incidental music he wrote for Jean Cocteau's version of Sophocles' drama and used ancient Greek modes and tropes in a wind-dominated score. The 2nd, *Sinfonia India* (NY, 23.i.36), contains themes recognizable to any lover of cowboy movies, relying on authentic Amerindian sources and intriguingly arrayed in cross-rhythms and counterpoint in a single 11-minute movement. The 4th, *Sinfonia Romantica* (Louisville, Kentucky, 11.ii.53), used a mosaic of small melodic fragments to create a coherent whole. His 5th (Los Angeles, 1.xii.53) is for strings alone.

Although he favoured declamatory titles – like *Sinfonia proletaria* (Mexico City, 29.ix.34), a choral setting of revolutionary songs – and wore socialist credentials on his sleeve, Chávez was anything but a realist or propagandist composer. The latest techniques were at work even in primitivisms like the Aztec ballet, *Xociphilli-Macuilxochitl* (1940), which used a Varèsian array of four wind and six percussion. His abstract music was cleanly conceived; the violin concerto (Mexico City, 29.ii.52) presents a perfect mirror image: ABCD-DCBA.

He endowed the national stage with a folk ballet *El fuego nuevo* (Mexico City, 4.xi.28) and an opera, *The Visitors* (1957), written with Chester Kallman, Auden's partner, but he remained essentially a concert composer who excavated a nation's heritage – and had the courage and tenacity to liberate himself from it.

b. Calzada de Tacuba, Mexico, 13.vi.1899, as Carlos Antonio de Padua Chávez y Ramirez; orphaned at age three; st with *Ponce (1909–14) and *Varèse (1926–8); prof. at Harvard 1957; *d*. Mexico City, 2.viii.78. *other works*: *Dark Meadow*, ballet for Martha Graham (NY, 23.i.46); concerto for 4 horns (Washington, 11.iv.37), piano concerto (NY Phil. 1.i.42); three string quartets (1921–44); much piano music.

Cheltenham Rural festival founded in 1945 to present the latest in English symphonies, it became a term of abuse among the *avant-garde for representing a safe and traditional style. *Berkeley, *Rawsthorne, *Crosse and *Bainbridge were favoured composers.

Chicago Windy city of many musical attributes. Chicago jazz was the name given to the 1920s urbanization of Dixieland simplicity, centred on bootleg clubs and replete with white imitators. Chicago blues held sway in the 1950s with Muddy Waters band and Bo Diddley, both ancestors of the *Rolling Stones. The Chicago Symphony Orch., founded 1891, was ruled with rods of iron by Fritz Reiner (1953–63) and Georg Solti (1969–90).

Chichester Psalms *Bernstein's Hebrew-text creation for boy's voice, chorus and orchestra, commissioned by Chichester Cathedral. fp: NY, 15.vii.65.

Paul CHIHARA US-Japanese composer, interned as a child in the Second World War, he studied with *Boulanger in Paris but turned to serial and aleatory forms except in choral music, which he writes like a Renaissance scribe.
b. Seattle, Washington, US, 9.vii.38; taught UCLA 1966–74; *works include*: Forest music for orchestra (1968), two symphonies, *Grass* concerto for double-bass and orchestra (1971), saxophone concerto (1981), *Missa carminum* (1976).

A Child of our Time *Tippett oratorio inspired by the shooting of a Nazi diplomat, it uses Negro spirituals to celebrate human integrity. fp: London, 19.iii.44, cond. Walter Goehr.

Children's corner Six English-titled piano pieces by *Debussy for daughter,

Chouchou; the *Gollywogg's Cake Walk* parodies *Tristan. fp: Paris, 18.xii.08.

China The five-pitch (pentatonic) scale of indigenous Chinese music intrigued Mahler while writing *Das *Lied von der Erde* and Puccini during *Turandot*. Western music was encouraged in China before the communist takeover but was violently expunged during the 1960s Cultural Revolution perpetrated by the 'Gang of Four' surrounding Chairman Mao's wife, Jiang Qing. The anti-intellectualism of this oppression proved irresistible to *Cardew and *Wolff. Peking-style *socialist realism planted proletarian exhortations in traditional theatre, opera and popular song. A few works were officially sponsored, generally by composer collectives. Of these, the *Yellow River Concerto* by four composers enjoyed a vogue in the West and the *Butterfly Lovers' Concerto* by Chen Gang and He Zhan Hao, a sickly-sweet romance, was a hit in East Asia. Around 1980, young composers at the Beijing central conservatory attempted a synthesis in which indigenous Taoist sources predominated over Western. Their ideas were shelved after the 1989 Tienanmen Square students massacre, but persist among expatriates, such as the composer Tan Dun of Columbia University. Music in China has been inextricable from politics.

Chinese Flute Chamber symphony by *Toch for soprano and 14 instruments using ancient Chinese poetry. fp: Frankfurt, 24.vi.23.

Chinese string quartet 12-tone work by *Hauer, dated 1953.

Osvald CHLUBNA Pupil of Janáček, he helped revise the early *Sarka* and posthumously completed his tone-poem *Danube* (Brno, 2.v.48) and the opera *From the House of the Dead* (Brno, 12.iv.30). In the latter he fleshed out the score and added an upbeat hymn to freedom that held the stage for 30 years. He composed pastoral, patriotic tone-poems and five string quartets.
    b. Brno, 22.vii.1893; *d.* there, 30.x.71.

choral music Modern masters include Stravinsky, Kodály, Janáček, Bernstein and Berio. The medium was corrupted by totalitarian regimes which demanded hymns of praise to steelworks and military conquests.

chôros Brazilian street music, refined by *Villa-Lobos in series of 14 works.

Chout *The Buffoon* – ballet by *Prokofiev. fp: Paris, 17.v.21.

CHOU Wen-Chung *Varèse's executor completed his teacher's *Nocturnal* (1968) while in the ascendant at *Columbia University. Academic duties absorbed his creativity, which once promised a delicate fusion of advanced western sonorities and Chinese principles based on the I Ching.
    b. Cherfoo, China, 29.vi.23; fled to Shanghai 1937; graduated as civil engineer 1945 and st architecture at Yale; st with *Slonimsky, Martinů, Varèse, *Luening; joined Columbia 1957, vice-dean 1976-; works: *Landscapes* for orchestra (San Francisco, 19.xi.53), *7 poems of the T'ang dynasty* for tenor and ensemble (NY, 16.iii.52), *And the Fallen Petals* for orch. (Louisville, 9.ii.55), *Riding the Wind* for wind (1964), *Yun* for wind, two pianos and percussion (1969).

Christophe Colombe Discovery opera by Milhaud, using film inserts. fp: Berlin 5.v.30, cond *Kleiber.

Jani CHRISTOU Adventurous Greek who read philosophy with Wittgenstein and psychology with Jung before returning to the family estate on Hios and exploring his creative psyche in unconventional ways. Overcoming a *serialist choral 2nd symphony (1958), he invented a *notation that embraced music, stage direction and lighting. These works were meant to 're-vive primeval rituals' in performances that combined psychic seances with psycho-analytical group therapy. *Anaparastasis* (re-enactments, 1965–66), a series of 140 rites, left room for *aleatory improvisations and were littered with curious symbols, some of which proved indecipherable after his death, in an Athens car-smash on his 44th birthday.
    b. Heliopolis, Egypt, 8.i.26; *d.* Athens, 8.i. 70. *performable works include:* opera, *The Breakdown* (1964), Pentecost oratorio, *Tongues of Fire* (Oxford, 27.vi.64); six songs on poems by T.S. Eliot for mezzo-soprano and orchestra (1955); *The Strychnine Lady*

for viola, five actors, two instrumental ensembles, tapes, metal sheet, toys, red cloth, other objects (1967).

Jan CIKKER Slovak opera composer drawing on world literature – the Dickensian *Mr Scrooge* (1954), Tolstoy's *Resurrection* (1962), Shakespeare's *Coriolanus* (1972) and *The Play of Love and Death* (1969) after Romain Rolland.
   b. Banska Bystrica, 29.vii.11; st with *Novak; *d.* Bratislava, 21.xii.89.

Francesco CILEA The Italian *verismist came to the fore with *Adriana Lecouvreur* (Milan, 6.xi.02), the true romance of a French soprano poisoned by a jealous princess. It proved magnificent for divas, but its successor *Gloria* (Milan, 15.iv.07) failed, driving Cilea to despair of opera and he slunk off to run conservatories at Palermo (1913–16) and Naples (1916–35).
   b. Palmi, Calabria, 23.vii.1866; *d.* Varazze, 20.xi.50. *other works*: opera *L'Arlesiana* (1897), symphonic poem for soloist, chorus and orch. (1913), violin and piano variations (1931).

Cinderella Three-act ballet by *Prokofiev. fp: Moscow, 21.xi.45.

Circus polka Orchestral piece by *Stravinsky to accompany marching elephants. fp: Cambridge, Mass., 13.i.44.

clarinet Amenable to new sonorities, it appealed to Berio, Birtwistle and Boulez; traditional concertos were added by Nielsen, Stravinsky and Copland.

Kenny CLARKE The outstanding US *jazz drummer virtually invented *bebop with his off-beat rhythms and veered further from exhausted traditionalism as a founder of the Modern Jazz Quartet in 1952. He moved to Paris three years later, playing there until 1973 with unflappable serenity.
   b. Pittsburgh, 9.i.14; *d.* Paris, 25.i.85.

Rebecca CLARKE The English viola player was not taken seriously as a composer, so she sailed to America where her viola sonata was pipped by *Bloch to the 1919 *Coolidge prize. She won outright with a charming piano trio two years later but could not change English opinion. In 1944, she married another unrecognized composer, James Friskin (1886–1967), and

emigrated to New York. She wrote deceptively penetrative chamber music – a Prelude, Allegro and Pastorale for viola and clarinet is deliciously poignant – and lived to win acclaim from feminists.
   b. Harrow, 27.viii.1886; *d.* NY, 13.x.79.

Classical Symphony First symphony by 28-year-old *Prokofiev, in homage to Haydn and expiation of his previous musical savagery. fp: St Petersburg, 21.iv.18.

Aldo CLEMENTI The Italian avant-gardist focussed on the end of music which, he argued, justified any means. His dense works proceed momentously to an ineluctable conclusion.
   b. Catania, Sicily, 25.v.25; st at *Darmstadt (1955–62); *stage works*: *Blitz* (1973), *Collage 4* (1979); *instrumental works*: three *Informels* (1961–3), violin concerto (1977), viola concerto (1980).

click sheet/click track What film composers and conductors use to give them cues for action.

Clocks and Clouds Quintessential *Ligeti piece for 12 women's voices and orchestra, evoking an atmosphere of nebulously shifting rhythms and harmonies. fp: Graz, 15.x.73, cond. *Cerha.

Albert COATES Whirlwind conductor, he assisted at the birth of Russian modernism as conductor at St Petersburg's Maryinsky Theatre (1911–19), cultivating a public taste for Skryabin and encouraging Prokofiev to write operas. After the revolution, he wandered far and wide, deputizing for *Beecham in London, forming the Rochester SO and teaching at the Eastman School (1923–25), finally settling in South Africa. He composed colourful operas on *Samuel Pepys* (Munich, 21.xii.29) and *Pickwick* (London, 20.xi.36) and what must have been the first Afrikaans opera, *Tafelberg se Kleed* (Capetown, 7.iii.52).
   b. St Petersburg, 23.iv.1882 of English and part-Russian parents; st with *Nikisch; cond. Elberfeld 1906–10, Dresden, 1910–11, St Petersburg 1911–19, emigrating on political and economic grounds; *d.* Milnerton, nr Capetown, 11.xii.53.

Eric COATES English composer of a breezy *London Suite* (1932) that yielded a hugely popular *Knightsbridge March*, his wealth was founded on *Sleepy Lagoon* through which 1930s dancing couples dreamed of distant serenity.

b. Hucknall, Notts., 27.viii.1886; *d.* Chichester, 21.xii.57.

code When composers were unable for personal or political reasons to speak their mind, they buried the truth in secret codes. *Shostakovich used the notes equivalent to his German *initials – DSCH (S = E-flat, H = B-natural) – to voice dismay at Soviet totalitarianism, primarily in the string quartets and occasionally in the later symphonies. Alban *Berg expressed his passion for Hanna Fuchs-Robettin in the *Lyric Suite and violin concerto by intertwining their initials – AB (B = B-flat) and HF – and playing complicated rhythmic and structural games with the numbers 10 and 23, which he regarded as personally fateful. Elgar scattered unresolved clues in the title pages and themes of the Enigma Variations and the violin concerto about an old, unrequited love.

Composers would reward patrons with works based on their initials – the Swiss Maecenas Paul *Sacher was amply blessed in this way – and Parisians in particular composed lettered suites to congratulate and commemorate one another. *Fauré delighted in such tributes.

The German conductor Karl Muck (1859–1940) was arrested in Boston in 1917 for supposedly encoding military secrets into orchestral scores that he was taking back to Europe. During the Second World War, Elizabeth *Poston was one of several composers employed by the Allies to devise musical ciphers. None has ever been cracked.

Ornette COLEMAN Alto-saxophonist, inventor of 1960s 'free jazz' that returned to group *improvisation against the trend of intellectualism and European gloss. He struck sparks off his partner John *Coltrane, after whose death he formed a quartet and turned to formal composition. His *Skies of America* was played by quartet and full symphony orch. at the 1972 Newport Festival. He ventured into fusions with *rock and *electronics and came to be regarded as the last of the great jazz innovators, though none of his music had the

wide appeal of *Ellington's or the raw sensuality of *Parker's.

b. Fort Worth, Texas, 19.iii.30;

Samuel COLERIDGE-TAYLOR The son of a West African doctor and English mother, he shone at the Royal College of Music, married a fellow-student and settled into a suburban composer's life at Croydon. He hit the limelight with *The Song of Hiawatha* (1900), an American Indian epic composed in a style that combined Sibelian sagas, the lilt of Dvořák tone-poems and the singalong solemnity of Mendelssohnian oratorio. It played annually in London until 1939, prompting amateur choristers from all over the land to dress up as braves and squaws for their big night in thew Royal Albert Hall. In the US, Coleridge-Taylor was dubbed 'the black Mahler' on three conducting tours and was celebrated in Washington and Baltimore with three-day festivals of his music. He publicly demanded black liberation, composed Symphonic Variations on an African Air (1906) and a suite, *Toussaint L'Ouverture* (26.x.01), on the leader of Haitian independence. His ascent was cut short by the English climate. Waiting for a train on the platform of West Croydon Station, he collapsed with pneumonia and struggled home unaided, to die at the age of 37.

b. London,15.viii.1875; st with *Stanford; prof. at Trinity College 1903, Guildhall School 1910; *d.* Croydon, 1.ix.12. *other works*: opera *Thelma* (1909), oratorios *Kubla Khan* (1906) and *A Tale of Old Japan* (1910), violin concerto in G minor (1911).

Michael (Charles) COLGRASS Percussive composer in Chicago, he won the 1978 Pulitzer prize for *Déja vu*, a concerto for four percussionists and orchestra.

b. Chicago, Illinois, 22.iv.32; st with Milhaud, Foss, Riegger; *other works*: *Letter from Mozart*, collage for piano and orch. (NY, 3.xii.76), viola concerto (Toronto, 26.ix.84).

collage The collation of pieces of existing works into a new creation stemmed from the early Cubists who pasted newspaper cuttings on to canvas. In music, it was initially indistinguishable from traditional forms of quotation. *Mahler stuck a Carinthian song by Thomas Koschat into the 5th symphony and a snatch of *Merry Widow* into the 7th; he was accused of pastiche and unoriginality, when his intention was to use and distort familiar objects to comment on social evils. *Berg pasted folksongs and Bach chorales into his operas to ease the pain of atonality and into his violin concerto for private and sentimental reasons. The entire option of classicism was essentially a collage of music from one era into works of another.

Collage ultimately came of age in the no-man's land between conflicting ideologies. In the post-Stalinist USSR, where the official doctrine was *realism and the opposing line was astringent radicalism, Shostakovich made his 15th symphony into a disturbing patchwork of Rossini, Wagner, Mozart, Berg and others. *Schnittke's symphonic works, especially *(K)ein Sommernachtstraum*, lull the listener with a block of derivative romanticism that implodes unpredictably into cacophony – a technique he designated *polystylism. *Berio's *Sinfonia* similarly marched between Western late romanticism and avant-gardism. It employed a chunk of Mahler's 2nd symphony and phrases by Ravel, Strauss and others, as well as a speech by the black liberationist Martin Luther King to achieve a multi-layered effect. *Gerhard called his 3rd symphony 'Collages for tape and orchestra' and many electronic composers pieced together strips of pre-recorded tape in an orthodox collagist manner.

Phil COLLINS The most successful British rock act in the US since the Beatles, he is basically an old-fashioned balladeer with up-to-the-minute, high-tech accompaniments and stage paraphernalia. A former drummer in the intelligent rock group Genesis, his number one hits have included 'You Can't Hurry Love' (1982), 'Against All Odds' (1984), 'One More Night' (1985). As a child he played Artful Dodger in the musical *Oliver!*
   b. London, 31.i.1951;

Cologne The Rhineside cathedral city was the first to build an *electronic music studio in 1953. With *Stockhausen and *Kagel in residence, it became a year-round hive of charismatic *avant-gardism.

colour The idea that shades of tonal intonation are parallel to visual hues was mooted since medieval times. In the art nouveau era, modernists sought to define that correlation. *Skryabin ascribed specific keys to certain colours and invented a colour keyboard to change the lighting according to shifts of musical mood in his *Prometheus* symphony (1911). *Bliss named each movement of his *Colour Symphony* (1922) after a different hue and *Schoenberg specified precise changes of colour as a vital ingredient of the atonal opera *Die glückliche Hand* (1913/24). *Messiaen, much later, composed the colours of exotic birds and the heavenly hosts.

Colour perception remained, however, a subjective judgement. Skryabin saw F♯ as bright blue, while Messiaen composed clear skies in A major. Schoenberg, himself a gifted painter, absorbed a concurrent idea of Wassily Kandinsky (1866–1944) that colour, words and tone were elements in their own right and need to accord with nature. Grass need not be green, nor red happy, since green and red were self-defining. In *Die glückliche Hand*, Schoenberg wrote an enigmatically sparse text, illuminated by intensive stage and lighting directions that used colour as a Wagnerian leitmotiv, a device that found its way into modern theatre. Schoenberg, in the same period, gave the name 'Farben' (colours) to the central movement of his Five Pieces for Orchestra and coined a term, *Klangfarbenmelodie* – sound-colour melody – to define how a tune could be altered by timbre rather than picth. The same note played by different instrumental combinations changes the sound-picture more radically than another note or key. This discovery proved seminal for *Webern and ultimately for *Stockhausen and electronic composers. Many *Cologne taped compositions were named after colours of the rainbow.

John COLTRANE Saxophonist with Miles *Davis and Thelonious *Monk, he was a vital catalyst in the confused search for a modernist jazz. He introduced time-shifts between melody and harmony and helped *Coleman on the road to neo-

improvisatory 'free jazz' before dying at 40 of liver cancer and the after-effects of prolonged drug addiction. His record *A Love Supreme* sold a quarter of a million copies.
b. Hamlet, N. Carolina, 23.ix.26; d. NY 17.vii.67.

Columbia Records The Columbia Phonograph Company was incorporated in NY in 1890 and split into sundry ownerships of which the CBS media group was largest. CBS Records dominated the US classical market. It was sold to Japan in 1987 and renamed Sony Entertainment.

Columbia-Princeton Electronic Music Center Founded in NY by *Luening and *Ussachevsky in 1959, it enabled *Varèse to finish his *Déserts* and occupied the vanguard of electronic experimentation, attracting *Babbitt and *Davidovsky among others.

compact disc The introduction of a digitally-encoded, undamageable sound carrier in 1982 reversed a long decline in record sales and yielded an unforeseen plurality in art music. CDs soon became so cheap to manufacture that esoteric music could be painlessly released and unfashionable composers were able to find a domestic audience. By 1990 more art music was available on record than ever before. In addition, the clarity of a system that eliminated hiss and crackle enable the delicate sonorities of 12th-century plainchant and 20th-century introspection to achieve satisfactory reproduction. The technology was pioneered by Philips of Holland in conjunction with Sony of Japan.

combinatoriality A technique patented by *Babbitt, using half of a 12-note *row together with one of its permitted transformations. Babbitt ascribed the principle to *Schoenberg's 4th string quartet (1936); it had little impact beyond US academia.

combo A small jazz band of three to six players.

Company Sondheim musical, staged by Hal Prince. fp: NY (Alvin Theater), 26.iv.70.

composers There were a number of attempts to redefine the role of a composer away from the romantic image of artist-in-a-garret and the late-romantic, Wagnerian idealisation of a titanic thinker who communes with eternal forces. Marxist-Leninism viewed the composer as an 'art-worker' who was paid by the state to deliver entertainment, propaganda and uplift to the people. Free-market capitalism required uncommercial composers to undertake other occupations, whether in the public eye as conductors and soloists or humbly serving as a publisher's copyist. The composer-as-thinker image survived in Germany and the US where composers could expect professorial chairs, and their music would retreat into ivory towers. The Wagnerian ideal of the composer as catalyst of all the arts persisted to the end of the century in the ambitions of *Boulez and *Stockhausen and the cross-cultural appeal of *Cage and *Glass.

computers The messianic hopes vested in *electronic music after 1945 switched to information technology in the 1970s. Here, potentially, was a means of calculating musical ideas and details, storing them and reproducing or transforming them in concert. *Xenakis used a processor to compute probabilities in his *stochastic compositions and *Cage computerized the Chinese I Ching for his *chance operations. The most exciting option was that computers could split tones unachievable by human means. *Boulez declared that computers held the key to the future of music and built his *IRCAM around Giuseppe de Giugno's massive 4X mainframe. His major work, *Répons* (1981–), involved live participation of the 4X and its technicians but the machine was so bulky that performances were scarce. It was also rendered obsolete by inexpensive home computers. Although computers have been used in a range of experimental compositions, their most significant application to date is in copying musical parts, a drudgery that traditionally provided employment for hungry composers.

concert The content and atmosphere of concerts changed appreciably. At the turn of the century, it was acceptable for ticket-holders to drop in and out of long programmes that ran to a dozen items. Beer was served to patrons at their tables in Berlin's Philharmonie and smoking was actively encouraged. Heavy symphonies would be given in the first half, followed by sweetmeats and virtuosity after the interval. Programmes started to shrink after the First World War, assuming a standard triptych of overture, concerto and symphony. Although formal dress declined, the distance between public and performers was preserved by a raised platform and separate facilities. *Boulez tried to break down barriers in 1970s *rug concerts that brought both sides together during and after a concert.

concert party A group of friends attending a concert, or a party of light entertainers giving a seaside show. The term came to be applied to 1980s business fraudsters who bought large tranches of shares together to raise their price artificially.

concerto While the shape, size and very survival of the symphony was continually challenged, the concerto flourished almost unchanged as a contest or collaboration between soloist and orchestra, and a box-office opportunity to add star quality to a concert. The major 20th-century concertos are: piano: Rachmaninov 2, 3, 4, Paganini Rhapsody; Bartók 1–3; Gershwin *Rhapsody in Blue*, concerto in F; Falla *Nights in the Gardens of Spain*; Ravel G major and left-hand concertos; Poulenc; Szymanowski *Symphonie concertante*; Schoenberg; Prokofiev 1, 3, 5; Shostakovich 1 and 2, Ireland, Ligeti, Lutosławski.

   violin: Barber, Bartók 2, Berg, Elgar, Glazunov, Larsson, Martinů 2, Nielsen, Prokofiev 1 and 2, Schnittke 4, Schoenberg, Shostakovich 1 and 2, Sibelius, Stravinsky, Szymanowski 2, Walton, Weill.

   viola: Bartók, Hindemith, Schnittke, Walton.

   cello: Barber, Bloch *Schelomo*, Britten *Cello Symphony*, Elgar, Kabalevsky 1, Korngold, Lutoslawski, Penderecki, Prokofiev *Sinfonia Concertante*, Rodrigo, Shostakovich 1&2, Zimmermann.

   bassoon: Panufnik.

   clarinet: Copland, Corigliano, Finzi. Nielsen, Stravinsky *Ebony Concerto*

   oboe: Carter, Strauss, Zimmermann.

flute: Arnold, Nielsen.
horn: Hindemith, Strauss.
trumpet: Birtwistle, *Endless Parade* (1987), Jolivet 2.
tuba: Vaughan Williams.
saxophone: Glazunov, Larsson.
harpsichord: Falla, Gerhard, Gorecki.
harp: Ginastera.
organ: Poulenc.
guitar: Catselnuovo-Tedesco, Rodrigo *Concierto de Aranjuez*, Villa-Lobos.
harmonica: Villa-Lobos.
double concertos:
flute/oboe: Ligeti.
oboe/harp: Henze, Lutosławski.
two violins: Arnold.
piano/harpsichord: Carter.
triple concerto: Tippett.

concerto for orchestra Composition in which most instruments get a chance to show off. Invented by *Hindemith (1925), it was made famous by Bartók's Boston masterpiece (1943). The concerto for orch. was conceivably the century's most successful new musical form.

   other concertos for orch. are by: Piston (1933), Petrassi (seven concertos 1934–64), Stravinsky (*Dumbarton Oaks*, 1938), Kodály (1939), Morton Gould (1944), Baird (1953), Lutoslawski (1954), Bacewicz (1962), Tippett (1963), Gerhard (1965), Schuller (1966), Musgrave (1967).

concerto grosso Baroque form re-examined by Bloch, Martinů, Malipiero, Vaughan Williams.

Concord Sonata Ives' pianistic everest with tone-*clusters in the 2nd movement and a flute obbligato in the finale. It was nominally his 2nd sonata for piano, in four movements titled 'Emerson,' 'Hawthorne', 'The Alcotts' and 'Thoreau'; composed 1909–15; published 1919; fp: NY, 20.i.39.

conducting Leading an orchestra became a separate profession when Hans von Bülow (1830–94) was expelled from the Wagner circle and carved himself a charismatic niche at Meiningen. He became the first figurehead of the Berlin Philharmonic Orchestra, where he was succeeded by the hypnotic *Nikisch and the mystical *Furtwängler. Others, imitating *Mahler at Vienna and *Toscanini in Milan, seized administrative power at state institutions as music directors. In the media age, conductors saw the chance to add wealth to executive power, an ambition exemplified by *Karajan and promoted by increasingly powerful agents. With the accretion of might and money, there was a parallel decline in the depth and spirituality of symphonic interpretation.

Technically, there were few advances in the art. The myopic Toscanini set a trend for conducting from memory and the modernist *Boulez dispensed with the baton. Furtwängler abhorred precision and pursued a shimmering glow by fluttering his stick indeterminately; *Abbado devoted long stretches of rehearsal to a miniscule instrumental detail; the expressive Russian Gennady Rozhdestvensky was contemptuous of over-rehearsal. A handful of conductors applied themselves to the advancement of new works. The most convincing were *Klemperer, *Koussevitsky and *Stokowski; the Germans Hans Rosbaud (1895–1962) and Hermann Scherchen (1891–1966) premièred cornerstones of 12-tone and *avant-garde music, including Schoenberg's *Moses and Aron* and Boulez's *Le marteau sans maître*. Modern Czech music was fathered by Václav Talich (1883–1961); five of the Shostakovich symphonies were premièred by Yevgeny Mravinsky (1903–88) and Schnittke's oeuvre was promoted by Rozhdestvensky.

> *Bib*: Norman Lebrecht, *The Maestro Myth*, London (Simon & Schuster), 1991.

Justin CONNOLLY US-oriented Englishman, primarily influenced by *Babbitt and *Carter but latterly veering to simpler forms.

> *b*. London, 11.viii.33; taught Yale U. 1963–66; RCM, London 1966–; *works include*: *Antiphonies* for 36 instruments (1966), oratorio on William Blake's *Marriage of Heaven and Hell*.

Marius CONSTANT A member of the hybrid breed of composer-administrators cultivated in France – see *Liebermann, *Landowski – this Romanian pupil of *Boulanger, Honegger and Messiaen, became musical director of French radio in 1953 and ran the Opéra de Paris from 1973 to 1978. His music is fearlessly eclectic, moving from Debussyist impressionism through serial and aleatory techniques to a collage represented by a succession of concertos. *Choruses and Interludes* for horn and orchestra (1990) and the saxophone concerto (1978) are pure Franco-jazz; the concerto for barrel-organ and orchestra contains an amusing attempt to meld in a modern work music that Mozart and Beethoven wrote for mechanical organ. Constant collaborated with Peter Brook on *La tragédie de Carmen* (5.xi.81), a production that received some 1000 performances worldwide.

> *b*. Bucharest, Romania, 7.ii.25; graduated local conservatory 1944, st Paris 1945–49; lecturer in composition at Stanford and Hilversum; *other works*: *Candide*, 'mimodrama' for Marcel Marceau (Hamburg Opera, 24.i.71); Oratorio on the Rights of Man (1989), many ballets, piano concerto (1954), 24 Preludes for orch. (cond. *Bernstein, 1958), Symphony for Winds (1978), *Pelléas-et-Mélisande* symphony (1983).

Paul CONSTANTINESCU Late-romantic Romanian composer of two operas, a symphony and concertos.

> *b*. Ploesti, 13.vii.09; st with *Schmidt; *d*.Bucharest, 20.xii.63.

The Consul *Menotti's opera about an attempt to flee a fascist country. fp: Philadelphia, 1.iii.50.

Contrasts Foot-tapping country-dance piece by *Bartók for Benny *Goodman (clarinet), Joseph Szigeti (violin) and himself (piano). fp: NY, 21.iv.40.

Frederick Shepherd CONVERSE Composer of a machine-age hymn to the ten-millionth automobile that rolled off Ford's production line. It was titled *Flivver Ten Million* and performed by the Boston SO on 15.iv.27. He was the first American to write an opera for the Met, with *The Pipe of Desire* (1906), and completed four late-romantic symphonies.

> *b*. Newton, Massachusetts, 5.i.1871; *d*. Westfield, Massachusetts, 8.vi.40.

Barry CONYNGHAM Under the aegis of his teacher *Sculthorpe, Conyngham made the front page of the *Sydney Morning Herald* by going to study with *Takemitsu in Japan rather than following the trail to

Oxford or New York. It signified a Pacific and Antipodean awareness that has echoed in his compositions, though not so assuredly as in his teacher's.

b. Sydney, 27.viii.1944; taught Melbourne U. 1975– ; *works*: operas *Edward John Eyre* (1973) *Ned* (1978), *Fly* (1984), double-bass concerto: *Shadows of *noh* (1978), cello concerto (1984).

Arnold (Atkinson) COOKE *Hindemith's British apostle composed two operas, six symphonies and five quartets. He wrote a piano trio while anchored off the Normandy coast during the Allied invasion.

b. Gomersal, Yorks., 5.xi.06; R.N. lieutenant 1941–5; *other works*: opera, *Mary Barton* (1954).

Deryck COOKE BBC radio producer who, with *Goldschmidt's help, created the best performing version of *Mahler's 10th symphony; fp: London, 13.x.64.

b. Leicester, 14.ix.19; *d.* nr. London, 26.x.76.

cool jazz Clear, cerebral jazz of 1950s provenance, originating on the American West Coast with Dave Brubeck, Gerry Mulligan, Chet Baker.

Elizabeth Sprague COOLIDGE US maecenas and musical activist, she founded Berkshire festivals of chamber music and a concert series at the Library of Congress for which she commissioned key works by Stravinsky (*Apollon Musagète*), Copland (*Appalachian Spring*) and Bartók.

b. Chicago, 30.x.1864; *d.* Cambridge, Massachusetts, 4.xi.53.

Aaron COPLAND The independence of American music was, to a very considerable extent, proclaimed by the fifth son of a pair of Russian-Jewish immigrants who escaped to Brooklyn from murderous pogroms. In the city where Copland grew up, Charles *Ives was silently imagining a new American music, strong, quirky and unbeholden to the old continent. After counterpoint studies with the ex-Viennese Rubin *Goldmark, he went to Paris for the finishing touch of Nadia *Boulanger who, rather than smoothing his edges, gave him the confidence to express his originality.

A prototype American in Paris, he came home with an organ symphony (NY, 11.i.25, Boulanger soloist; revised as 1st symphony) that forced its conductor, Walter Damrosch, to apologize to his audience, declaring that anyone who composed such a work at 25 would be capable of murder by the age of 30. Boston voted with its feet over the hot jazz rhythms of the two-movement piano concerto (28.i.27, cond. Koussevitsky). His spiky pianism reached its apogee in the taxing Piano Variations of 1930 in which he attempted a personal form of *serialism. Everything Copland did was without American precedent and, when he turned to indigenous American subjects, he was able to do so with the integrity and ingenuity that Ives had foreshadowed.

Having absorbed European tradition and modernism, he arrived at a simplicity that was easy only on the ear. Its creation was a matter of great sophistication. It took something approaching genius to invent the shimmering A-major serenity that opens the Martha Graham ballet *Appalachian Spring* (Washington, D.C., 30.x.44), music that pleased farmers and professors alike. His *Fanfare for the Common Man* (Cincinnati, 12.ii.43) amounted to a credo: Copland believed good music should belong to everyone and devoted his life to reaching out, as a composer and writer, conductor and teacher. He was the Father of American Music in a highly practical sense.

His folklore suites opened the American west for exploration by many other composers, while preserving an individual, humane and somewhat prophetic outlook. His balletic portrayal of *Billy the Kid* (Chicago, 16.x.38) as feckless rather than evil, a victim of corporatism rather than the rule of law, anticipated Bob *Dylan's version 40 years later for Sam Peckinpah's film. He laid ground-rules for a jazz-symphonic synthesis in the early concertos and in *Quiet City* (NY, 28.i.41), a jazz trumpeter's moody reflection on modern urban life. His extraordinary piano sonata (Buenos Aires, 21.x.41), ranging from chordal novelty to a conclusion of meditative transcendence, was the starting-pistol for a decade of sonata writing by *Barber,

*Carter and other Americans. He was role model to his countrymen, most of all to Leonard *Bernstein, who shared an identical background. *Vitebsk* for piano trio (NY, 16.ii.29) is his only musical acknowledgment of his Jewishness, a klezmer-like memory of stepmother Russia.

Maturity came around 1930, when he abandoned the subversive harmonies that, in *Nocturne* for violin and piano (1926), delighted a Paris salon attended by James Joyce. He gave advanced new music concerts in NY with Roger *Sessions, but at the same time joined the communist party and wrote a First of May workers' song. An invitation from *Chávez gave him the chance to gather material for the colourful ballet, *El Salón México* (Mexico City, 27.viii.37), that set the style for *Billy the Kid*, *Rodeo* (1942) and ultimately *Appalachian Spring*. That suite made Copland the first US composer to win global recognition and popularity. He used its tonality to open the enriched 3rd symphony (Boston, 18.x.46), one of the most performed of all American symphonies; its finale contains the *Fanfare for the Common Man*, as does the *Lincoln Portrait*, a patriotic recitation of democratic values for speaker and orchestra (Cincinnati, 14.v.42). Untroubled by accusations of self-borrowing, he was careful to avoid self-caricature and stagnation.

Hollywood claimed him for *Of Mice and Men* (1939), *Our Town* (1940) and *The Red Pony* (1948) but Copland belonged to the East Coast and returned quickly to its concert halls. The eloquent clarinet concerto for Benny *Goodman (NY, 6.xi.50) married a multitude of sources. Its sombre opening recalls *Mahler's 9th symphony; it then lightens into a *Vaughan Williams-type pastoral, before jiving into Brazilian rhumba and ending in ripples of jazz riffs. Fifteen minutes long and scored for strings, harp and piano, it is an endearing masterpiece.

His populism – allied to his socialism, Jewishness and homosexuality – became suspect in the McCarthy era when the *Lincoln Portrait* was banned from President Eisenhower's inauguration ceremony and Copland felt for the first time a stranger in his homeland. The stigmas he encountered

prompted a return to more recondite music. Twelve-tone incursions in the Piano Quartet (1950) and the orchestral *Connotations* (NY, 23.ix.62, opening Lincoln Center's Philharmonic Hall) and *Inscape* (U. of Michigan, 13.ix.67; both cond. Bernstein) impressed neither common man nor highbrows. His only full-length opera, *The Tender Land* (NY, 1.iv.54), was a dramatic failure despite dazzling musical passages.

Having composed all his life with apparent ease, he became depressed by negative criticism and an ascetic musical climate. He ceased composing at 70 and, though he lived another two decades, said he never missed it. 'I must have expressed myself sufficiently,' he reflected.

b. Brooklyn, NY, 14.xi.1900; *d.* NY, 2.xii.90. *other works*: Dance Symphony (1930), Short Symphony (aka 2nd symphony, Mexico City, 23.xi.34); *Letter from Home* (NY 17.x.44), *Danzon Cubano* (Baltimore, 17.ii.46), *Music for a Great City* (London, 26.v.64), 12 Poems of Emily Dickinson (voice/piano, 1950), Nonet (1960), *Threnody 1: in memoriam Igor Stravinsky* (flute and string trio, 1971); *Night Thoughts (Homage to *Ives*, piano, 1972).
Bib: A. Copland, *Copland on Music*, 1960; A. Copland and V. Perlis, *Copland* (2 vols.), 1982–89.

John CORIGLIANO On Bernstein's death in 1990, Corigliano led the race to inherit his mantle as America's musical spokesman. Having failed to make an appreciable foreign name by the age of 50, he won the important *Grawemeyer award in 1990 for his first symphony (Chicago, 15.iii.90, cond. Barenboim), commemorating in a patchwork quilt of sombre melodies and crashing sonorities a number of friends who died of AIDS. It was the first musical statement on the subject and, while simplistic in utterance, had many moving and impressive moments.

The following year, Corigliano was the first composer for quarter of a century to present a new opera at the Met. His *Ghosts of Versailles* (18.xii.91, cond. Levine) seemed new in name alone, revisiting the Beaumarchais of *Figaro* in a pastiche somewhere between *Rosenkavalier* and The *Threepenny Opera*. It was a great night out, but hardly a momentous work of music theatre.

Prior to these achievements, Corigliano had various concertos to his credit. The best was a Pied Piper fantasy for James Galway that sent the flautist traipsing through the auditorium trailed by kids. The 30-minute clarinet concerto (NY, 6.xii.77) consisted of three contrasting, unconnected movements – don't leave after the noisy *Cadenzas*, you might love the hushed *Elegy*, a clarinet-violin dialogue in memory of the composer's father, or the Renaissance-inspired *Antiphonal Toccata*. Shamelessly eclectic, the concerto pretended to be all things to all men. The oboe concerto (NY, 9.xi.75) opens with a movement entitled 'Tuning Game'. As expected, it involves the sound of an orchestra tuning up, ha-ha; the finale is a Moroccan arabesque picked up on a visit to Marrakech. A setting of Dylan Thomas's *Poem in October* (NY, 25.x.70) for tenor and eight instruments sounds like Dudley Moore's strangulated parody of the pieces *Britten wrote for his consort, Peter Pears.

b. NY, 16.ii.38, son of the NY Philharmonic concertmaster; st with *Creston; *other orch.* **works**: *Fern Hill* after Dylan Thomas (NY, 19.xii.61); *Elegy* for orchestra (San Francisco, 1.vi.66), piano concerto (San Antonio, Texas, 7.iv.68).

Cotton Club Harlem nightclub that was New York's jazz centre from 1920–40, with Duke *Ellington, Cab Calloway and Bojangles Robinson in residence.

country (or country-and-western, or hillbilly) music American prairie tunes that combined with *jazz, *blues and gospel music to form the basis of Western *pop, retaining its integrity as a folk art in an era of mass communication. Its mecca is Nashville, Tennessee, home of the Country Music Hall of Fame and annual jamboree. Bob *Dylan was heavily indebted to its modes.

cover Recording of a pre-existing hit; have been more than 100 cover versions of the *Beatles song 'Yesterday'.

(Sir) Noël COWARD No-one defined middle-class fears and febrility of the interwar years as bitingly as this fay English entertainer, heir to the laconic, self-mocking wit of W. S. Gilbert and a composer of no mean skill. *Bitter Sweet* (London, 12.vii.29) was a full-blown operetta, equal in most musical respects to *Léhar's and superior in its dramatic relationships. Like Cole *Porter and Irving *Berlin he could only play piano in a couple of keys but his lyrics touched a universal chord and entered common parlance: Don't Put your Daughter on the Stage, Mrs Worthington; Mad Dogs and Englishmen; Someday I'll Find You; Don't Let's be Beastly to the Germans. He sang off-key, rolled his rs and played cameo roles in many movies and in life, but as a social commentator with musical obbligato he was, in his genre, without rival.

b. Teddington, Middlesex, 16.xii.1899; *d.* Port Maria, Jamaica, 25.iii.73.

Henry COWELL Some of the most radical innovations ascribed to John *Cage were actually the work of his teacher, Cowell. It was Cowell who, in 1923, began tampering with the insides of a grand piano. In the 1930s he allowed performers *aleatory freedom of choice in works that had parallel passages of varying length for different players. A Californian by birth and disposition, he felt closer to Asia than to Europe and was drawn to Indian and Japanese sonorities and rhythms. He was involved with Theremin's *electronic experiments. Any one of these ventures would secure his place in the modernist pantheon. His principal discovery, however, preceded them all. In 1912 at the irreverent age of 15 he alighted, by striking the piano keyboard with his fist or forearm, on tone-*clusters – which became an integral element of *Bartók's piano music.

In 1919, he wrote a book on *New Musical Resources*. Soon after, he crawled beneath the lid of a grand piano in *Aeolian Harp* (1923) to pluck its strings while pressing the keys. In *Suite for Solo String and Percussion Piano with Chamber Orchestra* (Boston, 11.iii.29, cond. *Slonimsky), he tickled the strings with drumsticks and inserted a darning egg between them. This was the fore-runner of Cage's *prepared piano.

Aside from his own advances, Cowell founded a *New Music* magazine and record label in 1927 to support fellow-progressives. He was the first to proclaim the genius of *Ives; others he promoted were *Antheil, *Chávez and *Ruggles. He endured a painful breach with the puritanical Ives, for whom he felt a filial love, when a monstrous injustice sent Cowell to San Quentin jail for four years in 1937, without trial or benefit of attorney, for allegedly impairing the morals of a 17-year-old boy. With boundless courage he organized a prison band, started a music education program and composed a *United Quartet* that purported to dissolve the harmonic differences between nations. On his release, he married the folklorist Sidney Robertson, was reconciled to Ives and served as secretary to the exotic Percy *Grainger. He taught at Columbia U. from 1951 to his death. Among his private pupils, Cage apart, were George *Gershwin and Lou *Harrison; *Nancarrow named him as a formative antecedent. He was beyond question the founder of US experimentalism, a tradition snubbed by the East Coast establishment and central to the vitality of multi-media *happenings and 1980s *minimalism.

Cowell wrote a vast amount, including 20 symphonies. This was designed, said Slonimsky, to confuse his enemies but left admirers equally bemused. Little of his music is ever revived, nor is due credit given to his precedence. While his works lack the concentrated certainty of *Varèse, there is pleasure and aural titillation aplenty in such pieces as *Pulse* for five percussion players (1939). *Saturday Night at the Firehouse* (1948) and *Tales of our Countryside* for piano and orch. (Atlantic City, 11.v.41, cond. *Stokowski) combine US folklore with his own solo piano pieces.
  b. Menlo Park, California, 11.ii.1897; *d.* Shady, NY, 10.xii.65. *other works*: *Madras Symphony* for orch. and 3 Indian instruments (Madras, 3. iii. 59), harmonica concerto (1960), harp concerto 1965); 2 koto concertos (1962–65); *Tides of Manaunaun* (1st work to use clusters, 1912); 1st biography of Ives (1965).

Edward COWIE The contrasting landscapes of England and Australia are depicted in Cowie's excellent paintings and varied compositions, which include three symphonies and a 1982 opera on the outback bandit, Ned Kelly.
  b. Birmingham (UK), 17.viii.43;

Cowpat music Disparaging term coined by *Lutyens for English pastoralities of *Vaughan Williams and his flock.

Robert CRAFT Attaching himself to *Stravinsky in 1947, Craft converted the master to serialism and promoted a personal view of his ideas and history. He published conversations with Stravinsky and edited his selected correspondence.
  b. Kingston, NY, 20.x.23;

Ruth (Porter) CRAWFORD-SEEGER A 1931 string quartet of astonishing prescience achieved an almost static harmony to convey a sense of space. *Cowell published her music and she emerged as a seer of modern harmony. She married her composition teacher Charles Seeger (1886–1979) and became stepmother to his folksinger son, Pete.
  b. East Liverpool, Ohio, 3.vii.01; *d.* Chevy Chase, Maryland, 18.xi.53. *other works*: violin sonata (1926), *In Tall Grass* (Amsterdam *ISCM, 15.vi.33), wind quintet (1952).

La Création du Monde *Milhaud's dazzling jazz suite. fp: Paris, 25.x.23.

Paul CRESTON Born among poor Italian immigrants, Creston left high school to earn a living and made his name near the end of the War with a 2nd symphony that expressed tragedy and triumph in a flowing street pageant, full of vitality and blues, as vibrant as late Gershwin (NY, 15.ii.45). He caught the ear of top conductors but was spurned by intellectuals for his humble status as church organist and for writing music that was melodic, rhythmic and unpretentious. Among some 200 works are six large symphonies and 15 concertos, as well as several pieces inspired by Walt Whitman and some devoutly Catholic derivations from scripture. He did not experiment with modernist techniques, regarding Bach and Ravel as the borders of his tonal universe.
  b. NY, 10.x.06 and christened Giuseppe Guttoveggio (Creston was a schoolyard nickname); organist at St Malachy's Church NY 1934–67, composed first piece, 5 *Dances*,

at 26 years old and won Guggenheim Fellowship; *d.* San Diego, 24.viii.85. *other orch. works*: saxophone concerto (1941), *Chthonic Ode (homage to Henry Moore)* (Detroit, 6.iv.67), *Sadhana* (inspired by *Tagore) (1981).

crooners The most successful 1940s male singers – Bing Crosby, Perry Como, *Sinatra to some extent – earned their living by smooch.

Gordon CROSSE Studies in Rome with *Petrassi sent Crosse home a *serialist with a pechant for rude medievalism, rather like Maxwell *Davies', voiced in a one-act 1966 opera on Yeats' *Purgatory*. Under Britten's sway, however, he turned lyrical, almost late-romantic.
 b. Bury, Lancs., 1.xii.37; taught Birmingham U. 1964–69, U. of Essex, 1969–76; *works*: five operas of which *The Story of Vasco* (1974) staged at London Coliseum, two symphonies, cello concerto (1979), piano trio (1986).

crossover Pop musicians playing classics, and vice-versa. Prime examples are street ballads recorded by Caruso and Pavarotti, Broadway shows by *Weill and *Bernstein, the requiems of Andrew Lloyd Webber and Paul McCartney (written with Carl Davis), Frank Sinatra singing 'September Song'.

George (Henry Jr.) CRUMB In *Black Angels* (Ann Arbor, Michigan, 23.x.70), Crumb conceived a personal range of sonorities to express his despair at the state of America during the Vietnam War. Scored for conventional string quartet amplified by stage microphones, it requires the players periodically to strike or stroke gongs, count aloud to seven in various languages, shake maracas and draw their bows hauntingly across the rims of half-filled glasses. Interweaving fragments of the Russian Orthodox funeral mass, an Elizabethan madrigal and Schubert's *Death and the Maiden*, it is as moving a requiem for lost verities as Elgar's cello concerto or Shostakovich's sixth symphony. Despite an inherent pessimism, it points ahead progressively.
 Crumb achieved sonic breakthroughs in *Vox Balacnae (Voice of the Whales*; Washington, D.C., 17.iii.72), pitching four

eletronic instruments against submarine recordings of the great mammal with a naturalism as heart-warming as *Messiaen's. In *Sun-Child* (NY, 5.v.77, cond *Boulez) for two children's choruses and huge orchestra, he employed household utensils and their noises.
 Some of his music has been directed primarly towards sound-seeking, but there are works of extreme traditionalism. The sonata for solo cello (1955) has a pleasing Bachian structure and is a standard repertoire piece for graduate cellists. Crumb's innovations have not received due recognition and he has been derided by some critics as dilettantish. Closer study of his music reveals progress and originality in each succeeding work.
 b. Charleston, W. Virginia, 24.x.29; st with *Finney, *Blacher; won 1968 Pulitzer Prize for *Echoes of Time and the River*; taught U. of Colorado 1959–64, U. of Pennsylvania 1965–.

César CUI The last of Russia's Mighty Five lived to witness the Bolshevik Revolution. He composed two insignificant adult operas and four for children in the 20th century and completed Mussorgsky's opera, *The Fair at Sorotchinsk* (1916). His 3rd string quartet (1913) and three piano Scherzos (1910) are typical of his diminutive composing gifts; Cui wielded his fiercest pen as a newspaper critic.
 b. Vilna, Lithuania, 18.i.1835; *d.* Petrograd, Russia, 26.iii.18.

cultural bolshevism *Kulturbolschewismus* – term coined by the Nazis for modern music and used to suppress it. It was loosely applied to high art in general, prompting Hans Johnst's widely-quoted aphorism, 'When I hear the word "culture" I reach for my pistol.'

cultural diplomacy Statesmanlike 1970s policy aimed at bridging political differences by exchanging orchestras and works of art. Even as they waved at each other weapons of mass destruction, Soviet and American negotiators spent evenings yawning through one another's music.

cummings ist der dichter Boulez piece for 16 voices and 24 instruments based on unpunctuated verses by the American poet e e cummings and taking its title from a telephonic misunderstanding. Asked in German what he was going to call the work, Boulez said, 'I don't know, but cummings is the poet' – a phrase that duly appeared on the title page. fp: Stuttgart, 25.ix.70.

Cunning Little Vixen Comic-strip nature-opera by *Janáček tracing the life-cycle of female fox and lamenting the human ageing process. fp: Brno, 6.xi.24.

Curlew River Britten's church parable, based on a Japanese noh-play. fp: Aldeburgh, 12.vi.64.

Alvin CURRAN Rome-based American celebrated for a 1984 outdoor work using foghorns and shiploads of sailor-singers, *Maritime Rites*. Other environmental titles include: *Light Flowers, Dark Flowers, Natural History. Electric Rags II* for saxophone quartet (1989) is a psychedelic throwback to happier, smokier times.
   b. Providence, Rhode Island, 13.xii.38; co-founded Musica Elettronica Viva, Rome, 1966.

Czechoslovakia For 20 years from independence to the Nazi invasion (1918–1938), Prague was a great capital of modernism. *Zemlinsky, who directed its German Theatre from 1912, introduced operas by Hindemith, Schreker, Strauss, Korngold, and the world première of *Erwartung* (1924). With the Czech Philharmonic he conducted Mahler and works of the *Schoenberg circle, *Berg in particular. *Janáček's late flowering was stimulated. *Hába developed microtonality at the conservatory; *Weinberger produced a worldwide operatic hit. Beside them, the traditionalists *Suk, Novak and *Foerster flourished and outstanding conductors emerged in Erich Kleiber, Karl Rankl, Georg Szell, Rafael *Kubelik, Karel Ančerl.

The curtain fell on the world première of *Krenek's opera *Karl V* (15 vi. 38), after which the Nazis and post-War Stalinism all but quelled the spark. Those who could, chose exile; Ullmann, Haas and Schulhoff perished in the Holocaust. The lone, stubborn voices of *Eben, Kalabis and Slavický began to emerge after the collapse of communism. The *Slovakian region produced significantly less talent.

dada The short-lived anti-art nonsense genre ('dada' literally means hobby-horse) arose in Zurich and New York around 1916 and was exemplified by Marcel Duchamp's moustachioed Mona Lisa with an obscene caption. It had echoes in *Satie's music and habits but no profound musical repercussions until *Cage's assaults on grand pianos and 1960s *happenings. The smashing of instruments, seen in some avant-garde concerts and copied by hyped-up rocked musicians, recalled the Cologne exhibition of 1920 where spectators were offered axes to destroy the exhibits.

Dalcroze method Also known as Eurythmics, it teaches musical skills and understanding through rhythmic movements. Pupils start by clapping hands, stamping feet and swaying their bodies, progressing to solfège singing and improvisation at the piano. The method was devised by a Bruckner pupil, Emile Jaques-Dalcroze (*b.* Vienna, 6.vii.1865; *d.* Geneva, 1.vii.50), who in 1910 founded a school near Dresden, soon moved to Geneva, launching a worldwide movement. He composed five operas and a folksy operetta.

Luigi DALLAPICCOLA Just as Marx never dreamed that his revolution would start in Tsarist Russia, so Arnold Schoenberg was amazed to discover in 1945 that his ideas had taken root in, of all countries, melomanic Italy. Luigi Dallapiccola was the first musician outside Schoenberg's immediate circle to compose *12-note music and did so with an imme-

diacy that others longed for but never attained. He made his decision emotionally in September 1938 and had no personal contact with the Second Viennese School until a 1942 encounter with *Webern and a post-war exchange of letters with the delighted Schoenberg.

The 34-year-old Florentine professor, previously enamoured with the regenerative promise of fascism, was propelled into modernism on hearing Mussolini announce on the radio new laws for racial discrimination. Dallapiccola resolved to marry his Jewish girlfriend, Laura Coen Luzzato, and began composing a prayer by Mary Stuart that he had just read in a best-selling, newly-banned biography by Stefan Zweig. With mounting emphasis on the imprisoned queen's words 'libera me!', he constructed a 12-note row and wound it around the mordant chords of the Russian Dies Irae, aiming 'to address myself to a vast audience, speaking to all sufferers'. The 27-minute *Canti di Prigionia*, for mixed chorus, pianos, harps and percussion was augmented with an apocalyptic passage by the sixth-century philosopher Boethius and a deathbed meditation by Girolamo Savonarola on the Psalmist's words, 'In You, God, I put my trust.' It was sung in Rome (11.xii.41), the day Mussolini declared war on the US, and was immediately prohibited. Its next performance, to international admiration, was at the 1946 ISCM Festival in London, announcing Dallapiccola as a modernist capable of instantaneous emotive appeal.

In the years between, he went intermittently into hiding with his wife and wrote a

12-note one-act opera on a similar topic, titled *Il prigioniero* (Florence, 20.v.50). It told of a prisoner apparently allowed to escape by a friendly jailer, only to run smack into the waiting Grand Inquisitor outside. A torment worse than loss of liberty, implied Dallapiccola in lyrical, haunting tunes, was the kindling of false hope. Together with his 1939 one-acter *Volo di Notte (Night Flight)* (Florence, 18.v.40), *The Prisoner* established Dallapiccola as an operatic reformer, combining a gift for communication with advanced composing techniques. He never repeated operatic success, however, perhaps because in the course of time he conformed increasingly to Webern's rigidities. He wrote a two-act *Ulisse* (Berlin, 29.ix.68) and a corps of choral works that were praised by the avant-garde for their 'floating rhythms' but never reached a wider public. He was the doyen of post-war Italian modernism and his choral style anticipated *Nono's. The sweetest of his concert works was the Little Night Music or, in its self-evoking Italian title, *Piccola musica notturna* (Hanover, 7.vi.54).
  b. Pisino (Pazin), Istria, Austro-Hungary, 3.ii.04; exiled to Graz 1917–18 to escape anti-Italian tide; prof. at Cherubini Conservatorio, Florence, 1934–67; taught *Tanglewood 1951, Berkeley 1962 and other US campuses; *d.* Florence, 19.ii.75. *other orch. works*: *Tartiniana* for violin and small orch. on themes by Giuseppe Tartini (1692–1770) (in two parts, 1951/56), *Piccolo concerto per Muriel Couvreux* for piano and chamber orch. (Rome, 1.v.41), Variations for orch. (Louisville, Kentucky, 2.x.54), *3 Questions with 2 Answers* (New Haven, Conn., 5.ii.62), Songs of Liberation for chorus and orch. (Cologne, 28.x.55).

Jean-Michel DAMASE Commercially successful French composer writing with great fluency for wind instruments and harp, somewhat recalling *Milhaud.
  b. Bordeaux, 27.i.28; won Grand Prix de Rome 1947; *works include*: seven operas, seven ballets, various concertos, 17 Variations for wind quintet.

dance – see ballet.

Dance around the Golden Calf Orgy scene from *Schoenberg's *Moses and Aron*.

Dance of the seven veils *Salome's strip-tease as she demands John the Baptist's severed head on a plate. Pseudo-exotic, intentionally erotic, in $3/4$-time, the dance was written as a late afterthought to Strauss's opera.

Dance Suite Important orch. work by Bartók for jubilee of Budapest, 19.xi.23.

DANIEL-LESUR Midway man in French music, he joined *Messiaen in the *Jeune France movement but retreated in his only opera, *Andrea del Sarto* (Marseilles, 24.i.69) to wagnerizing *Pelléas.
  b. Paris, 19.xi.08 (as Daniel Lesur);

Richard DANIELPOUR Lyrical US symphonist.
  b. NY, 28.i.56; *works*: three symphonies, including No.2 'Visions', for soprano, tenor and orch. (San Francisco, 19.xii.86, cond. *Wuorinen), and No. 3 'Journey Without Distance' for soprano, chamber chorus and orch. (Akron, Ohio, 24.ii.90); ballet *Urban Dances* (NY, 6.iv.90).

Danse sacrée et danse profane Piece for harp and strings by Debussy. fp: Paris, 6.xi.04.

Dantons Tod Von *Einem's break-through opera, libretto by *Blacher after Büchner's 1835 drama of French Revolutionary strife. fp: Salzburg, 6.viii.47.

DAO Meditative Vietnamese protégé of *Messiaen.
  b. Hanoi, 1940 as Nguyen-Thien Dao; st in Paris, 1968; *works include*: opera *My-chau Trong-thuy* commissioned by Rolf *Lieber-mann (1978); *Ba Me Vietnam* (1974) for double bass and 20 instruments, percussion concerto (1980), piano concerto (1985), violin concerto 'Thien Thai' (Paris, 8.viii.88), Concerto 1789 for string sextet and orch. (Moscow, 10.xi.89), *Voie-concert* (Paris, 13.iv.92).

Daphnis et Chloë *Ravel's sensuous ballet for Diaghilev. fp: Paris, 8.vi.12.

Darmstadt Cultured city in western Germany, near Frankfurt, that became the incubator of *avant-gardism from 1946 when Wolfgang Steinecke (1910–61) founded International Summer Courses for New Music in the castle of Kranichstein. His aim was to awaken young German musicians to music that was forbidden in the Hitler years, primarily to *serialism. For the first couple of years, the course had hardly any foreign teachers and students; the star pupils were *Henze and *Stockhausen. *Leibowitz joined the faculty in 1948 and the following year *Messiaen began to develop his own strand of serialism. Maderna arrived in the same summer.

From 1950 onwards, Darmstadt represented the cutting edge of musical thinking, a place where that latest experiments in *electronics, *aleatory music and dadaism were discussed and performed. Stockhausen (1953–72) and Boulez (1956–65) were key teachers; Cage came in 1958. Never before had musical progress been so concentrated in a single spot. Darmstadt became a byword for all that was adventurous and iconoclastic in music, rejecting past legacies and facing the future with boundless confidence in the discovery of new musical languages. Its students carried the gospel to all corners of the Western world and the name Darmstadt characterized works of music that existed primarily in the laboratory. From 1979 the fearsome *Ferneyhough took up a teaching post but time was running out for the avant-garde generation, which had produced little of public consequence to justify its dictatorship of style. The German modernist *Rihm attacked the summer school, saying 'only people with a weak ego go to Darmstadt' and his colleague Walter *Zimmermann declared: 'we don't need this overdose of originality any more.' The arrival of Morton *Feldman in 1984 signalled a softer, more approachable policy as Darmstadt drifted towards marginality.

Dartington School of Summer Music British course fashioned in Darmstadt's image and run from 1951 to 1979 by William *Glock. It introduced many Darmstadt figures and their works to the UK, as well as music by *Carter. The menu was mixed, however, with a wide range of older music.

Johann Nepomuk DAVID Fluent composer whose polyphonic mastery and reverence for tradition aroused a powerful nostalgia in German audiences and tedium elsewhere. David rose during the Nazi era as teacher and organist in Leipzig and after the war was professor of composition at Stuttgart. His music, which includes eight numbered symphonies, is mainly neo-Baroque (between the 5th and 6th he inserted a 'symphonia pre-classica'). He toyed with *12-note rows in his 2nd violin concerto (1957) and wrote his last symphonic fantasy, *Magische Quadrat* (1959), on a counterpointed version of *Schoenberg's method, basing the work on a mathematical conundrum and Albrecht Dürer's *Melencolia*.
  b. Eferding, Upper Austria, 30.xi.1895; *d.* Stuttgart, 21.xii.77.

His elder son, **Thomas Christian DAVID,** taught music in Vienna and conducted the Iranian television orchestra in Teheran. His travels enriches a 3rd concerto for string orch. and percussion (1974) with charming near-eastern sonorities.
  b. Wels, Austria, 22.xii.25; *other works*: piano, violin and guitar concertos.

Mario DAVIDOVSKY NY *electronic evangelist, his central work was a set of 8 *Synchronisms* (1964–73) for tape and varied combinations of live instruments, of which the 6th for symphony orchestra (or piano) and electronics won the 1971 Pulitzer Prize and was widely imitated for a while. Between the plops and jerks of manufactured sound, his music possessed a clear structure and discernible emotional content.
  b. Buenos Aires, 4.iii.34; moved to US 1960 to work at *Columbia-Princeton electronic music centers, of which he became director; prof. at Columbia U. 1981–; *other works*: *Scenes from Shir Hashirim* for chamber ensemble and four voices (1976); 2 string quartets (1954, 58).

(Sir) Peter Maxwell DAVIES The death of *Britten in 1976, though premature, found British music in a state of fertile promise. *Tippett was moving into his second stride; *Arnold was in full flow; and Aldeburgh acolytes were coming smoothly to maturity. Although Britten abhorred *serialism and the *avant-garde, his presence encouraged heterodoxy and expectations now shifted to the *Manchester trinity of *Goehr, *Birtwistle and Maxwell Davies.

'Max', as he was demotically known, was the pacesetter. His college-days trumpet sonata opus 1 (1955) was smack-in-the-face dramatic, almost operatic in its mood swings and declamations. Soloist and audience had barely time to breathe through seven eventful minutes. The opening theme was recycled in *Taverner, his first opera, recounting a Tudor composer's confrontation with a changing church, staged and restaged at Covent Garden (12.vii.72), noisy, unsettling and brimful of youthful challenge. Max's rough edges were the antithesis of Britten's polish; the musical future, from a 1970s perspective, belonged to the guerrillas.

He possessed, moreover, a formidable technique that switched easily from medievalism to Mahlerian orchestration, atonality to Me-Generation *pop. His chamber opera *Eight Songs for a Mad King (London, 22.iv.69) veered from Handel arias through Schumann and foxtrots to the Beatles' valediction 'Let it Be' in its depiction of a besmeared lunatic who imagined himself, or maybe was, King George III, loser of the American colonies. It stood in the genre of *Pierrot Lunaire and the epigrammatic theatre of Beckett and Pinter. This was a composer of untold cultural and continental awareness. In the year of Britten's death he composed A Mirror of Whitening Light (23.iii.77), an acute and unsettling landscape.

Fifteen years later, Maxwell Davies was writing ten Haydn-like concertos for the Scottish Chamber Orchestra, as radical a reversion to convention and commercialism as any composer in the century. He seemed, wrote a perplexed contemporary, 'intent on restoring those *Sibelius-plus-*Berkeley values that his early pieces rebelled against'. The reasons for this retreat were locked in a complex character that, while sociable, preferred self-isolation in the storm-swept Orkney Isles. He hid deeper behind borrowed themes and a bewilderingly profuse output.

Almost all his interesting works predate 1976. The chamber operas Miss Donnithorne's Maggot (Adelaide, 9.iv.74) and The Martyrdom of St Magnus (1976) belong to the Mad King's world as does Vesalii Icones (London, 9.xii.69) for naked dancer, solo cello and ensemble. Worldes Blis (London, 28.viii.69) presaged orchestral turbulences that were fulfilled only in the first symphony, composed 1973–76 (London, 2.ii.78, cond. *Rattle). Among many concerted works, the half-hour concerto for trumpet and large orchestra (Hiroshima, 21.ix.88) harked back without detectable anger or personal progress to that earliest sonata; the violin concerto (St Magnus, 21.vi.86) for Isaac Stern conveyed Orcadian atmosphere with little intellectual substance. He wrote copiously for children's voices, while unmarried and childless. Maxwell Davies was also to be found in the neo-medievalism of the ballet Caroline Mathilde (Copenhagen, 14.iii.91), courtly dances recomposed in a style not greatly advanced from that of Peter *Warlock. Like many frustrated composers, he took up conducting posts in mid-life.

b. Manchester, England, 8.ix.34; formed Pierrot Players with *Birtwistle, 1967, dir. Fires of London 1970–90; moved to Orkney island of Hoy 1970; knighted 1987; other works: opera Resurrection (Darmstadt, 21.ix.88), chamber opera The Lighthouse (Edinburgh, 2.ix.80), 2nd symphony (Boston, 26.ii.81, cond. *Ozawa), 3rd symphony (Manchester, 19.ii.85), 4th symphony (London, 10.ix.89); An Orkney Wedding with Sunrise (Boston Pops Orch., v.85), Ojai Festival Overture, Ave Maris Stella (Bath, 27.v.75), Canon in memoriam Igor Stravinsky (BBC, 6.iv.72); ten 'Strathclyde' concertos for every instrument of a chamber orchestra; scores for two Ken Russell films, The Devils and The Boyfriend (1971); much vocal and instrumental music.

(Sir Henry) Walford DAVIES Elgar's successor as Master of the King's Music was a Welsh warbler who delivered dulcet reactionary commentaries on the wireless. His specialty was sacred choruses and he wrote an anthem for the Royal Air Force.
b. Oswestry, 6.ix.1869; d. Wrington, Somerset, 11.iii.41. other works: symphony (1911).

Anthony DAVIS X (NY City Opera 28.ix.86), a compassionate life-story of the urban insurrectionist, Malcolm X, presented the unsettling image of a violent, black Siegfried, knitted out with street-credible music and dialogue, while classically through-composed. Son of the first black professor at Princeton, Davis's roots were in Afro-American literature and NY jazz, broadened by study trips to *India and *Indonesia. His violin concerto, *Maps* (Kansas City, 24.iv.88) melds Bartók-like asperities with gamelan sounds in a symphonic showcase of the kind Duke *Ellington once wrote.

> *b.* Paterson, New Jersey, 20.ii.51; *other works*: opera *Under the Double Moon* (St Louis, 15.vi.89); orch. *Notes from the Underground* (NY, 24.iv.88), piano concerto *Wayang V* (San Francisco, 15.xii.84, cond. *Adams).

Carl DAVIS Fertile film and TV composer with credits topped by *The World at War* (1973) and *The French Lieutenant's Woman* (1980), he longed for serious recognition. A 1980 symphony made little mark and the *Liverpool Oratorio* (29.vi.91) he wrote with Paul McCartney lacked the spark of original invention.

> *b.* NY, 28.x.36; *other work*: opera, *Peace* (1978).

Miles (Dewey) DAVIS (III) The most thoughtful of jazz musicians, the trumpeter tackled its creative crisis by interacting with *rock and *electronics, especially acoustic keyboards, in the phenomenon known as *free jazz. By pinning a mike to his horn, he perambulated the stage and produced distinctive wah-wah effects. Duke *Ellington dubbed him 'the Picasso of jazz' though Davis was less a maker of new forms than a brilliant improviser on old. His career was colourful and crossed many boundaries. The son of a ranch-owning dentist in East St Louis, he studied at Juilliard in 1944 but dropped out to join Charlie Parker's band in the heady excitement of post-War New York. Five years were sacrificed to heroin addiction, which he kicked in 1954, forming his first quintet with John Coltrane and others. He improvised a soundtrack for Louis Malle's movie, *Lift to the Scaffold*, and in an album titled *Kind of Blue* brought the perfectionism of chamber music and particular shades of modernism to the oldest of jazz

modes. His mind and music attracted collaborators of the calibre of Herbie Hancock, Chick Corea and Keith Jarrett, though Davis preserved his enigma behind a cloak of unapproachability. He retired in the 1970s after being shot at by gangsters and harassed by police, accusing the record industry of inbred racism. He made a famous comeback in 1981 as *The Man With the Horn* and attained a kind of apotheosis in his final decade. His hit albums were *Sketches of Spain* (1960) and *Bitches Brew* (1969).

> *b.* Alton, Illinois, 25.v.26; *d.* Santa Monica, California, 28.ix.91.

death Richard *Strauss on his deathbed in 1949 is supposed to have said: 'Dying is just as I composed it 60 years ago in *Tod und Verklärung* (*Death and Transfiguration*).' *Schoenberg described his own heart attack in the string trio op 45 and *Schnittke in his 5th symphony. *Mahler in his 9th and 10th symphonies, *Britten in his 3rd quartet, *Martinů in his nonet and *Debussy in his late chamber music confronted impending death with varying defiance or resignedness. Whether such explicit collisions with mortality were more effective than Beethoven's predominantly non-programmatic late quartets is a matter for continuing debate.

Death in Venice Valedictory opera by *Britten on Thomas Mann's novella of a homosexual artist obsessed by the beauty of a young boy on the beach.

> fp: Snape, 16.vi.73; libretto by Myfanwy Piper.

(Achille) Claude DEBUSSY In the German-occupied state of late romanticism, a senior conductor like Hans Richter could confidently declare 'there is no French music', knowing that in the quarter-century after the 1870 Siege of Paris, there was very little self-assertion in music written by Frenchmen. Then along came Debussy in his 20s, determined to invent a music that was specifically French and entirely new. On 20.xii.1894, he presented, almost unnoticed, a work that would define the sound of French music for most of the next century. It would also alter the world's perception of what constituted music. With *Prélude à l'après-midi*

Lindloff
'913

Like most of his contemporaries, Debussy fell under a *Tristan* spell during two visits to Bayreuth in 1888–89. Unlike the rest, he fought addiction with every alternative substance he could find. As a youth of 19 he became enamoured of Russian music while tutoring the children of Nadezhda von Meck, Tchaikovsky's unseen patroness. He became alienated from Italian opera while resident (1884–87) in Rome. In 1889 he discovered the plangent delights of the Javanese *gamelan at the Paris Universal Exhibition. He shared café tables with the symbolist poets Verlaine and Mallarmé and was smitten by the paintings of Monet and Cézanne. All of these ingredients contributed to a personal style that began to emerge with the G-minor string quartet of 1893, its middle movements echoing gamelan rhythms and Borodin.

The year 1893 was the turning point when he received permission from the Belgian symbolist Maurice Maeterlinck (1862–1949) to make an opera of his death-fixated play *Pelléas et Mélisande*. Its motionless account of the forbidden love between a princess and her brother-in-law is Wagnerian in content and imagery. Mélisande's long hair falling down from her window to envelop Pelléas is a variant on Parsifal cleansing his feet in Kundry's flowing mane. The illicit union and death aura are familiar from *Tristan* and *The Ring*. Yet Debussy had purged himself of the Wagnerisms that coloured his earlier Baudelaire settings and was able to compose a score that eliminated leitmotivs, symphonic development and disernible melody – the last of which, he memorably averred, was 'anti-lyrical' and only held up the action. 'My procedure, which consists above all in dispensing with Wagner, owes nothing to him,' he stated.

The music has a transparency that allows every word to be heard and a delicacy that can never be mistaken for Wagner. Contrary to the composer's protestations, there are identifiable themes and leitmotivs but they are not a driving force. Psychological subtlety is the source of the opera's hypnotic fascination, and its music mirrors changing moods with uncanny pre-Freudian perception. The première of

d'un faune, noted *Boulez, 'the art of music began to beat with a new pulse'.

In fact, it almost dispensed with rhythmic propulsion. Its uniqueness lay in a sultry languor that sacrificed motion for extended contemplation of momentary beauties. The piece described after-lunch reveries of a debauched faun, uncertain whether or not he had made it with two nymphs, but the Mallarmé poem on which it was based was not rendered explicitly until Nijinsky, to the composer's outrage, danced the auto-erotic faun 18 years later in Diaghilev's ballet production. Debussy had given only a hazy impression of the creature's fantasies in a score that inaugurated musical *impressionism. Flute and harp were well to the fore, mitigating sensuality with a certain coolness. Light and shade, shimmer and stillness, took the place of theme and variation; apart from the rippled opening, melody was almost immaterial. This was music of the highest procedural novelty. It threw off the pervasive spectre of Wagner and opened up a whole boulevard of compositional possibilities. For many composers, the 20th century would begin here.

Pelléas on 30.iv.02, after stormy rehearsals, objections from Maeterlinck and political intervention to remove the offensive word 'bed', was a landmark in operatic history. When Mélisande, dying, asks for the window to be opened, she let in not only sunlight but – said the conductor André *Messager – the whole of modern music. To German audiences, raised on Wagner, it was, and seemingly remains, the operatic anti-Christ. In accentuation and refinement of detail, it was quintessentially French.

Debussy composed the opera in two phases at either end of the 1890s, interrupted by domestic scandals. He finished a draft of *Pelléas* in the spring of 1895 and again in 1897 but withdrew the score each time, preoccupied by emotional turmoil. In 1892 he had set up home in a garret with green-eyed Gaby Dupont who accompanied him to bohemian haunts but was not accepted in the respectable homes of bourgeois musician friends. In 1894 he became engaged to a singer, Thérèse Roger, but he could not give up Gaby and the engagement was broken off, at the cost of Chausson's friendship. Her discovery of another affaire in 1897 prompted Gaby to attempt suicide. He broke with her in 1899 and married Lily Texier, a 25-year-old blonde, only to leave her after five years for Emma Bardac, a financier's wife and former mistress of *Fauré. This defection provoked outrage in *Ysaÿe, Gustave Doret and other intimates, and Debussy had to leave for England until the fuss died down. Emma gave birth to his adored only daughter, Chouchou, but their eventual marriage was dogged by naggings of dissatisfaction, boredom and lack of money.

All life long, he looked back at the 1890s as the acme of contentedness: 'I miss the C. Debussy who worked so happily on Pelléas,' he told a friend, 'because, between ourselves, I have never met him again.'

His character was neither firm nor pleasant, combining fickleness, a caustic tongue and self-obssessive depression. When his benevolent publisher died, he voiced 'a real sorrow – he was a lucky find for me'. During the Dreyfus Affair that divided France, the only political issue that provoked his attention was a postal strike that delayed his mail. His French nationalism verged upon rabid xenophobia. He hated Mahler and Schoenberg because they represented German music; during the First World War he took to signing himself 'CD, musicien français'. He was jealous of *Ravel and scornful of Fauré, writing newspaper criticisms and private comments of unnecessary virulence, but he extended a friendly hand to the young Stravinsky and Varèse, perceiving them correctly as a fellow-revolutionaries. He was personally unscrupulous, without ever compromising his compositions. He was a man of pleasure rather than passion, said his first wife, a remark that was relevant to his music.

Pelléas was the only opera he completed, though not the last of his stage attempts. *The Fall of the House of Usher* and *Le Martyre de Saint-Sébastien*, unfinished and unsatisfactory respectively, one after Edgar Allan Poe and the other a religious mystery by Gabriele d'Annunzio, lacked the dramatic certainty of Pelléas. Harmonically, however, the Martyrdom pre-echoed *Messiaen's modes, and there are passages in the ballet *Jeux* (Paris, 15.v.13) that could have been composed by *Boulez.

The first decade of the new century was taken up by orchestral and piano music. While sheltering at Eastbourne, on the Sussex coast, from the wrath of Parisian society he turned his ear to the English Channel and immortalized it as *La Mer* (Paris, 15.x.05). This was an impressionist work of high sophistication, blending the visual depths of the English painter Turner with the precisionism of a contemporary Japanese print, 'The Hollow Wave' by Katsushika Hokusai, that Debussy had printed on the cover of the orchestral score. After a harp opening that was almost Mahlerian, Debussy painted a still-life whose fearsome energy was implied but never declared.

He followed it with *Images* (Paris, 26.i. 13), which had an Ibéria movement but none of the literalness of *Rimsky-Korsakov or Chabrier's Spanish suites. Instead, it offered an alternative to musical *nationalism in a wash of exotically elusive images that include, in the initial Gigues section, a Northumberland folksong made morbid by discoloration. Interpretation of

Debussy's orchestral works demands a high level of preparation since, like the shop window of any Paris dressmaker, presentation is paramount.

Debussy's piano music is distinguished by its cloudiness, shrouding often explicit movement titles – 'Hommage à Rameau', 'The submerged cathedral' – behind a sonorous murk that lifts and descends unexpectedly. In the *Children's Corner* he wrote for his little daughter, he committed heinous musical heresy by wickedly parodying a phrase from the prelude to *Tristan* in the Golliwogg's Cakewalk. It was done so cleverly that Debussy had to explain the reference to dull-witted pianists. In 1904 he anticipated the advent of *jazz in a *Rapsodie* for alto-saxophone and piano, later orchestrated.

Debussy was afflicted by rectal cancer in 1909 and six years later underwent unsuccessful surgery. His last years, spent in wretched agony, produced three masterpieces of chamber music, rekindling the intimacy entombed in his string quartet. The 1915 sonata for flute, viola and harp reduced his instrumental colours to bare essentials. The sonatas for cello and piano (1915) and violin and piano (5.v.17, his last public appearance) admit an unsuspected warmth without in any way stooping to self-pity. The violin sonata seems to envy the freedoms of gypsy fiddlers. He contemplated a choral *Ode à la France* but died, aged 55, in his Paris apartment as German long-range guns pounded the city in the last throes of the war. 'Il est mort, Claude de France,' remarked the poet d'Annunzio. No French musician to this day has managed to escape his shadow.

b. St.-Germain-en-Laye, nr. Paris, 22.viii. 1862; *d.* Paris, 25.iii.18. *other works*: incidental music to *King Lear* (1904), *Danse sacrée et danse profane* for harp and strings (1904), *Nocturnes* (versions for piano and orch.), *Images* (1905–07, two series for piano, wholly different from the orch. work), 12 études for piano (1915), *En blanc et noir* for 2 pianos (1915).

Decadent music (*Entartete Musik*) Nazi term for music by modernists and Jews. Banned in 1933, it was the subject of a 1938 touring exhibition that backfired embarrassingly as the German public flocked to sample forbidden sounds.

deconstructionism Lit.-crit. term adopted by opera producers to justify demolishing (= deconstructing) a libretto and resiting it in another period – e.g. Peter Sellars' *Don Giovanni* among New York blacks and Puerto Ricans.

Maurice (Charles) DELAGE Awoken to music by *Pelléas, this ardent Debussyist became *Ravel's pupil and close friend. He travelled widely in the orient to write four delicious *Hindu poems* for soprano and nine instruments, as well as a ballet based on Kipling (see *Koechlin).
   b. Paris, 13.xi.1897; *d.* there, 21.ix.61. *other works*: 7 *Haï-Kaï* (1923), string quartet (1948).

Frederick (Fritz Theodore Albert) DELIUS A mess of a life that produced large works of even temperament but none that blazed with passion. The *impressionistic *On hearing the First Cuckoo in Spring* and *Summer Night on the River* have a timeless charm, as do the more tepid pastoralities, *In a Summer Garden* (London, 11.xii.08), *Brigg Fair*, 'an English Rhapsody' with 17 variations on a common theme (Liverpool, 18.i.08), *Eventyr* 'Once upon a time . . .' (11.i.19) and *A Song of Summer* (17.ix.32). It is not by such works that Delius wanted to be remembered, for his aspirations were Wagnerian or Debussyan in scale.

A Mass of Life (7.vi.09, cond. Beecham), after Nietzsche's *Thus Spake Zarathustra*, covers the gamut of German romanticism from Weber through Wagner to Strauss and Reger without offering a compelling reason for its existence beyond the ingenuity of its harmonies. The Nietzschean *Requiem* (23.iii.22) for artists fallen in the First War has more purpose but less musical invention. *A Song of the High Hills* (26.ii.22) for chorus and orchestra has no words at all, a relief after previous turgidities. His love-operas are unstageworthy, with the arguable exception of *A Village Romeo and Juliet* (Berlin, 21.ii.07). The best of *Fennimore and Gerda* (Frankfurt, 21.x.19) is its orchestral intermezzo.

None of these works possesses a compelling urgency. His concertos for violin (30.i.19) and cello (Frankfurt, 30.i.21) are inferior to *Elgar's; and the double concerto (21.ii.20) is simply tedious. Delius's acolytes, drawn to his music by its refreshing cosmopolitanism, included Percy Grainger, Philip Heseltine and Thomas *Beecham, the only conductor who could make Delius's music sound first-rate. German conductors *Nikisch, *Weingartner and *Klemperer enjoyed his slightly French timbre and he was published by the prestigious Universal Edition in Vienna.

Although English by birth, Delius lived in nomad's land. The son of German merchants, he was sent to Florida in his 20s to run an orange grove; American themes pervade the 1888 *Florida* suite and tone poem *Hiawatha*, as well as the massive orchestral *Appalachia*, with choral finale (Elberfeld, 15.x.04). Walt Whitman supplied the texts and Atlantic scenery for *Sea Drift* (Essen, 24.v.06). He went to study in Leipzig, was befriended by *Grieg and moved on to Paris where he mixed with impressionists and contracted the syphilis that blighted his last years. Marrying the painter Jelka Rosen, granddaughter of the composer Ignaz Moscheles, he moved into her house at Grez-sur-Loing, near Fontainebleu, where, from 1928, an English volunteer, Eric Fenby, received by dictation from the blind and paralysed composer the music he imagined but was unable to write down.

b. Bradford, Yorks., 29.i.1862; *d.* Grez-sur-Loing, France, 10.vi.34. *other works*: operas *Koanga* (Elberfeld, 30.ii.04), *Margot-la-Rouge* (1902); *Paris, the Song of a Great City* (orch., 1898), *North Country Sketches* (10.v.15); 3 string quartets, 3 violin sonatas and a 1916 mournful sonata for cello and piano.
Bib: Eric Fenby, *Delius as I Knew Him*, London (Faber), 1981.

Norman DELLO JOIO Son of an immigrant organist, he won the US Music Critics' Award in 1947 for a brace of premières. Fritz Reiner gave his *Concert Music* at Pittsburgh (4.i.46), George Szell conducted *Ricercari* for piano and orch., with the composer as soloist (NY, 19.xii.46). Like fellow-Italians *Creston and *Piston, he was devoted to ancestral harmonies and

liturgy, admitting just enough dissonance to keep pace with modern times.

A Joan of Arc opera and symphony, both entitled *The Triumph of Joan* (1950-1) were widely heard; a sequel, *The Trial of Rouen*, was made for television (NBC, 8.iv.56). Dello Joio opened a new line of work with small-screen documentaries, providing a soaring score for a 26-part CBS history of *Air Power* in 1956. His media success, allied to a steady conservatism, blunted his concert-hall appeal.

b. NY, 24.i.13; st with *Wagenaar and *Hindemith; taught Mannes College, NY, 1956-72, Boston U. 1972-9; *other works*: opera *Blood Money* (San Francisco, 18.ix.61); three ballets for Martha Graham; three masses; *Meditations on Ecclesiastes* for string orch. (Washington 17.xii.57; Pulitzer Prize); *Variants on a medieval tune* for band (1963); *Hommage to Haydn* (1969).

David (Walter) DEL TREDICI Californian composer who 'rediscovered' tonality – together with a fascination for Lewis Carroll's *Alice in Wonderland* that sparked a string of orchestral works. *Final Alice* (Chicago, 7.x.76, cond. Solti), for amplified soprano, folk group and orchestra, was an instant hit. It is riddled with gimmicks, from a tuning-up ritual that represents 'a time before time' to a 13-fold closing repetition of his own surname – the Italian word for 'thirteen' – and was rapturously received. None of its sonorities would have surprised the young Richard *Strauss. 'I certainly didn't sit down and decide to become a tonal composer – I fought it all the way,' insisted Del Tredici.

His *March to Tonality* (1985) was supposed to presage an era of musical confidence but Del Tredici's star waned as the novelty of his anachronisms wore off. *Steps* for orchestra, a New York Philharmonic commission (8.iii.90, cond. Mehta) introduced some dissonance but conceivably too little, too late.

b. Cloverdale, California; 16.iii.37; debut as pianist at 16 with San Francisco Symphony; st with Seymour Shifrin, *Kim and *Sessions; taught at Harvard 1962-72 and Boston U. 1973-; *other Alice works*: *Pop-pourri* (1968), *An Alice Symphony* (1969), *The Lobster Quadrille* (London, 14.xi.69, cond. *Copland), *Adventures Underground* (1971),

Vintage Alice (1972), *In Memory of a summer's Day* (St Louis, 23.ii.80, Pulitzer Prize winner), *Child Alice* (1981), *Haddocks' Eyes* (NY, 2.v.86).

Claude DELVINCOURT The student who shared the 1913 Prix de Rome with Lili *Boulanger was severely wounded in battle two years later, but recovered to head the conservatories at Versailles (1931–41) and Paris (1941–54). He wrote sinuous scores that recalled *Ravel's, mostly for the stage.
b. Paris, 12.i.1888; d. in car smash at Orbetello, Italy, 5.iv.54.

Chris DENCH *Microtonalist seeking mystic contact with earthly forces – not a lonely hearts ad, but a paraphrase of his publisher's leaflet. Dench has written shamanistic piano works for fellow-composer Michael *Finnissy and for the *Darmstadt coven, where he taught in 1986 and 1988.
b. London, 1953; autodidact; married flautist Laura Chislett, 1987; works: énoncé for 15 players (1983), string quartet (1985), 4 Darmstadt Aphorisms (1986–89), Topologies for solo piano (1980).

Edison DENISOV In the stagnant pond of Soviet music after Shostakovich, Denisov stood out for his daring, ever willing to make ripples and challenge official confirmity. Would-be rebels flocked to his Moscow classes and were introduced to avant-garde, underground techniques. The *Firsova-*Smirnov generation regarded him as a father figure and appointed him president of their revived Association of Contemporary Music.
Yet, when restrictions crumbled and communism disintegrated, the music that Denisov composed was in no sense equal to the historic occasion or to the size of his reputation. A symphony written for the Orchestre de Paris (2.iii.88) sounded like discarded sheets of *Messiaen, requiring a vast ensemble of considerable skill but signifying very little to the intellect or the emotions. As the Soviet state withered away, Denisov was seeking commissions in Switzerland.
Destined for a life of progress, he was named by his engineer father after the great American inventor. Appointed to the Moscow conservatory faculty at the age of

30, he appeased the authorities with political titles – *Ode in memory of Ché Guevara* (1968) – escape censure for impermissible atonalities that verged on 12-note technique but never fully embraced it. The *Crescendo e diminuendo* (Zagreb, 14.v.67) for harpsichord and 12 strings possesses a fashionable asceticism; the opera *L'écume des jours* (1981) is rowdily aggressive. A cello concerto of 1981 alternates between anger and a defeatist Russian morbidness, an affecting piece that – together with *Death is a Long Sleep* (Moscow, 30.v.82) for the same forces – casts Denisov in truest perspective.
b. Tomsk, USSR, 6.iv.29; other works: chamber symphony (Paris, 7.v.83), concertos for flute (1976), violin (1978), piano (1978), clarinet and viola; arrangements of music by Mussorgsky, Mosolov and Schubert.

Victor De SABATA Toscanini's successor at La Scala admired *Strauss and *Ravel and composed an opera *Il Macigno* (*The Rock*, Milan, 30.iii.17; revised as *Driada*, 1935), three symphonic poems and a ballet *1,001 Nights* (1929). He also provided fragrant incidental music for Max Reinhardt's 1934 production of *The Merchant of Venice*. He gave up composing when he took charge of the opera house from 1929 to 1953.
b. Trieste, 10.iv.1892; music director Monte Carlo Opera 1918–30; d. Santa Margherita Ligure, Italy, 11.xii.67.

Alfred DESENCLOS Just too young to join Les *Six, he wrote sinuous, Ravellian melodies. The sultry saxophone quartet (1962) and *Prelude, Cadence et Finale* (1956) for alto sax and piano found foreign audiences.
b. Le Portel, Pas-de-Calais, 7.ii.12; won Prix de Rome 1942; d. Paris, 3.iii.71.

Déserts Varèse's breakthrough into electronic sound, the first work for ensemble (wind/percussion) and pre-recorded tape, although he specified that it could be performed without the three electronic 'interpolations'. fp: Paris, 2.xii.54; cond. Scherchen.

Vladimir DESHEVOV Machine-Age Soviet composer, he created *Ice and Steel*, an opera intended to warm Stalin's heart, and *Rails*, a 1926 piano suite in praise of the locomotive. Most of his music was for film and theatre.

b. St Petersburg, 30.i.1889; st with *Lyadov and *Shtaynberg; *d.* Leningrad, 27.x.55.

Yvonne (Berthe Melitta) DESPORTES A French Suite for four clarinets that won her the 1939 Prix de Rome contains anticipations of *Copland's sublime concerto. In 1943, she set up a rival teaching institute to *Boulanger's.

b. Coburg, France, 18.vii.07; st with *Dukas; *works*: five operas, three ballets, two symphonies, two percussion concertos.

Paul DESSAU The last and least assertive of Bertolt *Brecht's composer-collaborators, Dessau provided incidental music for *Mother Courage* (1946), *The Good Woman of Szechuan* (1947) and *The Caucasian Chalk Circle* (1954), in which both instrumentation and thematic treatment are redolent of *Weill. Returning from US exile to communist eastern Germany, he turned out agitprop pieces – 'Workers of the World Unite!' for female chorus; 'To My Party' for baritone and string orch. – but hit trouble with the regime for his Brecht opera *The Trial of Lucullus* (17.iii.51, cond. Scherchen) that reopened the Unter den Linden opera house. He was made to tone down discordances and Brecht changed the title to *The Condemnation of Lucullus* (12.x.51). He composed another Brechtian opera, *Puntila* (Berlin, 15.xi.66) and a Marxist explication of *Einstein's* life and theories (16.ii.74).

The sincerity of his output in a totalitarian society is hard to assess, but the music is well-crafted and, later on, craftily experimental. The 1963 Bach variations for large orchestra possess a self-mocking wit. In 1960, he joined four composers from east and west Germany to write a *Jewish Chronicle*, warning against a revival of anti-semitism.

b. Hamburg, 19.xii.1894 (his mother perished in Terezin concentration camp); exiled 1933; st *serialism with *Leibowitz 1935; travelled to Palestine and US, where he wrote synagogue music, film scores and worked for a while as a gardener; back to eastern Germany in 1948; *d.* nr. Berlin, 28.vi. 79. *other works*: two symphonies; Requiem

for Lumumba (1964) and other Marxist cantatas; orch. elegy, In Memoriam Bertolt Brecht (1957); seven string quartets; piano piece 'Guernica' (1938), piano sonata (1955).

The Devils of Loudun Noisy Aldous Huxley opera by *Penderecki. fp: Hamburg, 20.vi.69.

Serge DIAGHILEV The ballet impresario preferred new music to familiar tunes and commissioned 30 years' worth of masterpieces, five by *Stravinsky, others by Debussy, Ravel, Les Six, de Falla, Satie, Strauss and Prokofiev – and many other composers whom he launched on the international stage. Improvident, homosexual and incorrigibly optimistic, he preyed on the aristocracy to pay for his Ballets Russes, formed in St Petersburg and regrouping in Paris after the Bolshevik Revolution.

b. Gruzino, Novgorod, Russia, 31.ii.1872; *d.* Venice, 19.viii.29.

Dialogues des Carmélites *Poulenc's opera in a nunnery. fp: La Scala, 26.i.57.

David DIAMOND US symphonist whose music won local awards but barely crossed national boundaries. A *Boulanger pupil, his hero was *Ravel. An *Elegy for Maurice Ravel* (1938) for string and percussion reveals the best of both composers – elegant, harmonically adroit, a memorable dirge that does not quite touch emotional depths. Diamond composed nine symphonies (1941–85), three violin concertos and ten string quartets. His prelude and fugues for piano (1939) were recorded by *Bernstein, a lifelong intimate.

b. Rochester, NY, 9.vii.15; *other works*: *L'âme de Claude Debussy* (1949), a vocal setting of *Debussy's correspondence.

Diary of one who disappeared Missing person's saga by *Janáček for five voices and piano, drawn from daily newspapers. fp: Brno, 18.iv.21.

Peter DICKINSON A British student at Juilliard, he met *Cage, *Carter, *Cowell and the aged *Varèse and envisaged a English-speaking union of new music. His musical orientation is audible; his emotive capacity less so. An organ concerto (1971), based on a blues setting of a Byron verse and the harmony (bars 53–61) of the first of Ravel's *Valses Nobles et Sentimentales*, liberates the soloist from alignment with the orchestra. His many-layered piano concerto (1984) attempts to musify James *Joyce. He has written amusing songs for his mezzo sister, Meriel, whom he accompanies on the piano.

b. Lytham St Annes, Lancs., UK, 15.xi.34; taught Keele U., 1974–84.

dictionaries of music George Grove, British inventor of the layman's companion to music, died as the century dawned. His four-volume compilation, shed some of its Germanic bias in the course of five editions that encrusted conservatism on to its initial enlightenment. A wholescale renovation, the 20-volume *New Grove* (1980, ed. Stanley Sadie) with manifold spinoffs, removed the enterprise from amateur perusal in terms of tone, scope and cover price and realigned it for English-speaking academics and institutions. Among single-volume reference works, the *Oxford Dictionary of Music*, devised by the jolly critic Percy Scholes, retained a little of its populism in Michael Kennedy's meticulous updatings.

Die Musik in Geschichte und Gegenwart (*Music in the past and present*, ed. Friedrich Blume) is a collective enterprise of German scholarship issued in facsimiles over 19 years (Kassel, 1949–68). It has been updated in further volumes and appears admirably methodical and sternly impersonal. Most subsequent dictionaries use *Grove* and *MGG* as basic sources, reiterating their occasional errors with touching fidelity. Reference works on modern music dating from the second half of the century were indoctrinated by *avant-gardism. They include dictionaries by John Vinton (editor, 1973), Paul Griffiths (1986) and a critical two-part survey of post-1945 music by Ulrich Dibelius (1966, 1988).

The US-originated *Baker* dictionaries (1900–92), edited since their 5th edition by *Slonimsky, are the liveliest biographical references, challenged by Alain Pâris's French opus on musical performers. Dictionaries of opera and popular music have proliferated and specialist trends in

*musicology have given rise to specific dictionaries of terminology, individual instruments and other paraphernalia.

Alphons DIEPENBROCK *Mahler's host in Holland was a classics teacher and philologist who turned to music in his late twenties. Knowledge of Greek drama, Latin liturgy and painting gave him cultural resources that he set to music in a late-Wagnerian mode. Serious to the point of depression, his output is intriguing rather than life-enhancing. The major work is a *Hymn to Rembrandt* (1906) for soprano, women's chorus and orch; a hymn for violin and orch. (1905) is a little lighter. Diepenbrock wrote incidental music for many plays, of which his most cherished project was the last – a suite for Sophocles' *Electra* (1920) that lacks *Strauss's venom but adds an ominous aura of its own.

b. Amsterdam, 2.ix.1862; *d.* there 5.iv.21. *other works*: *Hymn to the Night* (after Hölderlin, for soprano and orch. 1911), incidental music to Goethe's *Faust* (1918) and Aristophanes' *The Birds* (1917).

James DILLON *Ferneyhough follower, entirely self-taught, he is obsessed by extreme complexity and problem creation. He has experimented at *IRCAM with combinations of instruments and *electronics in a multi-part work, *Nine Rivers* (1982–).

b. Glasgow, Scotland, 29.x.50; *other works*: flute concerto (1992), *Le Rivage* (wind quintet, 1984), two string quartets (1983, 91), *Come Live with Me* (1981), *Windows and Canopies* (1985), *Spleen* (piano, 1980).

Dire Straits UK rock group whose *Dylanite founders, singer-guitarist Mark Knopfler and drummer Pick Withers, were recruited by their idol for his albums *Slow Train Coming* (1979) and *Infidels* (1984).

direction (opera) At the turn of the century, stage direction did not exist in opera outside of Bayreuth, where Wagner had stipulated every twist and turn. Elsewhere, singers were shown where to enter and exit, and that was it. *Mahler introduced elements of stage production at the Vienna Court Opera and *Toscanini followed suit at La Scala, Milan. In 1910, Richard Strauss summoned the theatre director Max Reinhardt (1873–1943) to Dresden to help with the intractable 3rd act of *Rosenkavalier. Reinhardt went on to establish a production style at *Salzburg; his pupil Carl Ebert (1887–1980) became general director at Darmstadt and Berlin State Opera, before joining Fritz Busch to create *Glyndebourne. The age of the opera director, also known as regisseur, had dawned.

Abstract productions, first seen at the *Kroll in the late 1920s, acquired a moral impetus when Wieland Wagner cleansed his ancestor's operas of nationalist trappings after 1945 by presenting them on an almost bare stage. His style was taken to a sanitized extreme in the centenary *Ring* of 1976, staged by Patrice Chéreau and conducted by Pierre *Boulez.

Political revisionism penetrated opera from East Berlin, where *Brecht built a socialist theatre and Walter Felsenstein (1901–75) at the Komische Oper (1947–75) adduced a contemporary relevance from operas that were intended to amuse rather than provoke. His disciples Götz Friedrich (*b*. 1930), Joachim Herz (*b*. 1924), Ruth Berghaus (*b*. 1927) and Harry Kupfer (*b*. 1935) dictated production style in German opera from the 1970s, often opting for dark-brown sets and costumes to imply the corruption and ultimate doom of capitalism.

Italian opera drew on the filmic extravagance of Luchino Visconti (1906–76) and Franco Zeffirelli (*b*. 1923). Peter Brook (*b*. 1925) and Peter Hall (*b*. 1930) introduced Shakespearian devices to Covent Garden. Hal Prince added Broadway gloss in Vienna. Jean-Pierre Ponnelle (1932–88) designed insubstantial magniloquences for Herbert von *Karajan's showy Salzburg productions.

The 'dictatorship of directors' of the 1980s began when producers *deconstructed operas by shifting their time-zone and relationships. They demanded nudity and athleticism from singers, often to their vocal detriment, in attempts to rejuvenate timeworn works. London was the centre of this trend. At English National Opera, Jonathan Miller (*b*. 1934) set Verdi's *Rigoletto* among New York mafiosi and production director David Pountney (*b*.

1947) cast the mother and witch frighteningly as the same person in *Hansel and Gretel*. David Freeman at Opera Factory stripped singers to the buff in Mozart and Monteverdi. The American *minimalist theatre of *Glass and *Adams threw up the directors Bob Wilson and Peter Sellars, who took traditionless views of Mozart. Some considerable vocal talents were shunted off-stage by directorial demands for shapeliness and youth, but the novelty palled after a decade or so and a traditionalist backlash was threatened by music directors.

disco 1970s dance craze centred on discothèques and typified by the movie *Saturday Night Fever* (1977); its thump-thump music was mindless even by current pop standards.

Hugo DISTLER German church musician, committed conscientious suicide under the Nazis and is commemorated in Berlin musical institutions.
  b. Nuremburg, 24.vi.1908; *d*. Berlin, 1.xi.42. *works include*: cembalo concerto (1936), several cantatas.

Divine Poem Skryabin's 3rd symphony. fp: Paris, 29.v.05.

Dixieland Traditional jazz made by New Orleans musicians from 1917 to 1929, when Depression threw most of them on to the streets. Key players were King *Oliver, Louis Armstrong, Jelly Roll *Morton.

Andrzej DOBROWOLSKI Poland's earliest *electronic adventurer, moved to Austria in 1976.
  b. Lvov, Poland, 9.ix.21; taught Cracow 1947–51, Warsaw 1954–76, Graz 1976–; *works include*: *Music No 1* for tape (1962), **Musiken** (orch., 1968–79).

dodecaphony Technical term for *12-note music or *serialism.

Charles DODGE Dodge's *electronic composition based on *Earth's Magnetic Field* (1970) seemed to touch a new kind of naturalism. His synthesized version of Caruso's disc of 'Vesti la Giubba' (1980) became a fringe icon, but he found no takers for his *computer adaptation of a Samuel Beckett play.

b, Ames, Iowa, 5.vi.42; st with *Beeson, *Chou, *Ussachevsky; president, American Composers Alliance 1971.

Ernö (Ernst von) DOHNÁNYI Three misconceptions dog Dohnányi: that he was Hungarian as goulash, that he collaborated with Nazism and that his best work was a childish prank. The so-called *Variations on a Nursery Song* (Berlin, 17.ii.14) is a concerto in which, after a monumental introduction, the pianist chimes in with 'Twinkle, twinkle little star'. A joke written, he said, 'for the enjoyment of fun-lovers and the annoyance of others', it parallels the unintentional 'Three Blind Mice' adagio of *Rachmaninov's 4th concerto.

Although joined in a Hungarian trinity with Bartók and Kodály, Dohnányi did not share their interest in folk music and nationhood. He composed Germanically, his most gratifying ideas coming in chamber music, notably a violin sonata (1912) and jolly sextet (1935). He wrote three operas in Hungarian and an orchestral *Ruralia Hungarica* (Budapest, 17.xi.24) that was no more authentic than Brahms' whipped-cream Hungarian Dances.

Raised in polyglot Pressburg – Bratislava to the Slovaks, Pozsony to Magyars – he went to the same secondary school as Bartók and presided over the Budapest music scene for music for half a century as pianist, composer, conductor and teacher at the Academy of Music. He headed the Academy twice, in 1919 under Bela Kun's Soviet regime and from 1934–41 under fascism, resigning in protest over anti-Jewish laws. He fled in 1944 to Austria, then on to Argentina and the US. One of his sons died fighting on the Russian front, the other was hanged in Germany for plotting against Hitler. One grandson was elected mayor of Hamburg, another is the German conductor Christoph von Dohnányi (*b*. Berlin, 8.ix.29), who presided over the Hamburg State Opera (1977–84) and Cleveland Orch. (1984–).

b. Pressburg, Austro-Hungary, 27.vii.1877; professor at Berlin Hochschule 1908–15, then in Budapest until 1944; composer in residence at Florida State U., 1949; *d*. New York, 9.ii.60. *other works*: two symphonies (D minor, Manchester, 30.i.02; E major, London, 23.xi.48), two concertos for piano and one for violin; *Festival Overture* for Budapest's 50th anniversary (19.xi.23), American Rhapsody (Athens, Ohio, 21.ii.54), many choral works and piano pieces, including *Nocturne: Cats on the Roof*.

Doktor Faust *Busoni's operatic apogee, bypassing Goethe and reverting to folk legend and Kit Marlowe's 1589 English play to examine the compact between man and devil. The richly expressive score was posthumously completed by Philipp *Jarnach (fp: Dresden, 21.v.25); a more comprehensive ending was compiled 60 years later by Antony Beaumont. fp: London, 25.iv.86.

Doktor Faustus Novel by Thomas Mann in which the devil gives composer Adrian Leverkühn a limited span of genius as a modernist messiah. The composer is drawn as a totalitarian ideologue opposed to German tradition; Schoenberg took violent offence. The book was written during the last years of War, published in German in 1947, and woodenly translated the following year.

Die Dollarprinzessin (*The Dollar Princess*) Hit-operetta by *Fall. fp: Vienna 2.xi.07.

Domaine Musical Parisian concert series co-founded in 1954 by *Boulez at the Théâtre Petit Marigny to present contemporary music mostly cond. by himself. Premieres included Messiaen's *Oiseaux exotiques* and Stockhausen's *Zeitmasze*; the series was dissolved in 1973.

Plácido DOMINGO Spanish tenor of unparalleled dramatic range – Puccini to *Parsifal*. He commissioned *Menotti's opera, *Goya* (1986).

b. Madrid, 21.i.41;

Franco DONATONI The Beat poet William Burroughs helped extricate Donatoni from dead-end *serialism into a hippyish radical simplicity that was not afraid to use classical and baroque expressions. He became, after *Berio, the most accessible of living Italians

b. Verona, 9.vii.27; st with *Pizzetti and at *Darmstadt; prof. at Milan 1969–; *major* *works*: two *Puppenspiels* for orch. (1951, 61), four string quartets (1950–60), Doubles II for orch. (1970), *To Earle Two* for 11 insts. (1972), *Duo pour Bruno (Maderna)* (orch., 1975), *Le ruisseau sur l'escalier* for cello and 19 instruments (1980).

Donaueschingen Festivals Rhine-side summer festival founded in 1921 by Prince Max Egon zu Fürstenberg, it served twice as a midwife to modernism. In its first cycle from 1921 to 1930, the festival introduced, among various world premières, Schoenberg's 12-note Serenade Op 24, Webern's six Bagatelles for string quartet, Weill's *Mahagonny Songspiel*, Hindemith's *Hin und Zurück* and the Weill-Hindemith radio cantata, *Lindbergh's flight* – the last three at a new venue in Baden-Baden. After a 20–year quietus, the festival resumed in 1950 under 50–50 sponsorship of Fürstenberg and Southwest German Radio. It became a haven of *avant-gardism and gave important premières by *Stockhausen – Momente (1964), Mantra (1970) – and *Boulez – Pli selon pli (1962), Répons (1981).

Cornelis DOPPER *Mengelberg's deputy conductor at the Concertgebouw orchestra composed eight symphonies, the 3rd named 'Rembrandt' and the 6th 'Amsterdam' (1912).
b. Stadskanaal nr. Groningen, 7.ii.1870; *d*. Amsterdam, 18.ix.39.

Antal DORATI The accomplished conductor created a pot-pourri of Johann Strauss waltzes for a long-running 1940 pageant *Graduation Ball*. His weightier compositions were melodic, civilized and idealistic, latterly concerned with dreams of world peace. His 2nd symphony is titled *Querela pacis*. A busy recording artist, he directed the first complete Haydn symphony cycle for Decca and performed many modern works on the Mercury label.
b. Budapest, 9.iv.06; st with Bartók, Kodály; cond. Ballets Russes de Monte Carlo 1933–40, American Ballet Theater 1941–49, Minneapolis SO 1949–60, BBC SO 1963–66, Stockholm Philharmonic 1967–74, National SO, Washington, D.C., 1970–75, RPO London 1975–78; *d*. nr.Berne, Switzerland, 13.xi.88. *other works*: opera *The Chosen*, cello concerto, string quartet, Variations on a Bartók theme for solo piano.

Down in the Valley American folk-opera by *Weill. fp: Indiana U., 15.vii.48.

Jacob (Raphael) DRUCKMAN While running the electronic music studio at Yale, Druckman lost his taste for technology and composed an orchestral work, *Windows* (Chicago, 16.v.72), that won a Pulitzer Prize for tuneful allusions to earlier music. Druckman kicked off the *neo-romantic revival and wrote further pieces – *Mirage* (1976), *Aureole* (NY, 6.vi.79) and *Prism* (Baltimore, 21.v.80) – that blend quotations from historic works into a modern bombastic score. The effect is pastiche-like and intermittently illuminating, close to Maxwell *Davies' later style.
b. Philadelphia, 26.vi.28; st with *Persichetti and *Copland; professor at Yale 1975–; composer in residence to NY Philharmonic 1982–6; president, Koussevitsky Foundation 1980–; *other orch. works*: The Sound of Time for soprano and orch. to Norman Mailer texts (1965); viola concerto (1978), *In memoriam Vincent Persichetti* (1987); *Shog* (Paris 21.ii.91).

drugs Narcotics caused the deaths of rock and jazz stars Charlie Parker, Jimi Hendrix, Janis Joplin, Mama Cass. Concert performers were less tempted by addictive drugs, though marijuana was whiffed backstage at Carnegie Hall and alcohol and tranquillizers were widely used to combat preconcert anxiety. In one London study, one-third of orchestral players admitted taking pills for their nerves.
The drug culture of the 1960s gave rise to hazily psychedelic pop music, heralded by the *Beatles' Sgt. Pepper album and rooted in repetitive *Indian ragas. These shimmering sounds fed into early *minimalism and thence into concert music.

Dean DRUMMOND An assistant to the inventor *Partch, Drummond devised a 'zoomoozophone' for which *Cage wrote a pretty Haikai (1984). Based in NY, Drummond composes *microtonally for odd instruments and implements.
b. NY, 1949; *other works*: Columbus (1980), *Then or Never* (1984).

Hugues DUFOURT French philosophy professor who joined *Boulez to synthesize

electronic and orchestral sound at
*IRCAM. His music is slow and massive,
in the manner of *Varèse; *Antiphysis* (1978)
for flute and chamber orch. is the pick.
> *b.* Lyon, 1943; st philosophy and music at
> Geneva U.; *other works*: *Erewhon* for six
> percussion (1976).

Paul (Abraham) DUKAS Withdrawn
and insecure Parisian Jew, unsurprisingly
in the Dreyfus era, he composed sparingly
and would not allow his picture to be published. The piece that made his name was
The Sorcerer's Apprentice, after a Goethe
story; his dreams for the eloquent, prematurely Freudian opera *Ariane et Barbe-bleu*
(*Ariane and Bluebeard*, Paris, 10.v.07)
were unrealized. It took Bartók to bring
the gory uxoricide to operatic life.
> *b.* Paris, 1.x.1865; *d* there, 17.v.35. *other
> works*: ballet, *La Péri* (Paris, 22.iv.12); piano
> Variations on a theme by Rameau.

Duke Bluebeard's Castle One-act opera
by Bartók. fp: Budapest, 24.v.18.

Dumbarton Oaks Concerto in E♭ for
chamber orch., named by Stravinsky after
the Washington estate of Mr and Mrs
Robert Woods Bliss, who commissioned it
and paid for a private first performance on
8.v.38.

Marcel DUPRÉ A catalyst in French
organ music, he was star pupil of the venerable *Widor and teacher of the momentous
*Messiaen. Much of his music was impro-
vised before being published as three organ
symphonies, the 3rd (1938) with orchestra,
and 76 chorales containing remarkable
dissonances.
> *b.* Rouen, 3.v.1886; won Prix de Rome 1914;
> organist at Notre dame (1916–22), Ste-
> Sulpice (1934–71), taught Paris Conserva-
> toire (1926–54); *d.* Meudon, nr. Paris, 30.v.
> 71.

Louis DUREY The least of Les *Six
turned communist in 1936, was active in
the anti-Nazi resistance, became music critic of *L'humanité* and devoted his prime to
choral polemics against US power. His
initial conversion to music, after studying
engineering, came about on seeing *Pelléas*
in 1907.
> *b.* Paris, 27.v.1888; *d.* St Tropez, 3.vii.79.

works: comic opera, *L'Occasion* (1925), *Ile
de France* overture (1955), Sinfonietta (1966),
string quartets, much piano music.

Zsolt DURKÓ Driest of Hungarians, his
orchestral sound from *Organismi* (1964,
violin/orch.) onwards was unmistakable,
though not invariably agreeable. He
acquired from his teacher in Rome a flexible *serialism and applied it impressionis-
tically in *Turner Illustrations* (1976) for 15
players that suggest the English painter's
unsullied landscapes on an array of modern
percussive instruments.
> *b.* Szeged, Hungary, 10.iv.34; st with Farkas
> and *Petrassi; *other works*: opera, *Moses*
> (Budapest, 15.v.77), piano concerto (1981),
> two string quartets, *3 English Verses* for
> mezzo and 12 instruments. (London,
> 16.ix.91).

Joannes Martin DÜRR Composer of a
monumental *Cathedrale* (1984–) in
memory of his late wife, a Viennese edifice
150 minutes long and still incomplete.
Dürr was previously editor of Janáček's
scores at *Universal Edition.
> *b.* Vienna, 1931.

Maurice DURUFLÉ French Catholic
composer, second to *Messiaen in devotional output but less adventurous in tone and
texture. His 1947 Requiem, with echoes of
*Fauré, and a gregorian-modelled Mass
(18.xii.66) became popular.
> *b.* Louviers, France, 11.i.02; st with *Dukas;
> organist at St Etienne du Mont, Paris, 1930–
> 68; prof. at Paris Conservatoire 1942–69; *d.*
> Paris, 16.vi.86. *other works*: four motets
> (1961), various organ solos.

Pascal DUSAPIN The only musician
whom *Xenakis acknowledged as a pupil,
he has depicted a violent world in immaculate structures. His 80-minute opera
Romeo and Juliet (Montpellier, 10.7.89)
employs a huge orchestra and half-spoken
dialogue in fragmented romantic imagin-
ings and diverse tonalities.
> *b.* Nancy, France, 29.v.55; *works include*: *La
> rivière* (orch. 1979), *Fist* for eight players
> (1982), *Niobé* for soprano, 12 mixed voices
> and eight players (Paris, 16.vi.84), *La
> Conversation* for eight players (1986), *If* for
> clarinet (1984), *To God* for soprano and clar-
> inet, after William Blake (1985), two string
> quartets, *Musique fugitive* for string trio
> (1980).

Henri DUTILLEUX Determined orchestral composer, economical of utterance in an unpropitious time and place, he limited himself to a few works that simply had to be written. For a living, he could always teach. His mission, noted a sympathetic critic, 'is to be a civilized artist, defending a certain elevated and refined notion of beauty'. This unpretentious objective was sublimely realized in his cello concerto for *Rostropovich, *Tout un monde lointain . . . (A whole distant world)* (Aix-en-Provence, 25.vii.70), in which the soloist acts as mystical intermediary between the composer and some unquoted Baudelaire poems. *L'Arbre des songes (Tree of dreams)* (Paris, 5.xi.85), a violin concerto for Isaac Stern, grafts the soloist graphically on to the trunk of an orchestral tree, whose roots and branches extend in every direction. Grace and lyricism abound, sometimes languidly. Two symphonies (Paris, 7.vi.51; Boston, 11.xii.59) virtually complete his orchestral oeuvre. *5 Métaboles*, written for George Szell (Cleveland, 14.i.65), splits the orchestra into little groups while retaining a simple expressive clarity. A ballet, *Le Loup (The Wolf*, Paris, 18.iii.53) is slightly reminiscent of Prokofiev, musically as well as in its lupine hero.

In a modest corps of chamber music, the string quartet *Ainsi la nuit* (1976) stands out; there are also sonatas for oboe and flute strongly redolent of Ravel. He destroyed almost everything written before 1950. His output is concentrated, distinctive and durable, the Honegger-like 1st symphony fluttering insistently on the fringe of the permanent concert reportoire.
>   *b. Angers*, 22.i.16; st Paris; won Prix de Rome 1938; worked for French radio 1943–63, professor at Paris Conservatoire 1970–;

Antonín DVOŘÁK Back from his American interlude, Dvořák devoted his last energies to opera. *Rusalka* (Prague, 31.iii.01), the fairy-tale of a water nymph and the Prince who betrayed her, supported by a richly symphonic score, was delightful. *Armida* (25.iii.04), a story previously set to music by Lully, Gluck, Handel, Haydn and Rossini, was a flop. His repute rests on nine earlier symphonies, a cello concerto and 14 string quartets.
>   *b.* Nelahozeves, nr Prague, 8.ix.1841; *d.* Prague, 1.v.04.
>   *Bib*: J. Clapham, *Antonín Dvořák*, Newton Abbot, 1966.

Bob DYLAN Folk-rock troubadour, he was the conscience and prophet of pop music, breaking record industry taboos on sexual relations and political protest with numbers like 'It Ain't Me Babe' and 'Talkin' World War III Blues'. He moved through rhythm-and-blues, country music and gospel-Christianity ('When He Returns'), before rediscovering Jewish roots and balladry. His songs, nasally and often tunelessly declaimed to guitar and mouth-organ accompaniment, had poetic lyrics of intense immediacy. He took his name from the Welsh poet; terrorists took theirs from a mumbled word 'weatherman' in the 1970 song 'Subterranean Homesick Blues'
>   *b.* Duluth, Minnesota, 24.v.41, as Robert Allen Zimmerman; changed name to Bob Dylan, 1962; starred in Newport Folk Festivals 1962–64 alongside Joan Baez; toured worldwide; married Sara Lowndes 1965, divorced 1977; *other hits*: 'Like a Rolling Stone', 'Lay Lady Lay', 'Knockin' on Heaven's Door', *Blood on the Tracks*, *Slow Train Coming*.

Ivan DZERZHINSKY A composer remembered only for negative reasons. His opera *And Quiet Flows the Don* (Leningrad, 22.x.1935), after Sholokhov's plagiarized Cossack novel, was declared by Stalin to be a paragon of socialist art and was used as a stick to beat *Shostakovich. Dzerzhinsky's remaining six operas and three piano concertos were in the same realist vein.
>   *b.* Tambov, Russia, 9.iv.09; *d.* Moscow, 18.i. 78.

ear music Music that is learned and performed by listening to others, rather than read off a score. The term is particularly applied to jazz musicians and improvisationists.

early music Pre-classical music first intrigued conservatives like D'*Indy and Pfitzner who sought moral alternatives to modernism. Its revival took off in the 1960s when British and German academics began playing ancient music on original instruments at informal concerts. They brought to life such important composers as Schütz and Monteverdi, and opened a vigorous *authenticity debate on how classics should be played. Leaders of the so-called Early Music Revolution advocated faster speeds and lower pitch for Bach and Mozart.

Pre-classical sounds appealed to composers of all persuasions from *Messiaen to *Stockhausen. Harrison *Birtwistle used treble voices in both his major operas and by-passed polyphony altogether in his musical outlook. His generation found common factors between ancient and modern musics, especially in their reliance on rhythm and volume, rather than melody and harmony.

Ears Open (Korvat auki) Rebellious group of 1980s Finnish composers, led by *Kortekangas, *Lindberg, *Saariaho and *Salonen, rejecting both Sibelian and modernist orthodoxies and pressing for closer links with rock techniques and avant-garde trends. Primary influences were *Berio and *Zimmermann. The group brought about a revitalization of Finnish music.

Earth Dances *Birtwistle's orchestral roar, nicknamed Earthquake Dances. fp: London, 14.iii.86.

Earthly Life Delicate enchantment for soprano and small ensemble by *Firsova. fp: London, 10.x.87.

Peter EBEN Imprisoned by the Nazis, oppressed by the communists, Eben's story is that of his native Czechoslovakia. Through half a century of tyranny, his religious faith held firm and found expression in numerous organ works and crafted concert pieces.

b. Zamberk, E. Bohemia, 22.i.29; taught Charles U., Prague, 1955-; *works include*: *Apologia Sokrates* banned oratorio on Plato's defence of his fellow-philosopher (1967), ballet *Curses and Blessings* (Holland Festival, 1983), two organ concertos (1954, 1982), *Prague Nocturne* (orch. 1983), nonet (1988), *The Windows* for trumpet and organ, on Marc Chagall's Jerusalem masterpiece (1976), harpsichord sonata (1988).

Ebony concerto Stravinsky's contribution to jazz clarinet. fp: NY, 25.iii.46.

Echo Symphony *Malipiero's 5th. fp: London, 3.xi.47.

eclecticism Using other people's ideas is accepted musical practice where the intention is to pay homage to a colleague – as, for example, Mozart did to Johann Christian Bach in the andante of his 12th piano concerto, K414. It can also be a synonym for plagiarism.

The whole of *neo-classical music is

founded on unabashed eclecticism, reset-ting ideas by composers of a previous generation. *Bernstein, *Penderecki and *Holloway were eclectic to shock or satir-ize. Andrew *Lloyd Webber went to the limits of intellectual tolerance.

Eclecticism was the basis of *collage composition exemplified at its most ex-treme in the *Sinfonia* written by Berio to texts by Claude Lévi-Strauss, Martin Luther King and Samuel Beckett and musi-cal fragments by Mahler, Bach, Schoen-berg, Debussy, Ravel, Strauss, Berlioz, Boulez, Stockhausen, Stravinsky, Beet-hoven and others too numerous to list.

Ecuatorial *Varèse's musical discovery of the Americas, replete with *electronic in-struments. fp: NY, 15.iv.34, cond. *Slonimsky.

Helmut EDER Austrian composer who worked in most modern techniques from neo-classic to aleatory, but failed to achieve a distinctive sound. His opera *Mozart in New York* (Salzburg, 15.viii.91), while striving to appear wittily up-to-date, lapsed into self-parody and lacked any musical coherence.

> *b.* Linz, Austria, 26.xii.16; st with *Orff and *David; founded Linz electronic studio 1959, professor at Salzburg Mozarteum 1967-; *other works:* six operas, five symphonies, cello concerto (1981), Haffner concerto for flute and orch. (1984).

Ross EDWARDS Australian *mini-malist.

> *b.* Sydney, 23.xii.43; st with *Sculthorpe, Maxwell *Davies; *works include:* piano con-certo (1988), *Maninya series* for various instruments.

Henry EICHHEIM Amateur US orien-talist who composed only on far eastern themes. His travelogues include: Chinese Legend (1925), Malay Mosaic (1925), Impressions of Peking (Venice, *ISCM, 3.ix.25), Java (1929) and Bali (Philadelphia, 20.iv 33), the last two integrating a *game-lan with Western orchestra. Eichheim played violin in the Boston SO, 1890–1922.

> *b.* Chicago 3.i.1870; *d.* nr Santa Barbara, Calif., 22.viii.42.

Eight Songs for a Mad King Maxwell *Davies mini-opera on demented George III, quoting eclectic range of sources from Handel to *Beatles. fp: London, 22.iv.69.

Herbert EIMERT Influential protago-nist of electronic music who founded a Cologne studio with *Stockhausen in 1951 and directed it for a decade. Before that, he wrote an important early analysis of 12-tone music back in 1923. Outlawed in the Nazi era, he became something of a cult figure for the post-War *avant-garde. Apart from a 12-tone string quartet (1925), his own compositions are mostly taped works, such as *Chimes* (1954).

> *b.* Bad Kreuznach, Germany, 8.iv.1897; *d.* Cologne, 15.xii.72.

Gottfried von EINEM Viciously criti-cized – 'nicht von Einem, sondern von Vielen' ('not by one man but many') – his *eclecticism was transparent and self-defeating. Listeners can play 'spot the com-poser' in works like the Concerto for Orch., Op. 4, ticking off obvious influ-ences from Strauss to Rachmaninov. The Concerto's merit lies in clever orchest-ration and a Broadway breeziness that uncannily anticipates *Bernstein. The Nazis banned it after *Karajan's Berlin pre-mière (3.iv.44).

From 1938 Einem worked at the Berlin State Opera but, with his mother, secretly aided fugitives. The pair were held for months by the Gestapo, an experience explored in his major opera of Franz Kafka's *The Trial* (Salzburg, 17.viii.53). After the War he married a Bismarck and moved into a Salzburg Schloss, becoming a director of the Festival and, with his first opera, *Danton's Death* (Salzburg, 6.viii. 47), Austria's foremost composer. Both early operas and his fourth, *The Old Lady's Visit* (Vienna, 23.v.71), gained real popu-larity with German audiences but little elsewhere. *Jesus' Wedding* (Vienna, 18.v. 80), depicting Christ with a wife, was a seven-day scandal. He has been active in many local musical causes, notably the Mahler revival, and is an accomplished Lieder writer.

> *b.* Berne, Switzerland, 24.i.18, son of Austrian military attaché; grew up in Germany; st with *Hindemith, *Blacher; vocal coach at Berlin State Opera and Bayreuth, 1938–44; *other works:* Vienna Symphony, op. 48; five string quartets.

Einstein on the Beach *Glasswork to text by director Robert Wilson. fp: Avignon, 25.vii.76.

Hanns EISLER Bertolt *Brecht's replacement for the alienated *Weill was a composer who habitually subordinated his personality to greater causes yet preserved a distinctive sound in all his mature works. As *Schoenberg's pupil, he wrote spare atonalities; as a communist, he churned out partyline songs; as Brecht's partner, he was faithful to the poet's cadences. Each of his scores, however, was subtly hallmarked. Although he opened the *Pierrot-like cantata *Palmström* (1924) with four notes representing Schoenberg's initials and his own, he modified its *sprechgesang to a laconic, *cabaret-like delivery. In *Die Massnahme* (Berlin, 13.xii.30), Brecht's ideas of revolutionary justice are made to sound humane and reasonable. He was the only musician whom Brecht fully trusted to tamper with his texts.

Eisler was an outsider – a Viennese sophisticate among bluff Berliners; an intellectual in Hollywood, where he worked for Charlie Chaplin and wrote a text-book, *Composing for the Films*; a

humanist in the East German police-state, whose deceptive national anthem he composed. His plan for a Faust opera was thrown out by the Berlin communist hierarchy in June 1953 and Eisler unavailingly sought Austrian citizenship.

The son of an Austrian philosopher, Eisler returned from the trenches to spend four years with Schoenberg, spurning 'art for art's sake' but acquiring lifelong respect for the *12-note method which he perceived as the basis for 'a new social music'. Music, he believed in Weimar fashion, needed to be useful. It must help create a better world. Schoenberg accused him of betrayal, but Eisler felt that the progressive thrust of his ideas paralleled the march of Marxist progress. Many of his exile songs used aspects of Schoenberg techniques.

It was characteristic of Eisler to set complex thoughts to a simple tune and simple emotions to advanced harmonies. His 600 songs can be categorized as either populist chansons or serious Lieder. The *Ballad of the Wife and the Soldier* that opened his account with Brecht in 1928 defined the first genre; *On the Duration of Exile* and *Two Elegies* that they wrote in mid-War set the more contemplative tone. Both styles filtered into the post-War Viennese music of *Schwertsik and *Gruber. The *Ballad of Nigger Jim, Back to Nature* and *German Chanson* are among his finest inventions; his weakest were those Brecht songs that echoed the inimitable Weill.

Eisler wrote incidental music for Brecht's later plays and many film scores, notably Steinbeck's *Forgotten Village* (1941), *Hangmen Also Die* (Brecht/Lang, 1943), *None but the Lonely Heart* (Odets, 1944) and Alain Resnais' *Nuit et brouillard* (1956). Some of his theatre scores were adapted for concert performance – the 1940 chamber symphony and graphic 1957 *Sturm* suite – but the major concert works had a vocal message. Brecht wrote texts for the German Symphony (1939) and Lenin Requiem (1937); Goethe's *Faust* provided the soprano solo in the reflective Rhapsody for large orchestra (1949).

b. Leipzig, 6.vii.1898; moved to Vienna 1901; soldier 1916–18; st with *Weigl 1918, Schoenberg 1919–23; concert debut with piano sonata, Vienna 1.x.24; lived in Berlin

1925–33, Vienna, Paris and London 1933–38, NY 1938–42, Hollywood 1942–48, deported by order of House Committee on Unamerican Activities; thrice married; *d.* Berlin, 6.ix.62. *other works: Kleine sinfonie* (1932), *5 Orchesterstücke* (1938), Nonet (1939), Variations on American nursery songs for flute, clarinet, bassoon and string quartet (1941), septet no. 2 (1947), string quartet (1938), three piano sonatas.
Bib: Albrecht Betz, HE, *Political Musician*, Cambridge, 1982.

Viktor EKIMOVSKY Author of the first Russian study of *Messiaen, he composed a map of the stars as *Up Among the Hunting Dogs* for three flutes (1986). Less than entirely serious, he has written a *Balleto* (1974) for conductor and optional ensemble in which the maestro's every motion is hilariously choreographed.
b. Moscow, 12.ix.47; *other works: The Trumpets of Jericho* for 30 brass (1977); Double chamber variations for 12 players (1989).

Halim EL-DABH Egyptian musician teaching in the US who wrote a caustic drama, *Opera Flies* (Washington, D.C., 5.v.71), on the 1969 police killing of students at Kent State, where he was on the faculty. His three symphonies (1950–56) and much his music are infused by Arab sonorities and rhythms.
b. Cairo, 4.iii.21; st with Copland and Fine; taught Haile-Selassie U. Addis-Ababa, 1962–5, Howard U. 1966–9, Kent State 1969–; *other orch. works: Fantasia-Tahmeel* (1954), concerto for darabukka, clarinet and strings (1981).

electric and electronic instruments The Telharmonium, built in Massachusetts from the 1890s, was first; it was too heavy to be moved and was used for relaying concerts and operas down the telephone. In the 1920s, Martenot and Theremin designed new concert instruments that attracted top composers; Friedrich Trautwein's 1930 trautonium was taken up by Hindemith and Strauss.
The first electric organ appeared in 1929. Named after its builder, the American Lorens Hammond, it became a cinematic fixture. The electric guitar arrived in 1937, altering the acoustic of *country music and getting a walk-on part in Stockhausen's *Gruppen*. Other stringed and wind instruments were hooked up to the mains with the object of amplification or sound manipulation. They provided staple backing for *rock and *pop music from the mid-1960s. A *synthesizer, which could simulate any sound by electronic synthesis, was invented in America around 1958 and fathered keyboards and computer games.

electronic music The dream of making music out of thin air without manual intervention was made real in 1876 by Alexander Graham Bell's discovery that sound can be converted into electric signals and decoded back through the telephone. The following year, Thomas Alva Edison invented recording, adding a second means of electronic sound generation. Neither was used systematically to create music for three-quarters of a century. By the 1990s, electronic music had penetrated every corner of musical life. It extended from ethereal sound-waves played by esoteric experimenters to the thumping syncopation that accompanies every pop record.
It took almost 50 years after Edison's brainwave for a composer to work recorded sound into a concert work when *Respighi introduced bird-sound into *Pines of Rome*. Advances were made in building *electronic instruments but they were generally impractical. In 1906 Thaddeus Cahill built a 'telharmonium' in Holyoake, Massachusetts that weighed 200 tons and emitted little sound. Leon *Theremin intrigued Lenin with his look-no-hands thereminovox and Maurice Martenot prompted *Messiaen to write for his *ondes. At the same time, intellectual demands mounted for new sonorities to resolve the tonal crisis. *Busoni became increasingly impatient with the means at his disposal and his visionary pupil, *Varèse, told a reporter in 1916: 'I refuse to submit myself to sounds that have already been heard.'
Although Germans developed magnetic tape, it was an American who made compositional use of recorded sound. In 1939, John *Cage played three test records of pure frequencies simultaneously but at different speeds. He called his experiment *Imaginary Landscape 1* and it changed the definition of music since it was a work that consisted neither of written notes nor manipulated instruments.

After the war, electronic music took off in Europe among young composers with access to military-made technology and with a burning urge to eradicate the cultures that bred conflagration. *Musique concrète was created in Paris in 1948 from edited *collages of everyday noise. It sounded as ugly as its name, but impressed *Boulez and *Stockhausen.

Once domestic tape recorders became available around 1950, composers were free to record what they liked, and distort tapes at will. The resultant creations were ear-splitting but evolutionary. Ambitions quickly spread to tackle the raw roots of sound – sine tones, electronic signals and frequencies. Composing studios sprang up at radio stations and universities, the first at Northwest German Radio in Cologne (1953), where the term 'electronic music' was coined to distinguish their pure experiments from musique concrète, followed by Milan (1955) and Columbia and Princeton universities in the New York region (1959). More than 500 such centres were active by 1975. These were the laboratories where music of the future would be made, proclaimed Boulez to President Georges Pompidou when persuading him to build him the state-of-the art *IRCAM centre in Paris. Helmholtz, the 19th-century physical theorist, was disinterred as a modern hero and his writing became essential textbooks. Modernist doctrine dictated that composers had to know as much about physics and *computer sciences as they did about harmony. The passion for empirical truth mirrored the *avant-garde's adherence to *Webern's precise rules of *serial composition.

The sounds that emerged initially were scratchy and unpalatable. *Ussachevsky and *Luening, a Busoni pupil, presented the first public concert of electronic music at the Museum of Modern Art in New York (28.x.53). *Eimert at Cologne laboured over one-minute compositions until Stockhausen broke through with *Gesang der Jünglinge (1956) where a boy's treble voice was hauntingly transformed by sound-manipulation. *Xenakis began to combine electronic tapes with live instruments in a fetchingly modern synthesis. The aged *Varèse realized a lifelong dream in *Déserts (1954) for wind, percussion and tape, and *Poème éléctronique for a trade pavilion designed by Xenakis. For *Krenek, another European refugee, electronic music assumed the status of divine mission in *Spiritus Intelligentae Sanctus* (1956). *Zimmermann devised a role for tape in his opera, *The Soldiers* (1958–64).

In the late 1960s more channels appeared on tape-mixing desks and the *synthesizer became ubiquitous in *pop music. Live electronics took their place on the concert stage. Boulez in his self-vindicating *Répons (1981–) placed computer technicians at the centre of his orchestra. *Birtwistle worked co-ordinated electronic sounds into his opera, *Mask of Orpheus* (1986); electronic instruments were integral to the scores and operas of Philip *Glass. Quartets written for *Kronos frequently called for amplification or sound transformation. As the novelty wore off, however, electronic music became less central to the concerns of major composers and some, like Birtwistle, renounced it as a transient distraction. Nevertheless, by the end of the century there were likely to be a million electronic pop and art works in existence. Among the more durable are:

Ashley: *Purposeful Lady, Slow Afternoon* (1968); Babbitt: *Composition for Synthesizer* (1961), *Philomel* (1963); Beatles: *Sgt. Pepper's Lonely Hearts Club Band* album (1967); Behrman: *Wave Train* (1967); Berio: *Mutazioni* (1956), *Omaggio a Joyce* (1958), *Diario Immaginario* (1975); Boulez: *Répons* (1981–); Cage: *Radio Music* (1956), *Music for amplified toy pianos* (1960), *Cartridge Music* (1960), *HPSCHD* (1969); Carlos: *Switched-on Bach* (1968); Crumb: *Black Angels*; Eimert: *Webern variations* (1958); Gerhard: 3rd symphony (1960); Harvey: *Mortuos plango, vivos voco* (1983); Kagel: *Unter Strom* (1969); Krenek: *Pfingstoratorium* (1956); Luening/Ussachevsky: *A Poem in Cycles and Bells* (1956); Maderna: *Notte in Città* (with Berio, 1956), *Continuo* (1958); Nono: *Como una ola del fuerza y luz* (1972); Reich: *Come Out* (1966), *Different Trains* (1989); Riley: *A Rainbow in Curved Air* (1969); Stockhausen: *Kontakte* (1960), *Kurzwellen*

(1968) *Hymnen* (1967), *Mantra* (1970);
Varèse: *Déserts* (1954); Xenakis: *Persepolis*
(1971).

> *Bib*: Paul Griffiths, *A Guide to Electronic
> Music*, London (Thames & Hudson), 1979.

electro-acoustic music   Alternative name
for *electronic music.

Elegy for Young Lovers   *Henze opera
to Auden/Kallman libretto about a poet
who sends his mistress and stepson to their
deaths. fp: Schwetzingen, 20.v.61

Elektra   The first of five operas *Strauss
wrote with Hugo von Hofmannsthal elab-
orates the Greek myth of a daughter's
revenge on the mother and lover who murdered her kingly dad in the bath. Strauss's
most heavily scored opera, with a 109-
piece orchestra, requires deft conducting to
allow the singers to make themselves heard
without shrieking. In addition to violent
assaults, the music contains passages of
erotic decadence and ironic charm, prefacing the bloody act of matricide with a waltz
motif. The single 100-minute act ends on a
C-major chord, signalling the composer's
retreat from the brink of atonality.

> premières: Dresden, 25.i.09; New York,
> 1.ii.09; Berlin, 15.ii.09; Vienna 24.iii.09;
> London, 19.ii.10.

(Sir William) Edward ELGAR   The
rebirth of music in the Land without Music
is commonly dated from Hans Richter's
fin-de-siècle première of Elgar's Enigma
Variations, a work that swept across
Europe in five years, winning the respect of
Richard *Strauss and *Rimsky-Korsakov.
This version of history, while chronologi-
cally accurate, actively distorts the character of a deceptive composer and his mildly
catalytic role.

It is true to say that the Variations on an
Original Theme, to give its official title,
was the first concert music by any
Englishman since Henry Purcell to enter
the repertoire. Its reception gave confidence to younger composers and its format
foreshadowed two outstanding British
works, Holst's *Planets suite and *Britten's
Bridge Variations.

In no other sense, however, was Elgar a
progressive or determinant force in the
nation's artistic regeneration. The Enigma
(London, 19.vi.1899) was cast in a traditional Brahmsian mould with a discernible
Mendelssohn quotation in the 13th variation and echoes throughout of other
German and French composers. Its portentous beauties and instrumental sheen belonged to the fading Victorian era, as did its
celebration of asexual friendship and its
buried clues. Twelve variations bear the
initials of known friends, the 14th represents the composer himself. The penultimate variation is starred with three
asterisks, possibly in memory of a long-
lost fiancée Helen Weaver, a whimsy repeated in the anonymous dedication of his
violin concerto. There was, additionally, an
unnamed, underlying musical theme,
which might have been Auld Lang Syne.

These extra-musical contrivances were
the mark of a creative personality insecure
in his artistry, his Englishness and his status. A Roman Catholic from middle
England, a shopkeeper's son in a small
town where traders knew their place, Elgar
was an outsider in a society he regarded
with ambivalence. The emotional shudder
of those of his works that appear to vaunt
imperialism – the *Pomp and Circumstance*
marches, in particular – resides in a faint
undertone of doubt that haunts the jingois-
tic theme. Conversely, the fervour of three
fine oratorios – *The Dream of Gerontius*
(1900), *The Apostles* (1902), *The Kingdom*
(1906) – is integrally maimed by Elgar's
admitted loss of faith. Here was a paradox
of an English unbeliever writing religious
music in an old-fashioned Franco-German
romantic mode.

Unlike Mahler, who acknowledged his
place on the fringe, Elgar was motivated by
a need to belong. He ascended a social rung
or two in 1889 by marrying a general's
unmarriageable daughter, Alice Roberts,
who provided a discipline and domesticity
that underpinned his creative work. When
she died in 1919, he dried up.

In the decade before the Enigma, he
turned out a string of oratorios for flourishing choral festivals, as well as a *Dvoř-
ákian Serenade in E minor (1892) that
anticipated the shimmering textures of his
Introduction and Allegro for strings (London, 8.iii.05), the first of many works he
conducted with the newly-formed London
Symphony Orchestra. He got on well with

working musicians and their co-operation enabled the self-taught Elgar to acquire instrumental nuances for a symphony that he began writing days after his 50th birthday.

Beset by self-doubt and eye-strain, he had endured a barren two years and talked of giving up music and going into the coal business. Yet the symphony in A-flat major (Manchester 3.xii.08, cond. Richter) began with a woodwind and lower-string tune of total serenity that blossomed into a march of imperious optimism. It received 100 performances in just over a year, capturing as it did the sublime certainties of pre-1914 Europe. Its sentimental flaws became apparent in more worldly times.

The second symphony, in E-flat major (London, 24.v.11, cond. Elgar), was a comparative failure, unable to strike a clear attitude in the opening phrases and dedicated, with evident sycophancy, to the memory of the late monarch, Edward VII. The larghetto contains a lovely lament. Elgar toyed for years with a third symphony but achieved nothing performable.

The violin concerto (London, 10.xi.10) won the allegiance of discerning interpreters – Kreisler, Ysaÿe, Menuhin, Heifetz. Its strength and weakness is a tenderness that is unaffected at the outset but settles in the andante to self-pity. The cello concerto (London, 27.x.19) on the other hand, is Elgar's masterpiece, arguably the finest of its kind. Here, for once in his life, Elgar expressed himself without fear or favour, and certainly without regard for the poor soloist who plays almost without a bar's break. Regret for a world ruined by war is audible throughout. It is made all the more poignant by a nostalgia not for what had been lost but for a society in which he had never been accepted. Not for him the affectionate reminiscences of Proust, more the white-lipped anger of Orwell. A string quartet and piano quintet of the same year give vent to the same emotions. Months later, his wife died at 71 and his last 14 years were sterile. He was named Master of the King's Musick in 1924 but was denied the peerage that would have signalled his acceptance among the great and the good.

Much in Elgar is a matter of interpretation. Performed by Englishmen as a quintessential Edwardian – bluff, expansive, somewhat lachrymose – his music is clad in a mask of his own making. A more likeable, and genuine, Elgar was discovered by foreign conductors – Nikisch, Monteux, Bernstein, Solti – who perceived the loneliness of his position and the intensity of his unfulfillable yearnings.

b. Broadheath, nr. Worcester, 2.vi.1857; married Alice Roberts 1889; knighted 1904; *d*. Worcester, 23.ii.34. *other works*: overtures *Cockaigne* (Lon, 20.vi.01), *In the South* (Lon, 16.iii.04); *Falstaff* (Leeds, 2.x.13), symphonic prelude *Polonia* (Lon, 6.vii.15); *Elegy* for string orch. (Lon, 13.vii.09), *Sospiri* for strings, harp, organ (Lon, 15.viii.14); *Sea Pictures* for mezzo and orch. (Norwich, 5.x. 1899); *Coronation Ode* (Sheffield, 2.x.02), *Coronation March* (Lon, 22.vi.11); E minor violin sonata (1918); various masques, dramatic and choral pieces.
Bib: Michael Kennedy, *Portrait of Elgar*, Oxford (2nd edn), 1982.

Brian (David) ELIAS Meticulous post-*Bergian, he wrote an appealing setting for orchestra of five poems by the Russian prisoner of conscience, Irina Ratushnis-kaya (London, 23.iv.89). Beneath plinkings of late modernism and some sinuous hints of *Ravel, the work was underscored by Judeo-Christian religious sonorities from eastern Europe. A similar religio-erotic timbre enlivens his ten minute Solomonian *Song* (London, 14.vii.86) for soprano and hurdy-gurdy.
b. Bombay, India, 30.viii.48; st with Lutyens; *other works*: *L'Eylah* (orch., 1984), *Tzigane* (solo violin, 1978), ballet, *The Judas Tree* (Covent Garden, 19.iii.92).

Anders ELIASSON Swedish dissonant on the road back to tonality.
b. Borlänge, Sweden, 3.iv.47; st with *Lidholm; *works include*: church opera *One of Us* (1974), symphony (1986), *Ombra* for clarinet and string quartet (1980), 1st string quartet (1988).

elitism Populist accusation that *art music is monopolized by the moneyed classes.

Fred ELIZALDE Band-leader at London's Savoy Hotel, he volunteered to fight in the Spanish Civil War, during which he conducted his *Sinfonia concertante* at the Barcelona *ISCM (23.iv.36). The cause lost, he went home to the Philippines to run the Manila Broadcasting Co. and compose an

opera, *Paul Gauguin* (1943), for the painter's centenary.
b. Manila, 12.xii.07; *d*. there 16.i.79.

Heino ELLER Foremost composer of the independent, inter-War Estonian Republic, Eller wrote folkloristic symphonic poems that flickered like the northern lights. *Videvik (Twilight*, 1917) presaged liberation, while *Koit (Dawn*, 1981) announced its fulfilment in heart-tugging crescendi. National aspirations had to be supressed under Soviet rule, but Eller raised a new generation of composers – chief among them *Tubin and *Pärt – who would carry the flame into a newly autonomous era.

In addition to three symphonies (1936, 1947, 1961) and a violin concerto, Eller left a beautiful Elegy for harp and strings (1931). Although he studied in St Petersburg, his outlook was firmly Western and predominantly Scandinavian; stylistically his music falls somewhere between Grieg and Vaughan Williams.
b. Dorpat, southern Estonia, 7.ii.1887; st with Steinberg in St Petersburg; tauaght at Tartu 1920–40 and Tallinn 1940–60; *d*. Tallinn, 16.vi.70. *other works*: five string quartets, 180 piano pieces.

'Duke' (Edward Kennedy) ELLINGTON The symphonist among jazzmen, Ellington broke the straitjacket of the three-minute 'set' and cut loose on extended, structured *improvisations that lasted more than half an hour. The shifting harmonies and striking tonal colours of accompanying instruments in his band, not least his own pianism, were every bit as compelling as the lead voice, usually his trumpeter, Bubber Miley. Their jazz was 'hot' but clever and sensual. At the first of what became an annual Carnegie Hall concert (23.i.43), they premièra a 50-minute composition, *Black, Brown and Beige: Tone Parallel to the American Negro*. Ellington never wrote down a note of his music. He stood imaginatively head and shoulders above his field and wore his genius with the dignity and charm that were the trademark of jazz masters. Miles *Davis once said: 'All the musicians should get together one day and get down on their knees and thank Duke.'

The son of a former White House butler, Duke acquired his 'title' for teenaged elegance. At the age of 24 he took a five-man dance combo to New York. It grew to 11 men by 1930 and 19 by 1946. Unusually intensive rehearsals lay behind their coordinated invention. 'East St Louis Toodle-oo' (1927), their first big hit, was recorded in eight different arrangements as Ellington tinkered compulsively with his music. 'Creole Love Call' (1927) used a wordless vocalist. 'Mood Indigo' (1930) was an unmistakable calling-card. He introduced *electronic amplification and Latin rhythms. There were also the expected spate of smoochy ballads but among them crept 'Mr Bojangles' and 'Concerto for Cootie' with original and memorable music. 'Take the "A" Train' was the pulsating theme of the wartime years.

When the *swing era started to decline, Ellington became all the more symphonic in his music and ducal in his manner, mixing with kings and presidents. In 1959 he wrote *The Queen Suite* for Elizabeth II, one copy only and none other released until after his death at the age of 75. His son, Mercer, kept the band alive.
b. Washington, D.C., 29.iv.1899; *d*. NY, 24.v.74. *other work*: *Liberian Suite* (1948).

Jean-Claude ELOY *Boulez disciple who turned away from avant-garde to eastern mysticism.
b. Mont-Saint-Aigan, Seine-Maritime, France, 15.vi.38; st with *Milhaud before Boulez conversion at *Darmstadt; taught analysis at Berkeley 1966–68; *works include*: *Kamakala* for three orchestras and chorus (1971), *Kshara-Akshara* for soprano, chorus, triple-orch. and 3 conductors (1974), *Shanti*, two hour electronic meditation (London, 6.iv.75), *Gazu no Michi* (1978).

Maurice EMMANUEL *Neo-classical Frenchman whose music was outshone by his eminence as an art historian. Unabashedly eclectic, he wrote six piano sonatinas, the first, *sonatine bourguignonne* (1893), in folkish style, moving towards *Fauré with a *sonatine pastorale* (1897), to *Debussy in the third sonatina (1920) and in *Ravel's direction in a fourth that same year. The last two, dated 1926, are infected by the jazz age. Beneath these borrowings stood a capable musician. He wrote a two-volume history of musical language and a seminal work on Greek dance.

b. Bar-sur-Aube, Burgundy, 2.v.1862; *d.* Paris, 14.xii.38. *works include*: opera, *Salamine* (Paris, 28.vi.29), two symphonies (1919, 1931), two string quartets.

The Emperor of Atlantis (*Der Kaiser von Atlantis*)

One-act opera written by *Ullmann in 1943 in the Nazi camp of Theresienstadt to text by Peter Kien (1919–44). It describes a war in which death goes on strike and no-one dies. The SS banned its performance and sent the authors to Auschwitz. fp: Amsterdam, 16.xii.75, cond. Kerry Woodward.

Georges ENESCO (French transcription of Gheorghe ENESCU)

The only Romanian of musical eminence, Enesco's posthumous reputation has been confined to a pair of folkish *Romanian Rhapsodies* (Bucharest, 8.iii.03), all squeaky fiddles and whirring skirts, and a few instrumental showpieces. This categorization cruelly distorts one of the compelling personalities in 20th-century music, a brilliant violinist, pianist, conductor, conversationalist and, for most of his bifurcated life, composer of versatile and challenging art – 'the greatest musical phenomenon since Mozart', according to his concert partner Pablo Casals.

That the fiery Rhapsodies remain popular is unsurprising. More than any Balkan music before Bartók, they avoid touristic voyeurism to reflect savage emotions and daily hardship on the borderless plains. A pair of contemporaneous violin sonatas (1897–9) and a *pièce de concert* (1906) for viola were refined by residence in Paris, but ethnic self-assurance and a tinge of melancholy underlie almost everything Enesco wrote.

Towering above all else is the opera *Oedipe* (Paris, 13.iii.36), inspired by Sophocles' tragedy at the Comédie Française in 1906 and occupying him for the next 30 years. Written with a French-Jewish poet Edmond Fleg, who provided the libretto for *Bloch's Macbeth, its tonal colour runs from *Tristan* through *Massenet yet the Hellenism sounds ululatingly authentic and the composer's hallmark is stamped on every bar of a pulsating score. As a musical experience, it contains infinitely more stimulus than Stravinsky's stab at the same source. Rarely staged outside Romania, *Oedipe* can be heard on a 1990 EMI recording and in some closely related chamber works, the 1st piano sonata (1924) and 3rd violin sonata 'in the popular Romanian style' (1926).

After studies in Vienna with 'serenaden-*Fuchs' and in Paris with *Fauré and Massenet, Enesco divided his life between his native land and *belle époque* Paris. He was a charismatic performer, teacher and social magnet, whose pupils included Yehudi Menuhin and whose lovers numbered the soprano Maggie Teyte. For seven prime years, he was barely able to compose because his manuscripts, shipped by the Romanian government with its gold reserves for wartime safe-keeping in London, were detained in Moscow by the Bolsheviks. They were finally released on Bruno *Walter's intercession in 1924.

The 3rd symphony in C major (1919) mourns the ravages of war. Its language seems stranded tonally between Brahms and Debussy until Enesco shows a burst of resourcefulness in the finale introduces a wordless chorus as a supplementary instrument, giving the music a sense of missing mystery.

Exiled and impoverished by the Second War, he suffered renewed creative impotence that lifted in his last year in the Chamber Symphony for 12 solo instruments, It shares a morose atmosphere with *Schoenberg's but has a voice and beauty all of its own, mourning the bleakness of a culture riven by murderous conflict. At its first, posthumous, performance in Bucharest, the entire work was repeated.

b. Liveni (renamed George-Enescu), northern Moldavia, 19.viii.1881; gave concert of own music in Paris, 11.vi.1897; patronized by Queen of Romania; married Princess Marie Cantacuzino in 1939 after a 20-year affair; *d.* Paris, 4.v.55 and buried in Père Lachaise cemetery. *other works*: three mature symphonies (1906, 1915, 1919); two unfinished late symphonies; chamber symphony (1954); two string quartets, two piano quartets.

Bib: Noel Malcolm, *George Enescu*, London, (Toccata Press) 1990.

L'Enfant et les Sortilèges (*The Child and Magic Objects*) Dream-opera by *Ravel. fp: Monte Carlo, 21.iii.15.

(Sven) Einar ENGLUND The end of the Second World War left Finland facing its former enemy, the USSR, with tremulous uncertainty. The anxiety of that bleak period is conveyed in two grey symphonies by Englund, closer to *Shostakovich than Sibelius. The War Symphony (Helsinki, 17.i.47) masks its joy at the nation's miraculous survival in a cloud of individual fear; the Second Symphony (8.x.48) looks ahead to joyless industrialization and vigilant defence. Englund wrote five more symphonies, lacking the same immediacy.
  b. Ljugarn, Finland, 17.vi.16; *other works*: two piano concertos, clarinet concerto (1991), concerto for 12 cellos (Helsinki, 4.ix.82).

Brian ENO Restless avant-gardist of *rock music, he was among the first to espouse synthesizers and explore advanced *electronics. He viewed most *popular music as *aural wallpaper and devised 'Ambient Music' albums called 'Music for Airports' and 'Music for Films' in an engagingly *Satie-an gesture. Some of his ambient pieces played insistently at La Guardia and St Paul (Minnesota) airports, and at the Berkeley Art Museum in California. Apart from his own music, Eno has produced and influenced records by David Bowie and U2.
  b. Woodbridge, Suffolk, UK, 15.v.48; formed Roxy Music group c. 1970, departed 1975.

Ensemble InterContemporain Parisian ensemble modelled on *London Sinfonietta, founded in 1976 and answerable to Boulez.

environmental music Charles *Ives wanted his last symphony to be played from mountain tops. The Muzak company pumped tunes into elevators. Various multi-media artists have taken live performance into unlikely venues. Max *Neuhaus wrote *Water Whistle* (1971) for swimming pools, indoor or outdoor. Such phenomena, to name just three, reflected the declining musical centrality of the concert hall.

Peter EÖTVÖS One of the most effective conductors of post-*Boulez music, he has composed various electronic works and 'clowneries' – such as *Harakiri* (Bonn, 22.ix.73) for three musicians and three actors, *II Maestro* for pianist and 2 Steinways (Budapest, 6.x.74) and *Leopold & Wolfgang* (Oeldorf, 22.vii.76), comprising extracts from the Mozart correspondence. His *Chinese Opera* (Paris, 17.xi.86) for orchestra and amplified instruments contains an open invitation to six named directors – among them Peter Brook, Luc Bondy and Jacques Tati – to take his music and make a movie of it.
  b. Szekelyudvarhely, Hungary (now Romania), 2.i.44; worked with *Stockhausen from 1966; producer at WDR Cologne electronic studios 1971–9, music director Ensemble InterContemporain, Paris, 1979–91; premiered Stockhausen's *Licht* opera and *Birtwistle's Earth Dances in London.

Donald (James) ERB Cleveland-based composer of agreeable, at times jazz-tinged, concertos. His most performed piece is *The 7th Trumpet*, 1971 UNESCO award winner.
  b. Youngstown, Ohio, 17.i.27; st with Boulanger; composer in residence at Dallas SO 1968–69, St Louis SO 1988–90; *concertos include*: keyboards (1978), trumpet (1980), contrabassoon (1984), clarinet (1984), brass (1986).

Frédéric d'ERLANGER British banker who wrote operas under the anagrammatic pseudonym of Ferd. Regnal and used his position on the Covent Garden board to have them performed. His notable work was *Tess* (Naples, 10.iv.1906), after Thomas Hardy's novel.
  b. Paris, 29.v.1868; *d.* London, 23.iv.43.

Erwartung (*Expectation*) Dream-opera for solo soprano by Schoenberg, overlaid with Kandinskian visual imagery, in which a woman finds her lover's body in a wood. fp: Prague, 6.vi.24, cond. *Zemlinsky.

Oscar ESPLA (y Triay) Spanish composer active in the short-lived republic, his career suffered when he was expelled by the fascists. His 1909 opera *Sleeping Beauty* was once staged in Vienna and his *Levantine suite* was widely known. Eschewing nationalism, he explored medieval and moorish music and produced his major work in the tone poem *Don Quixote Guarding his Arms*, commissioned in 1924 by de *Falla. After Espla had spent 15 years in Belgian exile, Franco named him Spanish representative at UNESCO.

> *b.* Alicante, Spain, 5.viii.1886; *d.* Madrid, 6.i.76.

Essays Three ten-minute works that Samuel *Barber wrote as substitutes for symphonies. He employed the Oxford definition of Essay as 'a composition of moderate length on any particular subject'. fps: First Essay NY, 5.xi.38, cond. *Toscanini; Second Essay NY, 16.iv.42, cond *Walter; Third Essay NY, 14.ix.78, cond. Mehta.

Etudes Debussy's impressionistic study-pieces for pianists. fp: Paris, 14.xii.16.

exile Many musicians fled political oppression. Jews, socialists and liberals escaped Nazi Europe, Christians and democrats left the Soviet bloc, others escaped totalitarianism in Latin America and east Asia.

The experience was inhibiting. Schoenberg and Bartók died poor in the US, Rachmaninov all but lost his creativity after leaving Russia and Prokofiev was emotionally tugged back home. Weill and Stravinsky succeeded only by rejecting their former musical personalities and adopting a new style.

The Excursions of Mr Brouček Lunar-probe comic opera by Janáček, fp: Prague, 23.iv.20.

experimentalism Every creative act involves risk, no matter how safe its idiom. The bold concept of experimentation was hijacked by the post-1945 *avant garde to distinguish between themselves and traditionalists. *Cage, who defined experiment as 'an act of which the outcome is unknown', declared that it was unnecessary to refine the outcome of an experiment in order to create art. Experimentation alone justified a composer's existence.

expressionism A visual arts term applied to Edvard Munch (1863–1944), Vassily Kandinsky (1866–1944) and their *fin-de-siècle* generation, who deliberately exaggerated line and colour to produce a keener sense of expression. The term was loosely attached to Kandinsky's friend and collaborator, *Schoenberg, who vented an extreme expressiveness in the vocal works of his atonal period, notably *Die *glückliche Hand* and *Erwartung*. The connection was tenuous, however, and broke down altogether with the advent of *serialism. Certain individual composers with a strong affinity to visual stimulus – *Birtwistle, perhaps, and *Henze – might more be aptly deemed expressionist in the manner of Munch, but the term really has no musical meaning.

eye music The bizarre new notations of *avant-gardists gave rise to *graphic scores of striking, Kandinsky-like beauty. The huge blobs and perfect geometrical lines of *Cardew's Treatise, the paintings of *Haubenstock-Ramati, the crazy lines of *Cage and *Feldman, the comic strips of Cathy *Berberian – all constituted music that pleased the eye as much as it did the ear, and sometimes more. The idea of notational visuality has classical origins. Haydn in *The Creation* wrote music resembling rising and falling waves to represent the ocean. Beethoven has lightning bolts in the violin parts of the storm scene in the *Pastoral* Symphony.

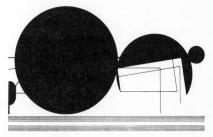

Cornelius Cardew *Treatise (1967)*

Façade Quirky English entertainment by Edith Sitwell and young *Walton, later danced as ballet. fp: London, 12.vi.23.

Leo(pold) FALL Operetta composer of Vienna's Silver Age with 20 shows to his name; *Die *Dollarprinzessin* (1907) was his international calling card.
    b. Olmütz (Olomouc), Austro-Hungary, 2.ii.1873; *d.* Vienna, 16.ix.25.

Manuel (Maria) de FALLA (y Matheu) The soul of Spanish music for half a century, he flew the flag alone after the early deaths of *Albeniz and *Granados. Castillian by birth and Parisian by training, his music was periodically snubbed at home as too cosmopolitan; abroad, it was disdained as tiresomely Iberian.

The work that set him on the map was *Nights in the Gardens of Spain*, conceived as three nocturnes for solo piano but worked into a concerto (Madrid, 9.iv.16, Arthur Rubinstein soloist). Liberated from literalism by *impressionist techniques picked up from *Debussy and *Dukas and a *neo-classicism that parallelled *Stravinsky's, he evoked a Moorish atmosphere without resorting to shallow description.

*Diaghilev rejected the score, whereupon Falla responded with the vivid *Three Cornered Hat* (London, 22.vii.19), based on the same novel as Wolf's *Corregidor*, recounting a miller's rescue of his wife from the clutches of a lascivious magistrate. A previous ballet, *El Amor Brujo* (*Love the Magician*, 15.iv.15), more plangently Iberian, entered concert repertoire by way of its ululating soprano solo. With these three works, de Falla invented a means by which successors such as *Gerhard and *Halffter could present Spanish folklore for external consumption. *El retablo de maese Pedro* (Madrid, 23.iii.23), a marionette children's play, resorts to Spanish idioms without adornment.

Settling in Granada he composed sparingly and sparsely. His dry concerto for harpsichord (Barcelona, 5.xi.26; Landowska soloist) is accompanied by just five instruments. *Homenajes (Homages)* for Debussy, Dukas, Arbós and Pedrell were written for solo guitar or piano, and bound together with orchestration as an afterthought (Buenos Aires, 18.xi.39).

Dismayed by the Spanish Civil War and the death of the poet Lorca, a close friend, he emigrated in fragile condition to Argentina and died there after seven lean years. Ernesto Halffter completed his opera *L'Atlantida* and younger composers formed a Manuel de Falla Group to study in secret European currents of modernism, of which he had been the nation's foremost practitioner.
    b. Cadiz, 23.xi.1876; st with *Pedrell, *Dukas; named president of the Spanish Institute by General Franco in 1938; emigrated 1939; *d.* Alta Gracia, Argentina, 14.xi. 46. *other works: La vida breve* (opera, 1905), *Fuego fatuo* (comic opera, part-lost, 1919); some piano pieces and popular songs; cantata *Psyché* (1924).

Fanfare for the Common Man *Copland's proclamation of wartime ideals, commissioned by *Goossens in a series of fanfares to open his Cincinnati concerts. fp: 12.iii.43.

David FANSHAWE British ethnomusical explorer, his nomadic voyages on three continents yielded an *African Sanctus* (Toronto, i.78) and, after sailing with Bahrain pearldivers, *Salaams* (London, v.70).
   b. Paignton, Devon, 19.ii.42;

Fantasia Classical music cartoon by Walt Disney and *Stokowski, premiered 1939.

Fantasia Concertante on a Theme of Corelli *Tippett's string orch. variations on Italian master's Concerto Grosso Op.6 no.2 fp: Edinburgh, 29.viii.53.

Fantasia Concertante on a Theme of Handel Tippett again, for piano and orch. fp: London, 7.iii.42.

Fantasia Contrappuntistica *Busoni's attempt at a new Art of Fugue for one or two pianos. fp: Berlin, 16.xi.21. (2nd vers.)

Fantasia on a Theme by Thomas Tallis *Vaughan Williams' great wash of sound for two string orchs. and string quartet, based on Elizabethan psalm tune. fp: Gloucester, 6.ix.10.

Fantasia on British Sea Songs Henry Wood's compilation to celebrate centenary of Trafalgar victory (1905), performed annually at Promenade Concerts.

Fantasia on Greensleeves Vaughan Williams, back in Elizabethan vein (1934).

Fantaisies symphoniques. Martinů's title for his 6th and last symphony. fp: Boston, 12.i.55.

Ferenc FARKAS Teacher of a generation of Hungarian radicals, his music consisted of mildly Stravinskian cantatas and an opera, *The Magic Cupboard* (1942).
   b. Nagykanisza, Hungary, 15.xii.05; st with *Weiner, taught Budapest Academy 1949–75.

Ernest (Bristow) FARRAR Organist at English Church in Dresden, killed by Germans on the Somme.
   b. London, 7.vii.1885; *d.* France, 18.ix.18. *orch. works*: *The Open Road, Lavengro, The Forsaken Merman*; variations on an old English song for piano and orch.

Arthur FARWELL Early collector of American Indian and Black folksong for symphonic use, and *Cowell-like publisher of music by composers less fortunate than himself on hand-cranked Wa-Wan Press.
   b. St Paul, Minnesota, 23.iv.1872; st with *Humperdinck; *d.* NY, 20.i.52. *orch. works*: *Symbolistic Study No. 3* (after Walt Whitman, 1905), *Symphonic song on 'Old Black Joe'* (1923).

fascism Aside from its geo-political meaning, the term was directed musically against post-1945 *serialists of the *Darmstadt school who claimed their method as the only acceptable form of composition for the modern era. Their admiration of Webern's ordered rows of notes was deemed to be fascist. *Webern had been attracted to Nazism and German composers were said to have adopted his style as a surrogate for lost ideals. The debate was opened around 1968 by Otto M. *Zykan, a Viennese polemicist, and countered by the Darmstadt crowd with the assertion that serialism was *a priori* antifascist since *Schoenberg had viewed Nazism as the negation of law and his teaching was meant, Moses-like, to uphold justice and humanity.

Gabriel-Urbain FAURÉ The Requiem for which Fauré is famed was written in 1887–8 and much revised before its present score was performed (Paris, 12.vii.1900). Since the composer was agnostic and never met the man it mourned, it was a masterpiece of objectivity rather than religious sincerity.
   He composed music for Maeterlinck's *Pelléas et Mélisande* (London, 21.vi.1898) ahead of Debussy, Sibelius and Schoenberg and made an orch. suite of it in 1909. It was out of character for Fauré to be in advance of the times. He was, like his friend *Saint-Saëns, a conformist and conservative yet, as director of the Paris Conservatoire (1905–20), he reformed the structure of French musical education and nourished the progressive talents of *Ravel, *Enesco and the *Boulanger sisters with his own recognizable delicacy. Administration absorbed his energies and he was reduced in his prime to the status of summer composer, seeing his music eclipsed by the denigratory Debussy and his own pupil, Ravel.
   A débâcle with the lyric tragedy *Prométhée*, staged outdoors at Béziers

(27.viii.1900), was not redeemed by the lyrical *Pénélope* (Monte Carlo, 4.iii.13), which took him six summers to write. Its heroic theme and heroine were well-received in Paris, but war intervened before the opera was fully established and by 1919 it looked anachronistic and was sidelined.

Fauré's chamber music is quietly spoken. The deathbed string quartet (1924) is darkly E minor but makes no forceful statements. His piano music, arranged in nocturnes, barcarolles and the like, is painless art for the bourgeois parlour, absolutely adored by Marcel Proust.

In one style, though, Fauré was paramount. Throughout an uneventful life he gently reinvented French art song, matching his beautifully crafted vocal lines to the pale flavours of modern poetry. He wrote 96 songs in all, including a cycle of 16, *La Bonne Chanson*, to poems by Paul Verlaine, intended for Fauré's lover, Emma Bardac, who later married Debussy. Verlaine's *Clair de Lune* (1887) was his most popular number. Three post-1914 sets, *Le Jardin Clos, Mirages* and *L'Horizon Chimérique* are strangely impersonal, provoking faint comparisons with late Beethoven while more substantially recalling glories of the Provençal landscape.
   b. Pamiers, Ariège, 12.v.1845, son of a schools inspector; settled in Paris 1871 as organist-choirmaster at the Madeleine; engaged 1877 to Marianne, daughter of mezzo Pauline Viardot, married 1883 Marie, daughter of sculptor Emmanuel Fremiet; *d.* Paris, 4.xi.24. *other works*: Music for a comedy, *Masques et Bergamasques* (Monte Carlo 10.iv.1919), two piano quintets (1895, 1921), two pianos quartets (1879, 1886), piano trio (1923), two cello sonatas (1918, 1921), two violin sonatas (1876, 1917).
   Bib: J. Barrie Jones (ed.) *Gabriel Fauré: a life in letters*, London (Batsford), 1989.

Faust The man who mortgaged his soul to the devil remained relevant in modern times, when entire nations sold out. *Busoni warned of current dilemmas in *Doktor Faust* and Hindemith told a similar tale in *Cardillac*. In recent times, Pousseur and Birtwistle have toyed with the theme.

Jindrich FELD Anti-communist Czech symphonist, he taught in Australia after the crushing of the Prague Spring but returned home in 1970 to write music in total disregard of political and compositional orthodoxies. With the collapse of communism, he became head of music on Czech radio. His two symphonies, four string quartets and various concertos for small orchestra are imbued with baroque traditions and Janáčekovian rhythms.
   b. Prague, 19.ii.25;

Morton FELDMAN Death promoted Feldman from *avant-garde obscurity to mainstream appeal. Suddenly it became apparent that this quiet, witty New Yorker had been a powerful undercurrent in the flow of musical thought away from abstruse serialism back towards audience communication. He saw himself as an heir to the early-20th-century European tradition embodied by Busoni and Strauss; as a young man he visited *Varèse weekly. His friends were the painters Mark Rothko and William de Kooning and he came of age in a city where the cream of Europe's creators had sought refuge.

Feldman was drawn initially in the late 1940s to *Cage and excelled in new forms of *graphic notation. Yet even mathematical formulae like *The King of Denmark* for solo percussion had a direct and often beautiful simplicity. *Structures* (1951) for string quartet sounds like a dotted line with just enough cohesion to sustain attention across the spaces.

His music was very quiet and insistent, often graced by self-mocking titles – *I met Heine on the rue Fürstenberg* (1970); *False Relationships* (1968); *Crippled Symmetry*; *The Viola in my Life* (1970–1). The most haunting is *Madame Press Died Last Week at Ninety* (1970), a soulful invention for chamber ensemble wound around the repeated cuckoo-calls of two flutes, in a manner reminiscent of Schoenberg's tolling Op 19/6, written on his return from Mahler's funeral; Mme. Maurina-Press was Feldman's piano teacher. *The Turfan Fragments* (1980), a Swiss radio commission, is deathly quiet, dwelling like all his music 'in the area between piano and pianissimo', between the hypnotic and the soporific.

In 1967, the aptly-named *In Search of an Orchestration* signalled an attempt at mass communication through sounds that had much in common with early *minimalism. It sparked off two fertile decades that yielded concertos for cello, piano, oboe, flute, violin and string quartet, the choral *Elemental Procedures* and *Neither*, a one-act opera by Samuel Beckett for soprano and orchestra. Feldman felt that the Irishman's way of nagging away at a line with infinite tiny variations until a deeper meaning became apparent was analogous to his own musical method. His penultimate composition was named *For Samuel Beckett* (1987).

His anti-*Webernism and omni-culturalism struck chords at *Darmstadt in 1984 and *Birtwistle considered him to be the composer whose ideas ran closest to his own. Young Germans like Zimmermann declared themselves as Feldman disciples. Just as recognition was dawning, he died.
    b. NY, 12.i.26; st piano with a *Busoni pupil and composition with Riegger and Wolpe; taught at SUNY, Buffalo; *d*. NY, 3.ix.87.

Philippe   FENELON   *Messiaen-like colourist.
    b. Sèvres, France, 23.xi.52; st with Messiaen; *works*: *Diagonal* for 14 players (Paris, 10.xi.83), *Du blanc le jour son espace* (Paris, 20.ii.88).

Howard FERGUSON Ulsterman who flared with a violin sonata op. 2 (1931) that *Heifetz played as if it were late Brahms – which it nearly was, mellow, moody and finely-wrought. His Octet (1933) recalled Brahms' clarinet sonatas; a 2nd violin sonata (1946), in the same vein, started to seem like too much of a good thing. At 50 Ferguson gave up composing and took to editing old keyboard music. One other notable work is *Discovery*, a song-cycle to five Denton Welch poems – uncommonly aphoristic for a British composer, and ominous as a November love-affair: 'When you get this/I'll be dead.'
    b. Belfast, 21.x.08; taught London RCM 1948–63; *other works*: Partita for orch. (1936), 4 diversions on Ulster Airs (1942) and a splashy piano concerto (London, 29.v.52) reminiscent of John *Ireland's.

Der ferne Klang (*The Distant Sound*) Erotic opera by *Schreker, left its mark on *Berg, who edited the vocal score. fp: Frankfurt, 18.viii.12.

Brian FERNEYHOUGH A recent historian of the string quartet named Ferneyhough as heir to the genre that Haydn invented. This was true perhaps in the sense that the émigré British composer was fixated on foursomes, but any audible resemblance between Haydn's drawing room music and the plucks and plinkings of a Ferneyhough creation was purely imaginary. Ferneyhough was not remotely for domestic performance or consumption. His 42-minute *Sonatas for String Quartet* (Royan, 24.iii.75) demanded total absorption from listeners and players alike and repayed very little by way of reward, beyond fragments of theme and a sense of forward momentum. Three subsequent quartets – 1980, 1987, 1990 – were no more ingratiating. The 3rd is almost static, 'rather autistic' in his words, with 23 types of texture that appear in ordered formation. The 4th is modelled on Schoenberg's 2nd quartet, with soprano solo. The *Carceri d'Invenzione* series of seven works for small ensembles and solo instruments (1982–86) elicits outlandish sonorites from familiar instruments.

Fernehough's music is never as grating on the ear as the squeaks of lesser serialists, but is plainly designed for a coterie of confirmed believers – music for the new music *ghetto. It was defined as the 'new complexity' and, while intentionally esoteric, left a mark on some younger contemporaries like *Rihm. Ferneyhough rejected *experiment for its own sake. 'A truly "experimental" music,' he asserted, 'is not necessarily one that juggles half-digested ideas and materials in order to be surprised by what comes out; rather, it is a form of living discourse which, at every moment, offers many possible paths towards its own future.'

He was embraced by the *avant-garde at the 1968 Gaudeamus composers' contest in Holland, where the unfinished Sonatas for String Quartet won a prize. His teacher, *Huber, won him stipends from Swiss and German sources; he began teaching at Freiburg (1973–86), *Darmstadt (1976–), Milan (1984–), The Hague (1986–) and became professor at the University of California, San Diego, in 1987. His music is not remotely English, nor has he connected with his homeland for many years, but Ferneyhough credited the British musical infrastructure with giving him access to a formative range of sources. He is regarded by a small band of loyalists as 'our king across the water'.

b. Coventry, England, 16.i.43; st with de *Leeuw, *Huber; *other works*: Sonata for two pianos (1966), *Time and Motion Studies* (1971–77), I for bass clarinet, II for cello and *electronics, III for 16 solo voices with percussion and electronics; *La chute d'Icare* for solo clarinet and seven players (1988), *Menmosyne* for bass flute and tape (1986).

Luc FERRARI After radical *musique concrète beginnings, Ferrari launched into comic dialogues and *happenings with audiences, live and on film, in which the very purpose of composing was questioned.

b. Paris, 5.v.29; st with Messiaen, Honegger; dir. (with *Schaeffer) Groupe de Recherche Musicale, 1958–66; *works include*: *Interrupteur* for nine instruments (1967), *Tautologos III* (1969), *Presque rien (almost nothing*, tape, 1970), *Sexolid* for soprano, 15 instruments and tape (1983).

festival A meeting point of artistic imagination and marketing skill, designed to trap an audience in provincial location – such as *Salzburg in summertime – or in a concert series larger than it might naturally want. Alternately, it consists of a gathering of clans – modernists at *Donaueschingen, the *avant-garde at *Darmstadt, cowpat collectors at Cheltenham. Such festivals are conspicuous by their lack of festivity. Joy is only to be found at youth-oriented sleep-ins like *Tanglewood, *Dartington and *Woodstock.

Jacques FEVRIER Frenchman who ruined *Rachmaninov's hopes of composing Maeterlinck's *Monna Vanna* by signing the playwright to an exclusive contract. Reputedly the best of his five operas (fp: Paris, 13.i.09), it was not seen abroad.

b. Paris, 2.x.1875; *d.* there, 6.vii.57.

Fiddler on the Roof Long-running Jerry Bock musical on Jewish village life on old Russia. fp: NY, 22.ix.64.

film music In 1908, the 73-year-old *Saint-Saëns in his opus 128, written for H. Lavedan's *L'Assassinat du Duc de Guise*, inaugurated an unequal alliance between music and 'the 20th century's most important art form'. It enabled a few composers – *Korngold, *Previn, *Williams – to earn untold wealth in movieland and created a minor cult for film music. The conductor Leopold *Stokowski became a Disneyland star in *Fantasia*. The high-minded *Schoenberg admired Chaplin and wrote an imaginary *Accompaniment for a film scene* (1930); he declined, though, to compose a straight soundtrack for Irving Thalberg's *The Good Earth*.

Film music as such began with the talkies. Korngold, a Viennese opera composer, was brought to Hollywood in 1934 by Max Reinhardt to arrange his production of *A Midsummer Night's Dream*. He set the standards for the art in scores for *Captain Blood* and *Anthony Adverse*. His principal followers were Dmitri *Tiomkin (*High Noon*; *Guns of Navarrone*), Miklos *Rozsa (*Spellbound*; *Julius Caesar*) and Max *Steiner (*Gone with the Wind*; *Casablanca*). The rich sonorities of *Rachmaninov, endlessly imitated, made a mushy backdrop for love films; *Stravinskyish sounds supposedly indicated modern values. *Copland and *Thomson contributed prairie tunes.

In Europe, symphonists from *Walton (*Henry V*) to *Auric (Cocteau's *Orphée*) were drawn to the screen. Malcolm *Arnold in *Bridge on the River Kwai* led a post-War generation of specialists. *Prokofiev gave Soviet cinema a touch of class with scores for Eisenstein's *Alexander Nevsky* and *Ivan the Terrible*. Shostakovich was forced to write film scores to atone for symphonic offences against the people's tonality. Hanns *Eisler wrote a 1947 textbook, *Composing for Films*. Some composers became attached to particular filmmakers. Bernard *Herrmann added chill to Alfred Hitchcock thrillers, Nino *Rota had just the right blend of mischief, nostalgia and menace for Federico Fellini. The Polish radical Wojtech Kilar added indispensable atmospherics to Andrzej Wajda's films. *Takemitsu made an invaluable contribution to Japanese cinema.

These were rare oases, however, in a generally mediocre and unvalued medium. *Vaughan Williams used music from *Scott of the Antarctic* for his 7th syphony and Korngold himself recycled soundtrack material into his violin concerto but the creative traffic was pretty much one-way. From time to time a movie theme became so popular that it briefly entered concert repertoire. Richard Addinsell's 1941 *Warsaw Concerto*, a Rachmaninov pastiche for the British film, *Dangerous Moonlight* was played by splashy pianists; John Williams' *Star Wars* became a showpiece for orchestra.

A movie hit could spectacularly revive the fortunes of a neglected concert work. Key beneficiaries were *Ligeti's *Lux Aeterna* and Strauss's *Also Sprach Zarathustra*, used in Stanley Kubrick's 1968 space fantasy *2001*, the Adagietto from Mahler's 5th symphony (in Visconti's *Death in Venice*) Ravel's *Boléro* (in the Bo Derek sex-vehicle *10*) and the entire corpus of Mozart's piano concertos from the use of the Andante of K467 in the 1968 Swedish romance *Elvira Madigan*.

Irving FINE   The shy Bostonian trailed *Copland through *neo-classicism and *neo-romanticism to a tentative *serialism that found dramatic expression in an 'almost operatic' Symphony (Boston, 23.iii.62). Months later, he was killed by a massive heart attack. Fine's appealing middle style yielded a *Notturno* for strings and harp (28.iii.51) reminiscent of Mahler's *Adagietto, and some delightful songs. His string quartet (NY, 18.ii.53) was orthodox *12-note but in the succeeding string trio (1957), he dictated some original rules and resonances. 'His music was both sweet and strong,' eulogized Virgil *Thomson.

b. Boston, 3.xii.14; st with Boulanger; taught Harvard, 1939–50; co-dir. Salzburg Seminar for American Studies, 1950, prof. at Brandeis, 1950–62; *d.* Boston, 23.viii.62. *other works: Serious Song*: a lament for string orch. (Louisville, 16.xi.55), *Diversions for Orch.* (children's entertainment, 5.xi.60), partita for wind quintet (NY 19.ii.49); *The Hour Glass*, choral cycle to Ben Jonson poems (1.v.52); two-minute *Hommage à Mozart* for piano (1956).

Vivian FINE   Middle-American tonalist, she won a National Endowment for the Arts grant to write a feminist opera, *The Women in the Garden* (San Francisco, 12.ii.78), featuring a colloquy between Isadora Duncan, Emily Dickinson, Gertrude Stein and Virginia Woolf.

b. Chicago, 28.ix.13; married sculptor Benjamin Karp 1935; *other works: A Guide to the Life Expectancy of the Rose* for soprano, tenor and chamber ensemble (NY, 16.v.56).

Fidelio   (Fritz)   FINKE   The once-prominent Finke was destined for music from birth. Raised among German settlers in Bohemia, he studied in Prague with *Novák and taught composition there until the collapse of Nazi rule, when he moved to Dresden and became a figurehead of the German Democratic Republic. Conservative and self-restrained, he composed four operas and eight orch. suites, as well as many pedagogic pieces that carried his name into the world's classrooms. The Concerto for Orchestra (1931), from his happiest period, finds him alert to contemporary trends but persisting with solid counterpoint and some sentimentality in the central *Nachtstück*.

b. Josefsthal (Josefuv Dul), Austro-Hungary, 22.x.1891; *d.* Dresden, East Germany, 12.vi.68. *other works*: piano concerto (1930), five string quartets.

Ross Lee FINNEY   Minnesotan pupil of *Berg and *Malipiero, he kept a folksy style going until 1950, when he attempted a kind of 12-note individualism that retained semblances of melody. Several works were choreographed by Martha Graham's husband, Erick Hawkins.

b. Wells, Minnesota, 23.xii.06; won Purple Heart for wartime bravery in France; professor at U. of Michigan 1948–73; *works include*: four symphonies, two piano concertos two violin concertos (1935 and 1973), solo *Fantasy* for *Menuhin (Brussels, 1.vi.58), piano *Variations on a Theme by Alban Berg* (1952), eight string quartets.

Michael   (Peter)   FINNISSY   English iconoclast, he clung to *avant-garde ideals assimilated in boyhood, yet wrote communicative music. In an hour-long piano suite *English   Country   Tunes* (London, 18.xii.79), he ranged from sultry, un-

English eroticism to wild violence, fearsome virtuosity to provocative silence. With the exception of *World* (Royan, 23.ii.75) for six voices and large orch., his best music is for keyboard solo. It includes jazz, tango and imaginative transcriptions of Verdi and Gershwin.

b. London, 17.iii.46; st with *Stevens, *Searle and *Vlad; taught Sussex U. 1989–90; *other works*: opera *The Undivine Comedy* (London) 4.vii.88), string quartet (Huddersfield, 21.xi.85), string trio (1986), three piano miniatures *Ives, Grainger, Nancarrow* (1974–80).

Gerald (Raphael) FINZI English composer of few works, a confluence of *Elgar without bluffness and *Vaughan Williams at his most delicate. His concerto for clarinet and strings (Hereford, 9.ix.49) is a light and lovely lament for lost times; *Dies Natalis* Wigmore Hall, (London 26.i.40) for high voice and strings is modelled on Bach cantatas with a flow and sweetness that eluded Britten in similar essays. *For Saint Cecilia* (London, 22.xi.47) showed he could write an effective fanfare and blazing chorus, but Finzi was at his best when quietly introspective.

b. London, 14.vii.01; st with *Farrar; *d*. Oxford, 27.ix.56. *other works*: cello concerto (1955); Interlude for oboe and string quartet, Thomas Hardy songs for braitone and string quartet (1922).

Firebird *Stravinsky's first ballet, commissioned by *Diaghilev, choreographed by Fokine and composed in simple Russian folk style. fp: Paris, 25.vi.10.

Fireworks Festive orchestral score that Stravinsky wrote for the wedding of *Rimsky's daughter. fp: St Petersburg, 17.vi.08.

Elena FIRSOVA The cantata *Earthly Life* (London, 10.x.87), written amid the stagnancy of Brezhnevite repression and performed outside the USSR, brought to light a fragrant talent of untold promise. The daughter of a nuclear physicist who longed to travel abroad, she absorbed cosmopolitan tastes in childhood and was drawn to forbidden poets. She wrote two pieces for voice and verses by Osip Mandelstam, Stalin's victim – *Tristia* (Moscow, 17.x.81) and *The Stone* (1983) – before tackling the five poems that constitute

the 20-minute *Earthly Life* for soprano and small ensemble. Starting as a post-*Bergian lament, its serenity and intimacy intensify with each passing phrase. 'Don't wipe away the sweet design,' implores the central verse, to a harmony of heartbreaking beauty.

Misterioso (Moscow, 14.iv.82), her 3rd string quartet, written in memory of *Stravinsky, uses notes with astonishing economy. Its silences speak volumes. A protégée of *Denisov, Firsova married a fellow-composer Dmitri *Smirnov, with whom she left Russia in 1991, fearing for the health of her children in particular, and of musical life in general.

b. Leningrad, 21.iii.50; *other works*: two cello concertos, two violin concertos, flute concerto, piano concerto – all for small orch.; *Augury* for chorus and orch. (London, 4.viii.92); piano sonata (1986); Shakespeare Sonnets for voice and organ (English text, 1981), vocal Romances on poems by Pasternak and Mayakovsky (1967–9).

First of May Title of *Shostakovich's 3rd symphony. fp: Leningrad, 21.1.30.

Dietrich FISCHER-DIESKAU The outstanding operatic and Lieder baritone sang in many languages and represented the humane, progressive character of a renascent German nation. He inspired major works by Britten (*War Requiem, William Blake Songs*), Henze (*Elegy for Young Lovers, Raft of the Medusa*), Reimann (*Lear*), Lutosławski (*Les Espaces du Sommeil*) and many others.

b. Berlin, 28.v.25; army service 1943–5, POW 1945; prof. at Hochschule der Kunst, Berlin, 1982–9.

Bib: D. Fischer-Dieskau, *Echoes of a Lifetime* (1989).

Luboš FIŠER Czech emigré in Pittsburgh, his output ranges from a musical on Hasek's comic novel, *The Good Soldier Schweik* (1962), to a vast cantata on texts taken from ancient Sumerian tablets, *Lament over the destruction of the city of Ur* (1969). A single-movement solo cello sonata written on his 40th birthday is affectingly melancholic.

b. Prague, 30.ix.35; emigrated 1971; *other works*: *15 prints after Dürer's Apocalypse* (Prague, 15.v.66), *Albert Einstein*, portrait for organ and orch. (1978).

Gregor FITELBERG The Polish revivalist conducted first performances of almost everything *Szymanowski wrote for orchestra. His compositions include two symphonies (1903, 1906) and two populist Polish Rhapsodies (1913, 1914).

> *b.* Dunaburg, Latvia, 18.x.1879; chief cond. Warsaw Philharmonic 1907–11, 1923–4, Warsaw Radio Orch. 1934–9, Katowice Radio Orch. 1947–53; *d.* Katowice, 10.vi.53.

His son and pupil, **Jerzy FITELBERG**, composed two neo-classical violin concertos and five string quartets.

> *b.* Warsaw, 20.v.03; *d.* NY, 25.iv.51.

Graham FITKIN Middle-of-road British *minimalist, a disciple of *Andriessen, his static sound blocks for small ensembles resembled presyncopated programs on personal keyboards. Their subliminal appeal won him a cult following and recording contracts.

> *b.* West Cornwall, 1963; *works*: *Huoah* (1988), *Slow* (1991); many pieces for single and multiple pianos.

Ella FITZGERALD Doyenne of jazz singers, she was the only female vocalist to sustain the unsullied dignity of *Armstrong and *Ellington, or to match them note for note in serious repertoire. Her recording with Armstrong of *Porgy and Bess* has high voltage and classic simplicity. She was equally adept at *scat singing and could bop with the best. An orphan child in Virginia, she was adopted at 16 by the bandleader Chick Webb and inherited the band on his death five years later. Her international solo career began directly after the War and lasted into the 1980s.

> *b.* Newport News, Virginia, 25.iv.17.

Nicolas FLAGELLO Lyrical US composer; his 5th opera *The Judgement of St Francis* (NY 18.iii.66) contains an 'Adoration' intermezzo hauntingly reminiscent of *Barber's Adagio.

> *b.* NY, 15.iii.28; *other work*: opera *Beyond the Horizon* (1983), four piano concertos.

(Ernst) Heinrich FLAMMER Probably the first German composer since Wagner to make the front page of *The Times* (2.xii.88), he achieved that unwanted glory when the *BBC Symphony Orchestra's principal cellist smashed his instrument to pieces after having to play through Flammer's piano concerto, *Zeitzeichen-Zeitmasse*. Players complained that their instruments had been abused by the composer, in a work that sound like a throwback to 1968 student protests.

> *b.* Heilbronn, 1949; *other work*: *Building the Tower of Babel* for three choirs, three orchs., soprano, baritone, speaker and *electronics (1982).

flexatone A kind of musical saw introduced to the orchestra by *Honegger and *Schoenberg (Op. 31 Variations) and taken up by Henze, Penderecki and many others.

Flight of the Bumble-Bee All the buzz in Rimsky-Korsakov's 1903 suite from opera *Tsar Saltan*.

The Flood Biblical pageant by *Stravinsky. fp: CBS-TV, 14.vi.62.

Florence Italian town renowned musically for its Maggio Musicale, a May festival founded in 1933 by Vittorio Gui. It premiered operas by *Dallapiccola and *Pizzetti and rekindled international interest in Weimar opera.

A Florentine Tragedy *Zemlinsky's one-act opera after Oscar Wilde's infidelity story. fp: Stuttgart, 30.v.17.

Marius FLOTHUIS As the Concertgebouw Orch.'s deputy manager, he was deported by the Nazis in 1943 for hiding Jews. He later served successfully (1955–74) as artistic director. His compositions are mainly neo-classical.

> *b.* Amsterdam, 30.x.1914; *works include*: concertos for flute (1944) and clarinet (1957).

Carlisle FLOYD Composer of ten American operas adapted from books by John Steinbeck – *Of Mice and Men* (Seattle 22.i.70), Robert Penn Warren, *All the King's Men* (renamed *Willie Stark*, Houston, 24.iv.81) – and lesser authors. Two non-US sources, *Susannah* (from the Bible, Houston, 24.ii.55) and *Wuthering Heights* (Santa Fe, 16.vii.58) made greatest impact. His music is melodious and eclectic, less flamboyant than *Menotti's.

> *b.* Latta, South Carolina, 11.vi.26; st with *Bacon; taught Florida and Houston Us.; *other operas*: *The Passion of Jonathan Wade* (1962), *Bilby's Doll* (1976).

flute *Debussy and *Ravel spotlighted the instrument in chamber works and it remained a favourite with French composers down to *Boulez.

Josef Bohuslav FOERSTER A formative figure in Czech music, Foerster's six operas and colourful suites have largely lapsed. A Dvořák pupil who became Mahler's close friend, he wrote rich, sometimes ponderous pieces on the general theme of love. His first three operas – *Deborah* (1893), *Eva* (1899) and *Jessica* (Prague, 16.iv.05) – bear women's names and his best suite celebrates the romantic martyr *Cyrano de Bergerac* (Prague, 3.iii.05). Six heroines are vividly depicted in *From Shakespeare* (21.xi.11); he composed incidental music for *Julius Caesar, Twelfth Night* and *Love's Labour's Lost*. His 4th symphony in C minor (*Easter Symphony*, 22.xi.05) flatters Mahler by imitation. He admired Goethe and, less nationalist than his compeers, wrote many German songs.

Foerster composed prolifically throughout a Methuselan existence; the later contemplations – notably a Sonata quasi fantasia for violin and piano (1942), written under Nazi occupation – are wise and warm.

b. Prague, 30.xii.1859, descendant of famous organists; married star soprano Berta Lauterer (1869–1936) 1.ix.1888; teacher and critic in Hamburg 1893–1903 and Vienna 1903–1919; married Olga Dostál, 1937; *d.* Novy Vestec, 29.v.51; *other works*: operas *The Conquerors* (19.xii.18), *The Heart* (15.xi.23), *The Simpleton* (28.ii.36); two violin concertos for *Kubelik (1911, 1926), cello concerto (1931), 5th symphony (2.xi.29), autobiographical suites *My Youth* (1900) and *Enigma* (1909; four string quartets 1882–1944), piano trio in memory of his only son, 1921.
Bib: J. B. Foerster, *Der Pilger*, Prague (Artia), 1955.

folk music The source of 19th-century symphonic music was given a rebarbative edge by *Bartók and *Stravinsky. Instead of smoothing down peasant tunes, they emphasized primeval elements in folk music and travelled far in search of exotic primitivism. Bartók's excursions to Transylvania, Turkey and North Africa instilled a wanderlust in composers whose local resources had been overworked. Late and latent nationalisms looked to their own backyard. The English musical renaissance was fuelled by the folk researches of *Holst and *Vaughan Williams; Spain found its voice in local tunes collected by Albeniz and de Falla. In the USSR and its satellites, folksong was the basis of Socialist Realism, the people's voice in music, and symphonists were expected to flourish literal quotations. Towards the end of the century, *Berio and *Reich contrived abstract applications of raw folk material in *Coro* and *Tehillim*.

In popular music, the folk revival started out as a rebellion and ended as a wealthy adjunct. The dustbowl songs of Woody *Guthrie and Pete Seeger carried left-wing political messages that survived the ravages of McCarthyism to attract a 1950s protest following. Smoothed down by the likes of Joan Baez and Peter, Paul and Mary, folk music briefly graced the hit parade. In its raw state, it captivated Bob Dylan and gave rise to a lucrative fusion of folk, rock and alternative society.

Jacqueline FONTYN Belgian impressionist, unafraid to express strong images and emotion. *Colinda* for cello and chamber orch. (1990) set a Romanian Christmas song in memory of a friend killed in the December 1989 uprising against the Ceaucescu regime.

b. Antwerp, 27.xii.30; prof. at Antwerp Cons. 1963–70, Brussels, 1971–90; *other works*: piano concerto *Reveries and Turbulence* (1987), *Scurochiaro* (septet, 1989), *L'orée du songe* for viola and orch. (1991).

Arthur (William) FOOTE Boston romantic composer of Hiawatha and Omar Khayyam sketches.

b. Salem, Massachusetts, 5.iii.1853; *d.* Boston, 8.iv.37.

formalism Meaningless term that Stalin coined to define music he did not like. It became an article of Soviet cold-war cultural policy.

Wolfgang FORTNER A prominent phoenix in post-1945 German music, he spent a quiet war as instructor in church music at Heildelberg and emerged as a *12-

note convert, perhaps as a personal act of repentance. He joined *Darmstadt in 1946 as a model proselyte of modernism and in 1957 became head of the German section of the *ISCM. His music, initially *Hindemithian and damned by some Nazi critics for atonality, applied a Weber type of serial, Bachian counterpoint. His turning point, the 1947 Symphony, was succeeded by highly emotive oratorios, *The Creation* (1955) and *Pfingstgeschichte nach Lukas* (1963) for tenor, chorus and 11 instruments.

> *b.* Leipzig, 12.x.07; taught Heidelberg 1931–54, Detmold 1957–64, Freiburg 1957–82; founded Musica Viva series in Heidelberg 1947 and dir. Munich series 1964–87; *d.* Heidelberg, 5.ix.87. *other works*: *Ein deutsche Liedmesse* (1934), concerto for strings (1935), violin concerto (1946), ballet *The White Rose* (1950), Fantasy on B-A-C-H for two pianos, nine solo instruments and orch. (1950), *Impromptus* for orch. (1957); *Triplum* for orch. and three pianos (1967); five operas including *Blood Wedding* (after Lorca, Cologne, 8.vi.57), *Elizabeth Tudor* (Berlin, 23.x.72) and *That Time* (after Samuel Beckett, Baden-Baden, 24.iv.77).

Lukas FOSS A poor man's *Bernstein, he shared his friend's easy eclecticism without his charismatic communicativess. He began composing music at seven years old and had it published at 15, was *Koussevitsky's blue-eyed boy at *Tanglewood, played piano with leading orchestras and was music director of the Buffalo (1963–70) and Brooklyn (1971–) Philharmonics. Composing copiously, not one of his works lodged in the repertoire. He was fated to hit fashions at the wrong time, discovering Ives and aleatory music too early, medievalism and romanticism too late. Bernstein depicted him sparkily in one of *5 Anniversaries* (1951), entitled 'For Lukas Foss'.

> *b.* Berlin, 15.viii.22 (as Lukas Fuchs); emigrated to US 1937; *works include*: operas, *The Jumping Frog of Calaveras County* (after Mark Twain, Bloomington, Indiana, 18.v.50), *Griffelkin* (NBC-TV, 6.xi.55); two piano concertos, oboe concerto, *Renaissance* concerto for flute and orch. (1986), *Folksong* for orch. (1976); *Time Cycle* song collection (1960); three string quartets.

John (Hebert) FOULDS The first Englishman to flirt with *microtonality in the 1890s, and with exoticism while head of European music on All-India Radio (1937–39). Much of his huge output was lost in transit.

> *b.* Manchester, 2.xi.1880; played in Hallé Orch. 1900–10; cond. in London 1910–35; went to India, 1935; *d.* Calcutta, 24.iv.39; *works include: A World Requiem* (1921), two cello concertos (1909), 3 *Mantras* (1919), Chinese Suite (1935).

Four Last Songs (Vier letzte Lieder) Richard Strauss's, valedictory elegy for soprano and orchestra to three poems by Hesse – 'Frühling', 'September', 'Beim Schlafengehen' – and one by Eichendorf, 'Im Abendrot'. The order of the four songs can be varied; a fifth, of inferior quality, was found decades later in the estate of Maria Jeritza (1887–1982). fp: London 22.v.52; Kirsten Flagstad (sop), cond. *Furtwängler.

Four Saints in Three Acts Opera by Virgil Thomson to Gertrude Stein's nonsensical libretto. fp: Ann Arbor, Michigan, 20.v.33.

Four Seasons Vivaldi's title, borrowed by Milhaud's publishers for a quartet of concertos (1934–53).

Four Temperaments i. Title of Nielsen's 2nd symphony. fp Copenhagen, 1.xii.02.

ii. Moody ballet by Hindemith; also concert piece for piano and strings. fp Boston, 3.ix.44; Lukas *Foss soloist.

Jean FRANCAIX By name and nature the quintessential French composer, contemptuous of foreignness, elegant as a cravat and conservative to the core. When Saint-Saëns died in 1921, the nine year-old Françaix declared, 'I will replace him.' Nadia *Boulanger groomed him for the role.

His music is at best witty and light as a soufflé. A jolly piece for five instruments called *L'heure du berger* (*The Shepherd's Hour*, 1947) delicately parodies French pastoral types. He was good at picking out the individual character of wind instruments, and his flute concerto (1967) is a model of its kind. The 1958 horn *Divertimento* is a showpiece and the saxophone quartet of 1939 is good clean fun.

He wrote gracefully and classically for strings, typically in *Sei Preludi* (1964).

His limitations are exposed in large works. The *St John's Apocalpyse* oratorio (Paris, 11.vi.42) has no bang and much whimper. His first opera, *Le diable boiteux* (Paris, 30.vi.38) was conducted by his doting teacher but did not travel. Françaix's music demonstrates what happens when a modern composer denies the existence of Wagner, Mahler, Schoenberg and Stravinsky. No matter how rich he may be in themes, his lack of engagement with contemporary ideas means that many of his works live only as examination pieces.

b. Le Mans, France, 23.v.12; *other works*: ballet after Hans Christian Andersen's tale of the Emperor's new clothes (1936), symphony (1932) piano concerto (1936) and concertino (1932) two piano concerto (1965), violin concerto (1970), piano sonata (1960).

France The French contribution to 20th-century music was greater than in any other epoch, although focused on fewer individuals. Four innovators left an indelible mark; *Debussy originated the first numerical *impressionism; *Ravel produced an easily imitable sinuous sound; *Messiaen married modern technique with natural elements; and *Boulez bestrode the post-war scene with Napoleonic hauteur. The majority of French composers were backward-looking, however, emulating d'*Indy's nostalgia for past glories. Despite massive government funding for showy projects like *IRCAM and the *Bastille Opera, music education was perfunctory, orchestral standards were generally pathetic and a minister of culture, André Malraux, was able to declare with impunity that 'France is not a musical nation'.

Alberto FRANCHETTI Known as the Italian Meyerbeer, his family wealth enabled him to write and stage operas on a grand scale. *Caruso sang in *Germania* (La Scala, 11.iii.02) and recorded some arias; otherwise Franchetti might have been remembered only as the composer who lost *Tosca* to *Puccini.

b. Turin, 18.ix.1860; *d.* Viareggio, 4.viii.42. *other operas*: *Asrael* (1888), *Cristoforo Colombo* (1892).

Benjamin FRANKEL Anglo-Jewish son of immigrant parents, Frankel was a jazz violinist and witty film composer before he turned earnest in a post-Mahlerian mode. A string trio (1944), that paved the way for five quartets, is intimate, propulsive and elegiac. An intense violin concerto (19.vi.51) grew out of the 4th quartet and an ineluctable preoccupation with the Holocaust. Frankel left the Communist Party during the Prague show-trials and was the focus of a notorious slander action brought against him by *Lutyens' husband, Edward Clark. Although exonerated, Frankel suffered a heart attack and was never the same again. He turned *serialist and wrote eight symphonies but lost the élan of his chamber music.

b. London, 31.i.06; *d.* there 12.ii.73. *other works include*: *The Aftermath* (1946) for tenor, off-stage trumpet and strings (q.v. Britten's Serenade); *Sonata ebraica* for cello and harp; more than 100 movie scores.

Die Frau ohne Schatten *(The Woman Without a Shadow)* *Strauss's and Hofmannsthal's 4th opera, replete with oriental themes. fp: Vienna, 10.x.19.

free jazz An attempt to resolve the creative crisis in jazz by engaging with *rock, *electronics and other media. Ornette Coleman experimented with noise; John Coltrane hit high speeds; the Art Ensemble of Chicago introduced Mahlerian irony and Miles Davies went his own sweet, fertilizing way without, however, providing a solution.

Betty FREEMAN Maecenas of modern art in Los Angeles, she commissioned works by a range of composers from *Cage to *Young, especially boosting *minimalism and preserving such rare flowers as *Partch, *Nancarrow and *Rudyhyar. She gave monthly Sunday brunch concerts in her living room, made an award-winning film on Partch, posed for David Hockney and gave exhibitions of her own perceptive photographic portraits of modern iconoclasts. Cage composed 16 *Freeman Etudes* for violin; she is the dedicatee of *Adams' opera, *Nixon in China*.

b. Chicago, 1921, moved to LA 1950, remarried and established dual residence in Italy 1979.

Frescoes of Pierro della Francesca Delightful orch. work by *Martinů, inspired by seeing his brother restoring paintings in a church near their birthplace. fp: *Salzburg, 28.viii.56, cond. Kubelik.

Tibor FREŠO Obeisant chief of Slovak National Opera.

    b. Spissky Stiavnik, Czechoslovakia, 20.xi. 18; *d.* Bratislava, 1987. *works include*: *Martin and the Sun* (children's opera, 1974), *A Bug is Born* (ballet), *After the Peace* (1949), *Song on Woman* (1975).

Peter Racine FRICKER A descendant of the great French dramatist, Fricker wrote five post-War British symphonies in a free atonal style though with high emotional voltage. The last (1975) is for organ and orchestra. He became visiting professor at the University of California in 1964 and emigrated six years later. His *Sinfonia in memoriam Benjamin Britten* (1977) is unfailingly moving.

    b. London, 5.ix.20; st with *Seiber; *d.* Santa Barbara, California, 1.ii.90. *other works*: oratorios *The Vision of Judgement* (1958) and *Whispers at those Curtains* (1984), 2nd violin concerto (1954).

Oskar FRIED Late-romantic German composer, he adored Mahler and Nietzsche in equal measure and wrote a *Verklärte Nacht* and similar extravagances for large orch. Expelled by Hitler, he settled in the USSR.

    b. Berlin, 10.viii.1871; *d.* Moscow, 5.vii.41.

Robert FUCHS Known as 'Serenaden-Fuchs' for five much-played string pieces in the manner of Brahms, he wrote more than 100 other derivations including a mild, late piano quartet, Op. 75. The pupils of this genial copyist included *Mahler, *Wolf, *Sibelius, *Schmidt, *Schreker and *Zemlinsky.

    b. Graz, 15.ii.1847, professor at Vienna Conservatory 1875–1912; *d.* Vienna, 19.ii.27. *other works*: two operas, symphony, piano concerto.

Julius FUČIK Czech bandmaster whose marches, especially 'Entrance of the Gladiators', became world-popular overtures, encores and programme fillers.

    b. Prague, 18.vii.1872; *d.* Litomerice, 25.ix. 16.

Anis FULEIHAN Cypriot-American who lived in the eastern Mediterranean while writing music that became steadily less oriental. The work that caught most attention was a concerto for *theremin, premiered by *Stokowski (NY, 26.ii.45).

    b. Kyrenia, Cyprus, 2.iv.1900; studied in the US 1915–16; worked as editor for G. Schirmer 1932–39, taught at Indiana U. 1947–51, Beirut conservatory 1953–60, cond. Orchestre Classique de Tunis 1962–65; *d.* Palo Alto, California, 11.x.70. *other works*: opera *Vasco* (1960), Mediterranean Suite (1930), two symphonies (1936, 1962), three concertos for piano and violin, Symphonie concertante for string quartet and orch. (NY Phil., 25.iv.40).

furniture music (musique d'ameublement) *Satie's concept of a music to be played but not attentively heard, the forerunner of *Muzak (see *aural wallpaper).

Beat FURRER Rising comet on the *Universal list, he seems preoccupied with structure and percussion. His 80-minute music drama *Die Blinden* (Vienna, 25.xi.89), on decadent texts by Maeterlinck, Hölderlin and Rimbaud, with Platonic interpolations, was commissioned by the Vienna State Opera.

    b. Schaffhausen, Switzerland, 1954; moved to Vienna, 1975; st with *Haubenstock-Ramati; formed Societé de l'art acoustique ensemble; *other works*: *Risonanze* for large orch. in three groups (1988), *Face de la Chaleur* for five instrument groups (Vienna, 27.x.91); two string quartets, *Music for Mallets* (1985).

Wilhelm (Gustav Heinrich Ernst Martin) FURTWÄNGLER Iconoclastic conductor of the Berlin Philhamonic (1922–54) and Leipzig Gewandhaus (1922–28) orchestras. Furtwängler disdained to give a clear beat, asking musicians to share a mood implied by his wavery bodily movements. Uncertainty raised the tension of his performances and blurred entries added depth to the musical ambience. He was the antipode of *Toscanini, pursuing the spiritual in music at the expense of the literal. They clashed politically over Furtwängler's decision to stay in Germany under Hitler – in order, he insisted, to rescue the German soul. He fought the Nazis over *Hindemith's opera *Mathis der Maler*, and lost. Only Hitler's favour saved him from retribution.

Abroad, he was named Toscanini's successor at the New York Philharmonic in 1936 but withdrew after an anti-German campaign. He conducted opera regularly at Covent Garden, Bayreuth and Berlin and recorded unwillingly for EMI and DG, maintaining that the performance of music must be founded on momentary inspiration, and was distorted by recording. Conservative by inclination, he premièred Bartók's first piano concerto and Schoenberg's Orchestral Variations.

He saw himself, like Mahler, as primarily a composer, yet his music is of little consequence. In three symphonies (1941–54), he seems repeatedly to linger and luxuriate in the sound he has created, though none of it bears the mark of an original mind. The works lack momentum, daring and, above all, anything personal to say – an unbelievable neutrality, given the times and the composer's musical stature. The third in C-minor is classically formed and derivative of Bruckner. There is also a piano concerto that does a thematic tour around the great composers.

b. Berlin, 25.i.1886, son of eminent archaeologist; cond. Munich, Strasbourg, Lübeck, Mannheim; married twice and fathered five children (four out of wedlock); *d.* Baden-Baden, 30.xi.54.

futurism Artistic movement started by Italians, in which painters and musicians sought to express the spirit of the modern age in mechanical imagery. The roaring motor-car, wrote Filippo Marinetti in 1909, was more beautiful than anything by Michelangelo. A futurist musical manifesto advocated the concert injection of industrial noises. Francesco Pratella (1880–1955) composed *Musica futurista* for conventional orchestra (Rome, 1913); his radical comrade Luigi *Russolo replaced musical instruments with *intonarumori* – noise intoners – and presented two of his works in London in 1914 under the titles *The Awakening of a Great City* and *A Meeting of Motorcars and Aeroplanes.*

Futurism subsided with the outbreak of war but left a substantial Parisian residue in the thinking of Varèse, Satie, Prokofiev and Honegger (Pacific 231). Marinetti became an ardent Fascist and the movement linked hands with triumphant totalitarianism. In the Soviet Union it became a guiding light for *socialist realism, inspiring symphonies of steel and hymns to hydro-electric dams.

gagaku Japanese court music, imitated by *Britten in church parables.

Hans GAL Austrian refugee in Edinburgh, he helped found the international festival and was a guiding musical light in the Scots capital. As a youth, he played Brahms' clarinet sonatas with Richard Mülhfeld, their dedicatee. In 1964 he composed a sonata for clarinet and piano that shares their timeless melodic elegance. He had several operas staged in Weimar Germany; *Der Arzt der Sobeide* was composed in the Carpathian First War trenches; *Rich Claus, Poor Claus* had its Dresden première scrubbed by the Nazis and was not performed for half a century.
  b. Brünn (Brno, Czechoslovakia) 5.viii.1890; dir. Mainz conservatory 1929–33, taught Vienna 1933–38, settled Edinburgh 1938; prof. at Edinburgh U. 1945–65; *d.* there, 3.x.87. *other works*: three symphonies, *Pickwickian overture* (1939), cello concerto (1944), serenade for strings, four string quartets.

Blas GALINDO(-Dimas) Mexican composer of Indian descent, his early works were mistakable for *folk music. Stung by accusations of unoriginality, he went *avant-garde and wrote what must have been the first concerto for electric guitar (Mexico City, 12.vi.77). He ran the national conservatory (1942–61).
  b. San Gabriel, Jalisco, Mexico, 3.ii.10; st with *Chávez, *Copland; *works include*: seven ballets, three symphonies, *Erotic litany for peace*, for orchestra, organ, soloists, narrator and tape (Mexico City, 2.v.69).

The Gambler Compulsive Prokofiev opera after Dostoyevsky; composed in St Petersburg between 1917 revolutions, fp: Brussels, 29.v.29.

gamelan The gentle patterns of Javanese and Balinese orchestras entered French music and modernism via *Debussy. See: Indonesian music.

Henry Balfour GARDINER Wealthy Frankfurt Gang member, he paid for the private première of Holst's *Planets, launched *Bax and *Grainger in a 1912 concert series and bought *Delius a roof over his ailing head. His *Overture to a Comedy* (London, 28.xi.06) was a jolly piece of Edwardiana and *Shepherd Fennel's Dance* enjoyed a folkish vogue. He gave up composing at the age of 48 and destroyed most of his scores.
  b. London. 7.xi.1877; *d.* Salisbury, 28.vi.50.

His great-nephew, **John Eliot GARDINER,** is an aggressive *early music pioneer who crossed the gulf into conducting symphony orchestras.
  b. Fontmell Magna, Dorset, 20.iv.43; formed Monteverdi Choir, English Baroque Orch. and English Baroque Soloists; mus. dir. Lyons Opera 1983–89, NDR Orch. Hamburg, 1991–.

Gaspard de la nuit Macabre piano suite by Ravel. fp: Paris, 9.i.09.

Gayaneh Khatchaturian's sabre-rattling ballet. fp: Perm, 9.xii.42.

Gebrauchsmusik (Ger. = useful or utility music) A democratic initiative by *Hindemith, Weill and other Weimar idealists to write music that anyone could play or sing. Hindemith won greatest attention with *Lehrstück*, a music drama written with *Brecht in 1929 and a children's opera *Wir* *bauen eine Stadt* (*We are building a city*, 1930). *Orff took up the educational challenge by writing school pieces with modern harmonies. *Eisler wrote workers' choruses that *Copland imitated in America. Britten's *Let's Make an Opera* was a British application of *Gebrauchsmusik*.

Bob (Frederick Zenon) GELDOF Irish *punk singer whose band, the Boomtown Rats, had passed its sell-by date when he was so shaken by a BBC-TV report on Ethiopian famine that he organized a rock summit on record and a 1984 Band Aid concert, raising more than £50 million for Africa. His initial bash was followed by the 1985 Live Aid and similar spin-offs for worthy causes, none of which touched quite the same chord. Geldof, ironically, scored his first hit with a song called 'Looking After Number 1' (1979).

b. Dublin, 5.x.52;

Harald GENZMER Weighty German pupil of *Hindemith, he attempted, like his teacher, two concertos for the *electronic trautonium (1939, 1952) but for the rest confined himself to conventional instrumentation. His 20-minute concerto for four horns (1984) is modelled on Schumann's odd Konzertstück; his 2nd trumpet concerto 'im alten Stil' is *neoclassical. Professor at Freiburg (1946–57) and Munich (1957–74), his many pupils included *McCabe.

b. Bremen, 9.ii.09; *works include*: three symphonies, three piano concertos, concertos for viola, organ, cello, harp, two clarinets and percussion; ballet *The Magic Mirror* (1965), *German Mass* (1973).

Roberto GERHARD If history was fair, Gerhard would rank with *Berg as a founder of modern opera. A penniless Catalan refugee in Cambridge, he spent the two post-war years (1945–7) writing a work that synthesized Spanish and English cultures with the spirit of the *Second Vienna School. *The Duenna*, a setting of Robert Brinsley Sheridan's 1775 comedy of manners, was to be the first contemporary-sounding operetta, or zarzuela. Breaking the convention of strung-together numbers, this was a through-composed, structurally impressive three-act comedy in which the rhythms were irresistible and the songs could be whistled all the way home, but the scoring was intricate and multi-dimensional. Gerhard applied *12-note passages selectively to intensify the emotional background and believed he had found a balance between tradition and progress, populist satisfaction and cerebral stimulus.

To his dismay, *The Duenna* was rejected by both sectors. British admirers of his colourful hispanic themes – *Alegrias* (1942) and *Don Quixote* (1944) – were deterred by dissonances, while the *ISCM concert audience at Wiesbaden in 1949 berated the former Schoenberg pupil for bowing to popular taste and muddying the master's dogma. *The Duenna* was not staged for 45 years (Madrid, 21.i.92) when Spain discovered it as lost national heritage – albeit sung in English. Had its case been made sooner, it might have bridged the gulf between art and popular musics and helped accustom the public ear to *serial procedures.

Gerhard treated folk culture with laconic affection. He was a European without frontiers and national complexes. Born of Swiss-German and Alsatian parents in northern Spain, he studied in Berlin and Vienna, returning to Barcelona as professor of music and cornerstone of new music. It was at his home that Schoenberg in 1931 composed the 2nd act of *Moses und Aron*; *Webern premièred his *6 Catalan Folksongs* (Vienna, *ISCM, 16.vi.32). After the fascist victory in the civil war he fled to Paris; Edward J. *Dent set him up on a tiny stipend at Cambridge, where he remained for the rest of his life.

The Duenna's dismissal, followed in 1952 by a mild heart attack, prompted him to link up hands again with the modernist vanguard. His 3rd symphony *Collages* (1962) and 4th symphony *New York* (1967) interpolated electronic tape; the 2nd string quartet used some of *Penderecki's fearsome effects. There are parallels to be found with *Busoni and *Bartók, also with *Hába and *Hauer. Yet Gerhard was consistently his own man, bringing the richness of many cultures to both light and abstract works. No other composer could have got away with slipping Chopin's funeral march into the balletic whirl of *Alegrias*.

The violin concerto (1943), austere as Schoenberg's, admits Iberian melodies. The concerto for piano and strings (1951), his first fully 12-note composition, recalls the Spanish baroque keyboard masters and pulls the Viennese technique off to his own patterned tangent. The first symphony (Baden-Baden *ISCM, 21.vi.55, cond. Rosbaud) was melodic enough for Bernstein to claim its US première. In some works of his last decade the asceticism sounds dated, for Gerhard was at his best when combining popular material with advanced methodology.

b. Valls, Catalonia, 25.ix.1896; st with *Granados, *Pedrell, *Schoenberg; married Leopoldina Feichtegger in Vienna, 1930; founded Independent Composers of Catalonia group 1931; visiting prof. at U. of Michigan 1960, Tanglewood 1961; d. Cambridge, England, 5.i.70. *other works*: ballets *Ariel* (Barcelona, 18.v.36), *Don Quixote* (Covent Garden, 20.ii.50), *Pandora* (Cambridge, 24.i.44) – all arranged as concert suites; symphony *Homenage a Pedrell* (1941), harpsichord concerto (1957), concerto for orch. (1965), *Leo*, chamber symphony for ten players (1969); *The Plague* for speaker, chorus, orch. (after Camus, 1964); radio incidental music for *Don Quixote* (1944), Camus' *The Outsider* (1954), film score for Lindsay Anderson's *This Sporting Life* (1963); nonet (1956), wind quintet (1928), *7 *Haiku* for voice and five instruments (1922).

(Sir) Edward GERMAN (Jones) Theatrical composer whose mock-Tudor hit music for Henry Irving's *Henry VIII* (1892) freed him from the need to compose. He completed *Sullivan's unfinished *Emerald Isle* (1901) and followed it with operettas *Merrie England* (1902) and *Tom Jones* (1907). He wrote two symphonies and a Coronation March for George V (1911).

b. Whitchurch, Shropshire, 17.ii.1862; d. London, 11.xi.36.

German music Like most European hegemonies, Austro-German music reached its zenith at the turn of the century and was starting to disintegrate. Bach's tonal and structural corsets were wearing thin and the extreme chromaticism of Wagner's operas left little for successors to build on. The symphony could grow no larger than the armies amassed by *Mahler and *Strauss. Musicians who perceived the crisis were decried as revolutionaries and pushed to the fringe. Yet, when *Schoenberg crossed into *atonality and invented the *12-note system, his aim was still to find a method that 'would assure the dominance of German music for the next 1,000 years'.

It was not to be. Although the *Weimar ferment produced a several fresh options – the historical ideas of *Busoni, *Hindemith's practicalities and *Weill's jazzy populism – they were expunged by Nazism, pledged to cleanse the continent of *decadence, and German music never recovered from the ravages.

After the War, *Henze led a handful composers who regained international exposure, while *Cologne and *Darmstadt were world centres of *avant-gardism, built around *Stockhausen's problematic personality. The communist experiment in eastern Germany produced no music of great consequence and composers in reunified Germany – *Rihm, von *Bose – either looked elsewhere for stimulus or became so preoccupied with German problems that their contribution was marginal.

George GERSHWIN The song-plugger who became a symphonic composer: an apotheosis of the American dream in a peculiarly insecure prism. The comparisons with Franz Schubert are obvious. Both were youthful founts of melodic energy, borrowing their styles from the surroundings and forever seeking self-improvement from senior composers. But whereas the Viennese composer was grounded in an established tradition from which he could draw guidance, Gershwin operated in a rootless society. He had to invent a tradition and knew himself to be

Long Live Jazz!!!!

George Gershwin.

unequal to the task. What others saw as success was, in reality, the tragedy of a sensitive individual cast in a role he neither wanted nor could hope to fulfil.

*Rhapsody in Blue was a milestone in music history, the first concert work to fuse *jazz with concerto form and the first US composition to enter the standard concert repertoire. It was by no means the earliest attempt to join jazz to mainstream music – such solid European figures as Ravel, *Milhaud and Hindemith had preceded him by a couple of years – nor was it intended for a stuffed-shirt audience. It was dashed off at Schubertian speed in less than four weeks for a Paul *Whiteman band concert at Aeolian Hall, NY (12.ii.24) and orchestrated for the occasion by Ferde Grofé, with Gershwin featuring as piano soloist. Instant success led to a Carnegie Hall date in April and a nationwide tour with slightly modified orchestration and a loss of riffs in the indelible clarinet wail that makes its opening perhaps the most distinctive in all modern music. The clarinet cadenza was written by its instrumentalist, Ross Gorman, but the work was sustained beyond this initial thrill by the propulsive vitality of a 25-year-old composer-pianist who defined his talent as 'I Got Rhythm'. His own piano roll performance seems to capture the metropolitan melting pot as assuredly as the Viennese depicted their golden woods.

Gershwin was booked by the NY Philharmonic to write a Concerto in F (NY, 3.xii.25) and attempted a 2nd Rhapsody at Boston (29.i.32, cond. *Koussevitsky) but neither possessed the same shock of novelty. To dispel rumours that he was unable to orchestrate, he composed a symphonic poem, An American in Paris (NY, 13.xii.28) that expressed something of the spirit of the age. The Cuban Overture (NY, 16.viii.32) on *salsa beats he retrieved in Havana presaged a decade of US musical fascination with Latin America and helped introduce Latin rhythms to the New York jazz scene.

All the while, he turned out Broadway musicals and a bejewelled string of hits – 'Swanee', 'The Man I Love', 'Fascinatin' Rhythm', 'Lady Be Good', ''S Wonderful', 'Strike Up the Band' – many of them with

lyrics by his devoted brother, Ira (1896–1983). He went to study with *Cowell, *Riegger and *Schillinger and applied unsuccessfully for lessons to Ravel.

In 1931 he attempted to define American music theatre in Of Thee I Sing, the first musical comedy to win a Pulitzer Prize. Dissatisfied, he returned to an operatic idea that occupied him for nine years, an unusual application in a life of fleeting involvements. *Porgy and Bess (Boston, 30.ix.35) represented in its composer's mind a combination of the drama and romance of Carmen and the beauty of Meistersinger. Conceived in its entirety, though not through-composed or without slack moments, it is powered by knockout set-piece numbers like 'Summertime', 'A Woman is a Sometime Thing', 'I Got Plenty of Nuttin' and 'Bess, You is My Woman'. Sympathy for southern US blacks and their indigenous art pervades every bar of the score. The love-tangle is a simple tale and the opera has overwhelming emotional punch when staged with appropriate conviction. It took half a century to reach the Met, an era of half-cocked productions and copyright wrangles. It was brought off for the first time, said Ira's widow, in the 1986 Glyndebourne staging conducted by Simon *Rattle. A recording by Louis *Armstrong and Ella *Fitzgerald manifests how close Gershwin got to black gut-feelings.

Bored with *Broadway, he moved to Hollywood to try his hand at the movies. He sought composing lessons with Schoenberg but they settled for playing tennis together and painting each other's portraits.

'Let's Call the Whole Thing Off' and 'A Foggy Day in London Town' were his last gems. Plagued by headaches, he visited several psychiatrists before collapsing with a brain tumour and dying on the operating table, aged 38. 'George Gershwin is dead,' wrote novelist John O'Hara, 'I don't have to believe it if I don't want to.' Never again would a composer walk with such apparent ease on the tightrope between populism and high art.

b. Brooklyn, NY, 26.ix.1898, of Russian-Jewish immigrant parents; plugged songs at 16 on Tin Pan Alley; st rudimentary har-

mony with Rubin *Goldmark; at 19 sold quarter of a million copies of his own song 'Swanee' sung by Al Jolson; wrote 1st musical, *La, La Lucille*, v.19; many girlfriends, never married; *d.* Beverly Hills, California, 11.vii.37. *other works*: *I Got Rhythm Variations* for piano and orch. (Boston, 14.i.34), preludes for piano solo (1936), George Gershwin's Song Book (piano solo, 1932).
Bib: Edward Jabloński, *Gershwin*, NY (Simon & Schuster), 1988.

Ottmar GERSTER Neo-classical German who modified his tune twice when the Nazis and communists seized power.
b. Braunfels, 29.vi.1897; succeeded Hindemith as concertmaster in Frankfurt 1923–27; taught at Essen, 1927–39, army service 1940–45, taught Weimar 1947–52, Leipzig 1952–62; *d.* Leipzig, 31.viii.69; *works include*: opera *Enoch Arden* (1936), Thuringian symphony (1952), Leipzig Symphony (1965), *Ballad of Karl Marx and the World's Transformation* (1961).

Gesang der Jünglinge *Stockhausen's electronic transformation of a young boy's singing voice – hence the title – into the smoothest of early taped compositions. fp: Cologne, 30.v.56.

Gordon (Peter) GETTY Sometime head of Getty Oil, one of the richest men since Croesus, is a part-time mathematician and composer. He wrote a semi-staged opera on Shakespeare's *Falstaff* called *Plump Jack* (Spoleto Festival, 1989) and a song cycle to poems by Emily Dickinson (1988). The music is cautious, correct and bewilderingly faceless, written in anachronistic mid-19th-century tonalities.
b. San Francisco, 20.xii.33;

(Giorgio) Federico GHEDINI *Neoclassic Italian, among eight operas he composed Melville's *Billy Budd* at the same time as *Britten. *De Sabata propagated his 1931 *Pezzo concertante* for two violins, viola and orchestra. He was Berio's principal teacher.
b. Cuneo, Piedmont, Italy, 7.vii.1892; dir. Milan Conservatory 1951–62; *d.* Nervi, 25.ii.65.

ghetto Term for tighly-knit *new music audience, current in Paris and Berlin.

Vittorio GIANNINI Son of an Italian tenor, he composed bel canto operas that were staged in 1930s Germany. He wrote an IBM Symphony for the 1939 World Fair and four untitled symphonies. His elder sister, Dusolina, was a celebrated Aida.
b. Philadelphia, Pennsylvania, 19.x.03; *d.* NY, 28.xi.66. *operas include*: *Lucedia* (Munich, 20.x.34), *The Scarlet Letter*, (Hamburg, 2.vi.38), *The Taming of the Shrew* (NBC TV, 13.iii.54), *The Servant of 2 Masters* (NY, 9.iii.67).

Remo GIAZZOTTO Italian Baroque scholar whose reorchestration of an adagio by Tomasso Albinoni (1671–1751) became a classical pop. He wrote biographies of Albinoni, Busoni, Viotti and Vivaldi.
b. Rome, 4.ix.10;

Michael GIELEN German modernist of high pedigree – his father was a noted stage director, his uncle was Eduard *Steuermann – he played Schoenberg's complete piano works in public before taking up the baton. He promoted contemporary works as chief conductor of Stockholm Royal Opera (1960–65) and Netherlands Opera, (1977–87) and music director at Frankfurt (1977–82) and Cincinnati (1980–6). His major première was *Zimmermann's *Die Soldaten*.

His compositions are omni-cultural. The 1983 string quartet was written while reading Walter Benjamin's philosophical discourse on Charles Baudelaire and took as its main theme the French poem *Le Cygne* (The Swan) which members of the quartet declaim in the language or languages of their choice in the course of their playing. The second violin walks in with a theme from *Zemlinsky's Lyric Symphony, hinting at its importance to *Berg, and in the finale the players turn away from one another in a gesture of alienation. The work is intended as live theatre but its terms of reference are too oblique for all but eggheads to guess.
b. Dresden, 20.vii.27; *other works*: *four poems of Stefan George* (1955), Variations for 40 instruments (1959), *The Bells are on a False Trail* (1969).

Dizzy (John Birks) GILLESPIE Jazz trumpeter, second only to *Armstrong, he was among the originators of *bebop, of which his 'Night in Tunisia' (1942) is a classic. He overcame youthful clowneries to contribute materially to abstract modern jazz.

b. Cheraw, South Carolina, 21.x.17; founded own band 1944;

Alberto GINASTERA   Argentina's leading composer was forever in and out of trouble with his government. Success at 19 with a *Concierto argentino*, followed at 21 by the ballet *Panambi* (Buenos Aires, 27.xi.37) won him a Guggenheim fellowship to study in the US but the military junta delayed his departure until the war was over. Returning in 1948 he was named head of the national conservatory, sacked by Juan Peron four years later and reinstated in 1956 after the dictator's downfall. His music had matured meanwhile from naïve nationalism to imaginative *serialism in the highly tuneful piano sonata (Pittsburgh, 29.xi.52), and exotic magic realism in *Cantata para America magica* for soprano and percussion ensemble (1961). His piano concerto (Washington, D.C., 22.iv.61) was sensationally effective – Bartók on the pampas. Much of his music was commissioned and staged in the US by the Coolidge, Fromm and Koussevitsky foundations.

His first opera, *Don Rodrigo*, opened in Buenos Aires (24.vii.64) and moved to New York City Opera with the young *Domingo in the title role. *Bomarzo* (Washington, D.C., 19.v.67) was intended for his home town but banned by the mayor because it contained too much sex, violence and dissonance. Ginastera left the country for good, settling in Switzerland with his second wife, the cellist Aurora Natola, for whom he wrote a sonata and concerto (Buenos Aires, 6.vii.81). The most enchanting of his concertos was for harp (Philadelphia, 18.ii.65).

b. Buenos Aires, 11.iv.16; *d*. Geneva, 25.vi.83. *other works*: 3rd opera *Beatrix Cenci* (Washington, 10.ix.71), 2nd piano concerto (1973), violin concerto (NY, 3.x.63, cond. *Bernstein), *Popul Vuh* on pre-Colombian themes, for orch. (St Louis, 7.vii.89), *Glosses* on a theme of Pau *Casals, for string orch., and string quartet (San Juan, Puerto Rico, 14.vi.76), four string quartets.

Umberto GIORDANO   The composer of *Andrea Chénier* (1896) and *Fedora*

(1898) scored no further success in the next century though he tried seven more times with the same *verismo mix of sex and violence.

b. Foggia, Italy, 28.viii.1867; *d*. Milan, 12.xi.48. *other operas*: *Siberia* (La Scala, 19.xii.03), *Madame Sans-Gêne* (NY Met, 25.i.15, cond. Toscanini), *Il Re* (La Scala, 10.i.29).

Girl of the Golden West   (*La Fanciulla del West*) Puccini's opera of the American mid-West, with Humperdinck's *Königskinder* and Granados' *Goyescas*, the Metropolitan Opera's only significant world première. fp: NY, 10.xii.10.

Glagolitic Mass   Irreligious Slavonic rite by *Janáček. fp: Brno, 5.xii.27.

Detlev GLANERT   With a symphony premiered by the Berlin Philharmonic when he was 25, Glanert was showered with German honours and study scholarships. He has since written *Mahler/Skizze* (1989), a retro-aural contemplation of *fin-de-siècle* symphonic frangments.

b. Hamburg, 1960;

Peggy GLANVILLE-HICKS   Australian deputy to Virgil *Thomson, whose concert reviews she set to music in *Thomsoniana* (1949), she ran a new music forum in 1950s NY. In 1959 she moved to Greece, where she staged a hellenic opera, *Nausicaa* (Athens, 19.viii.61) to a text by Robert Graves. She went blind in 1969, fell silent and returned home.

A pupil of *Vaughan Williams, *Boulanger and *Wellesz in Vienna, she searched far and wide for a personal idiom, favouring the harp in several works – *Gymnopédies, Concerto antico* for harps and string quartet – and attempting to define a new Australian style in *Sinfonia da Pacifica* (1953). *Stokowski premièred her *Letters from Morocco* for voice and orch. (NY, 22.ii.53), a melismatic setting of notes she received from Paul *Bowles.

b. Melbourne, 29.xii.12; married to composer Stanley Bates 1938–48; music critic *NY Herald Tribune* 1948–58; lived in Greece 1959–76; *d*. Sydney, 25.vi.90. *other works*: operas *The Transposed Heads* (1954), *The Glittering Gate* (NY, 14.v.59); ballets *Postman's knock* (1940), *The Witch of Endor* (1959), *A Season in Hell* (1967); *Etru-*

scan concerto for piano and chamber orch. (NY, 25.i.56).

Philip GLASS The first composer since *Stravinsky to be exclusive to a particular record company, Glass showed that new music could be commercial if it borrowed mass-culture methods. Snobs might deplore his repetitive simplicity, but Glass pulled a new audience to opera without pandering to soft-porn stage gimmicks. There was actually an educational aspect to his trilogy of 'profile operas', based on the lives of Albert Einstein, Mahatma Gandhi and a mythical, hermaphrodite pharaoh.

What made his music easy listening was an unchanging four-note groundbass, which served as patterned wallpaper for foreground music that was only slightly more varied. There were no discords, no heroism or passion. A synthesizer played in the opera pit, alongside the orchestra, simulating the syntax of popular music. The effect was as soothing as a warm bath.

Glass travelled a long road to find simple truths. Raised in Baltimore, a great-nephew of Al Jolson, he was a star pupil at *Juilliard and had written 70 performable works when he joined the well-beaten trail to Nadia *Boulanger's door. In Paris, he was alienated by 'creepy' European *avant-gardism and discovered enlightenment at the feet of Ravi *Shankar, the sitar player, while scoring his music for an American underground movie, Chappaqua.

The equality of notes and subtle shifts of rhythm in *Indian music had a Eureka-like impact. He travelled to North Africa and the Himalayas. Back in Greenwich Village, he found affinities (later denied) with *Reich's repetitive tapes and ethnicities and Joan *LaBarbara's flexible vocalities. He formed his own ensemble and record label, but drove cabs and waited tables to survive until *Einstein on the Beach (Avignon, 25.vii.76), an opera devised with the stage-wizard Robert Wilson, gave minimalism a theatrical dimension.

It was followed by Satyagraha (Rotterdam, 5.ix.80), sung in Sanskrit, and Akhnaten (Stuttgart, 24.iii.84), a fable of an Egyptian boy-king who invented an abstract god. None of these was natural fodder for opera; their success was achieved by clever staging and movie-like music that often merely underscored the drama. Modernists damned him for mindlessness; the Philadelphia Orch. played an act of Akhnaten in concert alongside Die Walküre.

There was a sameness about the operatic trilogy that impeded further progress. A science fiction fantasy, The Making of the Representative for Planet 8 (Houston, 8.vii.88), was a washout and his orchestral creations did not demand undiverted attention. While *Adams and Reich emerged from minimalism, Glass remained stuck in a rut of his own making. The most charming of his absolute works was a 1984 quartet, Company, written for *Kronos and sounding like Brahms without the bite.

b. Baltimore, 31.i.37; formed Philip Glass Ensemble 1968; married (1) Jo-Anne Akalaitis, (2) Luba Burtyk; exclusive to CBS Records 1986–; other works: Mishima quartet (1985, extracted from Mishima film score); Phaedra, ballet from same movie; violin concerto (NY, 4.iv.87); cadenza for Mozart piano concerto K467 (1987); Passages (1990), a setting of Ravi Shankar ragas.

Alexander GLAZUNOV An attractive symphonist, Glaznov's greatest contribution was as bravely reformist head of the St Petersburg Conservatoire (1905–28), protecting leftist and Jewish students from Tsarist expulsion and later talent, notably *Shostakovich, from communist interference.

Appointed as a composition teacher in 1899, he quit in 1905 over the dismissal of *Rimsky-Korsakov, returning nine months later as director with extraordinary guarantees of autonomy. Under his aegis, Leopold Auer (1845–1930) continued to produce a stream of Jewish violin virtuosi many, like *Heifetz, registered illegally by Glazunov. Administrative burdens and alcoholism diminished his appetite for composition.

The A minor violin concerto (St Petersburg, 4.iii.05, Auer soloist), is a brilliant, melodic and wholly unreflective showpiece. Another brief concertante work, the lovely Chant du Ménéstrel for cello and orchestra, dates from 1901. Two piano concertos (1911, 1917) proved negligible but a last-ditch saxophone concerto (Nyköping, Sweden, 25.xi.34) recaptures an effortless melodism that shows its regret for *temps perdu* in a passing quotation from Tchaikovsky' *Pathétique* Symphony.

Of his eight symphonies (1881–1906), the 7th (3.i.03) was his Pastoral and palpably his finest. An indifferent conductor, he was blamed by *Rachmaninov for the failure of his first symphony. Unsettled by the revolutions, frozen, lonely and alcoholically deprived, he fled to France to spend his last years in dismal exile. His remains were returned on 13.xi.72 and buried beside other great composers in the Alexander Nevsky cemetery.

b. St Petersburg, 10.viii.1865, son of a book publisher; had 1st symphony performed at 16 by *Balakirev; met Liszt at Weimar; two ballets, *Raymonda* (1896) and *The Seasons* (1899) proved enduringly successful; lived all his life with mother but married Olga the housekeeper at 63 and adopted her pianist daughter; *d.* Neuilly-sur-Seine, France, 21.iii.36. *other works*: Volga Boatmen's Song orchestration (1905); two string quartets (1930–1).

Reinhold GLIÈRE (Glier)   A Russian of the old school, he wrote the revolutionary ballet *The Red Poppy* (Bolshoi Theatre, Moscow, 14.vi.27; renamed *The Red Flower* to avoid opiate connotations) in which a Chinese working girl gives her life to save rebel leader from vile capitalists. Composed in pseudo-exotic pentatones but with Russian dances and the 'Internationale' to underpin political points, it was staged 200 times in two years and was the cornerstone of the Soviet ballet until relations soured with Mao's China. An early revolutionary, Glière went to study in Berlin after signing an anti-government manifesto in 1905; his 3rd symphony (Moscow, 23.ii.12), named *Ilya Muromets*, relates the exploits of a Russian folk-hero in weighty late-Wagnerian mode with lots of *Rimskian tunes. He taught the young *Prokofiev, Miaskovsky and Khatchaturian.

Under Lenin, Glière went to organize cultural life in Azerbaijan. He returned with an ethnic-flavoured opera, *Shah-Senem* (1927) that invoked the Soviet style of 'colourful' regionalism. During Stalin's purges, he was held up as a model composer but stood apart from the persecutors. His music won two Stalin prizes (1948,

1950) and was boomed from loudspeakers at railways stations.

b. Kiev, Ukraine, 11.i.1875, son of a Belgian instrument-maker; st Moscow with Arensky and Taneyev; st conducting in Berlin with Oskar *Fried, 1905–7; dir. Kiev Conservatoire 1914–20, prof. at Moscow Conservatoire 1921–56; chairman of USSR Composers, Union organization committee, 1939–51; *d.* Moscow, 23.vi.56; *other works*: ballets *Chrysis* (1912), *Comedians* (1931), *The Bronze Horseman* (Leningrad, 14.iii.49); five operas; 2nd symphony (Berlin, 23.i.08, cond. *Koussevitsky); harp concerto (1938), concerto for coloratura soprano and orchestra (Moscow, 12.v.43), cello, horn and violin concertos, five string quartets and some 200 songs.

Vinko GLOBOKAR   Trombone player to the official *avant-garde, he received solo works from Berio (*Sequenza V*), Kagel (*Atem*) and Stockhausen (*Solo*). He was on the team that founded *IRCAM and composed ugly virtuosities for individual instruments. More interesting were his semi-staged works for voices and instruments on specific social issues.

Les Emigrés (1982), with a text that is in part multi-lingual documentary collage and part written by the Austrian Peter Handke, examines European motives and fears of inward and outward migration. The whole resembles a flickering early newsreel of half-familiar ominous scenes with accompaniment that veers from noise to jazz, often out of synch with the events depicted.

b. Anderney, France, 7.vii.34; worked as jazz trombonist in Yugoslavia 1947–55; st with *Leibowitz, *Berio; *other dramatic work*: *L'armonia drammatica*.

(Sir) William GLOCK   To supporters, Glock was a visionary who revitalized *BBC music with a large dose of serialism and appointed his friend Boulez as chief conductor. Detractors saw him as a bureaucrat who banned music that was not, in his view, progressive. Chief victims were *Panufnik and *Arnold.

b. London, 3.v.08; founded Dartington summer school 1948–79; BBC controller, music, 1959–73; dir. Bath Festival 1979–84.

Die glückliche Hand   (*The Lucky Hand*) *Schoenberg opera. fp: Vienna, Volksoper, 14.x.24.

Glyndebourne Sussex country opera festival launched by John Christie in 1934. Its premières are few, including Britten's *Rape of Lucretia* and *Osborne's Electrification of the Soviet Union*.

Mikhail GNESSIN *Rimsky pupil, he went in 1921 to study Palestine-Jewish folklore but returned a loyal Soviet. With his four sisters he founded a Moscow music school that still bears their family name.
   b. Rostov-on-the-Don, Russia, 2.ii.1883; *d.* Moscow, 5.v.57. *works include*: opera *Abraham's Youth* (1923), tone poem *1905–1917* (1925), *Jewish Orchestra at the Town Bailiff's Ball* (1926).

Leopold GODOWSKY Polish pianist who found Chopin so easy that he set his Etudes contrapuntally against one another and dashed them off two at a time.
   b. Soshly, Lithuania, 13.ii.1870; *d.* NY, 21.xi.38. *piano works*: 30-piece *Triakotameron*; the 11th 'Alt-Wien' is popular.

Alexander GOEHR The transformation of a rampant Euro-rebel into a pillar of the establishment showed that the British system had lost none of its power to emasculate iconoclasts. Goehr was the guiding light of the 1950s *Manchester School that fought English insularity, infusing his generation with the unsettling ideals of *Schoenberg, *Messiaen, *Stravinsky and *Eisler. The son of a Berlin refugee conductor who gave seminal *Britten and *Tippett premières, he fired *Birtwistle, Maxwell *Davies, *Ogdon and friends with a curiosity for continental trends.

   He was an enfant terrible in the 1960s, fluttering the dovecotes with a *Little Symphony* (York, 1963) in none-too-affectionate memory of his severe father and causing disturbances at Hamburg State Opera with *Arden Must Die* (4.iii.67), written with the Marxist poet Erich Fried and accusing federal Germany of complicity in Nazi crimes, or complacency at very least. Its political agenda obscured a credible drama and some love-music of flagrantly *Janáčekovian intensity. Goehr made no excuses for using prime cuts from music history. He next wrote a triptych of 'dramatic madrigals' – *Naboth's Vineyard* (1968), *Shadowplay* (1970) and *Sonata*

about Jerusalem (1971) – which were meant to herald a new form of music theatre but went little further than Britten's church parables. Goehr began lecturing at Leeds that year and in 1976 accepted the chair at Cambridge, where no major composer ever taught. He was an erudite and inspiring instructor, and no more a threat to society. In 1987 he was invested with the honour of giving the BBC's Reith Lectures; in 1989 he was elected to the American Academy and Institute of Arts and Letters.

   Goehr professed faith in the symphony but barely attested it. His contribution amounts to the ambivalent paternal tribute, a one-movement symphony of 1970, *Sinfonia* (1979) and a *Symphony with Chaconne* (1987). His music was assimilably tonal and terribly knowledgeable, lacking the grit of Birtwistle or the easy eclecticism of Maxwell Davies, both of whom eclipsed him in performances and public favour.
   b. Berlin, 10.viii.32; *other works*: opera *Behold the Sun* (1984); violin concerto (1962), *Romanza* for cello and orch. (1968), piano concerto (1972), *Metamorphosis/Dance* for orch. (1974), Concerto for 11 instruments (1970), *Eve Dreams in Paradise* for soprano, tenor and orch. (1988), *Das Gesetz der Quadrille*, a setting of Kafka texts for baritone and piano (1979); three string quartets.

Karel (August) GOEYVAERTS Belgian composer who alerted *Stockhausen to his teacher, *Messiaen, and the serialism of *Webern. Stockhausen claimed Goeyvaerts' two-piano sonata of 1951 as his personal starting point and defended it against the intellectual critique of *Adorno. It has been claimed as the first work written in *total serialism; another of his pieces featured in the first broadcast of electronic music in 1954. In the late 1950s he became disenchanted with the *avant-garde and went to work for the national airline as a translator. His music gravitated towards religion and the theatre, retaining an element of aleatory chance.
   b. Antwerp, Belgium, 8.vi.23; st with Milhaud, Messiaen and Martenot; taught at Antwerp Conservatoire 1950–57; *other works*: *Opus 3 aux sons frappés et frotté (with striking and rubbing sounds)* (1952), *Opus 5 aux sons purs (with pure*

sounds) (1953), *Improperia*, Good Friday cantata (1958), Mass in memory of Pope John XXIII (1968).

The Golden Cockerel Last opera by *Rimsky-Korsakov. fp: St Petersburg, 7.x.09.

Friedrich GOLDMANN East German symphonist, tentatively *serial and *aleatory by method, his intentions obscured by discretion necessitated by totalitarianism.

b. Siegmar-Schonau, nr. Chemnitz, 27.iv.41; st with *Wagner-Régeny; *works*: three symphonies (1968–86), two *Essays* (1968–71), *Exkursion* (1984).

Karl GOLDMARK Genial Viennese composer of Hungarian-Jewish origin who achieved operatic fame with the *Queen of Sheba* (Vienna, 10.ii.1875) and wrote further late-romanticisms for the next 40 years. His 20th-century works include the operas *Gotz von Berlichingen* (after Goethe, Budapest, 16.xii.02) and *A Winter's Tale* (after Shakespeare, Vienna, 2.i.08).

b. Keszthely, Hungary, 18.v.1830; *d.* Vienna, 2.i.15. *other works*: *Rustic Wedding* symphony (1896), violin concerto (1878).

His American nephew **Rubin GOLDMARK** was educated in Vienna, returning in 1902 to New York where he taught *Copland and *Gershwin. From 1924 until his death he was head of composition at Juilliard School. His music includes a *Negro Rhapsody* (NY 18.i.23) and a Requiem on Lincoln's Gettysburg address (NY, 30.i.19).

b. NY, 15.viii.1872; *d.* there 6.iii.36.

Berthold GOLDSCHMIDT In 1990, at the age of 87, a frail composer in London's Belsize Park district was presented with the first recording of his life and the news that German opera houses were planning to stage *Der gewaltige Hahnrei (The Mighty Cuckold)*, last seen at Mannheim in 1932. Goldschmidt was one of the bright hopes of German music until the Nazis seized power and he was exiled into obscurity. Living in London, he helped Deryck Cooke prepare the performing version of *Mahler's 10th symphony, conducted its première, and gave grandfatherly guidance to young *Rattle. His music, however, was ignored and for 20 years he gave up composing until, in the 1980s, German interest was rekindled in the doughty survivor.

His first quartet, with an ironically Mahlerian waltz, was praised by *Schoenberg. The 1926 piano sonata anticipated Bartók's tone-*clusters. A 1930 setting of Erich Kästner's poem 'Last Chapter', predicting air raids on civilian targets, is redolent of *Weill. He planned to compose Leskov's *Lady Macbeth of Mtsensk* but gave up on hearing that *Shostakovich had started. While awaiting emigration papers, he wrote a vigorous set of piano variations on a Palestine shepherd's theme (1934) Ensconced in London, his 2nd string quartet and orchestral *Ciaconna Sinfonica* (1936), overflow with anxieties, vitality, compassion and some of the most riveting music written anywhere that year. The quartet's inner movements relate the horrors of Hitler's Germany without specificity or self-pity, while the *Ciaconna* weaves masterly variations around a 32-note theme, somewhat in the manner of *Hindemith. His second opera, *Beatrice Cenci*, after Shelley's verse drama, was picked for the 1951 Festival of Britain but not staged; its soprano arias are splendid.

Aged 85, he wrote a 3rd string quartet that amounts to a kind of autobiography, weaving a Jewish prayer tune around a tramping theme of godless conquerors in his choral *Belsatzar* (1985).

b. Hamburg 18.i.03; st with *Schreker; as Kleiber's assistant, played celesta in *Wozzeck* première; won Mendelssohn Prize for Passacaglia (1925); composer in residence at Darmstadt (1929); emigrated 1935; cond. at BBC; *other works*: anti-fascist ballet *Chronica* (1938); concertos for cello (1953), clarinet (1954), violin (1955); Mediterranean Songs (1958); clarinet quartet (1983); piano trio (1987).

Benny (Benjamin David) GOODMAN Master-clarinettist and band-leader played jazz with greater conviction than classics but kept trying; commissioned Bartók's *Contrasts and *Copland's concerto.

b. Chicago, 30.v.09; *d.* NY, 16.vi.86.

(Sir) Eugene GOOSSENS Member of Belgian family of many musical talents, Goossens composed two symphonies and the operas *Judith* (Covent Garden, 25.vi.29) and *Don Juan de Mañara* (Covent Garden, 24.vi.37) in a style somewhere between Debussy and Delius. *Two Sketches* (1916) for string orch. enjoyed ephemeral popularity and the Variations on a Chinese Theme (20.vi.12) was quite a hit in its day. He wrote an oboe concerto for his brother, Léon (London, 2.x.30) and a piano concerto for José Iturbi (Cincinnati, 25.ii.44). While conductor at Cincinnati, Copland and nine others wrote variations on one of his themes. His podium career ended in disgrace when he was expelled from Australia for allegedly smuggling in a smutty magazine.

b. London, 26.v.1893; st with Stanford; cond. with Beecham's company 1915–20, Rochester (NY) Philharmonic 1923–31, Cincinnati SO 1931–46, Sydney SO 1947–56; d. London, 13.vi.62. *other works*: Silence for chorus and orch. (1922); *Fantasy* string quartet (1915); *A Memory of the Players in a Mirror at Midnight*.

Henryk Mikolai GORECKI The 3rd symphony of Górecki, written in 1976, amounted to a premature requiem for communism. That music of such intense religiosity could be composed in a totalitarian state testified to the state's failure to control creativity.

Living in the notoriously polluted city of Katowice, Górecki drew on a millennium of rural and spiritual heritage to write a slow, winding, ethereal work with soprano solo, entitled 'Symphony of Sorrowful Songs.' Its release on record a decade later turned the reclusive composer into an international personality.

A flower of the 1956 Warsaw Autumn, he began writing *serialism so extreme that commissars cut the finale from his first symphony in 1959. *Scontri (Collisions)* for large orch. took Boulez aback with its aural violence, wilder even than *Penderecki's. Three years later, he parted with the avant-garde in three slow-moving *Pieces in the olden style* for string orch. Two decades later this was acclaimed as a forerunner of 'new simplicity', whereas it had no agenda other than Poland and itself. The 2nd symphony (Warsaw, 22.vi.73), named after the astronomer Copernicus, and the *Amen* chant of the same year confirmed his spiritual retreat. Yet Gorecki was able, when necessary, to summon the most ferocious of sounds in *Already it is Dusk*, a string

quartet for *Kronos (Minneapolis, 21.i.89) combining folk and religious themes with political and industrial decay. He had demonstratively resigned as head of the Katowice music college in 1979 and suffered hardships and ill health during the period of martial law, emerging frail and undaunted as a moral beacon for new Polish music.

b. Czernica, Poland, 6.xii.33; st with Boleslaw Szabelski; *other works*: *Old Polish Music* (1969), harpsichord concerto (1980), *Lerchenmusik* (1984) for clarinet, cello, piano.

Gothic Symphony 'Largest-ever' symphony by Havergal *Brian, combining elements of Goethe and Lutheran liturgy in cathedral-like architectonics. Composed in aftermath of the First War it was not performed for 40 years. Amateur fp: London, 24.vi.61; professional fp: London, 30.x.66, cond. Boult.

Jakov GOTOVAC Master of Croatian opera, running the Zagreb opera house (1923–58) and composing seven dramas in the local tongue.

b. Split, Austro-Hungary, 11.x.1895; d. Zagreb, 16.x.82.

Glenn GOULD Eccentric Canadian pianist who, at 32, gave up live concerts, playing only on radio and record. He composed a string quartet.

b. Toronto, 25.ix.32; d there, 4.x.82.

Morton GOULD Skilful orchestrator, whose *Negro Spirituals* (NY, 9.ii.41) for string choir and orch. and *Symphony of Spirituals* (Detroit, 4.i.76) treated religious folklore sensitively and without sensation-seeking. He rifled Americana in un-Hollywoodish ways – *Cowboy Rhapsody* (1943) – and scored difficult themes for TV, notably *Holocaust*, a 1978 soap on the murder of six million. In concert, he succeeded with *Derivations* (Washington, 14.vii.56), for Benny *Goodman, in which jazz and blues are given a formal setting that preserves their improvisatory air. *Stokowski was enamoured of his *Chorale and Fugue in Jazz* (1934) and *Toscanini of his *Lincoln Legend* (1942) but his three symphonies (1943–7) missed the mark.

b. Richmond Hill, NY, 10.xii.13 of immigrant parents; played piano in jazz bands;

music director of CBS Chrysler Hour 1943; ASCAP president 1986-; *other works*: musical *Billion Dollar Baby* (1945); ballet *Fall River Legend* (1947); Latin American Symphoniette (1941), Tap Dance concerto (1952), Jekyll and Hyde Variations (1957), Vivaldi Gallery (1968), American Ballads (1976), Concerto Grosso (1988).

Goyescas Opera by Granados formed from eponymous piano suite. fp: NY Met, 28.i.16.

Paul GRAENER German late-romantic who became an active Nazi in the interest of self-advancement. As vice-president of Goebbels' Reich Chamber of Culture from 1933, he took a leading role in purging German music of Jews and modernists but reaped scant reward and died destitute in a Salzburg pension in the final months of war. Apart from many affable Lieder in a Straussian vein, Graener wrote seven operas, of which *Friedemann Bach* (Schwerin, 13.xi.31), on the life of Johann Sebastian's eldest son, made greatest impact and acquired brief notoriety when its librettist was discovered to have been Jewish. Graener beseeched Hitler to attend *Der Prinz von Homburg* (Berlin, 14.iii.35), which he envisaged as the model for German national opera, but his wish was spurned.
  b. Berlin, 11.i.1872; taught London Royal Academy of Music 1897–1902, then in Vienna, at Salzburg Mozarteum, Munich, Leipzig (as *Reger's successor) and Berlin; *d.* Salzburg, 13.xi.44. *other works*: orch. suite, *The Flute of Sanssouci*, on Frederick the Great's instrumental pastime; six string quartets, 130 Lieder.

Percy (Aldridge) GRAINGER Anguished Australian, he wasted a modest compositional talent on pianistic miniatures and orchestrations of folksongs. He treated jolly country frolics with utmost solemnity, offset by glimpses of harmonic originality. *Molly on the Shore* (1908) and *Handel in the Strand* (1911) became popular; the celebrated *Country Gardens* (1918), he said, was filled with turnips, not flowers.
  While collecting English, Irish, Nordic and Maori tunes, he developed notions of racial purity that extended beyond population control to exhuming the English language of alien elements: 'vegetarianism', for example, would become 'meat-shunment'. He dressed in multi-coloured towelling cloths and practised sexual masochism. His mother committed suicide in 1921, depressed by whispers of incest. He married a Swede, Ella Viola Ström, in the Hollywood Bowl in front of 20,000 people, before the première of his cantata *To a Nordic Princess* (9.viii.28). He wanted his skeleton to be displayed posthumously at the University of Melbourne's Grainger Museum, but had to settle for a life-sized papier-mâché model of himself.
  b. Melbourne, 8.vii.1882; st with James Kwast and Ivan Knorr in Frankfurt (1895-9) and *Busoni in Berlin; toured UK, Scandinavia, S. Africa and Australia; lived in US from 1915; head of music department, NY University 1932–3; *d.* White Plains, New York, 20.ii.61 and buried in Adelaide, Australia. *other works: Arrival Platform Humlet, Blithe bells* (variations on Bach's *Sheep may safely graze*), *Mock Morris*, My Robin is to the Greenwood gone, *The Gumsuckers' March* and much else in similar vein; the choral technique of *Shallow Brown* (1927) was admired by Britten.
  Bib: John Bird, *Percy Grainger*, London (Faber), 1976.

(Pantaléon) Enrique GRANADOS (y Campiña) The Iberian revivalist was an innocent victim of a war in which his nation was neutral. Delayed in America by a White House invitation after a successful Met première, he was sunk by a German torpedo while sailing home and drowned trying to rescue his wife, his clothes weighted with the gold paid him by the Met management.
  Unlike his friend *Albéniz, he was self-taught and industrious, writing six operas, numerous symphonic poems and a plethora of piano pieces and songs, though conspicuously nothing for the native guitar. Possessed of a visual imagination and gift for painting, he created his finest work in the opera *Goyescas* (NY Met, 23.i.16) on the painter Goya's life and work, and two eponymous piano suites that provided its framework. An intermezzo from the opera has enjoyed independent existence.
  b. Lerida, Catalonia, 27.vii.1867; st with Pedrell; founded Academia Granados, 1901; *d.* English Channel, 24.iii.16, leaving six orphans;

other works: operas *Maria del Carmen* (1898), *Picarol* (1901), *Follet* (1903, *Gaziel* (1906) and *Liliana* (1911); Suite arabe; string quartet, piano trio, three large collections of songs.

Le Grand Macabre *Ligeti's bizarre and only opera, a tale of sexual and political intrigue with an overture played by 12 motor horns. fp: Stockholm, 12.iv.78.

Stéphane GRAPPELLI Foremost exponent of European 'hot' jazz and violinist co-founder of the Quintette du Hot Club de France (1934). Endowed with a formidable technique, he matched *Menuhin effortlessly on best-selling duets.
   b. Paris, 26.i.08;

graphic notation When dots between staves were inadequate to express a composer's vision, he might draw pictures or abstracts. Kagel, Cardew and Cage were masters of *eye music. *Haubenstock-Ramati sold his scores as works of art.

the GRATEFUL DEAD Californian band that developed over 20 years from the mid-1960s a form of symphonic rock, playing extended thematic intermezzos that linked their loud and heavy numbers in a continuous sequence. The bassist Phil Lesh (*b*. Berkeley, California, 15.iii.40) was a *new music freak who secretly subsidized recordings by UK composers, *Brian, *Simpson, *Stevens, *Finnissy.

Grawemeyer award Annual $150,000 prize for living composers that saved several from penury. Founded in 1984 at the University of Louisville, the winners include Lutosławski, Ligeti, Birtwistle, Corigliano and Penderecki.

Cecil GRAY Would-be reformer of British music, he fell into the dissolute company of *Delius, Van *Dieren, Philip *Heseltine and D. H. Lawrence and never satisfied his compositional ambitions. Nor did his new music concerts in London go far after First War critics stigmatized them as pro-German. He figured as a character in novels by Lawrence and Anthony Powell and did not see his voluptuous operas, *Deidre* and *The Trojan Women*, staged.
   b. Edinburgh, 19.v.1895; *d*. Worthing, Sussex, 9.ix.51.

Alexander GRECHANINOV *Rimsky-Korsakov pupil who sought to broaden the tonal scope of Russian Orthodox singing; his liturgies offended the episcopate but won him a Tsarist pension in 1910 – soon terminated by revolution. His unoriginal first symphony was conducted by Rimsky in 1895; the 2nd (Moscow 14.iii.09) reminds one of *Rachmaninov without the melancholy. Three further symphonies of slight substance followed in American exile.
   b. Moscow, 25.x.1864; emigrated 1922; *d*. NY, 3.i.56; *other works*: operas, four string quartets, many songs.

Greece Like much else in a turbulent land, music divided on partisan lines. The romantic nationalism of *Kalomiris and his school fiercely resisted 12-tone cosmopolitans like *Skalkottas. Progressives and intellectuals, in turn, rejected the 'street music' of *Theodorakis that won Greece its widest musical renown. In a climate of intolerance verging on violence, leading composers, *Xenakis at their head, emigrated and performing standards declined, leaving Greece at the periphery of the musical map.

Edvard (Hagerup) GRIEG The Norwegian wrote little in his last years beyond simple piano pieces – Norwegian Peasant Dance (1902), Moods (1903) – and Four Psalms (1906). His major work completed before the age of 35, he lived to see musical *nationalism erupt and evanesce.
   b. Bergen, 15.vi.1843; *d*. there, 4.ix.07.

Karl-Rudi GRIESBACH Pupil of *Jarnach, he wrote a politically-inspired *African Symphony* (1963) in memory of the murdered Congolese leader Patrice Lumumba.
   b. Breckerfeld, Westphalia, 14.vi.16; professor at Dresden; *other works*: three symphonies, *Blues Impressions* for piano and strings.

Charles Tomlinson GRIFFES American prodigy of Mozartian lifespan, he studied in Berlin but gravitated to French impressionism in *The Pleasure Dome of Kubla Khan* (Boston SO, 28.xi.19, cond. Monteux) and to oriental exoticism in the ballet *Shojo* (1917). Walter Damrosch premièred the flute concerto in NY (16.xi.

19) and *Stokowski conducted four pieces in Philadelphia, but Griffes died of pneumonia at 35.

b. Elmira, NY, 17.ix.1884; d. NY, 8.iv.20. other works: songs to German, French and English texts, including 5 poems of Ancient China and Japan.

Gérard GRISEY *Boulezian composer of clashing sound-bergs; were it not for occasional collisions, his Modulations (1978) would lull its 33 players to sleep.

b. Belfort, France, 1946; other works: Dérives (1974) for two orchs.; Partiels for 18 players.

Ferde (Ferdinand Rudolph von) GROFÉ A musical landscape gardener, Grofé devised a Grand Canyon Suite (Chicago, 22.xi.31) that erred on the wrong side of kitsch. Finding himself on to such a good thing that even *Toscanini conducted him, he composed a Mississippi Suite, New England Suite, Hollywood Suite – ad nauseam.

His main gift was as an arranger; his 1920 setting for the Paul Whiteman band, 'Whispering', was one of the record industry's earliest million-sellers. He orchestrated Gershwin's hurriedly-written *Rhapsody in Blue for Whiteman and earned himself a name as ancestor of the big-band sound. Late in life, he turned out a smoochy piano concerto (1959).

b. New York, 27.ii.1892; d. Santa Monica, California, 3.iv.72. other work: Requiem for a Ghost Town (Virginia City, Nevada, 10.viii.68).

H(einz) K(arl) ('Nali') GRUBER A wacky Viennese, indirect descendant of the Gruber who composed the Christmas hymn Silent Night, his main attraction is Frankenstein!! – a pan-cultural 'pandemonium' for baritone (himself) and orchestra, as near as dammit to a concert cabaret. With Schwertsik, he formed a Third Viennese School to poke fun at the official *avant-garde. A sometime member of the Vienna Boys Choir, he earned his living playing double bass in the radio orchestra.

b. Vienna, 3.i.43; st with Jelinek and von Einem; other works: violin concerto (1978), cello concerto (Tanglewood, 3.viii.89); Bring me the Head of Amadeus, TV opera for the Mozart bicentenary, 1991.

Louis GRUENBERG Had his moment with a Eugene O'Neill opera, The Emperor Jones, at the Met (7.i.33). Its percussive scoring was impressive but not enough to get a second run in the depression, or after.

b. Brest-Litovsk, Russia, 3.viii.1884; d. Los Angeles, 9.vi. 64. other works: five symphonies, Jazz Suite (1929), Daniel Jazz for tenor and nine instruments (1925).

Gruppen Spatial work by Stockhausen for three orchestras and conductors. fp: Cologne, 24.iii.59.

Carlos GUASTAVINO Instinctually direct Argentine songwriter with the fluidity of *Poulenc and the hit-quotient of Jerome *Kern. You don't need a word of Spanish to find a song like 'Hermano' unforgettable at first hearing, naive yet thematically intriguing. He has composed music for poems by Jorge Luis Borges and a 1952 Romance de Santa Fé, his birthplace, for piano and orch.

b. Santa Fé, Argentina, 5.iv.12;

Sofia GUBAIDULINA Of all the composers who emerged from the murk of Soviet stagnation, Gubaidulina seemed the most self-assured. Her mentors, she said, were Shostakovich and Webern – not for their sound but because they 'taught me . . . to be myself'. She wrote contemplative music of a religious intensity and symbolism. The two instruments of In Croce for cello and organ (Kazan, 27.ii.79) are metaphors: man and cross. A similar analogy is used in Seven Words (Moscow, 20.x.82) for cello, bayan and string orch. A 25-minute sonata for violin and cello entitled Rejoice! (1981) is mournfully morose until its fidgety, irresolute finale, concealing its inner meaning. Garden of Joy and Sadness for flute, harp and viola (Moscow, 9.ii.81) ruminates solicitously around two mordant themes.

Of Tatar origins and broad culture, Gubaidulina was drawn to ancient Egyptian and Persian poems and turned in major works to two literary soulmates – Marina Tsvetayeva and T. S. Eliot. Hour of the Soul (1974) for mezzo-soprano and large wind orch. features verses by the tortured Russian poetess; Hommage à T. S. Eliot (Cologne, 25.iii.87) is self-explanatory. Her outstanding successes were a 42-minute symphony in 12 movements called *Stimmen . . . Verstummen* (Berlin, 4.ix.86) and a violin concerto, *Offertorium*, that underwent three fundamental revisions with Gidon Kremer from its première in 1981 until it achieved perfection.

> *b*. Chistopol, Tatar republic, 24.x.31; st with *Shebalin, moved to Moscow in 1963; founded Astreya group in 1975 with *Suslin and *Artyomov to explore Caucasian and central Asian folk instruments; *other works*: Concerto for symphony orch. and jazz band (Moscow, 16.i.78), bassoon concerto (6.v.76), *Introitus*, piano concerto (22.ii.78), *Night in Memphis* for mezzo-soprano, chorus and orch. (1968), three string quartets, many chamber works with percussion, *Tsvetayeva* for *a capella* choir (1984).

Jean-Pierre GUEZEC *Messiaen disciple, he agitated orchestral colours in small ensembles, reflecting social unrest and personal disquiet. *Messiaen commemorated him in the horn solo of *Des canyons aux étoiles*.

> *b*. Dijon, France, 29.viii.34; *d*. Paris, 9.iii.71. *major works*: *Architectures colorées* (Paris, 20.i.65, cond. *Maderna), *Suite for Mondrian* (Paris, 23.ii.65), *Ensemble multicolore* (Royan, 1.iv.66), *Formes-Couleurs* (St-Paul-de-Vence, 22.vii.69), Suite for *Much Ado About Nothing* (1969).

guitar Introduced by *Mahler to the concert hall in 7th symphony and by *Rodrigo to the standard repertory in *Concierto de Aranjuez*. The playing of *Segovia, more than any compositional factor, was responsible for its concert respectability. It was the indispensable accompaniment of 1960s American folk music. The electric guitar was the groundbass of *rock.

Friedrich GULDA Cultish pianist-improviser, fond of *jazz, multi-coloured headgear and shocking TV audiences by appearing with unclothed aides. He has composed jazz musicals and many short pieces and organized a Eurojazz Orchestra.

> *b*. Vienna, 16.v.30;

GURDJIEFF – See de *HARTMANN

Ivor (Bertie) GURNEY British war victim, gassed and shellshocked in 1917, a vagabond after the war when he wrote his best poetry and music, committed to an insane asylum in 1922. His verse, song-cycles and piano pieces are nurtured in the rich soil of Gloucestershire. French timbre prevails over German and there is constant melodic interplay between voice and piano.

> *b*. Gloucester, England, 28.viii.1890; st with *Stanford, *Vaughan Williams; committed 1922; *d*. City of London Mental Hospital, Dartford, Kent, 26.xii.37. *major cycles*: 'Eliza' songs (1912–19); Houseman settings (1920–21).

Gurrelieder Last and largest of *Schoenberg's Tristanisms, it was begun (1900) in the heat of pre-marital passion and finished 11 years later in total disillusion with both subject and style. Its impact was irresistible, given its *Mahlerian forces – five soloists, four choruses, speaker, huge orchestra – and Wagnerian chromaticism. By the time of its première (Vienna, 23.ii.13, cond. *Schreker), Schoenberg was immersed in atonality.

Woody (Woodrow Wilson) GUTHRIE Gravelly dustbowl singer, he aligned the gloomy ballads of a depressed midwest with a left-wing political agenda, providing the basis for 1950s protest music. His most celebrated song was 'This Land is Your Land' and his style and message were decisive for Pete Seeger and Bob *Dylan.

> *b*. Okemah, Oklahoma, 14.vii.12; *d*. NY, 3.x.67.

gypsy music *Bartók opened a can of worms when he asserted that there was no such thing as gypsy music, merely indigenous Hungarian tunes played by gypsy bands. There was, however, a paramount gypsy style that conditioned the performance of dance music in various lands, from flamenco to czardas, and, while little may have been composed by gypsy bands, theirs was the medium by which the music became widely known.

Joseph HAAS A *Reger disciple pursuing contrapuntal elaboration and Catholic piety in operas, 'folk oratorios' and many fine Lieder. He revived music education in Munich after 1945.

> b. Maihinger, Germany, 19.iii.1879; d. Munich, 30.iii.60. *operas include*: *The Mountain Queen* (a Christmas tale, 1927), *Tobias Wunderlich* (1937) and *Job's Wedding* (comedy, 1944).

Pavel HAAS Czech-Jewish composer, incarcerated at Theresienstadt and exterminated at Auschwitz. A *Janáček pupil, he developed a rare blend of Moravian, Hebraic and Parisian neo-classical sounds, introduced in an engaging wind quintet of 1929. In between its insistent rhythms, there emerges an intriguing melancholia. Economical in output, Haas left one opera, *The Charlatan* (Brno, 2.iv.38), three film scores, an unfinished symphony, two string quartets, a Hebrew male-voice chorus *Al S'fod* (1942) and four tragic Chinese Songs in the bass register, written and sung in the concentration camp (22.vi.44). A fellow-inmate, the conductor Karel Ančerl, reconstituted his *Study for Strings* from fragmentary parts.

> b. Brno, Moravia, 21.vi.1899; murdered Auschwitz, Poland, 17.x.44.

Alois HABA The father of *microtonality used quarter-tones as the basis of his 2nd string quartet (1922) and issued a much-admired manifesto on the subject. Taking up *Busoni's challenge to seek new forms of music, he ventured further into fifth- and sixth-tones. His masterpiece was a broken-home, quarter-tone opera, *Matka*

(Mother), staged at Munich (17.v.31) and deemed unsingable by its cast.

Hába was not the first nor the most effective tone-splitter but he was the leading propagandist for the idea that the future of music lay somewhere in between the notes – a notion that persisted down to *Boulez and computer music, via *Messiaen who picked it up in *Deux monodies en ¹/₄ de ton* (1937). Hába founded a department of microtonality at Prague University and built a piano, clarinet and other instruments to play his music. His brother Karel (1898–1972), composer of a microtonal violin concerto, was an early graduate; other students included *Ullmann and the conductors Karel Ančerl and Walter Susskind.

He got the idea from listening to his father's village band as a child in Moravia. His music shares common ground with Bartók and *Janáček but is hard to play accurately and somewhat remorseless to the ear.

> b. Vizovice, Austro-Hungary, 21.ix.1893, st with *Novák, *Schreker; taught Prague Conservatory 1923–53; d. Prague, 26.xi.73. *works include*: concertos for violin (1955) and viola (1957), two unperformed operas, 15 string quartets, many tonally composed.

Manos HADJIDAKIS Concurrent with *Theodorakis, his renown rests mainly on an Oscar-winning score for the film *Never on a Sunday*. It was Hadjidakis who, in 1949, claimed the *rebetiko*, or urban song, as equal to the rural folk material that fuelled Greek musical nationalism – and was duly ostracized by a staid establishment. He founded an Athens Experimental

Orchestra to play his kind of music. Many of his songs are unwittingly carried around the world by humming tourists.

> *b.* Xanthi, Greece, 23.x.25; self-taught; self-exiled during colonels' regime to New York 1967–72; deputy head, Greek National Opera, 1974; *other works*; six ballets, theatre and film scores, numerous songs.

Reynaldo HAHN Marcel Proust's male lover cut a fashionable figure in French music for half a century, writing exquisite *mélodies* for Paris salons that he would also sing in a sweet, light baritone while reclining in a Venetian gondola. A capable conductor, he revived a taste for Mozart as director of the Paris Opéra in 1945–46; he wrote a musical comedy called *Mozart* for Sasha Guitry and Yvonne Printemps (Paris, 2.xii.25).

His greatest hit was *Ciboulette* (7.iv.23), an operetta set in the Paris fruit and vegetable market, Les Halles. His orchestral music includes the charmingly episodic *Bal de Béatrice d'Este* (11.iv.07) and an elegant piano concerto (4.ii.31). Dandified and decadent, he dismissed musicians who appeared unkempt at his rehearsals. In the Gay Nineties, he revealed to Proust the 'petite phrase' from Saint-Saëns' D minor violin sonata that runs through *A la recherche du temps perdu* and bestowed aspects of his personality on several of its central characters.

> *b.* Caracas, Venezuela, 9.viii.1874; taken to Paris aged five to study with *Massenet; music critic for *Le Figaro* 1934; *d.* Paris, 28.i.47. *other works*: a violin concerto (1927) and a biography of his friend Sarah Bernhardt (1930).

Alexei HAIEFF US composer of Russian birth and neo-classical tendencies, he had a penchant for busy rhythms and once conducted the Woody *Herman Orch. His piano concerto created a minor stir (NY, 27.iv.52, cond. Stokowski) but most of his career has been spent in academia.

> *b.* Blagoveschensk, Siberia, 25.viii.14; came to US 1931; st with *Goldmark, *Boulanger; taught American Academy in Rome and Us. of Buffalo and Utah; *works include*: three symphonies, violin concerto, *Caligula* (after Robert Lowell) for baritone and orchestra (NY, 5.xi.71).

haiku Epigrammatic Japanese poem favoured by epigrammatic composers.

Rodolfo and Ernesto HALFFTER Sons of a German immigrant from Königsberg, Rodolfo (*b.* Madrid 30.x.1900; *d.* Mexico City, 14.x.87) sailed in 1935 for Mexico City, founded a music magazine and wrote three ballets and various orch. pieces in the manner of Manuel de *Falla. Ernesto (*b.* Madrid, 16.i.05; *d.* there, 5.vii.89) studied long and hard with de Falla and initially copied the neo-baroque style of his harpsichord concerto in the ballet *Sonatina* (1927). His frankest imitation was the *Portuguese Rhapsody* for piano and orch. (1941), a take-off of *Nights in the Gardens of Spain*. But his completion of Falla's cantata *Atlantida* aroused controversy for it showed just how far he had abandoned his teacher's style in favour of *Ravel's and particularly *Poulenc's.

His many film scores were clear and light and his guitar concerto (1969) has delicate attractions. Neither brother was particularly prolific.

Cristobal HALFFTER Nephew of Ernesto and Roberto, he started out in the family Falla style with *Antifona pascual* (four voices, chorus and orch., 1952) but joined a budding avant-garde that flowered as the fascist grip weakened. He moved into *Stravinsky terrain with *Dos movimientos* for timpani and string orch. and by the mid-1960s was composing abstract and electronic works like a true *Darmstadter. His opera *Don Quichote* was staged at Düsseldorf and he became a frequent conductor of German orchestras. In 1990 he signalled a possible return to centreground with a 3rd string quartet that, while rich in tuneless flutterings, showed some pull towards tonality.

> *b.* Madrid, 24.iii.30; st with Conrado del Campo and *Tansman; *other works*: piano concerto (1953), *Anillos* for large orch. (1968), Plaint for victims of violence (18 inst. and electronics, 1970), Requiem for imagined liberty (1971), cello concerto (1975), much vocal spiritual music.

Half-time Martinů's football interlude. fp: Prague, 7.xii.24.

Bengt HAMBRAEUS Dissonant doyen of Swedish electronic music, adding religious mysticism to *Darmstadt-learned discords in many organ and choral works.

b. Stockholm, 29.i.1928; moved to Canada, 1972.

Peter Michael HAMEL German meditator on Asiatic timbres in high-tech settings. *b.* Munich, 1947; *works include*: opera *Ein Menschentrau* (1980), *Voices for Peace* for chorus, piano and orch.

Iain (Ellis) HAMILTON Eclectic Scot, he underwent typical phases of romantic *Variations* for string orch. (1948) and serial *Sinfonia* for two orchestras before giving rein to a natural dramatism. His second opera, *The Royal Hunt of the Sun* after a Peter Shaffer play, was staged at English National Opera (2.ii.77). Visits to the West Indies brought a slight calypso flavour to his later works, particularly the 2nd string quartet of 1965.
b. Glasgow, 6.vi.22; taught Duke U., North Carolina, 1961–81; *other works*: operas *The Catiline Conspiracy* (1974) and *Anna Karenina* (1981), 2nd symphony (winner of Koussevitsky award, 1950), two piano concertos, two violin concertos.

Howard HANSON A split American personality who preached progress to his pupils while practising decadent romanticism in his symphonies. The first, *Nordic* Symphony (1923), recalled his ancestral Sweden in an idiom not far removed from Grieg. The 2nd, *Romantic* Symphony (Boston, 28.xi.30), was favourably compared during the Boston Symphony's jubilee to recent astringencies from Europe. The big tune of its central andante was unforgettable and his homespun 3rd symphony (26.iii.38) was premièred live over the NBC network; his 4th (3.xii.43) won the Pulitzer Prize. His opera, *Merry Mount*, was staged at the Met (10.ii.34). *Koussevitsky championed his music as a cornerstone of US culture.

Hanson, however, led a double life at Rochester, New York, where in 1924 he persuaded the Kodak inventor, George Eastman, to found a School of Music and a festival of American music. Both were hotbeds of modernism; graduates included Dominick Argento and Ulysses Kay.

He continued composing through a long life, achieving *A Sea Symphony* (7.viii.77), his seventh, when past 80. He wrote a choral *Song of Democracy* (1957), followed by *A Song of Human Rights* (1963), and took his Eastman Orch. on State Department missions all over the northern hemisphere. An excellent concert hall bears his name in Rochester, but his bright and optimistic music barely stands the test of time.
b. Wahoo, Nebraska, 28.x.1896; spent three years at the American Acadamy in Rome; headed Eastman School 1924–64; married Margaret Nelson 1946; *d.* Rochester, NY, 26.ii.81. *other notable works*: *Lux aeterna* for viola and orch. (1923), Lament of Beowulf for chorus and orch. (1926), concerto for organ and orch. (1926), string quartet (1926), Elegy for Serge *Koussevitsky (20.i.56), *Mosaics* (Cleveland, 23.i.58).

Jan HANUS Deeply religious Czech whose first symphony was banned by the Nazis and communists alike for its patriotic fervour. The choral finale was lost after a 1943 première and was reconstituted from memory by the composer after the 1989 revolution, when he became head of the reformed Union of Czech Composers. He has written four more symphonies, concertos, stage works and much choral music, including an outstanding *Glagolitic Mass* (1986). His style is richly traditional, reminiscent of Dvořák and Fibich.
b. Prague, 2.v.15;

happening A spontaneous substitute for formal concerts, possibly devised by *Cage around 1952, it flourished in flower-power California when a piece of music could consist a musician drawing a razor across his wrists, or two people copulating inside a grand piano. More sedate occasions involved reading, slide shows and unchoreographed dance.

Harawi, chant d'amour et de mort Song-cycle by *Messiaen, linked in his *Tristan* triptych with *Turangalîla* and *Cinq rechants*. fp: Mâcon, 24.vi.46.

John (Harris) HARBISON Eclectic American, his style varying with his subject matter, he won the 1987 Pulitzer Prize with an orchestral tone-poem, *The Flight into Egypt*. His most affecting piece is

Mirabai Songs (1982) for soprano and chamber orchestra, a setting of verses by a 16th-century Indian widow who refused to die on her husband's pyre. Grief, ecstasy, sexuality and defiance mingle in a fiery and lovely dirge reminiscent of the young *Messiaen. *Variations* (1982) are also rooted in Asian ritual dances, reviving the unusual trio of Bartók's *Contrasts in varied combinations.

> *b.* Orange, New Jersey, 20.xii.38; st with *Blacher, *Sessions and *Kim; taught M.I.T. 1969–82; *other works*: operas *The Winter's Tale* (San Francisco, 20.vii.79), *Full Moon in March* (Cambridge, Massachusetts, 30.iv. 79); violin concerto (1980), symphony (1984).

Die Harmonie der Welt (*Universal Harmony*) *Hindemith's symphony (1951) and opera (1957) on the life of the astronomer Johannes Kepler and his theory linking the movement of planets with the relation of musical tones.

Harmonielehre *Schoenberg's 1911 textbook of diatonic harmony codified a topic that he had lately rendered obsolete. He believed in a new harmonic order by which each composer drew up his own pitch-relations. Some replaced the term harmony with *Babbitt's 'simultaneity', arguing that harmony was indefinable in a modern context.

Harnasie Ballet-pantomime by *Szymanowski. fp: Prague, 11.v.35.

(Le)Roy (Ellsworth) HARRIS The high point of Roy Harris' life was *Koussevitsky's première of his 18-minute 3rd symphony (Boston, 24.ii.39). With war looming over Europe, it affirmed a muscular Americanism, slow and open as the prairies. The work had five phases: tragic, lyric, pastoral, fugue-dramatic and dramatic-tragic. It became the most performed American symphony and, in 1973, the first to be played in China. Together with 3rd symphonies from Harris' pupil *Schuman and his friend *Copland, it formed the centre of a new American concert repertoire.

Harris failed to repeat its success, though he lived another 40 years and wrote 15 symphonies in all. Born in an Oklahoma log cabin on Abraham Lincoln's birthday, he grew up on a farm near Los Angeles and studied in Paris with Nadia *Boulanger, who let him roam free and find his own metier. A concerto for piano, clarinet and string quartet (Paris, 8.v.27) was well received, but Harris broke his back on a flight of stone stairs and was invalided out of Europe.

Koussevitsky, seeking 'a great symphony from the West',, claimed his first three for Boston. The 4th went to Cleveland (26.xii.40) and marked the onset of decline. It was called a *Folksong Symphony* and grew out of contacts with Woody *Guthrie, Burl Ives and fellow folk-revivalists. In symphonic terms, it regressed towards a simplicity not far removed from *Stalin's musical formula. Harris reverted to literal patriotism in the 6th symphony, *Gettysburg Address* (14.iv.44), and the 10th, his *Abraham Lincoln* Symphony (Long Beach, California, 14.iv.65), but his moment had passed. What was best in his music were its confident Americanism, its Protestant work ethic and hymnody, and its boundless optimism.

> *b.* Lincoln County, Oklahoma, 12.ii.1898; married pianist Beulah Duffey 1936; *d.* Santa Monica, California, 1.x.79. *other works*: symphonic overture *When Johnny Comes Marching Home* (Minneapolis, 13.1.35); *Kentucky Spring* (Louisville, 5.iv.49); concerto for two pianos (Denver, 21.i.47), concerto for amplified piano, brass and percussion (1968); four string quartets; chamber cantata, *Abraham Lincoln walks at Midnight* (1953).

Lou HARRISON Associate of *Cowell and *Cage, he pursued the percussive qualities of Asian instruments and household objects, such as flowerpots. Two concertos for flute and percussion are ingeniously attractive and short. His piano concerto (1985) was premièred by jazzman Keith *Jarrett. His vocal works had texts in the would-be universal language, Esperanto.

> *b.* Portland, Oregon, 14.v.17; *other works*: *La Koro Sutro* for 100 voices, harp, organ and gamelan (1971), *Schoenbergiana* for sextet (1945).

Karl Amadeus HARTMANN Pivotal figure in German music, its conscience and continuity through the Hitler era and the post-War schism. An instant foe of

a turbulent *marche funèbre* to a ferocious finale.

It is the symphonies, however, most of them for outsized orch., that are the core of his work. The first, titled 'Essay for a Requiem' (Vienna, 22.vi.57), has a contralto singing harrowing verses by the American poet Walt Whitman. The first movement is called Misery, the second Spring ('When lilacs last in the dooryard bloom'd . . .'), the third consists of instrumental variations on a theme from Hartmann's anti-war opera *Simplicissimus* (1935), the fourth is named Tears and the finale is a Supplication delivered in mordant *sprechgesang.

The 2nd symphony (Donaueschingen, 10.ix.50) is a 15-minute adagio composed around a Russian-Jewish lament. The 3rd (Munich, 10.ii.50) comprises two slow movements strongly redolent of late *Berg and is partly derived from an abandoned 1940 *sinfonia tragica*. In the 4th (Munich, 2.iv.48) he dropped an intended vocal finale and wrote for strings alone. The 5th (Stuttgart, 21.iv.51) is a happier 15-minute miniature described as a 'symphonie concertante', while the 6th (Munich, 24.iv.53) employs a large orchestra for just two movements.

All of these symphonies were reconstituted from existing manuscripts and all, in some way or other, bear a Mahlerian imprint, in either their shape or themes, and always in their philosophy. The symphony, Mahler ordained, must be all-embracing.

The 7th and 8th symphonies (Hamburg, 15.iii.59; Munich, 25.i.63), the only ones composed without reference to earlier scores, adopt an agitated polyphonic, almost *neo-classical manner, interspersed with grave melancholy. The symphony, Hartmann indicated, had a secure future – though its future and Germany's were not necessarily bright. The opening movement of the 8th was his most personal utterance.

Although he studied briefly with *Webern, he rejected 12-tone rules and was considered a dinosaur by *Stockhausen. A gregarious, cultured and popular man, he would liked to have been a painter like his brother. Weeks after the end of hostilities, he founded a *Musica Viva concert series in

Nazism, Hartmann risked his life helping others escape. He withdrew his music from performance in Germany in a protest known as 'inner emigration', sending it abroad to signal the survival of a moral resistance. In wartime, he went periodically into hiding to avoid the draft and the Gestapo. Much of what he composed was recycled into his seven post-War symphonies. These, scarcely played outside Germany, constitute the missing link in the nation's culture between *Mahler and *Hindemith on the one hand, *Henze and *Rihm on the other. They are indispensable to any understanding of the thread of German music.

Hartmann did not try to conceal human and political sentiments in his music. He wrote a string quartet in 1933 around a Jewish Sabbath-night melody, *Elija-hu hanavi*. In 1935 he sent to Prague an orchestral *Miserae* about the Dachau concentration camp. The disturbing *Concerto funèbre* for violin and string orchestra, premièred in Switzerland in 1940 and revised 20 years later, uses a Czech Hussite chorale to reflect the three phases of Hitler's demolition of a free nation. Its 4th movement, citing an anti-Tsarist Russian song, restores a modicum of hope.

As the war ended, he wrote a piano sonata titled *27 April 1945* which described a line of prisoners leaving Dachau, a sight from which other neighbours averted their eyes. 'Unending was the stream . . . unending was the misery,' mourned Hartmann. He opened the sonata with the bassoon melody of Stravinsky's *Rite of Spring*, perhaps referring to the Russian inmates (it is quoted again in the middle movement of his 5th symphony), and advanced through the ruins of his native Munich that, annually and uncoercively, introduced his fellow-Germans to the modern music they had missed under totalitarian rule. It became the archetype of contemporary music festivals, despite the avant-garde's view of its founder.

b. Munich, 2.viii.05; *d*. there, 5.xii.63. *other works*: viola concerto (Frankfurt, 25.v.56), *Gesangszene* for baritone and orch. (Frankfurt, 12.xi.64), *Ghetto* for baritone and small orch. (part of joint *Jewish Chronicle* composition with four fellow-Germans), two string quartets, jazz and burlesque piano pieces.

Thomas de HARTMANN Russian nationalist with modernist and mystic leanings he set songs of Proust and Joyce and worked with Wassily Kandinsky in Munich from 1908–12 on the development of 'a total work of art for the stage'. He composed music for the painter's play, *Der gelbe Klang (The Yellow Sound)*; the score has been reconstituted by *Schuller (NY, 9.ii.82). A devotee of G. I. Gurdjieff, he preached rural self-sufficiency while earning his keep from film scores. He left a volume of music collected or invented by Gurdjieff and adored by his followers.

b. Khoruzevka, Ukraine, 21.ix.1885; *d*. Princeton, New Jersey, 26.iii.56. *works include*: three symphonies, concertos for cello, piano, double-bass and harp; *12 Russian Fairytales* for orch. (Houston, 4.iv.55, cond. *Stokowski).

(Sir Herbert) Hamilton HARTY The Irish conductor wrote orchestral pieces with a romantic, rural outlook – *With the Wild Geese* (1910) and a soprano setting of Keats' *Ode to a Nightingale* for his wife, Agnes Nicholls. Josef Szigeti espoused his violin concerto. His best-known pieces were obese reorchestrations of Handel's *Water Music* and *Fireworks Music*. As conductor of Manchester's Hallé Orch. (1920–33), Harty gave UK premières of Mahler's 9th symphony and Shostakovich's 1st.

b. Hillsborough, Ireland, 4.xii.1879; *d*. Hove, Sussex, 19.ii.41.

Jonathan (Dean) HARVEY Pensive English cathedral musician, he was drawn to *Babbitt's radicalism at Princeton and to *Boulez's dream of a new universe of sound. Working at *IRCAM, he produced in 1980 what may be the most haunting composition to emerge from an electronic studio. *Mortuos Plango, vivos voco* (Lille, 30.xi.80) combines the tolling bell of an English cathedral and the treble voice of the composer's young son, both real and synthesized, in a 14-minute tape of slow, sensual dimensions, somehow recalling the eastern *minimalism of *Pärt and *Gorecki. Its equally beautiful *IRCAM successor, *Bhakti* (Paris, 3.xii.82), followed Boulez's current line of combining live ensemble with pre-recorded tape. Spirituality is always at the foreground of Harvey's work, often a Steinerist Christian belief infused with Indian philosophy. He has written many devotional vocal works and two surging string quartets (1977, 1989).

b. Sutton Coldfield, Warwicks., 3.v.39; st with Erwin Stein, Hans Keller and Babbitt; taught U. of Southampton 1964–77, U. of Sussex 1977– ; *other works*: *Smiling immortal* (1977) and *Easter orisons* (1983), both for chamber orchestra; *Madonna of Winter and Spring* (1986) for orchestra and tape; *Come, Holy Ghost* for chorus (1984).

Háry János Opera by *Kodály with universally popular suite. fp: Budapest, 16.x.26.

Roman HAUBENSTOCK-RAMATI Stravinsky's scores were calligraphed so neatly they looked like works of art. Haubenstock's were exhibited and sold in Vienna galleries, their *graphic notation delicately offset by background shades of blue, yellow and grey. On paper, it looks appealing and innovative. To the ear, his numerous 'mobile' compositions sound drearily *avant-gardist, many of them scored predictably for percussion and electronic tape. His 1977 second string quartet, however, is a work of pure emotion, mourning the death of a Viennese prima ballerina with explicitly expressive markings – 'bitter-sweet', 'passionate', – and two canons as elegiac as Berg's.

b. Cracow, Poland, 27.xi.19; head of music on Cracow Radio 1947–50; music librarian in Tel Aviv 1950–56; moved to Vienna 1957; *works include*: opera *Amerika* (after Kafka, Berlin, 8.x.66), *Symphonie 'K'* (1967), ballet *Ulysses* (1967), *Mobile for Shakespeare* (1960), two string quartets, two string trios.

Josef Matthias HAUER Alternate inventor of the *12-note method, Hauer lived in Viennese obscurity while Schoenberg and his disciples hogged the notoriety. During an analysis of his own music, he discovered the 'law of the 12 notes' at least a year ahead of Schoenberg, albeit less workably, divided into units of six *tropes. The two composers met in 1917 and Schoenberg programmed Hauer's music in his *private concerts, but ties were cut when Hauer demanded acknowledgement of his dodecatonal primacy. Banned in the Nazi era, his sage-like presence in post-1945 Vienna gave heart and courage to embattled modernists. His music has a spherical, mystic character, lacking the practicality and despotic certainty of Schoenberg's compositions. He once said 'in my whole life I have written only one work' – a work that stretched from *Nomos* of 1919 to a succession of *Zwölftonspiele* – 'games' for orchestra and differing combinations of instruments.

> *b*. Wiener Neustadt, Lower Austria, 19.iii. 1883; *d*. Vienna, 22.ix.59. *other works*: cantata *Der Menschen Weg* (1934–52), Sinfonietta (1927), violin concerto (1928), Slow Waltzes for orch. (1953); operas *Salambo* (1930) and *Die Schwarze-Spinne* (1932).
>
> *Bib*: W. Szmolyan, *J. M. Hauer*, Vienna (Lafitte), 1965.

Siegmund von HAUSEGGER Austro-German late-romantic, son-in-law of Alexander Ritter (Wagner's nephew, *Strauss's teacher), Hausegger achieved his heyday in the Nazi era, when he was portrayed as protoype of the New German Composer. His works include a Nature symphony with choral finale, a Dionysian Fantasy for orchestra and two symphonic poems.

> *b*. Graz, Austria, 16.viii.1872; cond. Frankfurt Museum concerts 1903–10, Hamburg's Philharmonic concerts 1910–20 and the Munich Konzertverein 1920–38; *d*. Munich, 10.x.48.

heavy metal Excruciatingly loud form of rock music, a testament of creative poverty and a *punk-age reaction against ultra-smooth *Beatles style. The term originated in Steppenwolf's 1968 song, 'Born to be Wild', and was itself a quotation from William Burroughs' novel, *Naked Lunch*. The music grew ever noisier and the stage antics more violent in the acts of groups like Black Sabbath and AC/DC until, early in the 1980s, the rock TV network MTV pulled the plug on heavy metal plays and the genre subsided for a decade.

Hebrew The language of ancient and modern Israel appealed to *Stravinsky in *Abraham and Isaac* and *Stockhausen in his *Licht* cycle as a device of Biblical immediacy. *Bloch, *Milhaud, *Castelnuovo-Tedesco and *Weill created liturgical settings; *Bernstein included prayers in two symphonies and *Schoenberg in *A Survivor from Warsaw* and *Kol Nidrei*. *Reich founded *Tehillim* on the Davidian Psalms. The gutturals of spoken Hebrew were ill-suited to Western music and most settings,

*Chichester Psalms excepted, were unidiomatic.

Jascha HEIFETZ The supreme violinist, flawless and imperturbable, his technique and ice-clear textures were inexplicable wonders. Rivals consoled themselves with the allegation that Heifetz lacked warmth, when what he really missed was depth. On the road from age 11, when he made a Berlin debut in the Tchaikovsky concerto under *Nikisch, he reached Carnegie Hall at 16 (27.x.17) before an aghast audience of famed virtuosi. 'Hot in here,' said Mischa Elman to Leopold *Godowsky. 'Not for pianists,' retorted his keyboard colleague. He toured further in both hemispheres than any predecessor, and in the course of his travels had little pause for reflection. Once settled in Hollywood, he embraced glamour at the expense of gravitas. His Bach and Beethoven were too slick for most tastes, but his playing of the Glazunov and Prokofiev concertos were above reproach and it was his recording in 1936 that fixed the Sibelius concerto in the concerto repertoire.

He commissioned concertos without much success. *Schoenberg's he paid for but refused to play; others by *Korngold, *Castelnuovo-Tedesco, Rozsa and Gruenberg were revamped film music. Apart from the Schoenberg concerto, only the *Walton (1939) made lasting impact. Physically attacked in Israel for playing *Strauss, Heifetz retorted: 'I recognize only two kinds of music – good music and bad. Good music is for all those who have ears to listen.'

> *b*. Vilna, Lithuania, 2.ii.01, taught by father, Reuven, and Leopold Auer; emigrated 1917, US citizen 1925; married (1) Florence Vidor, silent film star, 1918–46; (2) Frances Spiegelberg, 1947–63; retired reclusively, 1970; *d*. Los Angeles, 10.xii.87.

Werner HEIDER German mediator between *serialism, *rock and *jazz in a large corpus of individualist works.

> *b*. Fürth, Bavaria, 1.i.30; formed Ars Nova ensemble in Nuremberg, 1968–; *works include*: symphony (1975), *Rock-Art* for symphony orch. (1981), *Commission* on poems of Ezra Pound for baritone/chamber orch (1972), *D.E. Memorial* homage to Duke Ellington for solo trombone (1975).

Paavo HEININEN Father-figure to an international generation of Finnish composers, Heininen is scarcely known abroad. His major work, *The Damask Drum* (Helsinki, 5.iv.84) is a stylized opera based on a 14th-century Japanese Noh-play. Orch. works, including four symphonies and three piano concertos, are relentlessly technical, using serial methods acquired from Bernd Alois *Zimmermann. He was able, however, to help *Lindberg, *Salonen and friends overcome avant-gardism and find their true voices.

> *b*. Helsinki, 13.i.38; st also with *Rautavaara, Persichetti and Lutosławski; taught Sibelius Academy 1966–; *other works*: cello concerto (Helsinki, 26.ii.86), saxophone concerto (29.viii.83); *Musique d'été* for chamber ensemble (Tampere, 11.x.67).

Jimi HENDRIX Guitarist and singer whose impact on rock music was as brief and explosive as Charlie *Parker's on jazz. Playing the guitar upside down because he was left-handed and yelling his songs at top volume, he brought *Woodstock to a standstill with 'Purple Haze' – subsequently reinvented by *Kronos as an electrified string quartet. He burned out on drugs at 27.

> *b*. Seattle, Washington, 27.xi.42; *d*. London, 18.ix.70.

Pierre HENRY Taking over the simple experiments of the engineer Pierre *Schaeffer, Henry founded and ran a *musique concrète research department at French state radio (1949–58). In 1958 he founded the first private electronic studio at Apsome and dropped out of the official *avant-garde. His taped creations were choreographed by Maurice Béjart and danced as a paradigm of abstract modernism. The most famous were *Symphonie pour un homme seul* (Symphony for a Loner) (with Schaeffer, 1950) and *Orphée* (1958). He provided *Temptations of St Anthony* (1967), *Mass for the present time* (1967) and *Nijinsky, Clown of God* (1971) for George Balanchine.

> *b*. Paris, 9.xii.27; st with *Messiaen, *Boulanger; *other taped works*: *Messe de Liverpool* (1968), *Futuristie I* (1975), reviving noisemaking instruments of *futurists.

Hans Werner HENZE The outstanding German composer after 1945 spent his creative life and energies in conflict with the society that created him. A last-ditch conscript to Hitler's army, he shunned the conformism of the successor federal republic, emigrated in his 20s, campaigned for homosexual causes and supported communist militancy – all the while continuing to compose for subsidized German institutions and bask in German applause. He was, by his own definition, an outsider, but one who flagrantly enjoyed the ear of the German establishment and its unstinted patronage.

At 27 when he moved to Italy, he had written three symphonies, five operas and a ballet. He composed fluently in the meticulous manner of Stravinsky and Hindemith, though at such high pace that his instrumentation sometimes looked second-hand. He mastered *serialism at *Darmstadt but abandoned it as insufficiently communicative. Teaching at Darmstadt in 1955 alongside Boulez, he preached the supremacy of melodism and was demonized by the *avant-garde as a dangerous heretic.

His first operas tackled themes and writers suppressed in Hitler's Germany. *Boulevard Solitude* (Hanover, 17.ii.52) reset the Manon Lescaut story among urban drug addicts in a *jazz-*Weill score. Two radio operas, *A Country Doctor* (NDR, 29.xi.51) and *The End of a World* (NDR, 4.xii.53) had stories by Kafka and Wolfgang Hildesheimer. His European reputation was founded on the very German fairy-tale of *König Hirsch* (*King Stag*, Berlin, 23.ix.56, cond. *Scherchen), a kind of Hansel and Gretel for grownups. He wrote the ballet *Maratona* (Berlin, 24.ix.57) with Luchino Visconti and, more lastingly, *Undine* with Frederick Ashton for Covent Garden (27.x.58).

Two partnerships cemented his operatic success, a double collaboration with the German writer Ingeborg Bachmann in *Der Prinz von Homburg* (Hamburg, 22.v.60) and *Der Junge Lord* (Berlin, 7.iv.65) – and, around the same time, a dual venture with *Auden and his companion Chester Kallman. *Elegy for Young Lovers* (Schwetzingen Festival, 20.v.61) told of a poet whose art feeds off the destruction of his loved ones, a parable told in some delicately affecting music. Auden demanded of Henze that he study *Götterdämmerung* before tackling *The Bassarids*, (Salzburg, 6.viii.66, cond. Dohnányi), a Greek tragedy that displayed the composer at his most Stravinskian and that he ultimately considered 'my most important opera'. Like *The *Rake's Progress*, it contains wonderful lines and static drama. Henze composed as readily to English and Italian texts as to German and could pass for a landed gentleman in either land.

In the mid-1960s, he shook off what remained of his German restraint and shifted from soft socialism to radical Marxism, and from discreet relationships to gay liberation. He backed Rudi Dutschke's student riots, wrote an *Essay on Pigs* (baritone/chamber orch., London, 19.ii.69) against the Berlin police and spoke of 'the necessity of creating the greatest work of art of mankind: the world revolution'. He went to live for two years in Cuba, writing a 6th symphony (Havana, 26.xi.69) and an anti-slavery pageant *El Cimmarón*, in which he simplified his music to the point of puerility. His next operas were agit-prop disasters: *La Cubana* (Munich, 28.v.75) and *We come to the River* (Covent Garden, 12.vii.76). The oratorio *Raft of the Medusa* (stage première Nuremberg, 15.iv.72) adopted texts by the guerrilla leader Che Guevara and a percussive finale chant of 'Ho Chi Minh'. In *The English Cat* (Schwetzingen Festival, 2.vi.83) Henze attempted contemporary social parody against a *Rakeish neo-classical backdrop, unimpressively.

Continuous performances in both Germanies made him rich; he was untroubled by communist tyranny. While his views did not falter until the Berlin Wall collapsed, in the mid-1980s his music underwent a perceptible change. *Das verratene Meer* (Berlin, 5.v.90), after Yukio Mishima's novel *The Sailor Who Fell From Grace with the Sea*, was straightforward narrative opera with no social axe to grind and a rich, post-romantic score. The 7th symphony (Berlin, 1.xii.84), by far his finest, conjured in a stridently confident opening a vision of Germany revitalized and resurgent. Two of its four movements were elegiac but the underlying message was unmistakable: power. This exciting, amusing, eloquent symphony seemed spiritually vacant at its centre, perhaps a reflection of the composer's perplexing duality, perhaps of the new Germany itself. As close friends died of old age and AIDS, his music turned inwards towards, as his followers put it, 'a liberation of the spirit'. A Requiem (1992) for Michael Vyner of the *London Sinfonietta promised profound utterances on art and life. He was the guiding light of the Munich biennale and in 1990 proudly accepted an award from the Siemens Foundation, kings of German industrialism.

> *b*. Gütersloh, Westphalia, 1.vii.26; military service 1944–45; st with *Fortner and at *Darmstadt; ballet cond. at Wiesbaden 1950–52; moved to Italy 1953; taught at Salzburg Mozarteum 1962–67, founded Montepulciano summer workshops 1976; *other works*: 7 Lovesongs for cello and orch. (Cologne, 12.xii.86), two violin concertos, two piano concertos, double concerto for oboe, harp and strings (Zurich, 2.xii.66), *Telemanniana* for orch. (Berlin, 4.iv.67), *Tristan* (1973), preludes for piano, orch. and *electronics; five string quartets; much vocal and chamber music.
> *Bib*: H.W. Henze, *Music and Politics*, London (Faber), 1984.

Victor HERBERT   Serious music took second place when Herbert made it big on Broadway. Foremost among some 40 operettas were *Babes in Toyland* (1903) and *Naughty Marietta* (1910), both filmed. He wrote a score to accompany a silent film, *The Fall of a Nation*.

His 2nd cello concerto (1894) was a model for Dvořák's and two of his operas, *Natoma* (Philadelphia, 25.ii.11) and *Madeleine* (NY Met, 24.i.14), were staged. His most lasting creation was ASCAP, the American Society of Composers, Authors and Publishers, founded in 1914 to fight for creative rights. He is credited with the immortal songline 'A Woman is Only a Woman, But a Good Cigar is a Smoke'. He died of a heart attack on his doctor's staircase after a generous lunch.

> *b*. Dublin, 1.ii.1859, worked in Germany 1867–86, married Viennese soprano Therese Förster; played cello in New York Philharmonic, 1887; cond. Pittsburgh Symphony, 1898–1904, formed Victor Herbert NY Orch. 1904; *d*. NY, 26.v.24.

Woody (Woodrow Charles) HERMAN   Jazz clarinettist and alto-saxophonist, commissioned Stravinsky's *Ebony concerto, had a lifelong rivalry with Benny *Goodman and was destroyed by a federal tax investigation.

> *b*. Milwaukee, Wisconsin, 16.v.13; *d*. Los Angeles, 28.x.87.

Bernard (Benny) HERRMANN   The man who put the chill into Alfred Hitchcock's movies was a hypertense Anglophile who wrote an opera on *Wuthering Heights* and introduced Americans to the music of Walton, Rubbra, Rawsthorne and many others. Herrmann joined CBS as head of educational programmes in 1934 and from 1942–59 was chief conductor of the network orchestra. In 1950 he composed a TV musical on Dickens' *A Christmas Carol*.

His principal achievement, though, was 60 movie scores. Rejecting explicit accompaniments, he invented a genre for Orson Welles, a former CBS workmate, with a tremulous tapestry of opposing string themes that gave *Citizen Kane* (1940) its ominous undertone. He introduced electric violins in a sci-fi thriller, *The Day the Earth Stood Still* (1951). His style reached its summit in a ten-year partnership with Hitchcock for whom he provided a Prokofiev-like ambience for *North by Northwest* (1959) and a Mahler-Tenth mournfulness for *Psycho*, punctuated by the squeaky violins of nerves strained to breaking point. *Vertigo* (1958) and *The Birds* (1963) were equally macabre; he finally broke with the director over *Torn Curtain*, for which Herrmann required an orchestra with 16 horns and nine trombones. In 1966 he joined Hitchcock's French admirer François Truffaut for *Fahrenheit 451* and *The Bride Wore Black*. His last score was a blues-rich track for Martin Scorsese's *Taxi Driver*.

> *b*. New York, 29.vi.11; st with *Goldmark, *Grainger; settled in London, 1965; *d*. Los Angeles, 24.xii.75. *other works*: symphony (NY, 12.xi.42), clarinet quintet (1967).

Philip HESELTINE – See Peter WARLOCK

Hans-Joachim HESPOS Self-taught outsider of the German *avant-garde, he has written extremely abstract works for single instruments and small combinations that stand and fall locally on the strength of his considerable personality.
   b. Emden, 13.iii.38; *music theatre works*: *itzo-hux* (1981), *za'khani* (1984).

L'heure espagnole (*Spanish hour*) One-act opera by Ravel on the wiles of a watchmaker's wife. fp: Paris, 19.v.11.

Volker HEYN A busker for 12 years, roaming Australia with guitar in hand, he returned home to give symphonic expression to his experiences.
   b. Karlsruhe, Germany, 1938; *major work*: *TEM* for orch. (1980).

Alfred HILL Pioneer of modern Australasian music, he studied Maori and aboriginal music for his eight operas, ten symphonies and 17 string quartets.
   b. Melbourne, 16.16.xi.1870; st in Leipzig; *d.* Sydney, 30.x.35.

Edward Burlingame HILL Harvard stalwart whose grandfather was college president, he was music prof. 1908–40, claiming *Bernstein as his star pupil. His compositions were was Francophone rather than Germanic; he awoke to jazz in 1920s with Jazz studies for two pianos (1924) and a piano concertino (1931).
   b. Cambridge, Massachusetts, 9.ix.1872; st with *Paine and with *Widor in Paris; *d.* Francestown, New Hampshire, 9.vii.60. *other works*: tone poem *Lilacs* (1926).

Wilfried HILLER Munich-based composer of an opera for actress and four percussion players, *An diesem heutigen Tage* (Munich, 15.vii.79), based on Mary Stuart's dying words, 'en ma fin est mon commencement'. He has also staged Lewis Carroll's nonsense verse 'The Hunting of the Snark' as *Die Jagd nach dem Schlarg* (Munich 16.i.88).
   b. Weissenhorn, Swabia, 15.iii.41; st *Darmstadt with Boulez, Stockhausen, Maderna; editor at Bavarian radio 1971–81.

Hiller Variations Ingenious orch. work by *Reger. fp: Cologne, 15.x.07.

Paul HINDEMITH Proof that Nazism was a ragbag of individual prejudices rather than a coherent ideology was provided by the notorious Hindemith case. Here was a composer who was German by ancestry and attitude, who mined the national heritage for musical inspiration, who worked harder than anyone to bring music back into ordinary German lives – and whose opera was banned in 1934 because the propaganda minister took a personal dislike to his intellectualism and his Jewish friends.

   Hindemith was attacked by Goebbels as an atonalist when he was, in fact, a German craftsman working in traditional materials of Bachian counterpoint and Lutheran chorale. *Furtwängler, admiring his high-mindedness, performed a symphony from the opera *Mathis der Maler* in Berlin (12.iii.34), triggering official protests, his own resignation and the composer's emigration. *Mathis* revealed the randomness of Nazi cultural oppression. A parable on an artist's role during medieval social unrest, it made a hero of the painter Matthias Grünewald (1470–1528) in a score rich in spirituality but short on contrast that was staged, with great success, in Zurich (28.v.38). Hindemith wandered from Switzerland to the US and back again,

earning respect as a violist, conductor and educator, but never regaining the status of innovator that he enjoyed in *Weimar.

His next opera, 20 years later, broached another cerebral-mystical topic. *Die *Harmonie der Welt* (Munich, 11.viii.57), recounts the troubles of the astronomer Johannes Kepler, whose planetary theories had musical origins. Hindemith was convinced that music contained secrets of the universe, but his cultivated scores lacked Schoenberg's messianic fervour, Bartók's rhythmic primitivsm or Stravinsky's wicked humour and he slipped out of the front rank of modernists.

His creative facility was phenomenal. Sitting in a BBC studio when news arrived of King George V's death, he dashed off *Trauermusik* in an hour and performed it the following day. He could compose a sonata movement on a short train journey. To avert boredom while writing down the notes, he played structural games within a score. In the theatre piece *Hin und Zurück* (*There and Back*, Baden-Baden, 17.vii.27), the music reverses itself; in *Ludus Tonalis* for solo piano (Chicago, 15.ii.43) the postlude consists of the prelude turned upside down.

He emerged from the First War worried about the continuing relevance of music. A dip into the novelty of *jazz in *Kammermusik* 1 (1921) provided no lasting solutions. Opera was an obvious vehicle for social comment and he embarked on the Kokoschka collaboration, *Murderer, Hope of Women* (Stuttgart, 4.vi.21), the Faustian legend *Cardillac* (Dresden, 9.xi.26) and the newspaper satire *Neues vom Tage* (*Daily News*, Berlin, 8.vi.29). The edge of his operas was blunted as he became the professional model of Germanic seriousness. Privately, he doodled funny self-caricatures.

To address the role of music in society he came up with *Gebrauchsmusik* – utility music that amateurs could play – and *Hausmusik* to revive the habit of domestic music making. 'People who make music together cannot be enemies, at least while the music lasts,' he wrote. His simplified pieces are fun to play but do not stand up to repeated listening. Several items in this vein were entitled *Konzertmusik* and

intended for large ensembles, including brass band.

Much of his chamber music was written for domestic consumption. The clarinet quintet (1923), a pleasing work of early maturity, opens with a parody of instruments tuning up before moving into folktunes and Twenties swing. The finale is the opening played backwards.

On a higher plane of endeavour he produced sonatas for individual instruments, several of which are classics of their kind. The trumpet sonata (1939) takes its theme from the dark times and fades out in a funereal chorale; he wrote the words 'Alle Menschen müssen sterben' (All men must die) over the finale.

In a profusion of concertos, he wrote three for his own instrument, the viola, among which the folk-based *Der Schwanendreher* (Amsterdam, 14.xi.35) is charming despite over-civilizing its source material. An accomplished virtuoso, he played the première of *Walton's viola concerto and his own violin concerto (Amsterdam, 14.iii.40). Further concertos for Benny Goodman's clarinet (Philadelphia, 11.xii.50) and Dennis Brain's horn (Baden-Baden, 8.vi.50) are inappropriately straitlaced; *The Four Temperaments* (Boston, 3.ix.44) for piano and string orch. steps out in livelier fashion. The catchiest of his orch. works is the 20-minute *Symphonic Metamorphoses of Themes of Carl Maria von Weber* (NY, 20.i.44) based largely on Weber's original music for Gozzi and Schiller's play, *Turandot*.

Hindemith is often considered dry, though he was not without wit and performers like *Bernstein and Glenn *Gould discovered ecstasy in the Mathis music and the 3rd piano sonata. He is performed in Germany with leaden respect and rarely elsewhere. His pupils were numerous, especially in the US where he taught at *Tanglewood and Yale (1940–53).

The son of a house painter who was killed in the First War, Hindemith was called up but avoided seeing action by forming a string quartet that played nightly to ease the nerves of his commanding officer. Back in Frankfurt, he was concertmaster of the opera orch. (1915–23) and married the conductor's daughter, Gertrud

Rottenberg. Based on his experience, he wrote *Concerto for Orchestra (1925) long ahead of Bartók, as well as a *Philharmonisches Konzert* (Berlin, 15.iv. 32) for Furtwängler's ensemble and sundry unnumbered symphonies (E-flat, 1940; Serena, 1946; B-flat for concert band, 1950; and Pittsburgh Symphony, 1958).

b. Hanau am Main, near Frankfurt, 16.xi. 1895, of mixed Protestant and Catholic ancestry; US citizen 1946; settled in Switzerland 1953; *d*. Frankfurt, 28.xii.63. *other works*: six string quartets; much music for voice and orch., notably *Lindbergh's Flight* (German text, 1929) and *When Lilacs Last in the Dooryard Bloom'd* (after Walt Whitman, 1946).
Bib: Paul Hindemith, *A Composer's World*, Cambridge, Mass., 1952. Geoffrey Skelton, *Hindemith: The man and his music*, London, 1975.

hip-hop   Alternative term for *rap music.

René HIRSCHFELD   German composer of a lyrically lascivious, one-act *Bianca* (Salzburg, 16.viii.91), based on the Oscar Wilde story from which *Zemlinsky composed *A Florentine Tragedy*.
b. Dresden, 1965; st with Udo Zimmermann.

Histoire du soldât   – see Soldier's Tale

hit   A late-19th-century term implying audience success was monopolized by popular music when US radio launched a weekly 'hit parade' in 1935.

Joseph HOLBROOKE   British nationalist who gained early recognition in Europe but faded into the mist of a Celtic operatic trilogy, *The Cauldron of Anwen*.
b. Croydon, nr. London, 5.vii.1878; *d*. London, 5.viii.58. *other works*: symphonic poems *The Raven, Queen Mab, Byron* (1900–06).

Billie HOLIDAY   Although the story of her life was filmed as *Lady Sings the Blues* (with Diana Ross, 1972), Holiday was a pure jazz singer with a grating voice whose 'torch songs' relied more on personality than music.
b. Baltimore, Maryland, 7.iv.15; *d*. NY, 17.vii.59.

Holidays   Symphonic movements on US festive occasions by *Ives, comprising Washington's Birthday (1913), Decoration Day (1912), 4th of July (1913),

Thanksgiving and/or Forefathers' Day (1904).

Heinz HOLLIGER   The Swiss oboe virtuoso attracted important concertos and sonatas from *Martin, *Henze, *Penderecki and *Berio, adapting his technique to suit the most extreme avant-gardist demands. His own compositions are highrisk and admirably unsqueaky, while failing to impress as more than instrumental exercises. He married the harpist Ursula Hänggi and attracted a lovely double concerto from *Lutosławski and further compositions for their combined skills.
b. Langenthal, 21.v.39; st with *Boulez; prof. at Freiburg-am-Breisgau and co-cond. with *Sacher of Basle Chamber Orch.; *works include*: chamber opera *What Where* (Frankfurt, 17.v.89), *Scardanelli cycle* for flute, chamber orch., choir and tape (1975–85); *Improvisation* for oboe, harp and 12 strings (1963), Duo for violin and cello (1982).

York Georg HÖLLER   Close disciple of *Stockhausen and *Boulez, he made strenuous efforts at *Cologne and *IRCAM to make electronic music easily assimilable. His taped works – *Horizont* (1972), *Klanggitter* (1976) and *Antiphon* (1977) for string quartet and tape – had an agreeable smoothness that recalled the dimension which set his two teachers apart from their 1950s contemporaries. But it was with wholly conventional forms that Höller achieved his self-proclaimed aim of audience communication. His piano concerto (London, 3.xii.85) was a 20-minute chain of ambient music in which the piano works with the orchestra rather than against it and there are no offensive noises. There are meditative episodes at the start and towards the end and there is an improvisatory feel to some of the instrumental riffs.

In 1989 he closed the old Salle Garnier in Paris – the *Bastille was about to open – with a debut opera, *Der Meister und Margarita* (20.v.89), on a long-suppressed Russian novel by Mikhail Bulgakov. Moving between Stalin's Moscow and the Jerusalem of Jesus Christ it crossed religious disquisition with fantastic vaudeville on a grand scale presaged by *Zimmermann in *The *Soldiers*. Its 31-note basic melody was shared with two parallel works, *Schwarze Halbinsel* (1982) and *Traumspiel* for soprano, large orch., tape (after Strindberg, Metz, 18.xi.83). Höller embarked on a second opera, *Caligula*, for the Vienna State Opera and has composed *Aura* (1992) for the Chicago Symphony Orch. at the behest of Daniel Barenboim, a keen interpreter of the piano concerto. He remains nevertheless committed to electronics as an integral element of the musical future. He has composed a pleasant *Résonance* for chamber orch. and computer tape at IRCAM and in 1990 took over as director of the Cologne electronic studios. Rooted in the teachings of *Adorno, he remains touchingly loyal to 1950s *Darmstadt doctrine.

    b. Leverkusen, Germany, 11.i.44; st with B.A.*Zimmermann, *Eimert and *Boulez; worked with Stockhausen 1971–72; won *Liebermann Prize for best opera written between 1987–90; *other works: Topic* for large orch. (1967), *Fanal* for trumpet and orch. (Paris, 17.vi.91), *Pensées* for piano, large orch. and tape (1992), *Improvisation sur le nom de Pierre Boulez* for 16 instruments (Baden-Baden, 31.iii.85); *Diaphonie: hommage à Béla Bartók* for two pianos (1965/74), two piano sonatas, cello sonata.

Robin   (Greville)   HOLLOWAY

Holloway's passion was Samuel Richardson's 1740s novel, *Clarissa*, epic in both structure and tragedy as it follows an immaculate heroine driven to madness by her vicious family and the libertine Lovelace. He began the opera, without commission, in 1971 and saw it staged two decades later, with moderate success, at English National Opera, (18.v.90). The music re-imagines 18th-century manners without resorting to *neo-classical pastiche, tonally closer to *Rosenkavalier and with a *Lulu-like twist to the tale. Holloway remained at heart an antediluvian romantic whose gentilities for small orch. – *Serenata notturna* (London, 9.xii.84) – possess a timeless appeal.

    b. Leamington Spa, England, 19.x.43; lecturer at Cambridge 1975-; *works include*: concertos for horn, harp, oboe, bassoon, saxophone, viola; violin concerto (Manchester, 27.iii.92); double concerto for saxophone and clarinet (London, 20.v.88); *Clarissa Symphony* (Birmingham, 9.xii.82); symphonic poem *Seascape and Harvest* (Birm-

ingham, 29.iv.86) and the choral *Spacious Firmament* (Birmingham, 21.i.92, all cond. *Rattle); *Inquietus* for chamber orch. (London, 3.iv.87) in memory of *Pears.

Vagn HOLMBOE

Denmark's foremost composer after *Nielsen is a mainstream artist who modelled himself on Haydn and Hindemith, writing 11 symphonies and 14 string quartets in an accessible neo-classical manner. Far from being a dour northerner, Holmboe was an eclectic cosmpolitan who collected folk tunes in the Faroes and Romania, his wife's homeland, and immersed himself in medieval church music. He won international attention with the 5th symphony, performed at the 1947 *ISCM festival in Copenhagen, and received various commissions across Europe. The 7th (18.x.51) and 9th symphonies (19.xii.68) are his most intense, the 4th quartet (1952) his most intimate. His music is sometimes dark but rarely morose. As professor at the Royal Danish Conservatory (1950–65), he wielded a benevolent influence over national progress.

    b. Horsens, Jutland, 20.xii.09; married Romanian pianist Meta Graf 1931; *other major works*: three operas, *Requiem for Nietzsche* (1964), 13 chamber concertos, symphonic *Epilogue* (1962), much chamber music.

Gustav(us Theodorus von) HOLST

Was Holst more than a one-work wonder? His astrological suite, *The Planets* (London, 29.ix.18, cond. Boult), is the most widely performed piece of British music, though he never counted it among his best. Its topical bombast ('Mars, the Bringer of War' composed viii.14), astral mysticism and the timeless spiritual quest evoked by the wordless women's choir of 'Neptune' proved universally irresistible – especially on record and as advertising jingles. Of its seven movements, Holst was proudest of reflective 'Saturn, the Bringer of Old Age'.

    Nothing in his orchestral writing shared its immediacy. Much is coloured by the English folksongs he collected with *Vaughan Williams. *A Somerset Rhapsody* (1907) is polished and simplistic; *Egdon Heath* (1927, after Thomas Hardy) distils a desolate Dorset landscape into something more surreal. Applying the method to other cultures produced the orientally ridiculous *Beni Mora* (1910), fruit of a cycling holiday in Algeria.

A youthful fascination with Hinduism led to a chamber opera *Sāvitri* (5.xii.16) that served as a model for *Britten's church parables. *The Perfect Fool* (Covent Garden, 14.v.23), an unwitting *Parsifal* parody, was stupefyingly incomprehensible; its dances survive in a concert suite. The orchestral suites *St Paul's* (1913) and *Brook Green* (1913) – were written for the girls of the London school where he taught.

The only work of Planetary stature is the revolutionary *Hymn of Jesus* (25.iii.20), a departure from stuffy Anglicanism into ghostly Gregorian rhythms and ear-catching discords, more striking than anything to be heard in Elgar's oratorios. Its textures intrigued as violent a radical as Harrison Birtwistle. Britten (*War Requiem*), *Tippett and even *Birtwistle took their cue from Holst more than any other compatriot; His analytical influence was far-reaching; Elliott *Carter was one of his pupils on two teaching tours to the US.

The son of a Swedish piano teacher, Holst failed exams to music college. He learned socialism from William Morris and love from a soprano in his Hammersmith choir, Isobel Harrison, with whom he had a daughter, Imogen.
> *b*. Cheltenham, Glos., 21.ix.1874; *d*. London, 25.v.34. *other works*: ballets *The Golden Goose* and *The Morning of the Year* (1926–27), mystery play *The Coming of Christ* (1928), Japanese Suite for orch. (London, 19.x.19), *Fugal Concerto* for flute, oboe and strings (London 11.x.23), *Capriccio* for *jazzband (1932).

Imogen HOLST   Gustav's daughter and biographer, became Britten's amanuensis at Aldeburgh (1952–76), and a conductor of modest repute. Her string quartet (London, 20.v.46) is serious and lyrical, though entirely unsentimental, suggesting a strength of purpose that she subjugated willingly to male masters.
> *b*. Richmond, Surrey, 12.iv.07; *d*. Aldeburgh, 9.iii.84. *other work*: string quintet (1981).

Simon HOLT   Lyrical English composer absorbed in the Spanish emotions of Federico Garcia Lorca (1898–1936).
> *b*. Bolton, Lancs, 21.ii.58; st with Anthony Gilbert, *Henze; *works include*: *Cappricio spettrale* (1989, *Lilith, Ballad of the Black Sorrow*, (1990), *Tangra* for soprano/ ensemble (Vienna, 16.x.91); *Palace at 4 a.m.* for flute, oboe, clarinet, cello (1980), *Burlesca Oscura* for clarinet quintet (1985).

Arthur (Oscar) HONEGGER   Geographical coincidence accounts for Honegger's presence among 'Les *Six', for there was none of *Satie's wit or wickedness in him. A sober Swiss of Protestant faith his involvement with post-War Paris rebels amounted to playing viola and tambourine at a couple of Cocteau scandals. Stravinsky was his idol and *neo-classicism, combined with solid rhythms and dark colours, won him recognition with the 'dramatic oratorios', *King David* (Mézières, Switzerland, 11.vi.21) and *Joan of Arc at the Stake* (Basle, 12.v.38), both attempts at almost-theatre.

Honegger's seriousness was questioned when he wrote a pair of symphonic movements that became instant hits. *Pacific 231* (Paris, 8.v.1924), a thundering portrait of trans-American locomotion, was followed by *Rugby*, a violent sporting metaphor performed during an England-France international match. They were partly responsible for the 'machine music' of Socialist Realism and showed Honegger in wholly untypical light. He recanted with a first symphony (Boston, 13.ii.1931), written for the Boston SO jubilee and gained respect with the 2nd (Zurich, 18.v.42, cond. Sacher) a masterly response to the trauma of War – two anguished movements for strings alone with a trumpet bringing relief in the finale. The 3rd (Zurich, 17.viii.46), named 'Liturgique' because its movements mirror the Catholic Mass for the Dead, offered welcome visions of post-War tranquillity in a 'Donna nobis pacem' that culminated in birdsong. The 4th symphony, 'Deliciae Basiliensis' (Basle, 21.i.47), celebrates the city of Basle with fragments of birdsong and local tunes; the 5th symphony (1950) is stylized and weak.

Bach provided many of his best ideas. Both *King David* and the 2nd symphony end in great chorales, while the Prelude, *Arioso and Fughetta on the name of BACH* (1936) is a delightful chamber piece with a central tune recalling 'My Funny Valentine'. Honegger was openly eclectic, enjoyed jazz, and wrote 40 film scores, including music for Abel Gance's silent movie, *Napoleon* and *Les Misérables* (1934).

b. Le Havre, France (of Swiss parents), 10.iii. 1892; st with D'Indy and Widor; served Swiss army 1914; debut, Paris, 15.i.18; had son by mezzo-soprano Claire Croiza (1882–1946) before marrying pianist Andrée Vaurabourg (1894–1980); visited US 1929 and 1947, suffered heart attack there and returned an invalid; *d*. Paris, 27.xi.55. *other works*: seven operas, inc. *Antigone* (1927) and *Judith* (1925); 14 ballets; cello concerto (1934), chamber concertos, ten vocal orch. works, three string quartets, much piano music and 60 songs.
Bib: Arthur Honegger, *I am a Composer*, London, 1966.

honky-tonk Derogatory term for ill-tuned piano played in *ragtime, also for the low dives where it was played.

Lightnin' (Sam) HOPKINS Last of the country-*blues singer-guitarists.
b. Centerville, Texas, 15.iii.12; *d*. Houston, 30.i.82.

horn The outstanding 20th-century concertos were by *Strauss and *Hindemith.

Joseph HOROVITZ Mainly a film and ballet composer, Horovitz wrote his 5th string quartet (London, 9.x.1969) as a delayed response to Nazism by a near-victim. A lush chromatic opening, reminiscent of Schoenberg's *Verklärte Nacht*, is fissured by parodies of a waltz and the *Horst Wessel song before finding resolution in unintentional echos of the dying *ewig . . . ewig* of Das *Lied von der Erde*.
b. Vienna, 26.v.26, moved to London 1938; st with *Jacob and *Boulanger; *other works*: two comic operas, *The Dumb Wife* (1953) and *Gentleman's Island* (1958), ballet *Alice in Wonderland* (9.vii.53), trumpet concerto (1965), Toy Symphony (for strings and toys, 1977).

Vladimir HOROWITZ Magical pianist whose plangent tone provoked allegations that he tampered with the strings. Renowned for idiosyncratic Mozart, inimitable Skryabin and composer-endorsed Rachmaninov, he performed only at 4 o'clock on propitious afternoons.
b. Berdichev, Russia, 1.x.04; debut Kiev, 30.v.20; sent abroad with Milstein as ambassadors of Soviet culture (Horowitz returned in 1986, Milstein never); US debut with NY Philharmonic, *Beecham cond., 12.i.28; US citizen 1942; married Wanda *Toscanini 1933, one daughter; retired 1953, returned 1965, withdrew 1969, back again 1974; *d*. NY, 6.xi.89.

Karl HORWITZ One of Schoenberg's earliest pupils, his devotion to *Mahler was expressed in an orchestral song-cycle for baritone, *Vom Tode (Of Death)*. Completed on 1.x.1922 and self-published, it is modelled closely on the Resurrection Symphony and *Das Lied von der Erde*. Horwitz was among the founders of the *Donaueschingen Festival and enjoyed brief success there and at Salzburg before his untimely death.
b. Vienna, 1.i.1884; *d*. Salzburg, 18.viii.25. *other works*: Symphonic overture (1921) and string quartet.

Alan (Vaness Scott) HOVHANESS US composer of Armenian-Scottish parentage, he indulged the melismas of his paternal ancestry in a wearisome profusion of 65 symphonies and 23 concertos. Most are named after geographical locations or landscapes, *Ararat* and the like. *Talin* (1952) for viola or clarinet and string orchestra is fairly typical: a blend of routine *neoclassicism and Lebanese souk songs, pleasant enough but lacking food for thought or emotion. He joined the *environmental brigade with *And God Created Great Whales* (NY, 11.vi.76), a symphonic piece integrating underwater tape recordings of humpback leviathans.
b. Somerville, Massachusetts, 8.ii.11.

Elgar HOWARTH Member of the British *Manchester school, he became a versatile conductor of modern opera, giving premières of Ligeti's *Grand Macabre* and *Birtwistle's *Mask of Orpheus* and

Gawain. He wrote a trumpet concerto for the Swedish virtuoso Håkan Hardenberger and many transcriptions for brass band, including one of Mussorgsky's *Pictures at an Exhibition*.
    b. Cannock, Staffs, 4.xi.35; studied RNCM 1953–7; played trumpet in ROH and RPO orchs., 1963–68.

Herbert (Norman) HOWELLS Conservative choral composer, his profoundest work was the 1938 *Hymnus Paradisi*, written to overcome three years of mourning the death of meningitis of his son. In Howells' output – indeed, in the entire cadre of modern Anglican cathedral music – the *Hymnus Paradisi* stands out as an expression of deep emotion, rounded by craftsmanship and dignity. Howells was not religious in a formal sense but stood, like his friend Vaughan Williams, in awe of the church and its legacy. Apart from vocal and organ works, his music falls into the *cowpat category – fragrantly pastoral and cerebrally undemanding.
    b. Lydney, Glos, 17.x.1892; succeeded Holst as music director at St Paul's School, 1936, prof. of music, London U., 1952–62; *d*. Oxford, 24.ii.83. *other works*: Requiem (1936, partly reworked into *Hymnus Paradisi*), *Take Him Earth, for Cherishing* – motet on death of President Kennedy (1964); two piano concertos; In Gloucestershire string quartet (1923).

Leonid HRABOVSKY Ukrainian experimentalist who, depressed by official Soviet culture, gave up music in the late 1970s and became a night-watchman. He resumed in more liberal times with the chamber vocal cycle *When?* (1987) and eventually emigrated. He was one of the first Soviet *minimalists.
    b. Kiev, 28.i.35; st with *Liatoshinsky; *other works*: *The Sea* for speaker, chorus, organ and orch. (Rotterdam, 10.ix.71), symphonic poem *St John's Eve* (1976).

Jenö HUBAY Hungarian violinist of conservative tastes, he clashed with *Bartók while running the Budapest conservatory (1919–34) on reactionary lines. He wrote eight operas, four symphonies and four concertos that were propagated by his loyal pupils Szigeti, Telmanyi and Franz von Vecsey.
    b. Budapest, 15.ix.1858 and christened Eugen HUBER; st with Joachim in Berlin; formed eponymous quartet; *d*. Vienna, 12.iii. 37. *works include*: opera *Venus de Milo* (1935).

Klaus HUBER Swiss precisionist applying *Webern's rigorisms to mystical ideas from the German renaissance. His seriousness was admired in Germany, where his pupils included *Ferneyhough and the rising *Rhim.
    b. Berne, 30.xi.24; st with *Burkhard, *Blacher; prof. at Freiburg-im-Breisgau 1973-; *works include*: opera *Jot* (1973); *Tenebrae* (1970 bicentennial Beethoven prize); *James Joyce chamber music* (1967).

Nicolaus HUBER Politically conscious German, he managed to work an air-raid siren into the finale of an otherwise austere and mathematically calculated *Trio with stabpandeira* – as well as various works with leftist-revolutionary titles and themes (see: *Henze).
    b. Passau, 15.xii.39; st with *Bialas, *Nono; prof. at Essen 1974-.

Bronislaw HUBERMAN Virtuoso violinist who assembled exiled Jewish musicians from Hitler's Germany in 1936 into the Palestine Symphony Orchestra. His floridly expressive playing style offended ascetic musicians.
    b. Czestochowa, Poland, 19.xii.1882; *d*. Corsier-sur-Vevey, Switzerland, 15.vi.47.

humour Music is no laughing matter for its makers; modernists took themselves especially seriously. Some ascetics, however, allowed an occasional wintry smile. Schoenberg caricatured Stravinsky as 'der kleine Modernsky' in *Three Satires* (1925). Shostakovich wickedly sent up Soviet apparatchiks in comic instrumental obbligatos.
    Music and humour are essentially incompatible. Where good music grows with repeated hearing, jokes go stale on repetition. Past attempts at musical wit relied on absurdly wrong notes and simulated bodily noises. Modern musical humour veered subtly towards self-mockery and in-jokes. Debussy's interpolation of the *Tristan* theme in his Golliwogg's Cakewalk made a monkey of Wagner; Dohnányi's thunderous orchestral introduction to a common

nursery rhyme comments wryly on the inegalities of concerto playing. Schnittke's cadenza for conductor in the middle of his fourth symphony takes a poke at the maestro profession. The wit of Erik Satie was too painful to draw many laughs, while Cage and Feldman often mystified those they meant to amuse. Ligeti, possessed of a charming Hungarian whimsy, mocked musical exactitude in a symphonic poem for 100 metronomes and politicians' self-righteousness in Le *grand macabre. *Kagel played jokes at the audience's expense. Der *Rosenkavalier, an intentional anachronism, was the acme of 20th-century comic opera.

Engelbert HUMPERDINCK (1) Orthodox Wagnerian famed for his children's horror opera Hänsel und Gretel (Weimar, 23.xii.1893, cond. *Strauss), he invented a kind of *sprechgesang in the opera Königskinder (Royal Children, NY, 28.xii. 1910) – a serious attempt to develop the music of everyday speech. His four remaining operas were makeshift works.

b. Siegburg, nr Bonn, Germany, 1.ix.1854; d. Neustrelitz, 27.ix.21. other works: incidental music to Berlin productions of The Merchant of Venice, The Winter's Tale, Romeo and Juliet, Twelfth Night, The Tempest and Aristophanes' Lysistrata; many Lieder.
(2) British *pop singer; no relation.
b. Madras, India, 2.v.36 (as Arnold George Dorsey);

Hungary The restoration of an independent Hungary in 1918 coincided with the emergence of a composer of global significance in *Bartók, and two associated figures of national stature, *Kodály and *Dohnányi. The country's subsequent musical development was coloured, but not crushed, by political repression. Home-made fascism in the late 1930s forced Bartók into American exile. Communist tyranny prompted *Ligeti to flee west after the 1956 uprising, and *Kurtág to stay silent for many years. But the culture survived and evolved and, when the repression eased, Hungarian composers led eastern Europe out of modernist isolation. A new music studio was opened in 1970, yielding talents of the quality of Eötvös, *Marta and *Sary.

The traditions of conducting, founded by *Nikisch, continued through Fritz Reiner, Antal *Dorati, Georg Solti and Istvan Kertesz. For a nation of fewer than 15 million, Hungary's musical contribution in the 20th century is out of all proportion to its size.

Karel HUSA Czech exile in Baltimore, he persisted with *Hába's microtonality and in Music for Prague (1968) pioneered aleatoric techniques for brass and wind band. The core of Czech hymns amid a densely fragmented atonality was a rare instance of sophisticated modernism yielding a cathartic response. He won the 1969 Pulitzer Prize with his 3rd string quartet.

b. Prague, 7.viii.21; st with Talich and in Paris with Boulanger and Honegger; lecturer at Cornell University, 1954-; other works: Sinfonietta (Prague, 25.iv.47), 1st symphony (Brussels, 4.ii.54), Mosaiques for orch. (Hamburg, 7.xi.61), concerto for brass quartet and string orch. (Buffalo, 15.ii.70), An American Te Deum (Cedar Rapids, Iowa, 4.xii.76), trumpet concerto (1974).

Hymnen Electronic reprocessing of the world's national *anthems by *Stockhausen. fp: Cologne, 30.xi.67.

Ibéria 12 piano suites by Albéniz (1906–08); 2nd section of Debussy's orchestral *Images* (1908).

Jacques IBERT French composer of the old school – suave, elegant and tart as citron – Ibert is at his most seductive in the central movements of a curvaceous flute concerto (Paris, 25.ii.34) and a raunchy chamber concerto for saxophone (2.v.35). He made his name with *Escales* (6.i.24), reporting on a wartime tour of duty in the Mediterranean with the French Navy. It sounds like Debussy on vacation, though the master-*impressionist might not have stooped to the pseudo-Arabisms of its Tunis docking. Ibert's facility as a colourist was brought out to the full in *Divertissement* (30.xi.30), a suite from the Labiche farce *An Italian Straw Hat*, complete with a Johann Strauss pastiche waltz. In 1932 he beat Ravel and Milhaud in a contest to compose a Don Quixote movie score for the ageing bass Feodor Chaliapin, composing four songs before shooting was abandoned. Ibert spent much of his career in Rome as director of the Academie de France. Returning home in 1955 he ran the Paris opera house inefectually for two years. *Honegger, with whom he wrote two operas, greatly admired his style.
  b. Paris, viii.1890; *d.* there 5.ii.62. *operas and operettas include: Angélique* (1927), *Persée et Andromède* (1929), *Le roi d'Yvetot* (1930), *Bluebeard* (for radio, 1943); and, with Honegger, *L'aiglon* and *Les petites cardinal* (1937–8); five ballets; *orchestral works: The Ballad of Reading Gaol* (after Oscar Wilde, 22.x.22), concerto for cello and wind instruments (28.ii.26), *Paris* (Venice,

15.ix.32), Elizabethan suite (1944), Louisville concerto (Louisville, 17.ii.54).

I Ching Ancient Chinese short-straw game, used by *Cage in calculating *aleatory and chance music.

Toshi ICHIYANGI Japanese Cage follower.
  b. Kobe, 4.ii.33;

Abraham Zevi IDELSOHN Field researcher into the diasporan diversity of Jewish music, he unearthed direct links between Gregorian chant and Yemenite synagogal music, indicating a common source in Temple worship. His ten-volume *Thesaurus of Hebrew-Oriental Melodies* remains definitive.
  b. Filzburg nr Libau, Latvia, 14.vii.1882; st Königsberg, Berlin and Leipzig; cantor at Regensburg 1903; emigrated to South Africa, 1904; lived 1906–21 in Jerusalem, where he founded an Institute for Jewish Music; professor at Hebrew Union College, Cincinnati, 1924–34; *d.* Johannesburg, South Africa, 14.viii.38. *works include*: two string quartets and a musical play in Hebrew on the Biblical tale of Jephtha (self-published, Berlin, 1924); *writings include*: *Jewish Music in its Historical Development* (NY, 1929), *The Kol Nidrei Tune* (Cincinnati, 1932).

Les Illuminations Rimbaud settings by Britten for high voice and strings. fp: London, 30.i.40.

Images Debussy's title for two separate works: (1) six piano pieces in two sets; (2) three linked symphonic poems of which the second, *Ibéria*, has three named movements (fp: Paris, 26.i.13, cond. Pierné).

Imaginary Landscapes John *Cage, playing gramophone records at varying speeds. The first IL (1939) ran three turntables of radiophonic test-signals in one of the earliest *electronic works; the 3rd (1942) added oscillators, and a buzzer to an ensemble of six percussionists; the 5th (1952) employed 52 turntables and was probably the first taped composition in America.

imitation As man imitates God, so lesser composers have always copied their superiors. *Zemlinsky, for example, mimicked Mahler in the *Lyric Symphony and Schoenberg in the 2nd quartet, his two finest works. *Rimsky-Korsakov was the model for early Soviet composers, *Hindemith for many post-1945 Germans, *Debussy for the French. In *neo-romantic circles it was common for a composer to announce unashamedly, 'this is my Bruckner symphony', or 'listen to my Brahms quartet'.

impressionism Art movement in late-19th-century France that attached greater value to subtleties of light, colour and atmosphere than to the painting's central subject. The canvas might be blurred, giving an 'impression' of its content rather than a vivid image. In music, the term was applied to Debussy, after *Prélude à l'après midi d'un faune*, and subsequently to *Delius, *Messiaen and *Ligeti.

improvisation Until the middle of the present century, soloists were the only concert performers licensed in limited *cadenzas to make up their own music. In jazz, on the other hand, almost all music was improvised. This threw down a challenge to which few composers responded creatively. Some, following the *aleatory lead of Cage and Ligeti, offered performers specific choices within a piece of music. Others, like *Carter, tightened up their instructions to deny players any room for manoeuvre. Although a few idealists and jazz fans, like *Cardew and *Foss, left gaps in some works for players to extemporize, composers in general did not trust musicians to express their own feelings and viewed improvisation as antithetical to art. 'A musical score is written to keep the performer from playing what he already knows,' wrote Carter. Scores with improvised passages include: Berio, *Circles*, Cardew, *Solo with Accompaniment*, Donatoni, *Black and White*.

Improvisation sur le nom de *Boulez 60th birthday tribute by *Höller. fp: Baden-Baden, 31.iii.85.

In C Idea of Terry *Riley's that marked the birth of *minimalism. It involved any number of players chiming in *ad libitum* on a tiny phrase around the tone C in a simulated psychedelic trance. fp: San Francisco, 21.v.65.

In the Mists Evocative 1912 piano suite by Janáček.

In Memoriam Dylan Thomas *Stravinsky's 12-note requiem for an admired poet, scored for tenor, string quartet and trombones. fp: Hollywood, 20.ix.54.

indeterminacy Cage's term for *aleatory music.

Indian music Rabindranath *Tagore excited European imaginations with sounds of another world to win the 1913 Nobel Prize for Literature. *Zemlinsky set seven of his poems, *Janáček composed a chorus, *The Wandering Madman*; Tagore later figured as a character in Glass's opera *Satyagraha*. *Holst translated Sanskrit verses in *Hymns from the Rig Veda*, (1907) and composed his opera *Sāvitri* on an episode from the Mahabharata. *Messiaen studied Sanskrit and furnished Hindu ideas in the *Turangalîla* symphony.

The greatest single impact was made by the insistent ragas of Ravi *Shankar who, discovered by Yehudi *Menuhin and John *Coltrane, became guru in the mid-sixties to Philip *Glass and George Harrison of the *Beatles. In the psychedelic era, Indian imitations became all the rage in Western popular and art music. Few troubled to study authentic raga disciplines, entwined with Indian art and dance, that range from rhythmic cycles of three beats to 108-beat units. Once assimilated, the culture enabled initiates to improvise freely. LaMonte *Young, who established a US school of Indian music after studies with Pandit Pran

Nath, felt that his compositions existed in a state of continuous flux.

Indonesian music An inspiration to *Debussy at the 1889 Paris exhibition, the percussive potential of the gamelan orchestra drew many westerners to Bali, Java and Madura. Colin *McPhee's researches enriched the music of *Britten, *Cage and *Harrison; *Messiaen heard a gamelan at the 1931 Colonial Exhibition in Paris and decisively changed his timbre, passing on the idea to his pupils, *Boulez and *Stockhausen.

The gamelan uses two scales of five and seven notes respectively on tuned percussion instruments ranging from low drums to high chimes. A flute, two-string fiddle, zither and singers are optional extras. The leader sets a basic tune and rhythm and the rest of the village, old and young, join in with accompaniments and embellishments.

(Paul - Marie - Théodore-) Vincent D'INDY Nationalist musician of noble Catholic descent, d'Indy was the Marshal Pétain of French music. Acknowledging the weakness of France, he blamed the Jews and proclaimed a reversion to peasant values behind a shield of Wagnerian-German bombast. Although his music was not infectious, he was hugely influential.

D'Indy dominated music education, succeding his teacher César Franck as head of the Société Nationale de Musique (1890–1931) and forming a Schola Cantorum to advance the study of plainchant. He was appointed in 1892 to reform the syllabus at the Paris Conservatoire and taught there until his death; three generations of composers sat at his feet.

An enemy of *Pelléas and all things modern, he composed contrapuntally in strict sonata form tinged by romantic chromaticism. His *Symphony on a French mountain song* for piano and orchestra (Paris, 20.iii.1887) was rooted in his native locality, as was *Jour' d'été sur la montagne* (*Summer's day on the Mountain*, Paris, 18.ii.06). Much of his chamber music is pseudo-Baroque. His 5th opera and magnum opus, *La Légende de Saint-Christophe* (Paris, 9.vi.20) was reputedly antisemitic.

b. Paris, 27.iii.1851; *d.* there, 2.xii.31. *other works*: symphonies (1875, 1904, 1919),

concerto for piano, flute and string orch. (Paris, 2.iv.27), two piano trios, much vocal, keyboard and organ music, 100 opus numbers in all.

Inextinguishable Symphony Nielsen's 4th. fp: Copenhagen, 1.ii.16, cond. composer.

Intermezzo Opera by *Strauss based on a stormy episode in his marriage. fp: Dresden, 4.xi.24.

initials Users of musical *code often reverted to the simplest. The first seven letters of the alphabet correspond with notes A to G. In German the letter B denotes B-flat, H becoming B-natural. The letter S sounds like the German 'es', meaning E flat. Thus Alban Berg was able to twine his intials secretly around those of Hanna Fuchs-Robettin in the Lyric Suite and Dmitri SCHostakovich invested his 8th quartet and many other works with a personal signature.

Intimate Letters *Janáček's 2nd string quartet, addressed to his love, Kamilla Stösslová. fp: Brno, 11.ix.28.

Introitus Stravinsky memorial to the poet, T. S. Eliot. fp: Chicago, 17.iv.65.

inversion Turning inter-note intervals upside down in a *12-note work. If the original *row of notes contained a rising third, it became a falling third in the inversion.

Invisible City of Kitezh Gaudy opera by *Rimsky-Korsakov. fp: St Petersburg, 20.ii.07.

Yannis IOANNIDIS Greek *serialist, settled in Venezuela after the 1968 colonels' coup.

b. Athens, 8.vi.30; prof. at Caracas U. 1971–; *works include*: two string quartets, *Nocturno* for piano quartet.

Ionisation All-percussive piece by Varèse. fp: NY, 6.iii.33, cond. *Slonimsky.

Mikhail IPPOLITOV-IVANOV Antediluvian Russian liberal, he ran the Moscow Conservatoire through three regimes and wrote the same folkish scores for the commissars as he had done under the Tsars.

> *b.* Gatchina, Russia, 18.xi.1859; st with *Rimsky-Korsakov; dir. Moscow Conservatoire 1905–22, cond. Bolshoy Theatre 1925–35; *d.* Moscow, 29.i.35; *works include*: operas *Asya* (1900), *Treason* (1909); orch. *Caucasian Sketches* (1895/1906), symphony (1908), *Armenian Rhapsody* (1909) *On the Volga* (1910), symphonic poem *The Year 1917* (1934).

IRCAM   The *Institut de Recherche et de Coordination Acoustique/Musique* was conceived by Pierre *Boulez as a place where composers, scientists and computer experts could unlock the future of music. Opened in 1977 in an underground cavern beside the Pompidou Centre in Paris at a cost of 90 million francs, it was soon attacked for failing to produce anything of artistic worth. Boulez responded with *Répons* (1981) for musicians and 4X computer, but the mainframe was too large to be transported to concerts. Similarly, *Birtwistle's electronic music in *The Mask of Orpheus* became a rarity because of its unwieldiness and expense. In the late 1980s, IRCAM focused on the musical potential of desktop personal computers.

John (Nicholson) IRELAND   Ireland's piano concerto (London, 2.x.30) was England's answer to Rachmaninov's second. It was a perennial at London's Promenade Concerts for two decades before fading suddenly like a summer's mist. Ireland had a feel for his locality. Three *London Pieces* for solo piano have a distinct Cockney charm and his *London Overture* (1936; originally *Comedy Overture* for brass band), is a breezily grimy evocation of a much-loved city woven around the call of a bus-conductor, 'Piccadilly! Piccadilly!'

For the rest, he havered between German romanticism and French modernism, English ruralism and Celtic mysticism. His sonatas for violin (1909/17) and cello (1923) warrant an occasional hearing, as does his drawing-room ballad, 'If there were dreams to sell', a 1918 lament of a man left behind while his friends die at the front. The pre-War *Songs of a Wayfarer* cycle (1903–11) left a mark on his pupil, *Britten. He lived the blameless life of a church organist at St Luke's, Chelsea (1904–26).

> *b.* Bowdon, Cheshire, 13.viii.1879; st with Stanford; taught at RCM London 1923–39; *d.* Rock Mill, Sussex, 12.vi.62. *other works*: symphonic rhapsody *Mai-Dun* (1921), glorious *Downland Suite* (1932) for brass band, *Legend* for piano and orch. (1933), Thomas Hardy songs (1925–6), two piano trios (1906, 1917).

Isabeau   Peek-a-boo nudist opera by *Mascagni. fp: Buenos Aires, 2.vi.11.

ISCM   The International Society for Contemporary Music, founded in 1922 by

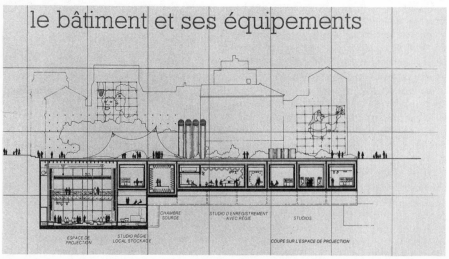

The underground world of IRCAM

the British scholar Edward J. Dent, gave annual festivals at different venues of the newest and bravest in music. Under Dent's presidency until 1938 the society was eclectic and relatively non-aligned, embracing everyone from *Walton to *Webern – who shared premières in Zurich one day of *Portsmouth Point* and *Five Pieces for Orchestra*. It was also a meeting place for opposing and like-minded musicians, an event where Schoenberg could meet Puccini and Britten could discover, in a Barcelona park, common ground with his fellow-countryman, Berkeley.

After the War, the ISCM was monopolized on one hand by the avant-garde and on the other by communist regimes, which dictated which composers would be performed. Bitter disputes ensued, in and out of lawcourts, as the ISCM became a ghetto of vested interests.

Kan ISHII Modern Japanese dance composer with nine ballets and four operas to his name.
   b. Tokyo, 30.iii.21; st with *Blacher and *Orff; president of All-Japan Chorus League, 1970-.

Maki ISHII, Kan's younger brother, also studied in Germany, where he began to experiment with *serial and *electronic theories on traditional Japanese instruments. He wrote *Sogu II* for gagaku and symphony orch. (Tokyo, 23.vi.71) and an all-percussive *Concertante* (1988).
   b. Tokyo 28.vi.36; st with *Blacher and Josef Rufer.

Isle of the Dead Rachmaninov's symphonic realization of a Böcklin poem, also set by *Reger. fp: Moscow, 1.v.09.

Italy Verdi was an impossible act to follow. The *verismists added a lurid coda to two centuries of Italian operatic glory, which ended with Puccini's death in 1924. Attempts by *Respighi, *Menotti and others to revive the corpse have signally failed, the only glimmers of potential being shown by the chamber operas of *Dallapiccola and *Berio. *Casella and *Petrassi raged against the stifling legacy of an encrusted national art and turned their attention primarily to concert music, with variable degrees of success. *Malipiero envisaged a neo-Baroque millennium rooted in the legacy of Monteverdi and Vivaldi.

Political interference in Italian music, endemic in Verdi's day, was solidified by Mussolini and endured in the coalition carve-ups of postwar Italy that ceded one city and its opera house to the communists, another to the christian democrats. The inseparability of politics and music was exemplified by the communist compositions of *Nono and Manzoni, and the craven fascism of Mascagni and *Pizzetti.

Ivan the Terrible Second of *Prokofiev's great film scores for Eisenstein, reworked into concert suite with narrator (1962) and without (London, 28.i.1991).

Charles (Edward) IVES A figure of supreme importance in America and curiosity value elsewhere, Ives was dismissing tonal music as irrelevant long before *Schoenberg embraced atonality. He was bored by conventional rhythms and straight-forward themes, preferring a clash of materials – a fascination that stemmed from hearing rival town bands play against one another in his Connecticut boyhood. In *Three Places in New England* (NY, 10.i.31, cond. Slonimsky), his undoubted masterpiece, the conductor has to beat different time with either arm as commonplace songs burst through a thicket of orchestral undergrowth. The finale, however, represents the tranquility of a Sunday morning walk in rural Massachusetts with his wife, named Harmony. Taxed with inconstancy – the central section is a shameless collage of previous scores – Ives said: 'Just like a town meeting – every man for himself!'

He discovered *microtonality when his father, a former bandleader in the American Civil War, built himself a quarter-tone piano to explore quirky sonorities. Professors at Yale struck out illicit tone-clusters and micro-tones from two youthful symphonies that ended up resembling Dvořák's *New World*. Although he graduated in music, Ives went into life insurance, believing he could help protect widows and orphans. He formed a successful agency, Merrick & Ives (part of Mutual Life), and became a millionaire, composing for pleasure and with no apparent desire for performance until heart disease and diabetes reduced him to prolonged invalidity around 1920. It was said that *Mahler studied the score of his 3rd symphony, but this has never been substantiated. Ives eventually allowed *Cowell, *Carter and other enthusiasts to clean up his illegible scores. Carter arranged premières at Columbia U. (11.v.46) of two captivating works *The Unanswered Question* and *Central Park in the Dark*, that were once played as interludes in a New York theatre around 1907. A belated première of the 3rd symphony (NY, 5.iv.46) won Ives a Pulitzer Prize. He spurned it muttering, 'prizes are for boys – I'm grown up!'

*Stokowski performed the choral 4th symphony (NY, 26.iv.65) whose percussive complexities are mitigated by a fugal third movement of unaffected beauty. His music was demonstrably ahead of its time although, truth be told, it sounds mawkily amateurish unless the performers are convinced of its greatness.

Many of his best ideas are found embryonically in vocal and chamber music, especially the ragbag of *114 Songs*, published at his own expense in 1922 and veering from tender lyricism (*Like a Sick Eagle*) to the toughest of dissonances. Several were used in ballets by George Balanchine and Jerome Robbins.

He wrote two piano sonatas. The first (1909), reminiscences of rural Connecticut, exudes the sense of a world power in the making amid the awkwardness of its structure and the gawkiness of its sounds. The 2nd, known as the *Concord Sonata* (1920), depicts the literary giants of Massachusetts – Emerson, Hawthorne, the Alcotts and Thoreau – with affection and wit, but little reverence. Fearfully hard to play, it needs a strip of wood to be placed over certain keys to produce a *cluster. The 'fate' theme of Beethoven's 5th symphony pops up here and in the knockabout *Three-Page Sonata* (1905), for no obvious reason.

These few works established Ives as father to every category of American modernism. Copland inherited his folk fancies, Varèse his percussionism, Cage his anti-traditionalism and disdain for instruments. When *Boulez came to America, Ives was the only US composer he was prepared to recognise. *Bernstein performed *The Unanswered Question* in Moscow and used it as the leitmotiv for his Harvard lectures, while *minimalists claimed descent from its simple, winding theme.

b. Danbury, Connecticut, 20.x.1874; st with Horatio Parker; became insurance broker, 1898; played organ at NY Presbyterian Church, 1899–1902; married Harmony Twichell 1908, suffered severe heart attack 1918, retired from business 1927; *d.*NY, 19.v.54. *other works*: unfinished *Universe* Symphony (1911–16), *Lincoln, The Great Commoner*, for chorus and orch. (1912), *A Holiday Symphony* in four parts, comprising: *Washington's Birthday* (1913), *Decoration Day* (1912), *4th of July* (1913), *Thanksgiving* and/or *Forefathers' Day* (1904); three Orchestral Sets; two string quartets, four violin sonatas.

Bib: Charles Ives, *Essays Before a Sonata*, NY, 1920; Vivien Perlis, *Charles Ives Remembered*, Connecticut (Yale), 1974.

Michael JACKSON Last star of black soul singing, he lightened his skin, promoted Pepsi Cola on TV, acquired the *Beatles' copyrights and in 1991 sold his future career to Sony for a reported one billion dollars. What the Japanese bought was a song-and-dance man with a surreal detachment from the rest of humanity: too rich to care about money, asexual, unattached. The youngest brother and lead belter of the Jackson Five, he was a top ten star at the age of ten and never overcame the premature exposure. His voice retained its high pitch and steadiness in maturity. His music was marketed in themed albums that took three years to produce, immaculate concepts of inhibited naughtiness. Top hits included 'Billie Jean', 'Beat It', 'I Can't Stop Loving You'.
   b. Gary, Indiana, 29.viii.58;

Gordon (Percival Septimus) JACOB Esoteric wind instruments get short shrift from composers. Jacob's *Five Pieces* for harmonica and orch. contain a Threnody of transparent beauty and a Russian Dance that sends players home smiling. He also wrote concertos for horn, bassoon and clarinet. His *Passacaglia on a well-known theme* (1931) used the nursery rhyme 'Oranges and Lemons' to such effect that critics likened it to the *Enigma Variations*.
   b. London, 5.vii.1895; st with Stanford; taught London RCM 1926–66; *d.* Saffron Walden, Essex, 8.vi.84. *other works*: two symphonies, Sinfonietta.

Max(ime) JACOB A *Satie disciple, Jacob turned to religion and became a Benedictine monk in 1929. Fifteen piano

sonatas came forth in the next 20 years, followed by eight string quartets.
   b. Bordeaux, 13.i.06; *d.* Tarn, 26.ii.77.

Frederick JACOBI A string quartet (1924) and orch. suite (1927) on American Indian themes made Jacobi the first American to be published by Vienna's prestigious *Universal Edition. His Assyrian symphony (San Francisco, 14.xi.24) was less interesting.
   b. San Francisco, 4.v.1891; *d.* NY, 24.x.52.

Otto JAEGERMEIER Composer with a premature ecological awareness, he sailed off in a huff to Madagascar when publishers refused to print his scores on handmade paper. Neighbour of *Strauss, whose symphonic poems he imitated.
   b. Munich, 29.x.1870; st Rheinberger and Thuille; emigrated to Africa winter 1905, repatriated 1932; *d.* Zurich, 22.xi.33. *works include*: four tone poems: *Psychoses* (1900), *Titanic Struggle* (1901) *The Seabed* (1902) and *Im Urwald* (*In the Primeval Forest*) (Baden-bei-Wien, 17.v.21, cond. Fried).
   Bib: M. Steinitzer, *Jägermania*, Stuttgart, 1910.

Die Jakobsleiter *Jacob's Ladder*, *Schoenberg's First War oratorio, was interrupted by army service and left unfinished at his death. fp: Vienna, 16.vi.61.

jam session Jazz musicians messing about usually in private, not without purpose but to sharpen their *improvisational responses.

Leoš JANÁČEK A phenomenon without parallel in the history of music. Dismissed as a country bumpkin until past

retirement age, he was triply rejuvenated by late recognition, an illicit love and the rebirth of Czech nationhood.

His are the only non-Italian operas in which dialogue is set to music without a hint of artifice. Janáček spent his spare time tracing the musical cadences of everyday speech, notating as precisely as he could the conversations he heard while shopping in the marketplace or drinking in a tavern. The commonplace remarks of ordinary people, rich in platitudes, repetitions and hesitations, produced an overwhelming sensation when applied to real-life tragedies in opera – a genuine *verismo that dissolved audiences and musicians alike in unforced tears.

Since his language was Czech, it took the greater part of the century for the world to appreciate the extent of his achievement. Several operas were sung in Max *Brod's translation in Weimar Germany and *Jenůfa was staged at the Met in German in 1924, but 67 years elapsed before *Katya Kabanova was seen in New York and Paris and Janáček's stature was confirmed as one of the century's handful of operatic geniuses. London was the source of this recognition, staging important productions from 1951 on under *Kubelik and Charles Mackerras.

The orphaned tenth child of a village schoolmaster in eastern Moravia, he was born a couple of miles up the road from Sigmund Freud and was sent to board at a monastery school in the provincial capital, Brno. In his cantata Amarus (Bitterness;

1897–1906), the work in which Janáček parted from *Dvořák's folksiness, the hero is a lonely foundling brought up by monks. Asked on his 70th birthday for a recollection of childhood, he composed the sour-toned Mládí (Youth, Brno, 21.x.24) for wind sextet.

After studies in Prague, Leipzig and Vienna, he returned to Brno as a music teacher, married a 15-year-old girl of Germanic stock and lived unhappily ever after. Both their children died prematurely. Apart from holidays in his home village and brief visits to Prague, he hardly ever left the market town in which his art was rooted.

In 1904, just before his 50th birthday, Brno provided his first operatic staging, an epic titled Jeji pastorkyra (Her foster-daughter, but better known by the name of its heroine, Jenůfa). Completed while his only daughter, Olga, lay dying of typhoid in the next room – he assiduously notated her death-sigh – Jenůfa recounted the dilemma of a religious functionary, the Kostelnička, who snatches and kills a baby to preserve her adopted daughter's marital prospects. The music as she takes the child is among the most visceral in operatic history.

Due to regional and personal animosities, the opera was spurned by the National Theatre in Prague for another 12 years, and accepted only after extensive revision by its chief conductor, *Kovařovic. The cosmopolitan Brod was transfixed by the opera and aroused Austro-German attention; the Brno-born soprano Maria Jeritza (1887–1982) made her name in the title role in Vienna and New York. Janáček, revived by success and his secret love for a young Jewish housewife, Kamilla Stösslova, began composing feverishly. No musician has written so much, so late and of such astonishingly high quality. There is nothing old-mannish about his music, no hint of nostalgia or compromise.

His ensuing operas – with the exception of The Excursions of Mr Brouček (Prague, 23.iv.20), a peculiar time-warp space comedy – have heroines modelled on Kamilla.

In *Katya Kabanova (Brno, 23.xi.21), he sublimated Kamilla's predicament in the story of a young wife's desire for a student visitor. Katya's descent into madness is unforgettably harrowing and the overture alone is enough to induce tears. *The Diary of One who Disappeared* (Brno, 18.iv.21) is infused by erotic desire and a sympathy for tormented lovers. Written for tenor, soprano, three women's voices and piano, it was posthumously orchestrated by his former copyist, Vaclas Sedlaček (Plzen, 26.vi.43), as a half-hour chamber opera.

The farmyard fable *Cunning Little Vixen* (Brno, 6.xi.24) is an anthropomorphic comedy for all ages about growing up and growing old, with a flouncing little feminine teaser in the title-role. In the macabre *Makropoulos Case* (Brno, 18.xii.26) the 339-year-old, sexually alluring Elena fends off young suitors in a comic reversal of the Janáček-Kamilla affair. Her soaring vocal lines parody the lubricity of *Strauss's vapid leading ladies. Janáček's sombre last opera, *From the House of the Dead* (Brno, 12.iv.30), based on Dostoyevsky's prison diaries, underlines his strong Slavonic orientation but lacks the drama and erotomania of his strongest works.

In contrast to Dvořák who Germanized his folk heritage for external consumption, Janáček refused to soften his gritty Moravian modes. His raw originality offended westerners like the critic Ernest Newman, who called *Jenůfa* amateurish, but Janáček's integrity was immovable and he was gratified at the 1925 *ISCM in Venice when *Schoenberg, *Schreker and fellow-modernists greeted him, a retired country schoolmaster, with collegial respect. His longest trip abroad was a 1926 visit to London for a concert of his chamber music attended by the Czech ambassador, Jan Masaryk, son of the nation's founder-president, who on one occasion shared his opera box in Prague with the delighted old composer.

Apart from his innovations in the music of speech, Janáček used rhythm with great ingenuity, inventing contradictory beats that pull the ear in opposing directions. The blazing first bars of *The Makropoulos Case* and the *Glagolitic Mass* (Brno, 5.xii.27) are pounded out by brass chorales that return with fragments of leitmotiv to tauten the unfolding theme.

In the years between *Jenůfa*'s première and its acclaim, Janáček toyed with a one-act opera, *Fate (Osud)* (Brno, 25.x.58), but was consumed with a frustration that constrained his output. This dark and lonely period yielded fine instrumental works. *Fairy Tale* (Brno, 13.iii.10) uses the cello as a human voice to relate a tender love story against a pianistic backdrop. The piano suites, *On an overgrown path* (1901–11) and *In the mists* (1912) are magically descriptive, brimming with impotent rage. The sonata *Street Scene* (1.x.05) reports with rising fury the death of a Czech worker killed during a nationalist rally in Brno. Janáček was gravely shaken by the event and, just before the performance, burned the third movement; he later drowned the other two in the Vlatava River but the pianist saved copies. The 3rd sonata for violin and piano – its predecessors were destroyed – went through four revisions during the First War and early independence years, balancing fear against hope in a composition of radiant warmth and stubborn non-conformity.

His two string quartets are compelling and tough to play. Both stemmed from his autumnal love. The *Kreutzer Sonata* (Prague, 17.x.24), took its title not from Beethoven (whom Janáček despised) but from Tolstoy's novella of marital misery and sexual jealousy. Its clashes of themes are suspended by sullen instants of eerie serenity, played perilously close to the bridge of the violins. *Intimate Letters*, the 2nd quartet (Brno, 11.xi.28), is a tapestry of 600 notes to Kamilla, embracing a variety of emotions yet structured so tautly that it might have been written by a dispassionate third party. Janáček knew that, without discipline, great love produces weak art.

His orchestral music includes the *Dunja* (Danube) Symphony, a portrait of riverside Bratislava which uses the voice as a sensual wordless instrument in an audible resemblance of *Katya*. *Taras Bulba* (Brno, 9.x.21), a tone poem about a Cossack revolutionary, expressed joy at Czech independence. In the *Sinfonietta* (Prague, 29.vi.26), a huge brass chorale signals the liberation of Brno from cultural oppression. Both metrically and tonally – pentatonically –

it is advanced and innovative, rude Czech rhythms overcoming smooth Austrian civilities with a battery of virtuosic brass. He would have written more but, while searching for Kamilla's lost son in the Hukvaldy woods, he caught cold and died at 74 of pneumonia. She was consumed by cancer six years later.

b.Hukvaldy, Moravia, 3.vii.1854; st with Pavel Krizkovsky in Brno and Franz Krenn in Vienna; founded organ school and conservatory in Brno; married Zdenka Schulzova 1881, met Kamilla Stösslova 1917; d. in hospital at Ostrava, 12.viii.28. *other works*: early operas, *Sarka* (Brno, 11.xi.25) and *Beginning of a Romance* (Brno, 10.ii.1894), *Elegy on the death of Olga* (in Russian, 1904), incidental music for Gerhardt Hauptmann's play *Schluck und Jau* (the last music he wrote; Prague, 13.ix.79); Capriccio for piano, chamber orch., sketches for a violin concerto (realization performed Brno, 29.ix.88).
Bib: B. Stedron, *Leoš Janáček, Letters and Reminiscences*, Prague, 1955.

Japan While other countries underwent westernization without embracing alien culture, Japan evinced an vast appetite for European art music which it imported at great expense and on a massive scale. *Suzuki taught infants to play it by rote. Early composers like *Yamada imitated symphonic poems. From the 1950s, influenced by *Messiaen and *Cage, younger artists began blending techniques and instruments from both cultures. The films of Akira Kurosawa carried music by *Takemitsu, the first Japanese to win a Western following.

By a reverse process, Japanese music and drama attracted Western admirers. Britten drew his second operatic breath from watching Noh plays and Stockhausen borrowed their stylized ceremonies for the *Licht* cycle and much else. Messiaen composed 7 *haïkaï*.

Philipp JARNACH *Busoni's pupil rendered vital service to posterity by completing his final opera, *Doktor Faust*. His inconclusive ending has been challenged by scholars and repaired by Antony Beaumont with lost sketches in 1985. But Jarnach made the best of the script at his disposal and kept the opera alive as a 20th-

century masterpiece. His own works were well-made but of little consequence.
b. Noisy, France, 26.vii.1892; prof. at Cologne 1927–49; d. Bornsen, Germany, 17.xii.82. orch. *works include*: *Winterbilder* (1915), *Sinfonia brevis* (1923).

Arne JÄRNEFELT Sibelius' brother-in-law wrote two pieces for small orchestra – *Praeludium* and *Berceuse* – that caught on like wildfire. His symphonic epics in the national style, however, never left their native land. He was conductor of the Royal Stockholm Opera, 1907–32, and Helsinki Opera, 1932–36.
b. Vyborg, Finland, 14.viii.1869; d. Stockholm, 23.vi.58.

Maurice JARRE Played with *Boulez in the Renaud-Barrault theatre pit before writing Oscar-winning scores for *Lawrence of Arabia* and *Doctor Zhivago*.
b. Lyons, 13.ix.24; orch. *works*: *Passacaille*, in memory of *Honegger (Strasbourg, 15.vi.56), *Mobiles* for violin and orch. (Strasbourg, 20.vi.61).

Keith JARRETT Jazz pianist and composer who drifted through Miles *Davis' 'free jazz' phase to a spaced-out New Age minimalism that provided excellent aural wallpaper. He also plays Bach and mystical works by Gurdjieff, humming aloud in concert like Glenn *Gould.
b. Allentown, Pennsylvania, 8.v.45;

Neeme JÄRVI Estonian conductor with astonishingly large recorded repertory, he was responsible for the promotion of *Pärt and the rediscovery of *Tubin.
b. Tallinn, Estonia, 7.vi.37; chief cond. Estonian Radio and TV 1963–80, when he emigrated; music dir. Scottish National Orch. 1984–87, Detroit SO 1988–.

Maurice JAUBERT Killed during the 1940 German invasion, he was the leading film composer in France, scoring for Jean Vigo, René Clair and Marcel Carné's classic *Le jour se lève* (*Daybreak*). He also wrote music for a Georges Simenon play, and a *Suite française* premièred in St Louis (10.xi.33).
b. Nice, 3.i.1900; wounded at Azérailles, d. Baccarat, 19.vi.40.

jazz The music of urban black Americans acquired its instrumentation in the first decade of this century and its name in the second. Its heyday, the so-called *jazz age, was between the two wars, when the middle classes danced to hot and heady rhythms in faintly naughty venues. The impact of jazz was universal, its influence on art music was profound and its decline was prolonged and apparently irreversible. In many ways, the crisis in jazz mirrored the communicative breakdown in concert music.

The origins of jazz are obscure and multifarious: slave-plantation songs, 'field hollers', West African drumming, gospel singing and a distinctive and still-undefined soundworld called *blues, latterly recognized as an art separate and distinct from mainstream jazz. Blues became the main tributary of *pop music, while jazz carried weight with serious composers.

Blacks and their music began to impinge on white commercial consciousness in the 1890s with a shortlived *ragtime craze centred on ill-tuned pianos played intentionally off the beat. Two of its stars, Jelly Roll *Morton and 'King' *Oliver, moved on into the brass-led Dixieland or New Orleans style that assumed inter-war dominance. The front line, providing melody, consisted of cornet, clarinet, slide-trombone and saxophone. The rhythmic rearguard was made up of a combination of piano, banjo, drums, sousaphone, tuba and double-bass. The bands comprised anything between ten and twenty players. The lead trumpeter was often a charismatic figure whose unimpeachable dignity offset the flagrant sensuality of the music. Louis *Armstrong and Duke *Ellington looked and sounded like diplomatic emissaries for a people and its culture.

The term jazz was reputedly coined in a San Francisco newspaper column in 1913; four years later it appeared on a record label in the title 'Dixieland Jass One-Step'. The word had no intrinsic meaning beyond an implicit suggestiveness of forbidden sexual liaisons.

The vitality of jazz resided less in tunefulness than in irresistible dance rhythms and the improvisatory character of the music. Most jazzmen were musically illiterate. They played from memory and inspiration. To northerners, taught to slave over music, their freedom was enviable and the spontaneity of their music-making had an instinctual flair long absent from sophisticated art. Each performance was new and fresh.

Emerging from New Orleans, additional genres flourished in the 1920s bootlegger era. Bix *Beiderbecke led smoky Chicago jazz; Count *Basie and Bennie Moten formed Kansas City style; Paul Whiteman, the first of many white interlopers, paraded a 'symphonic jazz' that gave *Gershwin his break. Club jazz cracked up under the dual pressures of Depression and police clean-ups, throwing musicians on to the street and driving Dixie and its progeny into desuetude. A tamer kind of *swing prevailed in the 1930s.

The Second War livened up the scene with *bebop rhythms. Post-1945 New York saw a second flowering in the varied talents of Charlie *Parker, Dizzie Gillespie and the *Modern Jazz Quartet. Dissonances were endemic and experimentation rife but drugs took a heavy toll and the hand of McCarthyism crushed the life out of US art. *Cool jazz in the 1950s focused on clarity. Cuban *salsa, eastern ragas and *electronic devices were desperately adopted as additional sources. Miles *Davis and John *Coltrane advocated a '*free jazz' of untrammelled sonorities. By the mid-1970s it became apparent that jazz had run into a cul-de-sac and, like art music, saw no way out. Its fans became faddists and grew fewer by the year. Great personalities died and were not replaced. Urban black talent turned to the easy money of rock music and the facile rhythms of *rap. The crisis seemed insoluble.

European jazz was nurtured in Paris, particularly by Django Reinhardt and Stéphane Grappelli at the Hot Club de France, and spread like wild-fire across the continent. A jazz textbook was published in Czech (E. F. Burian, 1928) before any work appeared in English. In Hitler's Germany, Stalin's Russia and communist-ruled eastern Europe, jazz belonged to the political undergound. In the Czech novels of Milan Kundera and Josef Skvorecky, it amounts to a vibrant metaphor for individual freedom.

Eminent composers noted the existence

of jazz from the dawn of the century. *Mahler dismissed ragtime in a 1909 interview as 'crude and unoriginal'; *Debussy used it in Golliwogg's Cakewalk to parody *Tristanism; Ives wrote a couple of rags. It was not until mid-War, however, that jazz began to penetrate concert music. Parisian bands, reinforced by the arrival of US troops, intrigued *Ravel though he made no compositional use of *blues until the violin sonata and piano concertos of the following decade. *Milhaud visited Harlem hotspots on his way home from Brazil in 1918, combining the feral experience of Latin jazz with northern urbanities in La *Création du Monde, and providing a foil for his friends in Les *Six.

Between the wars, Paris was the European capital of jazz and resident composers like *Martinů (Le jazz) and *Honegger (Concertino) were open fans. *Satie and *Stravinsky wrote *ragtime movements in, respectively, *Parade and A *Soldier's Tale; the Russian flirted through the 1920s with jazz rhythms but, when he wrote the *Ebony Concerto for Woody Herman in 1945 deliberately emasculated the jazz band by removing its 'swing' mechanism.

The response in Weimar Germany was no less excited. A curiosity in all things American prompted *Hindemith and *Krenek to dabble in jazz, the former trying out dance rhythms in his *Kammermusik I (1922), the latter sweeping the boards with the jazz-opera, *Jonny spielt auf. Kurt *Weill was converted somewhat later, though his use of jazz in *Mahagonny and The *Threepenny Opera was the most sophisticated yet. The craze even penetrated the austere Schoenberg circle, *Berg flicking eclectic jazz passages into the *12-note scores of *Lulu and Der Wein (1929).

US composers, in retrospect, were slow off the mark. Gershwin's *Rhapsody in Blue did not arrive until 1924, when it became the first jazz-based concert work to attain repertoire status, while neither *Copland's piano concerto with its Dixieland pulsation nor *Carpenter's jazz ballets found much of a foreign audience. It was Americans, however, who provided the most durable fusion. *Porgy and Bess was a jazz opera in substance as well as name and the musicals and symphonies of Leonard *Bernstein assimilated jazz culture with a panache that Europeans could merely envy.

Although jazz went through an abstract phase after the war, it was disdained by the European *avant-garde and the two musics drifted apart. *Schuller and *Foss sought a reconciliation, *Liebermann and *Penderecki composed jazz episodes, but there was no real resumption of relations until the 1980s when *minimalism broadened the base and expectations of the traditional concert audience and individuals like *Gulda, *Jarrett, *Rattle, Nigel Kennedy and the Labèque sisters performed jazz on equal terms with Western classical music.

Viewed across the century, both forms have left lasting marks on one another. Jazz turned symphonic in the works of Duke Ellington and his imitators. Technical skills improved in both sectors and an increasing number of performing musicians were able and willing to cross the invisible barrier. Even the ascetic *Boulez and *Stockhausen composed for typical jazz instruments such as tenor sax and vibraphone, and the improvisatory freedoms of the jazz club found their way into *aleatory compositions. Once the initial fascination wore off, the two musics achieved an informal co-habitation with prospects of further procreation.

jazz age   Term defining the inter-war era, especially in Paris and Berlin.

jazzband   Combo used by, among others, *Liebermann in concerto for jazzband and orchestra (1954) and *Holst in concertino (1932–68).

The Jazz Singer   The first sound movie, starring Al Jolson. fp: NY, 6.x.27.

Jeanne d'Arc au Bûcher   (*Joan of Arc at the Stake*) Dramatic oratorio by Honegger. fp: Basle, 12.v.38.

Hans JELINEK   Apostle of Schoenberg's 12-tone method, Jelinek played piano in Vienna cafés and wrote nothing during the Nazi era. His major work is a set of nine linked chamber pieces entitled *Zwölftonwerk* (1949). Less severe works

include a *Sinfonia ritmica* for jazz band and orchestra (Vienna, 14.iiii.31) and an operetta, *Bubi Caligula* (1947).
b. Vienna, 5.xii.01; *d*. there 27.i.69.

Zoltán JENEY The first crack in communist control allowed a new music studio to be opened in Budapest in 1970. Jeney was its first activist to catch the ear with flagrant imitations of western avant-gardism, using *Reichian repetitions in *Four Pitches* (1972), a *Stockhausen-like meditation in *OM* (1979) for two electric organs and pure *musique concrète in *For glass and metal* (1979). *Endgame* for solo piano consists of a *ffff* chord sustained for a long time, followed by a succession of plinks. More substantial were the orchestral *Alef – hommage à *Schoenberg* (1972) on a phrase from the Viennese master's *Five Orchestral Pieces* and *Laude* for large orchestra, which reorders the materials in the adagio of *Mahler's tenth. Jeney's eclecticism was outstripped by his studio colleagues *Márta and *Sáry.
b. Szolnok, Hungary, 4.iii.43; *st*. with Farkas, *Petrassi; *other works*: *Quemadmodum* for string orch. (1975).

Jenůfa (or: Her Foster-child) A church dignitary murders her foster-daughter's

Jenůfa

illegitimate baby to save her marital prospects. *Janáček's 3rd opera, written as his own daughter lay dying, presents in music of throat-catching immediacy the tragedy of two honest women overcome by maternal love. fp: Brno, 21.i.04.

Jeremiah *Bernstein's 1st symphony, with mezzo-soprano vocal finale. fp: Pittsburgh, 28.i.44.

Jesus Christ Superstar *Lloyd Webber's first smash-hit musical. fp: NY, x.71.

Jeux de Cartes Card-sharpers' ballet by Stravinsky. fp: NY, 27.iv.37.

Jeune France – See Young France.

Jeux Debussy's ballet for Nijinsky. fp: Paris, 13.v.13.

Jingle Short piece of music written for advertising film. At times, an existing piece of art music would be exploited to conjure nostalgia or manliness, Dvořák's New World theme covering home-made bread and Orff's *Carmina Burana* serving aftershave.

Karel (Boleslav) JIRAK Czech romantic, transplanted to Chicago.
b. Prague, 28.i.1891; st with *Novák, *Foerster; head of music, Czech Radio 1930–45; left 1947; *d*. Chicago, 30.i.72. *works include*: opera, *A Woman and God* (Brno, 10.iii.28), six symphonies, the 5th winning Edinburgh Festival prize in 1951; seven string quartets.

Jitterbug A lively 1930s dance, the name denoting sexual excitation.

Jive A derivative of *jitterbug used to describe prehensile forms of *rock dancing.

Job Masque for dancing by *Vaughan Williams. fp: London, 5.vii.31.

Robert Sherlaw JOHNSON British *Messiaenist whose output includes three piano sonatas (1963–76) and liturgical music in the Frenchman's footsteps.
b. Sunderland, NE England, 21.v.32; *other work*: Green Whispers of Gold for voice, tape and piano (1971).

Ben(jamin Burwell) JOHNSTON *Microtonal American who, steered by *Ives, *Partch and *Cage, developed a striking voice in the 2nd string quartet (1964) and, delightfully, in a contrapuntal quartet transcription of the hymn *Amazing Grace* (1973) that he blended surreptitiously with other folklorisms. He believed that listeners would only warm to fractured notes if they were presented tunefully. He became a Roman Catholic in 1970 and wrote devotional songs for the *Swingle Swingers.

b. Macon, Georgia, 15.iii.26; taught U. of Illinois, 1951– ; *other works*: opera *Carmilla* (1970), *Sonnets of Desolation* (1982), *The Demon's Lover's Doubles* for trumpet and microtonal piano (1985).

Betsy JOLAS Of literary parentage – her father published the first chapters of *Finnegans Wake* – she studied with *Milhaud and *Messiaen before accepting, like many Parisian composers, *Boulez writ. She ran new music output on French radio for 15 years and in 1970 replaced *Messiaen at the Conservatoire.

b. Paris, 5.viii.26; *works*: chamber opera *The Cyclop* (1986); orch. *Tales of a Summer Sea* (1977), piano concerto *Stances* (1978), *Trois rencontres* for string trio and orch. (1973).

André JOLIVET French anthology filler, rarely performed or recorded on his own merit. He wrote for neglected instruments – the first concerto for *ondes martenot (Vienna, 23.iv.48) and two for trumpet. He endowed the flute with an overplayed 1949 concerto and the hellenic lament, *Chant de Linos* (Paris, 1.vi.45). A penchant for rhythm, awoken by *Varèse, was demonstrated in a 1937 concert suite for flute and percussion. As a youth he joined *Messiaen and *Daniel-Lesur in a group, La Spirale, aimed at revitalizing chamber music. It turned inwards and became Jeune France, devoted to forming a national style free of 'impersonal' modernism.

Jolivet held key positions in Paris as music director of the Comédie Française (1943–59) and the Concerts Lamoureux (1963–68). He later experimented with serialism and electronics, without manifesting a striking individuality.

b. Paris, 8.viii.05; *d.* there 20.xii.74. *other works*: opera, *Le miracle de la femme laide* (1947); incidental music for classic French plays; three ballets; three symphonies; concertos and solo pieces for most instruments. The Sérénade for wind quintet with principal

oboe (1945) is astringently reflective and interesting to play.

Daniel JONES Schoolmate of the poet Dylan Thomas and composer of incidental music to his radio play, *Under Milk Wood*, Jones composed two operas, 12 symphonies and some appealing string quartets. His music is mellifluous and traditional; when he attempted a mathematical system of 'complex metres' it did not affect his Welsh lyricism. Outside the principality, he is almost unknown.

b. Pembroke, Wales, 7.xii.12; st in London with Henry Wood (cond.) and Aubrey Brain (horn), joined intelligence corps during War, edited Dylan Thomas' collected poems (1971); *other works*: *Capriccio* for flute, harp and strings (1965), violin concerto (1966), sonata for four trombones (1955).

Quincy JONES Jazz trumpeter and composer, mastermind of rock phenomena. He composed a Count *Basie LP in 1958, directed *Sinatra concerts, produced hit albums for Roberta Flack, Aretha Franklin, Ray Charles and invented the Michael *Jackson sound. In addition, he wrote sweaty film scores for *The Pawnbroker* (1965), *In the Heat of the Night* (1967), *The Getaway* (1972) and Bill Cosby's TV shows. His numbers included 'Summer in the City' (1973) but his chief contribution was as a conceptualist who could bridge the gulf between streetsounds and commercial music.

b. Chicago, 14.iii.33;

Joseph JONGEN The Belgian cosmopolit spent time in most European capitals and followed every style from romanticism to atonality in 241 works, of which he withdrew 104 at a final reckoning. His late-romantic *Symphonie concertante* for organ and orchestra (1926) has been widely recorded. His *Concert à cinq* (1923) is *Debussy by another name.

b. Liège, 14.xii.1873; dir. Brussels conservatoire 1925–39; *d.* Sart-lez-Spa, 12.vii.53.

Léon JONGEN Joseph's younger brother was conductor at the French opera house in Hanoi before succeeding Joseph as director of the Brussels Conservatoire (1939–49). At the age of 79 he wrote a violin concerto that became a compulsory test-piece at the Queen Elisabeth inter-

national competition. He travelled further than any of his music, which includes a picture-postcard orchestral suite called *Malaise (Malaysia, 1935).*
b. Liège, 2.iii.1884; *d.* Brussels, 18.xi.69.

Jonny spielt auf (Jonny strikes up) Jazz opera by Krenek, a hit between the wars but now sounding as dated as *The *Jazz Singer.* Its closing image of a black jazz fiddler sitting atop the world was used in Nazi propaganda as a dire portent of Aryan decline. fp: Leipzig, 10.ii.27.

Janis JOPLIN Self-destructive queen bee of white *blues, she fuelled sensationally vibrant performances with a cortège of female lovers and a narcotic addition, which killed her and made her a movie legend (Bette Midler starred in story of her life, 1979).
b. Port Arthur, Texas, 19.i.43; *d.* Hollywood, 4.x.70.

Scott JOPLIN Father of *ragtime, his *Maple Leaf Rag* of 1899, named after the Missouri club he played in, epitomized the entire genre. He followed up with a *Ragtime Dance* ballet which flopped in 1902 and cost him the publisher's confidence. An opera, *The Guest of Honour,* never saw print. His marriage failed, he moved to New York and worked on another opera, *Treemonisha.* He called a public rehearsal in 1915 but was in the tertiary stage of syphilis, on the verge of insanity, incarceration and death. Half a century later, a quickening of interest in ragtime saw *Treemonisha* staged in Atlanta (28.i.72) and made a hit of 'The Entertainer Rag', the theme of Paul Newman-Robert Redford's 1974 movie, *The Sting.* He was awarded a posthumous Pulitzer Prize.
b. Texarkana, Texas, 24.xi.1868; *d.* Manhattan State Hospital, NY, 1.iv.17.

Mihail JORA One-legged Romanian composer of *Moldavian Landscapes* orch. suite, (1924); also four ballets, a symphony and a ballad for baritone and orch. During the operation to amputate his leg without anaesthetic in the First War, *Enescu delayed the start of a Bucharest concert until news arrived of his survival.
b. Roman, 14.viii.1891; st with Reger; *d.* Bucharest, 10.v.71.

Wilfred JOSEPHS Film and TV composer with subsidiary line in two symphonies. His opera *Rebecca* (1983) was staged at Leeds and his ballet *Cyrano* at Covent Garden (1991). A 1963 Kaddish-Requiem for Holocaust victims was well received but his greatest success was with scores for UK television epics *I Claudius* and *The World at War.*
b. Newcastle upon Tyne, 24.vii.27;

Josephslegende (The Legend of Joseph) One-act ballet by Richard *Strauss for *Diaghilev, with scenario by Hofmannsthal and Count Harry Kessler. It flopped in pre-war Paris but contains sumptuous music. fp: 14.ii.14.

John JOUBERT South African-born academic composer.
b. Cape Town, 20.iii.27; taught at Birmingham U. 1962– ; *works include*: seven operas, two symphonies, bassoon concerto.

James Joyce The music of *Ulysses,* riddled with musical allusions and melodious wordplay, attracted composers almost immediately. An Irish critic, Herbert Hughes, assembled 18 early settings in 'The Joyce Book' (1933) and Samuel *Barber scored a sensation soon after with Three Songs (1936). The Italians *Dallapiccola *(Tre poemi)* and *Berio *(Ommagio a Joyce, Chamber Music, Epiphanie)* canonized Joyce for the *avant garde, neomodernists reclaimed him in Pulitzer-winning settings by Stephen *Albert. Others set off by *Ulysses* include: Bax, Bliss, Cage, Hopkins, Martino, Sessions and the French jazz writer André Hodeir.

Juilliard School NY school of music, founded 1924 with $20m left by cotton merchant; run by *Schuman 1945–62; famed for violin alumni.

Julietta Martinů's dreamy opera. fp: Prague, 16.iii.38.

Paul (Pavel) JUON Russian refugee teaching in Berlin until re-exiled by Hitler. His four romantic symphonies and concertos have fallen into disuse, but a delicate *Berceuse* for violin and piano survives as a recital encore.
b. Moscow, 23.ii.1872; st with Taneyev, Arensky; *d.* Vevey, Switzerland, 21.viii.40. *other works*: three string concertos.

Dmitri KABALEVSKY Amid the welter of worthless music provoked by Stalin's second reign of terror, Kabalevsky's cello concerto (Moscow, 12.v.49) was a rare exception of naïve hummability and emotional substance. When he attempted a more sophisticated 2nd concerto in 1955, his style came unstuck. He stood out as a figurehead of Soviet musical education.
  b. St Petersburg, 30.xii.04; st with *Miaskovsky; taught Moscow Conservatoire 1932–87, president of International Society of Music Education, 1969; *d.* Moscow, 14.ii.87. *works include: Colas Breugnon* (Leningrad, 22.i.38), after Romain Rolland's novel, and four other operas; four symphonies, three piano concertos (the last premièred by Vladimir Ashkenazy, Moscow, 1.ii.53), violin concerto (29.x.48), Requiem (1963), oratorio, *A Letter to the 30th century* (1970), and much film music.

Miloslav KABELÁČ A free mind that ranged over all forms of music from Gregorian chant to electro-acoustics, Kabeláč was banned in his native Czechoslovakia and smuggled his scores abroad. He wrote eight symphonies of diverse style and instrumentation, the last two concluding in Christian declamations. Ten years after his death, he was ceremoniously restored to grace with the Prague Spring première of *The Fateful Drama of Man* (21.v.90) for trumpet, percussion, piano and reciter, quoting Comenius' dictum, 'Return to thine heart'.
  b. Prague, 1.viii.08; worked at Czech Radio 1932–41 and 1945–55, taught composition at Prague conservatory 1958–62 and electronic music at Plzen 1968–70; *d.* Prague, 17.ix.79.

other works: Morvian lullabies (1951), *Eufemias mysterion (The Mystery of Silence)* (1964), both for soprano and chamber orch., eight Ricercari for percussionists (1967).

Kaddish Hebrew-Aramaic memorial prayer for the dead, title of *Bernstein's 3rd symphony, dedicated to John F. Kennedy (fp: Tel Aviv, Israel, 9.xii.63). There is no traditional tune to the prayer, whose text is quoted in many Holocaust commemorative compositions.

Pal KADOSA Pupil of *Kodály and admirer of *Bartók, Kadosa sustained their traditions in eight symphonies and three string quartets. He included *12-tone passages without loss of vitality or wit.
  b. Leva (now Levice, Slovakia), 6.ix.03; taught Budapest Academy of Music 1945–83; *d.* Budapest, 30.iii.83. *other works:* four piano concertos, four piano sonatas.

Mauricio KAGEL So much of Kagel's music is intentionally absurd that it is hard to know when to take him seriously. Certainly not in the 1960s stage pieces where actors meander around making meaningless noises, nor in a spate of films that are edited on musical techniques of variation, repetition and development but lack visual stimulus. *Repertoire*, a 1969 TV opera, has a man playing peek-a-boo with a screen. Its noises and atmosphere are less alarming than *Ligeti's in *Aventures* and the jokes quickly wear thin. *Sur Scène* (1960) is a shambolic lecture on contemporary music given against a backdrop of passing players and taped interruptions. In all of his music, Kagel plays games to which he alone knows the rules.

His antecedents are *Dada, Satie, *Cage and Samuel Beckett and his music is redeemed from mere experimentalism by a surprising melodiousness. The *Opus posthumum* for piano trio (Cologne, 5.iv.86) could almost be mistaken for *Schnittke were it not for a self-eulogizing title and an odd determination to stick to deadly low notes. The music was recycled from a theatrical epic about the devil, *Oral Treason* (1983), for three actors and seven instruments, perhaps the most sophisticated of his stage creations. One of his more obvious jokes is *Solo for Conductor*.

Argentine-Jewish by birth, Kagel was drawn to Cologne's *electronic studio in 1957 and stayed on as resident avantgardist and music professor. For the bicentenary of local hero Beethoven, he made a movie *Ludwig Van* (1972) with a score of optional instrumentation and duration. He has also written an unsynchronized score for Luis Bunuel's surreal film, *Un Chien Andalou*.

b. Buenos Aires, 24.xii.31; st with *Paz; *other works*: *Music for renaissance instruments* (1966), *Staatstheater* in nine scenes (1971), *2-man orchestra* (1973), *Kantrimusik* (1975), *Aus Deutschland* (lieder-opera, 27 scenes, 1981), *Rrrrrr.* (1982), *St. -Bach-Passion* (soloists, organ, three choirs, orch., 1985), three quartets.

Jouni KAIPAINEN A founder of Finland's *Ears Open movement, Kaipainen is essentially a romantic working with contemporary sounds. His 20-minute symphony (Helsinki, 7.iii.85, cond. *Sallinen) actually simplifies itself as it unfolds. Many of his chamber and vocal works have evocative titles – *Piping down the Valleys Wild* (1984) – and poetic texts.

b. Helsinki 24.xi.56; st with *Sallinen and *Heininen; *other works*: TV opera, *The Miracle of Konstanz* (in progress); clarinet concerto *Carpe diem* (Helsinki, 1.ix.90), three piano trios.

Victor KALABIS Introspective Czech who sank his religious faith into symphonies and concertos of unsettling immediacy. *Neo-classical on top, faintly recalling *Martinů, his piano concerto (1954) and *Sinfonia pacis* (1961) are charged with emotional undercurrents. The smaller his music, the darker it sounds. *Diptych for*

strings (Prague, 12.iii.88) seems unrelievedly pessimistic; the 6th string quartet (1989), written in homage to Martinů, offers a glimmer of dawning freedom.

b. Cerveny Kostelec, 27.ii.23; producer at Czech Radio 1953–72; *other works*: five symphonies, concerto for large orch. (1966), harpsichord concerto (for his wife, Zuzana Růžičková), Chamber music for strings (1963), three piano sonatas.

Vasili KALAFATI Stravinsky's harmony teacher, a musician of Greco-Russian ancestry, he composed in a national style and died in the siege of Leningrad.

b. Eupatoria, Crimea, 10.ii.1869; *d*. Leningrad, 30.i.42; *works include*: symphony, two piano sonatas.

Johannes KALITZKE Wildish young German who gets musicians to shout, whistle and put themselves about in a *Trio infernal* (Cologne, 12.ix.85), a musical commentary on individual behaviour in group situations. Even unseen, on record, it contains enough music to provoke thought.

b. Cologne, 1959; st with *Höller, *Globokar.

Emmerich (Imre) KALMAN Hungarian composer of Viennese operettas full of happy gypsies; he spent the Hitler era in New York and Hollywood.

b. Siófok, Hungary, 24.x.1882; *d*. Paris 30.x. 53. *hits include*: *Die Csardasfürstin* (*Gypsy Princess*, Vienna, 17.xi.15), *Princess Maritza* (Vienna, 28.ii.24), *The Circus Princess* (26.iii.26), *The Countess of Chicago* (6.iv.28).

Manos KALOMIRIS Westernizer of Greek music, Kalomiris applied outmoded ideas of musical nationalism to Hellenic heritage. What emerged was trite as a scenic postcard. His 1st symphony, 'Levendia' (1920), signifying youthful vigour and national liberation, collapses into a banality that is both decadent and unwholesome – the kind of triumphal finale that civilized Germans gave up writing after 1870. It was followed by an innocuous *Greek Rhapsody* (orch. *Pierné, Paris, 3.iv.26) that earned Kalomiris a foreign reputation. He founded a national conservatory in Athens, wrote 220 further works and was mercifully eclipsed by many pupils.

b. Smyrna, Turkey, 26.xii.1883; *d.* Athens, 3.iv.62. *other works*: five operas, two with texts by Kazantzakis; choral *Symphany of the Kind People* (1931), *Palamas* Symphony (1956), piano concerto (1935).

Kammermusik 'Chamber music'. Collective title of seven Hindemith works, 1921–27.

Ghiya KANCHELI As the Soviet Union fell apart, artistic attention moved from the centre to the outlying republics. The Georgian Kancheli resisted easy categorization. He wrote large-scale, melodic symphonies that used both ethnic and radical techniques yet seemed to contain hidden messages. The 3rd (1973) has a wordless tenor soloist at either end and a barbaric march in between, veering from the ethereal to the aggressive without a hint of explanation. The 6th symphony (1981) alternates between Asian melismas, a surreal silence and violent bursts of noise (his crescendi are unrivalled except by *Schnittke). His colleague *Schchedrin called Kancheli 'a restrained Vesuvius'. His music, though enigmatic, is original and unforgettably beautiful. As with Shostakovich, the listener is transfixed by oracular utterances. Kancheli has admitted to being influenced by *jazz, and by several US composers, chiefly *Copland, *Sessions and *Crumb.

b. Tbilisi, Soviet Georgia, 10.viii.35; *works include*: multi-media opera, *Music for the Living* (1984); seven symphonies; Concerto for Orchestra; viola concerto; *Morning Prayers* for chamber orch. and tape; *Sweet Sadness* for boys' choir and orch.; cantata *Mild Sadness* (1985).

Ernst KANITZ *Schreker pupil in Hollywood exile.

b. Vienna 9.iv.1894; taught USC 1945–59, Marymount College 1960–4; *d.* Menlo Park, California, 7.iv.78. works include: violin-piano sonata (1924), radio cantata *Zeitmusik* (1931), concerto for *theremin and orch. (1938), operas *Kumana* (1953) and *The Lucky Dollar* (1959), two symphonies.

Herbert von KARAJAN The Austrian conductor achieved unprecedented dominance of the music *business. He was music director simultaneously of the Vienna State Opera (1956–64), Berlin Philharmonic Orch. (1955–89), Salzburg festivals and

German repertory at La Scala, Milan, before scaling down his engagements to assert corporate control of record and film companies.

As a conductor, he pursued a 'beautiful sound' to the detriment of substance and confined himself mainly to the central ground of classical-romantic concert repertoire. His youthful Nazism and commercial imperialism provoked enduring hostility.

b. Salzburg, 5.iv.08; cond. Ulm 1928–33; Aachen 1934–38; Berlin State Opera and Staatskapelle 1938–42; Philharmonia Orch. 1947–55; Vienna SO 1951–5; Berlin Philharmonic Orch., 1955–89; dir. Vienna State Opera 1956–64, Salzburg Festival 1956–60, and board member thereafter; founded Easter and Whitsun festivals at Salzburg; *d.* Anif, nr. Salzburg, 16.vii.89.

karaoke 'Empty orchestra' – Japanese term for songs recorded with full backing but without vocal line, inciting amateurs to act Sinatra. Karaoke singing became popular in Tokyo bars in the 1970s and spread harmlessly across Asia and Europe.

Rudolf KAREL Czech victim of Nazi holocaust, he composed a children's opera, *3 Hairs of the Wise Old Man*, while in the Theresienstadt concentration camp.

b. Pilsen, 9.xi.1880; *d.* Theresienstadt, 6.iii.45. *other works*: two symphonies, chamber music.

Nicolai KARETNIKOV For two decades, while his serious works were banned by the Soviet Composers' Union and he was forced to write film music for a living, Karetnikov used spare time at the end of dubbing sessions and the goodwill of Moscow musicians to make a secret recording of his 2-hour collage opera, *Till Eulenspiegel*. Stylistically descended from *Lulu, it combined urgency with delicate expressionism.

b. Moscow, 1930; st with *Shebalin; *other works*: four symphonies, Chamber symphony (1968), ballet *Vanina Vanini* (1960).

Siegfried KARG-ELERT Paramount German organist, he composed profusely for harmonium and organ – as well as organ reductions of many symphonies, among them Elgar's first, and a *Symphonia Brevis* and piano concerto of his own. He took a romantic, Mendelssohnian view of the baroque masters and provided an alternative to the bottomless contrapuntal intricacies of *Reger.

> *b.* Oberndorf am Neckar, Germany, 21.xi. 1877 (as Sigfried Karg, which means 'stingy' and had to be changed); taught Magdeburg 1900–1919, Leipzig 1919–33; *d.* Leipzig, 9.iv. 33.

Karl V Krenek's opera, the first fully *12-note music drama to be performed. fp: Prague, 15.vi.38.

Mieczyslaw KARLOWICZ Passionate mountaineer whose ascent was terminated at 32 by an avalanche in the High Tatras, Karlowicz led *Young Poland into late romanticism. His violin concerto cheekily copies Tchaikovsky's, while the *Revival Symphony* in E minor (1900) echoes early Strauss with a hint of Mahler, lashings of folk-tunes and a fine chorale to finish (both fp: Berlin, 21.iii.03). The remaining six mature works are symphonic poems, of which *Stanislaw and Anna of Oswiecim* (Auschwitz) is highly evocative.

> *b.* Wiszniewo, Lithuania, 11.xii.1876, son of a musicologist; st with *Nikisch; cond. Warsaw Music Society 1904–6; *d.* nr Zakopane, Galicia, 8.ii.09. *other works*: Eternal Songs (1904) Lithuanian Rhapsody (1906).

Katerina Ismailova Sanitized version of Shostakovich's opera *Lady Macbeth of Mtsensk District*.

Katya Kabanova *Janáček's tragic opera after Alexander Ostrovsky's Russian play *The Storm* recounts the illicit love of a young wife in a village society dominated by her malicious, indomitable mother-in-law. Slightly less harrowing than *Jenůfa*, the score conveys waves of carnal and spiritual desire, the lovers coming together in a passage reminiscent of *Mahler's tonal resolution in *Das *Lied von der Erde*. fp: Brno, 23.xi.21.

Georg KATZER Economical *Eisler pupil in East Germany, he found expressive freedom in two Concertos for Orchestra (1975, 85) but was trapped into cold-war dialogues in his platonic opera, *Gastmahl* (1988).

> *b.* Habelschwerdt, Silesia (now Bystrzyen, Poland), 10.i.35; st with *Eisler, *Zechlin,

*Wagner-Régeny; *other work*: ballet, *A New Summer Night's Dream* (1980).

Ulysses (Simpson) KAY Relative of the jazzman King Oliver, Kay avoided overt ethnicity in compositions that mirrored the moderation of his teacher, *Hindemith.

> *b.* Tucson, Arizona, 7.i.17; *works*: four operas, oboe concerto, symphonic *Markings* in memory of US secretary-general, Dag Hammarskjöld (1966).

Milko KELEMEN Croatian folklorist drawn to modernism in 1960s Germany and combining both worlds in *multimedia shows. He co-founded Zagreb New Music Biennale.

> *b.* Podrawska Slatina, Yugoslavia, 30.iii.24; st with *Messiaen, *Fortner; moved to Germany 1965, prof. at Stuttgart 1973– ; *works include*: opera, *State of Siege* (after Camus' *La Peste*, Hamburg, 10.i.70), *Opéra bestiale* (1974), *Yebell* for narrator, pantomime and ensemble (Munich, 1.ix.72), *drammatico* (1985), *Surprise* for string orch. (Zagreb, 13.v.67).

Frederick Septimus KELLY Australian sacrifice of the First World War, he composed a tender orchestral Elegy *In Memoriam Rupert Brooke*.

> *b.* Sydney, 1881; *d.* on the Somme, France, 1916.

Rudolf KELTERBORN *Julia* (1991), a reworking of the Romeo story in Italian, Swiss and Palestinian settings, was well received for its plot and excoriated for a score that refused to yield modernist principles to emotional expression. Kelterborn has written four other operas and four symphonies.

> *b.* Basle, Switzerland, 3.ix.31; st with *Blacher; prof. at Detmold 1960–68, Zurich 1958–75, head of music at Swiss Radio 1975–80, dir. Basle music academy, 1983– .

Wilhelm KEMPFF German classical pianist, he played his own cadenzas in Beethoven and wrote three operas and two symphonies, of which the second was premiered by *Furtwängler. Unheard in London until 1951 or New York until 1964, he later sold 250,000 records of an authoritative *Emperor* concerto.

> *b.* Jüterbog, 25.xi.1895; *d.* Positano, Italy, 23.v.91.

Jerome (David) KERN A contributor to dozens of Broadway scores before venturing out on his own, he paired up with P. G.

Wodehouse and had an ephemeral hit with *Sally* (1920). His moment arrived with *Show Boat* (Ziegfeld Theater, NY, 27.xii.27), a precursor of **Porgy and Bess* that contained the bass song 'Ol' Man River' and struck a serious note amid the flapper frivolity of the genre. It gave Kern a passport to Hollywood and immortality.

Kern played a formative role in the evolution of American *popular music. His first hit, 'How'd you like to spoon with me?', dates from 1906 and he added a string of unforgettables including 'The night was made for love', 'Smoke gets in your eyes' and 'The last time I saw Paris'. Several songs were set by Charles Miller for string quartet.

b. NY, 27.i.1885; *d.* there, 11.xi.45.

Aaron Jay KERNIS Performed by the New York Philharmonic when he was just 23, Kernis impressed players both with the quality of his score and with his defence of it against deprecations by the conductor, Zubin Mehta. Freely drawing from every style, from baroque to rock, he wrote emotional, dreamlike music, often with creamy vocal topping.

b. Philadelphia, Pa., US, 15.i.60; *orch. works*: *Dream of the Morning Sky* (NY, 7.vi.83, cond. Mehta), *Mirror of Heat and Light* (NY, 24.ii.85), *Invisible Mosaic III* (NY, 5.ii.89), *Symphony in Waves* (St Paul, 3.xi.89, cond. *Adams); string quartet (NY 13.xi.90); *Songs of Innocence* for high voice (1991), 2nd symphony (NY, 15.i.92.).

Tristan KEURIS Introspective Dutchman, he has written bleakly autumnal Variations (1986) for string orch.

b. Amersfoort, 3.x.46; st with van Vlijmen, de *Leeuw; other works: saxophone concerto (1971), two string quartets.

Aram KHACHATURIAN Handcuffed to Shostakovich and Prokofiev as the 'Big Three' composers of Stalin's second purge, Khachaturian had done everything the party asked of him. He used folk sources from his ethnic heritage and wrote tunes that anyone could sing – as well as a *Song of Stalin* (Moscow, 29.xi.38) that glorified the great leader. His only sin was to have charmed the West with the excellence of his music.

Unlike the pseudo-orientalism of *Rimsky and his followers, Khacha-

turian's Asiatic melismas were the genuine article. He devised all the melodies himself and they sat securely in symphonic compositions.

His best music was written in the years 1936–46: a rippling piano concerto (Leningrad, 5.vii.37), an atmospheric, unmoody violin concerto (Moscow, 16.xi.40; reworked as flute concerto), the farmyard ballet *Gayaneh* (Perm, 9.xii.42) from which the popular *Sabre Dance* was extracted, a blazing 2nd symphony with bells and bits of Dies Irae (Moscow, 30.xii.43) and a reflective cello concerto (Moscow, 30.x.46). His populist touch faltered in the ambitious 3rd symphony (Leningrad, 13.xii.47), whose organ and 15 solo trumpets supposedly depicted village festivities. He was denounced for distortion and forced to atone with simplistic film scores. In 1954, he bravely denounced state interference in art, but was immediately forced to recant. The adagio of his third ballet *Spartacus* (Leningrad, 26.xii.56) hit the mark again, becoming a BBC television theme (*The Onedin Line*).

b. nr Tbilisi, Georgia, 6.vi.03, son of an Armenian book-binder; st biology in Moscow but in 1929 entered Conservatoire, st with *Miaskovsky, Vassilenko; married composer Nina Makarova, 1933; won Stalin Prize for violin concerto, 1940; *d.* Moscow 1.v.78 and buried in Armenian capital, Erevan. *other works*: Concerto-Rhapsodies for violin (1962), cello (1964) and piano (1968); *Ode to Joy* for 40 violins, ten harps, mezzo-soprano, mixed chorus and orch. (1955); self-assertive violin sonata, string quartet and trio for clarinet, violin and piano (all 1932); composition for solo clarinet (for Benny Goodman, 1966).

His nephew, Karen KHACHATURIAN
b. Moscow, 19.ix.20, composed *realistic orchestral scores.

Tikhon (Nikolaievich) KHRENNIKOV The quisling of Russian music, Khrennikov ran the USSR Composers' Union for 43 years, subjugating creative individualism to central political control. Installed as secretary general to instil Stalin's terror, he conducted the public humiliation of *Prokofiev and *Shostakovich and sent senior colleagues to the salt-mines of film studios. In later years, Khrennikov claimed to have acted altruistically to protect composers from the fate of exiled and executed writers. So polished were his bureaucratic skills that Khrennikov clung to office while Soviet Union collapsed and was among the last functionaries to be dismissed in 1991, when he was personally blamed for the mass emigration of composers.

His musicianship was modest. He emerged in 1937, aged 24, with a series of articles supporting *socialist realism and a folkish opera, *The Storm* (Moscow, 10.x.39), that depicted Lenin in saintly conversation with the same peasantry whom Stalin was busily massacring. It was a 'number opera' with many songs and no leitmotiv, and projected Khrennikov as a champion of popular song. He was rewarded with a seat on the Supreme Soviet and a place of honour in the Berlin Victory Day parade. In addition to tyrannizing Soviet composers, his writ determined which foreign modernists could be played in the country. He habitually basked in reflected glory when, for example, the *Rite of Spring* had its homeland première – half a century after it was composed.

b. Elets, Russia, 10.vi.13, tenth son of a small trader; secretary-general USSR Composers' Union, 1948–91; capable concert pianist; other works: four operas, three symphonies, three piano concertos.

Wilhelm KIENZL   A small talent by his own admission, Kienzl wrote an 'ethical' opera that stood halfway between early Wagner and the Italian verismists. With a showcase tenor role, *Der Evangelimann (The Evangelist*, Berlin, 4.v.1895) achieved enormous popularity and was briefly admired by Mahler and Strauss, who both conducted it. Kienzl never repeated its success. In 1919 he wrote a national anthem for republican Austria to words by its first Chancellor, Karl Renner; it was soon replaced by Haydn's old Kaiser theme.

b. Waizenkirchen, Upper Austria, 17.i.1857; cond. Hamburg 1890–2, Munich 1892–4, critic in Graz, 1897–1917, *d.* Vienna, 3.x.41; *other operas: Don Quixote* (Berlin, 18.xi. 1898), *Der Kuhreigen (The Cowherd's song*, Vienna, 23.xi.11), *Das Testament* (Vienna, 6.xii.16). He also completed a *Turandot* by Adolf Jensen (1837–79).

Wojciech KILAR   Unfrozen by the *Warsaw Autumn thaw, Kilar was allowed out to *Darmstadt in 1957 and again to Paris to study with Nadia *Boulanger. Armed with the latest Western knowhow, he was co-leader of the Polish revival with *Penderecki and *Baird. He composed two symphonies and pieces in diversely advanced styles, among them eulogies for *Bartók in the form of an *Ode* (1957) for violin, brass and two percussion groups, and a concerto for two pianos and percussion (1958). In the mid-60s he became the busiest composer in Polish cinema, writing important scores for Kieslowski, Zanussi and all of Ladislav Wajda's films. His serious music became religious and simplistic to the point of minimalism, though still extremely loud.

b. Lvov, Poland, 17.vii.32; *other works:* Exodus for orch. and choir, *Prelude and Christmas Carols* for four oboes and string orch. (1972), *Angelus* for soprano, chorus and orch.

Wilhelm KILLMAYER   Bavarian pupil of Carl *Orff, he symbiosed ancient and modern musics. His *Grande Sarabande* for strings (Zurich, 2.v.80) flickers in and out of a Baroque dance style, straying tonally into dissonance and rhythmically towards *bop. An ingenious variant on *neoclassicism, it lacks enough vim to reward repeated listening.

b. Munich, 21.viii.27; st with *Orff; ballet cond. Bavarian State Opera 1961–4; prof. Munich Musikhochschule 1974– ; *other works:* three symphonies, trumpet concerto, chamber music for jazz instruments, various pieces for percussion.

Yrjö KILPINEN   Prominent Finnish song composer.

b. Helsingfors (Helsinki), 4.ii.1892; *d.* there, 2.iii.59.

Earl KIM   Harvard professor (1967–) whose pupils include *Del Tredici and *Harbison, his few compositions are communicative in a deliberately theatrical way. The violin concerto (1979) employs the orchestra as backdrop and the instrument as an actor-substitute, its lines echoing the enigmatic, sometimes broken cadences of Beckett and Joyce, in a romantic plot resembling Mahler's *Adagietto.

b. Dinuba, California, 6.i.20; st with *Schoenberg, *Bloch and *Sessions; thrice married; plays poker; *other works: Footfalls* opera, 1981), *Earthlight* for soprano, violin, piano and spotlights to a mock-Beckett text; song settings.

Kindertotenlieder *Songs on the Death of Children* Mahler's setting for baritone and orch. of five poems by Friedrich Rückert; they reflect his own tragic childhood and recent brush with death rather than – as his widow would allege – prophesy the death of his own child. fp: Vienna, 29.i.05.

King David Honegger's 'dramatic psalm' for soloists, chorus and instruments, replete with pseudo-orientalism and *Salome-like sensuality. fp: Mézières, Switzerland, 11.vi.21. Revised with full orch., 1923.

The King Goes Forth to France *Sallinen's 3rd opera. fp: Savonlinna, 7.vii.84.

King Priam Greek tragedy by *Tippett. fp: Coventry, 29.v.62.

King Roger *Szymanowski's epic opera of a 12th-century Sicilian monarch who loses his wife and subjects to a Pied Piper-like mystic shepherd. fp: Warsaw, 19.vi.26, cond. Emil Mlynarski.

Leon KIRCHNER A *Schoenberg pupil in Los Angeles, Kirchner used *12-note music with other techniques. His palette ranges from an aggressively discordant 1st piano concerto (NY, 23.ii.56, cond. *Mitropoulos) to the discernibly sensual *Music for Orchestra I* (NY, 16.x.69) and a Pulitzer-winning 3rd string quartet with electronic accompaniment (27.i.67) written under the tuition of his former pupil, *Subotnick. His major work is the opera *Lily* (NY, City Opera, 14.iv.77) on Saul Bellow's novel *Henderson the Rain King*, deploring the destruction of one civilization by another and intended as an anti-Vietnam War allegory.
b. Brooklyn, NY, 24.i.19; st with *Toch, *Bloch, *Sessions; prof. at Harvard 1961–89; *other works: Music for Orchestra II* (1990), *Music for 12* (1985).

Giselher (Wolfgang) KLEBE Ex-avant-gardist who, like *Henze, drifted back to centre ground where he merged *12-note methods and the *variable metres of his teacher *Blacher in a romantic wash of sound. The 3rd of his five symphonies (1966) conceals advanced techniques in a work of traditional proprieties. His 11 operas include *Caesar's Murder* (after Shakespeare, Essen, 20.ix.59) and *Jacobowsky and the Colonel* (after Werfel, Hamburg, 2.xi.65).
b. Mannheim, Germany, 28.vi.25; taught Detmold music academy 1957– ; *other works*: five ballets, organ concerto, Masses, *La Tomba di Igor Stravinsky* for oboe, piano and 14 strings.

Erich and Carlos KLEIBER Father and son conductors – Erich premiered *Wozzeck and fought the Nazis; Carlos repeated his father's favourite works.
Erich: *b.* Vienna, 5.viii.1890; dir. Berlin State Opera 1923–34; composed violin concerto and other works; *d.* Zurich, 27.i.56. Carlos: *b.* Berlin, 3.vii.30.

Gideon KLEIN Conceivably the most gifted of the composers crammed into the Nazi show camp of Theresienstadt, Klein, unlike his fellow-inmates *Ullmann and *Haas, continued writing recondite atonalities under conditions of starvation and misery. Serving popular needs by transcribing familiar scores for the handful of available instruments, he wrote a boldly Schoenbergian piano sonata and unsentimental piano trio with a central Lento movement that plays rich variations on a Moravian folksong.
b. Prerov, Czechoslovakia, 6.xii.19; st with *Hába; *d.* Fürstengrube, Germany, 27.i.45; *other work*: Fantasy and Fugue for string quartet (1943).

Otto KLEMPERER The tempestuous *Mahlerian embraced operatic modernism while running the Kroll Theatre in Berlin, introducing to German audiences disturbing works by Stravinsky, Hindemith and Weill. Abstract stage design was inaugurated under his aegis. His world premières were relatively few, headed by Zemlinsky's *Der Zwerg* (Cologne, 28.v.22) and Schoenberg's orchestration of Brahms G-minor piano quartet (1938). Later in life, dogged by mental and physical illness, he slowed down to give statuesque accounts of symphonic masterpieces in London and on record. He composed six symphonies and nine string quartets, mostly in retirement.
b. Breslau, Austro-Hungary, 14.v.1885; cond. Hamburg Opera, 1910–12, Cologne

1917–24, Wiesbaden 1924–7, Berlin *Kroll Opera, 1927–31, Budapest Opera, 1947–50; from 1951 he worked with Philharmonia Orch. and in 1959 became principal conductor; *d*. Zurich, 6.vii.73.
Bib: Peter Heyworth, *Klemperer* (Vol. 1), Cambridge (CUP), 1984.

Alexander KNAIFEL Russian iconoclast, writing slow, quiet and unsettling music that passes from one instrument to another when it is good and ready. His orchestral piece, *Jeanne* (1978) is written in a single 80-minute movement for Mahler-sized orchestra. *Agnus* (1985) lasts two hours and is largely inaudible. *L'ange* for mixed choir is listed at four hours and a quarter. Many of his scores are unperformed, perhaps unperformable. Such gestures can be construed as a rejection of Soviet show-music and an emulation of the codes of Shostakovich, on whom Knaifel wrote a 1975 monograph.
b. Tashkent, Uzbekistan, 1943; st six years with *Rostropovich; *other works*: opera, *The Ghost of Canterville* (after Oscar Wilde, Leningrad, 26.ii.74), *Da*, for ensemble and unspecified soloists (Moscow, 31.i.81).

Lev KNIPPER In his 4th symphony, *Poem about the Komsomol Fighter* (1934), Knipper wrote a partisan song, 'Poliushko', that became so famous when sung by the Red Army Chorus that most thought it a folk melody. It squats uncomfortably in a grandiose Germanic orchestration that led one UK critic to dub Knipper 'the Soviet Mahler'. He was nothing of the sort, lacking irony or introspection. His *Far Eastern Symphony* (1933), on tunes collected in remoter Soviet republics, provoked Shostakovich to respond with his discordant Fourth Symphony, suppressed when Stalin imposed his musical tastes. Knipper broadened the debate with an abstract Sixth Symphony (1936), but was attacked as a *formalist and was forced back into conformist banality.
b. Tbilisi, Georgia, 3.xii.1898; st with Glière and in Berlin with Philipp Jarnach; *d*. Moscow, 30.vii.74. *works include*: 20 symphonies, nine concertos and two operas, *The North Wind* (1930, modernist) and *On the Baikal Lake* (1948, conformist).

Iwan KNORR *Frankfurt teacher whose pupils included *Pfitzner and *Scott. His symphonic music was based on Ukrainian folksongs that he heard while growing up in Russia.
b. Mewe, Germany, 3.i.1853; *d*. Frankfurt, 22.i.16.

The Knot Garden *Tippett's 3rd psychodrama. fp: London (Covent Garden), 2.xii.70.

Knoxville: Summer of 1915 *Barber's nostalgic song for soprano and orchestra, using a prose memoir by the theatre and movie critic James Agee. fp: Boston, 9.iv.48, cond. *Koussevitsky.

(Stuart) Oliver KNUSSEN Precocious son of a London orchestral player, he conducted his first short symphony at 15 (London, 7.iv.68) and his second at 19. A naïve penchant for Russian and American symphonic sounds was tempered by his tutor Gunter *Schuller with *serial techniques and *expressionist gestures in the second symphony (*Tanglewood, 18.viii. 81), in which a soprano sings elliptical verses by Georg Trakl. The 3rd symphony took him six years from start to première (London, 6.ix.79), depicting with commendable subtlety Ophelia's mad scene from *Hamlet*. It was 15 minutes long and easy enough on the ear to act as ambassador for a new generation of British composers, instinctively fluent in its control of orchestral nuances.
It ended Knussen's first creative phase. He moved into children's opera, writing *Where the Wild Things Are* (1981) and *Higgledy Piggledy Pop!* (1985), and applied himself to performing works by his contemporaries. He held posts at *Aldeburgh and Tanglewood and was much in demand as a conductor. His writing, though, became slower than ever and a mature masterpiece was long awaited.
b. Glasgow, Scotland, 12.vi.52; st with John Lambert and *Schuller; *other works*: *Coursing* for chamber orch. (1979), *Cantata* for oboe and string trio (1977).

Erland von KOCH Folksy Swede, successful with children's opera *Peter, the tailless cat* (1948) and Ingmar Bergman film tracks.
b. Stockholm, 26.iv.10; *orch. works*: 5th symphony (1977), saxophone concerto (1958), *A Swede in New York* (1973).

Zoltán KODÁLY Kodály was so close to *Bartók that many find them inseparable. In fact, their outlooks were diametrically opposed. Bartók searched persistently for new sounds, while Kodály was content to remain, in his friend's definition, 'the most perfect embodiment of the Hungarian spirit'. Bartók was universalist, Kodály more a nationalist. He composed in conventional tonalities, with a slight *Debussyan tinge.

A railway stationmaster's son, he picked up folk-tunes from servant girls and learned the cello in order to write an immature string quartet. The effort paid off eventually in a widely-played solo cello sonata (1915) and a rhythmic though reflective 2nd string quartet of 1918. Both conjure up recognizable moods but, unlike Bartók or *Janáček, fail to kindle strong emotions.

After the First War, Kodály became Dohnányi's deputy at the Budapest Academy of Music until a right-wing coup debarred him for two years. His frustration found voice in the *Psalmus Hungaricus* (Budapest, 19.xi.23), a choral setting of David's prayer to the Lord to deliver him from the persecution of his enemies (Psalm LX). It is probably the most effective of his works, impassioned and many-layered. Both the violent rhythms and fiercely sung locutions strike at the heart of human feeling. He struck a similar chord late in life with the Hymn of Zrinyi (1954), a medieval protest against oppression.

Kodály became famous abroad for his folklorisms. The *Háry János* suite (NY, 15.xii.27), extracted from a nationalistic Singspiel, is movietone without the images, adored by those who like fairy tales with their music. The *Dances of Galanta* (23.x.33) and *Variations on a Hungarian Folksong, The Peacock* (Amsterdam, 23.xi.39) are equally brilliant and harmless. His *Concerto for Orchestra* (Chicago, 6.ii.41) was no match for Bartók's.

He spent the Second War in Hungary, partly in hiding, and was honoured by the communists who adopted his educational method and propagated it abroad. Pushing 80, he married a 19-year-old pupil and wrote his first symphony (Lucerne, 16.viii.61), a failure.

b. Kecskemét, Hungary, 16.xii.1882; st briefly with *Widor in Paris; began helping Bartók collect folksongs, 1905, appointed to Academy of Music 1907; first all-Kodály concert, 1910; married 1910, remarried 1959; *d*. Budapest, 6.iii.67. *other works*: *Transylvanian Spinning-room* (opera, 24.iv. 32), *Summer evening* (tone poem, 22.x.06), *Dances of Marosszék* (Dresden, 28.xi.30), Missa Brevis (11.ii.45).

Kodály method The composer's way of teaching music to children, mainly by sight-singing, using many Hungarian tunes. The idea is to develop the ear and intelligence before attempting manual skills, the reverse of *Suzuki.

Charles (Louis Eugène) KOECHLIN Frenchman whose music mirrors a century of fluctuating style. Born in Berlioz's lifetime, he studied with Massenet and Fauré, mingled with Debussy and Ravel, taught Poulenc and Milhaud and heard Messiaen and Boulez. A dedicated composer with no other occupation or position, he built on a framework of Bachian counterpoint with the materials of each epoch. His first forty-odd works are late-romantic; the next batch turn impressionistic; while his triple-digit compositions, running up to opus 225, reflect multifarious elements from medievalism to jazz.

A long-bearded prophet of Protestant faith and communist sympathies, he lived reclusively and followed no conscious fashion, although Stravinsky was often in his mind. Rudyard Kipling was a source of inspiration, as were Hollywood movies. He wrote several major works on *The Jungle Book*, including four orchestral suites: *3 poèmes après Kipling* (1899–1910, with soloists and chorus), *Le course de printemps* (1927), *Le loi de jungle* (1939) and *Le Bandar-Log* (1940). His movie mania found expression in a Seven Stars Symphony (1933), its movements named individually for Douglas Fairbanks, Lilian Harvey, Greta Garbo, Clara Bow, Marlene Dietrich, Emil Jannings and Charlie Chaplin. There is also a saxophone *Epitaph pour Jean Harlow*.

Koechlin was a key witness to the evolution of French music and, in that capacity, is worth hearing, although record companies have largely overlooked his fastidious music. His viola sonata opus 92 (1915), dedicated to Milhaud, is bitonal and aurally intriguing. His second symphony (1944) makes pertinent use of the *ondes martenot. Foremost among French musicians, he fought the rise of fascism.

b. Paris, 27.xi.1867 of wealthy Alsatian stock; graduated from Conservatoire at 30; married 1903; *d*. Canadel, France, 31.xii.50. *other works*: La forêt, two-part symphonic poem (1897–1907); Symphony of Hymns (1936), *Hymne* for ondes martenot and orchestra (1942); *Offrande musical sur le nom de B.A.C.H.* for organ and orch. (1942), *Partita* for chamber orch. (1945); five Sheherazade Melodies for voice/piano (1922), 3 string quartets, wind trio (1924) sonatas for flute (1913), oboe (1916), cello (1917), bassoon (1919), horn (1925).

Gottfried Michael KOENIG *Electronics pioneer at Stockhausen's Cologne studios, he carried the gospel in 1964 to Holland, where he faded from the vanguard.

b. Magdeburg, Germany, 5.x.26; worked at West German Radio 1955–64, Utrecht University 1964– ; *works include*: *Klangfiguren 2* (1956), *Essai* (1957), *Terminus X* (1967), *Funktion Blau* (1969).

Josef KOFFLER *Schoenberg pupil shot dead with his wife and child during a Nazi roundup of Jews, near Cracow. His serialist, folktune-based 3rd symphony was premièred at the last *ISCM before the War (London, 17.vi.38).

b. Stryj, Poland, 28.xi.1896; killed Wieliczka, 1943. *other works*: 15 variations for string orch. (Amsterdam, 9.vi.33), string quartet.

Citrad KOHOUTEK Czech administrator who applied planned-economy principles to the art of composition, dictating the policy of each work before he put it into production. After *social-realist beginnings, he imported the dogmatism of *Darmstadt, where he studied in 1965, and was considered an authority in the communist states on Western avant-garde techniques. From 1980–87, he was artistic director of the Czech Philharmonic.

b. Zábreh na Morave, Czechoslovakia, 18.iii. 29; *works include*: symphonic poem *Munich* (1953), *Symphonic Newsreel* (1978).

Joonas KOKKONEN Post-Sibelian Finn, influenced by *Hindemith though

later works indicate an awareness of *Messaien. . . .*durch einen Spiegel* (1977) for 12 string instruments and harpsichord is raptly static.

b. Iisalmi, Finland, 13.xi.21; *other works*: opera *The Last Temptation* (1975), four symphonies.

Kol NIDREI Aramaic prayer for Jewish Day of Atonement, set for cello and orch. by the non-Jewish Bruch in 1881. It was reworked for rabbi, mixed chorus and orch. by *Schoenberg, retaining the traditional melody but prefacing the text with a cabbalistic legend. fp: Los Angeles, 4.x.39.

Barbara KOLB Kolb at first hearing can sound like demi-sec *Boulez but introductions are deceptive and her shyly ingratiating music conceals a sensuality and rhythms that have origins in *Debussy and jazz. *Soundings* (for two conductors, NY Philharmonic, 11.xii.75, cond. Boulez) plays games of depth and distance with a divided orchestra. *Millefoglie* for computer tape and ensemble (Paris, 5.vi.85) is an *IRCAM creation of almost-minimalist stasis.

b. Hartford, Connecticut, 10.ii.39; st with *Schuller, *Foss; *other orch. works*: *The Enchanted Loom* (Atlanta, 15.ii.90), *Voyants* for piano and chamber orch. (Paris, 23.ii.91).

König HIRSCH (*King Stag*) Dissonant opera in classical style by *Henze, following a Venetian fable in which the king becomes a stag. fp: Berlin 23.ix.56. Revised 1963, as *Il rè Cervo*.

Königskinder (*Royal Children*) *Humperdinck's follow-up to *Hansel und Gretel* kills off the princelings when the witch feeds them sweeties. It introduces a *Sprechstimme* (speaking voice) slightly ahead of Schoenberg's *sprechgesang. fp: Munich, 23.i.1897 (as play with music), NY, Metropolitan Opera, 28.xii.10.

(Count) Hidemaro KONOYE Princely brother of the imperial Japanese prime minister, he conducted the premier recording of *Mahler's 4th symphony in 1930 and composed, *inter alia*, *Etenraku* for large orch.

b. Tokyo, 18.xi.1898; st with d'*Indy, *Schreker; *d*. Tokyo, 2.vi.73.

Paul KONT Austrian post-1945 revivalist, Kont formed alliance of modernists to dispel Nazi-age prejudices.
b. Vienna, 19.viii.20; st with Messiaen, Milhaud; *works*: operas, *Lysistrata* (1957), *Traumleben* (1963), many concertos.

Kontra-Punkte (*Counterpoints*) Piece by Stockhausen for piano and nine instruments that fall out one by one, as in Haydn's Farewell Symphony. fp: Cologne, 26.v.53.

Marek KOPOLENT Abstract Czech composer working under severe constraints, he veered from *serial string quartets to the classical pastiche of *Art Nouveau* (1978).
b. Prague, 24.iv.32;

Nicolai KORNDORF Russian modernist fascinated by ancient Russia, has written three symphonies and two 20-minute *Hymns* (1987) for large orchestra, and a 30-minute string trio 'in honour of Alfred Schnittke' (1986).
b. Moscow, 23.i.47;

Erich Wolfgang KORNGOLD Hollywood's star composer won Oscars for *Anthony Adverse*, *The Adventures of Robin Hood* and *The Sea Wolf*, adding orchestral flair to the movies. Prior to that he wrote Vienna's longest-running inter-War opera. Earlier still he was hailed as the brightest musical prodigy since Mozart, with his *Snowman* pantomime (4.x.10) approved by Mahler and orchestrated by Zemlinsky, receiving its première at the Vienna Court Opera when the composer was just 12 years old.

He was pushed by his father, Julius, senior critic on the *Neue Freie Presse*, who presented him to Mahler with a juvenile cantata, *Gold*. Under unremitting paternal pressure, he produced in successive years a Straussian piano trio which Bruno *Walter performed, a glitzy overture for *Nikisch and a *Sinfonietta* that *Weingartner gave with the Vienna Philharmonic. By 18 he had staged two short operas, *Violanta* and *Polycrates' Ring* (Munich, 28.iii.16). His high water mark was *Die tote Stadt* (*The Dead City*, Hamburg and Cologne, 4.xii.20), libretto by Papa. The opera won Maria Jeritza worldwide fame in the twin roles of the hero's dead wife, Marie, and her surrogate, Marietta, whom he murders. It contains one aria 'Glück das mir verblieb' that Puccini might have envied and many orchestral ingenuities, but the plot is thin and, after an interwar rush, its appeal faded.

Lured to Hollywood by Max Reinhardt in 1934 to set Mendelssohn's music for his film of *A Midsummer Night's Dream*, he stayed to write music for 17 movies. His contract let him retain all rights over his movie music and from 1946 he started re-cycling it into concert works. A violin concerto for *Heifetz (St Louis, 15.ii.47) hints at higher things, but was critically damned as 'more corn than gold'; the symphony in F# lacks bite. The 3rd string quartet (1945) gives clearer indication of what-might-have-been, its sonorities fluctuating between Schubert and Schoenberg in a touching elegy for lost priorities.
b. Brno, Austro-Hungary, 29.v.1897; *d.* Hollywood, 29.xi.57. *other works*: operas, *Das Wunder der Heliane* (1927), *Kathrin* (1939); piano concerto for left hand (1923), cello concerto (1946), symphonic serenade (1949), Theme and variations for orch. (1953); three piano sonatas (1908–32).

Olli KORTEKANGAS Finnish rebel, a leader of the Ears Open movement, he blended rock techniques and advanced electronics in vocal compositions, most originally in the television opera, *Grand Hotel* (Helsinki, 12.ix.87), which is strung together like a batch of TV ads or rock videos.
b. Turku, 16.v.55; *other works*: three orch. songs to D. H. Lawrence poems (Oulu, 30.xi.89).

Arghyris KOUNADIS German-based Greek composer applying 12-tone style to Hellenic tunes.
b. Istanbul, 14.ii.24; st with *Fortner in Freiburg-im-Breisgau, where he settled as leader of new music ensemble; *principal works*: incidental music for classic Greek dramas; piano concerto; *3 Nocturnes after Sappho* (for soprano and instruments, 1960); one act opera, *Der Gummisarg* (1962); *Epitymbion in memoriam Charles *Ives* (for six percussionists, 13 flutes, 1965).

Serge KOUSSEVITSKY Perplexingly astute conductor who dictated paths of new music while barely able to read a modern score. A double-bassist in a Moscow orchestra, he married money, paid *Nikisch for conducting lessons and moved out to Paris where he founded a publishing imprint for rising Russians, Skryabin and Prokofiev at their head. In 1924 he became chief conductor of the Boston SO, where he commissioned major premières from Prokofiev, Stravinsky, Honegger and the dying Bartók and nurtured the first two internationally-known generations of US composers. His initial preference was for the romanticism of Harris and Piston, but his heart went out to Copland and especially the young Bernstein who revered his memory as long as he lived. The Koussevitsky Foundation, commemorating his second wife, commissioned important works from *Peter Grimes* onwards.

> *b*. Vishmy-Volochok, 26.vii.1874; double-bass player 1894–1905; own orch. in Russia 1909–15; State Symphony orch., Petrograd, 1917–20; Koussevitsky Concerts, Paris, 1922–24; Boston SO, 1924–49; *d*. Boston, 4.vi.51.

Karel KOVAŘOVIC, Chief conductor of the Czech national theatre (1900–20), he resisted Janáček's *Jenůfa* for 12 years, finally accepting it with his own revisions. The Kovařovic edition, universally accepted for half a century, deletes many of Janáček's distinctive repetitions and pauses and tones down violent orchestral colours, substituting trumpets for trombones; the final scene is notably smoothed over. Kovařovic also revised Dvořák's *Dmitri*. His own French-flavoured compositions have been forgotten, among them the faintly notorious 1884 ballet, *Hashish*.

> *b*. Prague, 9.xii.1862; wrote five operas, three ballets, piano concerto; chief conductor, Narodny Diavolo, 1900–20; *d*. Prague, 6.xii. 20.

William KRAFT Chief percussionist of the Los Angeles Philharmonic Orch., subsequently its composer in residence and founder of the city's New Music Group. His music has ranged from folksong variations to jazz and serialism.

> *b*. Chicago, 6.ix.23;

Hans KRASA In 1938, Krasa wrote a children's opera, *Brundibar*, for a Prague orphanage. Six years later, adapted to different circumstances, it was performed 55 times by the original cast in the Nazi camp of Theresienstadt (Terezin). Red Cross inspectors, enchanted by the show, ignored the bitter ironies in its score and story of two kids who scour merciless streets in search of milk for their sick mother. As soon as the visitors had gone, cast and composer were sent to their deaths at Auschwitz. *Brundibar* apart, Krasa was survived by a short string trio and *Theme with Variations* for string quartet (1942).

> *b*. Prague, 30.xi.1899; st with *Zemlinsky; murdered Auschwitz, 17.x.44.

Fritz KREISLER The velvety violinist wrote encores, of which *Liebesfreud*, *Liebeslied* and *Schön Rosmarin* can squeeze tears from reinforced concrete. He penned two Broadway operettas, *Apple Blossoms* (1919) and *Sissy* (1923). In 1905 he published 'transcriptions' of pieces by Baroque composers, causing a storm in the critical teacup 30 years later on revealing that they were his own music. He left cadenzas for the Beethoven and Brahms concertos and gave the première of *Elgar's (10.xi.1910). He was concert partner to *Busoni and *Rachmaninov, and one of the century's friendliest musicians.

> *b*. Vienna, 2.ii.1875; wounded in Austrian army in the First War, expelled from Germany 1933; *d*. New York, 29.i.62. *other works*: *Viennese Rhapsodic Fantasietta* (pure schmaltz), *Tambourin chinois* (eastern fakery), *The Old Refrain*, etc.

Ernst KRENEK (KŘENEK) No composer was more in tune with the century's shifting fashions than this nonagenarian child of Mahler's Vienna who lived into the era of Calfornian post-minimalism and attempted most techniques along the way. Married to Mahler's daughter, Anna, he joined the café society of post-1918 Berlin, forsaking romanticism for a fermenting cocktail of *utility music, *atonality and *neo-classicism.

His third and freshest opera *Orpheus und Euridice* (Kassel, 27.xi.26) was ahead of its time, post-*Bergian in its theatrical manipulation of tonal and atonal motifs. It did not pay the bills, so Krenek wrote a jazzy pot-boiler *Jonny spielt auf* (*Jonny strikes up*, Leipzig, 10.ii.27), which was staged in more than 100 European theatres.

Its tale of a bandleader who stole a Strad and set everyone dancing the Charleston was as insubstantial as the concurrent movie hit, *The Jazz Singer* – interesting only as the first of its kind. Its follow up *Leben des Orest* (Leipzig, 19.i.30) was intellectually too complex for the simplicity of its music.

Soon after, Krenek adopted *Schoenberg's method and clung to it for the rest of his long life. His *12-note opera *Karl V* was barred from Vienna by the Nazis and premièred in Prague (15.vi.38); it remains a neglected masterpiece of serial technique. Krenek went to America, settling in Palm Springs, California, and turning out some 250 works that were performed in repentant Germany but failed to enlarge standard repertoire. In 1956 he led US experiments in *electronic music with the taped *Sanctus* that in Europe conferred respectability on what was still an experimental pursuit. In all, he wrote 20 operas, five symphonies and four piano concertos, of which the dissonant 3rd was conducted from the keyboard by Dmitri *Mitropoulos (Minneapolis, 22.xi.46). His first string quartet (1921) has clear affinities with *Bartók; the 7th (1944) invented a new variant on serial rotation. The first piano sonata (1919) shakes up the serene manner of his teacher *Schreker with young optimism; the 7th (1988) looks coolly ahead with a *12-note theme and *Cageian stringpluckings. His continuous stylistic rejuvenation embodied the Mahlerian ideal of musical progress. Whatever he wrote, no matter how abstruse, it had a smoothness and charm that was eternally Viennese.

b. Vienna 23.vii.1900; *d*. Palm Springs, California, 23.xii.91. *other significant works*: *The Bell Tower* (Hermann Melville opera, Urbana, Ill., 17.iii.57), *Der goldene Bock* (Hamburg State Opera, 16.vi.64), *Sardakai* (Hamburg, 27.vi.70); *Lamentatio Jeremiae Prophetae* (mixed choir, Kassel, 5.x.58), *The Santa Fé Timetable* (mixed choir, Los Angeles, 20.ii.61), *Simeon der Stylit* (oratorio, composed 1938, fp: Salzburg, 29.vii.88); orch. *Circle, Chain and Mirror* (Basle, 23.i.58), organ concerto (Melbourne, 17.v.83), two cello concertos.

Kreutzer Sonata *Janáček's string quartet, named after Tolstoy's short novel of repressed sexuality. fp: Prague, 17.ix.24.

Kroll Opera Berlin company led by *Klemperer throughout its existence, 1927–31, on a determinedly modern course, presenting local premières of works by Janáček, Stravinsky and Weill, juxtaposing modern music in concert with Bach favourites, and creating abstract stagings of Beethoven and Wagner operas. An affront to reactionaries, it was closed down by a rightwing Prussian government.

KRONOS QUARTET After *Britten and *Shostakovich died, the string quartet was all but surrendered for a while to *Ferneyhough-type obscurantists. Kronos reversed the trend, cultivating a new audience with a provocative blend of cerebral music, rock transcriptions and ballet-designed outfits. Playing nothing written before 1900 and very little pre-1960, their recitals sandwiched ink-wet new works between a *Bartók quartet and a Jimi Hendrix number. Founded in Seattle by David Harrington in 1973 and re-formed five years later in San Francisco, the ensemble has premiered some 400 pieces including majorworksby*Carter,*Feldman,*Gubaidulina, *Reich, *Rihm, *Sculthorpe and *Volans.

Jan and Rafael KUBELIK The father, Jan, was a heart-throb violinist who married a fortune and lost it in ill-advised speculations, returning to Czechoslovakia under Nazi occupation to play his heart out in every village he could visit. He composed six virtuosic concertos and a symphony.

His son, Rafael, was an accomplished, undemonstrative conductor who internationalized Covent Garden in the 1950s and spent a brief spell at the Met in 1973. He composed three operas, three symphonies and a Requiem in modern sonorities and with frequent yearnings for the homeland from which he was driven by communism. Published by *Universal, his music deserves greater attention, especially the cello concerto and *4 Forms* for string orch. (1965).

Jan K.: *b*. Michle, nr. Prague, 5.vii.1880; *d*. Prague, 5.xii.40.

Rafael: *b*.Býchory, Czechoslovakia, 29.vi. 14; cond. Brno National Theatre 1939–41, Czech Philharmonic 1942–48, founded

Prague Spring Festival 1946, exiled after communist putsch in 1948, Chicago SO 1950–53, Covent Garden 1955–58, Bavarian Radio SO 1961–85, Metropolitan Opera NY, 1973–74; married (1) Czech violinist Ludmilla Bertlová for whom he wrote a concerto and (2) Australian soprano Elsie Morison; returned to cond. Czech Philharmonic at Prague Spring Festival, 12.v.90.

Gail KUBIK US composer of Czech and Irish stock, won the 1952 Pulitzer Prize for *Symphonie concertante* for piano, viola, trumpet and orch.
   b. South Coffeyville, Oklahoma, 5.ix.14; *d.* Covina, California, 20.vii.84; *works include*: three symphonies, two violin concertos, ballet *Frankie and Johnny* (1946), cantata *In Praise of Johnny Appleseed* (1961).

György KURTÁG Strong and almost silent during *Hungary's communist era, Kurtág emerged in the 1980s as a distinctive, disturbing voice. He had lived, after a year's tuition in France, within an intense inner cocoon that constituted both an escape from and a rejection of tyranny. The 14-minute string quartet of 1959, his opus 1, comprised six miniature images, unexplained and indefinable yet absolutely vivid in their imagery.
   Over the next 20 years he composed fewer than a dozen pieces. Then, as the political climate thawed, he brought forth extraordinary pieces for soprano and orchestra – *Messages of the late Miss R. V. Troussova* (Paris, 14.i.81, cond. *Boulez), followed by *Scenes from a Novel* (1984)

and the 70-minute *Fragments* (1987) from Franz Kafka's letters and diaries. Austere, sparing and not readily approachable, his was a *Webern-like self-absorption in a technique and environment entirely of his own making. There were echoes of *Bartók, in the quartet and in 15 songs (1982) for soprano and cimbalom, but his introspection ran closer to late-*Shostakovich, an affinity underlined by the Russian texts of the Troussova songs.
   b. Lugos, Hungary (now Lugoj, Romania), 19.ii.26; st with *Veress, *Kadosa, *Weiner; taught Liszt Academy 1959–81; *other works*: *Jaketok (Games)* for 2 pianos (four books, 1973–76), *The Sayings of Peter Bornemisza* (soprano/piano, 1968), *Homage to Luigi *Nono* (chorus, 1980), *. . . quasi una fantasia . . .* for piano and orch. (1988), *Requiem for a Friend* (London, 31.x.89), double concerto (piano/cello, Frankfurt, 8.xii.90); *Samuel Beckett: What is the Word . . .* (Vienna, 27.x.91, cond. Abbado).

His son, **György KURTÁG** junior (*b.* 1954), a member of the Budapest avant-garde, co-founded the New Music Studio and composed *Chamber Music Basic Cases – Please Don't Be Angry With Me* for trombone and piano (1978).

Jaroslav KVAPIL Brno's second composer, after *Janáček, he added contrapuntal mastery to command of vibrant Moravian rhythms.
   b. Frystak, Moravia, 21.iv.1892; *d.* Brno, 18.ii.58. *works include*: four symphonies, two violin concertos, six string quartets.

Joan LA BARBARA Vocal experimentalist in the manner of Cathy *Berberian, she sang avant-garde arias against an amplified background. Despite its weirdness, her music is soothing to the point of sleepiness and slipped easily into *minimalism and *New Wave categories. Natural images are close to her heart and she captured the Green mood in 1980s Europe. Before joining the artistic vanguard, she sang commercials on television.

> *b.* Philadelphia, 8.vi.47; *works include*: *October Music: Star Showers and Extraterrestials* (Paris, 28.x.80), *The Solar Wind* (Los Angeles, 7.ii.83), *Vlissingen Harbor* (Los Angeles, 6.xii.82).

Josef LABOR Blind Viennese seer who taught Alma Mahler and in 1894 urged *Schoenberg to become a composer. His works include a piano quartet and sonatas.

> *b.* Horowitz, Austria, 29.vi.1842; *d.* Vienna, 26.iv.24.

Helmut (Friedrich) LACHENMANN This sometime *Darmstadt director (1978–82) wrote dissonances for large orchestra with lots of percussion under such titles as *Air* (1969), *Kontrakadenz* (1971) and *Façade* (1973). His hardline asceticism is belied by a youthful set of five piano variations on a Schubert theme.

> *b.* Stuttgart, Germany, 27.xi.35; st with *David and *Nono; professor at Stuttgart 1981–.

Paul-Emile LADMIRAULT Breton prodigy whose three-act opera *Gilles de Retz* was staged in Nantes in 1893 when he was just 15, Ladmirault mined a rich seam of folklore in his Breton Suite (1903) and a symphony (1910). He wrote incidental music to the Arthurian legend of *Tristan et Iseult* (1929) and a symphonic poem, *In the Forest*, (1932).

> *b.* Nantes, 8.xii.1877; *d.* Kerbili, nr. Penestin, 30.x.44.

A Lady Macbeth of the Mstensk District Searing *Shostakovich opera after Nikolai Leskov's 1864 story of a merchant's wife who murders twice for her lover, who then betrays her. Both plot and score are sexually explicit; the trombone glissandi in a copulation scene were termed *pornophony. No composer so young had handled complex emotions more confidently. 'It's about how love could have been if the world weren't full of vile things,' he explained. The influence of *Mahler and *Berg is abundant.

But for *Stalin's attack on Shostakovich in 1935, this would have become the *Rheingold* of a Soviet *Ring* – four operas about modern woman. Instead, *Lady Macbeth* was withdrawn and watered down 25 years later as *Katerina Ismailova.

> fp: Leningrad 22.i.34, cond. Samosud; Cleveland, Ohio, 31.i.35, cond. Rodzinski; revised version Moscow, 26.xii.62.

László LAJTHA Custodian of *Bartók's and *Kodály's archival legacy at the Budapest Ethnographic Museum, he composed nine symphonies, the last of which (Paris, 2.v.63) is worked around echoes of Gregorian chant. The 4th symphony, titled Spring, was the most ethno-centred, composed in 1951 while he was shut away from society among Bartók's artefacts and cylinders; it displays the Debussyian gloss of an incurable francophile.

b. Budapest, 30.vi.1892; *d.* there 16.ii.63. *other works*: ten string quartets, many folk-song settings.

Constant LAMBERT An exotic, toxic growth in the English garden, Lambert wrote *Romeo and Juliet* for *Diaghilev while still at college and, as founder-conductor at Sadler's Wells, assisted at the birth of British ballet. Son of an Australian painter, he was a highly-sexed, heavy drinker, immortalized as 'Moreland' in Antony Powell's novelistic sequence, *A Dance to the Music of Time*. He died at 45 of undiagnosed diabetes.

Lambert shook British music to its foundations with a polemic, *Music Ho!* (1934), subtitled 'a study of music in decline', attacking English nationalism, German romanticism and French impressionism and pointing to a future that was eclectically jazz-tinted. His own music called to mind Les *Six, lusty hedonism and vibrant rhythms puctuated by movements of lugubrious melancholy – as in the Concerto for piano and nine instruments (London, 18.xii.31).

The Rio Grande (Manchester, 12.xii.29), a Sitwell poem set for piano, chorus, contralto and orchestra, was hugely popular for a while, taking insular ears on a grand tour of dangerous foreign parts. His creativity was haphazard. Infatuated with the actress Anna May Wong in 1926, he set *8 Chinese Poems* by Li Po. *Elegiac Blues* (BBC, 23.vii.28) commemorates a black actress. Watching Nazi troops parachute into Holland at dawn, he wrote an *Aubade héroïque* for the defenders. His final ballet *Tiresias* (Covent Garden, 9.vii.51) struggled manfully with his ambivalent, tormenting sexuality.

b. London, 23.viii.05; *d.* there, 21.viii.51. *other works*: ballets *Pamona* (1927) and *Horoscope* (1938); *Summer's Last Will and Testament* for baritone, chorus and orchestra (1935). *Bib*: Andrew Motion, *The Lamberts*, London (Chatto), 1986.

Land des Lächelns (*Land of Smiles*) Lehár's second greatest hit, after *Merry Widow*. fp: Berlin, 10.x.29, starring Richard Tauber.

Wanda LANDOWSKA Missionary of the harpsichord, which she revived in Bach recitals and with concertos written for her by Falla and Poulenc; and leader of a grand lesbian arts salon in inter-War Paris. *b.* Warsaw, 5.vii.1877; founded early music school near Paris 1927, emigrated to US 1941; *d.* Lakeville, Connecticut, 16.viii.59.

Marcel LANDOWSKI While *Boulez threatened to burn down opera houses, Landowski was head of music at the ministry of culture (1966–70), forming the Orchestre de Paris and writing symphonies of a conservative nature. A Gallic hybrid of artist and administrator, he was an agent of compromise between the reactionaries and avant-garde, whose electronic innovations he gradually assimilated. His four symphonies have *Honegger (whose biography he wrote) as their presiding influence, urbane but insufficiently urgent. The first (Paris, 1949) and 4th (15.iv.88) have metaphysical programmes attached to their movements; the 3rd (Strasbourg, 1965) takes the earth's 'wide open spaces' as its theme and is almost a concerto for orchestra. He also wrote two piano concertos, another for cello, and a concerto for *ondes martenot. *b.* Pont de l'Abbé, Finistère, 8.ii.15; m Jacqueline Potier 1941; dir. Conservatoire at Boulogne-sur-Seine 1960–65; music director Comédie Française 1962–66; *other orch. works*: *Le Rire de Nils Halerius* (Mulhouse, 19.i.51, in which the first act is an opera, the second a ballet, the third an oratorio), *Le Fou* (Nancy, 1971), *Wuthering Heights* (electronic/orch.), concerto for trumpet, orch. and electro-acoustic elements.

István LÁNG A Hungarian kind of *Schnittke – pluralist, unconfined, unafraid of flirting with banality. In his violin concerto (1977) for György Pauk the instruments fret and snap at each other like married couples while the soloist sustains a tiny melody that may represent lost affection; fragments of Bach and Beethoven flash through the finale. *The Concerto bucolico* for horn and orchestra plays macabre hunting games. In grimly serious vein, *In Memoriam NN* (1971) is a disjointed cantata on poems from the Ravensbrück concentration camp. Affinities to *Ligeti and *Mahler are never far removed. *b.* Budapest, 1.iii.33; music director National Puppet Theatre 1966–84, sec.-gen. Association of Hungarian Musicians 1978– ; *other works*: four symphonies, three string quartets.

Rued LANGGAARD The opera *Antikrist* (1936) summed up Langgaard's attitude to the state of music in Denmark. He opposed it, and offended it mortally with an ironic cantata entitled *Our Great Composer Carl *Nielsen*, 32 bars long and designated 'to be repeated for all eternity'. Propelled by rage he composed 431 works, of which 16 are symphonies of increasingly obvious late-romantic merit – though, since he kept renumbering and revising them, it is not yet possible to assess them individually.
> *b.* Copenhagen, 28.vii.1893; *d.* Ribe, 10.vii. 52.

Jean LANGLAIS Blind French organ composer working in the solid Catholic tradition of César Franck and *Tournemire.
> *b.* La Fontelle, Brittany, 15.ii.07; succeeded Tournemire as organist at Ste-Clothilde, Paris, 1938–76; *d.* Paris, 8.v.91. *works include*: Gregorian paraphrases for organ (1934), *Homages* to Frescobaldi, John Stanley and other masters of the instrument, etc.

Paul LANSKY A distant cousin of the celebrated gangster, Lansky taught unimpeachably at Princeton (1969–) and composed unexceptionally gentle tape and computer music. *As it grew dark* (1983) reprocesses the voice of an actress reading chapter 25 of Charlotte Brontë's *Jane Eyre*.
> *b.* NY, 18.vi.44; st with *Perle, *Weisgall, *Babbitt; *other works*: string quartet (1967), *mild und leise* (tape, 1976).

The Lark Ascending *Vaughan Williams romance for violin and orch. fp: London, 14.vi.21.

Lars-Erik LARSSON The first Swede to adopt *12-note music, Larsson flickered between the method *Berg taught him in Vienna and the pallid romanticism they loved back home. He was not much of a revolutionary. The mellifluous violin concerto (Stockholm, 11.i.53) manages a delicate balance between form, virtuosity and lilting melody. The saxophone concerto (Norrköping, 27.xi.34), an amiable oddity, arose from meeting the player Sigurd Rascher at the 1934 Florence *ISCM and finding they shared a birthday. When his opera *Princess of Cyprus* (29.iv.37) folded after 12 nights, Larsson tapped mass appeal with the Pastoral Suite (1939) and incidental music to Shakespeare's *A Winter's Tale* (1938). He would have been welcomed in Hollywood.
> *b.* Akarp, Sweden, 15.v.08; won state scholarship with 1st symphony (27.iv.29); worked for Swedish Radio, 1937–43, professor at State Academy, Stockholm, 1947–59; *d.* Danderyd, Stockholm, 27.xii.86. *other works*: three symphonies (1929–45, all withdrawn), Sinfonietta (1932), wartime propaganda songs, incidental music for plays by Shelley, Schiller and Strindberg, eloquent 12-tone Adagio for strings (1960), three string quartets.

James LAST Hugely commercial German leader of Glenn *Millerish big band for middle-class dance nights.
> *b.* Bremen, Germany 17.iv.29;

LEADBELLY The confluence in New York around 1938 of this Louisiana jailbird with Woody Guthrie's prairie folk and Pete Seeger's protest lyrics set the ball rolling on the American folk revival. Leadbelly, nicknamed for an abdominal bullet wound, had been jailed twice for murder and mayhem before he was found by folklorists to be a walking compendium of early *blues and southern stories. Freed in 1934, he worked his way into New York leftist chic, only to be jailed again for assault in 1939. The recordings he made between prison terms provided fodder for future hits by Seeger, the Weavers and Lonnie Donegan – 'Goodnight Irene', 'The Midnight Special', 'Pick a Bale of Cotton'.
> *b.* Mooringsport, Louisiana, 20.i.1889 (as Huddie William Ledbetter); *d.* NY, 6.xii.49.

Lear The Shakespearian tragedy that eluded Verdi and Britten was made into a tense, noisy opera by Aribert *Reimann (fp: Munich, 9.vii.1978). It also inspired a tone-poem by *Weingartner and an abandoned work by *Debussy.

Benjamin LEES Expressive American symphonist who keeps his dissonances under control and likes to open a large work with an instrumental solo. The 4th of five symphonies, *Memorial Candles* (1985), commemorates the Nazi Holocaust in a soprano recitation of Nelly Sachs poems.

b. Harbin, Manchuria, China, 8.i.24; *other works*: violin concerto (1958), concerto for string quartet and orch. (1965), concerto for brass (1983), horn concerto (1992).

Ton and Reinbert de LEEUW Dutch brother-composers, the elder more ethno-musicologically inclined, the younger a leading *Cageian and minimalist.

  Ton de Leeuw: *b.* Rotterdam, 16.xii.26; st with *Messiaen; sound director of Hilversum Radio 1954–59, then taught at Utrecht and Amsterdam; *works include*: radio oratorio *Job* (1956), opera *The Dream* based on 14 haiku (1965), *Symphonies for Winds* (homage to *Stravinsky, 1963), *Gending* for gamelan orch. (1975).

  Reinbert de Leeuw: *b.* Amsterdam, 8.ix.38; played the first recording of *Satie's *Vexations*; *works include*: *Rekonstructie*, 1969 anti-imperialist opera with *Andriessen, *Mengelberg, *Schat and Van Viljmen.

Paul LE FLEM Centenarian French neo-classicist and critic, composed 4 symphonies and an opera, *Le Rossignol de St-Malo* (Paris, Opéra-Comique, 5.v.42).

  b. Lézardrieux, 18.iii.1881; *d.* Trégastel, 31.vii.84.

Michel LEGRAND French composer of film music, his name used disparagingly by Boulezites to describe any music with tunes in it. His scores have yielded numerous hit ballads – 'Windmills of your Mind', 'Mon Amour', etc.

  b. Paris, 24.ii.32; *top movies*: *Bonjour tristesse* (1958), *Les parapluies de Cherbourg* (1964), *The Thomas Crown Affair* (1968), *The Go-Between* (1970).

Franz LEHÁR The operetta emperor wrote slower, smoochier dances than Vienna's waltz kings, founding his success on well-crafted melodramas with one hit per show. Librettists were told to keep the plot light and the characters credible; music would do the rest. It is hard to understand how a comedy of diplomatic manners as vapid as *The Merry Widow* (Vienna, 30.xii.05) could sweep the world for half a century, except by virtue of its appeal to bourgeois snobbery, its total unseriousness and one marvellous melody. Hitler loved the show; Mahler memorized the waltz. Its tune became Lehár's trade-mark; no-one complained of its affinity to the first of Brahms' Hungarian dances. It cropped up in several shows and raised the curtain in *Paganini* (Vienna, 30.x.25), his romancification of the diabolical fiddler.

  Lehár regularly reused songs, even entire shows. When *Yellow Jack* (1923) bombed at the Viennese box-office, he recycled it in Berlin six years later as *The Land of Smiles*. Although the 'golden tenor' Richard Tauber made hits of 'You are my Heart's Delight' from *The Land of Smiles* and 'O Mädchen, mein Mädchen' from *Friederika* (1928), nothing equalled *The Merry Widow*. *The Count of Luxembourg* (Vienna, 12.xi.09) and *Gypsy Love* (*Zigeunerliebe*, Vienna, 8.x.10) ran longer than the rest; *Giuditta*, (Vienna, 20.i.34), his last, required a Mahler-sized orchestra.

  Like most Viennese entertainers, Lehár was of non-Austrian origin. The Nazis overlooked his Jewish wife, but not his librettist, Fritz Löhner-Beda, whom they exterminated.

  b. Komorn, Hungary, 30.iv.1870, son of a Czech army bandmaster; st in Prague with *Foerster's father and *Fibich; joined military band 1889; operatic success at Leipzig in 1896 with *Kukuschka*; first operetta was *Wiener Frauen* (Vienna, 25.xi.02); *d.* Bad Ischl, Austria, 24.x.48. *works*: 28 operettas, Hungarian Fantasy for violin and orch.

René LEIBOWITZ Preacher of *Schoenberg's gospel in post-1945 Paris, his compositions were less significant than his revelatory impact on *Boulez.

  b. Warsaw, 17.ii.13; moved to Paris 1926; *d.* Paris, 28.vii.72. *works include*: five operas; violin concerto (1959), *Marijuana* for violin, trombone, vibraphone, piano (1960), eight string quartets.

Walter LEIGH British *Hindemith pupil killed in action at Tobruk. In 1932 he had the distinction of having an austere sonatina played at the *ISCM in Vienna while his show *Jolly Roger* was rehearsing in the West End.

  b. London, 22.vi.05; *d.* nr. Tobruk, Libya, 12.vi.42.

Kenneth LEIGHTON A cello concerto (1956) of precocious eloquence and Elgarian wistfulness was Leighton's break-through. After studying in Rome with *Petrassi he changed course into serialism and taught at Edinburgh U. His 2nd and 3rd symphonies (1977/85) have vocal soloists.

b. Wakefield, Yorkshire, 2.x.29; *d*. Edinburgh, 24.viii.88. *other works*: *Columba* (Glasgow, 16.vi.81); symphony for strings (1948), three piano concertos (1951/60/69), organ concerto (1970) choral suite *The Birds*; *Fantasia contrapuntistica* for piano (1956).

Artur LEMBA Composer of the first Estonian symphony, a 1908 romantic essay in C# minor whose national import overshadows its simple warmth.

b. Tallinn, 24.ix.1885; *d*. there, 21.xi.63. *other works*: five piano concertos.

Lenin Music commemorating the Bolshevik leader (1870–1924) includes Shostakovich's 12th symphony, Kabalevsky's third, Khrennikov's opera *Into the Storm*, Khachaturian's funeral ode, and countless cantatas.

Leningrad Symphony Shostakovich's 7th. The title was not his, nor was the popular image of a city resisting fascism. The composer intended the symphony to reflect Stalin's tyranny. fp: Kuibishev, 5.iii.42.

Lotte LENYA Sparrow-voiced actress wife of Kurt *Weill, she invented a half-spoken, half-sung style in *Mahagonny* and *The *Threepeny Opera*.

b. Vienna, 18.x.1898; married Weill 1926, divorced 1933, remarried 1935; *d*. NY, 27.xi. 81.

Ruggero LEONCAVALLO Co-founder with *Mascagni of *verismo opera, he scored with a single-act sex-and-murder saga called *Pagliacci* (*Buffoons*) (Milan 21.v.1892, cond. *Toscanini) that proved the perfect companion to Mascagni's outstanding *Cavalleria Rusticana*. He was beaten by *Puccini in a race to compose *La Bohème* (Venice, 6.v.1897) and, though initially preferred by Vienna, his version lacked a psychological dimension and strong tunes. His subsequent dozen operas were failures.

b. Naples, 23.iv.1857; *d*. Montecantini, 9.viii. 19. *other operas*: *Der Roland von Berlin* (commissioned by Kaiser Wilhelm II, Berlin, 13.xii.04), *La jeunesse de Figaro* (1906), *Maia* (1919), *Malbruk* (1910), *Gli Zingari* (London, 16.ix.12), *La candida* (1915), *Edipo rè* (Chicago, 13.xii.20).

Dmitri LEVIDIS Parisian Greek composer who wrote the first performable works for *ondes Martenot (Poème symphonique, Paris, 23.xii.28; *De profundis*, 5.i.30). He also composed *The Iliad* as a violin concerto (1927).

b. Athens, 8.iv.1886, *d*. there, 30.v.51. *other work*: *Chant payen* for oboe and strings.

Marvin David LEVY Composed *Mourning Becomes Electra* (17.iii.67) for the Metropolitan Opera and was tarnished by its failure.

b. Passaic, New Jersey, 2.viii.32;

Anatoli LIADOV Picturesque composer of symphonic tableaux: *Baba Yaga* (St Petersburg, 18.iii.04), *Enchanted Lake* (21.ii.09) and *Kikimora* (12.xii.09).

b. St Petersburg, 10.v.1855; *d*. nr. Novgorod, 28.viii.14.

Sergei LIAPOUNOV Despatched by the Imperial Geographic Society to collect folksongs in central Asia, he returned with materials for a symphonic poem, *Hashish* (1910). His two piano concertos (1890, 1909) and *Ukrainian Rhapsody* (Berlin, 23.iii.08, *Busoni soloist) have brilliant keyboard parts.

b. Yaroslavl, Russia, 30.xi.1859; *d*. Paris, 8.xi.24.

Boris LIATOSHINSKY Isolated composer in Kiev who encouraged his pupils *Silvestrov and *Hrabovsky to engage with forbidden Western *avant-gardism. His own scores were folkish and party-line but he earned a place as father to post-Soviet modernism.

b. Zhitomir, Ukraine, 3.i.1895; professor at Kiev conservatory 1920–68 and at Moscow 1935–38 and 1941–43; *d*. Kiev, 15.iv.68. *works include*: opera *Shchors*, celebrating Soviet partisan (Kiev, 1.ix.38); five symphonies; *Slavonic concerto*, piano and orch. (1953).

Licht Stockhausen's magnum opus: seven operas representing each day of the week, starting with *Donnerstag* (*Thursday*, Milan, 15.iii.81), and tracing the life-journey of a Siegfried-like hero.

Ingvar LIDHOLM A member of *Blomdahl's Monday Group, he forsook Swedish folkishness for *serialism, applying Swedish texts in vocal scores of surprising sensuality, most entrancingly in *Nausicaa alone* (1963) for soprano, chorus and orchestra.

b. Jönköping, Sweden, 24.ii.21; st with *Rosenberg and Matyas *Seiber; cond. Örebro orchestra 1947–56; *other works*: TV opera *The Dutchman* (after Strindberg, 1967), Bartókian *Music for Strings* (1952), *Stamp music* (a score intended to appear on a Swedish postage stamp).

Rolf LIEBERMANN

Power-player in European opera, he struck stylish blows for modernism as head of Hamburg state opera (1959–73) and the Paris Opéra (1973–80). At Hamburg, he premiered *Krenek and *Penderecki and presented new stagings of Berg, Britten and Janáček. Attacked by *Boulez for neglecting the *avant-garde, the wily Liebermann recruited him to conduct the complete *Lulu*. Before and after his administrative career, Liebermann was an unexceptional *serialist composer.

> *b.* Zurich, 14.ix.10; st with *Vogel; *works include*: operas *Leonore 40/45* (Basle, 25.iii. 52), *Penelope* (Salzburg, 17.viii.54), *Le forêt* (Geneva, 8.iv.87); concerto for jazzband and orch. (Donaueschingen) 17.x.54).

Goddard LIEBERSON

English-born composer who reached the top of a major record company, using his clout to promote contemporary work by Schoenberg, Webern, Stravinsky and Copland. At CBS he was known as 'God'. Among many premières, he recorded the first *Porgy and Bess*. Only two of his own scores got on to disc, a 1938 string quartet and *Piano pieces for advanced children or retarded adults*, written for his son, Peter.

> *b.* Hanley, Staffs., 5.iv.11; st Eastman School of Music, Rochester, NY; married ballerina Vera Zorina; joined Columbia Records 1939, president 1955–66 and 1973–5; president Record Industry Association of America, 1964; *d.* NY, 29.v.77.

His son **Peter LIEBERSON** was the youngest of 12 composers commissioned by the Boston Symphony Orchestra for its centennial. His piano concerto, performed (21.iv.83) by Peter Serkin and Seiji Ozawa ambles pacifically on a Buddhist-inspired 'journey'. A triplet of *Bagatelles* meanders with slightly greater purpose in its central section, *Spontaneous Songs*. Lieberson founded a Tibetan meditation programme in Massachusetts.

> *b.* NY, 25.x.46; st with *Babbitt, *Wuorinen, *Martino; performed by *Boulez in New York; ceased composing for a year on becoming Buddhist in 1973 and altered his style thereafter; *other works*: Concerto for four groups of instruments; Piano Fantasy, *Lalita* (Chamber Variations).

Das Lied von der Erde

(*The Song of the Earth*) Symphonic setting for two voices of German texts of eighth-century Chinese poems given to *Mahler in the summer of 1907, when shattered by his daughter's death and the diagnosis of his own fatal illness. The six songs for tenor, contralto and relatively small orchestra describe the fragility of life on earth. The consolatory ending, 'Ewig, Ewig . . .' (forever), marks a temporary coming to terms with terminality. Mahler feared some sections would be unperformable and did not live to conduct the work. *Webern described it as 'the most marvellous composition that ever existed'. It gave rise to numerous imitations, notably Zemlinsky's Lyric Symphony and Shostakovich's 14th, in which a poetic message is walled into the symphonic structure.

> composed Toblach 1908–9; fp: Munich, 20.xi.1911, cond. Bruno Walter, soloists William Miller and Sarah Charles Cahier.

Lieder

The final flickerings of German art-song came from Strauss, Pfitzner and Berg; *Vier Letzte Lieder* by Strauss amount to a virtual epitaph.

Revivalist attempts by *Blacher, *Eisler and von *Einem made no impact beyond German-speaking lands. The international art-song lingered longer in French (Poulenc), English (Britten) and Russian (Shostakovich). There is some substance to the assertion that popular ballads like *Weill's 'September Song' and the *Beatles 'Yesterday' are a modern incarnation of the Lied tradition.

Lieutenant Kijé

Concert suite lightly reorchestrated by *Prokofiev from his first film score, written on his return to the USSR. fp Paris, 20.ii.37.

Max LIFCHITZ

Mexican musician living in New York, he composed a series of 64 *Yellow Ribbons* for various instruments and ensembles, one for each hostage held by the Iranians in 1979 in the US Embassy in Tehran.

> *b.* Mexico City, 11.xi.48; taught Columbia U. 1977–86, NY State U. 1986– ;

other works: *Exceptional String Quartet* (1978).

György (Sandor) LIGETI On the night of 7.xi.56, while Soviet armour was pulverizing the Hungarian revolution outside his Budapest window, a 33-year-old composer crouched beside the radio and was literally transported by the crackly first broadcast of Stockhausen's *Gesang der Jünglinge*. Ligeti decided to risk an escape across the heavily-patrolled border and within two months was working at the forefront of *avant-gardism in Cologne. He settled in Vienna, forming a close creative friendship with *Cerha. In 1968 he became the first advanced composer to reach a mass audience when Stanley Kubrick spliced his ethereal *Lux aeterna* into the soundtrack of the space movie, *2001*. Its shivering chorus conveyed a much-imitated illusion of lunar alienation, a feeling with which Ligeti was tragically familiar.

In Hungary, his family was destroyed by the Nazis, father and brother murdered at Auschwitz and Ligeti himself sent into forced labour. The communists banned his radical music and as a lecturer in harmony at the Liszt Academy he was cut off from the *serial and *electronic experiments that he knew were taking place beyond the impermeable Iron Curtain. *Métamorphoses nocturnes*, his first string quartet (comp. 1953–4, fp Vienna, 8.v.58), used the rhythms and sonorities of *Bartók in an acutely individual way, rich in sardonic humour and sudden laments. The music scurries, then stops in static 'clouds' of sound. After a decade of modernist self-immersion, he wrote a second quartet (Baden-Baden, 14.xii.69) that reiterated the ideas of the first in more sophisticated terminology, but without loss of humanity or wit. Even in his greatest abstractions, there was always a hint of tongue-in-cheek. In ascetic *Darmstadt, he became a *Beatles fan.

Some of his more celebrated pieces were 'music about music', not to be taken entirely seriously however valid their message. *Poème Symphonique pour 100 Metronomes* (1962) made a statement about musicians' rigid adherence to tempo markings in a piece that – intentionally – provoked full-throated laughter. *0'00"*, the shortest composition on record, mocked Cage's *4'33"*; *The Future of Music* (1961) for non-speaking lecturer and audience was a parody of *performance art that raised issues of *musical communication. The weird glottal noises of *Aventures/ Nouvelles Aventures* (1962–65) had something comic and interesting to say about opera singers and their temperamental instrument; in due course, the pieces were staged together as a deadly serious mini-opera.

What he sought at Cologne, while living in Stockhausen's apartment, was the means to express a sound he imagined as a child in the Dracula land of Transylvania. He assimilated serialism by mathematically analysing *Boulez's *Structures 1a*, and *electronics by working with Gottfried Michael *Koenig on a piece called *Essai*. He then shrugged off the techniques and their associated ideologies to achieve *Apparitions* (Cologne, 19.vi.60, cond. Ernest Bour) and *Atmosphères* (Donaueschingen, 22.x.61, cond. *Rosbaud), two nine-minute orchestral pieces that introduced a particular soundworld of shifting, spiralling and motionless structures. Credited with inventing the glissando-*cluster, he shifted the credit to *Xenakis, whose ideas he disliked. He defined his own method as 'micropolyphony'.

For much of the 1960s he engaged with vocal effects in *Aventures* and a fearsome *Requiem* (Stockholm, 14.iii.65, cond. *Gielen). He refined his orchestral habit in a cello concerto (Berlin, 19.iv.67, cond. *Czyz) and *Lontano* (Donaueschingen, 22.x.67), and slimmed it down in the chamber concerto for 13 instruments (Berlin, 1.x.70). The next decade was taken up by his grotesque, erotic and anti-political opera, *Le *Grand Macabre* (Stockholm, 12.iv.78, cond. *Howarth), conceived as ominous but sometimes staged as comedy.

Throughout, there was a progression to what laymen would call 'beauty' and Ligeti dubbed 'transparency'. It was signalled in a delicate Double Concerto for flute, oboe and orch. (Berlin, 16.ix.72) and affirmed resoundingly in *San Francisco Polyphony* for large orchestra (San Francisco, 8.i.75, cond. *Ozawa) that created order from disparate sonic objects in a way that pleased the ear as much as the intellect. Ligeti became seriously ill with a heart condition in 1979 and had time to reflect with some bitterness on the impasse in modern music.

He eliminated static passages from his music and talked of finding new harmonic and rhythmic possibilities. The horn trio (1982) carried minimalist echoes of *Nancarrow, a stubborn loner whom Ligeti had lately discovered. Six Etudes for piano (1983) and the piano concerto (1985–88) are affectingly pleasant without yielding an iota of wit, bite or calculated precision. Ligeti had staked his territory on the fringe of modernism and prospected it continually for the oil of fluency that Mozart deemed to be the supreme musical virtue.

   b. Dicsöszentmárton, Hungary (now Tîrnaveni, Romania), 28.v.23; st with *Kadosa, Ference Farkas, Sándor Veress; taught Budapest 1950–56, guest professor Stockholm, Academy of Music 1961–71; married Vera Spitz, 1957; *other works*: *Ramifications* for string orch. (Berlin, 23.iv.69), *Melodien* for orch. (Nuremberg, 10.xii.71), *Clocks and Clouds* for women's chorus and orch. (Graz, 15.x.73, cond. *Cerha), *Hungarian Studies* for 16 voices (Stockholm, 26.ix.83), *Nonsense Madrigals* for six voices (1988), *Artikulation* (four-minute tape, 1957), *Continuum* (1968) and *Hungarian Rock* (1978) for harpsichord. *Bib*: Paul Griffiths, *György Ligeti*, London (Robson Books), 1983.

Douglas (Gordon) LILBURN   The first New Zealand composer to catch the limelight ran through the gamut of 20th century techniques, from the pastoralism of his teacher *Vaughan Williams to serialism and advanced electronics, in search of an internationally acceptable idiom. He might have done better to develop the intriguing Pacific sounds in the overture *Aotearoa* (1940), *A Song of Islands* (1947) and two early symphonies (1948–51).

   b. Wanganui, NZ, 2.xi.15; taught Victoria U. 1947– and founded electronic music studios there.

A Lincoln Portrait   *Copland's human-rights declamation, banned at President Eisenhower's inauguration. fp: Cincinnati, 14.v.42.

Magnus LINDBERG   Meteoric member of Finland's *Ears Open revolution,

Lindberg migrated to Paris at 23 to rediscover *musique concrète. His gloss on this defunct phenomenon was to submit the sounds of sea, rain, wind and fire to musical performance and electronic transformation in *Action – Situation – Signification* (1982), a composition dense to the point of intellectual pretentiousness, using Canetti's sociological treatise *Crowds and Power* as its underlying scheme. *Kraft* (1985), Lindberg's breakthrough work, is a piano concerto achieved with computer assistance, more soundscape than concert composition. *Xenakis and *Boulez were conscious influences. His most eloquent piece is *Kinetics* (Helsinki, 13.iii.89), which adopts the tinkling runs common to Messiaen's followers as a meeting-point with its public. 'I am a child of the times,' he once said. 'I like things that are complicated.'

   b. Helsinki, 27.vi.58; st with *Rautavaara, *Heininen, *Globokar; *other orch. works: Joy* (Frankfurt, 9.xii.90), *Marea* (London, 26.iv.90), *Metal Work* (1984, accordion and percussion).

Dinu LIPATTI   Delicate and dazzling Romanian pianist, noted for Chopin playing. His compositions were ethnically inspired and late romantic. They include a fiery symphonic suite, 'The Gypsies', a symphonie concertante for two pianos and strings, and Three Rumanian Dances for two pianos.

   b. Bucharest, 1.iv.17; st in Paris with Cortot, Boulanger and Dukas; *d.* Geneva (of leukemia), 2.xii.50.

Malcolm LIPKIN   Shy, austere English humanist, portraying in his first symphony (1965) the evils of city living and in his 3rd (1986) the span of modern life.

   b. Liverpool, 2.v.32; st with *Seiber; *other works*: piano concerto (1957), two violin concertos.

literature   Composers were always drawn to the written word but writers – even passionate music lovers like Goethe – disdained music as a literary subject. This attitude was reversed around the turn of the century. Marcel Proust (1871–1922) in *A la recherche du temps perdu* (published 1913–1921) modelled the fictional Vinteuil sonata on the Saint-Saëns D minor Op 75;

Proust structured his masterpiece with intricate inter-thematic relationships and a fastidious development of leitmotivs. In both style and construction, he imitated the process of musical composition more closely than any writer before him. Romain Rolland (1869–1944) introduced the composer as philosopher-hero in *Jean-Christoph* (1904–12).

The outstanding German writer Thomas Mann distilled his musical preoccupations into a powerful late novel of a composer's struggle with contemporary devils. The protagonist of *Doctor Faustus* (1949) was loosely based on *Schoenberg and its twelve-tone theory derived from Californian conversations with *Adorno and the conductor Bruno Walter. In post-1945 German literature the role of music was greatly diminished, although in Günter Grass's *The Tin Drum* (1959), the narrator's primitive musical lusts operate subversively in orderly Nazi society.

*Shaw, musically the most informed of British writers, avoided music in his plays. D. H. Lawrence (1885–1930) was influenced by Wagner, literally in *The Trespasser* (1909, first entitled *The Saga of Siegmund*), subliminally in many of the later works. He befriended the composers *Warlock and *Gray and drew them into *Lady Chatterly's Lover* and *Aaron's Rod*. The most musical of English writings, in both structure and subject matter, is *Joyce's *Ulysses*, itself an inspiration to many composers.

Anthony Powell (*b.* 1905), misleadingly likened to Proust, named his 12-novel cycle *A Dance to the Music of Time* (1951–75) after a painting by Poussin but used musical rhythm and structure to sustain its tension. The composers *Warlock, *Walton and *Gray are lightly fictionalized in *Casanova's Chinese Restaurant* (1960) and the concluding volume *Hearing Secret Harmonies* underlines the writer's aural concentration. J. B. Priestley (1894–1984) gave a vivid evocation of Brahms' First Symphony in his 1930 novel of London life, *Angel Pavement*, and was closely associated with two London orchestras. These were, however, exceptions: the mainstream of English writers remained resolutely tone deaf. Among American novelists, there is little evidence of musical interest; the poets were, of course, supremely musical.

Two Czechs, Milan Kundera and Josef Skvorecky, employ jazz musicians as symbols of resistance in a totalitarian society, their improvisatory gifts challenging rigid ideologies. Kundera's father was a *Janáček pupil; Skvorecky wrote a novel on Dvořák. In Kundera's discourses on the art of the novel, structure, economy and sonata form are paramount.

Tolstoy, though he employed a musical setting in the Kreutzer Sonata, disparaged most composed music. Lenin added weight to his prejudice by condemning music as a harmful distraction to revolutionaries. Between them they declared music off-limits to Russian prose writers. *Pasternak, with music in his blood, confined his allusions to poetry and, faintly, to *My Sister Love*.

The cross-fertilization between poetry and music remained active as ever. *Shostakovich and Anna Akhmatova saw themselves as allies against authority, *Britten's dramatic skills were discovered by *Auden, *Berg found his creative voice through the verses of 'Peter Altenberg' (Richard Englander) and *Boulez through René Char and Mallarmé. Allen Ginsberg and Bob Dylan are opposite sides of the same creative coin.

Little RICHARD Archetype rock'n'-roller, anarchic in performance, dress and sexual proclivity, he was a primary influence on Elvis Presley, the Beatles, the Rolling Stones and Jimi Hendrix. His self-defining hits were 'Long Tall Sally' (1956) and 'Good Golly Miss Molly' (1958). He survived puritan antagonism, physical deformities and a 1985 car smash to enjoy an uncommon longevity among his ilk.

b. Macon, Georgia, 5.xii.35 as Richard Wayne Penniman;

George LLOYD A Cornishman whose opera was staged and his 3rd symphony nationally broadcast by the time he was 22, Lloyd was then shellshocked in the war and retired for 20 years to grow carnations and mushrooms. Interest in his work resurged in the 1970s and he resumed composing.

Comparisons to Havergal *Brian are misplaced, for Lloyd wrote untaxing, sincerely old-fashioned music. *The Vigil of Venus*, an oratorio for chorus and orch., was performed in 1989 by Welsh National Opera, but could have been presented half a century before without alarm. The 11th symphony, written for the Albany Symphony Orchestra (Troy, NY, 31.x.86) has a second movement that sounds like a Mahlerian adagio written on a theme from Verdi's *Otello*; the rest shunts between Shostakovich and Vaughan Williams. His 1934 opera, *Iernin*, evokes the ruggedness of his native coastline; both his operas have librettos by his father.

b. St Ives, Cornwall, 28.vi.13; st violin with Albert Sammons; revival started with Edward Downes' 1977 BBC concert of 8th symphony. *other works*: operas, *The Serf* (Covent Garden, 20.x.38), *John Socman* (1951); four piano and two violin concertos.

Jonathan LLOYD Sometime street busker who achieved a kind of *minimalism by massive means, using electric guitar, jazz kit, saxophones and all manner of percussion in his 4th symphony (London, 26.vii.88), to arrive somewhere between *Tippett and Tommy Dorsey. Simon *Rattle is a keen interpreter.

b. London, 30.ix.48; *other works*: 1st symphony (Birmingham, 19.i.89), 2nd symphony (Baden-Baden, 12.ii.88), 3rd symphony for chamber orch. (1987), viola concerto (with huge percussion section, London 10.xi.81), *If I could Turn You On* for high soprano and chamber orch. (1981).

Andrew LLOYD WEBBER The glory of Broadway, or what little remained of it by 1980, was grabbed by the son of English church organist. Andrew Lloyd Webber's musicals allied simple-minded *pop songs to household themes. His unoriginal formula was unerringly commercial; whether it has lasting artistic merit needs to be judged work by work.

The first two shows were biblical and brimming with boyish irreverence. *Joseph and the Amazing Technicolor Dreamcoat* (Central Hall, Westminster, 12.v.68) had a psychedelic Sergeant Pepperish vitality. *Jesus Christ Superstar* was initially conceived with John Lennon in the JC role. This self-designated 'popera's' pretensions to higher art were confirmed by a lush instrumentation and André *Previn's involvement in the movie score.

It was released on record months before it was staged (Mark Hellinger Theater, Broadway, x.71), a familiarization trick that Lloyd Webber repeated with all his shows. Both lyrics and puerile tunes soon sounded dated by an era when *Time* magazine could demand 'Is God Dead?' and the Beatles claimed to be more famous than Christ.

Evita (Prince Edward Theatre, London, 21.vi.78) was paraded as an opera and derided accordingly, though its title song was the most memorable Lloyd Webber would ever write. Its story of the madonna-like wife of a corrupt Argentine dictator was emotionally flat and intellectually suspect. It ended his partnership with writer Tim Rice.

The next three shows dispensed with a storyline. Two described childish fancies, the third was mere contrivance. *Cats* (New London Theatre, 11.v.81) was a plotless song-and-dance show of T. S. Eliot felicities. *Starlight Express* (Apollo Theatre, Victoria, 27.iii.84) had roller-skaters simulating railway trains in an 'awesomely awful' presentation that lacked the faintest hint of a strong musical or cerebral idea. *Song and Dance* (Palace Theatre, London, 7.v.82) exploited the brazenly banal Paganini Variations he had previously written for his brother Julian's cello and rock ensemble, and sold as a theme for a long-running TV arts programme (LWT, South Bank Show).

By now, Lloyd Webber was among the richest men in showbiz and could have rested on gold-encrusted laurels. What drove him on was a desire for serious recognition as a composer, a frustration that embittered his father, whose death he mourned in a Requiem (St Thomas Episcopal Church, Manhattan, 24.ii.85, cond. Maazel) that was derivative enough to sound like a synthesis of untraceable bars by Puccini and Fauré. It was so sensually uninvolving as to raise questions about Lloyd Webber's human feelings. These he addressed in the autobiographical next show, *Phantom of the Opera* (Her Majesty's Theatre, London, 9.x.86), about an ugly composer who falls in love with a comely singer. His much-publicized marriage to its star, Sarah Brightman, lasted six years.

His last musical, *Aspects of Love* (London, 17.iv.89), was the ultimate bid to write an opera: composed throughout, with genuine arias and set-pieces that still, somehow, sounded as secondhand as Puccini in *The Girl of the Golden West* – a man who knew what he could do and persisted in trying to do something else. Shortly after the opening, Lloyd Webber, aged 41, announced on live television that he was giving up writing musicals and would concentrate on making movies.

    b. London, 22.iii.48;

Vassily LOBANOV Alfred Schnittke, his teacher, praised Lobanov's balancing act between *romanticism and *minimalism; Sviatoslav Richter, his concert partner, was drawn to his textural delicacy. Lobanov's 2nd piano sonata (1980) marked a libertarian breakthrough in Russian music by giving the soloist the freedom to decide how often to repeat each passage. Like much minimalism, it lacked an abundance of ideas, but the few displayed were sensitive. As a dedicated *poly-stylist, he employed *collage and quotations, many of them comprehensible only to his countrymen. Since 1990, Lobanov has lived in Germany.

    b. Moscow, 1947; *other works*: opera *Antigone* (1988), concertos for cello (1985) and viola (1989), symphony for chamber orch. (1977), five string quartets; three haikus for low voice and piano (1963).

Charles Martin LOEFFLER A musician who brought the bounties of many European cultures to Boston. Born in Alsace-Lorraine, between French and German cuisines, he followed his parents to Russia, the Ukraine, Hungary and Switzerland. He studied violin in Berlin and Paris. In 1881, aged 21, he crossed the Atlantic to play in Leopold Damrosch's New York band, then as first concertmaster of the new Boston Symphony Orchestra. He gave up playing in 1903 and applied himself to teaching and composing plush romanticisms under such exotic titles as *Hora mystica* (Boston, 2.iii.17, cond.

Muck), *Memories of my childhood* (*Life in a Russian Village*) (Chicago, 30.v.24) and a *Poem* for orch. after Verlaine's *La Bonne Chanson* (Boston, 1.xi.18).

    b. Mulhouse, 30.i.1861; *d.* Medfield, Massachusetts, 19.v.35.

Anestis LOGOTHETIS Vienna-based, mystical Bulgarian of Greek descent, his radical scores were so diagrammatic they were exhibited and sold as paintings.

    b. Burgas, Bulgaria, 27.x.21; st with *Uhl; *works include*: ballet *Odysee* (1963), stage work *Anastasis* (1969), many works for variable and optional instruments.

London A musical backwater following Handel's death, London's rebirth as a world centre for music was prompted by the growth of its record industry, the influx of Hitler refugees and the public response to Elgar's and Britten's success. The turning point was 1945 when government subsidy was passed through the Arts Council to two national opera companies and the number of full-time professional symphony orchestras leaped from three to five – more than any other metropolis could sustain. Proliferation bred commercial rivalry rather than perfectionism, but for the latter half of the century London musicians have prided themselves as being equal to any music that is put before them and London audiences have proved remarkably eclectic. Most major composers have spent time in the city. *Vaughan Williams wrote a symphony in its honour.

London Sinfonietta Small orch. founded 1968 to play late-20th-century music, it has given around 200 premières, among them major works by *Abrahmsen, *Birtwistle, *Carter, *Henze, Maxwell *Davies, *Osborne, *Takemitsu, *Xenakis.

Nicolai LOPATNIKOV St Petersburg refugee in Pittsburgh, he married the poetess Sara Henderson Hay, was elected to the National Institute of Arts and Letters and composed *neo-classically.

    b. Reval, Estonia, 16.iii.03; st at St Petersburg, lived in Germany 1920–33, London 1933–39, professor at Pittsburgh 1945–69; *d.* there, 7.x.76. *works include*: two operas, four symphonies, many concertos.

Los Angeles During the 1940s Los Angeles was home to the twin giants of

20th-century music, *Schoenberg and *Stravinsky. It also harboured refugees of the stature of *Adorno, *Korngold, *Klemperer, Alma *Mahler and Bruno *Walter. Anywhere else would have experienced a cultural renaissance, even an earthquake. But LA was a movie town and music was low on its scale of priorities. The titans lived in poverty and the moment passed.

Louise French *verismo opera by Charpentier; a seamstress gives up her family and virtue to live with an artist. fp: Paris, 2.ii.1900.

Arthur (Vincent) LOURIE Russian revolutionary who ran the music section of Lenin's Commissariat for Public Instruction and laid down the principles by which the art was harnessed to the needs of the party. He faced stiff resistance from fellow-composers and huffed off in 1921 into Parisian exile. A follower of *Skryabinesque and castigator of *Stravinsky's *neo-classical compromise, his music was little played until recent times. It includes a cubist *Formes en l'air* for piano, dedicated to Picasso, and much Orthodox liturgy.
   b. St Petersburg 14.v.1892; moved to France 1921, US 1941; *d.* Princeton, New Jersey, 13.x.66. *other works: Dithyrambes* for solo flute (1923), Dialectic Symphony (Philadelphia 17.iv.31), opera-ballet *The Feast during the Plague* (Boston 5.i.45), concerto da camera (1957).

Love for Three Oranges Comic opera by *Prokofiev about a prince who cannot laugh. fp: Chicago, 30.xii.21.

Lucerne Swiss lakeside town where Wagner composed much of *Tristan*, it offered a haven to many musicians from *Rachmaninov to *Kubelik. In 1939 the town established a summer festival that rivalled Salzburg in ostentation.

Alvin LUCIER His electronic experiments at Brandeis U. resulted in *Music for Solo Performer* (1965), the first piece ever to translate brainwaves into sound. It was achieved by attaching electrodes to the performer's skull. He subsequently performed

the same experiment on the earth's magnetic field, among other feats of *performance art.
   b. Nashua, New Hampshire, 14.v.31; st with *Berger, *Fine.

Otto LUENING The pioneer of US *electronic music was raised on a Wisconsin farm and educated in Munich, Zurich and Paris. He studied with *Busoni, brushed shoulders with Lenin and the Dadaists and worked in a theatre company run by James Joyce. Playing flute in US orchestras paled by comparison and academic life had little to offer until a job at Columbia University in 1944 provided an outlet for his varied talents. Luening promptly formed a number of key alliances to promote American music on record. He premièred several operas on campus, including Menotti's *The Medium*, Thomson's *The Mother of Us All* and his own Longfellow romance, *Evangeline* (NY, 5.v.48). More lastingly, he linked up with *Ussachevsky in 1952 to form a studio that grew into the *Columbia-Princeton Electronic Music Center, the Bayreuth of US futurism.
   Still tootling the flute, he recorded and mangled his own sounds on tape in the neanderthal phase of electronic music. *Sonority Canyon* (1952) received short shrift from critics, but *Stokowski was intrigued by *Fantasy in Space* and conducted it with orchestral accompaniment in New York (28.x.52). *Bernstein gave the first performance of *Concerted Piece* by Luening and Ussachevsky for tape and orchestra (31.iii.60) as Luening worked towards integrating pre-recorded sounds with orchestra.
   He never abandoned traditional instrumentation, however, writing a tuneful late-romantic *Lyric Scene* (1958) in memory of Busoni and returning to his hometown at 75 with *A Wisconsin Symphony* (Milwaukee, 4.i.76). In all, he wrote 300 pieces in many media, and an autobiography, *The Odyssey of an American Composer* (1980).
   b. Milwaukee, Wisconsin, 15.vi.1900, son of a German choirmaster; taught U. of Arizona 1932–4, Bennington College, Vermont, 1934–44, Barnard College 1944–47 and Columbia U. 1949–68; *other orch. works:* Concertino for flute and chamber orch.

(1935), Kentucky Concerto (1951), two Fantasias for Orch. (1925, 1957), Legend (1951); much chamber and instrumental music, notably for flute and oboe; *other electronic music* (with Ussachevsky): background music for *King Lear* produced by Orson Welles, NY, 1956) and G. B. Shaw's *Back to Methuselah* (1958); *A Poem In Cycles and Bells* for tape and orch. (Los Angeles, 18.xi.54).

Lulu *Berg's unfinished second opera, a lurid tale of an independent woman who comes to grief at the hands of Jack the Ripper, told in a *12-note score with some tonal lapses. fp: two acts, Zurich, 2.vi.37; three-act completion by *Cerha, Paris 24.ii.79, cond. *Boulez.

David LUMSDAINE UK-based Australian, adept in many techniques. *Aria for Edward John Eyre* (1972) recaptures the 19th-century exploration of outback Australia in a dramatization for soprano and double-bass soloists, narrators, chamber orch. and live electronics. He married the composer Nicola LeFanu, daughter of *Maconchy.
   b. Sydney, 31.x.31; st with *Seiber; taught Durham U. 1970– ; *other works: Looking Glass Music* for brass quintet and tape (1970), *What Shall I Sing?* for soprano and two clarinets (1982), *Fire in Leaf and Grass* (London, 31.x.91).

Witold LUTOSŁAWSKI Across the gulf of contempt that divided progressive and traditional composers after 1945, one figure was equally welcome in both camps. The soft-spoken Pole was an agreeable and unthreatening presence. He had endured the Nazi occupation and Stalinist oppression with stoicism and dignity. During the war he wrote four-handed Variations on a theme of Paganini and played them with his friend *Panufnik at underground conclaves. When the communists took over, he was forced to restrain his natural inquisitiveness and write Polish folksong settings. Avoiding the self-abasement of many colleagues, he obeyed instructions in a Concerto for Orchestra (Warsaw, 26.xi.54) that, while using a recognizable tune and the acceptable model of *Bartók, organized its material on symmetrical lines and smuggled in illicit dissonances. Through the dark ages, Lutosławski wrote slowly and little. He cited Chopin and *Roussel as primary influences.

With the coming of the cultural thaw at the Warsaw Autumn festival of 1956, he was among the first to borrow previously forbidden techniques in a wholly unforced and individual way. *Funeral Music* for string orchestra in memoriam Béla Bartók (Katowice, 26.iii.58) was composed on a *12-note row but sounded distinctly tonal.

He followed it with the antithesis of *Schoenbergian rules. On hearing a broadcast of *Cage's Piano Concert in 1960 he was struck by the need to restore freedom to the performers. *Venetian Games* for orch. (Venice, 24.iv.61) and the subsequent string quartet (1964) gave players options and choices they had never enjoyed before. 'Repeat 3 times, then make a sign to the others,' reads one score inscription. Remarkably, again the music was gentle on the ear – less broken than *Webern or Cage – and unlikely to frighten the commissars. What is more, it made an experimental idea work in ways its inventor had never imagined. Like many Poles, Lutosławski had learned to place safety first but his innate skill made his music acceptable to almost every taste.

Domestic security and international recognition did not make him compose any faster or differently, although his music showed signs of growing more tuneful with advancing age. The cello concerto for *Rostropovich (London, 14.x.70) is relatively severe. Ten years later, the concerto for oboe, harp and chamber orchestra (Lucerne, 24.viii.80) was sweetness itself, as was a *Chaine* (1985) for violin and orchestra. The 3rd symphony (Chicago, 29.ix.83, cond. Solti) was composed over a period of ten years. He wrote symphonies in two sections because listening to the regulatory three or four movements, he said, always left him feeling exhausted. Although he was explicit in placing himself in Stravinsky's camp rather than Schoenberg's, he kept his thoughts mostly to himself. Music for Lutosławski was a way to communicate when all other avenues were blocked. The objective of art, he once said, was 'unity of experience in which the creator and his recipient are basically two parts of one and the same instrument'.

   b. Warsaw, 25.i.13; *other works: Dance Preludes* for clarinet and chamber orch. (1955), 2nd symphony (Katowice, 9.vi.67), *Paroles Tissées* for tenor and chamber orch. (Aldeburgh, 20.vi.65), *Les Espaces du sommeil* for baritone and orch. (Berlin, 12.ii.78, *Fischer-Dieskau soloist), piano concerto (Salzburg, 19.viii.88).

Elisabeth LUTYENS Daughter of the famed architect of New Delhi, she composed *serially in an England that spurned modernism, foreign ideas and forthright women. After a conventional education and comfortable marriage, her Eureka moment arrived during Webern's *Augenlicht* (London, 17.vi.38), when she resolved to adopt *12-note technique. Weeks later she met and moved in with Edward Clark, a Schoenberg pupil and BBC music organizer, forming a modernist menage that turned notoriously foul-mouthed when Clark lost his job and her music failed to get performed. She ended up a raging ragdoll on the fringes of musical society, but her composition pupils were numerous, respectful and influential, among them *Bennett, *Saxton, *Bauld and *Elias.

   Her gift was setting poetry for voice and ensemble; the Rimbaud soprano cantata *Ô saisons, Ô chateaux* (London, 11.ii.47) was her most urgent work. *And Suddenly it's Evening* (London, 3.iii.67) and *Essences of our Happiness* (London, 8.ix.70), both for tenor voice and ensemble, provided a welcome alternative to the Pears-strained declamations of *Britten. The orchestral music of her early serial years includes *Three Symphonic Preludes* whose only performance was interupted by an air-raid (7.ix.40), five chamber concertos and a lyrical viola concerto (London, 8.ix.50). Her output was enormous, running to 160 numbered works.

   b. London, 9.vii.06; *d.* there, 14.iv.83. *other works:* chamber operas *Infidelio* (1954), *The Goldfish Bowl* (1975), *Time Off? Not a Ghost of a Chance* (1972); overture *Proud City* (in honour of London, 1946); 13 string quartets.

Lux aeterna (*Eternal light*) Chorus by *Ligeti, an unused fragment of his Requiem, that conveyed otherworldliness in Stanley Kubrick's space movie, *2001.* fp: Stuttgart, 2.xi.66.

Lyric Suite Coded six-movement string quartet by *Berg, intertwining his initials with those of his lover, Hanna Fuchs-Robettin, and giving heavy play to their 'fateful' numeral, 23. Although nominally written in *serial technique, Berg inserted the love theme from *Tristan* and the principal theme of the third song ('you are my own') of the Lyric Symphony by *Zemlinsky, the lovers' go-between, to underline the erotic secret, which was discovered only a half a century later. Three movements were transcribed for string orchestra in what became the work's familiar version. fp: (quartet) Vienna, 8.i.27; (orch.) Berlin, 31.i.29.

Lyric Symphony *Zemlinsky's setting for soprano, baritone and orchestra of seven poems by Rabindranath Tagore in what an admitted attempt to replicate *Das *Lied von der Erde.* fp: Prague, 4.vi.24.

Macbeth Epic opera by *Bloch. fp: Paris, Opéra-Comique, 30.xi.10. See also *Lady Macbeth*.

Edward (Alexander) MacDOWELL The first US composer to make it in Europe, he stayed in Germany after studying with Liszt and became famous with his second somewhat squishy piano concerto (1888) and suites of little songs. Rebasing in 1896 to found Columbia University's music department, he went mad after eight years' overwork. The $50,000 raised by a public appeal to pay for his medical care was invested a MacDowell Colony at Peterborough, New Hampshire, where composer and writers can spend their summers in the tranquillity that eluded its namesake. After 1900, he composed no more than a couple of choruses and some piano pieces
  b. NY, 18.xii.1860; *d*. there, 23.i.08.

François-Bernard MÂCHE *Messiaen pupil who matched tape-recorded natural sounds – the birds, the sea – with instrumental combinations. Aside from composing, he is a professor of classical literature and translator of Greek poetry.
  b. Clermont-Ferrand, France, 4.iv.35; *works include*: *Amargos* for sea waves and 12 instruments (1979); *Eridan* for string quartet (1986).

James MACMILLAN Anti-dogmatic young Scot, he attacked the elitist isolationism and outdatedness of most contemporary music and adopted pop rhythms and tunes in formal concert works. His piano sonata (1986) portrays a savage Highlands winter with hints of indigenous music.

b. Kilwinning, Ayrshire, 16.vii.59; *ensemble works*: *The Keening* for orch. (1986), *Visions of a November Spring* for string quartet (1988), *Confessions of Isobel Gowdie* (1990), *Tuireadh* (London, 2.x.91).

(Dame) Elizabeth MACONCHY Unlike many women composers who imitated masculine bombast, Maconchy expressed herself in the most domestic of media, the string quartet. She wrote 13 quartets from 1933 to 1984, all cogent and communicative, the first seven sharing a post-Brahmsian glow with occasional dissonant allusions. Something happened to Maconchy between 1957 and 1967, her most fertile period, ended by an 8th quartet that is fiercely wrought, searing away at Bartókian rhythms and sliding up and down the strings with great vehemence, softened by a *Lento* episode of grey introspection.
  Irish by ancestry and upbringing, she opted for a quiet country life to cope with a young family and severe bouts of TB. Her daughter Nicola LeFanu (*b*. 28.iv.47), herself a composer, married the Australian composer David Lumsdaine to form a modest dynasty.
  b. Broxbourne, Herts, UK, 19.iii.07; st with *Vaughan Williams and in Prague with Jirák; married William LeFanu 1930; *other works*: operatic trilogy – *The Sofa*, *The Three Strangers*, *The Departure* (1951–67); symphony for double string orch., bassoon concerto, serenata concertante for violin and orch., clarinet quintet (1957–67); clarinet concerto (1985).

Madama Butterfly Puccini's heartbreak opera of love among the geishas. fp: Milan,

La Scala, 17.ii.04, but extensively revised over next two years.

Maddalena Juvenile but not inconsequential opera by *Prokofiev. fp: BBC, 25.iii.79.

Bruno MADERNA The early death of Bruno Maderna dealt a crippling blow to the European *avant-garde. Apart from his pace-setting role as a composer, the gentle Venetian was a moral influence and a gifted interpreter – the only man of their generation apart from himself, said *Boulez, who could conduct new music. Boulez eulogized him beautifully in the *Rituel in memoriam Bruno Maderna* (1975). More demoralizing than his death, however, was Maderna's last work. His valedictory opera *Satyricon* (Scheveningen, Netherlands, 16.iii.73), was an indictment of modernism, forsaking abstraction and returning to ancient verities of lyricism, laughter and comprehensibity. It is not a literal tale but a commentary on the nature of drama with an essentially pessimistic outlook on the future of music. The opera was ostracized by fellow-modernists but constituted Maderna's verdict on their world.

Maderna was never a total rejectionist in the *Darmstadt mould, though he led classes there for 14 summers (1954–67). Despite co-founding Italy's first *electronic studio in 1953, he was bound to the neo-baroque conservatism of his teacher, *Malipiero, and to the hedonism of his native land. His music was *atonal and *12-tonal but never inelegant or jarring. Nor did he take it too seriously or promote it heavily. A characteristic lightness and geniality informs even sculptural edifices like *Quadrivium* for four percussionists and four orchestral groups (Royan, 4.iv.69). *Aura*, commissioned by the Chicago Symphony Orch. for its 80th anniversary (23.iii.72), was sensuous in a style somewhere between *Berg and Debussy. Hearing these works and his three graceful oboe concertos confirms Maderna's essential moderation. Along with *Berio's, his music withstood the excesses of the mid-century.

b. Venice, 21.iv.20; *d.* Darmstadt, Germany, 13.xi.73. *other works*: part-electronic opera *Hyperion* (Venice, 6.ix.64), electronic ballet *Oedipus-Roi* (Monte Carlo, 31.xii.70); violin concerto (1969), *Juilliard Serenade* for small orch. and tape (1969), *Biogramma* for large orch. (1972); electronic *Notte in città* (with Berio, 1956).

Leevi MADETOJA Finnish composer in Sibelian mould, he wrote three symphonies, tone poems and an opera, *Juha* (1935), not to be confused with the landmark work of the same name by *Merikanto. The 2nd symphony (1918) was a grim elegy in memory of his only brother and closest friend, both killed in the civil war; the 3rd (Helsinki, 8.iv.26), summery though introspective, views Finnish idioms in a wider European context. Madetoja's greatest Scandinavian success was achieved with the opera *The Ostrobothnians* (Bergen, Norway, 8.iii.23, cond. Kajanus).

b. Uleåborg (Oulu), Finland, 17.ii. 1887; *d.* Helsinki, 6.x.47.

Madness The fascination with insanity in *bel canto* and *verismo* opera waned in modern times. Mad scenes of 20th-century opera are found in *Elektra, Salome, Wozzeck, Turandot* and *Eight Songs for a Mad King*, all depicting earlier times. *Mahler felt he was going mad while writing the two last symphonies; *Macdowell, *Arnold and *Ogdon were institutionalized

MADONNA Aggressive sex-symbol, she asserted a provocative virginity before donning chain-mail costumes designed to exaggerate her erogenous attributes. Behind this was a dedicated musician, able to carry off a Kurt Weill song with ironic panache and sustain a tune and rhythm far better than her compeers. She aped Marlene Dietrich and Marilyn Monroe in Hollywood movies and projected herself as an icon of the times. Her concerts ceased to be rock gigs and became *performance art, combining dance, visuals and minutely-rehearsed music.

b. Rochester, Michigan, 16.viii.58 as Madonna Louise Ciccone;

Maggio Musicale Fiorentino Annual May festival in Florence with pronounced 20th-century content. Its premières have included *Dallapiccola operas.

magic realism Fantastic trend in Latin American literature, evident in *Birtwistle's

Gawain and some operatic productions of the 1980s.

Albéric (Lucien-Denis-Gabriel) MAGNARD It was acutely ironic that this German-romantic French composer should be among the first victims of the 1914 invasion, shot by German soldiers while defending his home. His house was then set on fire, destroying many scores. Magnard adored Beethoven and was supported by *Ysaÿe and *Busoni but his operas failed in Paris and the musical establishment recoiled from his pro-Dreyfus political stance. In the 1980s, his 3rd (1902) and 4th (1913) symphonies were discovered to be delightful, Schumann-esque in texture yet with a rare Gallic charm and delicacy.

> *b.* Paris, 9.vi.1865; *d.* Baron, Oise, France, 3.ix.14; *other works*: operas *Yolande* (1892), *Guercoeur* (Paris, 24.iv.31), *Bérénice* (Paris, 15.xii.11); string quartet (1904).

Mahagonny There was never a place called Mahagonny. It was an imaginary America devised by Brecht and *Weill for a semi-staged Songspiel, followed by a quasi-opera – *The Rise and Fall of the City of Mahagonny* – centred on the *Weimar pastimes of boxing, prostitution and litigation. The two eternal hits were 'Alabama Song' and 'Benares Song'. fp: (Songspiel) Baden-Baden, 18.vii.27; (*Rise and Fall*) Leipzig, 9.ii.30.

Alma (-Maria) MAHLER The great composer's wife and memoirist wrote *Tristanesque songs under *Zemlinsky's tuition. Mahler ordered her to desist, only to repent in his dying year and order their publication. His judgement was clouded, however, by love. Her music is slight and derivative. Alma earned notoriety by other means.

> *b.* Vienna, 31.viii.1879; *d.* NY, 11.xii.64.
> *Bib*: Alma Mahler, *Gustav Mahler, Memories and Letters*, London (John Murray), 1946.

Gustav MAHLER Irreconcilable dualities lie at the source of Mahler's hypnotic fascination. He was, at one and the same time, the last of the late romantics and the forger of modernism; a central Viennese figure and the most un-Austrian of musicians; a sensualist whose motives were cerebral; a naïve idealist who made unprecedented use of musical *irony; a self-obsessed sufferer whose music was universal in its scope and intentions. A decade ahead of Sigmund Freud, he discovered that he could trace the secrets of the human condition through creative auto-analysis.

He was first and foremost a composer, but always more than a composer. He established the conductor's prerogative to direct a state institution and, in a decade at the Vienna Court Opera (1897–1907), was the prime reformist force in a society where Freud, Schoenberg, Klimt, Mach and Wittgenstein were revitalizing western thought. He revolutionized the presentation of opera and reshaped the concert orchestra. He was among the first to proclaim that man's salvation lay in art, in short, one of the principal makers of modern culture.

Mahler was born of Jewish parents on the borders of Bohemia and Moravia and rose through provincial opera houses to become head of the royal opera company in Budapest at 29 and in Vienna at the age of 37. His folkloristic 1st symphony (Budapest, 20.xi.1889) left audiences uneasy at his sardonic treatment of familiar objects. In the 3rd movement, he turned a nursery rhyme, 'Frère Jacques' or 'Bruder Martin', first into a funeral march, then into a drunken orgy – a caustic comment on public indifference to infant mortality. In the insightful observation of Luigi *Dallapiccola, that movement was the source of Alban Berg's collagist technique and Kurt Weill's ribaldry. In four minutes of music, Mahler had foreshadowed the principal ascetic and popular streams of 20th-century music.

His 2nd symphony, titled *Resurrection* (Berlin, 13.xii.1895), strayed beyond the recognized boundaries of composing to tackle the religious conundrum of life after death. Mahler, who converted to Catholicism in 1897 in order to get a job in Vienna, believed that all mankind, regardless of merit or religion, would ultimately be redeemed. To sound the coming nemesis, Mahler scattered instrumental groups in the unseen distance, extending the *spatial dimension. The 3rd symphony (Crefeld, 9.vi.02) was drawn from nature, ending in a life-affirming *Adagio* of a kind that Mahler copyrighted. All three symphonies were unconventional in length, breadth – five or six movements – instrumentation and texture.

The 4th Symphony (Munich, 25.xi.01) that greeted the new century was a transitional work in classical format – just four movements, less than an hour long and standard-sized ensemble. It shocked audiences nevertheless with introductory sleighbells and a mocking gypsy fiddle, tuned a whole tone upwards, that turned the scherzo into a frightening dance of death. It was succeeded by a serene 20-minute *Adagio* that foreshadowed the profound contemplations of Mahler's last trilogy, although proclaiming apparent innocence in a child's vision of heaven, voiced by a limpid soprano.

Between writing the 4th and 5th symphonies Mahler, a confirmed bachelor, married the flirtatious Alma Schindler, a girl barely more than half his age. He returned to a dichotomy of domestic contentment and torture that had plagued his infancy. The 5th symphony (Cologne, 18.x.04) opened a middle period in which a façade of confidence and optimism is underpinned by forebodings of tragedy. Its opening funeral march twists the 'Fate' theme of Beethoven's Fifth, then crashes into the tramp of rampaging armies across a ravaged continent – a prescient intimation of world war. The fourth movement is Mahler's most famous piece of music, an 'Adagietto' for harp and strings, supposedly a love letter to his future wife yet strangely introverted and fatalistic. It is drawn from the most heartfelt of his orchestral songs, written around the same time to the words, 'Ich bin der Welt abhanden gekommen' (I am lost to the world . . .). Love, for Mahler, was inextricably linked to loss. His *Kindertotenlieder* (Songs on the death of children, Vienna, 29.i.05) voiced an acute foreknowledge of life's fragility.

The 6th (Essen, 27.v.06), also known as his Tragic Symphony, sounded a second warning of approaching war and delivered the most pessimistic finale in symphonic literature, a bleak prognosis penned in the summer of his greatest happiness. The 7th

(Prague, 19.ix.08) had three large movements separated by episodes of 'Night-music' and lightened instrumentally by a mandolin and guitar, instruments unknown to concert orchestras and inherited by modernists from Schoenberg to Boulez.

The 8th symphony (Munich, 12.ix.10) is often deemed an heroic failure, a hopeless attempt to weld into one vast piece the Pentecostal hymn *Veni Creator Spiritus* and the closing scene of Goethe's *Faust*. It requires eight vocal soloists, three full choirs and an immense orchestra – a 'Symphony of 1,000' performers that eludes the control of mortal conductors. Yet the score contains bold ideas and left marks on vital operas from *Pfitzner's *Palestina* to *Britten's *Peter Grimes*. Beneath its vocal mass lies orchestral writing of extraordinary sublimity.

It was his last great shout of self-assertion. In the summer of 1907 he suffered a triple disaster predicted, said his wife, in three awesome hammer-blows in the finale of the 6th symphony. A reactionary and racialist press campaign forced him to quit Vienna; his infant elder daughter died of diphtheria; and his own survival was threatened by a heart condition which, he was told, could kill him at any moment. He had to give up the pleasures of country exercise and accept a sedentary existence which, he feared, would impede the contact with nature that was essential to his music. Alma, offended at his loss of marital libido, consorted with lovers. His concluding trilogy was charged with the fear of losing her and his daily struggle with fate, death and God. His last four winters were spent in New York, conducting at the Metropolitan Opera and Philharmonic Orchestra. Each summer he returned to the solitude of a Dolomite mountain meadow to work on his triple epilogue.

*Das *Lied von der Erde* (Song of the Earth*, Munich, 20.xi.11) fought 'to find peace for my lonely heart' in eighth-century Chinese poems of nature and alienation. It was neither symphony nor orchestral song-cycle but a totally original hybrid. In six disparate sections, the mood swung wildly from maudlin to bacchanalian, until Mahler acheived a healing music in the last phase of the finale, fading away

CONTEMPORARY COMPOSERS
PORTRAITS BY BETTY FREEMAN

John Cage in his kitchen. New York, 1977

rton Feldman. California, 1987

Brian Ferneyhough. Darmstadt, 1988

Philip Glass (right) with Bob Wilson, planning *Einstein on the Beach*. New York, 1976

Hans Werner Henze.
Munich, 1990

György Ligeti.
Hamburg, 1990

Witold Lutosławski. Los Angeles, 1989

Arvo Pärt.
Berlin, 1990

Harry Partch surrounded by his instruments on the film set for *The Dreamer Remains*. San Diego, 1972

Steve Reich.
New York, 1985

Wolfgang Rihm.
Karlsruhe, 1990

sa Pekka Salonen.
os Angeles, 1988

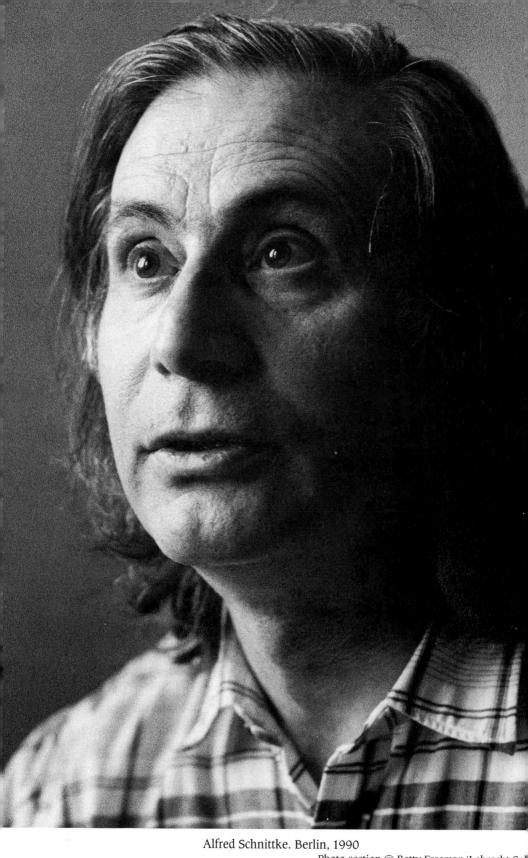

Alfred Schnittke. Berlin, 1990

on an eternal murmur of 'Ewig, ewig . . .' 'Is it bearable?' Mahler asked Bruno *Walter. 'Will people not want to do away with themselves on hearing it?' He had just written one of music's most cathartic episodes.

The opening of the 9th symphony (Vienna, 26.vi.12) seemed to have accepted the decree of fate, only for it to be resisted with controlled frenzy. The central movements contemplate the human dilemma with alternating humour and horror, affection and irony. A ghostly waltz is followed by a ghostly *Ländler*. Tonal and textural fragmentation, the portents of untold terrors, are relieved by a transcendent *Adagio* – 'music no longer of this world', said Berg. 'Ours is the century of death, and Mahler is its musical prophet,' commented Leonard *Bernstein.

He did not live to hear either work performed, dying in Vienna of a cardiac-related infection at the age of 50. Nor did he finish the 10th symphony, which his widow initially suppressed. Alma eventually permitted performances of the opening *Adagio* and central *Purgatorio* (Vienna, 14.x.24) and issued a facsimile of part of his manuscript, scrawled with agonized appeals for her love and God's help. Mahler's outline of the symphony's entire structure and development, along with all

available sketches, was finally made available in the 1960s to the British scholar Deryck Cooke (1919–76). His 'performing version' of the five-movement symphony has won acceptance, above more speculative, completions by US researchers Clinton Carpenter and Remo Mazzetti. Mahler would doubtless have made further alterations, but Cooke's version represents a freeze-frame of the his final thoughts and constitutes a shattering musical experience in its own right – more valid a realization than Süssmayr's completion of Mozart's deathbed Requiem.

The 80-minute work (London, 13.viii. 64, cond. *Goldschmidt), marks one last imaginative leap on Mahler's part. The opening *Adagio* in the key of F# is restless and morose – a far cry from his transcendent slow movements; it hovers on the very fringe of tonality and implodes into a nine-note dissonant chord after quarter of an hour of mounting tension. Some consider this proof of Mahler's breach with tonality and an endorsement or prediction of Schoenberg's experiments; the rest of the symphony, however, provides no substantiation of this view. The scherzo is less ominous; the *Purgatorio* opens with an ironic reminscence of innocent folkery, together with unresolved fragments of his life in music. The second scherzo is a diabolical dance – 'the devil dances with me,' he scrawled – studded with dissonance and ending on a muffled drum-stroke that, in Alma's account, Mahler overheard at the passing funeral of a New York fireman. The muted drum persists through a 25-minute finale that slowly restores a measure of peace and hope. The tenth symphony is a unique artistic document of mortal agony and a musical masterpiece in its own right.

Probably unknown even to himself, Mahler had taken the symphony beyond the Brahmsian endpoint and renewed it for posterity. After Mahler, a symphony could have any number of movements and instruments, and treat any topic from the personal to the political. The symphony, said Mahler to *Sibelius, 'is like the world: it must embrace everything'.

He was not, he asserted vigorously, writing for his own time. Both during his

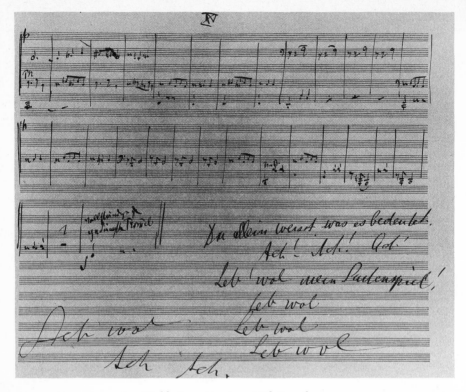

Mahler's manuscript – 10th Symphony

life and for half a century afterwards knowledge of his music was confined to curious musicians and a committted coterie. In the Nazi era it was banned in continental Europe. 'My time will come!' Mahler proclaimed. His revival began with centenary celebrations of his birth in London and New York and was confirmed by cyclical recordings by Bernstein and Rafael *Kubelik. By 1980 he was the most popular symphonist on the concert menu, recorded by the Vienna Philharmonic which once sacked him as conductor and acclaimed by audiences in Japan who had no conception of his ideas. Mahler was the commercial hit of the late-20th century.

This inherent acclaim obscured his singular influence on music and society. Of the major composers of the 20th century only *Stravinsky and *Debussy could claim to be wholly immune to Mahlerian innovations. Mahler towered over music as Beethoven and Wagner had done in the 19th century, Handel and Mozart in the

18th. He stamped his personality on a formative epoch in western art and science. More than just a musician, he was a monumental force in the 20th century, comparable to Einstein, Freud and Lenin.

b. Kalischt (Kaliště), Austro-Hungary, 7.vii. 1860; st with *Fuchs; assisted Bruckner with symphonic scores; cond. Laibach (Ljublana), Olmütz (Olomouc), Kassel, Prague, Leipzig, Budapest (1888–92), Hamburg (1891–97), Vienna (1897–1907), NY (1907–11); *d*. Vienna, 18.v.11.

Bib: Alma Mahler, *Gustav Mahler, Memories and Letters*, (fourth edition) London, 1990; Norman Lebrecht, *Mahler Remembered*, London (Faber and Faber), 1987.

The Makropoulos Case *Janáček's opera from Karel Capek's play about a 300 year-old woman who retains her youth by drinking a magic potion. Elena Makropoulos's relations with young lovers is a mirror image of the elderly Janáček's pursuit of a young married woman, Kamila

Stösslová. fp: Brno, 18.xii.26; cond. František Neumann.

Artur MALAWSKI A late start and early death pushed Malawski to the side-lines. He was 32 before he applied to enter a conservatory and only 53 when he died. By that time he had led the Polish section of *ISCM (1948–51) and made his mark with boldly *Bergian and *Stravinskian scores which ran counter to the Stalinist line. His major work is a *Toccata and Fugue in the Form of Variations* (1949) for piano and large orchestra. On his death, *Penderecki wrote a moving *Epitaph* for string orch. and percussion.
  b. Przemysl, Austrian Galicia, 4.vii.04; taught Cracow conservatory 1945–57; *d.* Cracow, Poland, 26.xii.57. *other works*: two symphonies, two string quartets.

Ivo MALEC Parisian composer rooted in *musique concrète, which he combined with orchestral sounds; he was commissioned to write the first new opera for the Bastille's 'salle modulable'.
  b. Zagreb, Yugoslavia, 30.iii.25; moved to Paris 1955 to st with *Henry; prof. at Paris Conservatoire 1972–; *works include*: *Sigma* (1963) for large orch., *Ottava Bassa* (1984) for double-bass and large orch., *Lumina* (1968) for 12 strings and tape, *Actuor* (1973) for percussion ensemble, *Examples* for orch. (1988).

Gian Francesco MALIPIERO Between the two wars, both of Italy's leading composers raged against a culture that said Malipiero, 'was suffocated by the tyranny of 19th century opera'. His friend *Casella composed *neo-classical concert music and promoted the regenerative myth of fascism. Malipiero courted favours from Mussolini but was too crabby an individualist to be useful to the regime. His music was banned as modernist in Nazi Germany and after the war he became godfather to the *avant-garde; his pupil *Dallapiccola called him 'the greatest Italian composer since Verdi'.

Yet Malipiero was essentially traditionalist, the excavator and editor of Monteverdi's neglected works and many of Vivaldi's. Spending the early years of the century in Venetian libraries provided him with a creative resource that bypassed *bel canto* opera. A spell in Paris under *Debussy's tutelage added impressionist technique to his palette. The First World War, particularly the humiliation of Italy's retreat, contributed to an essentially depressive, often paranoid personality.

Perhaps as an escape mechanism, he composed voluminously – more than 35 operas on classic literary themes, six ballets, 11 numbered symphonies, countless concertos including six for piano, eight string quartets and much vocal music. He was published in Vienna, Paris and London. His music was not typically neo-classical for, while grounded in history, it forsook sonata form for a process that consisted of what Malipiero termed 'free conversation' and Freud might have called 'free association'. This stream-of-consciousness evolved a structure that revealed itself only once the work was finished; it admitted occasional atonalities while keeping within diatonic lines. His 'dialogues', as various works were titled, were not readily definable. Proliferation, too, worked against him, as it did against *Milhaud and *Martinů. Unlike them, Malipiero was unable to write a single captivating *Création du Monde* or Rhapsody-concerto that caught the public ear and acted as an entry-point to the rest of his output. The music is therefore substantially neglected. Its summits are two operatic trilogies, *3 commedie goldoniane* (1926) and *L'Orfeide* (1925). The symphonic drama *Pantea* (Venice, 6.ix.32) dramatically foreshadows Dallapiccola's opera *Il Prigioniero*, as does another of Malipiero's ballets, *The Mask of the imprisoned princess* (Brussels, 19.x.24).

His piano music could be ominously luminous; the first of *Poemi asolani* written during the first war echoes the churchbells of Venice on the night of November first when the graveyards are illuminated and ghosts stalk the canals. Three ironic *Omaggi* (1920) for piano pay Alkan-like, or *Berners-like, tribute to a parrot, an elephant and an idiot.
  b. Venice, 18.iii.1882; *d.* Asolo, nr. Venice, 1.viii.73. *other orch. works*: violinistic ballet *Stradivario* (Florence, 20.vi.49); *Dityrambo tragico* (London, 11.x.19), *Pause del silenzio* (1927), orch. selections from stage works *La Cimarosiana* and *San Francesco d'Assisi*;

Concerto for orch. (Philadelphia, 29.i.32, cond. *Stokowski).

His nephew and pupil **Riccardo MALIPIERO** (*b*. Milan, 24.vii.14) was a prominent *serialist who organized the first International Congress of Twelve Tone Music (Milan, 1949).

Les Mamelles de Tirésias (Fr = Tiresias' tits) Transsexual opera by *Poulenc. fp Paris, 3.vi.47.

Manchester School Student composers who banded together in the mid-1950s to rid English music of deadening pastorality. Movers and shakers were *Goehr, Maxwell *Davies and John *Ogdon; Harrison *Birtwistle played clarinet and did not emerge for years as an equal composer.

Henry MANCINI If Puccini drove up a dead alley, the three Ms – Menotti, Mancini, Mantovani – applied variations on his sure-fire formula of simple tunes in soupy settings. Mancini devised memorable movie and TV themes upon three-bar ballads and inflated string sections with keyboard obbligato. A Clevelander of Italian descent, he played in the Glenn Miller and Mel Tormé bands, acquiring a gloss of sophistication from private studies with Krenek, Castelnuovo-Tedesco and the conductor Alfred Sendrey. His screen gems include 'Moon River' from *Breakfast at Tiffany's* (1961), *Charade* (1963), *The Pink Panther* (1964 et. seq.) and *10* (1979). He has conducted the tenor Pavarotti in popular programmes.
  b. Cleveland, Ohio, 16.iv.24, learning flute from his father; st Juilliard 1942–3; joined Universal Studios, Hollywood, 1952.

Philippe MANOURY Pupil of *Malec, he joined the Boulez circle at *IRCAM in attempts to synthesize a new music. His best-known work is *Zeitlauf* (Paris, 15.ii.83) for 12 voices, 13 instruments and live *electronics. Like Boulez, he continually revises pre-existent works.
  b. Tulle, France, 19.vi.52; *other works*: *Aleph* for orch. and four soloits (Strasbourg, 25.ix.87, 2nd version); *Le Livre de Claviers* for six percussionists (Strasbourg, 27.ix.88).

Tigran MANSOURIAN The Armenian composer sheltered from social upheavals in a Debussyan false tranquillity. His two

cello concertos and *Night Music* for orchestra resemble subdued *Shostakovich with strong Asian accents.
  b. Beirut, Lebanon, 27.i.39; moved to Soviet Armenia 1947; lecturer at Erevan Conservatory 1967-.

Annunzio Paolo MANTOVANI Birmingham bandleader who gave his name to a sickly-sweet string sound, sometimes emulated by eminent conductors.
  b. Venice, 15.xi.05; st Trinity College of Music, London; formed own band 1924; *d*. Tunbridge Wells, England, 29.iii.80.

Mantra Meditative trance by *Stockhausen for two amplified pianos, bells and woodblocks, marking his reversion to melody. fp: Donaueschingen, 18.x.70

Giacomo MANZONI Darmstadt (1952–56) Italian of leftist affinities, he made an opera of Thomas Mann's *Doktor Faustus* for La Scala (1989) and was an influential critic and teacher in Bologna and Milan. His East Berlin-commissioned *Mass* (6.x.77), subtitled 'homage to Edgard Varèse' was one of those plink-plonk works of the late *avant-garde that proclaimed universal sentiments in their technique and programme notes while signifying spectacularly little.
  b. Milan, 26.ix.32; *other works*: opera *Per Massimiliano Robespierre* (Bologna, 1975); symphonic scene from *Doktor Faustus* (1984); choral *Ombre* in memory of Ché Guevara (1968).

Tomás MARCO A Spanish *Stockhausen pupil, he synthesized avant-garde noises with native lyricism in *Deserted Mirrors*, a 15-minute string quartet (1987).
  b. Madrid, 12.ix.42; *other works*: five symphonies, violin concerto, *Tea Party* for two sopranos, trio for piano, tuba and percussion.

marimba Generic name for xylophone-like instruments originating in Africa and Latin America and used in orchestration, notably by Messiaen and Reich.

Antoine MARIOTTE Composed Wilde's *Salome* ahead of *Strauss and was accused of *plagiarism when he produced it later (Lyon, 30.x.1908).
  b. Avignon, France, 22.xii.1875; st with d'*Indy; dir. Orléans Conservatoire (1920–44) and Opéra-Comique, Paris, (1936–8); works include five operas (among them

Esther, Princess of Israel, 1925), songs and much pianistic pedagoguery; *d.* Izieux, France, 30.xi.44.

Igor MARKEVITCH

*Diaghilev's last protégé was a colourful young prodigy who performed his piano concerto at Covent Garden when just 16 (15.vi.29) and was known in his 20s as Igor the Second, the first being *Stravinsky. Bartók sent him a fan letter on seeing the ballet *Icarus' Flight* (Paris, 26.vi.33) and its reduced version for two pianos and percussion may well have instigated his own famous sonata five years later. But critical assaults for imagined dissonance led Markevitch to pursue conducting lessons with Hermann *Scherchen, and to devote most of his career to conducting in Stockholm, Madrid, Monte Carlo and Rome.

  b. Kiev, Russian Ukraine, 27.vii.12; *d.* Antibes, France, 7.iii.83. *other works*: *Cantate* (Cocteau text, Paris, 4.vi.30), *Concerto Grosso* (Paris, 8.xii.30), *Rebus* (ballet, in memoriam Diaghilev, Paris, 15.xii.31), *Psaume* for soprano and chamber orch. (Hebrew text, Amsterdam, 3.xii.33), *Paradise Lost* (oratorio, London, 20.xii.35), *Lorenzo the Magnificent,* sinfonia concertante for soprano and orch. (Florence, 12.i.41), *Variations, Fugue and Envoi on a theme of Handel* for piano (Rome, 14.xii.41).

Rudolf MAROS

Regarded in Hungary as a bridge between *Bartók and *serialism, Maros' music sounds relatively tame to western ears, and not unpleasant. *Musica da camera per 11* (1966) has the smoothness of Boulez at his most ingratiating; *Monumentum* (1969) for large orch. takes the notes number 1, 9, 4 and 5 from its serial row to construct a vision of the nation's year of doom and transfiguration. His son, Miklos (*b.* Pecs, 14.xi.43), is a sometime radical who moved to Stockholm in 1968 and rose to become vice-president of the Society of Swedish Composers.

  b. Stachy, Czechoslovakia 19.i.17; st with *Kodály, *Hába; prof. of chamber music at Budapest Academy 1949–77; *d.* Budapest, 2.viii.82. *other works*: seven ballets, two sinfoniettas, much chamber music for varied formations.

Ingram MARSHALL

US post-*minimalist, he used *electronics to create intriguing ambiences. The brass sextet *Fog Tropes* (1987) suggests a gloomy cityscape; *The Fragility Cycles* (1976) was played on Indonesian instruments; while *Gradual Requiem* used electronic sound-delay to create a churchy echo, acoustically transforming 16th-century mass into something quite contemporary.

  b. Mt Vernon, NY, 10.v.42; st with *Ussachevsky.

Istvan MARTA

Back to *Bartók – but with a difference. Marta went collecting folk music in the Balkans in 1973 and returned with evidence of Romania's systematic destruction of an ancient, indigenous Magyar culture. He combined two of his interviews with ambient noises and wrote around them a string quartet dirge for *Kronos. *Doom. A Sigh* (Los Angeles, 13.i.90) sounds initially exploitative of private grief but grows into a requiem for cultures eradicated by the march of 'progress'. This was music with a provocative political message, achieved by purely modern means. The same ominous view of social history pervades Marta's *Doll's House Story* (1985) for percussion ensemble.

  b. Budapest, 14.vi.52; st with *Lutosławski; *other works*: ballet, *Visions* (1984), *Our Hearts* for chamber choir and orch. (1983).

Le Marteau sans maître

(*The masterless hammer*) Boulez's breakthrough work. fp: Baden-Baden, 18.vi.55, cond. Rosbaud.

Frank MARTIN

The Swiss composer became continentally eminent when past 50 with an oratorio on the forbidden love of Tristan and Iseult. Entitled *Le Vin herbé (The tampered wine)* (Zurich, 26.iii.42) and sparingly scored for 12 solo voices, seven string instruments and piano, its ascetism contrasts sharply with Wagner's treatment of the ill-starred affair.

  Martin found his metier in reworking European myths. After *The Melody of the Love and Death of Cornet Christoph Rilke*, known for short as *Der Cornet* (Basle, 9.ii.45), he struck deep into German literature with *Six Monologues from [Hofmannsthal's] 'Jedermann'* for baritone and piano, or orchestra (1943). Celebrating the end of war chorally with *In terra pax – Peace on Earth* (7.v.45) – he moved to

Holland to enjoy fame as a supranational artist. Two operas he wrote there derived from Shakespeare – *Der Sturm (The Tempest)* (Vienna, 17.vi.56) – and Molière, *Monsieur de Pourceaugnac* (Geneva, 23.iv.63). His culture recognized no borders.

His music aroused respect rather than passion. Like his mentor *Ravel, who conducted the youthful *Les Dithyrambes* (1918), he produced scores of great precision and elegance. His *neo-classical orchestral pieces make a good hors d'oeuvre to something more substantial. The *Petite symphonie concertante* for harp, cembalo, piano and two string orchestras (17.v.46) and the intermittently 12-tone *Concerto for 7 wind instruments, timpani, percussion and strings* (Berne, 25.x.49) run like clockwork. Resorting often to antique instruments, his harpsichord concerto (Venice, 14.ix.52) has intriguingly anachronistic timbres. Past 80, he wrote a *Requiem* (Lausanne, 4.v.73) into which he put, like Mozart, everything he knew.

b. Geneva, 15.ix.1890; st in Zurich, Rome and Paris; taught at Jaques-Dalcroze Institute; *d.* Naarden, Netherlands, 21.xi.74. *other works*: two piano concertos (1936, 1969), violin concerto (1951), cello concerto (1967), seven-minute Ballade for flute (1939) and eight-minute Ballade for trombone (1940); very sprightly Etudes for string orch. (1956); eight piano preludes (for Dinu *Lipatti, 1948).

Donald (James) MARTINO It has been authoritatively asserted that if Martino was European his music would be widely known; that his *Pianississimo* (1970) sonata is a pinnacle of post-War modernism on a plane with *Boulez's and *Barraqué's; and that an enlightened government would sponsor him to spend the rest of his life composing Dante on the strength of *Paradiso's Choruses* (1974) for 12 soloists, two choruses, tape and orchestra. Meantime, Martino teaches at Harvard, plays excellent clarinet and writes chamber music to commission.

His music, while cerebral, is easy on the ear and intriguing to the mathematical mind. Although *serial, it possess a civility and humanity that recall *Dallapiccola (his teacher) and *Petrassi rather than the violent ravers of the *avant-garde. The piano

sonata apart, however, no single work seems to be stamped with the mark of greatness.

b. Plainfield, New Jersey, 16.v.31; taught Princeton (1957–59), Yale (1959–69), New England Conservatory (1969–81), Harvard (1983–); *other works*: piano conceto (1965), triple concerto for three types of clarinet and orch. (1977), string quartet (1983), *B,a,b,b,i,t,t* for clarinet (homage to his other teacher, 1966).

Jean MARTINON The distinguished French conductor found insufficient time to compose until he was thrown by the Germans into a Stalag in 1940. In two years of confinement he produced a *Psalm 136*, an orchestral *Musique d'exil* and various chamber pieces, all of which won him acclaim on release. He directed the Lamoureux orchestra in Paris (1951–57) and in 1960 was the first Frenchman to be appointed general music director of a German city, Düsseldorf. In 1963 he took over the Chicago Symphony Orch., offending patrons with modernist programmes and leaving after five years; from 1968 to his death he headed the Orchestre National de France and the Residente orchestra at The Hague. In addition to his prison scores, Martinon wrote four symphonies and an opera, *Hécube* (Strasbourg, 10.x.56). His most unusual work was a concerto for four saxophones and chamber orch. (The Hague, 5.iii.76).

b. Lyons, 10.i.10; *d.* Paris, 1.iii.76.

Bohuslav MARTINŮ The Czech composer spent his first 12 years 198 steps above the ground in a church steeple where his father was fire watchman. This perspective lent his music an unearthly breadth and detachment. He liked to let it undulate, like the hills and meadows that join Bohemia to Moravia. Such lack of incident can be soporific; in his case, it is often hypnotic.

Because he wrote over 400 works, including 16 operas, 11 ballets, six symphonies and seven string quartets, Martinů is commonly held to be an uneven composer. In fact, he was astonishingly consistent, incapable of composing badly. All the works after 1932 are polished, eloquent and individual. His personal motif of E♭ G B♭ F crops up at heartfelt moments

throughout his work and is blazed defiantly by a trumpet in his deathbed Nonet. Had he written less, the music might be more concentrated – but then it would not be Martinů.

The centre of his output is operatic, climaxing in *The Greek Passion* (Zurich, 9.vi.61) of Nikos Kazantzakis' controversial Crucifixion novel. *Julietta* (Prague, 16.iii.38), a dream study in alienation, is dramatically static but musically propulsive. Delicious melody in *The Miracles of our Lady* (Brno, 23.ii.35) evades any risk of sanctimony. *Comedy on a Bridge* (Czech Radio, 18.iii.37) is knockabout stuff at a border post.

He wrote the six symphonies after leaving France for the US in 1940. The 3rd (Boston, 12.x.45) was finished in June 1944 and concludes in a long-breathed coda of huge relief at news of the Normandy landings. The 5th (Prague, 27.v.47) has a middle movement that dances with an innocence reminiscent of Dvořák. Unsure of the symphonic character of the 6th (Boston, 7.i.56), he named it *Fantaisies Symphoniques*; it is dotted with references

to Dvořák's Requiem, Martinů's own *Field Mass* and a 14-bar theme from *Julietta*.

Among a hatful of concertos, the rhapsody-concerto for viola (Cleveland, 19.ii.53) opens with his signature tune and showcases the instrument with unforgettable mastery – a far lovelier work than Bartók's. The 3rd and 4th piano concertos are full of delights and the 2nd violin concerto (Boston, 21.xii.43) overflows with lyricism. There is a caustic concerto for string quartet and orchestra (1931), while the double concerto for two string orchs., piano and percussion (1938) is aurally challenging. Martinů's ear for instrumental combinations was acutely original. He did not shrink from dissonances and followed no preset rules. Some early ensemble works involved jazz (e.g. *Le Jazz* and the culinary ballet *La Revue de Cuisine*); others went down byways of Bohemian folklore. A boyish enthusiasm for football produced *Half-time* (Prague, 7.xii.24). The male choral *Field Mass*, written for Czech forces in France in 1939, has something of Janáček's ruggedness. The *Memorial to Lidice* (NY, 28.x.43) reflects on the Nazi annihilation of a Czech village.

His chamber music dips into a gamut of sources from medieval dance to *Honegger, a colleague he rated highly. The five pre-War quartets are conservative, almost anachronistic. The sixth (1946) bursts with energy, its themes working with and against one another over a pre-minimalist background. Cellists adore his three sonatas, the first of which (Paris, 19.v.40) contains an uncanny pre-echo of *Reich's *Endless Trains*.

Hearing Elizabethan madrigals sung in Prague by visiting Englishmen, he wrote four instrumental works with the linearity of a madrigal but without its vocal line. *Four Madrigals* for oboe, clarinet and bassoon (1937) and *Madrigal Sonata* for piano, flute and violin (1942) relate dreamily to *Julietta*; *Five Madrigal Stanzas* for violin and piano (1943) were written for the amateur fingers of the physicist Albert Einstein; *Three Madrigals* for violin and viola (1948) mirror Mozart's sinfonia concertante and Bach's preludes with wit, warmth and pleasing modernity. Beethoven is manifest in his beautiful 1944 trio for flute, cello and piano. But his chamber masterpiece is unquestionably the Nonet written on his deathbed, reflective yet unremorseful, in spirited Czech rhythms and with a spiritual self-assurance unheard since Janáček.

b. Policka, 8.xii.1890; played in Czech Philharmonic under *Talich (2nd violins), 1913–14; st with *Roussel; married and remained in France until 1940; returned to Prague in 1946 but left before the Communist takeover; prof. of music at Princeton, US, 1948–51; settled in Switzerland 1957; *d.* Liestal, 28.viii.59; reburied at Policka, 27.viii.79; *other major works:* Double concerto for two string orchestras (Basle, 9.ii.40); Sinfonietta *La Jolla* (1950), *Frescoes of Piero della Francesca* (Salzburg, 28.viii.56); *Epic of Gilgamesh* for narrator, soloists, chorus and orchestra (Basle, 24.i.58); five serenades.

Giuseppe MARTUCCI The conductor who premiered *Tristan* in Italy (Bologna, 1888) admired Brahms with equal fervour and was himself revered by *Toscanini, who premiered his two symphonies and B-flat minor piano concerto. His orchestral *Notturno*, Op 70/1, is an exquisite eight-minute delicacy reminiscent of the Siegfried Idyll and the *Adagietto of Mahler's 5th.

b. Capua, 6.i.1856, a trumpeter's son; prof. of piano at Naples 1880–6, dir. Bologna Cons. 1886–1902, dir. Naples Cons. 1902–9, *d.* there, 1.vi.09. *other works: La Canzona dei Ricordi* (Song of Remembrance) – an Italian equivalent of Mahler's folk-song cycles – a Mass, oratorio and much melodious piano music.

Martyrdom of St Magnus Chamber opera by Maxwell Davies. fp: Kirkwall, Orkney, 18.vi.77.

Le Martyre de Saint Sébastien Debussy wrote incidental vocal-orch. music for D'Annunzio's christian mystery play. fp: Paris, 22.v.11.

Joseph MARX As a youth Marx was entranced by *Mahler's orchestral songs and spent his creative life trying to emulate and improve on them. Friendship with the poet Anton Wildgans (1881–1932) provided him with a ready literary source, and his Lieder were swiftly taken up by top singers. Austrians consider him their outstanding lyrical composer since Hugo Wolf. In addition to songs, Marx composed an Autumn Symphony (Vienna, 5.ii.22, cond. Weingartner) on a similar scale to *Strauss's Alpine Symphony, and a Nature Trilogy (1926) of dionysian inclinations. His piano concerto (1920) is unabashedly titled 'Romantic' and contains no sound that might make Schumann wince. He was an influential teacher in Vienna and Graz and for three years advised the Turkish government on music pedagogy.

b. Graz, Austria, 11.v.1882; *d.* there, 3.ix.64. *other works: Verklärtes Jahr* for middle voice and orch. (1920), *Alt-Wiener Serenaden,* (Vienna, 14.iv.42, cond. *Böhm); *Quartetto in modo classico* (Vienna, 27.iv.42); Lieder with orch. and instrumental accompaniment.

Mary's Life (*Das Marienleben*) Soprano song-cycle by *Hindemith. fp: Frankfurt, 15.x.23.

Pietro MASCAGNI Famed at 26 years old for *Cavalleria rusticana* (1890), he failed to recapture its magic, wearing verismo paper-thin in the voyeuristic *Isabeau* (Buenos Aires, 2.vi.11) and prostrating himself before fascism in *Nerone* (Milan, 16.i.35). He died friendless in a fleapit hotel.

b. Livorno, Italy, 7.xii.1863; *d.* Rome, 2.viii. 45. *other operas: L'Amico Fritz* (1891), *Iris* (1898), *Lodoletta* (1917).

Mask of Orpheus *Birtwistle's unrepeated opera. fp: London (ENO), 21.v.86

Benedict MASON A voyage around his native coastline is described in the highly original *Lighthouses of England and Wales* (BBC, 28.iv.89), in which the orchestra is used almost filmically as flashing lights, foghorns and storms, and the conductor sweeps in a semi-circle like the tower itself. It sounds like a high-tech *La Mer*, only lonelier, and won the 1988 Britten prize, fittingly for an undoctrinal young composer. He has written a cantata, *Sapere Aude* (1989) for 18th-century period orchestra and synthesizers, a concerto for the viola section of a symphony orchestra (1992) and a football opera for the Munich Biennale with playwright Howard Brenton.

b. Budleigh Salterton, Devon, 19.iii.54; st with *Pousseur, *Ligeti; *other works:*

Imposing a Regular Pattern in Chaos and Heterophony (1990); string quartet (1987).

Daniel Gregory MASON The musical equivalent of Daughters of the American Revolution, his ancestors were Boston composers since George Washington's day. He used his pedigree to campaign against 'foreigners' – blacks and Jews – who were polluting the republic's culture. His racism was itself of foreign origin, imbibed in Paris as a pupil of d'*Indy; his compositions were Germanic and their textures unremarkable. For almost 40 years he was an influential faculty member at Columbia U. and chairman of its music department for a decade (1929–40).
  b. Brookline, Massachusetts, 20.xi.1873; *d.* Greenwich, Connecticut, 4.xii.53; *works include*: three symphonies (1916, 30, 37), *String quartet on Negro Themes* (1919).

mass Stravinsky and Bernstein wrote heartfelt Masses that irked the Vatican.

Jules (Emile-Frédéric) MASSENET The sensuous Frenchman shot his bolt in the *fin-de-siècle* with the evergreen *Manon* (1884), *Werther* (1892) and *Thaïs* (1894). Of his remaining 24 operas, *Le Jongleur de Notre Dame* (Monte Carlo, 18.ii.02) and *Don Quichotte* (MC, 19.ii.10) get an occasional showing. As professor of composition at the Paris Conservatoire (1878–1912), his pupils included *Bruneau and *Charpentier.
  b. Montaud, nr. St Etienne, Loire Valley, 12.v.1842; *d.* Paris, 13.viii.12.

Kurt MASUR Favoured conductor of East German communist rulers, he built a new Gewandhaus hall in Leipzig and applied discreet influence in humane causes. When the regime crumbled in October 1989, he helped avert bloodshed by throwing open his concert hall to demonstrators who would otherwise have run into tank fire. In 1991 he was named music director of the New York Philharmonic. His repertoire is predominantly 19th-century.
  b. Brieg, German Silesia, 18.vii.27; mus. dir. Komische Oper Berlin 1960–64, Dresden Philharmonic, 1967–72, Leipzig Gewandhaus 1970–; US début, Cleveland 1974.

Bruce MATHER Canadian *Boulezite, specialist in small-scale works.

b. Toronto, 9.v.39; st with *Milhaud, *Messiaen; taught McGill U. 1966–; *works include*: *Music for Organ, Horn and Gongs* (1973); Scherzo for orch. (1987).

William (James) MATHIAS Welsh tonalist of church and *Cheltenham repute, wrote royal wedding march for Prince Charles.
  b. Whitland, Dyfed, Wales, 1.xi.34; st with *Berkeley; prof. at Bangor 1970–88, president Incorporated Society of Musicians 1989; *d.* Menai Bridge, Wales, 29.vii.92. *works include*: opera *The Servants* (text by Iris Murdoch, 1980), three symphonies (1966, 83, 91), *Lux Aeterna* (1982).

Mathis der Maler Hindemith's totalitarian-era opera of an artist under pressure. fp: Zurich, 28.v.38. The *Mathis* Symphony caused Nazi ructions when *Furtwängler performed it (Berlin, 12.iii.34) against official orders.

Shin-ichi MATSUSHITA Japanese *electronic music pioneer, teaching music and mathematics at Osaka universities. His compositions include a Requiem for tape and traditional forces.
  b. Osaka, 1.x.22; founded Autumn in Osaka Festival 1962.

Colin and David MATTHEWS Musicians have understandable difficulty in telling the two brothers apart. Both were largely self-educated Londoners, drawn to music by hearing *Mahler, involved in the realization of his 10th symphony, active in the *Britten circle, both exceptionally able orchestrators and sharing the same publisher. Neither showed much interest in music theatre or modernist techniques. Both drew ideas from the English landscape, Colin in a half-hour 'sonata' for orchestra entitled *Landscape* (BBC, 17.xi.83, cond. Elder), David in a 25–minute mood-piece, *In the Dark Time* (BBC, 11.xii.85, cond. Elder). David has written four symphonies, Colin none. They often worked together on commercial projects and jointly orchestrated seven early songs by Mahler (Cardiff, 12.vi.81). Colin, the younger brother, is slightly more forthright; David veers to a more central European orientation. Both have a tendency to eclecticism; Colin's *Hidden Variables* (1989) is frankly *minimalist, David's *Romanza* (Buckingham Palace,

2.viii.90) for Rostropovich could almost have been written by *Elgar. If identity problems persist, they have only themselves to blame.

> David: *b.* London 9.iii.43; *other orch. works:* September Music (1979), violin concerto (1983); also 6 string quartets.
> Colin: *b.* London, 13.ii.46; *other orch. works:* Night Music (1977), cello concerto (1984); also two string quartets and oboe quartet (1981).

Siegfried MATTHUS Musical spokesman of the East German communist regime, he was dramaturg and composer in residence at the Komische Oper, Berlin, from 1964–89, turning out eight operas of tonally unexceptionable, socially upbeat character. He has composed copiously for orchestra – notably concertos for oboe and kettledrums (both 1984) – along with many vocal settings.

> *b.* Mallenuppen, East Prussia, 13.iv.34; st with *Wagner-Régeny; head of music at ruling German Arts Academy 1972–.

(John) Nicholas MAW In the 15 years that he pursued *Odyssey* (London, 20.iv.89), Maw acquired quixotic status among British musicians. Few imagined the work would be completed, let alone coherent and listenable at around 100 minutes of pure orchestral sound. *Odyssey* was astonishing as much for what it represented as what it contained – one man's dogged journey away from 20th-century ideologies and back to the essence of music. As the piece unfolds, the harmonies clarify and the texture expands to a Brucknerian scope, without resorting to pastiche or simple-mindedness, and remaining within a vastly preordained structure. Too straitlaced for frequent consumption, it stands out as a milestone in recent musical evolution.

Raised in Margaret Thatcher's birthplace, Maw was sucked into the Webernian vortex, rejecting it for melodism in *Scenes and Arias* (1962) but retaining the structural imperatives of serialism. His Irish insurrectionist opera *The Rising of the Moon* was staged at Glyndebourne in 1970.

> *b.* Grantham, Lincs, 5.xi.35; st with Boulanger and Max Deutsch; taught

Cambridge and Washington, D.C.; *other works: The World in the Evening* (London, 21.x.88, cond. Haitink), *Sonata notturna* for cello and strings (King's Lynn, 30.v.86).

Billy (Joseph William) MAYERL Cocktail lounge–pianist of the 1920s and 1930s, whose up-and-down keyboard pieces convey a certain period charm; *Marigold* is the best-known. He gave the first UK performance of Gershwin's *Rhapsody in Blue*.

> *b.* London, 1902; *d.* there, 1959.

Maxwell DAVIES – See DAVIES

Toshiro MAYUZUMI Buddhist music met Western avant-garde in Mayuzumi's hypnotic Prelude for string quartet (1961), mixing the repetitive chants and bells of religious ritual with disruptive dissonances of the modern age. He also composed a Mishima novel, *Kinkakuji*, as an opera for Berlin (1976). Winning a scholarship to France in 1951, he was drawn particularly to *Messiaen. He wrote scores for two Hollywood movies, *The Bible* (1965) and *Reflections in a Golden Eye* (1967).

> *b.* Yokohama, Japan, 20.ii.29; founded contemporary music festival at Karuisawa 1957; *other works: Nirvana Symphony* (1958), *Mandala Symphony* (1960), *Bugaku* ballet for Balanchine (1962), *X, Y, Z* musique concrète (1953), Perpetuum mobile for orch. (1989).

John McCABE While his generation took their gospel from *Darmstadt, McCabe opted for unfashionable Europeans, *Nielsen and *Hartmann. The first is heard lustrously in *Notturni ed Alba* for soprano and orch. (Hereford Cathedral, 26.viii.70), the latter in orch. *Variations on a theme of Karl Amadeus Hartmann* (1965), quoting the opening of the Munich composer's momentous fourth symphony. McCabe has written three symphonies of his own and a splendid Concerto for Orchestra (1983) but is best known for the orchestral suite *Chagall Windows* (Manchester, 9.i.75), responding to biblical images in the Russian master's stained-glass tributes to the 12 tribes at Jerusalem's Hadassah Hospital.

> *b.* Huyton, Lancs., 21.iv.39; st with *Genzmer; excellent concert pianist; dir. London College of Music 1983–; *other works:* opera *The Lion, the Witch and the*

Wardrobe (1969), ballet *Mary Queen of Scots* (1976), three piano concertos, two violin concertos, three string quartets, film music.

Paul McCARTNEY – See Beatles.

Colin (Cahart) McPHEE Canadian of Scots extraction, his enthusiasm for Balinese music infected *Britten and many Americans. After premiering a conventional piano concerto in Toronto, he took lessons from *Varèse in New York, attracted by his percussive notions. Disaffected by modernism, he was seduced by the recorded sound of gamelans and in 1933 sailed for Bali, settling there for six years. Summering in Mexico with *Chávez in 1936, he wrote his major symphonic work, the gamelan-flavoured *Tabuh-Tabuhan* for two pianos and orchestra. His output was modest – three symphonies, a concerto for wind orchestra and some keyboard pieces – but his books on Bali and his lectures at UCLA's Institute of Ethnomusicology (1958–64) had far-reaching resonances.
b. Montreal, 15.iii.01; *d.* Los Angeles, 7.i.64.

mbira African *marimba-like group of instruments.

Richard (Graham) MEALE Australian *Messiaen follower, also immersed in Indonesian music.
b. Sydney, 24.viii.32; *operas: Juliet's Memoirs* (1975), *Mer de Glace* (Sydney, 4.x.91).

The Medium One-act spiritualist melodrama by *Menotti; companion piece to The *Telephone. fp: NY, 8.v.46.

Nicolai MEDTNER The passing fancy of an Indian princeling, the Maharajah of Mysore, plucked this Russian émigré from English obscurity and paid to have his piano music recorded by EMI. Medtner briefly shared the celebrity of *Rachmaninov, who often wondered aloud why his friend's later music failed to achieve the concentration of his Russian scores. A casualty of *exile, Medtner retreated musically from *Skryabin-like adventurism to Brahmsian caution. Three piano concertos (1918, 1927, 1943) and a sheaf of sonatas and miniatures constitute his contribution.
b. Moscow, 5.i.1880; lived Berlin and Paris 1921–35, London 1935–51; *d.* London, 13.xi.51.

Wilfrid (Howard) MELLERS This unconfined musical commentator assessed Bob Dylan and the Beatles on the same terms as Bach and Vaughan Williams, in each book adopting an unorthodox thesis on moral high ground that he boldly defended against convention. Dylan, for example, was discussed as a symbol of Amerindian continuity. Mellers agitated the stagnant pond of musical dissertations and lectured engagingly on both sides of the Atlantic. His compositions tended to be English-traditional, albeit quirky as *Tippett.
b. Leamington, Warwickshire, 26.iv.14; st with *Rubbra and *Wellesz; prof. at Birmingham 1948–59, Pittsburgh 1960–63, York 1964–81; four times married; *compositions include: Life cycle* for three choirs and two orchs, *Yebichai* for soprano, scat singer, jazz trio, orch. and tape.

Willem MENGELBERG Dutch conductor of German descent and romantic sympathies, he led the Concertgebouworkest for half a century until sacked for working with the Nazis. A wayward and impulsive interpreter, he avidly espoused Mahler and Strauss, staging the first cycle of Mahler symphonies in May 1920.
b. Utrecht, Netherlands, 28.iii.1871; *d.* Chur, Switzerland 21.iii.51.
His nephew and biographer, Kurt Rudolf Mengelberg (1892–1959) had some impact as a composer with Symphonic variations for cello and orchestra (1927). Another nephew, Karel Mengelberg (*b.* Utrecht, 18.vii.02, *d.* Amsterdam, 11.vii.84), went to the USSR in the 1930s to run the music department at the Kiev film studios; he composed much chamber music, an orchestral *Requiem* (1946) and a horn concerto (1950). His son, Misha Mengelberg (*b.* Kiev, 5.vi.35), was an extreme experimentalist who wrote a piece for orchestra with electronic saw and excavating drills called *With the very Polite Greetings of the Camel* (1973) and became head of a Guild of Improvisers. He collaborated with *Andriessen and three others in an anti-imperialist collective opera, *Reconstructie* (Holland Festival, 29.vi.69).

Peter MENNIN(I) Regressive US educationalist of Italian origin, ran the Peabody Conservatory (1958–63) and Juilliard School (1962–83), and composed nine tonal symphonies.

b. Erie, Pennsylvania, 17.v.23; *d*. NY, 17.vi. 83.

Gian-Carlo MENOTTI The first opera designed for television was Menotti's finest. *Amahl and the Night Visitors* (NBC, 24.xii.51), a nativity tale with simple tunes, confronts the Bethlehem-bound Magi with a boy cripple. It was a class above the one-acters on which the Italian made his name. *The Medium* (NY, 8.v.46) depicted murder at a seance; *The Telephone* (18.ii.47) was an unconsummated conversation; the two are usually double-billed. *The Consul* (Philadelphia, 1.iii.50), an escape-from-fascism opera, cemented his neo-Puccinist style. The librettos were always his own.

As a teenaged overseas student at the Curtis Institute in Philadelphia, Menotti was tutored in sartorial and social graces by *Barber, forming a lifelong partnership. Barber loosened up under the Italian's influence; Menotti adopted three-piece suits. He also wrote librettos for *Vanessa and *A Hand of Bridge*. In 1958 he founded the Festival of Two Worlds at Spoleto, Italy; in 1974, he settled in Scotland with an adoptive son. Lasting success eluded him after Amahl, despite a productivity that continued into his seventies with operas for Plácido Domingo – *Goya* (Washington, D.C., 11.xi.86) – and for the 1988 Olympics, *The Wedding* (Seoul, Korea, 16.ix.88). An occasional sweet aria – 'What a Curse for a Woman is a Timid Man' (from *The Old Man and the Thief*, 1939) – did not redeem stretches of thinly concealed derivation in his 19 operas.

b. Cadegliano, Italy, 7.vi.11; *other operas*: Amelia Goes to the Ball (1937, *The Island God* (1942), *The Saint of Bleecker Street* (NY, 27.xii.54), *Le dernier sauvage* (Paris, 21.x.63), *Help, help, the Globolinks!* (Hamburg, 19.xii.68), *The Hero* (1976). He also wrote two piano concertos and a US bicentennial symphony (Philadelphia, 4.viii.76).

(Sir) Yehudi MENUHIN *Wunderkind* of the century, a world-famous violinist at 11 years old who suffered a crisis of technique in his thirties but endured in the public mind as an icon of spirituality. He inspired *Bloch's *Baal Shem* suite, *Bartók's sonata for solo violin and Malcolm *Arnold's concerto for two violins. Staid on the whole in his tastes, he formed a sparky duo with the jazz fiddler Stéphane *Grappelli and a meditative alliance with the sitarist Ravi *Shankar. He championed such thankless causes as *Furtwängler's post-war rehabilitation, Palestinian rights and the electric automobile. In 1959 he settled in England, founding a school at Stoke Mandeville for budding *Wunderkinder*; 30 years later he accepted citizenship and a knighthood.

b. New York, 22.iv.16 of Palestinian-Jewish parents; raised in San Francisco; st with Louis Persinger, *Enesco, Fritz *Busch; NY debut 17.i.26, Paris debut 6.ii.27, Berlin debut 12.iv.29; married twice; founder-director Gstaad Festival, Switzerland, 1956–, Bath Festival, England 1959–68.

La Mer Debussy's orchestral impressions of the English Channel, three linked sketches composed partly in England amid marital turmoil. fp: Paris, 15.x.05.

Pierre MERCURE A bassoonist in the Montreal Symphony Orchestra (1947–52), Mercure became involved with *musique concrète and *aleatory trends in Paris and devoted his short life to blending conventional instruments with electronics. As head of music on French CBC television, he ran a 1961 international Week of Avant-Garde Music in Montreal; he died at 38 in a road accident while driving from Paris to Lyon. His early compositions were neoclassical and published by Ricordi; from 1961 he wrote for combinations of tape and instruments.

b. Montreal 21.ii.27; *d*. Avallon, France, 27.i. 66. *works include*: Cantate pour une joie (1956, for soprano, instruments and orchestra), *Divertimento* for string orch. (1957), *Structure métalliques* for tape (1961), *Psaume pour Abri* (1963, for narrator, two choruses, orch., and tape).

Aarre MERIKANTO The upsurge of Finnish opera was prompted by the 1967 staging of an epic work, *Juha*, composed 45 years earlier by the frustrated Merikanto. Set in the northern wastes, the opera eschewed folksiness, depicting a modern, highly-sexed heroine in graphic *Janáček-like sonorities (the libretto, by soprano Aino Ackté, had sat untouched for two years on Sibelius' desk). *Juha* belonged strikingly to the era of *Katya and *Wozzeck* but demonstrated to the Sixties generation of *Sallinen and *Rautavaara how to write a contemporary opera without sacrificing national character.

Merikanto persisted with modernism through the 1920s, his Fantasy for Orchestra (1923) and Concerto for nine intstruments (1925) sharing a common language with *Berg. But rejection in Helsinki and the death of his father (himself the first composer of a Finnish-language opera) brought about a retreat into embittered conventionality. He destroyed several scores and did not live to hear his best music vindicated.

> *b.* Helsinki 29.vi.1893, son of Oskar Merikanto (1868–1924); st with *Reger; taught at Sibelius Academy 1936–58; *d.* Helsinki 29.ix.58. *other works*: *Konzertstück* for cello and orch. (1926), *Notturno* (1929); four violin concertos, three piano concertos.

The Merry Widow Silver-age Viennese operetta by Lehár. fp: Theater an der Wien, 30.xii.05.

Mersey Sound Collective name for the Beatles and their early imitators – Gerry and the Pacemakers ('You'll Never Walk Alone'), the Searchers, Cilla Black.

André (-Charles-Prosper) MESSAGER A key catalyst in French music, Messager came to attention in the last century as an operetta and ballet composer – *The Two Pigeons* (1886) *and Scaramouche* (1891). His grand opera *Fortunio* (1907) sounds like *Tristan* reworked by *Puccini – and none the worse for it. He wrote a four-handed Wagnerian *parody, *Souvenirs de Bayreuth*, with his friend *Fauré and urged *Debussy to refute Tristanism in *Pelléas et Mélisande*, whose première Messager conducted. He directed the Opéra-Comique (1898–1908), the Paris Opéra (1907–1915) and Covent Garden (1901–7) and commanded the Conservatoire concerts in Paris from 1908 to his death.

> *b.* Montluçon, France, 30.xii.1853; stage works include *La Béarnaise* (1885), *Madame Crysanthème* (1893, on same lines as Puccini's subsequent *Butterfly*), *Miss Dollar* (1893), *Véronique* (1898); married US songwriter Hope Temple (1858–1938); *d.* Paris, 24.ii.29.

Olivier (Eugène Prosper Charles) MESSIAEN The central figure in

modern French music arouses conflicting emotions. There is universal admiration for

his uncommon harmonies and huge wedges of static orchestral sound, alongside reservations about his narrow outlook and stubborn faith, a condition bordering on dogmatism. 'I wish I could be as sure of anything as Messiaen is of everything,' moaned a disgruntled colleague.

Messiaen spanned the permanent split in French culture between state/progress and church/reaction. He played the organ four times every Sunday and all feast days at the Paris church of La Trinité from 1931 into his eighties, representing in his office and compositions the granitic fundamentalism of Roman Catholicism. But by 1936, he was equally active in contemporary causes, forming a 'Jeune France' group with *Jolivet and others to advance a nationalist spirit in music. After the War, he became guru to a generation of revolutionaries and free-thinkers led by *Boulez, Xenakis and Stockhausen.

Whatever line he took, Messiaen's certainty was absolute. His musical tastes were overwhelmingly chauvinist, centred on *Debussy and extolling Honegger and Milhaud above superior foreigners.

He ascribed his creativity to three sources: 'the theological truths of the Catholic faith'; human love; and nature. As a church composer, his music is unrivalled in the entire century. Advancing beyond the modest fugues of his teacher *Dupré, Messiaen at 20 wrote the tantalizing *Celestial Banquet* and in 1935 produced an organ cycle of nine 'meditations' describing *La Nativité du Seigneur (The Birth of our Lord)*. They presaged a plenitude of organ and instrumental pieces, among which *Visions de l'Amen* (Paris, 10.v.43) for four-handed piano – composed as a reaction against German occupation – and the *Vingt Régards sur l'enfant Jésus* (1944) are popular recital works

His most trenchant wartime piece was the *Quatuor pour la fin du temps (Quartet for the end of time)*, written for himself and three fellow-prisoners in a German Stalag and played with freezing fingers on a broken piano, clarinet, cello and violin (Görlitz, Silesia, 15.i.41). Aphoristic in utterance, almost *Webernian, it aspires in propulsive rhythms and tranquil raptures to an uplifting faith in liberation. The apotheosis of his religious art was attained with the choral-orchestral *La Transfiguration de Notre Seigneur Jésus Christ* (Lisbon, 7.vi.69) and the static opera, *St François d'Assise* (Paris, 28.xi.83). In these and other large-scale constructions, Messiaen composed music in massive blocks that are laid before the audience without much development or continuity. This is existential music: I sound, therefore I am. It is a statement that has to be taken on its own terms, and which comes in long, very slow stretches that can seem interminable. Listening to Messiaen is itself often a confession of faith in his genius.

To attain monumentalism, Messiaen first traversed preoccupations with sex and ornithology. As a young man he pondered warmly on the delights of erotic love which, as a communicant, were forbidden to him outside wedlock. Marriage in 1932 to Claire Delbos, a violinist whom he called Mi, inspired a *Theme and Variations* for violin and piano, followed in 1936 by the *Poèmes pour Mi* for soprano, with piano or orchestra. In 1945 he wrote a lovely vocal cycle, *Harawi*, 'a song of love and death' which remodelled the Tristan legend on a Peruvian folktale and employed native South American tunes and bird sounds in its makeup.

It was the first of a so-called Tristan trilogy that ended with a set of *Cinq Rechants* for *a cappella* choir, consisting of love poems in his own invented language for his bespectacled pupil, the pianist Yvonne Loriod, with whom he became close while his wife wasted slowly away in hospital from a tragic disease. He capped his yearnings with the *Turangalîla Symphony* (Boston, 2.xii.49, cond. *Bernstein), the pivotal point of his life and work. It amounts to an 80-minute discourse on two Sanskritic themes – *Turanga*, or passing time, and *lîla*, the act of creation, or procreation, or destruction. Written in ten movements for large orchestra with glockenspiel and vibraphone, piano and *ondes Martenot, it is colourful, splashy, over-the-top – a limitless and at times literal hymn to the physical passions that led ascetics like Boulez to call it 'bordello music'. It expresses, in parts, frustrated desire for his beloved (soon to become his second wife) and possesses a definable appeal for young audiences; the best recordings are by conductors in their 30s. In practical terms, it is a quasi-piano concerto that rotates around the key of F# major with its dreamy centre in the 6th movement. *Turangalîla* extended Messiaen's reliance on pure rhythm – a tendency he derived from *Stravinsky – and helped ferment a number of musical theories and theoretical writings. His rhythmic techniques and 'non-retrogradable rhythms' entered the musical lexicon, a far cry in sheer simplicity from serial theory yet a distinct stage in the emergence of *total serialism.

In addition to dipping into varied exotic cultures, including Javanese gamelan, Turangalîla introduced Messiaen's third source of inspiration – the trill of birdsong. Over the next decade, instead of following the Pied Piper of Webern's serialism along with most of his pupils, Messiaen recorded and notated the birds of rural France and elsewhere, imitating their sounds pianistically in *Catalogue d'oiseaux* (1958) and utilizing them as the basis for large orchestral works, *Réveil des oiseaux* (Donaueschingen, 11.x.53) and *Oiseaux éxotiques* (Paris, 10.iii.56).

The shimmering *Colours of the Celestial City* (Donaueschingen, 17.x.64; cond. Boulez) contained the piercing cry of the Brazilian araponga and two New Zealand birds, as well as cowbells, Greek and Hindu rhythms, Gregorian chant, religious imagery and a musical rainbow. *Chronochromie* (1960) depicts a mountainside.

Des Canyons aux étoiles (*From the canyons to the stars*, NY, 10.xi.74), celebrating the vast expanses of rural America, is a 90-minute stop-start epic in which breathtaking sonorities sprout sporadically in an endless aural landscape. It calls to mind Rossini's comment on Wagner: 'Il a des beaux moments, mais des mauvais quarts d'heure' (He has beautiful moments, but dreadful quarter-hours). The town of Parowan, Utah, where *Canyons* was composed, named a nearby peak Mount Messiaen in his honour. A gentle and private man, Messiaen lived a relatively uneventful life, spoke no foreign language and travelled little but retained a catholic interest in exotic cuisine.

His impact on music is two-fold. As a teacher in Paris, Tanglewood (1948) and Darmstadt (1950–53), he helped students find their own way to diverse expressions, from the *musique concrète of Pierre *Henry to the Debussyist scores of George *Benjamin. Starting with *Turangalîla*, he broke down the traditional composition of the orchestra, forming an ensemble of 13 wind, xylophone, marimba, piano, four percussion and 8 violins for *7 Haïkaï* (Paris, 30.x.63), and using 43 players and a jamboree of instruments in Canyons.

His music is never miserly – audiences in austere communist societies adored its aural luxuries – and his appeal to sophisticated listeners surmounted the child-like simplicity of much of his material and ideas. Those who cannot stomach certainty in an artist should avoid Messiaen at all costs – but they should also beware of Wagner and Mozart. Messiaen possessed an essential attribute of a great composer – a sound that is unmistakably identifiable as his own. His plangent textures have

entered the lexicon of the 20th century and permeated the music of many cultures. The Messiaen message can be heard nowadays in advertising jingles and rock accompaniments.

b. Avignon, 10.xii.08; st at Paris Conservatoire with Dukas and Dupré; taught there 1941–78; organist at Ste Trinité 1931–88; *d*. Paris, 28.v.92. *other significant orch. works*: Les offrandes oubliées (Paris, 19.ii.31), Hymne au Saint Sacrement (23.ii.33), L'Ascension (1935), Et expecto resurrectionem mortuorum (7.v.65), Livre du Saint Sacrément (1985, organ).

Metamorphosen Personal regrets for 23 strings by Richard *Strauss, reflecting on the destruction of his homeland. fp: Zurich, 25.i.46, cond. *Sacher.

Ernst Hermann MEYER A Berlin Communist, he fled in 1934 to London, where he worked in the film industry and lectured at Bedford College while writing a definitive study of English chamber music from antiquity to Purcell (pub. 1946). Returning home, he was named professor of music sociology at Humboldt University (1948–70) and turned out cantatas of praise for the Stalinist regime, serving on the central committee of the ruling SED party. He succeeded *Eisler as president of the Academy of Arts. His violin concerto was premièred by *Oistrakh (East Berlin, 5.iii.65); his only opera, *Reiter der Nacht*, (17.xi.73) was hailed as 'a major contribution to international socialism'. An enduring friendship with Alan *Bush won the British Marxist renown in East Germany.

b. Berlin 8.xii.05; *d*. there, 8.x.88. *other works*: B major symphony in five movements (28.ii.69).

Krzysztof MEYER Polish composer who became preoccupied with mounting national crisis, naming his 6th symphony (1981) after his homeland.

b. Krakow, Poland, 11.vii.43; st with *Penderecki, *Boulanger; *other works*: Lyric Triptych for soprano and chamber orch. to *Auden texts (Aldeburgh, 22.vi.78), D major symphony 'in the style of Mozart' (Poznan, 1.iv.77).

Mi Messiaen's first wife, dedicatee of *Poèmes pour Mi*.

Nicolai MIASKOVSKY After the collapse of the USSR, the reputation of the 'Father of the Soviet Symphony' is undetermined. A 1917 supporter of Bolshevism, he fell foul of commissars with a dissident 6th symphony (Moscow, 4.v.24). Miaskovsky went unpunished but the work was not played again. He made amends with a derivatively romantic 7th symphony (8.ii.25) and intrigued *Prokofiev with the instrumental felicities of the large and lowering 8th (23.v.26), producing a symphony a year for the rest of his life. He made fulsome use of folk material and in the 10th symphony (7.iv.28) painted the history of Leningrad. Such literalisms failed nevertheless to please the party and Miaskovsky was twice terrorized by Stalin, alongside Shostakovich, for reasons none could fathom.

Was his music subversive? If so, it awaits decoding for, on paper and to the ear, it appears conformist – though never as dull as some western critics suggest. Apart from 27 symphonies, he wrote an *Elgarianly elegiac cello concerto near the end of the Second World War (17.iii.45) and much gentle chamber music. The cycle of nine piano sonatas (1907–49) contains essential clues to his inner world.

b. Novogiorgievsk, nr. Warsaw, 20.iv.1881; Army service 1915–21; taught Moscow Conservatory 1921–50; *d.* Moscow, 8.viii.50. *other works*: orch. poem, *Silence* (Moscow, 13.vi.11), violin concerto (Leningrad, 14.xi.38), Serenade and Sinfonietta for small orch., 13 string quartets, two cello sonatas.

microtonality Anything other than the whole tones and half-tones struck by the white and black keys respectively of a well-tuned piano is a microtone. To produce one, you need to retune or mistune a keyed instrument. *Quarter-tones, halfway between semitones, are fairly easily achieved on a violin. Eighths are elusive except on a double-bass and fractions like fifths and elevenths are manually unattainable and probably indiscernible by the ear with any degree of accuracy. Such fragments are possible only on an instrument tuned to their pitch, or when generated by *computer. Microtonal music possessed a messianic allure for some central Europeans aware of the finite options of the diatonic scale. *Bartók borrowed microtonal intervals from gypsy and balkan cultures in a number of major scores, most notably the early string quartets. Around 1920, the Czech visionary *Hába proclaimed that the future of music lay in fragmented tones, and invented instruments for that purpose. His important opera *Matka* proved virtually unsingable in the intervals he intended. The Mexican *Carrillo wrote a quarter-tone Concertino for *Stokowski's orchestra and toured central America in the 1930s with a microtonal ensemble. *Ives was another who relished the space between tones; *Partch composed on an eccentric 43-note scale. Enthusiasm for such ideas waned in the austere era after 1945, returning 30 years later when *Boulez declared that the solution to the century's musical conundrum lurked within the mind of a computer. Concurrent with his electronic quest, microtones became common in the simple-sounding compositions of *minimalists. Hába, in the medium term, may have been right.

Middle-of-road (MOR) Popular music that is not specifically youth-oriented and may be familiar to older listeners.

The Midsummer Marriage *Tippett's first opera. fp: Covent Garden, 27.i.55.

A Midsummer Night's Dream *Britten's Shakespearean opera. fp: Aldeburgh, 11.vi.60.

Francisco MIGNONE There is an awful lot of music in Brazil. Much of it was written by Mignone, applying the smooth lyricism he learned in Italy to rapid local rythms and melodies.

b. São Paolo, Brazil, 3.ix.1897; prof. there 29; *d.* Rio, 18.ii.86. *works include*: two operas, three ballets, *Suite brasiliera* (1933), *4 fantasias brasileiras* (1937), *sinfonia tropical* (1958).

Georges MIGOT The Havergal *Brian of French music spent a long life in murky corridors as curator of instruments at the Paris Conservatoire, writing slightly archaic music that no-one wished to hear. It included 13 symphonies, three operas to his own texts, six oratorios on the life of Christ and an incalculable amount of chamber music. A pupil of *Widor and d'*Indy, he detested the pastiche of neo-

classicism and opted to combine *Debussyan textures with baroque echoes of the Rameau era of national ascendance.
b. Paris 27.ii.1891; *d*. Levallois, nr. Paris, 5.i.76.

Edmund Odön von MIHALOVICH Hungarian mentor to Bartók and Kodály, though himself arch-conservative. He wrote four symphonies, two operas in German and a Wagnerian *Faust* overture
b. Fericance, 13.ix.1842; *d*. Budapest, 22.iv.29.

Marcel MIHALOVICI Parisian associate of *Enescu, he dissembled native Romanian melodies in elegant and fashionable settings. A convivial and civilized musician, his home was the centre of an école de Paris formed by east European émigrés.
b. Bucharest, Rumania, 22.x.1898; went to Paris 1919 to study with d'*Indy; married pianist Monique Haas (1909–87); *d*. Paris, 12.viii.85. *works include*: five operas, five ballets, five symphonies.

Minoru MIKI Japanese composer of stylized stage works, including a puppet-opera *Jōruri* (St Louis, 1985).
b. Tokushima, Shikoku, 16.iii.30; *other works*: Requiem (1963), concertos for marimba (1969) and koto (1974).

Mikrokosmos *Bartók's guide to playing the modern piano, 153 pieces arranged in six volumes of ascending order of difficulty; published 1940.

Darius MILHAUD The most productive composer since Schubert or Czerny, Milhaud could write music anywhere and in any medium. Confined to a wheelchair by rheumatoid arthritis for much of his life, he deplored sloth and constantly scribbled notes. Not composing was harder for him than composing. He turned out more than 400 works of fluctuating consistency, often vital and picturesque but at worst mere note-spinning around a minuscule idea. The 1st cello concerto (Paris, 28.vi.35), for instance, opens with a bold solo statement that melds into a delightful orchestral foxtrot; the joke, however, wears thin as the supporting material begins to exhaust its substance and the listener's patience.

Trail-blazer of Les *Six, Milhaud was a boy wonder of Mediterranean Sephardic

origin whose tastes were considered dangerously modern and foreign at d'*Indy's Conservatoire. Befriended by the writer Paul Claudel, he went as his secretary to the French embassy in Brazil, returning with an opera based on Claudel's translation of the *Oresteia* (*Les Choéphores*, Paris 15.vi.19) and a passion for samba rhythms and jazz. These elements, together with a facile polytonality, entered his oeuvre in the Parisian ballet *Le boeuf sur le toit* (*The ox on the roof*, 21.ii.20), which coined cliché for the frenzied age and set Milhaud at the centre of the ever-running cultural controversy known as Paris.

Saudades do Brazil (1921, for orch.) was a further product of the same voyage. He did not write glowing travel brochures, though. A parallel Debussyan sonata for flute, oboe, clarinet and piano (1918) captures some of the squalor that he saw in Rio, the bodies being trundled to mass graves after an outbreak of Spanish influenza.

His route to world fame came on a 1922 trip to New York, where he frequented Harlem bars and collected Black Swan 'race' records to assimilate the idioms of jazz and blues. These were fused into his phenomenally vivid score for the ballet *Le Création du Monde* (*Genesis*, Paris 25.x.23). The music was disparaged for its cabaret frivolity but its sheer energy and atmosphere proved irresistible. It was the world's first symphonic jazz score, years ahead of Gershwin, and Milhaud's most durable hit.

The remainder of his music aroused minor scandals but nothing like the storms and walkouts provoked by the initial concerts of Les Six. The accolade of respectability arrived with *Christoph Colombe* (Berlin, 5.v.30), a grand opera in 26 scenes to a text by Claudel.

During the Second War Milhaud found refuge in the US and taught for 25 years thereafter at Mills College in Oakland, California, where his pupils included *Reich, *Bolcom and the jazzman Dave Brubeck. He became a sage-like presence on the new music scene, willing to experiment with electronics and serialism but never losing his cheerful tunefulness. In later years he turned out laments for shorter-lived contemporaries – an elegiac 4th string quintet (1956) touchingly recalls Honegger – and music for every imaginable occasion. When a publisher asked him to stop writing symphonies after he had submitted 12, he wrote symphonic suites and named them after whichever place paid the commission fee – *Musique pour Prague, pour Lisbonne, for Boston*, and so on.

Of his 18 string quartets, the 4th (1918) is polytonal and inscribed to *Schoenberg, and the 14th and 15th can be played together contrapuntally as an octet (1949). It would be easier to assign Milhaud a place in posterity if he had exercised greater economy with his pen – but there was no containing Darius Milhaud, the gentle, intelligent, chubby, irrepressible composer of France's golden south.

b. Aix-en-Provence, 4.ix.1892; *d.* Geneva, 29.iv.74. *other important works*: operas *Maximilien* (1930), *Bolivar* (1943) and *David* (Jerusalem, 1.vi.54); ballet *L'homme et son désir* (1918); *Scaramouche*; 4th symphony (1948), 1st violin concerto (1919), concerto for flute and violin (1938), set of concertos entitled *The Four Seasons, Le Carnaval de Londres* (1937); much vocal music of which the *Cantique du Rhône* is singularly lovely; *Étude poétique* for seven tapes playing out of phase.

Glenn MILLER US big-band leader, famed for 'Moonlight Serenade', 'Little Brown Jug' and 'Chatanooga Choo-choo'.

Having waited until 1939 to make a mark on the charts, he broke up his band in 1942, enlisted in the USAAF and was lost with his plane over the English Channel.

b. Clarinda, Iowa, 1.iii.04; lost at sea, 15.xii.44.

million-dollar trio Press-hype for 1940s ensemble of Arthur Rubinstein, Jascha Heifetz and Gregor Piatigorsky. Forty years later, a conductor in Pittsburgh earned that amount in 14 weeks.

minimalism Minimalism began in medieval times with interminably repeated phrases of choral liturgy. It can be heard in Bach fugues, in the prelude to *Das Rheingold*, above all in the unvarying fragment of a phrase that constitutes *Ravel's Boléro*.

The modern cult started with Riley's *In C (San Francisco, 21.v.65), *Young's mantras and *Reich's experiments with tape loops. It peaked in the operas of Philip *Glass and began to die in *Nixon in China*, when melody reasserted control of rhythmic repetition. Its decline is still too recent to assess overall significance, except in two respects. It sparked a *new simplicity among young Europeans of the 1980s and it drew the techniques of art and rock music closer than ever before.

Miracle in the Gorbals Glaswegian ballet by *Bliss. fp: London, 26.x.44.

Miracles of our Lady Four-part devotional opera by *Martinů. fp: Brno, 23.ii.35

The Miraculous Mandarin Bartók's 2nd ballet depicting a plot by three pimps and a prostitute to murder a rich Chinaman. fp: Cologne, 27.xi.26.

Miss Julie Strindberg's drama fitted operas by *Rorem (1965) and *Alwyn (1977).

Dmitri MITROPOULOS Outstanding Greek modernist, he conducted at Athens in its only era of concert excellence (1924–36) before emigrating to the US where he headed the Minneapolis (1937–49) and NY Philharmonic (1949–58) orchestras. Huge, bald and homosexual, he was an impassioned interpreter of emotional scores, particularly Mahler and Berg, leaping high in the podium for added emphasis and heavily influencing his New York successor, Leonard *Bernstein. As a young composer, Mitropoulos impressed Saint-Saëns with the first modern Greek opera, *Sister Beatrice* (after Maeterlinck, Athens, 20.v. 1919).

> *b*. Athens, 1.iii.1896; *d*. La Scala, Milan, (while rehearsing Mahler's 3rd symphony), 2.xi.60.

Akira MIYOSHI Francophile Japanese composer.

> *b*. Tokyo, 10.i.33; *works include*: piano concerto (1962), marimba concerto (1969).

Mode de valeurs et d'intensités (mode of durations and volumes) 36-piece piano suite by *Messiaen that propelled *Stockhausen on the road to total serialism and provided *Boulez with the note-row for his first book of *Structures* (1952).

modernism If the modernist movement in art starts with Picasso and in literature with *Joyce, in music it is dominated by the dichotomy of *Schoenberg and *Stravinsky. For half a century, their opposing ideas offered clear alternatives to creative musicians, one pointing ahead to unexplored tonalities, the other aimed at modifying past traditions. Other options, like the *microtonality of *Bartók and Hába, were marginalized by the main struggle. When Stravinsky late in life accepted Schoenberg's *serialism, the divergent paths seemed to have united, but *serialism started to flag and towards the end of the century composers were facing the same uncertainty as they did at its start. (See *post-modernism.)

modern jazz Generic term for jazz written after 1945 and intermittently dissonant.

MODERN JAZZ QUARTET US ensemble (1952–74) of John Lewis, Milt Jackson, Percy Heath and Kenny Clarke, tinged by novel sonorities and Django *Reinhart's hot stuff.

Ernest John MOERAN Chunks of First War shrapnel in his head retarded Moeran's career and caused intermittent instability. He shared a house with hell-raising Philip Heseltine (Peter *Warlock) but was unsuited to bohemian ways and

unable to take a drop of alcohol. Instead, he whizzed around the country on his motorbike, collecting English folksongs. In 1930 he moved to the Norfolk wilds, where he wrote two impressionistic pieces for small orch.: *Lonely Waters* (London, 22.i.32), based on a pub song, and *Whythorne's Shadow* (1932), reflecting Heseltine's Tudor interests. A slight G minor Symphony (13.i.38) evoked nostalgia for the vanishing countryside, carved up by transport and mechanization. Unspoilt Ireland was his last destination; its dances and vistas coloured his dreamy violin concerto (8.vii.42) and the remainder of his music. He was found dead one winter's morning in the River Kenmare.

> *b*. Heston, Middlesex, 31.xii.1894, a parson's son, raised in Norfolk, wounded 1917, married cellist Peers Coetmore, 1945, and wrote her a lyrical concerto and sonata; *d*. Kenmare, Co. Kelly, 1.xii.50. *other works*: Sinfonietta, piano rhapsody (19.viii.43), orchestral Serenade (2.ix.48); G major string quartet; piano pieces and songs.

Richard MOHAUPT Anti-Nazi German, emigrated in 1939 to NY, where his symphony (5.iii.42) and violin concerto (29.iv.54) were premièred by the Philharmonic.

> *b*. Breslau, Austro-Hungary, 14.ix.04; *d*. Reichenau, Austria, 3.vii.57. *other works*: four operas, four ballets, *Town Piper Music* (London, *ISCM, 7.vii.46).

Federico MOMPOU Reclusive Spaniard, he wrote almost entirely for the piano. Following de *Falla to Paris in 1911, his initial suite *Intimate Impressions* (1911–14, revised 1959) recalls *Janáček's pianistic introspections. Five *Scenes with Children* (1915–18) are anthropological vignettes, the last of which was used in a John Lanchberry ballet. *Dialogues* (1923) was a counter-thrust to Satie's games. Economical with notes, his music requires a large hand and liberal rubato; a brilliant pianist himself, Mompou performed only for friends.

> *b*. Barcelona, 16.iv.1893; lived in Paris 1911–14, 1921–41, and received many honours there; *d*. Barcelona, 30.vi.87.

José Pablo MONCAYO (GARCIA) Mexican nationalist composer discovered by *Chávez as a percussionist in his orchestra. His opera, *La Mulata de Cordoba*

(1948), was staged by his mentor and he wrote two symphonies, but he is best known for a foot-tapping piece of anachronistic tourist folkery, *Huapango* (1941).
> *b.* Gudalajara, Mexico, 29.vi.12; *d.* Mexico City, 16.vi.58. *other works*: *Homage to Cervantes* for two oboes and strings (1947).

Meredith MONK Experimenter with vocal effects who, even in her throat-clicks and howls, rarely forsook musicality. As an accomplished film-maker and choreographer, she also made her music tell a good story. From *16mm Earrings* for voice and guitar (1966) to the Chagall-like *Book of Days* (1989) there is a narrative thread that sustains her albums and *performance art and enables her to cross with impunity from medievalism to minimalism, from outlandish noises to folk melody.
> *b.* Lima, Peru, 20.xi.43; *other works*: opera *Quarry* (1976), albums *key* (1971), *Recent Ruins* (1979), *Dolmen Music* (1981), *Turtle Dreams* (1983), *The Games* (1983).

Thelonious MONK Reclusive, eccentric, skullcapped black pianist, he was – with Charlie Parker – one of the prime movers in *modern jazz with numbers like 'Round Midnight' and 'Misterioso' that were instantly distinctive. He was something of an icon to oddball art musicians, Friedrich *Gulda adopting certain of his mannerisms and Gunter Schuller composing Variations on one of his themes.
> *b.* Rocky Mount, North Carolina, 11.x.17; *d.* Englewood, New Jersey, 17.ii.82.

Mona Vanna Opera that *Rachmaninov was unable to finish because Maeterlinck had sold his play to a Frenchman, Jacques Février (fp: Paris, 13.i.09).

Italo MONTEMEZZI Eclectic Italian whose great success was the opera *L'amore dei tre re* (La Scala, 10.iv.1913), which added a Wagnerian touch to the prevailing fashion for *verismo. In later operas, this mellowed into a Straussian timbre. Montemezzi lived in the US between 1939 and 1949 and wrote a symphonic suite *Italia mia!* (1944) to express his homesickness.
> *b.* Vigasio, nr Verona, Italy, 4.viii.1875; *d.* there 15.v.52. *other operas*: *Giovanni Gallurese* (1905), *Hellera* (1909), *La Nave* (Milan, 1.xi.18), *L'incantesimo* (NBC Radio,

9.x.43); he also wrote a symphonic poem, *Paolo e Virginia* (1930).

Montezuma Mexican opera by Sessions. fp: West Berlin, 19.iv.64.

Emmanuel MOOR Inventor of a double-keyboard piano, for which he composed four concertos.
> *b.* Kecskemét, Hungary, 19.ii.1863; *d.* nr Montreux, Switzerland, 20.x.31. *other works*: five operas staged in pre-1914 Germany, eight symphonies.

Douglas (Stuart) MOORE American folk-opera had a short vogue. It consisted of Moore's nine operas – principally the wild-western *Ballad of Baby Doe* (Central City, Colorado, 7.vii.56) and *The Devil and Daniel Webster* (NY, 18.v.39) and *Weill's *Down in the Valley*. Moore also wrote a 1927 symphonic poem on *Moby Dick*.
> *b.* Cutchogue, NY, 10.viii.1893; st with *Boulanger and *Bloch; taught Columbia U. 1926–62; *d.* Greenport, Long Island, 25.vii.69.

Charlotte MOORMAN Amply endowed cellist who was arrested in mid-concert by two New York policeman on 9.ii.67 for playing her instrument topless. She was simply following the score of Nam June *Paik's *Opéra Sextronique*, which also required her to run her bow over the composer's naked spine. Convicted and jailed by a district court, her sentence was suspended and she earned momentary celebrity for a milestone in *performance art. She repeated the feat unremarked in Berlin, roomed with fellow-exhibitionist Yoko Ono and played another Paik piece, *TV Bra for Living Sculpture*, with small screens over her breasts, which the audience could watch when the music bored them. In 1963 she founded the New York Avant-Garde Art Festival.
> *b.* Little Rock, Arkansas, 18.xi.33; *d.* NY, 8.xi.91.

John MORAN Protégé of Philip *Glass, he has staged two experimental operas in New York. *The Jack Benny Show* consisted of an electronic collage of excerpts from a defunct television comedy. *The Manson Family* (1990) disturbingly reconstructed the story of a murderous cult in 1969 California, in relatively conventional

narrative with *minimalist, mainly taped score.
  b. 1965;

Robert MORAN The gentler slopes of post-*minimalism were explored in Moran's operas, *Desert of Roses* (Houston, ii.92) and *From the Towers of the Moon* (Minnesota, ii.92). Both dispensed with the heavy beat of *Glass's works and trailed pleasant curlicues around a constant theme. Moran came out of the anything-goes Haight-Ashbury culture and achieved his greatest 'performance art' triumph with *39 Minutes for 39 Autos*, a spectacle that required 100,000 performers and a large part of downtown San Francisco on 29.viii.69. In a *neo-classical phase he wrote a *Pachelbel Promenade* for the Austrian town of Graz and a *Waltz in memoriam Maurice *Ravel* (1977). He worked with Glass on *The Juniper Tree* and describes his own music as 'disgracefully pretty'.
  b. Denver, Colorado, 8.i.37; st with *Apostel, *Milhaud, *Berio; composer-in-residence West Berlin 1975–7. *other works: Hallelujah* (for 75,000 participants, Bethlehem, Pennsylvania, iv.71); chamber opera *Let's Build a Nut House* (in memoriam *Hindemith, 1969), ballet *Ten Miles High over Albania* (1983).

Jelly Roll (Ferdinand Joeseph de la Menthe) MORTON Colourful giant in jazz history, he claimed to have invented New Orleans traditional style and was certainly a leading composer. He was also at various times a pimp, tailor, boxing promoter and bookie, as well as a brilliant player on several instruments. His signature tunes were 'New Orleans Blues' and 'Jelly Roll Blues'.
  b. Gulfport, Louisiana, 20.x.1890 of Afro-French parentage; *d.* Los Angeles, 10.vii.41.

Moses und Aron *Schoenberg's mighty opera of visionary leadership. Two acts were composed in 1930–32, but the 3rd was left incomplete. fp (stage): Zurich, 6.vi.57.

Alexander MOSOLOV Early hero of Soviet music, his Iron Foundry ballet (Moscow, 4.xii.27) set the tone for industrial imitations. The 'mighty hymn to machine work' was performed by fellow-travellers all over the world until Mosolov's explusion from the Composers' Union in 1936, allegedly for drunkenness and rude behaviour in restaurants. He was readmitted after a penance of collecting folksongs in Turkestan, but never regained official approval.
  b. Kiev, Ukraine, 11.viii.1900; *d.* Moscow, 12.vii.73. *other works*: operas, six symphonies, cello concerto (1946), patriotic cantatas and contritely folkish symphonic poems.

Alexander MOYZES A leading Slovak composer, his folkish early works have something of *Janáček's rhythmic vitality; post-1945 pieces are more reflective and eclectic, coloured by Stravinsky, jazz and political considerations.
  *b.*Klástor pod Znievom, Austro-Hungary, 4.ix.06; st with *Novák; *d.* Bratislava, 20.xi.84. *orch. works include*: nine symphonies, Concertino (1933), *Janosik's Rebels* overture (1943), *Down the River Vah* (1945), violin concerto (1958), flute concerto (1966), *Tale about Janosik* (1976).

Dominic MULDOWNEY *Birtwistle's heir in 1976 as music director of the National Theatre in London, he was much influenced by his predecessor. Jazz and *Brecht were other preoccupations, the former sensitively adapted in a saxophone concerto (1984), the latter manifested in numerous verse settings, such as the late-romantic *Duration of Exile* (1983) for voice and septet.
  b. Southampton, England, 19.vii.52; st with *Harvey, *Birtwistle, *Rands and D. *Blake; *other works*: piano concerto (1983), percussion concerto (1991), film scores for *The Ploughman's Lunch* and *1984*; violin concerto (1992).

Detlev MULLER-SIEMENS German neo-traditionalist, applying *Ligetian irony in a short opera, *Genoveva* (1978), and quoting Schubert *Ländler* in Variations for small orch. (1978).
  b. Hamburg, 1957; st with *Ligeti; *other works*: symphony (1981), viola concerto (1984), *Under Neonlight* for piano solo (1983).

multi-media Music plus video, audience participation and stage gimmicks, usually contrived to mask the paucity of the music.

Gordon MUMMA Robert *Ashley's radical partner in theatrical experiments, he wound up designing the Pepsi-Cola pavilion at the 1970 EXPO at Osaka. He has made a serious study of seismic tapes of earthquakes and nuclear tests.

b. Framingham, Massachusetts, US, 30.ii.35; formed ONCE festival with Ashley 1961–8; joined Merce Cunningham Dance Co. 1966; *works include*: *Megaton for William Burroughs* (1963), *Conspiracy* (1970) for computers.

Vano MURADELI The unfortunate trigger of Stalin's second musical terror was a fellow-Georgian whose two folkish symphonies pleased the Kremlin's archcritic. However, his opera *The Great Friendship* (Moscow, 7.xi.47) contained mild dissonances and Muradeli was charged, along with *Shostakovich and *Prokofiev, with the crime of *formalism. He made amends with a *Hymn to Moscow* that won the 1951 Stalin prize and spent the rest of his days in artistic and political safety.

b. Gori, Georgia, 6.iv.08; *d.* Tomsk, Siberia, 14.viii.70. *other works*: opera *October* (Moscow, 22.iv.64).

Tristan MURAIL French apostle of *Messiaen and *Boulez, he pursued *microtonal harmonies by both conventional and *electronic means. His music is elegant and non-violent. *Désintégrations* (1982) for 17 instruments and tape is among the most erudite works created on the *IRCAM computer.

b. Le Havre, 1947; *orch. works include*: *Gondwana* (Darmstadt, 21.vii.80), *Sillages* (Kyoto, 9.ix.85, cond. *Ozawa), *words of Christ on the Cross* (London, 28.x.89, cond. *Eötvös).

Thea MUSGRAVE Any woman composer who arose in Scotland would have to confront the national trauma of the beheaded queen. Musgrave's opera *Mary, Queen of Scots* (Edinburgh Festival, 6.ix.77, cond. composer; also staged in London, NY and Bielefeld) was the most trenchant and dramatically coherent of many versions since Donizetti's Schiller adaptation in 1834.

Theatricality informed much of Musgrave's work. After a brief *serialist excursion, she resorted to a ruggedly ecec-

tic traditionalism, akin to *Bartók's, allied to strong central characters in the operas *A Christmas Carol* (after Dickens; Norfolk, Virginia, 7.xii.79) and *Harriet, the Woman Called Moses* (after Harriet Tubman; Norfolk, Virginia, 1.v.85). Her concert works are comparably active. In the viola concerto (London, 13.viii.75), written for her husband, Peter Mark, the soloist wanders around the orchestra interacting with different groups of players. Since 1970, she has lived in the US.

b. Edinburgh, 27.v.28; st with *Gál, *Boulanger; *other orch. works*: Concerto for Orch. (1967), *Orfeo* for flute and tape or string orch. (1975), *From One to Another* for viola and tape or string orch. (1980), *Moving into Aquarius* in honour of *Tippett's 80th birthday (London, 23.i.85).

music Until the present century, no-one questioned what constituted music. Music was anything that was sung, or played, or written down in an accepted notational form. Doubt crept in when Schoenberg abandoned the laws of tonality and Stravinsky substituted rhythm for melody. The cry went up: 'that's not music!' Satie wrote 'furniture music' that was meant to be played but not paid attention. Mechanical noises were presented as music by the Futurists and endorsed by as traditional a composer as Hindemith. Cage proposed that silence was music.

His extremist followers, like Paik, argued that any kind of theatrical *happening counted as musical experience. Instruments were smashed in both art and pop concerts. In one of the more outrageous instances, a man cutting his skin with a razor blade featured on a Californian concert programme. At the end of the century, no definition had been coined to express the totality of the art in terms that were acceptable to a majority of musicians and listeners.

music theatre Term usually aplied to small-scale, unacted operas on the lines of Stravinsky's *Soldier's Tale*, Weill's *Mahagonny* and Davies' *Eight Songs of a Mad King*.

music therapy Gentle background music, Mozart in particular, was found to ease the pains of childbirth and reduce tension during surgery. Playing and teaching music helped stimulate retarded children. Clinical research is still at an early stage. Some researchers believe music may yet be found to have intrinsic healing powers.

musical Anglo-American theatrical entertainment with music that sometimes crossed the frontiers of high art, most markedly in Bernstein's *West Side Story*. Chief inventors were Jerome Kern, Irving Berlin, Cole Porter, Rodgers and Hammerstein and Andrew Lloyd Webber.

Musica Viva Munich festival of contemporary music founded by *Hartmann in 1946. It led German audiences gently back into mainstream music that Hitler had banned and formed the model for many continental festivals of contemporary music.

musicology The self-designated 'science' of music (*Musikwissenschaft*) extended its remit from the study of music history to embrace theory, analysis, aesthetics and ethnic musics. At best, its researches have led to the revival of forgotten masters and introduced living composers to new resources. At worst, its pseudo-scientific methodology supported Nazi racial doctrines and justified Stalin's artistic persecutions. Scholarly writing became progressively more technical, less readable. It tended to substitute social and biographical research with a fundamentalist application to notational literalism.

musique concrète (Fr. concrete music) Everyday sounds, tape-recorded and then distorted by slowing or speeding up playback and editing the tape. The process was devised and named by Pierre *Schaeffer, a Radio France technician who on 5.x.48 broadcast a four-minute splicing of train noises. An alternative to pure electronics, it attracted composers who lacked access to high-tech studios. By the mid-50s the two streams were joined in *Stockhausen's *Gesang der Jünglinge*, in which a young boy's voice was technologically altered, and the distinction between them vanished.

Muzak Background music designed to soothe without being consciously heard. The industrial use of *Satie's idea, it plays half-noticed on eight-hour reels in more than 100 million locations worldwide, annoying only those who choose to listen to how real music has been destroyed by an overlay of strings and the removal of any emphatic statement.

My Fair Lady *Musical-theatre adaptation by Frederick Loewe and Alan Jay Lerner of George Bernard Shaw's play, *Pygmalion*, one of the longest-running musicals of all time. fp: Broadway (Mark Hellinger Theater), 15.iii.56.

mystic chord Block of fourths (C – F# – Bb – E – A – D) nominated by *Skryabin in his tone-poem Prometheus.

Nicolas NABOKOV A cousin of *Lolita's* author and fellow-refugee from Bolshevism, he roamed the Weimar Republic, studied briefly with *Busoni, then went to Paris to compose for *Diaghilev. In 1933 he emigrated to the US, where he formed an anti-communist Congress for Cultural Freedom that won support in Washington and took him back to West Berlin as artistic director (1963–68) of a music festival designed to outshine socialist efforts across the wall. A convivial bon-viveur, he was a friend of *Stravinsky and *Prokofiev and wrote of them engagingly in two autobiographies. His compositions were less memorable, adopting a *Petrushka-like bitonality to assert modernist sympathies but lacking a compelling originality.
  b. nr.Lubcha, Minsk region, Russia, 17.iv.03; taught Wells College (1936–41), Peabody Conservatory (1947–52), NY U. (1972–73); *d*. NY, 6.iv.78. *works include*: operas *Death of Rasputin* (Cologne, 27.xi.59), *Love's Labour's Lost* (*Auden libretto, 1973); ballet-cantata *Ode . . . on Aurora Borealis* (Paris, 6.vi.28), ballet *Union Pacific* (Philadelphia, 6.iv.34), oratorio *Job* (1933), three symphonies, flute concerto (1948), cello concerto (1953), five poems by Anna Akhmatova for voice and orch. (1964).

nail pizzicato Technique devised by Bartók for snapping a violin string with the fingernail, denoted by a circled dot above the note.

Conlon NANCARROW Nancarrow made music on an obsolete household gadget. From the late 1940s he composed only for the Ampico player-piano, a machine long eclipsed by the gramophone. Punching holes in piano rolls at the painful rate of a dozen notes an hour, he devised blends of notes and rhythm beyond the capacity of human fingers and sounding like abstract *jazz.
  His conventional early scores, Prelude and Blues for piano (1938) and a string quartet (1942) suggest *Ivesian cross-rhythms and a wistful kind of lonesomeness. A jazz trumpeter, Nancarrow fought on the losing side in the Spanish Civil War and lost his US passport. He settled quietly in Mexico City. Forty years later, his music was rediscovered by *Ligeti and he received a $300,000 'genius grant' from the Macarthur Foundation of Chicago. Some of his player-piano pieces were retranscribed for live pianists and he wrote a wispy quartet for the *Ardittis (Cologne, 15.x.88) in which each player was given the same motif with a different beat, yet ended up playing the same note.
  b. Texarkana, Arkansas, 27.x.12; st with *Slonimsky, *Piston, *Sessions.

Luis NAON Argentine composer of a desperate *Tango del Desamparo* (1987) for small ensemble and tape, in memory of his brother who euphemistically 'disappeared' during the military dictatorship.
  b. Buenos Aires, 1961;

nationalism The creation of art music from indigenous folk resources sustained many composers through the century, among them *Copland, de *Falla, *Kodály and *Vaughan Williams. *Bartók extended the search to other cultures, while *Janáček explored the riches of spoken dialect. Nationalistic tunefulness was derided by modernists and the concept acquired unfortunate political associations. Stalin forced Soviet composers to revert to anachronistic simplicities. Hitler and Goebbels ranted on about a unique Germanness in music, when what they meant was marching tunes and propaganda songs. Nevertheless, after a century of anti-nationalism, there remains something suavely French about *Boulez's music and grittily British in *Birtwistle.

Oskar NEDBAL A brilliant violist, founder-member (with *Suk) of the Bohemian String Quartet (1891–1906) and conductor of the Czech Philharmonic in many premières (1896–1906), he founded the Slovak National Theatre in Bratislava (1921) and composed ballets and operettas, of which *Polenblut (Polish blood)* (Vienna, 25.x.13) has the best tunes. Among many waltzes for piano or strings, the *Valse Triste* reveals a melancholic streak; Nedbal committed suicide when accused of financial malpractice.
   b. Tábor, Bohemia, 26.iii.1874; cond. Vienna Tonkünstler Orch. 1906–19; *d.* Zagreb, Yugoslavia, 24.xii.30. *other works*: ballets *The Devil's Grandmother* (1912), *Andersen* (1914); piano suites *Miss Butterfly* (1907), *Valses Silhouettes* (1914).

Mark NEIKRUG Piano accompanist to violinist Pinchas Zukerman, he composed a lyrical 1984 concerto that other soloists have taken up. His theatre piece, *Through Roses*, is a Holocaust reflection, and he has written an opera, *Los Alamos*, for Berlin.
   b. NY, 24.ix. 46; *other work*: 1st symphony (Houston, 14.iii.92).

neo-classicism Shaking off Romantic values that brought the world to the brink of war, modernism followed two divergent paths. In *Schoenberg's circle, it shunned the tonal laws that had lasted half a millennium and produced painfully new note-relations. *Stravinsky, for his part, resolved the impasse by leap-frogging backwards over romanticism to its predecessor. Neo-classicism re-imagined 18th-century music in modern dress. In Stravinsky's brutal metaphor, it courted classical style by raping it.

Although Prokofiev preceded him with a *Classical Symphony and *Busoni advanced similar ideas, Stravinsky was credited with the invention when he made *Pulcinella* out of old Neapolitan manuscripts. The style served him well for 30 years, culminating in The *Rake's Progress. It was modish in inter-War Paris and found exponents in Poulenc, Roussel and *Martinů. Hindemith in Germany leaned more austerely to Baroque style, though his *Kammermusik* pieces recall Bach's Brandenburg concertos.

Schoenberg was outraged by these anachronisms and lampooned Stravinsky as 'der kleine Modernsky' in his 1926 satire for chorus, *Der Neue Klassizismus*. He was tempted, however, to borrow Baroque rhythms (gavotte) and sonata form in grimly *serialist works.

neo-romanticism American 1930s symphonists like *Hanson and *Barber threshed the last grains of a genre thoroughly exhausted in European music. Half a century later, the concept acquired currency in America when *Rochberg and *Druckman rebelled against academic hegemonies and reverted to the language of Beethoven and Brahms.

Neue Sachlichkeit (*new objectivity*) *Weimar anti-romantic music embraced *Weill and *Krenek's populism and Hindemith's utilitarian *Gebrauchsmusik.

Neues vom Tage (*Daily News*) Tabloid-newspaper opera by Hindemith. fp: Berlin, Kroll, 8.vi.29.

Max NEUHAUS Dedicated *environmental composer, he wrote electronic music that was pumped underwater into swimming pools (*Water Whistle*, 1971–5, a two-hour metamorphosed phone-in (Radio Net, 1977) and created a sound environment for a glass conservatory in Como Park, St Paul, Minnesota.
   b. Beaumont, Texas, 9.viii.39; played percussion in Boulez and Stockhausen ensembles; artist-in-residence Bell Telephone Labs, 1968–69.

New Age A vague term for the middle of the road where disenchanted *avant-gardists met upwardly mobile rock and ethnic musicians in the 1980s to produce a passing genre that was gentle on the ear and environmentally aware. Key exponents were Jean-Michel Jarre, Keith Jarrett, Brian Eno, Mike Oldfield, Ingram *Marshall and several ex-*minimalists. The definition extended to such early meditations as Ives' *Unanswered Question*, dating from 1906, and the pseudo-gamelan music of *McPhee.

new music (1) Between the Wars, it distinguished the output of radical composers from conventionalists: Schoenberg wrote 'new music', Sibelius didn't. From 1945 to 1990, the term was monopolized by the *avant-garde. (2) Colophon of Henry *Cowell's publishing imprint for neglected composers.

New Orleans jazz The earliest band style, typified by King *Oliver and Jelly Roll *Morton.

new simplicity Gentle European euphemism for *minimalism.

New York The gateway to America for European immigrants was rarely a hive of new culture. Its Metropolitan Opera went quarter of a century without commissioning a new work; the Philharmonic Orchestra served up safe menus, except when a composer – Mahler, *Bernstein, *Boulez – was at its helm. Dependent on rich patrons, large institutions could not risk novelty. There was, however, a permanent counter-culture away from the Manhattan epicentre. *Copland and Sessions ran a seminal series of modern concerts (1928–30) in Greenwich Village, and *minimalism was later cultivated there.

New York did have a brief modernist heyday from 1933–48 when Hitler refugees mingled with lively local talent. Bartók, Weill and various Schoenberg and Stravinsky associates left imprints on musical activity from Juilliard to Broadway. Varèse was a looming presence. Copland, Bernstein and *Carter featured in a post-War symphonic flourish which, in its turn,

was mocked by the iconoclasts *Cage and *Feldman, who mixed with the New York visual arts scene led by Jackson Pollock and Mark Rothko. This creative moment was crushed by McCarthyism.

The sounds of New York percolate *Gershwin's music. *Carpenter's *Skyscrapers* ballet (1926) idealized the modern age; Villa-Lobos traced a picture of the *New York Skyline* on to music paper and made a suite of it (1940). Weill's *Street Scene* is a realist slice of brownstone life; Bernstein's *West Side Story* explores the underbelly of hispanic poverty and strife. The same composer wrote the city's signature tune 'New York, New York, it's a wonderful town' in his ballet *On the Town*.

Carl (August) NIELSEN Into the symphonic split between Mahler and Sibelius – one pursuing universality, the other total refinement – stepped the great Dane with an intriguing symbiosis. Nielsen gave his symphonies descriptive titles and big tunes, but developed them organically in total integration. The 4th (Copenhagen, 1.ii.16), which he named 'Inextinguishable' and wrote in mid-war, has a bombastic opening and morose interior, yet escapes the different glooms of Mahler's 6th and Sibelius' 4th by an underlying sense of hope. The 5th (24.i.22), from its initial interplay of strings and woodwind, through a flurry of transient motifs to its tranquil conclusion, is rather like watching the world walking its dog past your window. It flickers away from a firm tonality, is cast in two movements and suggests possibilities for an open-plan, stream-of-consciousness modern symphony. Nielsen, however, had little influence on musical development. Rarely venturing abroad, he was unrecognized until the 1960s; the British symphonists *Simpson and *McCabe are his sole followers.

Of his six symphonies, the 1st (14.iii. 1894) brims over with Brahms and half-digested folk tunes. The second, known as *The Four Temperaments* (1.xi.02), depicts in successive movements the emotions of anger, phlegmatism, melancholy and optimism – as inspired by a woodcut Nielsen spotted in a country pub. In the 3rd, dubbed *Sinfonia Espansiva* (28.ii.12), Nielsen reassembled folk songs in his own form (much as Mahler did in his Third), as a hymn to man and nature in which soprano and tenor soloists meld wordlessly with the orchestra in the second movement. The 6th symphony, named *Sinfonia semplice* (11.xii.25), is an introverted, somewhat bitter work, replete with in-jokes and jibes about more successful composers.

His popular flute and clarinet concertos originated in a witty wind quintet (9.x.22) that Nielsen wrote for an ensemble he heard over the telephone playing Mozart; its minuet is *neo-classical while the finale takes a church hymn to unsuspected dissonances. The colloquy between the flute, oboe, clarinet, horn and bassoon returns in the flute concerto (Paris, 21.x.26), where the soloist communicates less with the whole orchestra than with individual instruments. The one-movement clarinet concerto (14.ix.28) is simpler, melodic and paradoxically more 'modern'. Nielsen's violin concerto is peculiarly underplayed. This meandering, faintly Brahmsian work (28.ii.12) was composed in *Grieg's house and contains all the elements of *Elgar's concerto, except pathos. Add a number of tone-poems, of which the *Helios* overture (8.x.03) recalls 'what I did last summer on the Med', and his orchestral output matches Sibelius in scale.

His operas *Saul and David* (28.xi.02) and the raunchy folkloristic comedy *Maskarade* (11.xi.06) enjoy national status. His literary memoir of growing up on the island of Fünen ('My Childhood' – 1927, English pub. 1953) is a classic account of pre-mechanized farm life; musically he recalled his origins in the lovely fantasy for three soloists, chorus and orchestra, *Springtime in Fünen* (1922). He wrote relatively little chamber music, preferring plangent piano and organ preludes.

A gregarious man, as remote from Sibelius as E major from F minor, he played violin in the court orchestra (1889–1905), conducted the Royal Opera (1908–14) and the Copenhagen concerts society. His wife was an eminent sculptress. On his only visit to London, he split his trousers while taking tea with the Queen Mother.

b. Norre-Lymdelse, nr Odense, on the island of Fyn (Fünen) 9.vi.1865, seventh child of a rural fiddler and house painter; joined military band at 14; st with Niels Gade; made his name in 1888 with fetching *Little Suite* for strings, sharper-edged than Grieg's popular suites; *d.* Copenhagen, after succession of heart attacks, 3.x.31. *other orch. works:* *Saga-Dream* (6.iv.08), *Fantasy Journey to the Faroe Isles* (27.xi.28), *Paraphrase on Danish and Bohemian folktunes* (1930).

Serge NIGG One of the first *12-tone composers in France he became a fervent fellow-traveller, forming an Association of Progressive Musicians and hallowing the Soviet Union as heaven on earth. His music became progressively more realist.

b. Paris, 6.vi.24; st with *Messiaen, *Leibowitz; *orch. works include:* two ballets; *Hieronymus Bosch* symphony (Strasbourg, 21.vi.60), *Millions d'oiseaux d'or* (Boston, 20.iii.81); two piano concertos; *Song of the Dispossessed* (Strasbourg, 25.vi.64).

night music Mahler named the second and fourth movements of his 7th symphony *Nachtmusik*; Debussy wrote orchestral Nocturnes and Britten a song-cycle by the same designation. Bartók inserted 'night music' episodes into his chamber music and Ligeti named his first quartet 'nocturnal metamorphoses'. Few of these works have a perceptibly night-time character. Mostly, composers wanted to indicate darkness of the soul, rather than the textural lightness of Mozart's popular serenade for strings, the title of which was adopted by Stephen *Sondheim as *A Little Night Music* and presented on Broadway (fp: 2.ii.73).

The Nightingale Fairytale opera by Stravinsky, revised as ballet. fp: Paris, 26.v.14.

Nights in the Gardens of Spain De *Falla's delightful piano concerto. fp: Madrid, 9.iv.16.

Arthur NIKISCH Formative conductor, known as 'the Magician', he directed with tiny motions and an equable temper. He turned the Berlin Philharmonic into Europe's top ensemble, popularized Tchaikovsky's symphonies and premièred Bruckner's 7th (Leipzig, 30.xii.84) and

many works by Reger. He composed a
juvenile B minor symphony; his pianist
son Mitya (1899–1936) composed a
concerto.
  b. Lébényi Szent-Miklos, Austro-Hungary,
12.x.1855; cond. Leipzig Opera, 1878–89;
Boston SO, 1889–93; Royal Hungarian
Opera, Budapest, 1893–95; Leipzig
Gewandhaus concerts and Berlin Philharmonic Orch., 1895–1922; Hamburg
Philharmonic concerts 1897–1922; London
SO, 1905–13; *d.* Leipzig, 23.i.22.

John Jacob NILES The Kentucky folksinger claimed to have discovered two
affecting songs, 'Black is the colour of my
true love's hair' and 'I wonder as I
wander', taken up by concert singers and
recast by *Berio. In fact, Niles wrote them
himself. A crashed First War pilot, he
studied with d'*Indy in Paris and collected
folksongs back home. He composed some
art music, including an oratorio, Lamentations.
  b. Louisville, Kentucky, 28.iv.1892; *d.* nr
Lexington, Kentucky, 1.v.80.

Bo NILSSON Sweden's leading *serialist, he returned to diatonic harmony in the
woodwind quintet *Déjà connu* (1973).
  b. Skellefteå, Sweden, 1.v.37; *works include*:
instrumental series *Szenes I–IV* (1961), 20
Gruppen for any 3 instruments (1957),
Autumn Song for baritone and orch. (1984).

Joaquin NIN (y Castellanos) Composer
and scholar of Spanish piano music, lived
mostly in France.
  b. Havana, Cuba, 29.ix.1879; *d.* there, 24.x.
49.

Joaquin NIN-CULMELL Joaquin's son
emigrated to the US in 1936 and composed
concertos for piano and cello.
  b. Berlin, 5.ix.08; taught U. of California at
Berkeley 1950–74.

Nixon in China News-opera by *Adams
on the 1972 restoration of diplomatic ties
between Washington and Peking. fp:
Houston, 22.x.87.

Marlos NOBRE Brazil's leading composer after *Villa-Labos achieved near-
naïvety in his harmonies by sophisticated
serial and aleatory techniques. His
Yanomani (1970) is a fervent lament for an

Amazonia threatened with extinction by
the destruction of the rainforests.
  b. Recife, Brazil, 18.ii.39; st with *Ginastera
and *Ussachevsky; *other works: Mosaico* for
large orch. (1970), *Desafio* for viola and
string orch. (1974), *Cancioneiro de Lampiao*
(folksongs, 1980).

Les Noces Stravinsky's portrait of a village wedding for chorus, four pianos and
percussion. Paris 13.vi.23.

Nocturnes Three orch. pieces by *Debussy. fp: Paris, 27.x.01.

Noh The stylized Japanese music drama
was revelatory for *Britten and *Stockhausen.

Luigi NONO A committed communist
from 1952, elected to the Italian party's
central committee in 1975, Nono wedded
leftist politics to modern art. Although his
kind of music was banned in the USSR, he
was welcomed there as visiting comrade
and significantly helped local composers
keep up with western atonal and electronic
advances.
  His music declaims an agit-prop message, relieved of its banality by an innate
lyricism and naïve passion. *Coma una ola
de fuerza y luz (like a wave of strength and
light)* (1972) is typical: a tribute to a communist accidentally killed during Chilean
unrest. It is scored for soprano, piano,
orchestra and pre-recorded tape and gives a
graphic account of proletarian rebellion in
complex and intriguing sonorities.
  Other pieces of similar character include
the anti-American *A Floresta é jovem e
cheja de vida* (1967) an oratorio to words
by Vietnamese guerrillas and *Y entonces
comprendio* (1970) honouring the insurrectionist Ché Guevara. *Per Bastiana Tai-
Yang Cheng* (1967) exists on three parallel
planes. At one level it is a chromatic setting
of the Maoist hymn 'The East is Red'; at
another it is two streams of notes being
played semi-randomly; and behind these
creations plays a tape of electronic frequencies compiled by the composer at
Radio Milan. In *Contrapunto dialettico alla
mente* (1968), Nono drew on Venetian
church bells, passing gondolas and memories of medieval banquets to create a contrapuntal sound collage into which he worked

a poem on the murder of Malcolm X and a dedication to Venezuelan rebels.

He was formed politically as an anti-fascist partisan towards the end of the second world war. Musically he was led by the modernist *Maderna and by marriage to Schoenberg's daughter, Nuria, for whom he wrote a simple but charming choral *Liebeslied* (London, 16.iv.56). His commitment to 12-note composition was as firm as his Marxism and he would rigorously predetermine the cells of a work before composing it. The oratorio *Il Canto sospeso* (Cologne, 24.x.56) surmounts theoretical limitations by setting letters by condemned resistance fighters to highly emotive music. Two stage works, *Intolleranza 1960* (Venice, 13.iv.61), which provoked a première riot, and *Al gran sole carico d'amore* (La Scala, 1975, cond. *Abbado), argue that organized class struggle is the only way to defeat fascism. The severe sonorities were intended for performance in factories and social clubs where Nono's personal charm magnetized the audience more than his music did. Late in life he composed in *microtones. A string quartet, *Fragmente-Stille, an Diotima* (1980), is rapt, intimate and almost motionless.

b. Venice, 29.i.24; *d.* there, 8.v.90. *other works:* Canonic Variations based on Schoenberg's note-row in *Ode to Napoleon* (Darmstadt, 27.viii.50, cond. Scherchen), *Sul ponte di Hiroshima* (soloists and orch., 1962), . . . *sofferte onde serene . . .* for piano and tape (1976), *Con Luigi Dallapiccola* for six percussionists and live electronics (1979), *No hay caminos, hay que caminar . . .* for seven instrumental groups (1987).

Arne NORDHEIM Norwegian composer whose gift for creating dark, broody atmospheres was applied mainly to the advancement of *electronic music. Among his lasting inventions is a 'Sound sculpture' at a blind people's home in Skjeberg, a large structure with internal tape loops which are activated photoelectrically when daylight falls on them. He provided, by similar means, music for the Scandinavian pavilion at the 1970 Osaka World Fair, later produced as a concert piece, *Lux et tenebrae (light and darkness)*. His instrumental compositions include a taxing, sombre sonata for solo cello called *Clamavi* (1980).

b. Larvik, Norway, 20.vi.31; *pre-electronic works include:* Canzona per orch. (1960), inspired by the Venetian renaissance composer Giovanni Gabrieli.

Per NØRGAARD Trend-setting Dane, he went from *Holmboe to *Boulanger to the *avant-garde in search of new ways to express the ice-clear tonalities of Nielsen and Sibelius. In the course of playing with tiny tonal *cells he stumbled across something uncannily like US *minimalism in the ballet, *The Young Man Shall Marry* (1965). Much of his music is engagingly rhythmic. *Fragments* (1959-), a series of works for solo instruments and groups, traces his artistic progression, rather as the *Sequenza* set does *Berio's. His 1st symphony is justly titled 'Austere' (Danish Radio, 19.viii.58); the 4th is named *Indian Rose Garden and Chinese Witch Lake* (Hamburg, 30.x.81).

b. Gentofte, nr. Copenhagen, 13.vii.32; taught at Danish conservatories; *other works:* Four operas, *Voyage into the Golden Screen* for chamber orchestra (1968), cello concerto (1985).

Ib NØRHOLM Danish eclectic who, like the better-known *Nørgard, aimed to suffuse the textures of Sibelius and Nielsen with simplified modernist techniques. *Prelude to my Wintermorning* (1971) for flute, piano and string trio, pictures an icy vista vividly in nine minutes with Webern-like concentration and nordic tonal cells.

b. Copenhagen, Denmark, 24.i.31; st with *Holmboe; organist at Bethlehem Church, Copenhagen, 1964-; *works include:* four operas, seven symphonies (1959–83), symphonic fantasy, *Hearing Andersen* (1987).

Alex NORTH One of the most successful Hollywood composers – *A Streetcar Named Desire, Death of a Salesman, The Agony and the Ecstasy* – also wrote concert music and a 1938 ballet for Martha Graham. *Bernstein and Benny Goodman produced his *Revue* for clarinet and orchestra (NY, 20.xi.46); his 3rd symphony (1971) is made up of out-takes from the space movie *2001*.

b. Chester, Pennsylvania, 4.xii.10; st with *Toch and *Copland. *d.* Los Angeles, 8.ix.91.

The Nose Shostakovich opera to Gogol story. fp: Leningrad, 12.i.30.

notation Writing notes on or between the lines of a stave failed to satisfy many modernists. *Cage, *Feldman, Brown and others created *graphics with accompanying texts to convey their intentions. *Haubenstock-Ramati painted pictures that were art works in their own right. *Stockhausen developed graphs of *electronic notation. Musical scores increasingly resembled the choreographic notation used in ballet.

Notations One of Boulez's suavest efforts, for piano solo (1945) or orch. (1978).

note row A series of 12 tones and semitones set in a chosen order for composition by the *twelve-note method.

Vítězslav NOVÁK Second-best tone-poet of the post-Dvořák generation, Novák's pastel suites were more placid than *Suk's and his five operas less graphic than *Janáček's. The most impressive symphonic poem is *In the Tatras* (Prague, 25.xi.02, cond. *Nedbal), a sweeping mountainscape for full orchestra; the *Slovak Suite* for chamber orch. (4.ii.06) and *South Bohemian Suite* (22.xii.37; cond. Kleiber) are cloyingly affectionate. The *Autumn Symphony* (18.xii.34, cond. Talich) with mixed chorus is loud, lovely but not very meaningful. Other suites take their cue from fairytales – *Eternal Longing*, after a Hans Christian Andersen story (8.ii.05) and *Timan and the Wood Nymph* (5.iv.08). Both are heavily decadent and were performed together under the title 'Desire and Passion'.

He wrote *Boure (The Storm)* a sea fantasy for chorus and orchestra to a commission from Brno, which lies further from the sea than any town in Europe (17.iv.10). *De Profundis* (Brno, 20.xi.41), an ominous incantation for organ and orchestra, was his response to the German occupation; a choral *May Symphony* (5.xii.45, cond. Kubelik) marked the Soviet-led liberation. Among a small chamber output, his 1892 graduation piece, the mellifluous sonata for violin and piano, is the most played of all his works; a growling cello sonata (Brno,27.ii.42) depicts the Nazi years.

b. Kamenice nad Lipou, southern Bohemia, 5.xii.1870, a doctor's son; orphaned at 11; st philosophy and law with Tomas Masaryk and composition with Dvořák; married his pupil Marie Prásková 1912; *d.* Skutec, Czechoslovakia, 18.vii.49. *other works*: comic opera *Karlstein* (18.xi.16); *Lady Godiva* overture (24.xi.07), E-minor piano concerto (21.xi.15), *St Wenceslas* triptych for organ and orch. (5.xii.45); 2 string quartets (1905, 1938); Eroica sonata for piano (1.iii.05), many songs.

numerology The *Second Vienna School were transfixed by the meaning of numbers. Berg, in particular, believed devoutly in the fateful personal connotations of the figure 23 and, consciously or otherwise, worked his compositions around that numeral and its multiples. He ascribed 10 to his secret beloved Hanna Fuchs-Robettin and intertwined both figures in the Lyric Suite and violin concerto. Schoenberg, rational in all other matters, was afflicted by triskaidecaphobia, an irrational fear of the number 13. He predicted, rightly, that he would die on that date. Webern saw numbers as building blocks for a symmetric unity. Their faith in numbers was conceived during a sweeping Viennese craze for spirituality, ouija boards, tarot cards and other imponderables.

Seppo NUMMI As a boy of 12, Nummi was drawn to the eighth-century Chinese poems that Mahler composed in *Das Lied von der Erde*. Bleak affinities of landscape between ancient China and his native Finland yielded a variety of piano-accompanied song cycles in a conservative idiom that predates Hugo Wolf. In 1967 Nummi founded the Helsinki Festival and directed it for ten years.

b. Oulu, Finland, 30.v.32; st with Kilpinen; *d.* Tampere, 1.viii.81; *song cycles include*: *From Spring Roads, Songs of the Western Palace* (Li Tai-po), *Autumn Days* (1979).

Emmanuel NUNES The Paris-based Portuguese composer writes soft, slow, post-*Bergian textures that create tension by almost *minimalist repetition. Most of his works are linked to one another in two distinct cycles.

b. Lisbon, 31.viii.41; st with *Pousseur, *Stockhausen; settled in Paris 1964; prof. at Freiburg 1986-; *works include*: *Musik der*

Frühe for orch. (1987), *Wandlungen* for 25 instruments and live electronics (1986), *Esquisses* for string quartet (1983).

Michael NYMAN Disenchanted by the arid *avant-garde, this severe English ex-critic found resolution in his own form of *minimalism. A neurological chamber opera, *The Man who Mistook his Wife for a Hat* (London, ICA, 29.x.86), wove a repetitive web around the case history of an Alzheimer sufferer who recognises only musical phrases until his neuro-physician discovers a diagnosis in the perfect symmetry of a Schumann song.

Vital Statistics (3.vi.87), a mini-opera on the war of two tenors, was too noisy to kindle much humour. Nyman reached a mass audience in amplified semi-pop concerts and scores for Peter Greenaway's filmed mystifications. For the bicentenary of the French revolution, he wrote a portable audio companion to the sights of the capital, *La Traversée de Paris*; for the Mozart bicentenary, he made a 'Not-Mozart' film.

In fiery youth, he wrote the libretto for *Birtwistle's small opera, *Down by the Greenwood Side*, and played in *Cardew's Scratch Orchestra.

b. London, 23.iii.44; st with Alan *Bush; *other works*: three string quartets.

Gösta NYSTROEM The impressionist among Swedish composers – he was also a gifted painter, a follower of Braque – Nystroem was obsessed by the sea and created in its vicinity. *The Sinfonia del mare* (1948), his masterpiece, is an unbroken 35-minute expanse from which a soprano aria *Det Enda* rises like a shimmering Aphrodite. He wrote it on the then remote island of Capri, while in love with an Anglo-Scots girl. Sea themes pervade other of his six symphonies and five concertos; the cello in his most-played concerto (1945) is submerged by the orchestra. Over the final bar of the piano concerto (1959) he wrote (in French): 'God preserve me! The sea is so great, and my boat so small.'

b. Silverberg, deep inland in the Dalarna province, 13.x.1890; met *Nielsen in 1914 while exhibiting paintings in Copenhagen; st with d'*Indy and the Russian Leonid Sabaneyev in Paris, 1919–32, where Honegger and Stravinsky were important influences; music critic in Gothenburg, 1932–47; *d.* Sarö, nr Gothenburg, 9.viii.66. *other works*: incidental music to Shakespeare's *The Tempest*, symphonic poem *Arctic Ocean*, viola concerto 'Hommage à la France', and many Swedish songs.

Ode to Napoleon Byronic 1942 utterance by Schoenberg on the doom of dictators, scored for reciter, piano and string quartet, or string orchestra. Its 12-note row was the basis for his son-in-law *Nono's first performed work. fp NY, 23.xi.1944.

Oedipus Sophocles' family tragedy acquired oratorio by Stravinsky (1927), operas by Enesco (1936) and Orff (1959).

John OGDON British pianist, co-winner of the 1962 Tchaikovsky competition in Moscow, then tragically plagued by mental illness. A cornerstone of the *Manchester School, he could play any music at sight and championed the 'unplayable' *Busoni and *Sorabji. His compositions included a knuckle-cracking piano concerto.
   b. Manchester, 27.i.37; *d.* London, 1.vii.89.

Maurice OHANA A rebel against the dictatorship of fashion – a heretical stance in France – Ohana rejected *serialism, Parisian cliques and *avant-garde techniques. Returning to Paris after spending the war with *Casella in Rome, he used his Andalusian folk-heritage as a lever to free himself from the diatonic scale, fixed rhythms and *bel canto* singing. His music had the primitive wildness of a southern escarpment, tempered by intellectual urbanity and a relentless quest for new nuances. He paid homage to Andalusia in *Llanto por Ignacio Sanchez Mejias* (Paris, 22.v.50), a Lorca poem set for baritone, women's choir and instrumental ensemble. Quarter

of a century later he returned affectionately to Lorca in a cello concerto, *Anneau du Tamarit* (Orléans, 10.xii.77).
   Broadening his base, Ohana borrowed the meditative stillness of Eastern nature-worship in *Signes* (1965) and set figures from Greek mythology in a concerto for orchestra, *Livres des Prodiges* (1979). A triptych of chamber operas, *Trois contes de l'honorable fleur*, for the 1978 Avignon Festival added electronic sounds.
   The static timelessness of *Ogre mangeant des jeunes femmes sous la lune (An ogress easts young women beneath the moon)* is dispelled by feral dance episodes reminiscent of the *Rite of Spring*.
   Disliked by the *Boulez faction, Ohana neither taught nor cultivated acolytes. He nevertheless became the focus of a group of composers led by Edith Canat de Chizy, Ton-That Tiêt and Guy Reibel.
   b. Casablanca, 21.vi.14; *other works*: guitar concerto (1956), *Tombeau de Claude Debussy* for soprano, zither tuned in ⅓ tones, piano and chamber orch., *Silenciaire* for six percussionists and strings (1969), opera *La Célestine* (Paris, 13.vi.1988).

Oiseaux exotiques (exotic birds) Orchestral work by Messiaen. fp: Paris, 10.iii.56.

David OISTRAKH The Russian-Jewish violinist stood for all that was incorruptible in Soviet music. He inspired two concertos by *Shostakovich and others by Miaskovsky and Khachaturian. He also helped Prokofiev convert a flute sonata into a more eloquent work for violin. In 1967, together with Shostakovich, he risked punishment by refusing to sign an artists' declaration condemning Israel's victory in the Six Day War. His son Igor (*b.* Odessa, 27.iv.33) is a musician.

b. Odessa, 30.ix.08; *d.* Amsterdam, 24.x.74.

Joe 'King' OLIVER   Early jazz master, famed for his Creole cornet, sidekick to the young Louis Armstrong, his career was cut short by teeth trouble and he ended his days as a poolroom attendant. His classic themes include 'Snake Rag' (1923) and 'West End Blues' (1928).

b. Abend, Louisiana, 11.v.1885; *d.* Savannah, Georgia, 10.iv.38.

Pauline OLIVEROS   Seduced by oriental timelessness, she conceived drone-like music with a hypnotic charm and points of reference to the Hindu view of the mandala, or universe. She would introduce household objects like garden hoses and alarm clocks to her ensembles. In 1967 she formed an electronic music centre in San Francisco and gave a 12-hour concert of her own tapes.

b. Houston, Texas, 30.v.32; moved to San Francisco 1958; *works include*: *Bonn Feier* (for Beethoven bicentenary, 1970), *The Mandala* (1980s), *Deep Listening* (1989).

On the Town   *Bernstein musical based on his ballet *Fancy Free.* fp: NY, 28.xii.43.

ondes Martenot   Electronic keyboard instrument named after its French inventor, Maurice Martenot (1898–1980), it was utilized by Messiaen (notably in the *Turangalîla* symphony) and by horror-movie makers for its shivery effects. The earliest electronic device to produce accurate pitch, including quarter- and eighth-tones, it was first scored in a *Poème-Symph onique* (23.xii.28) by Dmitri Levidis, a Paris-based Greek. Messiaen apart, Honegger's *Jeanne d'arc* (1935) and concertos by Jolivet and Landowski lead its widespread application by Francophones; *Rozsa led the Hollywood experimenters.

opera   Opera in the 20th century faced dead ends at every turn. Italy's melodic fount dried up with *Puccini; Wagner's romantic rush to the precipice of tonality had left few avenues open for Germans. Operatic composers of genius tended to be isolated phenomena, often thwarted by circumstance. Janáček invented a realism so stark and individual that none could imitate or inherit his style. Shostakovich portended a Russian Ring cycle that was cut short by Stalin. Atonality and 12-note music were liberally adapted by Alban Berg but others dared not take the same licence with Schoenberg's technique.

For want of new operas, producers freshened up the old with political allusions. Pierre Boulez, disgusted at the intractability of opera, called for the opera houses to be burnt down.

Despite its difficulties, opera yielded as many durable masterpieces in the 20th century as it did in the 18th. Richard Strauss, Puccini, Britten and Janáček were no less appealing to the public than Mozart and Handel. Debussy, Schoenberg and Busoni invented new ambiences. Prokofiev, Hindemith and Pfitzner discovered different ways of presenting historical parallels, which were often more effective than straight theatre.

Landmarks in 20th century opera	
Pelléas et Mélisande (1902)	Debussy
Saul and David (1902)	Nielsen
Madama Butterfly (1904)	
Turandot (1926)	Puccini
Jenůfa (1904)	
Cunning Little Vixen (1924)	
Katya Kabanova (1921)	
The Makropoulos Case (1926)	
From the House of the Dead (1930)	Janáček
The Merry Widow (1905)	Lehár
Salome (1905)	
Elektra (1909)	
Der Rosenkavalier (1911)	
Die Frau ohne Schatten (1919)	
Arabella (1933)	
Capriccio (1942)	Strauss
Don Quichotte (1910)	Massenet
Palestrina (1917)	Pfitzner
A Florentine Tragedy (1917)	Zemlinsky
Bluebeard's Castle (1918)	Bartók

The Love for Three Oranges (1921)	
War and Peace (1946)	
The Fiery Angel (1954)	Prokofiev
Doktor Faust (1924)	Busoni
Wozzeck (1925)	
Lulu (1936)	Berg
King Roger (1926)	Szymanowski
Threepenny Opera (1928)	
Street Scene (1947)	Weill
A Lady Macbeth of the Mtsensk District (1934)	Shostakovich
Porgy and Bess (1935)	Gershwin
Mathis der Maler (1938)	Hindemith
The Emperor of Atlantis (1943)	Ullmann
Peter Grimes (1945)	
Billy Budd (1951)	
A Midsummer Night's Dream (1960)	
Death in Venice (1973)	Britten
The Prisoner (1949)	Dallapiccola
The Rake's Progress (1951)	Stravinsky
Moses und Aron (1954)	Schoenberg
West Side Story (1956)	Bernstein
King Stag (1956)	
The Bassarids (1966)	Henze
The Soldiers (1965)	Zimmermann
The Devils of Loudun (1969)	Penderecki
Le grand macabre (1978)	Ligeti
Lear (1978)	Reimann
Donnerstag (beginning of Licht cycle, 1981)	Stockhausen
St François d'Assise (1983)	Messiaen
Un re in ascolto (1984)	Berio
Nixon in China (1987)	Adams
The Mask of Orpheus (1986)	
Gawain (1991)	Birtwistle

operetta *Lehár's *Merry Widow* (1905) opened a Viennese silver age to succeed the gilt of Johann Strauss. It was sustained into the 1930s by his musicals and those of Oscar *Straus, *Fall and *Kálmán, and was transplanted to Broadway by Sigmund *Romberg. Elsewhere, *Coward flourished in England, *Hahn in France, *Benatzky in Germany and *Nedbal in Czechoslovakia. The Spanish zarzuela stayed popular and might have been modernized had *Gerhard's *Duenna* not waited 45 years for a production. Broadway musicals survived until the 1960s when television killed operetta as a living art and reduced its audience to diehard nostalgists.

Julián ORBÓN Latin *neo-classic who lived in New York and worked in novel forms of instrumental counterpoint.
b. Avilés, Spain, 7.viii.25; emigrated to Cuba 1939, then to Mexico 1959 and US 1964; *d.* Miami Beach, 20.v.91. *works include:* Concerto Grosso (1958), piano concerto (1987), string quartet (1951).

orchestra The 70-strong Brahms orchestra grew to 100 in Mahler and Strauss symphonies and reached the limits of aural tolerance. *Stravinsky required 111 players for the *Rite of Spring*. Their successors could only vary the instrumentation with exotic and *electronic additions. Mahler began distributing ensembles *spatially around the hall; Stockhausen cleaved the orchestra into three for *Gruppen*, requiring three conductors. The reaction to overblown romanticism was ascetic contraction as *Schoenberg cultivated the *Chamber Symphony*.

The social role of orch. players changed from silent wage-slaves to lively participants in musical debate. Enlightened orchestras encouraged members to compose and play chamber music. A leading administrator, Ernest Fleischmann of the Los Angeles Philharmonic, declared in 1987: 'The symphony orchestra is dead. Long live the community of musicians.'

Carl ORFF *Carmina Burana* erupted at the right moment in history and the wrong one for its composer. Orff's concatenation of medieval students' songs seemed to mirror Nazi ideology in its tramping rhythms, relentless camaraderie, banal harmonies, nature worship, sexual frankness and suggestions of an exclusive folk-community founded on bloodlines. It was staged at Frankfurt on 8.vi.37 and at La Scala in 1942 as a showpiece of fascist values. Its popularity has persisted and its themes are used in advertising.

Orff's ideal of artistic communality was, however, antithetical to Hitlerism, which banned his progressive teaching methods from German schools. His heavy beat and neo-baroque music derived from the outlawed *Stravinsky; his bid to create a non-operatic music drama took its cue from

Oedipus Rex. Orff lived a cloistered life and after the War married the anti-Nazi author, Luise Rinser. The aggressiveness of *Carmina Burana* was out of character and was not repeated in other works, apart from its companion piece, *Catulli Carmina* (Leipzig, 6.xi.43). He minimized its significance by describing it as the opening pageant of a trilogy which climaxed, flaccidly, in *Karajan's La Scala staging of *Trionfo di Afrodite* (14.ii.53), a compilation of Latin and Greek erotica.

Born into a Bavarian military family, Orff grew up with regimental bands and, after a year in the trenches, joined a eurhythmics school where he encouraged teachers and pupils to devise their own music from bodily rhythms and primitive harmonies. He invented easy-to-play percussion instruments and published his methods in a *Schulwerk* that formed the basis of a global movement. His ideas paralleled *Hindemith's in promoting music as a social activity in which anyone could participate.

While rediscovering and arranging works by Monteverdi, including *Orfeo* and *The Coronation of Poppea*, Orff developed the simplicity that won him overnight fame with *Carmina*. Two Grimm fairytale operas, *Der Mond (The Moon*, Munich, 5.ii.39) and *Die Kluge* (*The Wise Woman*, Frankfurt, 20.ii.43) used the tonality of *Carmina* stripped of its savagery.

He next turned to an operatic trilogy of Greek dramas, *Antigonae* (Salzburg, 9.viii.49), *Oedipus the Tyrant* (Stuttgart, 11.xii.59) and *Prometheus* (Stuttgart, 24.iii.68), and concluded with a choral contemplation of the end of time, *De temporum fine comoedia* (Salzburg, 20.viii.73). None of these works advanced much beyond elementary monodies and none found a following beyond Germany, where Orff is revered as a teacher and philosopher.
b. Munich, 10.vii.1895; co-founded Güntherschule 1924–43, cond. Munich Bach Society 1930–36; *d.* Munich, 29.iii.82. *other works:* Easter cantata, *Comoedia de Christi Ressurectione* (1956), Nativity play, *Ludus de nato infante mirificus* (1960), *Rota* for 1972 Munich Olympics (based on 'Sumer is icumen in').

organ *Reger, *David, *Messiaen and *Widor were the principal 20th-century solo repertoire contributors. *Poulenc wrote a celebrated concerto.

Leo ORNSTEIN Russian pre-revolutionary who outraged audiences with the ferocity of his pianism and the savagery of his discords. *Wild Men's Dance* (1912) seemed the epitome of futurism and he was invited to lecture at Oxford and the Sorbonne. Settling in America, his music became eclectic and civilized – *Impressions of Chinatown* for orchestra (1917), a *Hebraic Fantasy* for violin and piano, written for Albert Einstein's 50th birthday (1929). He helped form the League of Composers in 1923 and opened an Ornstein School of Music in Philadelphia, where he taught until 1955. As his notoriety faded, his music subsided into obscurity.
b. Krementchug, Russia, 11.xii.1892; emigrated to US 1907; concert pianist 1911–20; teacher thereafter; *other works: Dwarf Suite, Impressions of Notre Dame and the Thames* (discordant piano pieces, 1912), violin sonata (1917), piano concerto (Philadelphia, 13.ii.25), *Suicide in an Airplane* (for piano, 1940), 20 waltzes for piano (1955–68).

Orpheus The Greek myth of distraught lover entering Hades to retrieve his lover yielded operas by Malipiero (1925), Krenek (1926), Milhaud (1926), and Birtwistle (1986) and ballets by Stravinsky (1948) and Henze (1979).

Robin ORR Scots composer and activist. Not to be confused with C. W. Orr (1893–1976), prolific English songwriter, or Buxton Orr (*b.* 1924), composer and conductor.
b. Brechin, 2.vi.09; st with *Casella, *Boulanger; prof. at Glasgow 1956–65, Cambridge 1965–76; chairman Scottish Opera 1962–76; *works include:* three operas, three symphonies.

Juan ORREGO-SALAS Principal Chilean composer, he combined native Indian rhythms and melodies with *serial and *neo-classical techniques.
b. Santiago, Chile, 18.i.19; st with Humberto Allende, *Thompson, Copland; taught U. of Chile 1942–61, Indiana U. 1961–; *works*

include: opera *Widows* (1989), three ballets, two cantatas, four symphonies, violin concerto (1983), *Variaciones serenas* for string orch. (1971), string quartet (1956).

Nigel OSBORNE Englishman whose values of individual rights and artistic freedoms were cemented while studying in 1970s Poland. His most substantial work is *The Electrification of the Soviet Union* (Glyndebourne, 5.x.87), an opera after Pasternak for chamber ensemble and electronic tape with thrilling, sensuous arias; it concerns a poet who loves a prostitute in Siberia.

b. Manchester, 23.vi.48; st with *Wellesz, *Rudzinski; taught at Nottingham U. 1978; editor, *Contemporary Music Review*; *other works:* *I am Goya* (baritone and quartet, 1977), flute concerto (1980), *Pornography* for mezzo and ensemble (1985).

Otakar OSTRČIL Successor to *Kovařovich as conductor of the National Theatre in Prague (1920–35) he composed five operas and gave the première of *Janáček's *Excursions of Mr Brouček*. His music was late-romantic, almost Mahlerian.

b. Smichov, nr Prague, 25.ii.1879; *d.* Prague, 20.viii.35. *other works:* Sinfonietta (1921).

Osud (*Fate*) Shelved 1904 opera by *Janáček, fp posthumously: Brno, 18.ix.34.

Seiji OZAWA The first Japanese to make a world name in Western music, Ozawa was a protégé of *Bernstein and *Karajan who became conductor of the San Francisco Symphony (1970–7) and music director of the Boston Symphony (1973–). Flamboyant in dress and podium manner, his interpretations of central repertoire are unrevealing and players murmured at a lack of discipline. In programme music and some modernism, however, notably *Messiaen, whose only opera he premièred, Ozawa can be vivid and revealing.

b. Hoten, Manchuria, 1.ix.35.

Luis de PABLO Madrid's leading avant-gardist, he pursued *Webernian serialism, *aleatory devices and live *electronics for 30 years, arriving finally at the conclusion that a little beauty might not come amiss. His 15-minute *Fragmento* for string quartet (1986) amount almost to a requiem for modernism, its ragged cross-themes failing to obscure a poignant personal sound.

b. Bilbao, Spain, 28.i.30; st in Paris and *Darmstadt; worked for Iberian Airlines 1956–60, founded Tiempa y Musica (1959) and Alea (1965) ensembles; dir. Madrid's first New Music Biennial, 1964; *other works*: *Pointillistic Polar* for chamber ensemble (1961), *Quasi una fantasia* for string sextet and orch. (1969); Las Orillas (The Shore) for orch. (1991); *We* for tape.

Pacific 231 Orch. piece by *Honegger depicting an American locomotive at full steam. It was the only record owned by Graham Greene while writing his novel *Stamboul Train*. fp: Paris, 8.v.24.

Ignacy Jan PADEREWSKI The only professional musician to head a government, Paderewski in 1919 became the first premier and foreign minister of the Polish state for which he had campaigned throughout the First War. He was ousted in less than a year, became Poland's delegate at the League of Nations (1920–21) and spent the rest of his life abroad. In 1939 he was co-opted into the Polish government in exile.

As a young pianist, he aroused Lisztian hysteria with his dexterity and long blond hair. His Chopin playing was outstandingly charismatic and he donated record fees to the national cause. He gave up composing when he entered politics. *Manru*, his tragic opera of Tatra mountain folk, was staged at Dresden (29.v.01) and New York; a splashy symphony in B minor (Boston SO, 12.ii.09) was sentimentally titled 'Polonia'.

b. Kuryowka, Poland, 18.xi.1860; st in Vienna with Theodore Leschetizky, whose second wife premièred his first concerto; NY debut 17.xi.1891; established $10,000 trust fund for US-born composers in 1900; married twice; *d.* NY, 29.vi.41, buried at Arlington National Cemetry pending liberation, reburied in Warsaw state funeral, 30.vi.92. *other works*: piano sonata in E-flat minor (1903) and many songs.

Bib: Adam Zamoyski, *Paderewski*, London (Collins), 1983.

Jaime PAHISSA Adventurous Catalan exile, biographer of de *Falla. His opera *The Prison of Lerida* (1906) was long a Barcelona favourite; a *Suite Intertonal* for orch. (1926) proposed a polytonal compromise.

b. Barcelona, 7.x.1880; *d.* Buenos Aires, 27.x.69.

Nam June PAIK Creator of Californian *happenings, he presented 'compositions' that consisted of cutting a ten-inch incision into his own skin (LA, 2.xii.65) and jumping into a water-tub with a naked female cellist. In *Ommaggio a Cage* (Düsseldorf, 13.xi.59), he threw rotten eggs at the audience and smashed up a concert grand. Paik had his heyday in the psychedelic era with Charlotte Moorman; since then, he had occupied himself largely with video.

b. Seoul, S. Korea, 20.vii.32; st in Germany with *Fortner; *other works: Young Penis Symphony* (San Francisco, 21.ix.75).

John Knowles PAINE   Formative figure in American concert music, the first US composer to write symphonies in the romantic style he learned in Germany, a style he propagated at Harvard to generations of pupils who included *Ives, *Carpenter, *Mason and the critic H. T. Finck. His late opera *Azara* (1901) was performed posthumously in Boston.
> *b.* Portland, Maine, 9.i.1839; *d.* Cambridge, Mass., 25.iv.06. *works include*: two symphonies, Hymn to the West (1904).

Palestrina   Historical-fiction opera by *Pfitzner about a Papal attempt to retard musical progress by banning counterpoint. A masterpiece of German opera, it presaged *Hindemith's *Mathis der Maler* and anticipated *neo-classical usages. fp: Munich, 12.vi.17; cond *Walter.

Selim PALMGREN   Finnish composer in Sibelian style, he studied in Berlin with *Busoni, taught at the Eastman School in Rochester (1923–26) and married the soprano wife of *Järnefelt. He wrote piano études in wintry colours and five concertos with evocative names like *The Stream* and *April*.
> *b.* Pori, Finland, 16.ii.1878; *d.* Helsinki, 13.xii.51.

Andrzej PANUFNIK   In the summer of 1954, Poland's leading composer shook off his minders while on a recording trip to Switzerland and caught a flight to Britain. In an instant, he passed from celebrity to obscurity. His music was cold-shouldered by an establishment because he failed to fit its rigid categories. He was neither a traditional tonalist nor a serialist and the emotional appeal of his music was deemed un-British. For nine years not a note of his work was broadcast on the BBC and Poland wrote him out of its history.

During and after the Second World War, he kept alive the creative spark. He played duets with *Lutosławski in underground haunts and premiered a self-explicatory *Tragic Overture* in March 1944. His *Homage to Chopin* (for soprano/piano or flute/strings, 1949) was dance-like without being flippant or propagandistic. But Stalin's fist was descending heavily and Panufnik felt that free expression was impossible.

At his new home in Twickenham, beside the river Thames, he created symphonies from minute cells of three or four notes, often arranged in geometric patterns. *Arbor Cosmica* (1983) for chamber orchestra was, for example, tree-shaped. His method was akin to Webern's but lacked its dialectic and remained somehow tuneful and moving.

Almost all of his major works related somehow to Poland and its pain. The *Sinfonia Sacra* (Monaco, 12.viii.64), his first expatriate composition, celebrated his nation's millennium of Christianity. The *Katyn Epitaph*, premiered by *Stokowski in 1968, exposed the forbidden topic of Stalin's massacre of 15,000 Polish officers. The *Sinfonia Votiva* (Boston, 12.i.82, cond. *Ozawa), an offering to the Black Madonna of Czestochowa, celebrated the Solidarity uprising at the Gdansk shipyards; a bassoon concerto was dedicated to the memory of the martyred priest, Jerzy Popietusko. The concerto (Milwaukee, 18.v.86) converts the most comic of instruments to deadly serious purposes. The violin concerto for Yehudi *Menuhin (London, 18.vii.72) begins and ends its opening movement with a solo cadenza of Bachian assurance, unusually allowing the soloist to dictate the tempo and interpretation of the entire taut work. Panufnik seemed to be expressing the individual's prerogative.

When communism crumbled, he was fêted in Poland and his self-sacrifice was acknowledged as a factor in the liberalization that allowed the Warsaw Autumn to flourish from 1956 as Eastern Europe's gateway to modernism. Panufnik never shared the outlandish concerns or sounds of the *avant-garde. In person as in music he was neat and well-mannered, convinced of the need for many styles to flourish simultaneously. He was always looking to simplify his means of communication. His very last work was a cello concerto for *Rostropovich (London, 25.vi.92).
> *b.* Warsaw, 24.ix.14, son of leading violin maker; st with *Weingartner in Vienna, cond., Cracow Philharmonic 1945–46, City of Birmingham SO, 1957–59; *d.* London, 27.x.91. *other works*: Autumn Music (Paris, 16.i.68), *Sinfonia Elegiaca* (Houston, 21.xi.57, cond Stokowski), *Symphony of*

Spheres (London, 13.iv.76), 9th symphony (London, 25.ii.87), 10th symphony (Chicago, 1.ii.90), four string quartets.
Bib: A. Panufnik, *Composing Myself*, 1987.

Yannis (Andreou) PAPAIOANNOU Influential teacher at Athens conservatory, where he led the way in 12-tone composition. Of five symphonies, the 3rd (1963) onwards are serial.
b. Cavala, Greece, 6.i.11; st with Honegger; *d*. Athens, 11.v.89.

(Marie Joseph Léon) Desiré PAQUE Peripatetic early modernist, he went atonal soon after Schoenberg but failed to find a publisher for most of his 144 works. They include eight symphonies, ten string quartets and a challenging *10 pièces atonales pour la jeunesse* (1925).
b. Liège, Belgium, 21.v.1867; lived in Sofia, Athens, Lisbon, Geneva, finally roosting in Paris, 1914; *d*. Bessancourt, France, 20.xi.39.

Parade *Satie's ballet for Diaghilev. Paris, 18.v.17.

Paul PARAY The French conductor wrote an oratorio on Joan of Arc (1931) and a Mass for the 500th anniversary of her execution (1956).
b. Tréport, 24.v.1886; *d*. Monte Carlo, 10.x.79.

Paris The capital of fashion made a fetish of novelty and placed itself in the vanguard of new art. Picasso, Stravinsky and Samuel Beckett were seduced by its allure. Unlike clothes, however, art could not be discarded after a season's wear and the pursuit of novelty at all costs led into cul-de-sacs that jeopardized the city's cultural reputation. The French, said André Malraux, De Gaulle's minister of cultural affairs, were 'not a musical nation'. Performing standards were poor and politics intervened in every artistic enterprise. Style in music mattered more than content.

Public taste was notoriously reactionary before the First War when *Diaghilev's ballets, particularly the *Rite of Spring*, provoked violent revulsion. *Debussy and *Ravel innovated by dressing their radical works in exquisitely smooth textures.

A frantic chase for new experience arose from the wartime trauma and found expression in the shockingly explicit rhythms of imported jazz and the *neo-classical frisson of a violated heritage. Between the wars, Paris was dominated by these twin trends and the wilful iconoclasm of *Satie and Les *Six. It rejected the symphonic visions of Mahler and Sibelius and the disciplines of Schoenberg.

Serialism was promoted by *Leibowitz after 1945 and became a religion for *Boulez and his disciples. *Musique concrète was created from tape fragments on the floor of a radio studio; Barraqué pioneered the art of black noise; *Xenakis designed tower-blocks of sound. Supported by massive government investment and a public willing to follow ephemeral novelty, Boulez built the *IRCAM research and performing centre and helped devise a modern opera house at the Bastille. Both became bogged down in bitter recriminations when the promise of a genuinely new music failed to materialize. In the meantime, mainstream composers were ruthlessly sidelined and the quality of orchestral playing stagnated.

Paris: The Song of a Great City Orch. nocturne by *Delius, fp: Elberfeld, Germany, 14.xii.01.

Charlie 'Bird' PARKER Fabled, short-lived alto saxophonist, king of *bebop in post-1945 NY and progenitor of modern *jazz. He represented a new 'cool' sound in which dissonances abounded yet did not deplete the blues feeling. Heroin addiction punctuated his career, fuddled his thinking and provoked his early death.
b. Kansas City, 29.viii.29; *d*. NY, 12.iii.55.

Horatio (William) PARKER The American equivalent of *Parry in England, he was dean of music at Yale (1904–19) and a retrograde, widely-sung choral writer. He taught better than he composed, and *Ives respected his wisdom. His opera *Mona* won a nationwide competition at the Met (14.iii.1912). *The Lord is my Shepherd* led his long list of hymns.
b. Aburndale, Massachusetts, 15.ix.1863; *d*. Cedarhurst, NY, 18.xii.19.

Bernard PARMEGIANI A *musique concrète associate of Pierre *Schaeffer, he created a 100-minute realization, *La Création du Monde* (1982–84), which spurns big-bang theory in favour of an almost biblical evolution.

b. Paris, 1927.

(Sir) Hubert (Charles Hastings) PARRY With Parry as director of the Royal College of Music (1894–1918) and *Stanford its professor of composition, the hand of Brahms lay heavy on England. Where Stanford's symphonies were relieved by an Irish lilt Parry's were lumpenly English as sausage and mash. His 5th and best (London, 5.xii.12) has movements labelled 'Stress', 'Love', 'Play' and 'Now', strolling through an untroubled Edwardian life in around 23 minutes. An *Elegy for Brahms* (8.xi.18), premièred at his own obsequies, is as emotional as Parry ever got. He is famed for the 1916 choral setting of Blake's *Jerusalem*, a utopian dream of England's green and pleasant land that is sung, more as fantasy than expectation, at Women's Institute meetings and the Last Night of the Proms.

> *b*. Bournemouth, 27.ii.1848; st Oxford, Leipzig and London; joined RCM at its formation in 1883 and succeeded George Grove as director; professor of music at Oxford 1900–8.; *d*. Rustington, 7.x.18. *other vocal works*: Blest Pair of Sirens (1887), I Was Glad (for 1902 Coronation), Coronation Te Deum (1911); The Pied Piper of Hamelin (1905); A Vision of Life (1907); Songs of Farewell (1916).

Arvo PÄRT As a technicain at Estonian radio, Pärt pioneered an eastern brand of *minimalism, unaware of what *Reich and *Glass were doing in the west. The essential difference is that where the Americans took their repetitive rhythms from Indian ragas and rock music, Pärt turned back to Bach and Orthodox plainchant for spiritual and technical guidance. Baroque groundbass was the backing on which he erected scores of mounting religious fervour, culminating in a slow, 80-minute *St John Passion* (Munich, 28.xi.82) that is so regressively reverential that it hardly emerges from the 17th century. Other Baroque offerings are more tongue in cheek, like *Wenn Bach die Bienen gezuchtet hatte* (if Bach had raised bees, Graz, 7.x.83); there are also several discursions on the letters B-A-C-H.

The most moving of his minimalisms is the six-minute *Cantus in memoriam*

Benjamin Britten (1977), in which divided groups of strings descend slowly but at different speeds down the scale of A minor, to the tolling of a single bell. As both an act of homage and an independent musical invention, it is wholly successful. The most undendurable of his minimalisms is *Spiegel im Spiegel (Mirror in the mirror)* for piano and violin or cello, which does nothing remotely inventive with a tiny cantilena for eight and a half long minutes.

Pärt's developed four distinct periods. Until 1968, apart from a brief flirtation with neo-classicism, he wrote along *serial lines, an act of open rebellion in the USSR. His was the first 12-tone symphony in Estonia, subtitled *Polyphonic Symphony* (1964) and cramming note upon note in mounting tension until the chord crashes down beneath its own weight. The 13-minute Second Symphony (1966) is depressing and portentous; disaster seems unavoidable from the fluttering of strings and groans of brass until a fragment of Tchaikovsky's *Sweet Dream* provides an improbable happy ending.

This borrowing led Pärt into his second phase as a collage artist. A parallel cello concerto for *Rostropovich titled *Pro et Contra* spliced pretty bits of Baroque music with massive discordances, creating conflicts that supposedly illustrate the title. With the 3rd symphony (1971), he turned his back on the 20th century and took his cue from monkish chants and early polyphony, though the underlying language is essentially late-romantic – and quite beautiful, a Baltic rediscovery of the mood of *Pfitzner's *Palestrina* and Hindemith's *Mathis der Maler*. It was followed by five years of virtual silence until Pärt produced his own distinctive synthesis of old sounds and modern rhythms in the form that won him worldwide renown. He described his own life as a continuous search and rejected many of the works of his prematurity. Balding and bearded, he came to resemble a latter-day prophet.

> *b*. Paide, Estonia, 11.ix.35; st with *Eller (dedicatee of his 1st symphony), worked at Estonian Radio 1958–67; migrated to Vienna January 1980, settling 1981 in West Berlin; *other orch. works*: Nekrolog (1960), Perpetuum Mobile (1963, dedicated to Luigi *Nono, who smuggled it out); Credo (1968),

Tabula Rasa for 2 violins, strings and *pre-pared piano (1977), *Fratres* for string orchestra (1980), *Festina Lente* for string orchestra (1989).

Harry PARTCH A crackpot inventor, as American as gun law, he rode the rails as a hobo during the Great Depression and subsisted as an odd jobs man while developing the *Genesis of a Music*, a 1949 manual in which he outlined his idea of 'corporeal' music. Contrary to common assumption, Partch proclaimed there were 43 notes in an octave and built the instruments to play them – a 72-stringed 'kithara', a 'chromelodeon', 'cloud-chamber bowls' and the like. The resultant compositions yielded an exotic *microtonality, peppered with American and other folklores that he picked up on his journeys and generally set to words and dance in a weirdly effective mixed-media show. Once the peculiar tonality has settled on the ear, clear tunes and themes emerge as if from an urban jungle. The effect is medidative and hypnotic.

Barstow (1941) is actually a setting of railside graffiti daubed at Barstow, California. Most of Partch's music can only be played on his instruments, which are now museum pieces, but his ideas won academic credence and infected *Cage, *Johnston and other iconoclasts.

b. Oakland, California, 24.vi.01; *d.* San Diego, 3.ix.74. *other works*: *17 Lyrics by Li Po* (1930), *San Francisco Newsboy Cries* (1941), *Oedipus* (music drama, Mills College, 14.iii.52), *The Bewitched* (U. of Illinois, 26.iii.57), *Revelation in the Courthouse Park* (musical tragedy, U. of Illinois, 11.iv.61), *Delusion of the Fury* (1966).

Ödön PARTOS *Kodály pupil who played first viola in the Palestine SO (1938–56) and formed music academy in Tel Aviv with *Schoenberg as president. He composed three concertos for his own instrument and various Hebraic pieces.

b. Budapest, 1.x.07; dir. Rubin Academy of Tel Aviv Universiy 1951–77; *d.* Tel Aviv, 6.vii.77.

Passacaglia Webern's opus 1. fp: Vienna, 4.xi.08, cond. by the composer.

Paul (Leslie) PATTERSON *English electronic authority with accessible orchestral touch applied in setting Roald Dahl's

Revolting Rhymes (1992) as a latterday 'Peter and the Wolf'.

b. Chesterfield, Derbys., 15.vi.47; head of contemporary music at RAM, London, 1985-; *orch. works include*: *Upside-Down-Under Variations* (disquisition on the Australian ditty, 'Waltzing Matilda', 1983), Concerto for Orchestra (1981), *Mass of the Sea* (1983), *Europhony* (1985), *The End* (1989).

Jiří PAUER Communist chief of Prague's National Theatre until the 1989 revolution, he was accused of abusing power to promote his own operas, *Zuzana Vojirová* (1958), *Martial Counterpoints* (1961) and *La Malade Imaginaire* (1969, after Molière). Among various key roles in the totalitarian state, he was repressive head of the Czech Philharmonic Orchestra for 22 years. 'Pauer's artistic attitudes grew from his civil and political attitudes; that is the reason for his straightforward and concrete musical thinking,' wrote a fellow-apparatchik.

Objectively sampled, his music is better than his reputation suggests; the children's opera *The Prattling Snail* (1950) was deservedly popular. A miner's son, Pauer learned the composer's trade with the microtonalist Alois *Hába, for whom he wrote a symphonic movement, *Initials* (1974), around the notes A and H (B♮).

b. Libusin, near Kladno, Czechoslovakia, 22.ii.19;

Stephen (Harrison) PAULUS In the outmoded *Barber tradition, Paulus made a lyrical, lurid opera of James Cain's erotic novel *The Postman Always Rings Twice* (St Louis, 1982), then applied himself to writing functional pieces for conservative orchestras, fleshing out their programmes with 12- or 15-minute sinfoniettas designed to advertise instrumental brilliance.

b. Summit, New Jersey, 24.viii.49; composer in residence at Minnesota SO 1983–87, Atlanta SO 1987–91.

Bernhard PAUMGARTNER Co-founder of the Salzburg Festival and long-serving head of the Mozarteum (1917–1959, except 1938–45), he composed three operas, three ballets and a variety of instrumental music for the festival's plays, in-

cluding a score for *Twelfth Night* based on Elizabethan tunes.
> *b.* Vienna, 14.xi.1887; *d.* Salzburg, 27.vii.71.

Pavane pour une infante défunte (*Pavan for a dead infanta*) Delicate eulogy by Ravel for piano (fp: Paris, 5.iv.02) or orch. (fp: Paris, 25.xii.10).

Luciano PAVAROTTI Outstanding lyric tenor blessed with a technique that seems to summon sounds from his lowest ventricles. The top-selling opera singer since *Caruso and *Callas, he confines himself mainly to bel canto, Verdi and Puccini.
> *b.* Modena, Italy, 12.x.35;

Anthony PAYNE A thoughtful combiner of modern theory with middle-of-road Englishness, often writing for his soprano wife, Jane Manning.
> *b.* London 2.viii.36; married 1966; *orch. works include*: *The World's Winter* (sop. solo, *Cheltenham, 4.vii.76), *Spring's Shining Wake* (modelled on Delius' *In a Summer Garden*, BBC 21.xii.83), *Time's Arrow* (London, 24.vii.90).

Juan Carlos PAZ Mover and shaker in Argentine music, he founded a Grupo Renovación in 1929 with like-minded radicals and proceeded to compose in a succession of modern techniques from *neoclassicism to *serialism.
> *b.* Buenos Aires, 5.viii.01; *d.* there, 25.viii.72. *orchestral works include*: *Ritmica ostinata* (1942), *Continuidad* (1961).

(Sir) Peter PEARS *Britten wrote all his major tenor roles from *Peter Grimes to Aschenbach in *Death in Venice* for his lifelong companion, who possessed a high, thin tenor voice. He also wrote cycles and orchestral songs with his voice in mind. Pears was a formidably intelligent interpreter of Schubert Lieder and premièred new works by Henze, Walton and Lutosławski.
> *b.* Farnham, Surrey, 22.vi.10; met Britten 1937; *d.* Orford, East Anglia, 3.iv.86.

Felipe PEDRELL Instigator of the Spanish music revival, he was outshone by his pupils *Albéniz, de *Falla, *Granados and *Gerhard and is remembered in their music rather than his own. Gerhard wrote a delightful *Homenaje a Pedrell* (1941) based on themes from his forgotten opera, *La Celestina*. Pedrell's nephew Carlos (1878–1941) became Uruguay's foremost composer.
> *b.* Tortosa, 19.ii.1842; *d.* Barcelona, 19.viii. 22. *works include*: *Los Pirineos* (1890–1), a tripartite quasi-Wagnerian attempt to liberate Spanish opera of Italian dominance; editions of Spanish Renaissance and church music.

Flor PEETERS Catholic organ composer in the manner of *Tournemire.
> *b.* Tielen, Belgium, 4.vii.03; *d.* Antwerp, 4.vii.86.

Pelléas et Mélisande Maurice Maeterlinck's 1892 play of deathless love acquired incidental music from *Fauré (1898) and *Sibelius (1902), and gave rise to a graphic symphonic poem by *Schoenberg, along the lines of his wordless story *Verklärte Nacht*. Its most important musical setting was Debussy's opera, hailed as an antidote to Wagnerism but actually an alternative *Tristan*. Debussy abandoned set-piece arias in favour of a seamless symphonic structure. His use of speech rhythms and instrumental atmospherics was equally significant, opening a century-long new avenue for French music. fp: Paris, 30.iv.02.

Krzysztof PENDERECKI As a boy, Penderecki watched the Jews of his home town being rounded up for massacre by the Nazis. As a young composer, his *Threnody for the Victims of Hiroshima* (Warsaw Radio, 31.v.61) won him fame as an artist whose music overrode advanced techniques and vicious dissonances by dint of sheer compassion.
Threnody, a classic of late modernism, is scored for 52 string instruments that play a quarter-tone apart and are regularly tapped and beaten. The sound grows into clusters of unbearable tension, washed away at its peak by a wave of pure emotion. *Anaklasis* (Baden-Baden, 16.x.60, cond. Rosbaud), introducing him to the West, conducted a nine-minute dialogue between 42 strings and a battery of percussion in language that sounded recklessly radical but proved deeply moving. Music in the first string quartet (Cincinnati, 11.v.62) evolved from a flicking and plucking of instruments; it wound up in perfect harmony.

Penderecki was hailed as the first *avant-gardist to speak directly to audiences. He deliberately shocked them, especially with fornicating nuns in his Aldous Huxley opera, *The Devils of Loudun* (Hamburg, 20.vi.69) but, unlike *Stockhausen and *Boulez, was perpetually conscious of audiences' needs and concerns. He was also acutely sensitive to conditions in his native Poland even when, in the 1960s, he lived mostly in Germany.

Religious music that he wrote all the while snapped his ties with the avant-garde. The *St Luke Passion* (Münster Cathedral, 30.iii.66) celebrated the millennium of Polish Christianity in rapturous yet disturbing cadences that took their theme from Christ and Bach and their mood from a sombre contemplation of Auschwitz. The Passion was approved by his local archishop, Karol Wojtya, whose election as Pope John Paul II, followed by the Solidarity revolt against communism, heightened the immediacy of Penderecki's music.

His *Polish Requiem* (Stuttgart, 21.vi.84) was built in sections marking momentous national events. *Agnus Dei* mourned the death of Cardinal Wyszynski in 1981; *Dies Irae* was written on the 40th anniversary of the Warsaw Ghetto uprising; *Lacrimosa* was requested by Solidarity to commemorate shipyard workers killed in the 1970 uprising; *Libera me* was dedicated to Polish officers murdered on Stalin's orders at Katyn. More than merely a national epic, the Requiem is a portrait of European history that offers a unique artistic prospect of conciliation.

Ultra-romantic works like the *Christmas Symphony* (NY, 1.v.80) drew accusations of betrayal from radicals, but Penderecki emerged from this phase around 1980 and started seeking a fusion between adventurism and tradition. The 2nd cello concerto (Berlin, 11.i.83, *Rostropovich) and a parallel viola concerto (Caracas, 24.vii.83) recapture some *Threnody* tensions in a melodic and expressive mode. Clusters reappear in his third opera, *The Black Mask*, a complex melodrama that was altogether too violent for the Salzburg summer audience (15.viii.86) which had imagined the composer to be tamed.

b. Debica, Poland, 23.xi.33; st in Cracow; won UNESCO award for Threnody 1961; principal of Cracow Academy of Music 1972-; professor at Yale 1973-8; *other works*: operas *Paradise Lost* (Chicago 29.xi.78); *Solomon's Song of Songs* (Lisbon, 5.vi.73), Magnificat (Salzburg Cathedral, 17.viii.74); 1st symphony (Peterborough Cathedral, 19.vii.73), violin concerto (Basle, 27.iv.77); *Actions* for jazz ensemble (Donaueschingen, 17.x.71).
Bib: Wolfram Schwinger, *Penderecki, Leben und Werk*, Stuttgart, 1979.

Pénélope The last French lyric-tragic opera, Fauré's masterpiece failed to find an international following. fp: Paris, 10.v.13.

pentatonic A scale of five notes, corresponding to the black notes on the keyboard. It is common in many forms of ethnic music, especially Chinese and Javanese, and was applied to individual effect by *Mahler, *Puccini and *Vaughan Williams.

Barbara PENTLAND First Canadian to write 12-note music, Pentland composed four symphonies and various concertos of local resonance.
b. Winnipeg, Canada, 2.i.12; st with *Copland; taught at Toronto (1943-9) and Vancouver (1949-63); *other works*: News (1970, using live actuality) for narrator and orch.

Ernst PEPPING Neo-Baroque German composer of Lutheran liturgy, he also wrote three symphonies (1939-44) and a piano concerto (1950). His major contribution consists of the 20-volume Spandauer Chorbuch for two to six voices covering the entire religious year, a Matthew Passion for *a cappella* chorus (1950) and a Te Deum (1955).
b. Duisburg, 9.xii.01; *d.* Berlin, 1.ii.81.

percussion The range of things that went bang in a symphony was blown up in the first decade of the century by *Mahler and *Strauss, who introduced glockenspiels, thunder-machines, hammers, cowbells and every kind of drum to the symphony orchestra. From there, it was no imaginative distance for composers to write works for percussion alone, particularly when they could call on the precise sonorities of percussive keyboard instruments such as the *celesta, *marimba and xylophone.

*Stravinsky employed pianos in *Les *Noces* in a percussive capacity. Varèse played one set of rhythms against another until he was ready to write the first Western work for solo percussion, *Ionisations* (1931). *Cage, *Reich, *Marta and the *minimalists composed for percussion ensembles which enjoyed a vogue as reincarnations of a primitive form of music making.

performance art Music plus acting and other *happenings, typified by the genre of *Anderson and *Paik.

performance practice How to play music as its composer intended was the underlying cause of the *early music movement.

Moses PERGAMENT Lone Jewish composer in Scandinavia, his profoundest utterances were two responses to the Nazi Holocaust – a choral symphony, *The Jewish Song* (1944) and *Eli* (1958), a radio opera written with the Nobel-winning poetess Nelly Sachs. His concertos drew on synagogal cantillation and, like Bruch, he wrote a Kol Nidrei for cello and orchestra (1949).
b. Helsinki, Finland, 21.ix.1893; *d*, Gustavsberg, Sweden, 5.iii.77.

Thomas PERNES Composer of *Alpenglühn* (*Alpine warmth*) ballet for Vienna State Opera (17.vi.84), for a combo of piano, synthesizer, percussion and folksong.
b. Vienna, 1956; st with *Uhl, *Cerha; *other works*: violin concerto (1983), *Adagietto* for four saxophones (1985).

George PERLE Leading authority on Alban *Berg, whose intimacies he decoded from numeral clues in the scores, Perle wrote dry and difficult works for piano. His music is elegant and clear but rarely surprising and never fantastical. His piano concerto (1990) was claimed to be the largest ever written.
b. Bayonne, New Jersey, 6.v.15, to Russo-Jewish parents; st with *Krenek; taught at universities of Louisville (1949–56), California (Davis, 1957–61) and at Queens College NY (1961-); founded International Alban Berg Society; *other works*: two symphonies; eight string quartets (1938–89); 13 Emily Dickinson songs; Six Etudes for piano.

Vincent PERSICHETTI Philadelphia composer whose tone was conditioned by the sumptuousness of his local orchestra. His 160-odd works have a lush underlay, enlivened with intermittent grit. The 20-minute *Symphony for Strings* (Louisville, Kentucky, 28.viii.54) surmounts an arid 15-bar theme to communicate warmly. His piano concerto (Hanover, New Hampshire, 2.viii.64) cloaks scant substance in lavish romantic material.
  Persichetti seemed able to compose at will in almost any style, improvising an entire sonata at the drop of a hat. He lived all his life in Philadelphia, serving as organist and choirmaster at Arch Street Presbyterian Church (1932–48), teaching six years at the local conservatory and commuting to Juilliard in New York from 1947. He enjoyed a moment of notoriety when *A Lincoln Address* (1973), written for Richard Nixon's second presidential inauguration, was dropped because of imagined allusions to the Vietnam War.
b. Philadelphia 6.vi.15; *d.* there, 14.viii.87.
works include: nine symphonies, 13 serenades, 11 piano sonatas, three string quartets, much vocal music including the *Harmonium* cycle for soprano and piano after poems by Wallace Stevens (1952), and a four-hand piano concerto (1952).

Persymfans Orchestra of Russian revolutionaries who abjured conductors and played in a semi-circle facing one another. Successful enough for Prokofiev and Milhaud to write them new works, they were disbanded on Kremlin orders in 1932 as a manifestation of bourgeois democracy.

Peter and the Wolf Orchestral tale for children by Prokofiev. fp: Moscow, 2.v.36.

Peter Grimes Britten's breakthough opera about a misanthropic Aldeburgh fisherman accused of the death of apprentice boys. The first international British opera since Purcell, its tonal language derived from *Mahler and *Strauss but Britten uncovered unsuspected lyricism in English everyday speech.
fp: London, Sadler's Wells, 7.vi.45.

Goffredo PETRASSI The Roman modernist acted as godfather to new Hungarian music, whose composers from *Durko onwards came knocking at his door. His lure is easily understandable. Less aggressive than *Berio and *Nono, Petrassi belonged to a pre-war iconoclasm that survived the Mussolini years, just as Budapest music was struggling to maintain integrity under communism.

*Neo-classical at first, like his mentor *Casella, Petrassi was drawn to Bartók and Stravinsky while staging their operas at Venice (1937–40). He progressed slowly towards *serialism, which he adopted in the 3rd of his eight concertos for orchestra (1953). His preceding two operas, *Il Cordovano* (La Scala, 12.v.49) and *La morte dell 'aria* (Rome, 24.x.50) were respectively comic-lyrical and tragic-*Verklärte Nacht*-ian.

His elegance overcame any constraints imposed by the 12-note system. The *Poema* for 48 strings and trombome (1980) and *Laudates Creatorum* for reciter and six instruments (1982) are memorably agreeable without being strident or didactic. Most of his work is vocal or chamber music; he ranks with *Dallapiccola as a moral and forward-looking paragon of Italian art.

b. Zagarolo, nr Rome, 16.vii.04; taught at Santa Cecilia Conservatorio 1939–74; president *ISCM 1954–56; *other works*: *Passacaglia* for orch. (1931), piano concerto (1939), flute concerto (1961), *Beatitudines*, chamber oratorio in memory of Martin Luther King (Fiuggi, 17.vii.69), string quartet (1975).

Petro (John) PETRIDIS Classic Greek composer, imbued with Orthodox liturgy and Homeric literature.

b. Nigdé, Turkey, 23.vii.1892; *d.* Athens, 17.viii.77. *works include*: five symphonies (1929–51); two piano concertos; Chorale and variations on a Byzantine theme (1939).

Emil PETROVICS Composer of a Hungarian stream-of-consciousness 12-note opera based on Dostoyevsky's *Crime and Punishment* (1968). He was director of Hungarian State Opera 1986–90.

b. Nagybesckerek, Yugoslavia, 9.ii.30; *other works*: cantatas on heroic themes – 'Dying in Action' and 'We Shall Depart'.

Petrushka *Stravinsky's ever-popular 2nd ballet. fp: Paris, 13.vi.11.

Allan PETTERSSON In a *Scandinavian social system which cares for composers from kindergarten to grave, Pettersson was the one who fell through the net. Living in a slum and playing viola in the Stockholm Philharmonic (1940–52), he was unable to get his symphonies played and the rare performances of his chamber music were derided as 'lumpy' and 'screechy'. He went to Paris for 18 months to study with *Honegger, *Milhaud and *Leibowitz but rejected the lessons of neo-classicism and formalised atonality. He contracted crippling rheumatoid arthritis, probably from living in damp accommodation, and seemed destined for obscurity when Antal *Dorati discovered his 7th symphony and gave it a shattering première (13.x.68) in the capital, followed by a recording and international tour. It was the last concert that Pettersson was physically able to attend. Although accorded the finest medical treatment, a luxurious apartment and every honour in the kingdom, he lived out the rest of his days in painstricken immobility.

Pettersson is sometimes described as a Swedish *Mahler, reaching into his own agonies for solutions to the human condition. All 16 of his symphonies are single movements in which apoplectic anger gives way to episodes of consolation. The Mahlerian element is strongest in the 7th symphony, his 40-minute breakthrough work, where a passage of serene beauty arises at the halfway point, reminiscent of the *Adagios* of Mahler's 4th and 9th. This remains his most performable and accessible music, the most important Scandinavian symphony since Sibelius.

The analogy with Mahler, however, goes no further. Pettersson lacked Mahler's melodic facility, irony, wit and self-mockery. His symphonies slump all too easily into unrelieved melancholy. The 2nd symphony (9.v.54) is the prototype for the series, a cycle which has its high points in the 7th and hour-long 9th (Gothenburg, 18.ii.71) but which, in truth, shows scant artistic progress. The 16th and last (24.ii.83) is a saxophone concerto in all but name. Many of the works take their theme from a 1950 cycle of *24 Barefoot Songs*, written to his own words and later orchestrated by Dorati, forming a kind of hymn to the dispossessed. The 2nd violin concerto (25.i.80), written for Ida Haendel and running almost an hour, sounds like the unbroken wailing of an orphan child torn from its parents and refusing all sympathy. To appreciate Pettersson one needs to inhabit his world, a world as obssessive, agonized and ineluctable as Strindberg's. He once said of himself: 'I am not a composer, I am a voice crying.'

b. Västra Ryd, Uppland, 19.ix.11; *d.* Stockholm, 20.vi.80. *other major works*: 12th symphony for chorus and orch., text by Pablo Neruda (24.x.74), *Vox Humana* for four soloists, mixed chorus and orch. to Latin American texts (29.ix.77), three concertos for string orch.

Felix PETYREK Atonalist who in 1923 turned a Hans Christian Andersen fairytale into a *sprechgesang chamber opera, *The poor mother and death*.

b. Brno, Austro-Hungary, 14.v.1892; *d.* Vienna, 1.xii.51. *other works*: Sinfonietta, sextet (1922).

Hans (Erich) PFITZNER A major composer whose music, like *Reger's, does not travel easily. His opera *Palestrina* (Munich, 12.vi.17, cond. Walter) is revered by Germans as their 20th century masterpiece but has never been staged outside German-speaking territory. Based on the medieval confrontation between composers and church over the use of music in worship, it opens with a prelude of irresistible ethereality, reminiscent of the Good Friday music in *Parsifal*. *Palestrina* is music about music, immaculately wrought, vocally attractive and subtly spellbinding. It is also static, deadly serious and implausible in its imitations of early-music. As pure music it has absolute logic and integrity but, at three and a half hours' long, it can strain the credulity of non-believers.

Pfitzner was bred with the intense patriotism of an expatriate and the conservatism of the congenitally insecure. Son of a German violinist in Moscow, he professed a deathless ultra-Germanism and, though he found the Nazis uncouth, contributed works with nationalist titles. After slandering a Gauleiter, he was protected from punishment by the music-loving mass-murderer of Poland, Hans Frank, for whom he wrote a *Cracow Greeting* in 1944. Such accolades are not for the squeamish. *Von deutscher Seele (From the

German Soul*; Berlin, 27.i.22), the first of four related cantatas, is a self-congratulatory medley of 19th-century poetic fantasies, a celebration of 'German seriousness and high spirits' winding up to a nationalist exhortation, 'the land is free!'

Pfitzner violently rejected the extravagant orchestrations of Mahler and Strauss, the atonal modernism of Schoenberg and the classical theories of Busoni, going his own obstinate way along a flower-decked dream-path of imaginary romanticism. *Palestrina* apart, he was most effective in that most Germanic of forms, the Lied, of which he wrote around 100. At best, they are as bleakly melodic as Schubert in *Winterreise*, the op. 41 set of 1931 especially so.

His orchestral output includes concertos for piano (1923), violin (1924) and two for cello (1935, 1944), as well as three unnumbered symphonies of small merit. In the 4th and last of his string quartets (1942) and a sextet dating from 1945 he admitted flickerings of self-doubt.

b. Moscow, 23.iv.1869; st in Frankfurt with pianist James Kwast whose daughter he abducted, cond. Mainz 1894–5, Berlin 1897–1907, Strasbourg, 1908–18; *d.* Salzburg, 22.v. 49, buried in Vienna. *other operas*: *Der arme Heinrich* (Mainz 1895), *Die Rose vom Liebesgarten* (Elberfeld, 9.xi.01 – cond. in Vienna by Mahler), *Das Christ-Elflein* (Munich, 11.xii.06), *Das Herz* (Berlin, 12.xi.31).

Michel PHILPOTT Radio engineer in the first *musique concrète experiments, he became president in 1973 of French national television. His pleasantly conventional compositions include two piano sonatas, a trio and an octet.

b. Verzy, France, 2.ii.25; st with *Leibowitz.

piano The sonority and use of this domestic instrument was transformed in the first decade of the century by Debussy's pointillisms and Stravinsky's percussiveness, Schoenberg's atonalities and Bartók's barbarism. New salon works, even by popular composers like Rachmaninov, were no longer within the grasp of amateurs and the domestic habit declined. The flow of public prodigies, however, was abundant, Paderewski, Busoni, Rubinstein, Horowitz, Richter and Brendel being among the most prominent.

In 1940, *Cage attacked the inside of a concert grand to invent the *prepared piano. *Multi-media events were staged in, around and upon a piano without fundamentally altering its function. Towards the end of the century, *Ligeti and Birtwistle rediscovered its concerto potency.

Astor PIAZZOLLA Argentina's 'King of Tango' expressed emotions as contradictory as the Strausses in their waltzes: love and longing, satisfaction in a new world and regret for the old, sentiment and savagery. He abandoned conventional styles for a New Tango of his own making. He called it 'danger music' and his life was often threatened by reactionaries. He wrote mainly for the bandonéon, a hybrid of accordion and concertina that sounds little richer than a mouth organ. His Concierto (1979) for the instrument is consciously neo-classical and suffers from formal strictness. *Tres tangos* for bandonéon and orchestra (1987) are wistful, whimsical and alarmingly memorable. Some of his smaller pieces have been transcribed for string quartet and other concert combinations.
    b. Mar del Plata, Argentina, 11.iii.21; st with Nadia Boulanger; *d*. Buenos Aires, 5.vii.92.

Riccardo   PICK-MANGIAGALLI Composer of conformist Italian operas, *Pizzetti's successor as head of the Verdi Conservatorio in Milan (1936–49).
    b. Strakonice, Bohemia, 10.vii.1882; *d*. Milan, 8.vii.49. *operas include*: Casanova in Venice (La Scala, 19.i.29), *L'Ospitta inatesto* (25.x.31, the first opera to be premièred by radio).

Tobias PICKER Neo-romantic in the style of *Barber and young Copland, he appealed to middle America with three symphonies and three piano concertos by his mid-30s. A blind hearing of *Old and Lost Rivers* (1986) would place it in the mid-1930s. Picker was not, however, a nostalgist and some scores contained sonic surprises. In 1985, as composer in residence at Houston, he devised a fanfare project by which leading composers wrote short opening blasts for each of the orchestra's concerts that season.
    b. NY, 18.vii.54; st with *Carter, *Babbitt; *other works*: The Encantadas (1983), narrated account of Herman Melville's visit to the Galapagos islands; oboe concerto, *Romances and Interludes* (1990).

Pictures at an Exhibition Mussorgsky piano suite, brilliantly orchestrated by Ravel and others.

Gabriel (Henri-Constant) PIERNÉ César Franck's successor at the organ of Sainte-Clothilde (1890–8) was also a noted conductor of the Colonne Concerts (1910–34) but failed to make great impact with his civilized, unincisive compositions. Of six operas, the most lasting was a one-act comedy on the private life of the French soprano, Sophie Arnould (Paris, 21.ii.27).
    b. Metz, Alsace, 16.viii.1863; *d*. Ploujean, Finistère, 17.vii.37. *other works include*: concert piece for harp and orch. (1901); many ballets and pantomimes, oratorios and much instrumental music.

His cousin, **Paul PIERNÉ,** composed three operas, two symphonies and a variety of symphonic poems. He was organist at the Paris church of St Paul-St Louis.
    b. Metz, 30.vi.1874; *d*. Paris, 24.iii.52.

Pierrot lunaire The quintet to which *Schoenberg set this cycle of French poems seemed quintessentially modern – piano, violin/viola, flute/piccolo, clarinet/bass clarinet) with a female narrator who half-speaks, half-sings the text of the moon-struck parrot in *sprechgesang style. It marked a new form of chamber music and concert programme, the dawn of small music-theatre. *Stravinsky took note in *Renard*; *Boulez, *Birtwistle adapted the ensemble to their own purposes. fp: Berlin, 16.x.12.

Willem PIJPER The dominant Dutch composer mitigated the *Mahlerisms he absorbed at an early age with French impressionism and a knack for making big scores out of three or four-note cells. He named this method 'germ-cell theory'; he also invented a 'Pijper scale' of alternating whole tones and semitones, unaware that it was an established Russian patent.
    His first symphony, *Pan* (Amsterdam, 23.iv.18) came straight out of Mahlerian folklore, but the 3rd, subtitled 6 *Symphonic Epigrams* (12.iv.28) showed an individual style, though lacking great invention. He founded a music journal, headed the music

school at Rotterdam (1930–47) and presided over a minor renaissance in the nation's music. Most of his manuscripts were destroyed when the Germans bombed Rotterdam in 1940; about 100 published works survive.

> *b.* Zeist, Netherlands, 8.ix.1894; st with *Wagenaar; *d.* Leidschendam, 18.ii.47. *works include*: opera *Halewijn* (13.vi.33, violin concerto (7.i.40), four string quartets.

I Pini di Roma *(Pines of Rome)* The 2nd of Respighi's three orchestral tributes to his home town contained the *recorded sound of a nightingale. fp: Rome, 14.xii.24.

Pink Floyd Premier *psychedelic rock band, formed 1965, exemplified by ethereal album *Dark Side of the Moon* (1973), which sold in excess of 20 million copies and remained in the charts on and off for almost 20 years. The band took its name from early *bluesmen Pink Anderson (1900–74) and Floyd Council (1911–76) and its members from London student combos. The founders were Syd Barrett, Roger Waters, Nick Mason, Richard Wright.

pink noise *Electronic signal excluding high frequencies.

Lubomir PIPKOV French-educated Bulgarian who held key positions as head of opera in Sofia (1944–7) and subsequently as a vocal teacher; his music is tinged by Bartók and Stravinsky.

> *b.* Lovech, Bulgaria, 6.ix.04; st with Boulanger; *d.* Sofia, 9.v.74. *works include*: three operas, four symphonies, much liturgical music.

Paul (Amadeus) PISK A progressive force in inter-War Vienna, he wrote music criticism for a workers newspaper and co-founded with *Berg and Paul Stefan the modernist periodical *Musikblätter des Anbruchs*. In 1936 Pisk read the writing on the wall and fled to the US, where he taught at universities in California (1937–50), Texas (1950–63) and St Louis (1962–72). His copious compositions are mainly atonal and 12-tone, in the manner of his teacher, *Schoenberg.

> *b.* Vienna, 16.v.1893; *d.* Los Angeles 12.i.90. *works include*: Cantata *Die neue Zeit* (1926), Passacaglia for orch. (1944), *A Toccata of Galuppi's* for narrator and orch. (1947), *3 Ceremonial Rites* (1958).

Walter (Hamor) PISTON US symphonist of Italian descent and temperament, his finer works are steeped in lyricism and elegant craftsmanship. Like so many of his contemporaries he imbibed neo-classicism at Nadia *Boulanger's Paris studio and returned to apply European methods to local material. His 2nd symphony (Washington, D.C., 5.iii.44) overflows with sweetly turned American tunes and spirituals. His other symphonies lack the same assurance, though the 3rd (1947) and 7th (1960) won Pulitzer prizes. He devised a 12-note motif for the 8th symphony (Boston, 5.iii.65) and Variations for cello and orchestra (NY, 2.iii.67), but his sympathies never strayed from middle-period *Stravinsky, a style that *Koussevitsky encouraged among his US protégés. His most performed work was *The Incredible Flutist* (Boston, 30.v.38), a jazzy ballet with a distinctly French seasoning.

Piston taught at Harvard for a quarter of a century (1926–60), numbering *Bernstein and *Carter among his pupils and writing well-thumbed textbooks on Harmony (1941) and Orchestration (1955).

> *b.* Rockland, Maine, 20.i.1894; served US Navy in First World War, married Kathryn Mason 1921; *d.* Belmont, Massachusetts, 12.xi.76. *other works*: concertos for violin (1940, 1960) and viola (1957), five string quartets. He wrote a fanfare for the US bicentennial but died shortly before its performance.

pitch Technical name for what laymen call a note, it was the organizational terms used by *12-note composers. Pitch numbers denoted the order of notes in a row.

Ildebrando PIZZETTI Despite founding a periodical called *Dissonanza* in 1914, Pizzetti was essentially a late-romantic composer who looked to Mussorgsky and Debussy for wider inspiration. Of his 13 operas, only *Fra Gherardo* (La Scala, 16.v.28) enjoyed much of a run abroad. Late in life he composed T. S. Eliot's *Murder in the Cathedral* for La Scala (1.iii.58). He was director of the Verdi Conservatorio in Milan (1924–36), then taught at the Santa Cecilia academy in Rome (1936–58).

b. Parma, Italy, 20.ix.1880; *d.* Rome, 13.ii. 68. orch. works include: *Concerto dell'estate* and *Rondo veneziano* (NY, 28.ii.29, cond. *Toscanini), cello concerto (Venice, 11.ix.34), violin concerto (Rome, 9.xii.45).

The Planets Holst's sevenfold suite with Jupiter its guiding tune. fp: London, 29.ix. 18.

Pli selon Pli *Fold over fold.* Five Mallarme songs for soprano and orch. by *Boulez. fp: Donaueschingen 30.x.62, cond *Boulez.

Poem of Ecstasy *Skryabin's erotic and mystical 4th symphony. fp: NY, 10.xii.08.

Poème électronique Tape that *Varèse made for the 1958 Philips pavilion at Brussels designed by *Xenakis. fp: 2.v.58.

Poème symphonique for 100 metro-nomes Extended joke by *Ligeti, lasting from 20 to 100 minutes (1962). fp: Hilversum, 13.ix.63.

Poèmes pour Mi Soprano lovesongs by *Messiaen. fp: Paris, 28.iv.37.

Pohjola's Daughter Symphonic poem by Sibelius. fp: St Petersburg, 29.xii.06.

pointillism The isolated squeaks of *total serialism provoked comparisons with dot-by-dot painting, and the adjective 'pointil-listic' was applied to many *avant-garde works of the early 1950s. The connection was tenuous for, where Seurat's intended image was obvious to the casual viewer of his canvases, only an expert theoretician could discern the structure and meaning of *Boulez's *Structures*.

Poland When Warsaw founded a Philharmonic Orchestra in 1901, students rebelled at its reactionary and foreign pro-grammes. They formed *Young Poland in Music under *Szymanowski and *Karlow-icz to combine nationalism with late romanticism. War and tyranny retarded much further progress until the *Warsaw Autumn festival of 1956 created an East-West meeting point where Polish inven-tors, *Lutosławski and *Penderecki at their head, exchanged ideas and techniques with the *avant-garde. There followed a vibrant heterodoxy in which *Gorecki experi-mented with *serialism, *Bacewicz followed

*Bartók, and Lutosławski pioneered *alea-toric ideas. A powerful national-religious undercurrent became dominant with the election of a Polish Pope and the 1980s restoration of democracy.

politics Totalitarianism brought music under political control, just as the church had done in previous centuries. Under the Nazis, modernism and music by Jews were banned as 'degenerate' and musicians were murdered in concentration camps. The state demanded upbeat marches and sym-phonies that glorified Aryan supremacism. In fascist Italy, state interference was less organized.

*Stalin imposed a socialist writ on music in 1934 when he removed *Lady Macbeth of Mtsensk from the Moscow stage and attacked its composer. *Shostakovich was the main target again in 1948 when Zhdanov conducted a second purge of composers. Modernism was anathema; *The Rite of Spring* was not heard in Russia until the Khruschev thaw in 1963. The Brezhnev regime reimposed conservatism in the 1970s, forcing *Schnittke virtually under-ground. Similar strictures applied in Soviet-controlled East Europe.

McCarthyism in the United States savaged leading composers on grounds of alleged communism. *Copland's *Lincoln Portrait* was dropped from the inaugu-ration of president Eisenhower; Bernstein had his passport confiscated. In Britain, some composers were ostracized for politi-cal reasons. Alan *Bush, a redoubtable Red, was rarely played on the BBC, and Bernard *Stevens suffered certain constraints. Authoritarianism made it acceptable for the modern state to have a say in music and democracies adopted the prerogative when convenient.

Several statesmen were fine musicians, though none to *Paderewski's standard. Edward Heath, UK Prime Minister 1970-4, conducted orchestras in a limited reper-toire. Helmut Schmidt, West German Chancellor 1974-82, recorded Mozart's three-piano concerto. Viatautis Lands-berghis, first president of post-Soviet Lithuania, was a noted musicologist.

Polonia Elgar's orchestral tribute to a wartime ally. fp: London, 6.vii.15.

Leonid POLOVINKIN   Quirky Russian revolutionary who wrote what was meant to be the *Last Sonata* in 1928 and matched *Mosolov's progress-worship in orchestral *Telescopes* (1926–8). When Stalin imposed conformity, he was reduced to writing children's music and folk-settings.
  b. Kurgan, Russia, 13.vii.1894; *d.* Moscow, 2.ii.49. *works include*: nine symphonies, four string quartets, five piano sonatas.

polyphony   Music in many parts, a multi-layered form of composition that flourished in the choral middle ages. It experienced an unexpected revival in the frugal scores of *Webern and *Boulez, where separate lines of a 12-note series work with and against one another.

polystylism   The use of many styles in a single work, an idea propounded by *Schnittke though previously advanced by *Zimmermann and, to some extent, *Berg. According to Schnitte, 'polystylism guided the avant-garde out of its crisis'.

polytonality   The use of more than one key at the same time, a device patented by Darius *Milhaud in his exotic phase and adopted by some traditional composers trying to avoid the leap into full *atonality.

Manuel (Maria) PONCE   Discovered in mid-life by Andres Segovia who called him 'probably the best composer for the guitar', he produced a Valse (1937) as haunting as *Ravel's and a fine concerto (Montevideo, 4.x.41). But the Mexican was more than just a fretwork artist. He had the misfortune to write a ballad, 'Estrellita' (Little star), without protecting his copyright and heard it sung throughout Latin America while he struggled for subsistence; he ruefully quotes it in the central movement of a bittersweet, unsentimentally folkish violin concerto (Mexico City, 20.viii.43). Other orchestral works, such as the triptych *Chapultepec* (25.viii.29), convey the flavour and culture of his country with an objectivity that stems from travels and studies in Italy, Germany, France, Cuba and the US.
  b. Fresnillo, Mexico, 8.xii.1882; st with his sister – and in Bologna, Berlin and with *Dukas in Paris, graduated from the Ecole Normale de Musique at age 50; worked in Mexico as a music critic, piano teacher and briefly as orchestral director; married a singer, Clema Maurel; *d.* Mexico City, 24.iv.48.

Marcel   POOT   Belgian   composer, favouring tonality and lively rhythms.
  b. Vilvoorde, nr. Brussels, 7.v.01; *d.* Brussels, 12.vi.88. *works include*: seven symphonies, *Poème de l'espace* (inspired by Lindbergh's flight, *ISCM Festival, Liège, 4.ix.30).

popular music   The tunes people whistled on their way to work used to belong either to their folk heritage or to a locally successful show. The manufacture of popular music for worldwide consumption began with the rise of recording in the late 1880s and peaked in radio days when American crooners like Bing Crosby, Perry Como and Frank Sinatra attained international celebrity. *Tin Pan Alley and its song-pluggers worked round the clock to furnish fresh hits. The potential rewards were enormous. Irving *Berlin's soupy 'White Christmas' of 1942 sold 25 million copies as a Crosby single and 100 million in other versions. W. C. Handy's 'St Louis Blues' of 1914 was recorded in 1000 different versions, a feat not repeated until the *Beatles' Tchaikovskian ballad, 'Yesterday'.
  The market for such music crossed barriers of class but not age. Songs were targeted at the over-20s and backed by large bands in impeccable evening dress. There was no hint of rebellion before 1945, even in the supposedly subversive music of the jazz age. Broadway and the West End dictated the pop charts, often with infantile banality. In 1953, the number one slot was occupied for eight weeks by 'How Much is that Doggie in the Window?'
  The arrival of *rock'n'roll transformed the pop scene. The market moved down in age and the songs became sexually and socially explicit. The *Beatles and Bob *Dylan raised standards to heights of sophistication, only to provoke a nihilistic counter-reaction in the form of late-1970s *punk rock. New stars were never in short supply but ideas stagnated after the Beatles. Chart-toppers of the 1990s were the same Paul McCartney, Paul Simon and Mick Jagger who ignited the Sixties.

While pop borrowed shamelessly from art music, there was relatively little traffic the other way. The 1953 Broadway show *Kismet* was constructed from Borodin melodies; the 1939 hit 'Tonight We Love' brazenly stole the opening of Tchaikovsky's B♭-minor piano concerto; in the 1970s a popular hit lifted the big tune from the finale of Saint-Saëns' organ symphony. Some serious musicians paid lip service to pop-age values but the music they performed, *minimalism apart, showed no top ten resonances.

pop video Three-minute collage of manufactured images and mini-dramas designed to make chart music acceptable on television. Its invention is attributed to the British group Queen's split-screen production of 'Bohemian Rhapsody' (1975). Proliferation prompted a non-stop rock network, MTV. The generic spotlighting and cartoon-strip storytelling of pop videos were picked up by opera directors like Peter Sellars and, to some extent, by composers *Adams and *Reich.

Gavriil POPOV Soviet symphonist who raised social issues in music but was crushed by Stalin's detestation of dissonance. His first symphony was condemned in the 1935 purge, his second in 1948. Popov survived by writing film scores (*Leader of Electrification*) and attaching pompous titles and choral sections to his works. The 4th symphony (1949) is titled *Glory to the Fatherland*.
  b. Novocherkassk, Russia, 12.ix.04; *d.* Repino, nr Leningrad, 17.ii.72. *other works*: organ concerto (1970).

Porgy and Bess Gershwin's black opera of love rivalry. fp: Boston, 30.ix.35.

pornophony Critic's term describing the sexual congress in Shostakovich's opera *A Lady Macbeth of the Mtsensk District*.

portable music During the First World War, Decca's lightweight gramophone machine brought music to the trenches and established the idea that aural pleasure need not be kept indoors. Wireless radiograms and car radios took the concept a stage further. True portability arrived c. 1980 with Sony's *Walkman players.

Cole (Albert) PORTER The only non-Jew among top Broadway balladeers, he was born rich and married richer still, composing for pleasure rather than need. His finest inspirations required no great voice – 'Miss Otis Regrets', 'Night and Day', 'What is this Thing Called Love?' Enamoured of Paris, where he enlisted in the Foreign Legion and took composition lessons from d'*Indy, he caroused there through the 20s and 30s until a horse fell on him in 1937, shattering his legs and leaving him chairbound. The Parisian songs in *Can-Can* (1953) are tinged with regret; *Kiss Me Kate* (1948) was, bar for bar, his outstanding musical show.
  b. Peru, Indiana, 9.vi.1891; *d.* Santa Monica, California, 15.x.64. *other hits*: 'Beguine the Beguine', 'I Get a Kick out of You', 'True Love' (from the movie *High Society*).

Quincy PORTER US composer of ten clever contrapuntal string quartets.
  b. New Haven, Connecticut, 7.ii.1897; st with d'*Indy and *Bloch; taught Cleveland 1922–32, Vassar 1932–8 and Yale 1946–65; dir. Boston's New England Conservatory 1942–6; *d.* Bethany, Connecticut, 12.xi.66. *other works*: *Ukrainian Suite* for strings (1925), two symphonies.

post-minimalism *Adams and *Reich abandoned obsessive repetition in the mid-1980s, adopting disciplined melodism in *Nixon in China* and *Different Trains*.

post-modernism An anti-serialist reaction arose during the 1970s as composers sought less austere methods. Some reverted to *neo-romanticism, others to *minimalism, bringing diatonic scales back into common usage. Careers that were blighted by the Boulezian hegemony began to revive. *Panufnik, whose music was banned on the BBC for a decade, declared: 'I shall belong to the end of the century when no single style predominates.'

Elizabeth POSTON A senior BBC executive, she composed classified works in music code for transmission to Europe during World War Two. In peacetime, she edited folk and church songs and wrote neo-classical chamber music. She worked closely with the novelist E. M. Forster and the poet Dylan Thomas.

b. nr.Walken, Herts, UK, 24.x.05; *d.* Stevenage, Herts, 18.iii.87.

Francis POULENC A fabulous melodist, *Fauré's natural heir, his larger works are marred by flippancy. The piano concerto (Boston, 7.i.50) opens with an irresistible tune, skips around it for a few bars, wallows in a little kitsch, returns somewhat distractedly to the source, then wanders off in a Rachmaninov pastiche; its central movement is a five-minute frolic, the finale a 'rondeau à la française' that gets sidetracked into 'Way down upon the Swanee River'. There seems to be some fault with the composer's attention span.

Poulenc's light-headedness stemmed from *Satie, his eclecticism from *Stravinsky. He was a product of post-1918 Paris, a member of Les *Six and, by definition, an enemy of convention: *trois mouvements perpetuels* (1918) play merry havoc with the formal piano recital. But contrariness was more than just a matter of *Zeitgeist*; it was part of his nature – 'a mixture of triviality and nobility', according to the baritone Pierre Bernac. He was both ascetic and glutton, devout Catholic and sexual deviant; he courted the commonplace but was easily bored. He was the acme of elegance, whom *Cocteau caricatured (to his approval) as a pig. He once described himself as Janus-Poulenc: two-faced.

The concerto for organ, timpani and strings (Paris, 21.vi.39) was a burst of mid-life religiosity that avoided sanctimony with fierce wit and a feral allegro. Built on a fantasia by the Danish master, Buxtehude, it is the only work of its kind to achieve concert permanence. Among other sacramental works, the *Gloria* (Boston, 20.i.61), commemorating Serge *Koussevitsky, was more popular abroad than in France, where its gaiety, bebop rhythms and Vivaldi echoes were considered suspect.

A moneyed habitué of literary salons, Poulenc was 24 when *Diaghilev commissioned the ambisexual ballet *Les Biches* (Mont Carlo, 6.i.24), which flits musically from Scarlatti to Stravinsky with obeisances to Mozart, a fundamentally facile score infused with worldly melancholy.

Aubade (Paris, 19.vi.29), his next ballet, was a concerto for piano and 18 instruments. Written for a fancy-dress party, it arrives portentously, raises spirits in a skittish keyboard run and shimmies though a variety of impersonations to a trick ending. The *Sinfonietta*, his only substantial work for orchestra, has the weight and nutritional substance of a well-made soufflé.

His three operas veer from the androgynously satirical *Les Mamelles de Tirésias* (*Tiresias' Tits*, after Guillaume Apollinaire; Paris, 3.vi.47) to the irreproachably sublime *Dialogues of the Carmelites* (La Scala, 26.i.57). The third, *La voix humaine* (*The human voice*, after Cocteau; Paris, 6.ii.59), is a telephone monologue for a woman jilted by her lover, concluding when she strangles herself with the cord.

The acme of Poulenc's art is found in 137 exquisite *mélodies* and delicate pianisms like the *Soirées de Nazelles* (1930–36) and the lovely Novelettes (1927–8). His 32 cycles for light baritone or soprano, mostly use modern French poems – from the epigrammatic to the epic – of which he had an intuitive understanding. He rarely sings out loud; nastiness is implied in the interplay of voice and piano. He used to say: 'Above all, do not analyse my music. Love it!'

In his very last works for piano and flute (1956), horn (1957), oboe (1962) and clarinet, Poulenc touched the summits of chamber music. The flute sonata weaves arpeggios around his recent song on Robert Desnos' 'Dernière Poème', written before the poet's death in a Nazi concentration camp. Its themes pervade the *Elegie* for horn and piano (1957) composed in memory of the British virtuoso Dennis Brain. The clarinet sonata, commemorating *Honegger, quotes from *Gloria* while the oboe sonata mourns Prokofiev in a quote from *Romeo and Juliet*. Both sonatas contain premonitions of his own imminent death.

b. Paris, 7.i.1899, son of founder of Rhône-Poulenc chemicals conglomerate; st with *Koechlin and Debussyist pianist Riccardo Vines; Army service 1918–21; never married; *d.* Paris, 30.i.63. *other works: Concert champêtre* for harpsichord and orch. (Paris, 3.v.29), concerto for two pianos (Venice, 5.ix.32), Sinfonietta (London, 24.x.48);

Stabat Mater (Strasbourg, 13.vi.51); *Le Bal masqué* for voice, oboe, clarinet, bassoon, violin, cello, percussion and piano (1932); *Suite française* for nine winds, percussion and harpsichord (1935); *Babar, the little elephant* (1940–45), children's entertainment for voice and piano, orch. 1962 by *Françaix. *Bib*: Pierre Bernac, *Francis Poulenc, the man and his songs*, London (Gollancz), 1977.

Henri (Léon Marie Thérèse) POUSSEUR Early (1951) follower of *Boulez, he ran the Belgian branch of the *avant-garde. He attempted extreme contrasts of pitch and dynamics but had no single work to represent a personal style, with the possible exception of the laryngeal *Phonemes for Cathy* (*Berberian). In *Couleurs croisées* (1967) he wrote orchestral variations on the US civil rights song 'We Shall Overcome'. His opera *Votre Faust* (1969) has events that are governed by audience choice; many later works have been spun off from the opera, to give a Boulezian impression of a never finished work. Pousseur is known as much for his polemical writings as for his music.
b. Malmédy, Belgium, 23.vi.29; co-founded Brussels electronic studio, 1958; taught Darmstadt, Cologne, Buffalo (1966–69), Liège; *other works*: *Electre* – 'action musicale' after Sophocles (1966), symphonies for 15 soloists (1955), *Répons* for seven instruments (1960), quintet (1955), Ode for string quartet (1961), *Nuits des Nuits* for orch. (1985), *Traverser la forêt*, cantata (1987).

John POWELL Returning from piano lessons in Vienna with Theodore Leschetizky, Powell was engrossed by the Deep South. He composed a *Rapsodie nègre* (NY, 23.iii.18) for piano and orch., inspired by Joseph Conrad's *Heart of Darkness*, and spent the rest of his life collecting southern folksongs.
b. Richmond, Virginia, 6.ix.1882; *d*. Charlottesville, Virginia, 15.viii.63.

Mel POWELL Pianist and arranger in Benny Goodman and Glenn Miller bands, Powell took daytime composing lessons with *Wagenaar and *Schillinger. He sat in on *Hindemith's Yale class of 1948 and developed a *neo-classical style with a strong jazz undercurrent and occasional atonalities. As a Yale professor (1957–69), he set up an electronics studio and encouraged experimentation; in 1969 he founded the California Institute of the Arts. *Duplicates*, his concerto for two pianos, won the 1990 Pulitzer Prize on *Previn's recommendation.
b. NY, 12.ii.23; *other works*: *Haiku Settings* (1960) for soprano and piano; *Immobiles* (1966) for orch. and electronic tape; string quartet (1982).

prepared piano In 1938, while writing a ballet, *Bacchanale*, John *Cage was unable to get the percussive sound he wanted until he inserted screws, paperclips and other household objects between the strings of a concert grand. 'Very quickly I produced a whole new range of sounds. In fact, the piano had become a percussion ensemble controllable by one player,' he wrote.
The rape of a fine instrument outraged traditionalists and became a totem of post-War avantgardism. Cage wrote 16 Sonatas and four Interludes for prepared piano (1946–8), and a formal concerto (1950), but though *Boulez endorsed the prepared piano, few composed for it.

Elvis (Aron) PRESLEY Country crooner who blended Southern US courtesy with black rhythm-and-blues in a potent melodic mixture which, delivered with pelvic thrusts, aroused feminine hysteria in pre-*Beatles *pop concerts. Weaned from explosive Little Richard hits, he was channelled by a cautious manager and record company into smooch ballads ('Love Me Tender', 'Are You Lonesome Tonight') and trash films, dissolving slowly into a barbiturate stupor. Although eclipsed by Sixties bands, Presley led the first wave of teenaged musical rebellion.
b. Tupelo, Mississippi, 8.i.35; *d*. Memphis, Tennessee, 16.viii.77. *other hits*: 'Heartbreak Hotel', 'Blue Suede Shoes', 'Good Luck Charm', 'Return to Sender', 'In the Ghetto'.

André PREVIN Hollywood-trained musician who won Oscars for his film arrangements, Previn became a conductor of top orchestras and an eclectic composer. Aside from some blues and popular songs written with his second wife, Dory Previn, his works are mostly orchestral. The guitar concerto (London, ix.71; John Williams soloist) recalls his teacher *Castelnuovo-Tedesco; the virtuosic piano concerto (Cardiff, 12.vi.85; Vladimir Ashkenazy, soloist) falls in no-man's-land between Rachmaninov and Prokofiev. Other concertos are for cello (1967) and horn (1968). He produced symphonic accompaniment for a successful Tom Stoppard play on Soviet psychiatric abuse, *Every Good Boy Deserves Favour* (1977), its initials forming a famous musical mnemonic. His third wife (of four) was the movie star Mia Farrow.

> *b.* Berlin 6.iv.29 of Russo-Jewish parentage as Andreas Ludwig Priwin; st at Hochschule für Musik until 1938, then with *Dupré in Paris; moved 1939 to Los Angeles where his uncle was music director at Universal Studios; US citizen 1943; st conducting with Pierre Monteux; cond. St Louis SO 1962–67; Houston SO 1967–69; London SO 1968–79; Royal Philharmonic Orchestra 1985–91; Pittsburgh SO 1976–86; Los Angeles Philharmonic 1986–90; *other works*: *Principals* (for orch. 1980), *Reflections* (for orch. 1981), Divertimento (1982); piano preludes, chamber music, songs.

André PREVOST   A pupil of *Messiaen and Dutilleux, Prévost led French Canadian music with more than 60 compositions, among which a six-minute *Scherzo* for string orchestra (1960) belies its 12-tone seriousness with a self-mocking sense of instrumental fun.

> *b.* Ontario, Canada, 20.vii.34; prof. U. of Montreal, 1964– ; *other works*: *Fantasmes* for orchestra (1966), cello concerto (1976).

programme music Symphonic works with descriptive titles, rejected by *Mahler around 1900, persisted through Strauss, Skryabin and Nielsen. They were virtually extinct by the 1930s, when Stalin revived the principle for works of Socialist Realism.

programming The process of preparing *computer music.

progressive jazz The heirs of Charlie *Parker – Stan Getz, Dave Brubeck, Stan Kenton.

Carl PROHASKA Born in the house where Beethoven wrote his Missa Solemnis, Prohaska was a friend and fond imitator of Brahms. His son Felix (1912–87) was a well-known conductor.

> *b.* Mödling, lower Austria, 25.iv.1869; *d.* Vienna 28.iii.27. *works*: opera *Madeleine Guinard*, oratorio *Frühlingsfeier* (1913).

Sergei PROKOFIEV The music is unmistakable, the motives inexplicable. It is impossible to divine what Prokofiev

wanted from art or life, beyond the desire to be left in peace. He was a victim of Russian history and his own indecision – a torment that invests his intimate music with singular pathos.

Prokofiev's melodic gifts were unique. No-one else could have written *Romeo and Juliet* and the 5th symphony, or the tunes in his movie scores for Sergei Eisenstein's *Alexander Nevsky* (1938) and *Ivan the Terrible* (1945). That fountain of creativity was allied to a meticulous precision, a mathematical exactitude worthy of a *Webern. 'Prokofiev works like a clock,' noted Eisenstein. He planned his schedule of work a year in advance and kept to it come what may. The composing machine concealed his feelings and the man's character remains elusive.

He arose in St Petersburg just behind *Stravinsky, and showed an alternative, though no less savage, face of Russian paganism in the *Scythian Suite* (29.i.16). He offended delicate ears with a spiky piano concerto (Moscow, 7.vii.12) and assuaged them with the pastiche of a *Classical Symphony* (Petrograd, 21.iv.18), as

Bolshevism began to bite. Conflict between a need to explore and pressure to conform was the engine of his creative friction.

Days after his symphonic debut, he emigrated. For the next 15 years he lived mainly in France, spending extended periods in the US. He acquired tastes for jazz, gourmet food and expensive silks, but longed for Mother Russia and went home just as Stalin started to persecute the arts. His last two decades were lived in fear of a midnight knock at the door. His Spanish wife, Lina Llubera, whom he married in 1923 and left in 1945, was sent to Siberia and his sons were made wards of the state, apparently as hostages for his good conduct.

In the 1948 purge, he was accused with *Shostakovich and *Khatchaturian of the crime of *formalism after his sixth symphony failed to resound with victorious jubilation. Prokofiev abased himself before the party, but articulated a truthful musical credo: 'I never had the slightest doubt of the importance of melody and consider it by far the most important element in music. Nothing is more difficult than to discover a melody which would be immediately understandable even to the uninitiated listener and, at the same time, be original.'

He was both fertile and versatile, reaching a mass public with *Romeo and Juliet* (Brno, Czechoslovakia, 30.xii.38) and the children's entertainment *Peter and the Wolf* (Moscow, 2.v.36) without compromising his modernist principles. He would pile note upon note to build a huge orchestral chord whose timbre was both agreeable and intriguing. From *Lieutenant Kijé* (1934) onwards, his movie scores added a dimension to Soviet cinema, suggesting the emergence of a socialist *Gesamtkunstwerk*.

His taste for experiment found scope in opera, where he flitted from one style to another, evading classification and the credit he deserved. After four juvenile attempts, the earliest at nine years old, he adapted Dostoyevsky's morality tale *The Gambler* for the Maryinsky Theatre headed by the English conductor, Albert Coates. Completing it in early 1917 with such concentration that he failed to notice the revolution, he faced a singers' rebellion and new management and could not get the opera staged for a dozen years. It was finally performed in Brussels (29.iv.29) with a French text and scaled-down instrumentation, and was not seen in the USSR until 1963. What Prokofiev had aimed to produce was the first dialogue opera in Russian, devoid of hackneyed arias and underpinned by a rich orchestration whose themes introduce the individual characters – the tutor, Alexei, by a variant of 'Happy Birthday' – and the hypnotic spinning of the roulette wheel. The music, sprinkled with anti-Germanisms and sardonic Beethoven quotations, is more involving than the action and was subsequently made into a strong symphonic suite (Paris, 12.iii.32); it contains uncanny anticipations of Shostakovich's rowdy *Lady Macbeth* realism.

His next project, conceived with Meyerhold at Coates' home, was meant to smash the convention that opera audiences may not laugh out loud. *The Love for Three Oranges*, a 1761 *commedia dell'arte* in which a prince has to be shaken out of his hypochondria by a fit of giggles, employs ladies' knickers, faked citrus fruit and much flatulence – but not enough music to sustain the jokes. The opera was premièred in Chicago (30.xii.21) and is much enjoyed by children; its brilliant march was turned into another successful suite (Paris, 29.xi.25).

The third opera, which he considered his finest, waited 30 years for a posthumous production. *The Fiery Angel* (composed 1922–3; staged Venice, 14.ix.55) is a five-act Faustian parable of good and evil with an atmospheric score, much of which found its way into his 3rd symphony (Paris, 17.v.29; cond. Monteux). The summit of his dramatic ambition was *War and Peace*, which he started writing in 1941 and continued revising until he died, leaving a 13-scene epic (eight of the scenes premièred in Leningrad, 12.vi.46) and an 11-scene reduction (26.v.53). Both are burdened by dramatic inconsistencies and a huge cast which a committed director and enlightened subsidy can overcome; the music is magniloquent and the opera gains adherents with each infrequent appearance; it was chosen to inaugurate the Sydney Opera House in 1973.

Two of his Soviet operas are overtly propagandistic, though neither pleased his masters. *Semyon Kotko* (23.vi.40), based on a novel called *I, Son of the Working Class*, lost its director Meyerhold to the secret police in mid-rehearsal; *The Story of a Real Man*, about a legless aviator, was withdrawn after a private Leningrad showing in December 1948 and not seen again until 1960. Both are tuneful without being as simplistic as the craven efforts of other cowed composers, or indeed of Prokofiev's own 60th birthday offering to Stalin, entitled *Zdravitsa!* (21.xii.39).

In his only other opera, *The Duenna* (after Sheridan; Leningrad, 3.xi.46) and the Soviet-era ballets – notably *Cinderella* (21.xi.45) and *The Stone Flower* (12.ii.54) – Prokofiev walked the tightrope of populism without succumbing to musical simple-mindedness or kitsch. Never one to waste a good tune, Prokofiev recycled his ballets and operas into piano suites.

His popular appeal brought inevitable sneers from highbrow critics, who found ready ammunition in the unevenness of his symphonic output. For some reason, the odd-numbered symphonies and piano concertos are better than the even ones, and several works tail off in mid-movement, as if the composer had lost interest but was determined to fulfil his quota. The Classical Symphony is a tour de force for conductorless ensemble, written *à la* Haydn but with modern harmonies and fidgety rhythms – a style that was revived and parodied by *Schnittke.

The 2nd symphony in D minor (Paris 6.vi.25) represents Paris in the Roaring Twenties. It has two structured movements, an *Allegro* and theme and variations, on the lines of Beethoven's last piano sonata, but possesses the picaresque detachment of film music. The 3rd symphony (Paris, 17.v.29) quotes Beethoven and Chopin's funeral march sonata; the 4th, in both its revisions – op. 47 of 1930 and op. 122 of 1947 – is an unwholesome mess, piecing together used and unused bits of *The Prodigal Son* (Paris, 21.v.29), a ballet he wrote for *Diaghilev.

The 5th (13.i.45), his 100th opus, was written within sight of victory in Europe and hope in Russia; two *Allegro* movements sway to infectious rhythms and the *Adagio* recalls the captivating love-theme of *Romeo and Juliet*. Ostensibly a celebration of the human spirit in war, it betrayed a bitterness in the two *Allegros* that reflected Prokofiev's deepening disenchantment with the USSR. Despite the vivacity of his melodies, little optimism was to be heard.

In the 6th Symphony (Leningrad, 11.xi.47) darkness returns, all hope abandoned until a disconnected finale reverts to classical vivacity. The 7th (11.x.52), his response to the state attacks that ruined his health and reduced him to penury, is deeply touching in the understated tragedy of its opening – Shostakovich without the coruscating irony.

The five piano concertos were written before he was 40, four of them for himself to play as soloist. Both pre-1914 works terrified audiences. The 1st was condemned as the work of 'a musical madman who should be put in a straitjacket', its youthful vigour mistaken for nihilism. The 2nd (Pavlovsk, 5.ix.23) was angrier and less coherent; it left one critic 'frozen with fright, hair standing on end'. The score was burned in Russia and reconstructed in Paris.

The 3rd concerto was his international visiting-card (Chicago, 16.xii.21) rich in *Love for Three Oranges* lyricism and with an unforgettable clarinet introduction. The 4th (Berlin, 5.ix.56) was a left-hand concerto written for the disabled Paul Wittgenstein, who put it in a drawer for 25 years. The 5th, in five movements, was poorly received (Berlin, 31.x.32, composer soloist, Furtwängler cond.) and was not revealed until the Russian pianist Sviatoslav Richter took it up. It amounted to a summary and commentary on all he had written before, running the gamut of spiky cross-beats, violent marches, thumping chords and silken, song-like reflections.

Richter played a vital role in his late sonatas for solo piano. Of the earlier sonatas, the 2nd (1912) is scabrous, while the 4th (1917) broods on the memory of a pianist friend who committed suicide, lapsing into a Rachmaninov-like melancholy in the central movement. With the 6th (1940), Prokofiev began using the keyboard as a means of private introspection. The 7th sonata, begun at the same time and played by Richter on 18.i.43, is like entering a prison cell and fingering the absent occupant's meagre possessions, some sentimental, others dangerous. It was perceived in the same way as Shostakovich's secretly-coded quartets, although Prokofiev intended no defiance. The last of his war trilogy, the 8th sonata (1944), was premiered by Emil Gilels and amounts to a calm anticipation of better things. In the 9th sonata (1947), the last such illusions are definitively dispelled.

David *Oistrakh was similarly involved with his violin output. Two concertos were acknowledged as masterpieces by the time their friendship began – the romantic and virtuosic 1st (Paris, 18.x.23) stemming from the lyrical overflow of 1917 and the 2nd (Madrid, 1.xii.35), written just after his return to Russia and brimming with Mendelssohnian tunes and fiendish tricks for the soloist. Oistrakh gave the premières, in reverse order, of two sonatas for violin and piano (23.x.42 and 17.vi.44), the 2nd being a transcription of an unheeded sonata for flute and piano. Both works contain a warmth and wit long absent from his grander scores.

The last of his collaborators was the cellist Mstislav *Rostropovich with whom he revised a twice-aborted concerto into the majestic and contemplative Sinfonia Concertante (Copenhagen, 9.xii.54), one of the few important modern creations for cello and orchestra, though it, too, is not without meandering moments.

Both the worlds that Prokofiev inhabited claimed him as their own. Russians said that all his greatest works were made in the motherland; westerners underlined the abiding impact of Paris and jazz. He was certainly the most cosmopolitan and self-confident of Russian composers, secure enough in his identity to avoid the liturgical quotations of *Rachmaninov and *Stravinsky, and possessing greater inventive resources than *Shostakovich. A chess fanatic who played the world champions Lasker, Capabanca and Botvinnik, he had

marvellous attacking strategies and paid no heed whatever to defence.

b. Sontskova, Ekaterinoslav, 27.iv.1891; st with Gliere, Rimsky-Korsakov and Liadov in St Petersburg; lived abroad 1918–33; *d.* Moscow 5.iii.53, on the same day as Stalin. *other major works*: ballets *Ala and Lolly* (1914), *Chout* (Paris, 17.v.21), *Le Pas d'acier* (*The leap of steel* – a tribute to Soviet industrialization – Paris 7.vi.27), *Sur le Borysthène* (Paris 16.xii.32); *Autumn* (symphonic tableau, 1911), Sinfonietta (1914), suites from all the operas and ballets, Russian Overture (29.x.36), The Year 1941 (1943), *Ode on the End of War* (London 1946), *Festive Poem* (3.x.47), *Ivan the Terrible* suite (from Eisenstein film score, 1942–45), *The Meeting of the Volga with the Don River* (for completion of a canal, 22.ii.52); overture on Hebrew Themes for clarinet, string quartet and piano (NY, 26.i.20), two string quartets (1931, 1941), sonata for two violins (27.xi.32), *Visions fugitives* for piano (1915–17) and many keyboard transcriptions. *Bib*: Oleg Prokofiev, *Sergei Prokofiev, Soviet Diary and other Writings*, London (Faber), 1991.

Prometheus Symphony by *Skryabin subtitled 'The Poem of Fire' and intended to be performed with the accompaniment of a *colour organ that would change hue according to the musical mood: fp: Moscow, 15.iii.11.

Psalmus Hungaricus National-religious cantata by *Kodály. fp: Budapest, 19.xi.23.

psychedelic rock Music composed under the influence of marijuana and LSD.

publishing Music publishers once grew rich on the sale of songs and piano pieces for playing in the parlour. When domestic music-making declined, they relied on copyright and performing right royalties. Some, like Ricordi of Milan, were bolstered by enduringly popular operas. Others invested in new creativity. *Universal Edition was set up specifically to promote new composers in 1901 and built the largest and most prosperous catalogue of 20th-century music from Mahler and Janáček to Berio and Birtwistle. Its directors Emil Hertzka (1869–1932) and Alfred Kalmus (1889–1972) became midwives to modernism.

Composers like *Ives who could not find a publisher would sometimes publish their own scores. Henry *Cowell set up New Music, a co-operative venture for undiscovered US colleagues. Britten co-founded Faber Music (with Donald Mitchell), while Stockhausen started an imprint for himself.

Giacomo (Antonio Domenico Michele Secondo Maria) PUCCINI The last giant of Italian opera flourished in the *fin-*

de-siècle when everything he wrote turned ochre. After Wagner's irresistible potion of love and death, he devised an unsubtle mix of sex and sadism, darkened by two or three arias of unforgettable poignancy. Superior minds derided his lurid topics and harmonic naïvety, but Puccini was not accountable to sophisticates. His gift was

milk the last drop of tension from a melodrama by adding a pertinent musical ingredient. Scholars might mock, but *Mahler approved and *Berg admired and took note.

Descended from five generations of church musicians at Lucca, Puccini wrote his first opera, *Le Villi*, at the age of 24, and saw it staged within a year, to Verdi's acclamation. *Edgar* (1889) was a self-confessed 'blunder' but with *Manon Lescaut* (1893) he found the formula of taking a proven theatrical hit and turning it into an opera of oppressive decadence, attaining the kind of sexual tension for which *Strauss was still vainly searching.

The next three operas were masterpieces, forged in a combustible alliance with Luigi Illica (1857–1919), who reworked an existing stage-play with fresh scenes, and Giuseppe Giacosa (1847–1906) who versified the text. *La Bohème* (1896), adapted in a race against *Leoncavallo from Henry Murger's Parisian drama, perplexed audiences at first with its conversational manner and occasional dissonances. It became the most popular opera of the age, with every diva from Melba onwards dying to depict the consumptive Mimi.

Tosca (Rome, 14.i.1900) ventured into a gruesome *verismo*, replete with torture, rape and murder. Puccini scored the violence with pentatonic passages that foretold *Butterfly* and *Turandot*, and provided a coruscating first-act conclusion in which the villainous Scarpia plans his sexual assault against the backdrop of a choral Te Deum. Perpetually self-dissatisfied, Puccini talked of dropping the star aria, 'Vissi d'arte', because it delayed the action.

Madama Butterfly (Milan, 17.ii.04), the tale of a geisha girl and her American officer, was taken from a real-life incident dramatized for the London stage by David Belasco. Suspicions that Puccini was pandering to his audience's lowest instincts were again proved unfounded when the first night dissolved in uproar, partly inspired by rival composers but at root derived from public incomprehension. Puccini withdrew it for a swift revision to a taut three-act version; second time round, the delicate eastern melismas worked a tender magic.

Giacosa's death and a domestic tragi-comedy derailed Puccini at the height of his fame; he did not regain mastery until his dying year. The suicide of a servant girl, following charges by Puccini's wife that she was his mistress, led to prolonged court hearings and public scandal. *Strauss might have used it as soap-opera but Puccini was disconcerted and turned to America in *The Girl of the Golden West* (NY Metropolitan Opera, 10.xii.10, cond. Toscanini), based on another Belasco stage-play. It proved too remote from reality to hold the attention.

A breach with his publisher Ricordi led to another misadventure, writing an operetta, *La Rondine*, for Vienna, though it moved in wartime to Monte Carlo (27.iii.17). *Il trittico* (NY, 14.xii.18), a triptych of short operas, missed the mark in all but its comic central panel, *Gianni Schicchi*, which is often staged on its own. The antics of a medieval Florentine rogue had much in common with *Verdi's *Falstaff* and *Stravinsky's dawning interest in early Italian cultures.

Like other composers in the aftermath of war, Puccini sought a new path and found it in *Turandot*, the most unrealistic of all his plots. Based on an 18th-century Venetian play of an imaginary China, it told of a court in which suitors were beheaded unless they answered three riddles (shades of Gilbert and Sullivan's *Mikado*).

Puccini furnished *Turandot* with urgent yearnings in a score whose pentatonic plangency recalls something of Mahler's *Das *Lied von der Erde*. Its tenor aria, 'Nessun dorma', a contemplation of dawn and love, explodes in a proclamation of anticipated triumph. Its composer did not live to see it, dying after unsuccessful surgery for throat cancer. The opera was performed initially as he left it (Milan, 25.iv.26, cond. *Toscanini) and subsequently in a completion by *Alfano which many find too long.

b. Lucca, Italy, 23.xii.1858; *d.* Brussels, 29.xi.24. *other works*: *Crysantemi* string quartet (1890), *Capriccio sinfonico* (1883), songs and various fragments collated by Ricordi.
Bib: Mosco Carner, *Puccini*, London 1958/74.

Pulcinella *Stravinsky's *neo-classical breakthrough ballet, based on Pergolesi and other 18th-century scores and depicting a *commedia dell'arte* knockabout. fp: Paris, 15.v.20.

Punch and Judy *Birtwistle's first opera, based on fairground entertainment; its brutal sights and sounds made *Britten walk out. fp: Aldeburgh, 8.vi.68.

punk rock Nihilistic response to over-sophisticated *rock music, punk was loud, fast, foul-mouthed and tuneless. Originating in the US and reaching a mid-70s peak with UK bands like the Sex Pistols, performers and fans wore torn clothing, spiky hairdos and safety pins through their skin. Gothic lettering and Nazi regalia were intrinsic. The genre faded around 1980 with the heroin death of Pistols star Sid Vicious but survived in eastern Europe as an underground anti-communist phenomenon.

Tauno (Kullervo) PYLKKÄNEN *Verismist of Finnish opera with ten staged works, of which *The Shadow* (1952) was seen abroad. He was artistic director of Finnish National Opera throughout the 1960s.

b. Helsinki, 22.iii.18; *d.* there, 13.iii.80. *other works*: symphonic poems *Summer in Lapland* (1941) and *Kullervo Goes to War* (1942), symphony (1945), cello concerto (1950), various song cycles.

quarter-tone *Microtonal interval, half-way between two semitones on a violin and unattainable on a normal piano. *Bartók composed quarter-tones in his string quartets; *Hába used them as a basis for microtonal music.

quartet The string quartet in the 20th century moved from the drawing room to the concert hall as amateur musicianship declined and scores became tougher. Even in public, however, the quartet remained for many composers their most intimate means of expression. *Shostakovich, in his cycle of 15, voiced personal anxieties and political dissent more acutely than in his symphonies; for Soviet musicians, the quartet became a kind of samizdat, or secret writing. *Bartók, in his series of six, wrote some of his most intense and incisive music, altering the form in various respects. Their sets are cornerstones of the 20th century quartet, as Beethoven's and Schubert's were of the 19th.

The medium yielded manifold masterpieces. Among them: *Janáček's two letters to his love, Ravel's F-major, Zemlinsky's 2nd, Schoenberg's 4th, Britten's 2nd, *Schnittke's 3rd.

In mid-century, the tendency to introspection became technically ingrown as composers took their cue from Webern's opus 28. Carter and *Ferneyhough wrote quartets of crossword complexity, Cage and Ligeti played private games. This retreat was reversed in the 1980s by flamboyant mass-performance artists like *Kronos who played modern music of great immediacy. Their espousal of *Crumb, *Riley and *Reich revived the quartet as an instant medium, almost a living newspaper of new music.

Quatuor pour la fin du temps (*Quartet for the end of time*) *Messiaen's serenely apocalyptic vision written for clarinet, violin, cello and piano in a German prisoner-of-war camp and performed there on 15.i.41.

A Quiet Place Opera by *Bernstein, incorporating his previous opera *Trouble in Tahiti*. fp: Houston, 17.vi.83.

Roger QUILTER Member of the Frankfurt Gang, he wrote moody songs of pastel coloration, mostly rooted in English folklore. He also turned out high quality incidental music for the London theatre, most exquisitely for *Where the Rainbow Ends* (Savoy, 21.xii.1911). His orch. *Shakespeare Songs* (1905) are charming. Heir to a fortune, he lived a bachelor's existence in St John's Wood, north-west London.

    b. Brighton, 1.ix.1877; st with Iwan Knorr in Frankfurt alongside Graingner, Scott and Gardiner; *d*. London, 21.ix.53. *other works:* opera, *Julia* (1935); Children's Overture (1910).

Hector QUINTANAR Mexican avant-gardist, allegedly the first to write an electronic film score.

    b. Mexico City, 15.iv.36; st with *Chavez and at Columbia U.; *other works:* three symphonies, viola concerto (1963), string trio and various tape compositions.

Jan RÄÄTS Estonian symphonist, in the manner of *Shostakovich.
   b. Tartu, Estonia, 15.x.32; st with *Eller; head of music on Estonian radio 1958–66, TV 1966–; *works include*: eight symphonies, concertos, oratorio.

Henri RABAUD A figure of authority in Paris, he ran the Opéra through the First War and the Conservatoire into the Second (1922–41); he was conductor of the Boston Symphony Orchestra, 1918–19. He made his name as a composer with a pseudo-oriental opera, *Mârouf, Shoemaker of Cairo* (Paris, 15.v.14) and a popular orchestration of *Fauré's Dolly Suite. He wrote two symphonies and a symphonic poem, Nocturnal Procession (Paris, 8.i. 1898).
   b. Paris, 10.xi.1873; *d.* there, 11.ix.49.

Sergei RACHMANINOV (also spelt **RACHMANINOFF, RAKHMANI-NOV**) The most performed and most imitated concerto of the century was conceived in a four-year fit of depression and completed under the influence of a hypnotist, to whom it is dedicated. Shattered by the public failure of his first symphony (St Petersburg, 15.iii.1897, cond. *Glazunov) and dejected still further by a meeting with Tolstoy, Rachmaninov's mind was finally eased in the spring of 1900 by Dr Nikolai Dahl, a physician and amatur cellist. He rushed into a second piano concerto in C minor (Moscow, 9.xi.01, cond. Siloti), which became his calling-card as one of the most popular composers and pianists in history. Its lure lay more in mood than in melody, although there is no shortage of tunes; and, while the pianism was showy, it

too served as part of an all-enfolding ambience. The music seemed to tug in opposing emotional directions, invoking an unattainable ideal alongside a personal sense of loss. This made it the perfect backdrop for lovers' partings on the Hollywood screen where it was copied shamelessly, and a box-office draw at the concert hall where pastiches similarly abounded; the B♭ second theme of the finale was particularly envied.

   Like most great art, the concerto did not spring fully-formed from a void. The pounding chords of its unforgettable opening can be heard at the end of the 19-year-old Rachmaninov's first hit, the C♯-minor prelude of 1892 which, played backwards, sounds curiously like the concerto. A brooding Russianness, often expressed in snatches of Orthodox liturgy, pervaded much of his music. Whatever he wrote was instantly identifiable as Rachmaninov, always the test of a good composer. Yet many arbiters, among them successive editors of Grove's dictionary, found him impossibly lowbrow and concluded that his appeal was likely to fade. It shows no sign yet of abating among Anglo-Americans and East Europeans, although it never had the same grip on continental western Europe.

In Rachmaninov, the second of everything turned out best – the 2nd concerto, symphony, piano sonata. His first efforts, generally of the 1890s, were fallible and later heavily revised. His fertility began with the success of the 2nd concerto and was ended with the outbreak of war. The 2nd symphony in E minor, which staked his claim as a symphonist (St Petersburg, 8.ii.08, cond. Rachmaninov), wiped out memories of its predecessor with a morbidly compelling opening theme. Its pessimism is dispelled by a finale that hovers on the very borderline of kitsch.

The 3rd piano concerto (NY, 28.xi.09) was written for his first American tour and and conducted there by Walter Damrosch and Mahler, with the composer as soloist. It was determinedly upbeat, as if he knew that the US public would not tolerate defeatism. Its objectivity makes it, structurally and creatively, the most confident and accomplished of his concerted works. The main theme may have originated in a Kiev monastery.

Inextricably Russian, Rachmaninov enjoyed a complex relationship with his motherland. The son of hard-up nobility, he was sent as a child to board with the rigorist, probably paedophile, piano teacher Nikolai Zverev, and was helped early in his Moscow career by his cousin, the conductor Alexander Siloti. However, once his works became known abroad, Rachmaninov spent less and less time in Russia.

He moved his family to Dresden in 1906, back to Russia in 1910, out again to Rome and Berlin in 1913 and back for the duration of the War – until the revolution prompted permanent exile in December 1917. He refrained from criticizing bolshevism until 1931 and, apart from a two-year ban at that time, was consistently performed and admired in Moscow. In exile, he vacillated between Europe and America, finally building a villa on the banks of Lake Lucerne in Switzerland, but moving again on the eve of the Second World War to America.

Like Stravinsky, but for many years longer, Rachmaninov was rendered impotent by expatriation. In common with his compatriot, though less schematically, he found salvation in *neo-classicism. From 1917 to 1931, his only significant new score was a 4th piano concerto in G minor (Philadelphia, 18.iii.1927), which he had sketched out in Russia and held in readiness for a rainy day. Its brittle harmonies and unconcealed anxieties, wrapped around a central dirge that resembled the nursery rhyme 'Three Blind Mice', were too perplexing for its American audience, and he withdrew the concerto for drastic revision.

He emerged from writer's block with a set of piano variations on a theme from Arcangelo Corelli's 12th sonata (Montreal, 12.x.31). It was coolly received but, encouraged by its acclaim in Russia and contentment at his Swiss home, he swept into the *Rhapsody on a Theme by Paganini (Baltimore, 7.xi.34), which interlaced the wizard violinist's A-minor caprice with its unsuspected mirror-image, the Russian Dies Irae, in an engrossing musical dialogue between disparate cultures. The 18th (of 24) variation is his most sumptuous tune, a heart-warming effusion of love and yearning. If posterity ever takes its toll, the Paganini Variations will be the last of Rachmaninov's works to vanish. He followed it with a 3rd symphony (Philadelphia, 6.xi.36, cond. *Stokowski), which he felt made concessions to modernism that failed to register on critics' ears; it fell between two stools and attained neither popularity nor academic respect.

The Symphonic Dances (Philadelphia, 3.i.41, cond. Ormandy), his last orchestral work reverted, contrary to the jolly title, mostly to gloom with overt references to the principal theme of his failed first symphony and the Dies Irae.

In life, as in music, Rachmaninov rarely smiled. He made strenuous efforts to conceal depression and lacked a manic counterbalance to his personality. He managed, however, to cultivate warm friendships with artists of equal rank, notably with *Kreisler, *Horowitz and Arthur Rubinstein. Along with most concert virtuosi, he found private comfort in playing chamber music with close friends; he composed a pleasant trio élégiaque (1893) and lyrical cello-piano sonata (Moscow, 25.xii.01). Much of his solo piano music was designed for the drawing-room, where it stoked the dying embers of an age of leisure. His more formidable piano works were modelled consciously on Chopin, beginning with Variations on Chopin's op28/20 (Moscow, 23.ii.03), followed by two sets of Preludes opp 23 and 32 (Moscow, 23.ii.03; St Petersburg, 18.xii.11) and climaxing in a 2nd sonata (Moscow, 16.xii. 13) whose key of B♭ minor is the same as Chopin's sepulchral masterpiece. He simplified this score for players less dexterous than himself, but was reconvinced of the original version by Horowitz's interpretation. His own pianism was famed for its clarity.

Rachmaninov was, additionally, a capable conductor who led several seasons at the Imperial Theatre and the Bolshoy. He attempted to write no fewer than eight operas, achieving three of them – *Aleko* (1893), *The Miserly Knight* and *Francesca da Rimini* (both Moscow 24.i.06, cond. Rachmaninov) – and leaving a performable fragment of a Maeterlinck play, *Monna Vanna*, that he discovered halfway through had been promised to a French composer. His vocal writing is of traditional Russian character, sampled to best effect in the cantata *Kolokola* (*The Bells*, St Petersburg, 13.xi.13).

The scope of his ambitions alone confirm that Rachmaninov was not a composer who pandered to public taste, any more than Mozart was. Nor was he an empty-minded musician who chased from one stage to the next in pursuit of the highest dollar. He was a reflective man who thirsted after new ideas, relished the company of intellectuals and held a liberal humanist outlook. Much misunderstood, he belonged to the fraternity of pre-war idealists who believed that music could make a better world. Historically, he belonged with Skryabin, Prokofiev and Stravinsky to an extraordinary artistic renaissance that was stunted by the First War and dispersed by the revolution. When communism crumbled at the close of the century, it was to these giants that Russian musicians turned for self-redetermination.

b. Oneg estate, nr. Novgorod, Russia, 1.iv. 1873; first UK concert 1899, first US tour 1909; married his cousin Natalya Satina, 1902, two daughters; emigrated 23.xii.17; moved to US 23.viii.39; *d*. of cancer at Beverly Hills, California, 28.iii.43. *other orch. works*: The Rock (Moscow, 1.iv. 1894), *The Isle of the Dead* (after a painting by Böcklin, Moscow, 1.v.09), *Vesna (Spring)* cantata for baritone, chorus and orch. (Moscow, 24.iii.02, cond. Siloti), 3 Russian Songs for chorus and orch. (Philadelphia, 18.iii.27, cond. *Stokowski). Also many piano pieces for two and four hands and playable transcriptions of works by Bach, Mussorgsky, Rimsky-Korsakov (*Flight of the Bumble-bee*), Kreisler and others.

Aladar RADO Early casualty of the First War, he left two Hungarian operas: *The Black Knight* (1911) and *Golem* (1912).

b. Budapest, 26.xii.1882; *d*. in fighting nr. Belgrade, 7.ix.14. *other works*: Hungarian Concerto for cello and orch. (1909), settings of R. L. Stevenson children's songs.

raga Indian melodic scale borrowed by *Stockhausen, *Glass, *Beatles.

ragtime Keyboard ancestor of *jazz with a two or four-beat rhythm, it syncopated a melody at twice the speed of its accompaniment with occasional missed notes, creating a headlong excitement. Its percussive use of piano enthused *Stravinsky, who wrote a ragtime movement in *A Soldier's Tale*, and *Satie a ragtime dance in Parade. Its outstanding composer-performer was the shortlived Scott *Joplin, whose *Maple Leaf Rag* appeared in 1899.

Kaljo RAID Estonian émigré whose ambitious first symphony was written at the age of 21 while fleeing to Sweden from the Soviet invasion. It is a romantic conception that combines personal optimism with national mourning. The war over, he moved to the US and studied with Milhaud and Ibert before taking holy orders as a Baptist priest in 1954 and settling in Canada. His later music has been coloured by immersion in medieval chant.

b. Tallinn, Estonia, 4.iii.22; st there with *Eller in whose memory he wrote a Lacrymosa for violin and cello (1970).

Priaulx RAINIER South African émigrée who caught the ear with a *Barbaric Dance Suite* (1949) that added a distinctive dark-continent primitivism to the now-familiar pounding rhythms of Bartók and Stravinsky. Becoming steadily more atonal, her chamber music possessed a ferocious intimacy.

b. Howick, Natal, 3.ii.03; prof. at RAM, London, 1942–68; *d.* Besse-èn-Chandesse, Auvergne, France, 10.x.86. *other works*: string quartet (1939), clarinet sonata (1942); John Donne vocal settings.

The Rake's Progress Stravinsky-Auden-Kallman chamber opera after Hogarth. fp: Venice, 11.ix.51.

Günther RAMIN Organist at Bach's church in Leipzig from the age of 20, he was appointed Cantor under the Nazis (1940) and preserved his post and the integrity of the St Thomas chorus when the communists took over. His organ compositions were widely performed and recorded.

b. Karlsruhe, Germany, 15.x.1898; *d.* Leipzig, 27.ii.56.

James K(irtland) RANDALL Trailblazer in US *computer music

b. Cleveland, Ohio, 16.vi.29; st with *Sessions, *Babbitt; taught at Princeton 1958-; *works include*: Lyric Variations for violin and computer (1968).

Bernard RANDS One of many British composers who found security, though scant fame, in US academe. A Yorkshire lad, Rands walked in *Berio's footsteps, both in collagist and electronic techniques and in delicacy of utterance. He has written a series of *Memos* for individual instruments (cf. *Sequenza) and is transfixed by the syntax of James *Joyce.

b. Sheffield, England, 2.iii.34; st with *Vlad, *Dallapiccola, *Maderna, *Boulez, *Berio; taught York U. 1969–72, U. of California at San Diego 1976-; *orch. works*: Agenda (1970), Mésalliance (piano/orch. 1973), Ology for Jazz group (1973), Aum (harpsichord/orch. 1974), Serenata 75 (flute/orch. 1976), Wildtracks for soprano/orch. (1969–75).

Ture RANGSTRÖM Composer of Sweden's national opera *Kronbruden* (The Crown Bride, Gothenburg, 25.iii.36), after Strindberg's tale of a country girl who sacrifices her newborn baby to gain a bridal crown. Its oppressively moralistic theme has common strands with *Jenůfa* and the music hints at times of Janáček grit, though mostly it sticks in a rut of mid-romantic sentimentality. Rangström was Sweden's most prolific songwriter with more than 250 titles to his credit. He worked mainly as a critic but was press officer at Stockholm Opera for five years.

b. Stockholm, 30.xi.1884; *d.* Tornsholmen, 11.v.47; *other works*: four symphonies.

György RÁNKI History-driven Hungarian, he wrote large-scale works named after national years of destiny, *1514* and *1944*.

b. Budapest, 30.x.07, st with *Kodály.

Karl RANKL The conductor who restored Covent Garden to European rank after World War Two was a rigorist whose crabby personality won his music no friends. He left eight symphonies and an opera, *Deidre of the Sorrows*, which, though it won a Festival of Britain prize, was never staged.

b. Gaaden, lower Austria, 1.x.1898; st with Schoenberg and Webern; cond. *Kroll Oper 1928–31, Graz 1931–37, Prague 1937–38, music. dir. Covent Garden 1945–51, Scottish Nat. Orch. 1952–58 Elizabethan Opera Co., Sydney, 1958–60; *d.* nr. Salzburg, Austria, 6.ix.68.

rap New York-style black *sprechgesang in which verses are improvised in rapid, repetitive, half-spoken rhythms, often with a violent message.

Rape of Lucretia Britten's chamber opera fp: (with Kathleen Ferrier as victim): Glyndebourne, 12.vii.46, cond. Ansermet.

Günther RAPHAEL Berliner of faintly Jewish ancestry, he was evicted by the Nazis but returned as a distinguished teacher. He wrote five late-romantic symphonies, and a Divertimento that was premiered by *Furtwängler (Leipzig, 1.ii.33).

    b. Berlin, 30.iv.03; *d*. Herford, 19.x.60. other works: three violin concertos, organ sonata (1949).

rapsodie espagnole *Ravel's orch. tribute to his southern neighbour. fp: Paris, 15.iii.08.

Alexander RASKATOV Russian miniaturist, his settings for soprano and small ensemble – *Courtly Songs* (1976) on Japanese texts; Circle of Singing (1984); Let there be Night (1981) – revert to the purified world of *Pierrot Lunaire.

    b. Moscow, 9.iii.53; *other work*: piano concerto, *Night hymns* (1984).

Karl Aage RASMUSSEN Dissonant Dane. In *Genklang* (1972), he reset the *Adagietto from Mahler's 5th symphony for a mistuned honky-tonk piano, *prepared piano and celesta.

    b. Kolding, Denmark, 13.xii.47; *other works*: operas *Crapp's Last Tape* (after Beckett, 1968), *Jephta* (1977), *Mayakovski* (1978); *A Symphony in Time* (1981).

Karol RATHAUS Neo-romantic émigré, edited the Met's version of Boris Godunov. His opera-in-exile, *Strange Land*, has found a European audience.

    b. Tarnopol, Austria, 16.ix.1895; st with *Schreker; exiled from Berlin 1933; taught Queen's College NY 1940–54; *d*. NY, 21.xi.54. *works include*: Requiem with text by Robert Louis Stevenson (1941), three symphonies, *Polonaise symphonique* (1943), five quartets.

Simon (Denis) RATTLE Appointed conductor in Birmingham at the age of 25, Rattle innovated a programme of late and neo-romanticism that brought the world rushing to his doorstep. His premières include *Gruber's *Frankenstein!!* and symphonies by Maxwell *Davies and Jonathan *Lloyd, alongside which he introduced to Britain a range of US and Russian postminimalism. He favoured original instruments for Mozart and earlier music and has sidestepped most central symphonic repertoire between Beethoven and Mahler.

Principal guest conductor with the Los Angeles Philharmonic from 1981, he made his US operatic debut there with *Wozzeck.

    b. Liverpool, England, 19.i.55; married soprano Elise Ross 1979.

Einojuhani RAUTAVAARA Caught between the overpowering role model of *Sibelius and his oppressive, 30-year silence, Finnish mid-century composers were a confused and unhappy lot. Rautavaara worked his way out of impasse with five symphonies that were stylistically different from one another, groping among romantic and modernist techniques for a personal and collective solution. His first symphony recalled Shostakovich, the 2nd Stravinsky; both appeared in 1957. The 3rd (1962) sounded uncannily like Bruckner. The 4th (1963) was 12-tone, the 5th shimmeringly abstract (Helsinki, 14.v.86, cond. *Salonen). Rautavaara had arrived at a synthesis of all available methods.

    He laid the foundations for operatic revival with eight stage works of which *Thomas* (Joensuu, 21.vi.85) and *Vincent* (Helsinki, 17.v.90) quickly reached an international public. Both composed to his own librettos, one depicts a 13th-century bishop, the other the life of Van Gogh. The music is vividly dramatic, punctuated by bursts of birdsong – a device that became Rautavaara's hallmark ever since *Cantus Arcticus* (Oulu, 18.x.72), a 'concerto' for taped birds and orch. In *Thomas*, in particular, his collage of Gregorian, modern and natural sounds energizes an ostensibly dull topic.

    b. Helsinki, 9.x.19.28; st with *Merikanto, *Copland, *Vogel; *other works*: *The House of the Sun* (opera, Lappeenranta, 24.iv.91), two piano concertos, four string quartets, much vocal music.

Maurice RAVEL A man who resembled his music to a remarkable degree – small, fastidious, aloof – Ravel was a solitary figure who produced music of emotional objectivity and sinuous individuality. Shunning dogmas and positions of influence, he surreptitiously infiltrated the consciousness of countless composers, chiefly *Messiaen, *Vaughan Williams, *Martinů, Gershwin, *Bernstein and *Boulez.

    An outsider by ancestry and origin, born of Swiss and Basque parentage on the

rocky coast where the Atlantic meets the Pyrenean foothills, he was forever drawn to the savage south. As a babe in arms he was whisked off to Paris, where he lived for the rest of his life. Entranced by the exotic music that *Rimsky-Korsakov conducted and, like *Debussy, by gamelans at the 1889 World exhibition, he shocked Parisian sensibilities with the voluptuous *Pavane pour une infante défunte (Pavan for a long-dead princess, 1899), which, along with other piano pieces, he later (1910) orchestrated almost beyond recognition.

Four successive bids for the Prix de Rome were snubbed by reactionary professors who suspected the tumbling fountains of Jeux d'eau (1901) of reprehensible Debussyism; if at all, the suite recalled Liszt. His rejection provoked a public scandal – 'l'affaire Ravel' – which resulted in the cleansing of Conservatoire stables and the appointment of Ravel's teacher, *Fauré, as director.

Where Ravel briefly made common cause with Debussy was in his F major string quartet (1903), decorously formal to begin but dazzling in its quicksilver pizzicato second-movement. Although neither

composer wrote another work of this kind, Ravel used a string quartet in the scoring of two of his most delicate accomplishments, the Introduction and Allegro for harp, strings, flute and clarinet (Paris, 22.ii.07) and the three Mallarmé settings (14.i.14). He was bracketed with Debussy as an iconoclast but fell out with him over which of them made first use of hispanic themes. Debussy claimed precedence with Ibéria (1903), but his junior colleague got there first in Habanera (1895) and more effectively in *Rapsodie espagnole (15.iii.08). There is a shadow of shared concerns in the exquisitely scored Schéhérézade songs (17.v.05) and the pianistic Histoires Naturelles (1906), but the eclectic Ravel took very little from Debussy and by the age of 30 was established as a singular voice, albeit one that many critics found 'cool', 'serpentine' or simply unpleasant.

Rapsodie espagnole demonstrated his principal trademark, a needle-sharp command of orchestral nuance whose subtlety rescued the score from touristic banality. *Stravinsky envied the delicacy of his *Diaghilev ballet Daphnis et Chloë (8.vi.12), so different from his own orchestral sledgehammer. He was less generous in conceding that Ravel possibly preceded him to *neo-classicism in his earliest published work, the Menuet antique of 1895, and his piano (later orch.) suite, Le Tombeau de Couperin (1917), written to help him escape images of the raging War.

Yet Ravel could also use the orchestra rhythmically and percussively when he so chose, crumping away relentlessly in the empty Boléro (22.xi.28), mindless forebear of *minimalism. In his *Koussevitsky-commissioned orchestration of Mussorgsky's pianistic Pictures at an Exhibition (1922) he exhibited an astonishing facility for bright colours and human vignettes.

This master of orchestration was also the composer of essential piano repertoire – Gaspard de la nuit (1908), Valses nobles et sentimentales (1911) and Le Tombeau de Couperin. He urged every composer to seek 'influences' – hence five Greek melodies and songs of various other nationalities, among them Hebrew and Madagascan. Malayan rhythms lie at the heart of his 1914 A minor Trio, where an acquaintance with *Pierrot Lunaire* and Stravinsky are audible. He added *parody to his palette with *La Valse* (1919), a study of Vienna in disintegration. Behind these multiple styles the real Ravel was well-hidden. He never married and had few intimate friendships.

The absence of emotional engagement in his music is compensated by constant textural ingenuity: Ravel may not move listeners, but he never bores them. Neither of his operas – the watchmaker comedy *L'heure espagnole* (19.v.11) and the animal fairy-tale *L'enfant et les sortilèges* (Monte Carlo, 21.iii.25) – possesses great profundity.

The two piano concertos, his last large-scale works, were conceived side-by-side in 1931 in directly opposite styles. The concerto for the left hand, written for Paul *Wittgenstein (Vienna, 27.xi.31), has bombastic rhythms, morose contemplations and a floating bassoon line that recalls *The *Rite of Spring*, perhaps hinting at the lunacy of war. The pounding is never oppressive, though, and the rhythms are excitingly propulsive. The G major concerto (Paris, 14.i.32), on the other hand, was the most flagrantly jazzy concerto after *Gerwshin's, with a serene central movement modelled on Mozart's clarinet quintet. Gershwin promptly wrote to seek lessons. No Frenchman had ever written concertos of such universal appeal, for Ravel in these last works before he succumbed to a debilitating brain disease achieved his lifelong ambition of easy communication. 'I am not one of the great composers,' he said on his deathbed. 'All the great ones have produced enormously, but I have written relatively little and with great hardship.'

b. Ciboure, France, 7.iii.1875; *d.* Paris, 28.xii.37. *other works*: *Mother Goose* (piano suite, 1908; ballet, 1912); *Tzigane* for violin and piano (London, 26.iv.24).

Alan RAWSTHORNE The original composer of music for T. S. Eliot's *Cats* poems (Edinburgh, 26.viii.54), Rawsthorne was a gritty northerner with a predilection for rough textures, almost an early *Birtwistle. Sent to become a dentist, he escaped to music college in Manchester and then went to Berlin to study piano with Egon Petri and absorb *Hindemith's style. His moment came with a *Theme and Variations* for two violins (London, 18.vi.38) and *Symphonic Studies* for orchestra (Warsaw, 21.iv.39), abstract works performed at successive *ISCM festivals.

Not for Rawsthorne the easy pastorality of his southern English compatriots. Even the concerto for string orchestra (1949) interplays busy rhythms, with little melodic relief. Two piano concertos (1939, 1951) and the second of three symphonies, his *Pastoral* with soprano solo (Birmingham, 29.ix.59), provide readier access to a well-stocked mind.

b. Haslingden, Lancs., 2.v.05, married (1) violinist Jessie Hinchcliffe (2) Constant Lambert's widow, Isabel; *d.* Cambridge, 24.vii.71. *other works*: ballet *Mme Chrysanthème* (London, 1.iv.55), two violin concertos, clarinet concerto, three string quartets, four piano bagatelles.

recording The recording of music changed its nature forever. The most ephemeral of arts acquired a mass audience, an unnatural perfectionism and an unimagined permanence. Domestic playing and literacy declined as people let a machine make music; so, too, did spontaneity and improvisation, cowed by commercial examples of *authentic performance.

Between its invention by Thomas Alva Edison in 1876 and Enrico Caruso's debut rolls in 1902, recording lacked artistic credibility. The Italian's bell-like voice pierced the crackle of surface noise; the first symphony, Beethoven's 5th, was recorded in 1913 by Arthur Nikisch and the Berlin Philharmonic. Successive technical improvements whittled down the perceptible distinction between canned music and live. Electric recording arrived in 1925, magnetic tape in 1938, long-playing records in 1948, stereophonic sound in 1958, digital recording in 1979. The inception of compact disc in 1983 enabled the record industry to boast with some validity that it had finally achieved perfect reproduction.

As recorded products increased, however, interpretative variety waned. Performers began to derive their style from records rather than from their own imagination. Newcomers feared to offend against orthodoxies instilled by commercial caution rather than intellectual truth. The tradition, defined by Nikisch, that each performance should be 'a grand improvisation' was parodied by the unchangeability of records. Tricky tape editing led to a note-perfectness that musicians sought to emulate in the concert hall, often at the expense of inspiration.

Records could earn untold popularity and endow a work of music with near-ubiquity. Vivaldi's *Four Seasons* and Rachmaninov's 2nd piano concerto entered living rooms – not to mention airports and hotel elevators – where no other music existed. Best-seller lists dictated the contents of concert seasons, not always to their detriment. The record industry can claim some credit for the Mahler and Bruckner revivals and in the compact disc era explored ever more esoteric repertoire.

The impact of recording on *popular music was sweeping and enormously lucrative. Before Edison, popular tunes were ground out by barrel-organ monkeys and sold in sheets. From the dawn of the 20th century, they became an inescapable element of everyday life. Records and broadcasting turned simple tunes into worldwide currency, elevating American urban sounds, particularly the rhythms of black musicians, into a universal culture and, from mid-century, specifically into a youth cult. Less and less musicianship was required to make a pop record. The *Beatles could not read music, but employed a literate producer; *punk rock dispensed with all foreknowledge as bourgeois and corrupt. Accompaniment, once the province of skilled instrumentalists, was reduced to a mechanized beat pre-syncopated in a spotless Japanese factory. In an almost sci-fi scenario, the machine had taken over music.

The record industry, run from America until the 1970s, became multi-nationalized. By the 1990s only one major group, Warner, was still US-based, though partly Japanese-owned. CBS was sold in 1987 to Sony of Japan and RCA to Germany's Bertelsmann group. The other surviving giants were PolyGram, owned by Philips of Holland, and EMI in the UK.

As an academic aid, recording was invaluable for capturing and preserving vanishing cultures, as well as the legacy of composers performing their own music. The ethnographical recordings of *Bartók and Kodály not only fuelled their own music but set a precedent for *McPhee, *Reich and others to seek out remote resources for their compositions.

Max(imilian) (Johann Baptist Joseph) REGER It is easy to hear why Reger's huge reputation has never spread beyond Germany. His music lacked any spark of wit. It is erudite, efficient, eloquent, often heartfelt, but the effervescence of genius in full flow of inspiration is conspicuously absent.

His craft was counterpoint; many consider him Bach's last descendant and Brahms' lineal successor. His brilliance at pattern-making is shown off in two orchestral sets of *Variations and Fugue on a Theme by Johann Adam Hiller* (Cologne, 15.x.07) and another by Mozart (Berlin, 5.ii.15) – the former derived from an 18th century *Singspiel*, the latter from the piano sonata K331. He was unequalled at writing double-fugues for a Strauss-sized orchestra. For ideas, he looked grimly backwards. The *Concerto in Olden Style* (1912) attempts to revive the concerto grosso; there are various piano variations on themes by Bach, Beethoven and Telemann.

Although he was emotionally uncommunicative, the *Four Tone Poems after* [the Swiss painter, Arnold] *Böcklin* (Essen, 12.x.13) evoke poignant sensations in contemplative solos illustrating 'The Hermit Violinist' and the gloomy 'Isle of the Dead' – which his exact contemporary *Rachmaninov composed rather differently four years later. The Sinfonietta and Serenade (1905–6) are strictly disciplined works of craftsmanship. He never achieved a full symphony, claiming the F minor piano concerto (Leipzig, 15.xii.10) as 'a symphony with piano obbligato'.

The finale of his violin concerto (Leipzig, 13.x.08) is meant to depict 'the Devil's grandmother as a young girl going to the court ball'. Such mirth as he managed was heavy and alcoholic; he died of a heart attack in a Leipzig hotel at the age of 43, leaving 146 opus numbers and 200 organ pieces. 'In music, there can be no compromise,' was his motto.

Reger felt out of step with his times and caricatured his critics as monkeys and sheep in the fourth of his violin-and-piano sonatas (1904). He responded famously to the leading Munich critic: 'I am sitting in the smallest room in my house. I have your review in front of me. In a moment it will be behind me.'

> *b.* Brand, Bavaria, 19.iii.1873, a schoolmaster's son; st with Hugo Riemann, 1890–95; toured as pianist and conductor; married and settled in Munich 1902; professor at Leipzig 1907–16; cond. Meiningen court orchestra 1911–15; moved to Jena 1915; *d.* Leipzig, 11.v.16; buried in Munich. *other orch. works*: Symphonic prologue to a tragedy (1908), Romantic Suite (1912), Ballet Suite (1913), Psalm 100 for mixed choir, organ and orch. (1909); also four string quartets (1901–9).

reggae Jamaican-based popular music rooted in calypso rhythms and Rastafarian beliefs which deified the last emperor of Ethiopia. It enjoyed western vogue in the 1970s but declined after cancerous death of songwriter-figurehead Bob Marley (1945–81).

Steve (Stephen Michael) REICH As a small boy, Reich shuttled by train between divorced parents living on opposite coasts of America. In Europe, Jews were being shunted in cattle cars to the death camps. The concurrence of these rail journeys produced in *Different Trains* (1988), a summation of his lifelong preoccupations and personal techniques. A 27-minute creation for string quartet and pre-recorded sounds, it vindicates his path through *collage and *minimalism. Using train noises and speech fragments by his childhood governess, a Pullman porter and holocaust survivors, Reich pieces together a historical jigsaw over an insistent string background (four times over-dubbed by the quartet) that reflects the melodies and rhythms of speech.

Reich was ever the most inventive of the first-generation minimalists. His earliest essays were snatches of speech, *It's Gonna Rain* (1965) and *Come Out* (1966), the latter a phrase uttered by a Harlem kid beaten up by cops who wanted 'to, like, open the blues up and let some of the blues' blood

come out to show them'. Two repeating tape-loops of the aggressive phrase were set running steadily out of sync with each other, ascending from echo into something like an eight-part vocal canon. Reich called the method 'music as a gradual process' and set about examining at great length the inherent possibilities of a simple phrase or rhythm.

Drumming (1970), informed by a research trip to West Africa, goes on for more than 90 minutes, of which the first half-hour amounts to pure drum patterns before he adds colouring of marimbas, voices and glockenspiels. *Six Pianos* (1972; transcribed as Six Marimbas, 1983) is a kaleidoscopic dialogue of banality between inhabitants of a deserted keyboard store. A study of Balinese music produced harmonic variety in *Music for Mallet Instruments, Voices and Organ* (1973) and the 100,000-selling record *Music for 18 Musicians* (1975). He had begun to seek the refinement that led him out of mind-numbing minimalism.

'At a certain point around 1974, I began to think, "Well, I'm obviously not an African, nor a Balinese. I'm a Jew." ' He studied Hebrew, devotional cantillations for reading the Torah and the traditions of Jewish communities in Yemen and India, recording a variety of styles on visits to Israel. The resultant *Tehillim* (*Psalms*, Houston, 21.xi.81) for chorus and ensemble brought extended melody into his work. Its appeal is shared by the ensuing orchestral works, *Eight Lines* (an orchestration of his earlier Octet, NY, 10.xii.83) and the surprisingly lush *Desert Music* (Cologne, 1984) whose symphonic textures override its synthesizers. Around the same time, Reich licensed his music for anyone to perform, having previously reserved the rights for his own ensemble.

The son of a lawyer and lyricist (mum wrote 'Love is a Simple Thing', among other hits), he once drove a cab in San Francisco. He admits a West Coast debt to *Cage and Terry *Riley, whose landmark *In C* he helped perform in 1964; his own influence on *Glass is less readily admitted.

> *b.* New York, 3.x.36; st with Roland Kohloff (ex-timpanist of NY Philharmonic), Milhaud and Berio; formed NY ensemble 'Steve

Reich and Musicians', 1966; remarried 1976 to video artist Beryl Korot; *other works*: *Piano Phase* (1967), *Violin Phase* (1967), 4 *Organs* (1970), *Clapping Music* (four performers, 1972), *Music for pieces of wood* (1975), *Music for Large Ensemble* (1978), Octet (Frankfurt, 1979) and chamber works for virtuoso instrumentalists pitted against their own pre-recorded tapes: *Vermont Counterpoint* (for Ransom Wilson's flute, 1982), *New York Counterpoint* (for Richard Stoltzman's clarinet, 1985) and *Electric Counterpoint* (for Pat Metheny's electric guitar, 1987).

Die Reihe   German for 'row' or 'series', the basis of *12-note composition. It was the title of a *Universal Edition *avantgarde periodical (1955–62) and of a modernist Viennese concert ensemble formed by *Cerha and Schwertsik.

Aribert REIMANN   Dietrich *Fischer-Dieskau's devoted accompanist wrote the baritone a sequence of song-cycles and a titanic operatic part – the role of Lear (Munich, 9.vii.78) in an opera that Verdi dared not compose. Reimann was adept at tragedy, since much of his music is dark and laden with foreboding. *Lear* is noisy, too, but so is the play, and in its operatic version clears the clutter of minor personae to focus on psychological intensity and strong feeling. In the space of a decade, it became a staple of the modern repertoire.

Reimann's next opera was a Strindberg play, *Ghost Sonata* (Berlin, 25.ix.84). Schumann is his favourite composer and the deepest of his song cycles is *Joycean and titled *Shine and Dark* (Zurich, 31.v.91).
  b. Berlin, 4.iii.36; st with *Blacher, *Pepping; professor of contemporary song at Hamburg 1974–83, Berlin 1983–; *other works*: operas *Ein Traumspiel* (*A Dream Play*) (after Strindberg, Kiel, 30.vi.65), *Melusine* (Stuttgart, 29.iv.71), *Troades* (after Werfel, Munich, 7.vii.86); Symphony – from the *Traumspiel* opera (Darmstadt, 12.ix.76), Seven Fragments for orchestra, in memoriam Robert Schumann (Hamburg, 25.ix.88), violin concerto (Hanover, 13.ix.89), *Invenzioni* for 12 players (London, 16.vi.79), songs for baritone with piano or orch. after Célan, cummings, Shakespeare, Eichendorff, Sylvia Plath, Michelangelo, Baudelaire, Edgar Allan Poe, Louize Labé and Rilke.

Django (Jean Baptiste) REINHARDT   Spark-plug of European jazz, he formed the Quintet du Hot Club de France with Grappelli in 1934, playing his gypsy guitar unamplified before the war and electrified after.
  b. Liberchies, Belgium, 23.i.10; d. Fontainebleu, France, 16.v.53.

Josef REITER   Ardent Austrian Nazi, sometime director of Salzburg Mozarteum, he dedicated a *Goethe Symphony* (1931) to Hitler.
  b. Braunau am Inn, Austria, 19.i.1862; *d.* Bad Reichenall, 2.vi.39. *other works*: incidental music for Raimund's popular play *Der Bauer als Millionär* and four operas.

Franz (Theodor) REIZENSTEIN   *Hindemith pupil who transferred in 1934 to *Vaughan Williams, achieving a synthesis of severe counterpoint and tender whimsicality that suited the insular English climate of his time. His chamber music was highly refined; its summits are a piano quintet (1951) and violin-piano sonata (1945). He wrote a spoof *Concerto Popolare* and *Let's Fake an Opera* for Gerard Hoffnung's comic concerts and was professor of piano at the Royal Academy of Music (1958–68).
  b. Nuremberg, Germany, 7.vi.11; *d.* London, 15.x.68. *other works*: oratorio *Genesis* (1958); two piano concertos; *variations on the Lambeth Walk* for solo piano.

Répons   Boulez's integration of computer and orch. fp: Donaueschingen, 18.x.81.

Ottorino RESPIGHI   Composer who, unusually for an Italian, made his mark in concert rather than in opera, his three sets of Roman postcards, *The Fountains of Rome* (Rome, 11.iii.17), *Pines of Rome* (14.xii.24) and *Roman Festivals* (NY, 21.ii.29), were god's gift to hi-fi salesmen. *Pines* was the first concert work to include pre-recorded sounds – a nightingale song – but its proto-fascist Legionnaires march climax is disquieting, and *Fountains* is the finer piece.

Orchestration was Respighi's principal talent, for he possessed little originality. *Martucci's success prompted him to write a Notturno (1905); *Rimsky-Korsakov taught him instrumentation; hearing *Salome* led to a Straussian *Sinfonia drammatica* and, when all other sources failed, he fell back on tried-and-tested Italiana.

His ballet *La boutique fantasque* (London, 5.vi.1919) exploits Rossini melodies, as does the orchestral suite *Rossiniana* (1925). Rummagings in early Italian music resulted in three batches of *Ancient Airs and Dances* (1916, 1923, 1931) for string orchestra. His suite *The Birds* (1927) uses themes by Rameau and Pasquini; *Church windows* (Boston, 25.ii.27) is based on Gregorian chant; Hebraic themes decorate his ballet, *Belkis, Queen of Sheba* (1932). He also made a 'free transcription' of Monteverdi's *Orfeo* (Milan, 16.iii.35) that amounts to a travesty of period style.

His nine operas lack dramatic propulsion, though *Belfagor* (Milan, 26.iv.23) and *La fiamma* (23.i.34) have lyrical moments. His swansong *Lucrezia* (Milan, 24.ii.37) was completed by his wife, Elsa. He wrote well for voice. *Il Tramonto* (The Sunset, 22.ii.18), for mezzo-soprano and string quartet or orchestra, is a delicate setting of a Shelley poem in which singer and symphonic texture are blended in quasi-Mahlerian unity. The final lines are stunningly rendered:

'. . . Oh, that like thine, mine epitaph were –
Peace!
This was the only moan she ever made.'

Of his chamber music, he was proudest of a romantically young-Straussian violin sonata (Bologna, 3.iii.18).

b. Bologna, 9.vii.1878; played viola in orchs. of Bologna Teatro Communale and St Petersburg Imperial Opera, 1900–04; taught in Berlin 1908–09; professor at Santa Cecilia Academy, Rome, 1913–26, and its director 1924–26; married Elsa in Rome's smallest church, S. Sebastianello, 13.i.19; *d.* of heart disease, Rome 18.iv.36. *other works include*: operas *La campana sommersa* (The sunken bell) after a play by Gerhart Hauptmann (Hamburg, 18.xi.27), *Maria egiziaca* (one-act mystery opera, NY, 16.iii.32); orch: Brazilian impressions (São Paolo, 16.vi.28), Three Botticelli Pictures (Vienna, 18.ix.27), *concerto gregoriano* for violin and orch. (Rome, 5.ii.22), piano concerto (NY, 31.xii.25), *Lauda per la Natività del Signore* for soloists, chorus and orch. (22.xi.30).

Bib: Elsa Respighi, *Ottorino Respighi*, Milan (Ricordi), 1962.

Hermann REUTTER Vocal composer who learned his trade as a recital accompanist and wrote Lieder and twelve operas that presented a melodious foreground against often dissonant instrumentation. He cited *Walter's performances of Pfitzner and Schreker operas as a formative influence. An unassuming musician, he is overlooked in some German dictionaries. He composed a cycle for *Fischer-Dieskau and a radio opera after Thornton Wilder's novel, *The Bridge of San Luis Rey* (Frankfurt, 20.vi.54).

b. Stuttgart, Germany, 17.vi.1900; professor there 1932–36, 1952–66, running the Frankfurt Music Academy in the interim; *d.* Heidenheim an der Brenz, 1.i.85.

Silvestre REVUELTAS Assistant conductor to *Chávez at the Mexican Symphony Orchestra, he had an ear for local Indian tunes and a flair for orchestration. In 1937 he was sent to run cultural affairs in Republican Spain but returned poor and in broken health. He died of pneumonia, alcoholism and heartbreak at the death of two daughters, on the day his ballet was premièred. His major concert work is *La noche de los Mayas (Mayan night,* 1939), a suite drawn from a film of the same name and depicting in four vivid movements ritual, revelry, contemplation (of almost *Mahlerian immobility) and climactic orgy.

b. Santiago Papasquiaro, Mexico, 31.xii. 1899; st in Chicago and NY; cond. theatre orchs. in Texas 1926–8; *d.* Mexico City, 5.x.40. *other works*: Planos, 'geometric dance' for chamber orch. (1934), *Homage to Federico Garcia Lorca* for small orch. (Madrid 22.ix.37), *Sensemaya* for voice and orch. (1938); three string quartets.

Cemal Resid REY Palestine-born and Paris-educated creator of music for a modern Turkish state, he wrote pleasant westernizations of indigenous idioms. *Scènes turques* (1927) give the melodic substance of Anatolian dances stripped of their wildness. *Instantanés* (Paris, 12.ii.32) is self-confidently more ethnic, five vivid sketches of village life for piano and orch., each lasting a minute or two. A symphonic poem, *The Conqueror* (1958), marks the 500th anniversary of Sultan Mehmet II's capture of Constantinople and culminates in an Islamic hymn blended with the ringing of church bells. Rey's first symphony (1941) and major opera *Celebi* (1943) are devoted to national-religious causes. He also wrote several operettas and, in mid-life, a substantial body of abstract music including a second symphony (1969), 12 preludes and fugues (1968), three concertos for piano, two for violin and one for cello. He founded Istanbul's first professional orchestra and was head of music on Turkish Radio.

> *b.* Jerusalem, 25.x.04, son of Ottoman governor of the Holy City; st with Fauré and the pianist Marguerite Long, returning to Turkey in 1923 when republic was declared; *d.* Istanbul, 7.x.85.

Roger REYNOLDS Technical innovator in American music, he mastered engineering physics before he entered art. He cofounded the avant-garde ONCE festival in Ann Arbor, Michigan, wrote graphic scores and electronic extravagances, and made his name in 1962 with *The Emperor of Ice Cream*, a Wallace Stevens poem set for eight solo voices, piano, percussion and double-bass. Responding to literary images, he also set texts by Samuel Beckett, Jorge Luis Borges and Milan Kundera. In 1989 he became the first radical composer to win the Pulitzer Prize since *Ives in 1947. However, the prizewinning work, *Whispers out of Time*, signalled a return to the mainstream with ostensible quotations from Beethoven's *Les Adieux* sonata and *Mahler's 9th symphony. There is nothing audibly experimental about the music, which constitutes a traditional tone-poem assembled by partly microtonal and cross-rhythmic techniques.

> *b.* Detroit, Michigan, 18.vii.34; st with *Finney, *Gerhard; taught at U. of California, San Diego, 1970– ; *other works*: Graffiti for orch. (1964), *Transfigured Wind II and III* for flute, orch. and four-channel tape (1983–7), *Symphony (Vertigo)*, *Archipelago*, *The Dream of Infinite Rooms*.

Rhapsody in Blue Near-concerto for piano and jazz band by *Gershwin, rescored for full orchestra by *Grofé and claimed as the first symphonic composition to play the blues. fp: NY, 12.ii.1924.

Rhapsody on a theme of Paganini Set of 24 variations for piano and orchestra by *Rachmaninov, twined around Paganini's much-abused 24th caprice for solo violin and echoes of the Russian Orthodox Dies

Irae. The 18th variation yields Rachmaninov's most celebrated love-theme after the 2nd piano concerto. fp: Baltimore, 7.xi.34

rhythm By one of those inexplicable *Zeitgeist* coincidences, in 1911 *Bartók and *Stravinsky both produced works – *Allegro barbaro* and *Rite of Spring* – that were driven by rhythm rather than by melody and harmony. This was, in truth, no great innovation since primitive musics of every continent are rooted foremost in rhythm. But in the self-consciously sophisticated world of concert music it had the force of revelation and provided composers of the new century with an extra dimension. Some, like *Blacher, *Messiaen and *Webern, chained the beast to their formulae. Others, particularly *minimalists, copied the improvisatory rhythms of jazz and the syncopations of popular music to provide a throbbing pulse. Even ascetic serenities by *Boulez contain cross-rhythms and fragmented beats that sustain momentum. Much music was written for *percussion alone, a phenomenon unthinkable in any other century.

rhythm-and-blues The root force of *rock music, r&b was an urban blend of separate *jazz strains that enjoyed a 1940s heyday and germinated the seeds of rock'n'roll. With steamy beat and risqué lyrics, it caught on among white kids, especially white musicians. Bo Diddley, Lightnin' Hopkins, Memphis Slim and John Lee Hooker were the stars. Both the *Beatles and the *Rolling Stones acknowledged debts to r&b.

Emilios RIADIS (born KHU) Greek folklorist who studied in Munich with Mottl and in Paris with Ravel. He wrote three operas and many songs of an oriental inclination.

> *b.* Salonica, 1.v.1885; *d.* there, 17.vii.35.

Wallingford RIEGGER German-trained American, he swapped romanticism for a straitlaced atonality propelled by fractional shifts of rhythm. An avant-gardist in 1920s New York, he participated in *electronic experiments but confined his own work to conventional instruments, writing 35 orch. pieces, including a prize-winning 3rd symphony of 1948, and many folksong settings. Under various pseudonyms, he also wrote agitprop workers' songs.

b. Albany, Georgia, US, 29.iv.1885; *d.* NY, 2.iv.61. *other works: Study in Sonority* for ten violins, or any multiple of ten (1927); *Dichotomy* for chamber orch. (1932), 4th symphony (1957).

Vittorio RIETI A *Diaghilev composer in the 1920s, Rieti divided the rest of his life between France and the United States writing amiable, middle-of-road neo-classics that included seven operas, five symphonies and chamber music.

b. Alexandria, Egypt, 28.i.1898; moved to Italy 1917; wrote *Barabau* for Ballets Russes, 1925; US citizen 1944; taught Baltimore, NY; *other works: Second Avenue Waltzes* (two pianos, 1942), two-piano concerto (1951), triple concerto (1971).

Wolfgang (Michael) RIHM White hope of German music in the 1990s, Rihm freed himself from dogma and used every technique he could find, even resorting to tonality when he need to soften the rigours of his dramatic chamber opera *Jakob Lenz* (1979), based, like *Wozzeck*, on a Georg Büchner text. At the heart of his work are 8 string quartets, of which the 3rd (1981), titled 'Im Innersten' (From Deep Within), veers from rank aggression to flagrant sentiment in sequences that echo *Tristan and *Verklärte Nacht. A certain *dejà vu* pervades his music, heightened by his reversion in the 3rd symphony (1977) to 19th century texts by Nietzsche and Rimbaud. The French poet features again in *Départ* (1988), a 60th birthday tribute to his teacher *Stockhausen set for mixed chorus, speaking chorus and 22 players. It sounds overwhelmingly like middle-period *Ligeti but this may prove a misnomer for Rihm stands intellectually in the German line that runs from *Mahler and *Berg through Karl Amadeus *Hartmann to its present indeterminate state. Appointed head of the music theory faculty at Karlsruhe conservatory at the age of 21, Rihm has been seen ever since as the likeliest saviour of German modernism. In the early 1980s he took charge of the *Darmstadt summer courses but later retired to Freiburg-im-

Breisgau to devote himself entirely to composition.

b. Karlsruhe, Germany, 13.iii.52; st with *Searle, *Stockhausen, *Fortner, *Huber; *other works:* operas *Faust and Yorick* (1976), *Harlekin* (1977–), *Hamlet-Maschine* (1986), *Oedipus* (1987), *The Conquest of Mexico* (Hamburg, 9.ii.92); *Monodram* for cello and orch. (1983); various Lieder cycles and piano pieces; octet (Berlin, 16.ii.91); piano concerto (1992).

Knudåge RIISAGER An official in the Danish ministry of finance for 22 years, he explored musical sources that were regarded as dangerously unorthodox. The most celebrated of his ten ballets, *Qarrtsiluni* (Copenhagen, 21.ii.42), tells the tale of a polar squaw in indigenous Eskimo sounds; T-DOXC (3.ix.27), an orch. suite, was described as a 'poème méchanique' in the anarchic manner of the *futurists. Effectively, Riisager was an eclectic *neo-classicist with more than a tinge of inter-War Paris, where he studied briefly with *Roussel. He was made head of the Danish Composers' Union in 1937 and of the Royal Conservatory in 1956, writing five symphonies, an opera buffa and many small pieces.

b. Port Kunda, Estonia, 6.iii.1897; *d.* Copenhagen, Denmark, 26.xii.74.

Terry RILEY Father of *minimalism – which he sired in San Francisco on 21.v. 1965 with the first performance, among friends, of a work entitled *In C*. It contains 53 simple fragments of music rooted in the octave C, to be played at any speed by any number of players on whatever instruments they choose and for as long as they care to continue. The repetitive, hypnotic interaction of elementary melodic phrases, underpinned by a ceaseless intonation of a single C-note, produced a sense of communal equality, allied to a mild hallucinogenic intoxication; the recording was rightly advertised as 'a trip'.

While Steve Reich and Philip Glass exploited the monotonous formula, Riley indulged in multi-coloured speculations and dreams of world peace. He recorded *A Rainbow in Curved Air*, along with *Poppy Nogood and the Phantom Band* and *Persian Surgery Dervishes*, on a variety of electronic keyboards, the accompanying text envisaging a proliferation of organic vegetables on the verges of interstate highways. The music has the undemanding consistency of a late Beatles intermezzo.

In 1970 Riley followed the pop trail to India to study raga traditions with a guru, Pandith Pran Nath (whom he shared with La Monte *Young), returning to teach North Indian raga at Mills College, Oakland, 1971–80. His idiom slipped easily into mantra repetitions. An association with *Kronos produced nine string quartets, five of which formed the cycle Salome Dances for Peace (1988). Riley himself appeared frequently in concert as a keyboard performer and improviser. His first orchestral piece was commissioned for the 1991 centenary of Carnegie Hall, a testament to his sweeping influence on contemporary American music.

Of his own work it can justly be said that a little goes a long way, though it is always politely phrased and unquestionably well-meant. A modern vision of Hell might well contain an unbroken loop of In C.

    b. Colfax, California, 24.vi.35; st at Berkeley; worked at ORTF studios in Paris, 1962–3; other works: film soundtracks for Le Secret de la Vie and No Man's Land; Shri Camel for solo organ; Harp of New Albion for retuned piano; five songs for Bulgarian Radio women's choir; The Room of Remembrance; In Winter They Killed the Cocktail Pianist.

Nikolai RIMSKY-KORSAKOV

A less communicative artist than his contemporary Tchaikovsky (1840–93), Rimsky was significantly more influential. He served as a unique bridging figure between Glinka and Dargomizhsky, founding fathers of Russian music, and the modernists *Skryabin, *Stravinsky and *Prokofiev. His writings on instrumentation were the most perceptive since Berlioz's and his harmonies were subtly original, prompting Russian musicians to talk of a generic 'Rimsky-Korsakov scale:' His editions of Mussorgsky's operas Boris Godunov and Khovanshchina and of Borodin's Prince Igor made them into repertoire works and made a decisive impact on *Debussy and modern French music. His penchant for oriental melodies pre-figured the fashion for exoticism. His roster of pupils included

*Glazunov, *Miaskovsky, *Stravinsky and *Shtaynberg, Shostakovich's teacher. He stood in paternal relation to the young rebels as Mahler did to Schoenberg, encouraging and tolerant but stylistically detached.

By 1900, the compositions by which he is famed were long established. Sheherazade dated from 1888, Capriccio espagnol from 1887 and the opera Christmas Eve from 1895. He was now almost exclusively an opera composer, completing an ouevre of 12 stage works with Servilia (St Petersburg, 14.x.02), Kashchey the Immortal (Moscow, 25.xii.02), The Commander (St P., 16.x.04) and two folkish works that received wide reception abroad, The Legend of the Invisible City of Kitezh (St. P., 20.x.07) and Le coq d'or (Golden Cockerel, Moscow, 7.x.09).

Although of gentle birth, he deplored Tsarist tyranny. His son Andrei (1878–1940) was a Soviet musicologist; a grandson Georgi (1901–65) composed *microtonally until Stalin's crackdown on modernism.

    b. Tikhvin, nr. Novgorod, Russia, 18.iii. 1844; served in Tsarist navy 1856–65, prof. St Petersburg Conservatory 1875–08; d. Liubensk, nr. St Petersburg, 21.vi.08.
    Bib: N. Rimsky-Korsakov, My Musical Life, NY (Knopf), 1924.

Jean RIVIER

French neo-classicist who tried in the 1930s to steer a middle tonal way between *Messiaen's modernism and the tattered hedonism of Les *Six. In typical Parisian fashion, his clique was given an appelation – the Groupe du Triton; its other leading figure was Henry *Barraud. Rivier's seven symphonies and numerous concertos wavered from classicism to impressionism in a pleasant and elegant fashion rather like *Roussel; he is best remembered for a 1938 Grave et Presto for saxophone quartet.

    b. Villemomble, nr Paris, 21.vii.1896; gassed in First War; professor of composition at Paris Conservatoire from 1947; d. La Penne sur Huveaune, 6.xi.87.

Paul ROBESON

Black bass singer of bottomless range, victimized in the US and lionized in Europe. Many of the ballads he sang demanded rights for his race; as

Othello in London in 1930 he retuned the role as a manifesto for oppressed minorities.

b. Princeton, New Jersey, 9.iv.1898; *d.* Philadelphia, 23.i.76.

George ROCHBERG The death of his 20-year-old son switched Rochberg off *serialism in 1964. When he resumed composing with *Contra mortem et tempus* for violin, flute, clarinet and piano, he re-entered tonality with quotations from Haydn, Mahler, Bartók and Berio. Subsequent works became ever more romantic, the 3rd string quartet of 1972 containing a slow movement that Beethoven might have imagined and the 1974 violin concerto singing away like Mendelssohn. An oboe concerto (NY, 13.xii.84) alludes to Prokofiev and later works recapture a *Bergian flavour. Whatever the merit of individual works, Rochberg will be remembered as the man who broke the dissonant stranglehold of academia on American composers and freed them to write tunes once again.

b. Paterson, New Jersey, 5.vii.18; st with *Menotti and *Dallapiccola; professor, U. of Pennsylvania 1960– ; *other works*: opera *The Confidence Man* (after Melville, Santa Fe, 31.xii.1982), five symphonies, six *Concord* quartets.

rock music *Popular music was overwhelmed in the mid-1950s by a phenomenon known, for carnal associations, as rock'n'roll. In a relatively short space of time, 'rock' music took over the pop market, marginalizing middle-of-road balladry and middle-aged consumers and projecting itself stridently at rebellious urban youth. Its roots lay in *rhythm-and-blues and its appeal in a heavy beat and foreplay lyrics that some sociologists decried as anti-social.

The term rock'n'roll was borrowed in 1951 from a black sexual euphemism by a white disc jockey, Alan Freed. It entered the US charts in 1954 with 'Sh-boom' and went worldwide the following year with Bill Haley's 'Rock Around the Clock' used as backing for the school movie, *Blackboard Jungle*. Chuck Berry, Little Richard, Elvis Presley were instant stars.

Initially apologetic – 'I know it's only rock'n'roll, but I like it' – it became

increasingly aggressive with heavy amplification and anti-authority gestures. Jimi Hendrix in his fabled Woodstock appearance attacked 'The Star-Spangled Banner' with a venom that rattled Washington windows. The Beatles and West Coast bands ventured into curclicues of psychedelic rock and industry moguls tried to tame the beast by neutering Presley. But rock survived the attacks and spawned new acts – David Bowie, U2, *Madonna. Although Pink Floyd and the Grateful Dead pioneered a symphonic style of extended numbers with linked intermezzos, this was highbrow stuff for aging nostalgists.

At root, rock belonged to adolescents and ran in dangerous tandem with drugs, street crime and unprotected sex. Its impact on art music was tangential, absorbed through the culture of interpreters who were raised in the rock era rather than exerting a direct influence on composers.

Richard (Charles) RODGERS Bankable on Broadway, Rodgers had a string of successes on stage and screen with librettist Lorenz Hart but broke the box office only when he hitched up with Oscar Hammerstein. Their *Oklahoma* (NY, 31.ii.43) announced the heyday of the Broadway musical. It was followed by *Carousel* (19.iv.45), *South Pacific* (7.iv.49), *The King and I* (29.iii.51) and *The Sound of Music* (16.xi.59), a range that encompassed Reader's Digest-type pastiches of country-and-western, Balinese and Alpine ambiences. Much of his lush orchestration was done by Robert Russell *Bennett. Rodgers excelled at the sure-fire showstopper – 'Oh What a Beautiful Morning,' 'Younger than Springtime', 'Nothing Like a Dame', 'Hello, Young Lovers', 'Climb Every Mountain'. With Hammerstein's death in 1960 his fertility declined; his last show, *Do I Hear a Waltz?*, was scripted by Stephen *Sondheim.

b. Hammels Station, Long Island, NY, 28.vi. 02 of Jewish parentage; *d.* NY, 30.xii.79. *other musicals include*: with Hart – *Dearest Enemy* (1925), *A Connecticut Yankee* (1927), *On Your Toes* (1936), *Pal Joey* (1940); with Hammerstein – *Me and Juliet* (1953), *The Flower Drum Song* (1958).

Joaquin RODRIGO The most popular concerto of the mid-century was composed by a blind man who never played its instrument. The *Concierto de Aranjuez* (Barcelona, 9.xi.40), specifically its moody *Adagio*, propelled classical guitar into the concert menu. Evoking the chivalry and cruelty of 18th-century Bourbon courts, it set the instrument's thin twang against an orchestral army – forcefully in the first movement, languidly in the adagio and gracefully in the finale. The central theme was picked up by everyone from French crooners ('Mon Amour') to Miles *Davis in *Pictures of Spain*.

Rodrigo continued writing period pieces. A violin concerto (Lisbon, 11.iv.44) was 'conceived in the manner of Vivaldi', the cello concerto (Madrid, 4.xi.49) was 'in gallant mode', while the *Fantasia para una gentilhombre* (San Francisco, iii.58), written for Andres Segovia and second only to *Aranjuez* in its appeal, used 17th-century dance tunes. He wrote further concertos for harp (1963), four guitars (1967), two guitars (1968) James Galway's flute (1979) and Julian Lloyd Webber's cello (London, 15.iv.82). *Aranjuez* retakes in *Concierto de Malaga* (Los Angeles, xi.81) and *Concierto para una fiesta* (Fort Worth, Texas, 9.iii.83) failed to catch fire.

Rodrigo wrote extensively for solo guitar. *An Invitation to the Dance* contains surprisingly modern resonances. More typical are *Three Spanish Pieces* for Segovia, a Baroque passacaglia sandwiched between two flamencos and the *sonata giocosa*, his homage to Domenico Scarlatti. He never played the guitar for fear 'it might interfere with my fantasy'.

b. Sagunto, Valencia, 22.xi.01; blinded 1904; st in Paris with *Dukas and De *Falla; married Turkish pianist, Victoria Kamhi, 1933; returned to Spain 1939; professor at Madrid University, 1947– .

Jean-Jules (Aimable) ROGER-DU-CASSE *Fauré's favourite pupil wrote a bouncy two-piano suite for his master's 60th birthday but mainly followed Bach and *impressionism. Apart from a successful Orpheus ballet (1926) and the comic opera *Cantegril* (1931), he composed little for large forces.

b. Bordeaux, 18.iv.1873; *d.* Le-Taillan-Médoc, nr. Bordeaux, 19.vii.54. *other works include*: two string quartets.

Bernard ROGERS US traditionalist, composed three operas, *The Warrior*, *The Veil* and *The Nightingale*, that fed 1950s vogue for new American opera. As professor at the Eastman School for almost 40 years (1929–67), he had among his pupils *Bergsma, *Diamond and *Ussachevsky.

b. NY, 4.ii.1893; *d.* Rochester, 24.v.68. *orch. works include*: *To the Fallen* (1919), 5th symphony 'Africa' (1959), Variations on a Mussorgsky Song (1960), *The Musicians of Bremen* for narrator and 13 instruments.

Alexis ROLAND-MANUEL (Lévy) French *neo-classical theorist, he helped *Stravinsky define his terms of reference and wrote studies of *Ravel. His own light operas, two ballets and a piano concerto have lapsed.

b. Paris, 22.iii.1891; *d.* there, 1.xi.66.

Romain ROLLAND The Nobel-winning French novelist was a progressive force in music, siding with *Ravel against the Parisian reactionaries and organising German artists to join his anti-war campaign. He was professor of music history at the Ecole Normale from 1896 and wrote blockbuster biographies of Beethoven (1903) and Handel (1910), as well as incisive essays on contemporaries such as *Strauss and *Mahler. His major enterprises were a 10-volume musical novel, *Jean-Christophe* (1904–12), and a seven-volume study of *Beethoven the Creator* (1928–43), both of which boosted the myth of the composer as social revolutionary. He won the 1915 Nobel not for literature but for peace, and was himself a hero in the Soviet Union, where his play, *Colas Breugnon*, was made into an opera.

b. Claecy, Nièvre, 29.i.1866; *d.* Vézelay, Yonne, 30.xii.44.

Amadeo ROLDAN Short-lived Afro-Cuban violinist, he sought to meld tunes and rhythms of both heritages in westernized symphonic works.

b. Paris, 12.vii.1900; *d.* Havana, Cuba, 2.iii. 39. *works include*: Overture on Cuban themes (1925), Danza Negra for voice and septet (1929), *3 Toques* for chamber orchestra (1931), *Motivos de son* for soprano, chamber orchestra and percussion (1934), 2 sets of *Ritmicas* for sextet and percussion ensemble.

the ROLLING STONES Rock group
that rose in the *Beatles' slipstream to dispel popular music's last vestiges of bourgeois civility. To a *rhythm-and-blues base,
the Stones added a thumping beat and
amplified volume which – allied to angry
lyrics, sexual come-ons and flagrant abuse
of narcotics – won them worldwide fame.
Mick Jagger, Brian Jones and Keith
Richards narrowly escaped jail on drugs
charges thanks to a *Times* leader which
thundered the Alexander Pope reproach,
'Who breaks a butterfly upon a wheel?'

While the Beatles resorted to studio
sophistry, the Stones were wholly upfront
– quintessentially a live band, belting out
their all in numbers that mocked middle-
class moderation ('I Can't Get No
Satisfaction'), neuroses ('19th Nervous
Breakdown') and pharmaceutical pallia-
tives ('Mother's Little Helper'). 'I know
it's only rock and roll,' they yelled, 'but I
like it.' Jones, ousted in May 1969, was
found dead in his Sussex swimming pool
and was mourned in a free Hyde Park
concert. The group's creative energies
waned but they held together for comeback tours and marketing initiatives.
Richards survived heroin addiction and
Jagger, whose liaisons filled the tabloids,
married twice and amassed a battery of
image-men and lawyers.

> **Mick (Michael Philip) Jagger**, vocalist; *b.*
> Dartford, Kent, 26.vii.43;
> **Keith Richard(s)**, guitar, *b.* Dartford,
> 18.xii.43;
> **Bill Wyman** (William Perks), bass player; *b.*
> SE London, 23.x.36;
> **Charlie Watts**, drums, b Neasden, North
> London, 2.vi.41;
> **Brian Jones** (Lewis Brian Hopkin-Jones),
> rhythm guitar; *b.* Cheltenham, 28.ii.42; *d.*
> Sussex, 3.vii.69. He was replaced first by
> Mick Taylor, then by Ron Wood.

romantic music Art of an era that combined sentiment and extravagance. The
early romantic period, dating roughly from
Napoleonic to Crimean wars, yielded
nationalist and exotic trends in Weber,
Chopin, Berlioz; the middle period was
dominated by Wagner, *Brahms and Liszt.
Late romanticism, from around 1890 to
1914, pushed the means of expression to
the limits of symphonic endurance in
hugely scored works by *Strauss and

*Mahler. It was the point of departure for
20th-century modernism.

Sigmund ROMBERG Broadway's an-
swer to Franz *Léhar. Of his 70 shows,
Hollywood made hits of *The Student
Prince* (NY, 2.xii.24; filmed 1954 with
Mario Lanza) and *The Desert Song* (NY,
30.xi.26, filmed 1929, 44, 53).

> *b.* Nagy Kaniza, Hungary, 29.vii.1887;
> arrived US 1909; *d.* NY, 9.xi.51. *other oper-*
> *ettas: The Midnight Girl* (first hit, 23.ii.14),
> *Maytime* (16.viii.17), *Blossom Time* (with
> Schubert melodies, 29.ix.21), *The Rose of*
> *Stamboul* (7.iii.22), *Up in Central Park*
> (27.i.45).

Romeo and Juliet Shakespearian ballet
by *Prokofiev containing some of his most
sparkling tunes (1938); also operas by
Sutermeister (1940) and Blacher (1947).

Julius RÖNTGEN Brahmsian Dutchman, composer of 12 symphonies and three
operas.

> *b.* Leipzig, Germany, 9.v.1855; *d.* Bilthoven,
> Netherlands, 13.ix.32.

Guy (Joseph Marie) ROPARTZ Pupil
of César Franck, he wrote five symphonies
and six string quartets influenced by the
sounds of his native Brittany. He headed
the conservatoires at Nancy and
Strasbourg.

> *b.* Guingamp, Britanny, 15.vi.1864; *d.*
> Lanloup-par-Plouha, 22.xi.55. *major stage*
> *work: Le Pays* (Nancy, 1.ii.12).

Ned ROREM Sensualist, indiscreet
American, his elegant scores belied the
sharpness of his tongue. Like Gore Vidal in
US literature, he was famed more for what
he said than what he wrote; his epigrams
would fill a dictionary of quotations, and
doubtless will some day. Once seen as
America's Schubert for his outpouring of
songs by 200 well-chosen poets, he
acquired oracular status for attacks on living US composers whom he accused of
lacking individuality. To justify his own
neo-romantic style he said: 'Music does
not evolve; it revolves like a great wheel.'

Apart from hundreds of songs and four
operas, Rorem wrote three symphonies
and piano concertos – abstract music that
seemed to lack constant focus. What it
missed was highlighted by the symphonic
suite *Sunday Morning* (1978), where

Rorem wordlessly re-imagined a poem by Wallace Stevens but used evocative lines as titles for each of the eight movements. His literary impulse was probably more powerful than his musical urge, for without the stimulus of a text he was bereft of ideas.

b. Richmond, Indiana, 23.x.23; st with *Sowerby, *Thomson, *Copland; lived in Morocco 1949–51, Paris 1951–57, describing his hedonist experiences in amusing journals; taught at Buffalo (1959–61), Utah (66–67), Curtis Institute (1980–); *other works*: operas, *A Childhood Miracle* (NY, Punch Opera Co, 10.v.55), *The Robbers* (NY, 15.iv.58), *Miss Julie* (NY, 4.xi.65), *Bertha* (NY, 26.xi.73); *The Poet's Requiem* (1957); symphonic poem, *Eagles* (1959), double concerto (1979), piano concerto for left hand (Philadelphia, 2.xi.91).

Hilding (Constantin) ROSENBERG Known as Sweden's 'master gardener' for his horticultural hobbies and the young composers he nurtured, Rosenberg was the first Swede to reject musical nationalism and Sibelian conformity. He embraced ideas from the rest of Europe, notably from *Hindemith and Les *Six. His 2nd symphony, the *Sinfonia grave* (Gothenburg, 27.iii.35) suited the national mood; the 5th, titled *The Gardener*, with contralto solo and chorus, was his namepiece. In all, he wrote eight symphonies and 12 string quartets, of which the 4th and 6th are the most vital. The first of seven operas, *Journey to America* (Stockholm, 24.xi.32) was an immigrant saga that combined Swedish folklore with *Weill-style jazzery. Four opera-oratorios dramatized Thomas Mann's saga of *Joseph and his Brothers*. After 1945 he took up *12-note music, composing six serial quartets.

b. Bosjökloster, Sweden, 21.vi.1892; *d*. Stockholm, 19.v.85. *other works*: sinfonia concertante for cello and orch. (1945), three string concertos (1960) inspired by Henry Purcell, *Alone in the Silent Night* (1976) for tenor and string quartet.

Der Rosenkavalier Opera's last comic hit. *Hofmannsthal's libretto mixed sentiment with snobbery, while *Strauss's music was both erotic and anti-romantic. A bored noblewoman of 32, the Marschallin, pushes her 17-year-old lover (Octavian, a mezzo part) into the arms of a young virgin. The three hours are shortened by Strauss's sumptuous, waltz-riddled score. Composed May 1909–26.v.10. fp: Dresden, 26.i.11, cond. Schuch.

Nikolai ROSLAVETS The mystery man of Soviet music – a revolutionary leader of the late 1920s who was expunged for half a century. Dubbed 'the Russian Schoenberg,' he became a *cause célèbre* for Western modernists, but their postglasnost exhumations proved disappointing. True, Roslavets had written a pellucid, contrapuntal *Chamber Symphony in the manner of the great atonalist but it played uncomfortably melodiously. A supposedly atonal violin sonata of 1913 and an unorchestrated 1925 violin concerto were lamentably tame to modern ears accustomed to daily dissonance. Only his tone poems and string quartets showed much by way of individuality.

b. Suray, nr. Chernigov, Russia, 5.i.1881; *d*. Moscow, 23.viii.44.

Mstislav ROSTROPOVICH Inspirational cellist who drew two concertos from Shostakovich, a revised masterpiece from Prokofiev, a symphony and sonatas from Britten and dedications from dozens of others, including *Dutilleux, *Lutosławski, *Bernstein and Panufnik. Expelled from Russia by the Brezhnev regime in 1977, he flew back on the day hardline communists tried to depose Gorbachev, lending his presence to the resistance around Boris Yeltsin.

b. Baku, 27.iii.1927; married soprano Galina Vishnevskaya.

Nino ROTA Italy's finest film composer was Fellini's regular partner and wrote masterly soundtracks for Visconti (*The Leopard*), Zeffirelli (*Romeo and Juliet*) and Francis Ford Coppola (*Godfather I* and *II*), whose theme was fleetingly heard years earlier in *8½*). At Zeffirelli's behest, he composed incidental music for *Much Ado About Nothing* at the National Theatre in London. His lyricism was tempered by playfulness and irony that particularly suited Fellini's bittersweet childhood flashbacks.

Rota also composed 12 operas and many concert works, including four symphonies. A traditional craftsman in the manner of his teacher, *Casella, he kept an open mind for new techniques and wrote a tongue-in-cheek *Fantasia on a 12-note theme in Mozart's Don Giovanni* for piano and orch. (1961). His harp concerto (1948) and *Variations on a jovial theme* (1954) make brilliant use of orchestral resources. As head of the conservatory at Bari (1950–78), he spotted the conducting potential of the teenaged Riccardo Muti.

b. Milan, 3.xii.11; *d.* Rome, 10.iv.79.

Albert (Charles Paul Marie) ROUSSEL

Roussel's 3rd symphony in G-minor may be France's finest this century. Commissioned by *Koussevitsky for his Boston orchestra's jubilee (Boston, 24.x.30), its outer movements pulsate with dramatic tension and the adagio expands to a climax that provides a marvellous showcase for a virtuoso ensemble. The music is eloquent, memorable, momentous and just 25 minutes long.

The three other symphonies are rather faceless and fidgety, though the 4th (Paris, 19.x.35) sounded firmer when conducted by Germans like *Karajan. His ballet scores, notably *Bacchus et Ariane* (22.v.31), have much in common with *Ravel's, while *Le festin de l'araignée* (*The spider's feast*, 3.iv.13) is shimmeringly reminiscent of *Debussy.

Starting out as a naval officer, Roussel turned to music at 29, studying with d'*Indy until he was 37. He embraced impressionism, neo-classicism, exoticism and astringent modernism, each for a while. His earliest orchestral piece, *Résurrection* (17.v.04) was Tolstoyan. While honeymooning in India, he conceived *Evocations* (Paris, 18.v.12) of the mystic East in grand manner with three soloists and several choirs, but avoiding the ponderousness that this Germanic line up usually possesses.

A lack of charisma cost him status. He got caught in crossfire between rival styles in French music and never staked out a personal territory. The best Roussel is found among his chamber and instrumental pieces, which include a piano trio

(1902), string trio (1937) and a delightful serenade for flute, violin, viola, cello and harp (1925). His early piano works are imbued by naval experiences, while two Chinese poems op 12 (1908) and 'Jazz dans la nuit' (1928) stand out among his songs.

b. Tourcoing, northern France, 5.iv.1869; served with French navy in Indochina and north Africa; resigned 1894; taught at Schola Cantorum 1902–14; married 1909; rejected for wartime service on health grounds; visited US 1930; *d.* Royan, 23.viii.37. *other works*: opera *Aunt Caroline's Will* (opéra-bouffe, Olomouc, Czechoslovakia, 14.xi.36), *Padmâvatî* (opera-ballet, 1.vi.23), *Aenéas* (ballet) (Brussels, 31.vii.35); *Suite en fa* (Boston, 21.1.27), piano concerto (7.vi.28), cello concertino (6.ii.37), psalm 80 for tenor, chorus and orchestra (25.iv.29); string quartet (1932) two violin sonatas (1908, 1924), two works for flute and piano; three cycles of piano pieces.

Miklos ROZSA

Miklos **ROZSA** Hungarian composer who linked up in London with the film-maker Alexander Korda to bring Budapest cosmopolitanism to the big screen. He scored *The Jungle Book* (1942) for Korda, *Double Indemnity* and *The Lost Weekend* (1946) for Billy Wilder, *Spellbound* (1945) for Hitchcock, *Ben Hur* (1959) for William Wyler and two outstanding Roman epics, *Julius Caesar* (1953) and *Quo Vadis*, in which he drew on early Greek monody to adumbrate an authentic antiquity. He won three Oscars.

Each year he took time out to compose 'serious' music, more astringent than his movie scores. The violin concerto (Dallas, 15.i.56) he wrote for *Heifetz has the texture and understated irony of early *Bartók; its themes were later sanitized for reuse in Billy Wilder's *The Private Life of Sherlock Holmes* (1969). The double concerto (Los Angeles, 29.ix.63) for Heifetz and Gregor Piatigorsky is more broadly central European, with a neo-classical theme and variations as its agreeable centrepiece. Rozsa figured in Leonard *Bernstein's sensational debut concert with the unrehearsed première of *Variations on a Hungarian peasant song* (NY, 14.xi.43).

b. Budapest, 18.iv.07; st with Bartók and Kodály, then in Leipzig with Hermann Grabner; moved to Paris 1932, then London 1935 to write ballet, *Hungaria* for Markova-Dolin company; emigrated to US in 1939;

other concert works: Theme, Variations and Finale (Duisburg, 1933), concertos for piano (LA, 6.iv.67) and viola (Pittsburgh, 4.v.84, Zukerman soloist). *other movies*: *The Four Feathers* (1938), *The Thief of Baghdad* (1939), *Lady Hamilton* (1941), *The Naked City* (1948), *The Red Danube* (1949), *Madame Bovary* (1949), *The Asphalt Jungle* (1950), *Lust for Life* (1956), *A Time to Love and a Time to Die* (1958), *King of Kings* (1961), *El Cid* (1962), *Providence* (Alain Resnais, 1977).

(Charles) Edmund RUBBRA Unsung British symphonist, born on the wrong side of the tracks to parents who were poor but musical. He was sent to work as a railway clerk at the age of 14, gave concert of Cyril *Scott's music in Northampton, and was admitted by the composer to the Royal College of Music.

Dedicated to symphonism which, he insisted, had to stem from a melodic source, he rejected film work and a solo career, writing four symphonies until War forced him into uniform as a touring pianist. The break was crucial to his artistic and spiritual progress. He re-emerged newly converted to Roman Catholicism with a 5th symphony (London, 26.i.49) that calls to mind *Pfitzner's neo-baroque language for *Palestrina*, and Elgar at his most *nobilmente*. It set the tone for six more symphonies, among which the 7th (1957) is preoccupied with nature on a grander scale than *Vaughan Williams and the 8th (1968) is inscribed to the religious philosopher Teilhard de Chardin. The 9th (1973) relates the Resurrection story with chorus and soloists, while the last two symphonies reduce their message to a single movement and small orchestra. Like *Messiaen, Rubbra looked to eastern philosophies but never changed his basic conception that music must speak directly to the hearts of men and women. His is among the loveliest settings of Psalm XXIII.

b. Northampton, 23.v.01; lecturer at Oxford 1947–68; *d.* Gerrards Cross, Bucks, 13.ii.86. *other works*: concertos for piano, violin and viola, four string quartets, masses for both Anglican and RC rites.

Marcel RUBIN Eclectic Viennese symphonist, his 4th (of ten) was constructed around the strophes of a *Brecht poem,

'Kinderkreuzzug' and the Dies Irae. A pupil of *Milhaud, he was open to all ideas except serialism.

b. Vienna, 7.vii.05 (on *Mahler's 45th birthday); ran contemporary music concert series 1931–8, emigrated to Mexico; returned 1947; *other works*: opera, *Kleider machen Leute*; oratorio *Der Heiligenstädter Psalm* (after Beethoven's testament, for baritone, chorus and orchestra).

Poul RUDERS Danish promulgator of a medieval form of *minimalism, tiny phrases of older music repeated and variegated in a manner similar to Michael *Nyman. His first violin concerto (1981) is flagrantly based on Vivaldi's *Four Seasons*, that most widespread piece of classical wallpaper, but sets a hypnotic agenda of its own in the hushed Cradle Song of the central movement. He is also capable of fearsome atonalities, some like *Stabat Mater* (1974) absorbed from Maxwell *Davies' stage works, others – *Manhattan Abstraction* (1982), concerto for clarinet and twin orchestra (1985) – entirely his own nightmares. His dual mastery of populist and ascetic expression was unique, though pastiche-like.

b. Ringsted, 27.iii.49; self-taught, self-employed; *other works*: opera *Tycho* (1986), symphony (1989), *Tundra* (homage to Jean Sibelius, 1990), Drama-trilogy – three linked concertos for piano, percussion and cello; 2nd violin concerto (1991); *Medieval Variations* (1970); three string quartets, Dante sonata for solo piano (1970), 2nd piano sonata (1982).

Dane RUDHYAR French mystic who took a Hindu name and in 1916 settled in America, where he acted the part of Christ in the silent Hollywood version of *The Ten Commandments* and went on to become a big name in astrology. He wrote a couple of 'dance poems' that were played at the Metropolitan Opera (NY, 4.iv.17) and 5 'syntonies' for orchestra but his most original work was for solo piano – series of Tetragrams (1920–68) and Pentagrams (1924–6) that bear heavenly missives in a synthesis of *Skryabin and Indian sounds. He was a proficient painter, popular lecturer and best-selling author of a dozen books on 'astro-psychology'.

b. Paris, 23.iii.1895 (as Daniel Chevennière); *d.* San Francisco, 13.ix.85.

Zbigniew RUDZINSKI Composer of a successful Polish chamber opera, *The Mannekins* (1981), about a philosophical tailor and his brainless models.

b. Czechowice, Poland, 23.x.35; taught Warsaw 1973– ; *other work*: quartet for two pianos and percussion (1969).

Rugby *Honegger's orchestral impression of the *sport was performed at half-time during an international between France and England in Paris, on 31.xii.28.

rug concerts 1970s events devised by Boulez in New York and London, in which the audience sat on the ground and debated afterwards with the musicians.

Carl (Charles Sprague) RUGGLES True to his name, Ruggles wrote granitic, tough-hued music. Rowdy, dissonant and uningratiating, his few finished works have a slow, grinding logic amid evocative imagery. *Sun-treader* (Paris, 25.ii.32, cond. *Slonimsky), planned as the climax of a symphonic triptych, marches grimly to a solar destination. The movements meant to precede it exist, less performed, as *Men, Lilacs, Marching Mountains* (NY, 7.xii.24) and *Portals* (NY, 24.i.26). Together with a symphonic suite for five trumpets and bass trumpet called *Angels* (1922, revised 1938), they amount to almost his entire output.

Ruggles rejected tonality as too soft on the ear. His method, developed independently of Schoenberg, was never to repeat a note until it had faded from memory – generally an interval of nine intervening notes. Indomitable and reclusive like *Ives and *Varèse, his cultural sympathies were predominantly Germanic and he spent years writing an opera on a Gerhardt Hauptmann play, *The Sunken Bell*, before burning the score. He was a talented painter, conducted an orchestra at Winona, Minnesota, for four years (1908–12), taught at the University of Miami (1937–43) and had a farm in Vermont. He was, and will remain, a voice in the wilderness, after the title of his first performed work, *Vox clamans in deserto* (for voice and chamber orchestra, 1923).

b. Marion, Massachusetts, 11.iii.1876; st with *Paine at Harvard; married Charlotte Snell 1908; *d.* Bennington, Vermont, 24.x.71. *other works*: *Polyphonic composition* (for three pianos, 1940); *Evocations* (piano suite, orch. 1945); *Organum* (for large orch., 1949).

Russia As the century dawned, Russia seemed poised to overtake Germany as the musical pacemaker. Tchaikovsky, six years dead, was Europe's most popular symphonist and *Rachmaninov's appeal was equally direct. The music of *Skryabin, *Stravinsky and *Prokofiev fizzed with a vitality that conquered audiences despite atonalities and technical difficulty.

This renaissance was derailed by the Bolshevik revolution and destroyed by intellectual *emigration and Stalin's enforcement of *socialist realism. The 1960s Khruschev thaw produced a minor Russian resurgence, which found full voice under the Gorbachev liberalization, when *Schnittke, *Gubaidulina and their successors burst upon western music like a long-dormant volcano. As Soviet society disintegrated, however, many musicians migrated to Germany.

William RUSSO Pursuing a fresh synthesis between jazz, ethnic music and symphonies, Russo came up with an enchanting blues concerto called *Street Music* (1977) for harmonica, piano and instrumental group. Distinct from the noise pictures that American composers paint of their cities, this is several slices of cross-rhythmic life in a San Francisco neighbourhood whose occupants come from every corner of the globe. Russo has also written two symphonies and an *English Concerto* (1963) for violin and jazz orchestra – as well as a *Zeitgeist* series of late-sixties rock cantatas.

b. Chicago, 25.vi.28; trombonist with Stan Kenton Orch. 1950–4; formed London Jazz Orch. 1962–5.

Luigi RUSSOLO Musical führer of *futurism, neither his compositions nor his instruments survived the initial *succès de scandale*.

b. Portogruaro, Italy, 1.v.1885; *d.* Cerro di Laveno, 4.ii.47.

Peter RUZICKA *Mahler-led new German, his *Five Fragments* for full orchestra (1987) intersperse Mahlerian marches and adagios with *serial aphorisms. Derived from an abandoned symphony, the episodes work well together as a music-historical lecture. Less agreeable is *Rapprochement and Silence*, four fragments on Schumann for piano and 42 stringed instruments (1981), a collage of keyboard quotations and avant-garde flutterings.

> *b*. Düsseldorf, 3.vii.48; dir. Hamburg State Opera, 1988– ; *other works*: *Satyagraha, rapprochement and withdrawal* for orch. (1984), concerto for beat band and orch., *Stress* for a eight percussion groups, six piano preludes (1984).

Frederic RZEWSKI An un-Caged escapee from experimentalism, he gravitated around 1970 to agit-prop politics, setting inflammatory texts to odd accompaniments. He delivered a Homer recitation against the background of rubber flowerpots, and set texts by rioters at Attica jail to a couple of oft-repeated bars of minimalist jazz. His 36 variations for solo piano were composed on a Chilean revolutionary tune, 'The People United will Never be Defeated'. His idol was *Eisler.

> *b*. Westfield, Massachusetts, 13.iv.38; st with *Piston, *Sessions, *Babbitt, *Dallapiccola; co-formed Musica Elettronica Viva in Rome, 1966; prof. at Liège 1977– ; *other works*: Requiem (1968), *Coming Together* for speaker and instruments (1972), piano variation on 'No Place to go but Around' (1974), *Satyrica* for jazzband (1983), *The Invincible Persian Army* for low voice and *prepared piano (1984).

Kaija SAARIAHO Among the *Ears Open rebels who radicalized Finnish music, *Lindberg and Saariaho joined the Parisian avant-garde, seduced by *Boulez's merger of music and technology. Most of Saariaho's work combines live and taped sounds, tracing gentle, sensual patterns on a timeless parabolic landscape. *Verblendungen* (1984), *Lichtbogen* (1985) and *Io* (1987) have a serene aloofness unlike any other computer product. Her scores are equally beautiful to the eye.
  b. Helsinki, 14.x.52; st with *Heininen and *Ferneyhough; *other works*: *Laconisme l'aisle* for solo flute (1982), *Jardin secret II* for harpsichord and tape (1984).

Paul SACHER The Swiss conductor married an heiress to the Valium and Librium pharmaceutical patents and applied her fortune to commissioning masterpieces of music, including *Bartók's *Music for strings, percussion and celesta*, Hindemith's *Harmonie der Welt*, Honegger's 2nd and 4th symphonies, Strauss's *Metamorphosen*, Stravinsky's *Concerto in D*, Carter's oboe concerto, Birtwistle's *Endless Parade* and various works by Martinů, who died in his arms. To enhance his priceless collection of composer autographs, he bought Webern and Stravinsky archives at auction for the Sacher Foundation in Basle.
  b. Basle, 28.iv.06; founded Basle Chamber Orchestra 1926.

Sacre du Printemps – See Rite of Spring

Harald (Sigurd Johan) SAEVERUD The Norwegian symphonist expressed the grandeur of the fjords in rugged diatonic harmonies. *Sinfonia Dolorosa* (Bergen, 6.iii.41), the 6th of nine bemoans the Nazi occupation; the 8th was commissioned by and named for the US state of Minnesota (Minneapolis, 18.x.58); the 9th (Bergen, 12.vi.66) havers between Sibelius and Stravinsky. He wrote a 1947 suite for Ibsen's *Peer Gynt* with the intention of supplanting *Grieg's.
  b. Bergen,17.iv.1897; salaried state composer from 53; *d*. Bergen, 27.iii.92. *other works*: *50 Small Variations for Orchestra* (1931), incidental music for *The Rape of Lucretia* (1935), concertos for oboe, bassoon, piano and violin and many piano pieces, notably *Slätter* (1942).

Saint François d'Assise Messiaen's only opera. fp: Paris, 28.xi.83.

(Charles-) Camille SAINT-SAËNS His life's work done by 1890, Saint-Saëns whiled away his latter years collecting honours and fighting modernism. His 20th-century output amounts to four insignificant operas, an inferior 2nd cello concerto (Paris, 5.ii.05), a 2nd string quartet and sundry instrumental pieces. Then, in 1921, three wind-and-piano sonatas unexpectedly recaptured his old vitality, the luminous clarinet sonata in particular flourishing lively melodies and a sombre chorale. Late that year, after watching *Lakmé* in Algiers, he climbed into a hotel bed and died contentedly in his sleep, aged 86.
  b. Paris, 9.x.1835; debut there 6.v.1846; *d*. Algiers, 16.xii.21. *works include*: 13 operas of which only *Samson et Dalila* (Weimar, 2.xii.1877; cond. Liszt) succeeds; other operas are *Les Barabares* (1901), *Hélène* (1904), *L'Ancêtre* (1906) and *Déjanire* (1911); three

symphonies, five piano concertos, three violin concertos.

Luis Humberto SALGADO Ecuadorian composer of three national operas and seven symphonies.

b. Cayambe, Ecuador, 10.xii.03; taught Quito Conservatory 1934–68.

Aulis SALLINEN The most successful Finn since Sibelius, Sallinen managed the radio orchestra in Helsinki while searching for a personal, post-serial style. *Mauermusik* (1962), mourning the erection of the Berlin Wall, won marks for political acumen rather than personality. He rediscovered melody in a violin concerto (1968), followed by simplicity in a 3rd string quartet of frozen beauty. Written to acquaint school children with his music, it took a familiar tune 'Peltoniemi Hintrik's Funeral March' and adroitly subverted it by having violin and cello play the theme in unison but with different bowings. To this echo-chamber opening, Sallinen added contemplative tune-snatches and dissonances to create a quarter-hour work of decisive character. The same method provided the basis for his first symphony (1971).

It was in opera, though, that Sallinen broke through. *The Horseman* (*Savonlinna, 17.vii.75) was the first Finnish opera to win foreign respect, recounting the nation's struggle for freedom from powerful neighbours, in music with its own dramatic agenda as Sallinen subtly shifted rhythms from the rush of battle to almost-static moments of oppression. *The Red Line* (Helsinki, 30.xi.78), his second opera, was a village drama of the northern tundra; the third, *The King Goes Forth to France* (Savonlinna, 7.vii.84), jointly commissioned by Covent Garden and the BBC, deals with the descent into a new Ice Age. Widely performed, they lacked the *Horseman's* startling mastery; nor was a moodily propulsive 5th symphony, *Washington Mosaics* (Washington D.C., 10.x.85) a great advance on its predecessors. In 1981 Sallinen was given a lifetime salary by the Finnish state to allow him to compose without having to earn a living. His official status drew scorn from the *Ears Open rebels and Sallinen faced a mid-life challenge of having to prove himself all over again. He concentrated on an opera on the *Kullervo* saga intended for Helsinki's new opera house, but first staged in Los Angeles (25.ii.92).

b. Salmi, Finland (now Russia), 9.iv.35; st with *Merikanto, *Kokkonen; *other works:* cello concerto (1976); 5th string quartet 'Pieces of Mosaic' (Kuhno, 18.vii.84, by *Kronos), ballet, *Heavenly Delights* to music from symphonies 1, 3 and 4 (Swedish TV, 20.x.86).

Erkki SALMENHAARA Radical Finnish simplifier, his piano sonata is virtually minimalist.

b. Helsinki, 12.iii.41; st with *Kokkonen and *Ligeti; taught Helsinki U. 1963– ; *major orch. works:* 4th symphony (Helsinki, 13.x.72), *Adagietto* (23.xii.82), cello concerto (Lahti, 25.iii.88).

Franz SALMHOFER Echt-Viennese musician, boasting blood-ties to Schubert and tuition from *Schmidt, he wrote incidental music for 300 plays at the Burgtheater where he was chief conductor from 1929–39. Sacked by Nazis, he ran the State Opera (1945–55) and Volksoper (1955–63) after the war. His operas – *The Lady in the Dream* (1935), *Ivan Sergeievich Tarassenko* (1938) and *Das Werbekleid* (1946) – survive in local repertory and his Lieder and theatre suites remain popular.

b. Vienna, 22.i.1900; *d.* there 2.ix.75. *other works:* two symphonies, trumpet concerto, cello concerto.

Salome Oscar Wilde's fable of Herod's lust for his teenage step-daughter and hers for the saintly John the Baptist culminates in her self-debauchment and the prophet's decapitation. *Strauss milked the sexual, religious and necrophile sensationalism with a 100-piece orchestra in a 100-minute one-act opera that proved his first dramatic coup. fp: Dresden, 9.xii.05.

Esa-Pekka SALONEN Co-leader of Finland's *Ears Open rebellion against state-sponsored elitist modernism, his baton skills outstripped his composing as he conducted the Philharmonia, London, from 1985 and became music director at the Los Angeles Philharmonic in 1991. In a saxophone concerto (Helsinki, 22.ix.81) and *Floof* (1990), Salonen aimed to bridge the chasm between rock and concert music by using sounds and gestures common to both.

b. Helsinki, 30.vi.58; st with *Rautavaara and *Castiglioni; *other works*: cello sonata (1977), wind quintet (1982), ITA series for solo instruments.

salsa Literally: 'sauce'. Cuban band rhythms that reheated 1940s New York jazz.

Salzburg Mozart's birthplace was a cultural backwater until it found itself the second city in shrunken Austria after the First World War. Together with *Strauss and his librettists *Hofmannsthal and Zweig, the theatrical wizard Max Reinhardt (1873–1943) founded a summer festival in 1921 which provided a refuge for top musicians and actors from urban pressures, enabling them to devote time and affection to acknowledged masterpieces. The festival was a haven of liberty in the 1930s, yoked to Nazism 1938–44 and revived initially as a mildly modernist conclave by Bernhard Paumgartner and Gottfried von *Einem. Under the heavy hand of local hero Herbert von *Karajan from 1955, it was a showcase for overpaid stars in predictable roles and static stagings. A massive Festspielhaus was gouged into the mountainside and the festival turned into the music industry's trade fair.

Karajan added sub-festivals at Easter and Whitsun.

On his demise in 1989, a government commission recommended sweeping reforms under the Belgian director, Gérard Mortier, with a view to rejuvenating repertoire and audience. Despite the city's conservatism, several important operas were created at Salzburg. They include: Strauss's *Die Liebe der Danae* (1952), Von Einem's *Dantons Tod* (1947) and *Der Prozess* (1953), Orff's *Antigonae* (1949), Henze's *The Bassarids* (1966) Berio's *Un re in ascolto* (1984) and Penderecki's *The Black Mask* (1986).

Carlos (Léon) SALZEDO French harpist of Spanish descent, he migrated to New York in 1909 to play in the Met orchestra and founded the International Composers Guild with *Varèse. He advanced the capacity of his instrument in compositions that progressed from *Ravel-like delicacy to tough-minded dissonance.

b. Arcachon, France, 6.iv.1885; US citizen 1923; taught at Juilliard and Curtis; set up Salzedo Harp colony at Camden, Maine, 1931; d. Waterville, Maine, 17.viii.61. *works include*: The Enchanted Isle, symphonic poem for harp and orch. (1918), concerto for harp and seven winds (1926), harp sonata (1922), harp suite (1943).

Eric SALZMAN US musical activist, he staged contemporary concerts in New York and formed an American Music Theater Festival in Philadelphia, believing that *mixed-media shows were the way to bring new music to a broad public. His scores apply serial and electronic techniques.

b. NY, 8.ix.33; st with *Sessions, *Babbitt, *Petrassi; critic on *NY Times* (1958–62) and editor *Musical Quarterly* (1983–87); *theatre works include*: Foxes and Hedgehogs (1967), radio opera Boxes (1982), *Big Jim and the Small-time Investors* (1985).

El Sálon México *Copland's discovery of folk resources, while holidaying with *Chávez. fp: Mexico City, 27.viii.37, cond. Chávez.

Gustave SAMAZEUILH French critic who made arrangements of Debussy, Dukas, Franck and Fauré.

b. Bordeaux, 2.vi.1877; d. Paris, 4.viii.67.

orchestral works: Etude symphonique (1907), *Chant d'Espagne* (1926, also virtuosic violin/ piano version), *Le cercle des heures* (1934).

samba Brazilian dance of African origin, a kind of ²/₄ shuffle. Allied to *jazz it spawned the 1950s *bossa nova craze.

Lazare SAMINSKY A *Rimsky-Korsakov pupil, he became expert in Persian Jewish liturgy and used its tunes as the basis for his music. In NY from 1920, he co-founded the League of Composers and was music dir. of Temple Emanu-El (1924–58).
> *b.* Valegotsulovo, near Odessa, 8.xi.1882; *d.* Port Chester, NY, 30.vi.59. *works include*: choral 5th symphony, *City of Solomon and Christ* (1930), Hebrew Rhapsody (violin-piano, 1911), much vocal music.

Sven-David SANDSTRÖM There are numerous Swedish composers called Sandström; Sven-David is the only one of international significance. He wrote a 1980 opera on Eugene O'Neill's *Emperor Jones* and a two hour electronic Requiem for child victims of war (1982). Percussion predominates in his work and is exemplified in *Drums* (1980). His emotional side was released by the poetry of William Blake; his 1978 *a cappella* version of *A Cradle Song/ The Tyger* is a confrontation between infantile innocence and bestial evil.
> *b.* Motala, Sweden, 30.x.42; st with *Lidholm, *Ligeti; *other works*: guitar concerto (1983), three string quartets.

Lazslo SARY Founder of Budapest's new music studio, Sáry advanced from copying *Cage – *Sounds for Cimbalom* (1972) – to a primitive *minimalism represented by *Pebble in a Pot* (1978) for percussion ensemble. His repetitiveness barely suited *Socrates' Last Teaching* (1980) for voice and piano.
> *b.* Györ, Hungary, 1.i.40; *other works*: *Sounds* for any soloist or ensemble (1973), *Drop by Drop* for two prepared pianos (1975).

Erik (Alfred Leslie) SATIE Practical joker or musical prophet – the Satie paradox is unresolved. A man who gave such titles as *Desiccated embryos, 3 pear-shaped pieces* and *Things seen from right and left* (*without glasses*) to his scores; who wrote a *minimalist 18-note *Vexations* to be played

840 times without variation or pause for a day and a night; who dressed in pince-nez, velvet suit and bowler hat; who set up his own church; an eccentric of such extremity was surely no serious composer.

Yet Satie was, at one time, a seminal influence on *Debussy and Ravel and at another the captain of Les *Six. His *furniture music bred the virus of *Muzak and his mischief the quirkiness of *Cage. Like many who played the public fool he was a sad and lonely man, his vulnerability resounding through music of rare translucence.

Of middle-class French and Scottish parentage, he dropped out of the Conservatoire and occupied himself with Gregorian chant in preference to prevalent romanticism. He played piano at the Chat Noir café in Montmartre and wrote slow, enchanting *Gymnopédies* and bar-less *Gnossiennes* (1890) that Debussy delicately orchestrated. He weaned his friend off Wagner and encouraged his pursuit of tonal purity in *Pelléas*.

He advertised a non-existent opera, *Tristan's Bastard*. In his published piano music, he scattered unrelated chords and left them unresolved and pregnant with tension. Stung by accusations of incompetence, he returned to school at the age of 39, graduating from the Schola Cantorum with a certificate signed by d'*Indy and *Roussel.

He had short-lived affairs with socialism and one or two women, broke with Debussy when he became famous, insisting that he alone was 'the precursor and apostle of the musical revolution now in progress'. His ballet *Parade* (Paris, 18.v.17) caused a scandal with Picasso's cubist décor and a score that contained typewriters, a steamship whistle and pistol shots. Striking a hostile critic, he was sentenced to jail. *Socrate*, his 'symphonic drama' (14.ii.20), has passages of music-hall banality; the audience giggled when the great philosopher died. One by one, Satie alienated Les *Six; former friends were turned away as he lay dying of cirrhosis. His autobiography was to be called 'Memoirs of an amnesiac'.

His compositions number 70 works, half of them for piano. His significance, however, is greater than the substance of his music. He foresaw many of the social and artistic trends of the 20th century; and if his predictions were sometimes wild, so too were Jeremiah's. Virgil *Thomson considered him the most original mind in modern music; more is the pity that it was applied so inconsistently to musical creation.

b. Honfleur, Calvados, 17.v.1866, baptized in Anglican rite; lost his mother at age six, hated his step-mother; met Debussy 1891, Ravel 1893; moved in 1898 to a room in outlying suburb of Arcueil-Cachan; formed Ecole d'Arcueil of acolytes; *d*. Paris, 1.vii.25. *other works*: Jack-in-the-box (piano, 1900, orch. by *Milhaud), *Sports et divertissement* (piano, 1914), *sonatine bureaucratique* (piano, 1917), *Mercure* (ballet, 1924), *Relâche* ('instantaneous ballet', 1924).
Bib: O. Volta, *Satie seen through his letters*, London (M Boyars), 1989.

Somei SATOH Time vanishes in Satoh's trance-like compositions. Rooted in Shintoism and the static court music of Japan, Satoh borrowed European romanticism and electronic high-tech to create a lyrical music that seems to have neither beginning nor end. *Shiragasi (A White Heron)*, his 1987 string quartet for *Kronos, induces a sense of pleasantly suspended motion despite a thrusting, propulsive beat. *The Heavenly Spheres are Illuminated by Light* (1979), for soprano, piano, percussion and echo, is wound *Tristan*-like around a single chord. Satoh experimented in mixed media, stationing massive speakers on Japanese mountain tops and similar extravaganza, but his true métier was direct east-west communication within the confined space of a concert hall, something no Japanese other than *Takemitsu ever achieved.

b. Sendai, Japan, 1947; *other works*: *Sumeru* for chamber orch., *Birds in Warped Time* for violin and piano.

Satyricon *Maderna's opera on erotic Roman tales, signalled a modernist return to tonal and narrative truisms. fp: Scheveningen, 16.iii.73.

Henri SAUGUET The man who brought ballet back to Paris after the second world war was a prolific, unassertive composer with a vast oeuvre of 150 works and a total insouciance towards fashion. 'I feel I am neither behind nor in front; I advance only in the domain of my own music', he wrote. Born among the Bordeaux bourgeoisie, he was apprenticed to a wine merchant at 15 but was drawn to Paris by *Milhaud and joined the Ecole d'Arcueil around the eccentric *Satie. His father, outraged by his bohemian friends, ordered him to drop his given name, Jean-Pierre Poupard, and adopt his mother's maiden name of Sauguet. He was spotted by *Diaghilev and trained in dramatic arts. The summits of eight operas and 26 ballets were *La Chartreuse de Parme* (Paris Opéra 16.iii.39) and *Les forains (The Strolling Players*, 1945) with which he and Boris Kochno revived Parisian dance after the German occupation. His concert music was civilized and witty, climaxing in a *Mélodie concertante* (1964) for *Rostropovich.

b. Bordeaux, 18.v.01; *d*. Paris, 21.vi.89. *other works*: *Symphonie expiatoire*, in memory of innocent victims of war (1945), three piano concertos, *Garden concerto* for harmonica (1970), Crepuscular sonata (violin-piano, 1981), two string quartets, songs.

Saul and David *Nielsen's superb biblical opera. fp: Copenhagen, 28.xi.02.

Savonlinna Midsummer opera festival founded in 1907 by Finnish soprano Aino Ackté. Revamped in 1967, it yielded major works by *Sallinen and *Rautavaara.

saxophone Instrument family invented in Paris around 1840, they were brought back to the US 50 years later by *Sousa's military band and lent an essential sensual adornment to evolving *jazz. By the 1930s, four saxophones were *de rigeur* in a jazz band. Bizet and Massenet blended saxophones in orchestral scores; *Strauss ordered four for *Sinfonia Domestica*; *Glazunov wrote the outstanding saxophone concerto.

Robert SAXTON At the age of nine he wrote to *Britten for technical advice; by 16 he was familiar with *Boulez's latest techniques. Precocious to a fault, Saxton started to show individuality in the 1980s with orch. works on visual and literary themes, composed with an unerring sense of structure and distinctive internal harmonies. The *Concerto for Orch. (London, 13.viii.84) described a circular Kabbalistic route through life; the Chamber Symphony *Circles of Light* (5.iii.86, cond. *Salonen) took its cue from Dante's vision of paradise. Unassertive and shy, his music exerted a stealthy charm in works like *In the Beginning* (31.i.88) and the violin concerto (Leeds, 22.vi.90). He wrote an opera with Arnold Wesker on his play *Caritas* (Huddersfield, 21.xi.91), describing with inflexions of Gregorian chant the plight of a young girl walled up inside a medieval church.
  b. London, 8.x.53; st with *Lutyens; *other orch. works*: *Ring of Eternity* (London, 24.viii.83, cond. *Knussen), viola concerto (Cheltenham, 9.vii.86), Variation on 'Summer is Icumen In' (Aldeburgh, 13.vi.87), *Elijah's Violin* (London 13.ii.89), cello concerto (London, 1992). Chamber music includes piano sonata in memory of *Bartók (1981) and *Piccola Musica per Luigi *Dallapiccola* (Montepulciano 5.viii.81).

Ahmet Adnan SAYGUN The outstanding Turkish composer studied with d'*Indy in Paris and became expert in Gregorian chant; his foremost work is the oratorio *Yunus Emre*, commemorating the 14th-century poet, that *Stokowski premiered in 1958.
  b. Izmir, Turkey, 7.ix.07, st Paris 1928–31; accompanied *Bartók on Anatolian trip 1936, head of composition at Ankara and Istanbul conservatories 1946–91; *d.* Ankara, 6.i.91. *other works*: opera *Koroglu* (1973), 3rd symphony (Koussevitsky Fund commission, 1960), cello concerto (1987), three string quartets.

Scandinavia Grieg, Sibelius and Nielsen towered retardingly over the musicians of northern Europe. Fired by fading *nationalism and officially rewarded with state pensions for conformist work, Scandinavian composers pursued a safe and insular art. Deviants, like *Valen and *Pettersson, were ostracized; *avant-garde fevers were short-lived. The region produced no new composer of world stature this century. There was, however, a glint of renewal in the ascent of Esa-Pekka *Salonen, whose anti-establishmentarianism encouraged other young composers.

Scaramouche Two-piano suite by *Milhaud (1937); also pantomime by Sibelius (1922).

scat singing Improvisatory jazz style of stringing together meaningless syllables – babadabadou – as a vocal cadenza in the middle of a big number.

Giacinto SCELSI (Count Dayla Valva) Sicilian aristocrat, dismissed as a dilettante, he traversed most modern trends before finding a philosophy of inner peace. The first Italian to write *12-note music back in 1936, he discarded Schoenberg's method and travelled to Tibet. He spent the war in Switzerland, was left by his British wife Dorothy for whom he had written a sixth piano suite, *Il capricci di Ty* (1939), and suffered a breakdown involving years in a convalescent home. Amusing himself at the hospital piano, he hit upon a concept of one-note music – calming, sedative, hypnotic. *Four pieces, each one on a single note* for small orch. was played in Lausanne (4.xii.1961), a rare event since Scelsi did not favour performance.

He persisted with solemn, psychedelic pieces of intense spirituality. *Aion*, his longest orchestral piece at around 20 minutes, was written in 1961 but not heard for quarter of a century (Cologne, 12.x.85). His ancestral castello collapsed in the 1980 Naples earthquake just as composers began flocking to his door, recognizing that Scelsi had discovered monotony and *minimalism long before them. Scelsi redated his manuscripts to confuse would-be scholars, refused interviews and threatened to kill anyone who took his photograph.

b. La Spezia, southern Italy 8.i.05; *d.* Rome, 9.viii.88. *other orch. works: Pfhat* and *Konx-Om-Pax* (both fp Frankfurt, 6.ii.86); 11 piano suites; five string quartets.

Boguslaw (Julien) SCHAEFFER Composer of the first Polish 12-note work, *Music for strings* (1953) and the first Polish all-percussion piece, *Equivalenze sonore* (1959).

b. Lvov, Poland, 6.vi.29; teacher at Katowice U. 1963– ; *other works: Non-stop for piano* (eight hours long, 1964), piano and violin concertos, (both 1988).

Pierre (Henri Marie) SCHAEFFER French inventor of *musique concrète – everyday noises recorded on tape and re-arranged on an edit deck. He abandoned the process in the 1960s after it became an *avant-garde cliché, devoting himself instead to writing science fiction novels.

b. Nancy, France, 14.viii.10; technician and department head at French Radio 1936–75; *works: Etudes aux chemins de fer* (train sounds, aired 5.x.48), *Etude violette, Etude de bruit, Etude aux casseroles, Etude aux objects* etc.; *Symphonie pour un homme seul* (with Pierre *Henry, 1949–66).

Dirk SCHÄFER Music by the eminent Dutch pianist was obscured – like *Schnabel's – by his fame as a performer. He wrote piano pieces in the limpid styles of Skryabin and Ravel. There is also a *Rapsodie javanaise* for orch.

b. Rotterdam, Netherlands 25.xi.1873; *d.* Amsterdam, 16.ii.31.

R(aymond) Murray SCHAFER Creator of quirky soundworlds ranging from *Ra*, an un*Glassy evocation of ancient Egypt, to *Carnival of the Shadows* (1989), a TV opera set in a fairground with acrobats, fire-eaters and other amiable distractions. An avowed eclectic who listed Paul

Klee, Ezra Pound and Sergei Eisenstein as principal influences, he ridiculed concert solemnity in *Son of Heldenleben* (tape/orch., 1968).

b. Sarnia, Ontario, 18.vii.33; taught Simon Fraser U., British Columbia, 1965– ; *works: Apocalypsis* (music theatre, 1980), *Adieu Robert Schumann* (alto/orch., 1976), five string quartets; edition of Pound's opera *Le Testament de Francois Villon*; how-to interviews with 20 British composers (1963).

Peter SCHAT Dutch *Darmstadt disciple, he wrote *On Escalation* (1967) in honour of the Latin American guerrilla Ché Guevara and joined the collective that composed the 'non-individualist' anti-US opera, *Reconstructie* (Amsterdam, 29.vi.69). In the 1980s he reversed course with two expressive symphonies and a grey, autumnal Serenade for strings.

b. Utrecht, Netherlands, 5.vi.35; st with *Seiber, *Boulez; *other works: circus opera Houdini* (1976).

Schelomo 'Hebrew rhapsody' for cello and orch., by *Bloch. fp: NY, 3.v.17.

Schenker system Method of analysis devised by the Austrian Hermann Schenker (1868–1935) reducing all music to foreground (the composition itself), background (its structure) and middleground (everything else). Highly valued by modernists who used it to 'prove' that atonality was scientifically superior to Mozart and Beethoven.

Hermann SCHERCHEN The German conductor, exiled in the Hitler years, was a living link between Schoenberg – whom he assisted in *Pierrot in 1912 – and the post-war avant-garde. His world premières included the orch. fragments from *Wozzeck*, Dallapiccola's *Il prigioniero*, Henze's *König Hirsch* and *Nono's *Intolleranza*. He wrote an important handbook on conducting (1930) and composed a string quartet and other pieces.

b. Berlin, 21.vi.1891; *d.* Florence, 12.vi.66.

His daughter, **Tona SCHERCHEN-HSIAO,** whose mother was professor at the central music conservatory of Peking, studied with *Messiaen and *Ligeti and produced sensitive mono-syllabic titles on the mysteries of the universe – Shen (1968) for six percussion, Tzi (1970) for *a cappella* chorus, Tao (1971) for viola and orch.

> *b*. Neuchâtel, Switzerland, 12.ii.38.

Lalo SCHIFRIN Son of the concertmaster at Buenos Aires' Teatro Colon, he went to study with *Messiaen but was drawn to jazz and the movies. In Hollywood since 1964 he composed dozens of soundtracks and an oratorio, *The Rise and Fall of the Third Reich*, performed at the Bowl (3.vii.67).

> *b*. Buenos Aires, 21.vi.32; played piano in Dizzie Gillespie's band 1960–62.

Joseph SCHILLINGER Product of the October Revolution, which he lauded in a 1927 piano concerto, he emigrated in 1928 to the US where he gave lessons to *Gershwin. He was much admired by modernists for reducing the principles of composition to pure maths in his textbook, *The Mathematical Basis of the Arts* (1948/76).

> *b*. Kharkov, Russia, 31.viii.1895; *d*. NY, 23.iii.43.

Max (von) SCHILLINGS As reactionary as any composer in Germany, hating the Weimar Republic while accepting its commission as intendant of the Berlin State Opera (1918–25), he exulted in the rise of Hitler and immediately demanded Schoenberg's expulsion from Berlin. He died in July 1933 before he could do more harm. His four operas are decadently Wagnerian; the gruesome *Mona Lisa* (1915) survives in German repertory. A 1910 violin concerto is like deracinated Mendelssohn.

> *b*. Düren, Rhineland, 19.iv.1868; st law at Munich, taken to Bayreuth by his friend *Strauss; cond. Stuttgart 1908–19; married soprano Barbara Kemp 1923; *d*. Berlin, 24.vii.33.

Schlagobers (*Whipped cream*) Strauss's balletic portrait of frothy Vienna. fp there, 9.v.24.

Franz SCHMIDT Racialists rejoiced when a Vienna Philharmonic cellist wrote a symphony (Vienna, 25.i.02) that opposed the ironies of his conductor, *Mahler, with the smiling serenity of Schubert. Franz Schmidt wrote symphonies like Austrians had always written them, if slightly thicker in texture. He won a Beethoven prize but carried on playing in the orchestra for ten years until he completed an opera *Notre Dame* (1.iv.14), whose surging intermezzo (6.xii.03) found a niche in popular concerts. His 2nd symphony (3.xii.13) recycled romanticism in a skilful *allegretto* with ten variations and a slow, Brucknerian finale. The 3rd symphony (2.xii.28), winner of a Schubert centenary prize, has original melodies, interesting colours, plenty of pathos, some joy and a coherent argument, lacking only a sense of urgency and anything to place it in time. There was stronger stuff in the 4th (10.i.34), born of personal tragedy at the death in childbirth of his only daughter. A chilling trumpet opening introduces a masterpiece of symmetry that swells into a centre of stressed emotion and falls back perfectly into a trumpet solo. There is every reason to regard this as an important 20th-century symphony. A premonition of impending apocalypse prompted him to write *The Book of Seven Seals* (15.vi.38), a biblical oratorio for six soloists, mixed choir, organ and huge orchestra. Dying of cancer, he greeted Hitler's Anschluss with a *German Resurrection* cantata.

> *b*. Bratislava (Pressburg), 22.xii.1874 of Austro-Slovak parentage; st with Bruckner and Fuchs; played 1897–1911 in opera orch. and Vienna Philharmonic; appeared also as pianist and taught at the Akademie; *d*. Perchtoldsdorf, Austria, 11.ii.39. *other works*: opera *Fredigundis* (1922); two concertos for left-handed pianist Paul Wittgenstein: Concertante Variations on a Beethoven Theme (2.ii.24) and concerto for left hand alone (10.ii.35); Variations on a Hussar's Song; Chaconne for orch. (1933); two string quartets; two clarinet quintets; piano quintet; organ music.

Florent SCHMITT The baneful xenophobia of this critic, composer and administrator affected French music for half a century. He was a presiding member of central musical socieities, where he opposed all things foreign, especially escapers from Nazi Germany. His music was insipid. The ballet *Tragedy of Salomé* (Paris, 9.xi.07) won him modest notoriety soon after Strauss's opera. It is empty of eastern enchantment, although culminating in a huge crash and dedicated to Stravinsky. The *Psalm 47* setting for soprano, mixed chorus and orch.

(27.xii.06) has more modern textures and was recognized by Messiaen as a precursor of his *Petites liturgies*. A parallel piano quintet (1908) was his most polished piece.

   b. Blâmont, France (of German ancestry), 28.ix.1870; st with Massenet and Fauré, winning Prix de Rome at third attempt in 1900; director of Lyons Conservatoire 1922–24; *d.* Neuilly-sur-Seine, 17.vii.58. *other works*: four ballets, much choral music, two symphonies (1941, 1958), a symphonie concertante for piano and orch. (Boston, 25.xi.32) – a total of 137 opus numbers.

Artur SCHNABEL Paramount classical pianist who restored the Mozart concertos to modern circulation and was the first to record the Beethoven sonatas, Schnabel longed for applause as a composer. Living in Berlin and mixing with high intellectuals, he composed in an *atonal idiom with a marked forward propulsion. Serious musician though he was, he possessed a caustic humour and love of melody that occasionally pierced the compositional seriousness. In 1920 he took a three-year sabbatical from the concert platform to write music. A 50-minute solo violin sonata was written seamlessly without bar-lines or movement breaks. The sheer difficulty of his scores deterred performers and, since Schnabel played little modern music himself, he was ignored by the composing guild. Exiled by the Nazis, he wrote three virtually unperformed symphonies.

   b. Lipnik, Austro-Hungary, 17.iv.1882; st with Leschetizky; married soprano Therese Behr 1905; taught Berlin Hochschule 1925–33; *d.* Axenstein, Switzerland, 15.viii.51. *other works*: piano concerto (1901), violin-piano sonata (1935).

Dieter SCHNEBEL In the ruins of 1945, every German value was thrown into question. The very nature of music was challenged by Schnebel, a Lutheran pastor who argued that redemption required abandonment of past certainties. *ki-no* (1967) forsook the act of composing, substituting 'the counterpoint of beating hearts'. *mo-no* (1969), subtitled 'music for reading', eliminated performance; *nostalgie* for solo conductor consists of absolute *silence. He has also, however, composed arrangements of Bach, Beethoven and Webern, and a 1968 German Mass drawing on multiple religious traditions.

   b. Lahr, 14.iii.30; vicar at Kaiserslautern and Frankfurt 1957–70; prof. of musicology at Berlin 1977– ; *other works*: *Maulwerke* (1974), *Schubert-Phantasie* (1978), *Thanatos-Eros* for orch. (1982).

Alfred (Harrievich) SCHNITTKE Two lines of musical opposition formed against the mind-numbing dictatorship of the Soviet proletatirat. *Shostakovich, terrorized by Stalin, made it his duty to document the nation's sufferings in 15 symphonies that, at the same time, communicated a coded resistance. Schnittke, of part-German origins and a less stringent epoch, let it all hang loose, countering the conformity of Soviet artistic policy with a cornucopia of cultural influences, some permitted, others prohibited, a sonic kaleidoscope that bewildered apparatchiks and Western concert-goers alike with an inherent condemnation of one-party art. He called it *polystylism and regarded it as a metaphor and method for extracting music from dictatorships of all kinds, political and academic. It was also a means of analysis, taking apart musical history and putting it together in unusual juxtapositions.

   After the death of Shostakovich, he was the central focus of musical dissent. His symphonies were outlawed in the Brezhnev era and he was obliged to write 60-odd film scores, notably Yuli Karasik's version of Chekhov's *The Seagull* and several of Elem Klimov's movies. His First Symphony (Gorki, 9.ii.74), banned from Moscow, underpinned Mikhail Rom's morbid documentary 'The World Today'.

   He had the good fortune to find brave and brilliant interpreters. The conductor Gennady Rozhdestvensky paid his orchestra's fares to play the first symphony in faraway Gorki, and gave the 2nd in London (23.iv.80). The violinists Gidon Kremer and Mark Lubotsky, the violist Yuri Bashmet and the Swiss oboist Heinz Holliger stimulated a flow of concertos.

   Speaking German from his student days in Vienna, he had more access to the West than most Russians and was able to experiment with esoterica until he found his polystylist métier. He composed electronically when the means were not yet available in Moscow and introduced the first *prepared piano to Russia in Concerto

Grosso No. 1 (Leningrad, 21.iii.77), a hugely-entertaining Baroque parody. The interplay of simulated 17th-century bon-bons with concrete chunks of contemporary technology served several purposes, while remaining accessible to almost every ear. It reconciled divergent musical worlds, mocked their pretensions and underlined the malleability of audience taste.

Like Mahler, he took familiar tunes and turned them into nightmares. He even adopted a piano quartet by Mahler and wrote his own sequel to it, first as a chamber composition, then as part of the 5th symphony (1990), which also doubled as Concerto Grosso No. 4. It was characteristic of Schnittke to roll works of music into one another, probably meaning to confuse the bureaucracy. *(K)ein Sommernachtstraum – (No) Midsummer Night's Dream* (Salzburg, 1985) was a sardonic pastiche of tunes that could have been written by Mozart or Schubert except that, as Schnittke proclaimed, 'I faked them.' It is wickedly funny, a sprawl across history from minuets to minimalism. Nowhere was his *collage more notorious than in the 1977 cadenza for Beethoven's violin concerto, which quoted fragments of every significant fiddle concerto from Bach to Berg and beyond. Booed in Salzburg, it ascribes a disturbing relevance to a familiar masterpiece.

Few composers exploit a large orchestra as cleverly or as noisily as Schnittke. In *Ritual* (Novosibirsk, 15.iii.85), he commemorated Second World War victims with a simple eight-minute dirge that evolves from silence to a cantillated crescendo and returns again to nothingness. In *Passacaglia* (Baden-Baden, 8.xi.81), he wanted to use electronics to whip up a sea-storm but, lacking the means in Moscow, used percussion instead and with striking ingenuity.

Most of his concertos were written for solo instrument and string orch. Among them, the viola concerto (Amsterdam, 9.i.86) is the most instantly engaging and identifiably Russian. Finished ten days before he suffered a severe stroke, it is said to portend that disaster. The first cello concerto (Munich, 7.v.86) is daunted by the same experience. The oboe and harp concerto (Zagreb, 1.v.82) is a dirge for dead friends that draws the listener into dark and unsettling regions. When he uses full orchestra, as in the 4th violin concerto commissioned by the Berlin Philharmonic for its centenary (Berlin, 1.ix.82), he cannot resist a dig at its pretensions. In the finale, the tutti swell so loudly that the soloist is left mutely miming his part. The joke is lost, of course, on record – as is the cadenza for conductor that he wrote into the 4th symphony.

Although he doubted the durability of symphonies, he continued to write them eclectically. The 3rd (Leipzig, 5.xi.81) was developed from the monograms of more than 30 German composers from Bach to *Zimmermann; the finale is recognizably B-A-C-H. The 4th (West Berlin, 11.ix.84) is overtly religious and uses prayer chants from several faiths. In any major work of Schnittke, you do not have to wait long before he changes gear into a completely different era.

His 3rd string quartet (1983), probably the most recorded modern chamber work, is formed from three quoted themes: a cadence from a medieval Stabat Mater by Orlando di Lasso, the main tune of Beethoven's Grosse Fuge and the letters D-S-C-H that constituted Shostakovich's musical signature. As historical barriers tumble, Schnittke's technique is revealed in all its marvels. Shostakovich, rarely evident elsewhere in his music, pervades the 1978 sonata for cello and piano, a grim portrait of Brezhnev gloom. Two previous quartets are equally dolorous, the first (1966) unexplainedly austere and the second (1980) a chant-like dirge for the film director Larissa Shepitko. The *Requiem* (Budapest, 8.x.77) is another mighty work of mourning.

Amid the borrowing, it is difficult to discern a compelling personality and Schnittke has revealed little of himself in interviews and writings. It is also hard to tell important works from lesser ones, although the 3rd quartet and the *Requiem* certainly belong to the former category, with the 5th symphony is another obvious candidate. His first opera, *Life with an Idiot* (Amsterdam, 13.iv.92), with a Lenin lookalike in the title-role, conveys the anarchic energy of modern Russia. Having remained in the USSR through the worst years, Schnittke emigrated in poor health during the Gorbachev liberalization and went to live in Hamburg.

b. Engels, Volga Republic, USSR, 24.xi.34; st piano in Vienna 1946–8 and composition in Moscow 1953–8; *other works*: 2nd cello concerto (1990); piano quintet (1976).

Othmar SCHOECK Composer of 380 Swiss *Lieder regarded as the continuance of *Wolf's, though toning mad passion into affection. He produced eight stage works, including a pantomime *Das Wandbild* with a libretto by *Busoni (Halle, 2.i.21). His operas, like Wagner's, seek redemption in the Goethean 'eternal feminine'; *Penthesilea* (Dresden, 8.i.27) and *Massimilia Doni* (Dresden, 2.iii.37) endure in German repertory. Neutrally undisturbed by the century's upheavals, Schoeck had no cause to compose with the times. A 1912 violin concerto for Steffi Geyer, *Bartók's beloved, is harmonically sweet and texturally light. His 1945 orchestral suite has none of *Strauss's regrets, no hint of global strife, simply tranquillity composed for its own sake.

b. Brunnen, Switzerland, 1.ix.1886; *d.* Zurich, 8.iii.57. *other works*: cello concerto (1947), horn concerto (1951), two string quartets.

Arnold (Franz Walter) SCHOENBERG Schoenberg tore up and rewrote the rules of musical composition, not once but twice, each time proceeding into entirely uncharted territory with the unshakable

faith of a missionary. He believed that the composer's duty to art transcended his right to self-expression. The act of composing was divinely ordained and anyone who took the easy way out was offending against God and man alike. He stood, rock-like, as a moral example to musicians, whether or not they agreed with his compositional techniques. *Mahler admitted he did not understand his music, 'but perhaps he's right'; *Puccini was proud to shake his hand. More than four decades after his death, many composers still ask themselves: what would Schoenberg have done in my position?

He attracted devotion and revulsion in equal measure. Reactionary composers saw him rightly as a deadly threat and orchestral players hated the sounds he forced them to make. Audiences were outraged by sounds that were not only tuneless but audibly violated the long-standing relationships between one note and its neighbour on the diatonic scale. Schoenberg insisted that his music was not being played properly and that, one day, it would be whistled by milk-delivery boys, like Puccini's. Picasso, when he wanted, could sketch a lifelike portrait. Schoenberg could, and often did, write music of arresting beauty. Such considerations mattered to him less, however, than the need to save music from impending paralysis. 'I am a conservative who was forced to become a revolutionary,' he liked to say.

He perceived, along with many others, the impending bankruptcy of a tonal system that had served music well for half a millennium but was going no further. Mahler and *Strauss had pushed tonality and orchestration to their limits; Wagner had hinted in *Tristan* that something lay beyond. In a Vienna where Sigmund Freud was redefining human sexuality and Ernst Mach (1838–1916) was rejuvenating the philosophy of science to the point where Einstein could see into the future, it was not unnatural for a composer to contemplate full-scale revolution.

First, around 1908, he threw off the requirement to write in a specific key, endorsing free atonality as young socialists embraced free love. The lack of fixed relations between notes was unsettling, though, and the atonal period proved comparatively infertile for its inceptor.

A dozen years later, he reversed course with a rigorist method that gave each of the twelve tones equal value in relation to one another, none having the right to be 'tonic' or 'dominant'. By laying out a *row of notes in his own order, and following that order through an entire work, a composer could liberate his fantasy within a fresh framework. Schoenberg believed he had found 'a method of composition that will assure the supremacy of German music for 1,000 years' and, though this dream was confounded by public resistance and political reverses, his *12-note technique became the basis for what was perceived as musical progress for the rest of the century. Alive, Schoenberg relied on the devotion of *Berg, *Webern and a tiny clique of disciples. After his death, his great antipode *Stravinsky endorsed his discovery and *Boulez dictatorially proclaimed that no-one could call himself a composer until he had assimilated and practised the method of composing that Schoenberg had invented and Webern had refined.

The would-be saviour of music was the son of a Jewish shoeshop owner in Vienna, sent at 17 to work in a small bank. He acquired rudimentary skills on the cello and viola but never had a proper music teacher until Alexander *Zemlinsky, his future brother-in-law, weaned him informally from an excessive love of Brahms displayed in some early piano music, to a proper reverence for Wagner. This found expression in *Verklärte Nacht (Transfigured Night; Vienna, 18.ii.02), a sextet of extreme sensuality which was performed at *Mahler's behest by the augmented Rosé Quartet. Arguably the first and only tone-poem to be written for chamber ensemble – he made the more familiar string orch. version in 1917 – it wordlessly describes a woman telling her lover that she is pregnant after casual sex with a stranger. He replies that their love will make the child his own, and a D minor aura of acute anxiety is dispelled in rosy resolution of D major. An early critic described it, not unreasonably, as Tristan taken while the ink was still wet and smeared across the page. Latter-day listeners have been heard to demand, 'why couldn't he write more works like Verklärte Nacht?'

The sextet was one of three substantial essays on illicit love inspired by his troubling passion for Mathilde Zemlinsky, whom he married in 1901. Pelleas und Melisande (26.i.05), his first orchestral score, described Maeterlinck's fable of love and death in a washy D minor tonality obviously derived from its predecessor. One Viennese critic, by no means the most violent, described it as 'a 50-minute long protracted wrong note'.

The third panel in his triptych was begun before Pelleas and completed ten years later in a tonal idiom that he had by then formally renounced. Gurrelieder (Songs of Gurre, 23.ii.13; cond. *Schreker) outstripped Mahler's Symphony of 1,000 with an orchestral horde containing ten horns and seven trombones, eight percussion, 64 strings, with four choruses, five vocal soloists and a narrator. Telling of the secret love of a Danish king for a girl, whom the people named 'Little Dove', it is a coherent, comfortably romantic and, in its finale, cathartic cantata of the old school, sumptuously beautiful. There was very little in his first dozen pieces to offend anyone's sensibilities, yet offended they were. Schoenberg, unable to earn his keep in Vienna, moved to Berlin directly after his marriage to write *cabaret songs for a small theatre, the Überbrettl. These delightful ditties, the lightest he ever wrote, were counterpointed by four deeply sensual Richard Dehmel songs, presumably expressing his nuptial sentiments. It was later said that Schoenberg went atonal because he could not write tunes like his betters; these unaffected songs refute that canard.

He returned to Vienna no richer in 1903, eking a living from a part-time teaching job and the fees of two private pupils, Alban Berg and Anton von Webern, who would follow his every turn and serve as his life-long apostles. What Schoenberg taught was not so much music as a moral imperative.

He was befriended paternally by Mahler, who enjoyed his iconoclasm and watched as his first string quartet (5.ii.07) – D minor again – was booed to the rafters. In the first Chamber Symphony, performed three days later, he wilfully contradicted Mahler's orchestral aggrandizements with a symphonic work for just 15 instruments – a wholly new and highly vigorous hybrid that made its symphonic statement in a single 21-minute movement with insistent intimacy. Although still speaking the tonal language of *Verklärte Nacht*, it moved towards what he called 'the emancipation of dissonance' – the acceptance of unresolved discords – in sounds that understandably upset contemporary listeners. It stands at a turning point in the history of music and can be analysed to demonstrate what came before, and what upheavals would follow.

Months afterwards, during a crisis in his marriage, Schoenberg made the breach with tonality. Mathilde, depressed by their poverty and her husband's singlemindedness, ran off with their upstairs neighbour, a gifted painter called Richard Gerstl who had been helping Schoenberg with his hobby. In the month of her absence, before Webern and others persuaded her to return, Schoenberg wrote a quartet scherzo around a motif bearing the words 'alles ist hin' – 'all is lost' – from the Viennese streetsong 'Ach du lieber Augustin', a section that departed from all strictures of a key signature. The last two movements consisted of a soprano setting of poems by the symbolist Stefan George (who provided verses for Schoenberg's next songcycle, *The Book of the Hanging Gardens*). These were cornerstones of expressionism, displaying stark-naked emotions in music of enervating ethereality. The second quartet provoked a riot at its first performance (21.xii.08, Rosé Quartet with Marie Gutheil-Schoder as soloist) and Schoenberg was destined for a life of notoriety. What made musicians murmur was not so much the sounds themselves but an intuition that these works masked a phenomenal, dangerous capability to undermine the easy pleasurability of music for all time.

Schoenberg's atonalities were closely allied to the aphoristic utterances of the polemicist Karl Kraus and the violent imagery of the young painters Oskar Kokoschka and Gerstl, who disembowelled himself with a butcher's knife after

Mathilde returned home. Schoenberg's *Five Pieces for Orchestra* (London, 3.ix.12, cond. Henry Wood) were clipped, garish and swimming in sound-*colours that he called *Klangfarben*. Dismayed by previous disruptions, he inserted a programme note stating that 'Herr Arnold Schoenberg has promised his co-operation . . . on condition that during the performance of his Five Orchestral Pieces perfect silence is maintained'. Its range of emotions was startling and its rhythmic propulsion had a thrust more uplifting than the wintry gloom of Sibelius or Elgar's imperial bluff. In Six Little Piano Pieces, opus 19, he painted exquisite miniatures, including a one-minute memoir of the bells tolling at Mahler's funeral.

Deprived of his mentor and wretchedly impoverished, Schoenberg put his paintings up for sale, urged his pupils to raise some money and set off again for a job in Berlin, where Busoni provided intellectual support and his originality was finally recognized by an audience.

Pierrot Lunaire was a milestone in modernist symbolism, a free translation and setting of Albert Giraud's French poems, for half the instruments of the Chamber Symphony and a voice that neither sang nor spoke but attempted something midway between – a style that he dubbed *sprechgesang. Delivered by the Viennese actress who commissioned it, Albertine Zehme (Berlin, 16.x.12), *Pierrot* was warmly received, in both senses, and became a paradigm of style that was neither concert nor theatre but both, an ancestor, though he would not recognize it, of Stravinsky's *Soldier's Tale*.

Schoenberg realized that words and scenery could provide a framework for music that had lost its tonal corsets. He exchanged imageries with another painter, Vassily Kandinsky (1866–1944), over two operas, *Erwartung* (Expectation, Prague, 6.vi.24) and *Die glückliche Hand* (Lucky Hand, Vienna, 14.x.24), that pointed the way ahead without quite arriving in their own right. An oratorio, *Jacob's Ladder*, was left unfinished. With the outbreak of war, Schoenberg went home to Vienna and was conscripted in 1917. His output shrivelled as he wrestled, like the angel in his composition, with human intractabilities. Fed up with public incomprehension, he formed a Society for Private Musical Performances where selected music was heard by a subscribing audience without applause or criticism.

As Europe returned to a semblance of normality around 1920, Schoenberg embarked on his second road to Damascus, the one on which he abandoned atonal freedoms for the rules and disciplines of his 'method of composing with twelve notes', alternatively known as *serialism or *dodecatonality. It was up to the composer to assemble his own key signature and stick to it throughout a work. Instead of the natural progression of A to G with five sharps and flats in between, any sequence of notes could be set out, but then had to be obeyed and elaborated in its own mirror-images. Tested in the Serenade opus 24 (Donaueschingen, 20.vii.24), Schoenberg found himself composing 'with the freedom and fantasy of a youth, yet subject to a precisely definable aesthetic discipline'. The serenade itself was a remarkable work with none of the squeaks or shrieks of wilder modernisms and a guitar and mandolin providing depth and warmth to five other instruments and a bass voice. A *numerical symmetry was displayed in its seven instruments, seven movements and a sonnet of Petrarch's that Schoenberg claimed was his 217th (7 x 31) but was actually the 218th.

In 1923 he underwent further personal turmoil with the death of his wife Mathilde but the following decade turned out to be the happiest in his life. Busoni's death in Berlin left a vacancy at the Prussia Academy of Arts, to which Schoenberg was appointed with due remuneration. New music acquired cult status and he was honoured as its prophet. He married Gertrud, sister of his pupil Rudolf Kolisch, and had three children to join the two of his first marriage. The shimmering *Variations for Orchestra*, opus 31, was attempted by Wilhelm *Furtwängler and the Berlin Philharmonic Orch. (2.xii.28), signifying his admission to an establishment. All this proved chimerical, however, when the Nazis came to power, driving Schoenberg into penniless exile and ban-

ning his music from greater Germany. He had been anticipating something of the sort for a decade, and started work on a mighty opera, *Moses und Aron*, a parable of dichotomous brothers who would lead the Jewish people out of the wilderness and into a promised land. On leaving Germany for the last time, Schoenberg demonstratively re-embraced his ancestral Jewish faith and changed the spelling of his surname, dropping the Germanic umlaut forever. Names and numbers held high significance in his mind. He spelled the Aaron of his opera with one 'a' because a conventional rendering would have given the title 13 letters, which he deemed unlucky. This work, too, was left unfinished.

He wandered to America, where the foremost living theorist of music was reduced to teaching junior college students in California and resisting offers of hackwork from nearby Hollywood. 'For 30 years, bald, parchment-faced, Austrianborn composer Arnold Schoenberg has written music so complicated that only he and a couple other fellows understand what it is all about,' was *Time* magazine's trailer for his violin concerto, begun in 1934 ahead of *Berg's and possessing an unmistakably Jewish virtuosity amid its serial severities. *Stokowski conducted its première (Philadelphia, 6.xii.40, Louis Krasner soloist) and performed similar service for the less angry, more lyrical piano concerto (NY, 6.ii.44, *Steuermann soloist). He also orchestrated Brahms' G minor piano quartet – so deliciously that his score has been described as 'Brahms' 5th symphony' (Los Angeles, 18.v.35, cond. Klemperer). He, at least, considered it a great improvement on Brahms.

His religious faith and solidarity were voiced in a *Kol Nidrei choral setting and the *Survivor from Warsaw*, a shattering composition of textual fragments that conveyed his personal horror at news of the Holocaust.

Even more trenchant were two chamber masterpieces. The 4th string quartet (Los Angeles, 9.i.37) was a definitive statement of 12-note technique in his most authoritative style. The string trio opus 45 described his experience of almost dying from a heart attack and receiving artificial resucitation, down to a passage describing the entry of a hypodermic needle into his chest – proof of the literal applicability of his compositional technique. It was a measure of Schoenberg's astonishing consistency that the majority of his works had an opus number which corresponds with the year they were written. His fear of the number 13 was sadly vindicated by his death on 13 July 1951 at the age of 76 (7+6=13). His deathmask had the strength and determination of Napoleon's. His final words on a sheet of music paper were: 'And yet I pray.'

He remains, and will probably always remain, anathema to easy listeners. His music demands an effort of concentration and, like all great art, a certain suspension of disbelief. That it was great art cannot be denied. 'As a composer, I must believe in inspiration rather than mechanics,' he said. His music may have suffered from the mechanism of ascetic interpreters but its composer was one of the most passionate and imaginative creators of music at any time. You do not have to like his music in order to recognize the essential rightness of almost every stance he took. Schoenberg walked with the angels while his reactionary opponents danced with the very devil.

b. Vienna, 13.ix.1874; *d.* Los Angeles, 13.vii. 51. *other works*: domestic opera *Von heute auf Morgen (From today to tomorrow*, Frankfurt, 1.ii.30); orch. *Accompaniment to a Film Scene* (Berlin, 6.xi.30), cello concerto (arrangement of Baroque piece by Georg Monn, 1933), 2nd Chamber Symphony (NY, 15.xii.40), *Variations for Wind Band* (Boston, 20.x.44, cond. by an uncomprehending Koussevitsky); Suite for two clarinets, bass clarinet, violin, viola, cello and piano (Paris, 15.xii.27); wind quintet (Vienna, 13.ix.24). *Bib*: Erwin Stein (ed.), *Arnold Schoenberg Letters*, London (Faber), 1964.

Franz SCHREKER It was Schreker, rather than Schoenberg, who invented *expressionism and carried it to musical extremes. The founder of Vienna's Philharmonic Chorus and conductor of *Gurrelieder*, he wrote sexually-heated operas that made the Italian *verismists sound like eunuchs. While Strauss was writing *Salome*, Schreker sweated over *Der ferne Klang* (The Distant Sound, Frankfurt, 18.viii.12), in which the young

composer abandons his true love, Grete, only to meet up with again in a Venetian brothel and die in her arms. The opera was an instant sensation and remained in German repertory until 1933. *Berg, who prepared the piano score, applied its lessons in *Wozzeck* and *Lulu*; *Schoenberg quoted the opera in his textbook on harmony and depicted Schreker not unflatteringly in his own opera, *Von heute auf Morgen*. The musical idiom is late-romantic shimmer, stretching into banality.

As soon as he had finished the score, his malformed friend *Zemlinsky asked him for a libretto on the fate of deformed outcasts, along the lines of Wilde's 'Birthday of the Infanta'. Schreker thought this was such a good idea that he wrote the text and music himself as *Die Gezeichneten (The Marked Men*) (Frankfurt, 25.iv.18), musically superior to *Der ferne Klang* and introducing a percussive combination that percolated into the music of Boulez and Henze.. It tells of a Genoese nobleman who tries to overcome his ugliness by staging orgies on his islands and killing several girls. Its long, late-romantic overture, *Vorspiel zu einem Drama* was performed independently and Schreker was regarded as the dominant operatic modernist in the Weimar Republic. The Nazis attacked his work as Jewish decadence and sacked him as director of Berlin's main music college. Shattered, he returned to Vienna and died of a heart attack. His operas suffered a half-century hiatus, returning to the German stage in the reparatory 1980s and finally attracting international attention, though their stuffed-shirt eroticism was palpably passé.

His orchestral music never attracted as much notice, for the simple reason that it was heavily imitative. The Chamber Symphony (Vienna, 12.iii.17) for 23 instruments including harp, piano and harmonium, opens with undisguised Ravel and travels through Mahler, early Schoenberg and Brahms to resolve itself in the dissolution of *Tristan*. Zemlinsky, in similar terrain, was always more effective. Schreker got round to writing an opera of 'The Birthday of the Infanta' titled *Das Spielwerk und die Prinzessin* (Frankfurt and Vienna, 15.ii.13), along with several operas of lesser repute. He was a suggestive and benevolent teacher whose star pupils included *Krenek and *Hába; he appointed *Hindemith to his staff despite their polar differences in the theory and practice of music.

> *b.* Monaco, 23.iii.1878, son of Austrian court photographer; st Vienna with *Fuchs and Arnold Rosé; married 18-year-old Maria Binder, 1910; taught Vienna Akademie 1912–20, Berlin Hochschule 1920–33; *d.* Berlin, 21.iii.34. *other operas: Der Schatzgräber* (*The treasure hunter*, Frankfurt, 21.i.20), *Irrelohe* (Cologne, 27.iii.24, cond. Klemperer), *Der singende Teufel* (*The singing devil*, Berlin 10.xii.28, cond. Kleiber), *Der Schmied von Gent* (Berlin 29.x.32), *Christophorus* (1929, staged Freiburg, 1.x.1978).

Erwin SCHULHOFF Turning Marxist in the 1930s in reaction against the rise of Nazism, the Czech modernist set the Communist Manifesto to rousing music (composed 1932, fp Prague, 5.iv.62). He fled when the Germans took over his country but was captured by their invading forces in the USSR and sent to his death in a concentration camp. Before his political conversion, Schulhoff composed eclectically in an area between atonality and the microtones of Alois *Hába. His 1925 string sextet is appealingly melancholic, reminiscent of *Zemlinsky. The double concerto for flute, piano and strings (1927) combines busy Bartók with a flavouring of blues; a set of Jazz Etudes (1926) for piano solo that Schulhoff played at many recitals amounted to a homage to George Gershwin. As an obedient communist, Schulhoff tuned himself to Stalin's wavelength and wrote five cheerfully upbeat symphonies.

> *b.* Prague, 8.vi.1894; st with *Reger; *d.* Wülzburg concentration camp, Bavaria, 18.viii.42. *other works:* two operas, two ballets, jazz oratorio, piano concerto, two string quartets.

Gunther SCHULLER A conciliator at the centre of American music, Schuller proposed a union of concert music and *jazz in a mutually regenerative *Third Stream. The idea was spurned by both establishments, though some European composers took creative note. The son of a German violinist in the New York Philharmonic, Schuller played French horn at the Metropolitan Opera (1945–59) and in a Miles *Davis ensemble. He helped devise a cerebral style of *cool jazz and played a key role in resurrecting *ragtime. His output of more than 150 outreach scores fell between the cracks of the musical tributaries he tried to span, and his main impact has been as a polemicist and pedagogue.

> *b.* NY, 22.xi.25; head of composition at *Tanglewood 1964–84, president, New England Conservatory 1967–77; *principal works:* jazz opera *The Visitation* (based on Kafka's *The Trial*; Hamburg, 12.x.66), children's opera *The Fisherman and his Wife* (libretto by John Updike; Boston, 7.v.70); symphony (Dallas, 8.ii.65), three concertos for orch. and 20 for solo instruments.

William (Howard) SCHUMAN Archetype US powerbroker, Schuman was president of the Juilliard School (1945–62) and the Lincoln Center (1962–69), as well as heading the music publisher, G. Schirmer, and the Videorecord Corp. of America. His dictatorship was generally benevolent, with any favouritism directed towards the late-romantic middle course of *Persichetti and Robert *Ward. Schuman found enough time in his busy life to compose. His predilections were parochial, from an *American Festival Overture* (Boston, 6.x.39) to a baseball opera, *The Mighty Casey* (Hartford, Connecticut, 4.v.53, revised as a cantata) and culminating in an *American Muse* Symphony, his 10th, for the US bicentennial (Washington, D.C., 6.iv.76).

His timbre was urban and rowdy, a raucous far cry from the log-cabin Americanism of his teacher, Roy *Harris. The *Overture* begins with a three-note call to kids to come out and play in the streets; its rhythms are restless and urgent. The 3rd and finest of his symphonies (17.x.41) opens with a resplendent passacaglia which Schuman thows into frenetic disarray, as vivid as a movie-score. In the 5th symphony for strings alone (12.xi.43), frenzied leaps arrange themelves into an insistent rhythmic pattern.

The 7th (21.x.60) has a jazzy second movement; the 8th (NY, 3.x.68) eulogizes the martyred Martin Luther King and Robert Kennedy; the 9th (Philadelphia,

10.i.69) is a memorial to Italian resistance fighters murdered by the Germans in the Ardeatine caves outside Rome. The violin concerto (10.ii.50), taken up by Isaac Stern, is essentially two symphonic chunks with a wiry solo spinal cord, tough as a Bronx hoodlum. Schuman did not hear European art music until his sister dragged him to hear the New York Philharmonic when he was 20, by which time he had sold 200 songs on *Tin Pan Alley, mostly with lyricist Frank Loesser.

b. NY, 4.viii.10; st Columbia and Salzburg; married Frances Prince 1936; won the first Pulitzer music prize in 1943 for Walt Whitman cantata, *A Free Song*; *d*. NY, 15.ii. 92. *other works*: Martha Graham ballets *Night Journey* (1947), *Judith* (1950); *New England* triptych for orch. (1976), *Concerto on Old English Rounds* for viola, women's chorus and orch. (1976); four string quartets.

Gerard SCHURMANN A neighbour of the grotesque painter Francis Bacon, Schurmann conceived *Six Studies of Francis Bacon* (Dublin, 9.i.69) for large orchestra – a spasmodic, brooding work whose repressed violence illuminates the spirit of Bacon's work. One of the paintings describes Isabel, wife of a fellow-composer Alan *Rawsthorne; another, depicting screaming Popes, inspired a successful orchestral piece by Mark-Anthony *Turnage.

b. Kertosono, Java, 19.i.24; came to UK as a boy; st with Rawsthorne; Dutch cultural attaché in London 1945–47; *other works*: opera-cantata *Piers Plowman* (1980), piano and violin concertos, nine Slovak songs for high voice and orch. (1988).

Der Schwanendreher The organ grinder – Hindemith's half-ironic title for folktune-based concerto for his own instrument, the viola. fp: Amsterdam, 14.xi.35.

Joseph SCHWANTNER He won the 1979 Pulitzer Prize with his debut work, *Aftertones of Infinity* (NY, 29.i.79, cond. *Foss), which wanders in a Messiaen-Boulez direction across a pale parabola of nowhere in particular. His titles were often more evocative than the music that followed.

He was endorsed by US academics and orchestral players, an unusual alliance, and was showered with commissions which have not, as yet, made an overseas impression except on record.

b. Chicago, 22.iii.43; taught Eastman School 1970– ; *other orchestral works*: *Music of Amber, Distant Runes and Incantations, A Sudden Rainbow* (1986), *Magabunda* (1989), . . . *From Afar* for guitar and orch. (1987), piano concerto (1988), *A Play for Shadows* for flute and chamber orch. (1990), percussion concerto (1992).

Reinhard SCHWARZ-SCHILLING An organist who wrote motets like Bach and Lieder like Mendelssohn, he taught composition in Berlin 1939–69. His output contains two symphonies.

b. Hanover, 9.v.04; *d*. Berlin 1987.

Die schweigsame Frau Opera by *Strauss and Stefan Zweig after Ben Jonson. fp: Dresden, 24.vi.35. Banned by Nazis after four nights because of librettist's race.

Wolfgang von SCHWEINITZ A return-to-beauty movement in German music was prompted in 1977 by Schweinitz's *Variations on a Mozart Theme* for large orch., extending eight bars from the Masonic Funeral Music in Straussian fashion that narrowly avoided simple-mindedness. He followed up with a *Homage to Schubert* string sextet and a piano concerto (1979) written in Lieder format. His Mass (Berlin, 8.vii.84) was unfashionably emotional and his opera-ballet *Patmos* (Munich, 28.iv.90) was set to the entire monumental text of Luther's translation of St John's Revelation. As a religious edifice, it was unequalled in German music since *Schmidt's Book of Seven Seals; as a work of art, it provoked extremes of admiration and hostility.

b. Hamburg, 7.ii.53; st with *Ligeti.

Albert SCHWEITZER Christian musician who resigned his Strasbourg pulpit in 1912 to become a missionary in Africa, founding a remote lepers' clinic where he healed the sick and played Bach of an evening. A magnificent organist, he gave European and US recitals to raise funds for his mission; in 1952 he was awarded the Nobel Peace Prize. Schweitzer campaigned for simpler organs, wrote a seminal biography of Bach (1905) and edited his organ works.

b. Kayserberg, Alsace-Lorraine, 14.i.1875; st organ with *Widor; theology prof. at Strasbourg 1902–12; *d.* Lambaréné, Gabon, 4.ix.63.

Kurt SCHWERTSIK

Minor prophet of post-War Vienna, he came through *Darmstadt unconvinced of the necessity to alienate audiences. His idols were *Eisler and *Satie, and his favoured genre the chanson-Lied, laconic social comments with witty music to match. Irreverence set him beyond the pale of the modernist concert elite and he inhabited the workers'-café fringe of Viennese society writing songs in local dialect that is incomprehensible to non-Viennese. His 1989 singspiel, *Der verlorene Wut,* a comedy of office manners, falls musically between Kurt *Weill and Noël *Coward. *The Wondrous Tale of Fanferlizzy Sunnyfeet* (Stuttgart, 24.xi.83) is a wicked little children's opera with Roald Dahl-like sense of mischief. Schwertsik is nostalgic for lost simplicities. A concerto for alphorn (Vienna, 15.v.77) reconciles rusticism with urban rush and the violin concerto (Graz, 9.x.77) is billed as 'romances in black-tinted tones and flowering paradise-white'.

b. Vienna, 25.vi.35; st with *Marx and *Stockhausen; played horn in Graz orch.; formed ensemble Die Reihe with *Cerha; issued anti-*avant-garde manifesto 1965; identified in mid-80s as head of Third Vienna School; *other works:* opera *Der lange Weg zur grossen Mauer* (*Long way to the great wall,* Ulm, 13.v.75); orch. *Irdische Klänge* (*earthly sounds,* two parts, Vienna 16.iv.80, 16.xi.86), *Wiener Chronik* (ballet suites, 1976–7); Song cycles *Brautigan Songbook* (1971), *Cinq chansons cryptiques* (Satie texts, 1985), *Gedichte an Ljub* (Altenberg poems with one song by Eisler, 1986), *. . . & was ist dann Friede* (poems by Erich Fried, 1983).

Salvatore SCIARRINO

One of the first to make computer music sound truly lyrical, his opera *Perseo e Andromeda* (Stuttgart, 27.i.91) throws four unaccompanied singers against electronic sounds that amplify their dramatic situation. But in *Come vegnono prodotti gli incantesismi?* (1985), a piece for solo flute and tape supposedly marking *The Magic Flute* bicentenary, the tension built up by the instrument's cool prelude is shattered by scratchy computer noises.

b. Palermo, Italy, 4.iv.47; *other operas:* *Aspern* (after Henry James, 1981), *Lohengrin* (1983).

scordatura

Retuning a stringed instrument in mid-work to achieve high or low notes not normally accessible. The most famous instance is at rehearsal number 90 in *The *Rite of Spring* where the celli retune their C strings to B natural in order to play an F♯ harmonic. All four strings on the violin are retuned in the finale of Bartók's *Contrasts. *Mahler considered the option in the 3rd movement of his 4th symphony but instead ordered the concertmaster to exchange his normal instrument for a gypsy fiddle.

Cyril (Meir) SCOTT

English faith-healer and composer invited to Vienna in 1913 by Alma *Mahler. His music and mysticism were favourably compared to *Skryabin's. Although the melodies were generally folkish and the scoring self-indulgent, *Kreisler played his piano quartet, *Stokowski performed his 1st concerto in Philadelphia and an opera *The Alchemist* was staged in Germany (Essen, 28.v.25). He lived to a great age with the help of his herbal cures and a young female companion, his music long forgotten.

b. Oxton, Cheshire, 27.ix.1879; st in *Frankfurt with Humperdinck and Knorr; *d.* Eastbourne, S. England, 31.xii.70. *other works:* poetry and theosophical pamphlets; three symphonies, violin and cello concertos, four string quartets.

Scratch Orchestra

Band of enthusiasts formed by Anglo-Maoist Cornelius *Cardew to pool human resources in the service of world revolution. Performances involved players, some of whom could not read or play music, sustaining a tune of their choice on any instrument for an indefinite period.

Peter (Joshua) SCULTHORPE

The first of many composers who owed their fame to *Kronos: Sculthorpe's 8th quartet opened the Californian group's debut album and sold 25,000 copies almost overnight. The quartet, dating from 1969, placed the rice-pounding rhythms of Balinese peasantry at the centre of a whispering, unspecific lament. It was the most original sound to emerge from Australia since Nellie Melba and the first to show awareness of regional contexts; it established Sculthorpe as musical figurehead for the entire Pacific basin. He wrote a less surprising 11th quartet, *Jabiru Dreaming* (1990), for Kronos on aboriginal and animal noises from the Kakadu national park in northern Australia. His credo was articulated in four pieces of *Sun Music* (1965–69) for timpani, percussion and strings and a fifth for voices, stitched together and danced as a 45-minute ballet.

> *b.* Launceston, Tasmania, 29.iv.29; st at Oxford with *Wellesz, *Rubbra; taught Sydney U. 1963– ; *other works*: TV opera *Quiros* (1982), *Rites of Passage* (1973) for chorus, soloists, orch. and dancers, *Child of Australia* (1987, same forces), piano concerto (1983), *Lament* for cello and strings (1991).

Sea Drift Choral setting of Walt Whitman by *Delius. fp: Essen, 24.v.06.

Sea Interludes Four orch. extracts from *Peter Grimes*. fp: Cheltenham, 13.vi.45.

Sea Symphony Vaughan Williams 1st, to words by Whitman. fp: Leeds, 12.x.10.

Humphrey SEARLE *Webern's principal British apostle, he promoted serialist music as a BBC producer but havered for some time before fully adopting the 12-note technique in the first of five symphonies (1953). The 5th (1964) was based on episodes from the rather dull life of Webern. Searle was discovered by *Leibowitz and Scherchen, who performed his *Poem for 22 Strings* (1950) at *Darmstadt and commissioned a short Gogol opera, *The Diary of a Madman*, for Berlin (3.x.58). His *Joyce orchestral setting, *The Riverrun* (1951) was narrated by Edith Sitwell and Dylan Thomas; *Liebermann commissioned a *Hamlet* opera for Hamburg (5.iii.68). Despite his pedigree, Searle's reputation subsided quickly after his death, partly due to the waning of serialism but more perhaps because of the deadly seriousness of his music.

> *b.* Oxford, 26.viii.15; *d.* London, 12.v.82.

Second Viennese School The collective name given to *Schoenberg and his pupils Berg and Webern, the trinity that overturned tonality. The grouping was in some sense misleading, for each wrote music that reflected personal traits. Schoenberg's was lofty, unyielding yet humane; Berg's was ingratiating and erotic; Webern's was precise, neurotic, authoritarian. They were united only by a technique, a time, and a place which wholly rejected them.

There was never a First Vienna School. That name was assigned retroactively to Mozart, Haydn and Beethoven. A Third Vienna School arose in the 1970s around Schwertsik and Gruber, who ridiculed the established aristocracy of modernism.

Pete SEEGER Folk revivalist with left-wing political agenda, he was a vital link in the chain that led from *Leadbelly and Woody *Guthrie to Joan Baez and Bob *Dylan. The son of ethnomusicologist Charles Seeger (1886–1979), he dropped out of Harvard to go slumming in the dustbowl, leading community singsongs and writing such hits as 'If I had a Hammer' and 'Where have all the Flowers Gone'.

> *b.* New York, 3.v.19;

Leif SEGERSTRAM The Finnish conductor has composed an improbable amount of unheard music, including at least 25 string quartets and a series of numbered *Orchestral Diary Sheets* (1977–) whose total exceeds 50. He was chief conductor at Austrian Radio, 1975–82, Danish Radio from 1989.

> *b.* Vaasa, Finland, 2.iii.44; st with Kokkonen, Englund.

Andrés SEGOVIA The Spanish virtuoso restored the classical guitar to concert circulation with dedicated performances of Bach transcriptions, Baroque concertos and native tunes. *Roussel wrote him a suite titled Segovia (Paris, 7.iv.24) and *Villa-Lobos, *Castelnuovo-Tedesco and various of his countrymen contributed concertos. Remarkably, he did not première the most popular of the works he inspired, *Rodrigo's *Concierto de Aranjuez*. His concert career lasted 77 years (1909–86).

> *b.* Linares, 21.ii.1893; *d.* Madrid, 2.vi.87.

Mátyás SEIBER Although widely travelled and admiring Hindemith, Schoenberg and jazz, Seiber was unable to shake off his Hungarian wit and rhythms. His *12-tone Joyce cantata, *Ulysses* (London, 27.v.49), its nocturnal 4th section constructed reverentially from two Schoenberg motifs, cannot repress an occasional smile and springtime lilt. A *Fantasia Concertante* for violin and strings (3.xii.45, cond. Goehr) and *Concertino* for clarinet and string orch. (11.v.54) are even lighter in spirit.

Theory, he said, was unimportant: 'the only thing that interests me is whether I have succeeded in writing *real* music'. One could hardly deduce this from the academicism of Seiber's reputation as a modernist teacher at Frankfurt (1925–33) and London's Morley College (1942–60), where he co-founded the *SPNM and was prominent in a generation of refugees who converted London's musical scene to cerebral values. Three Fragments from *Portrait of the Artist as a Young Man* for speaker, chorus and ensemble (1957), a further Joycean adaptation, was a modest landmark in British serialism, as was the Quartetto Lyrico (1951), somewhat resembling Berg's *Lyric Suite. His music for the BBC film of George Orwell's *Animal Farm* (1953) was appropriately ominous. He contributed an attractive Kenneth Macmillan ballet to Covent Garden – *The Invitation* (30.xii.60) – but did not live to see it danced. He died in South Africa's Kruger National Park when a steering wheel came off in his hands and his car smashed into a tree.

b. Budapest, 4.v.05; st with Kodály; settled in England 1935; *d.* nr Johannesburg, South Africa, 24.ix.60. *other works*: opera *Eva plays with dolls* (1934), two operettas, *2 Jazzolettes* for chamber orch. (1929, 32), *Elegy* for viola and small orch. (1955), *4 French Folksongs* for soprano and strings (1948), Improvisations for jazzband and symphony orch. (with Johnny Dankworth, 2.vi.59), three string quartets.

Sequenza   Series of works for solo instruments including voice, (1958–) by *Berio.

Serenade   (1) Schoenberg's opus 24, his first concerted work using the 12-note method. Scored extraordinarily for clarinet, bass clarinet, mandolin, guitar and string trio, it introduces a bass voice in the 4th of seven movements to declaim the 218th sonnet by Petrarch (1304–74). fp: (private) Vienna 2.v.24, (public) Donaueschingen, 20.vii.24.

(2) *Bernstein's quasi-violin concerto modelled on Plato's *Symposium*. fp: Venice 12.ix.54; Isaac Stern soloist.

Serenade for tenor, horn and strings *Britten's youthful evocation of eventide, six songs to poems by Charles Cotton, Alfred Lord Tennyson, William Blake, Anon., Ben Jonson and John Keats. fp: London (Wigmore Hall), 15.x.43; Dennis Brain and Peter Pears soloists.

Serenaden-Fuchs   Nickname of Robert Fuchs (1847–1927), Viennese teacher whose pupils included Mahler and Wolf and whose composing reputation rested on five serenades for string orchestra.

serialism   Music composed by the *12-note method. The term is strictly applied to *Webern and his followers.

Tibor SERLY   Violist who completed the final page of *Bartók's 3rd piano concerto, then reconstructed a less-finished concerto by Bartók for his own instrument. A former pupil of the exiled master, Serly was his closest confidant in the US. A player in the Cincinnati and Philadelphia orchs., he composed imaginatively, rhythmically and tunefully on his own account and sought to update the medieval harmonic framework known as Modus Lascivus. Taken to America at four years old, his music harks nostalgically for Hungarian plains.

b. Losonc, Hungary, 25.xi.01; st Budapest Academy with Bartók and Kodály 1922–26; *d.* London, 8.x.78. *orch. works*: two symphonies (1931–33), viola concerto (1929), Rhapsody for viola and chamber orch. (NY, 27.ii.48), *Translyvanian Suite* (1935), *American Elegy* (1945), *Symphonic Variations* for audience and small orch. (1957), *Canonic Fugue for 10 voices on 10 tones* for string orch. (1972).

Kazimierz SEROCKI   He followed his friend Tadeusz *Baird through *socialist realism, *neo-classicism, *serialism and experimentalism as Polish music emerged from the grip of Stalin's terror. Serocki was nominally in the vanguard of new music activism but his compositions are less assertive than his contemporaries'.

b. Torun, Poland, 3.iii.22; *d.* Warsaw, 9.i.81. *works*: 2 symphonies (1952–53), trombone concerto (1953), *Segmenti* for 12 winds, six strings, 58 percusion, etc. (1961), *forte e piano* for two pianos and orch. (Cologne, 29.iii.68), *concerto alla cadenza* for recorder and orch. (1975), *Pianophonie* for piano, electronics and orch. (Metz, 18.xi.78).

Roger SESSIONS One of half a dozen men who made American music what it is today, Sessions switched US compositional emphasis from Copland's naïve nationalism towards a naïve internationalism. He believed in the unity of Western tradition and wanted America to take over its custodianship in a century of European turmoil. He welcomed waves of refugees from Stalin and Hitler and, after a *neo-classical first symphony (Boston, 22.iv.27, cond. *Koussevitsky), adopted serial and structural techniques as the basis for US modernism. He warned heatedly against divergence from these norms and established a climate in which his pupil *Babbitt wielded a dictatorship of East Coast academicism over concert creativity

Sessions' mind was well-stocked and his writings authoritative enough to resist individualist contradictions. He was an engaging man of patrician New England birth who achieved persuasion by charm as well as intellect. His fundamental wrongheadedness, in both conception and application, was not exposed in his long lifetime. There was, of course, no single tradition but a burgeoning plurality, and the notion that 'leadership' of music could shift summarily to a new continent was either quixotic or imperialist.

He held positions of influence from his early twenties, succeeding his teacher *Bloch as head of the Cleveland Institute, running a 1930s modern concert series with *Copland in New York, co-chairing the US branch of the *ISCM and teaching successively at Boston, Princeton (1935–45), Berkeley (1945–51, 66–67), Harvard and *Juilliard.

Sessions was fond of saying that 'music goes deeper than . . . emotion' into 'the energies that animate our psychic life.' His compositions are almost devoid of warmth, characterized by flowing lines and daunting structure that purport to represent vital energic forces. From the 2nd symphony (San Francisco, 9.i.47) onwards, he applied *12-note methods. The 4th symphony

(Minneapolis, 2.i.60) has movements titled Burlesque, Elegy and Pastorale, evidently an attempt at expressiveness. But, though its central Elegy mourns the death of his brother, serial leaps and fits deny the transmission of real feeling. In all, he wrote nine symphonies (1927–80) and a violin concerto (Chicago, 8.i.40) that Elliott *Carter considered formative. A last-gasp Concerto for Orchestra, written for the Boston SO centennial (23.x.81, cond. *Ozawa) won him a belated Pulitzer Prize.

His two operas were disappointments. *The Trial of Lucullus* (Berkeley, 18.iv.47) with a libretto by *Brecht, ought to have achieved cultural unity but lost the drama somehow in the sum of its music; *Dessau made a better fist of the script in East Germany. *Montezuma*, a three-act colossus, preoccupied him for 20 years but fizzled out at its West Berlin première (19.iv.64). Although he was respected in Europe, his music rarely travelled.
    b. Brooklyn, NY, 28.xii.1896; *d*. Princeton, New Jersey, 16.iii.85. *other works*: piano concerto (NY, 10.ii.56), concerto for violin and cello (1971), *When Lilacs Last in the Dooryard Bloom'd* (soloists, chorus and orch., Berkeley, 23.v.71; see *Hindemith), two string quartets (1936, 1951), 3 piano sonatas, *Pages from a Diary* for piano (1939), sonata for solo violin (1953).

Seven Deadly Sins (of the Petit-Bourgeois) Weill's last fling with Brecht in Parisian exile. fp: 7.vi.33.

Seven, They are Seven Prokofiev cantata for tenor, chorus and orch. fp: Paris, 29.v.24, cond. Koussevitsky.

Déodat de SEVERAC Shortlived composer from the southwest of France, he applied d'*Indy's teachings to the folklore of the Languedoc and Roussillon region. He wrote some charming symphonic poems – *Nausikaa, Les muses sylvestres* – and a failed opera, *Le coeur de moulin* (Paris, 8.xii.09).
    b. Saint-Félix de Caraman, Lauragais, 20.vii.1872; *d*. Céret, 24.iii.21.

the SEX PISTOLS Media darlings of the *punk era, they were violent in word and deed. Their bass player Sid Vicious (1957–79) was implicated in the death of a girlfriend and died while awaiting trial of a heroin overdose, ending the band's short run.

Ravi SHANKAR Indian sitar player who in the mid-Sixties became pundit to the *Beatles and Philip *Glass, altering the language of Western popular and art music. He played duets with Yehudi *Menuhin, Jean-Pierre Rampal and John Coltrane, and wrote four sitar concertos with symphonic accompaniment. He was director of music on All-India Radio, founded schools in Bombay and Los Angeles, wrote plangent film scores for Satyajit Ray's *Pather Panchali* and Richard Attenborough's *Gandhi* and an opera–ballet *Ghanashyam* (*A Broken Branch*) for City of Birmingham Touring Opera, 1989.
*b.*Benares, India, 7.iv.20;

Harold SHAPERO *Neo-classic US composer, his 2nd piano sonata (1940) carries an emotional sensation over a fragmentary texture.
b. Lynn, Massachusetts, 29.iv.20; st with *Hindemith, *Boulanger, prof. at Brandeis U. 1952– ; *works*: *Credo for orchestra* (1955), Concerto for Orchestra (1958).

Ralph SHAPEY For seven years, 1969–76, Shapey banned his music from performance or publication anywhere in the world in protest against difficulties facing new composers. A pupil of the indomitable *Wolpe and admirer of *Varèse, he struggled to make himself heard in a world dominated by pop, commerce and serialist orthodoxy. His music, while technically serial, was flagrantly romantic. He belonged to the expressive generation of artists that flourished in post-1945 New York.
b. Philadelphia, 12.iii.21; taught Chicago U. 1964–85, Queens College, NY, 1985– ; *works*: seven string quartets, symphony (1952), clarinet concerto (1954), double concerto (1983), concerto for piano, cello and strings (1986).

Yuri SHAPORIN Conservative composer of much-revised Soviet propaganda opera, *The Decembrists* (1925–53). His only symphony (1933) was described as 'Borodin inflated to the dimensions of Mahler'.
b. Glukhov, Ukraine, 8.xi.1887; *d.* Moscow, 9.xii.56. *other works*: cantata *The Battle for the Russian Land* (Moscow, 18.iv.44).

Cecil (James) SHARP Leader of English folklorists and country dancers, his collected songs are holy writ to folk revivalists. In 1916–18 he collected US folklore in the Appalachian Mountains.
b. London, 22.xi.1859; *d.* there, 23.vi.24.

Rodion SHCHEDRIN In the uncertain waters of Soviet music, Schchedrin did the best he could. He graduated a year after Stalin's death, with a first piano concerto that recalled *Shostakovich's college precocity. He nailed his colours to the mast in a daring 1955 article, 'For Creative Courage', that urged comrades to discover modernists (*sic*) like Mahler, Debussy and the still-banned Stravinsky, whose restoration he thus initiated. His Prokofiev-flavoured 2nd piano concerto (1966) was described by one critic as more motion than emotion; the 2nd symphony (1965) was a doom-laden partial atonality, signifying the assimilation of western ideas in an orthodox contrapuntal mode.

In 1965, alarmed at the liberties he had unleashed in others, he turned tack and spearheaded a violent Party attack on Edison *Denisov for 'imitating' the western *avant-garde. His 1969 oratorio *Lenin Lives in the People's Heart* harnessed Stravinskian rhythms to the cause, its cries of 'nyet! nyet! nyet!' failing to dispel deadly bathos. He voiced dissent, however, in *Chimes*, a commission for the NY Philharmonic's 125th anniversary (NY, 11.i.68, cond. Bernstein) that he based on Russian religious campanology. Married to a dancer, Maya Plisetskaya, he created for her a series of successful ballets, *The Humpbacked Horse* (1955), *Carmen* (after Bizet, 1967) and *Anna Karenina* (1972). In the glasnost era, Shchedrin produced *Stihira* (1987), a ceremonial hymn on liturgical themes for the millennium of Russian Christianity, commissioned by the exiled *Rostropovich at the National Symphony Orch. of Washington, D.C.
b. Moscow, 16.xii.32; st with *Shaporin; *other work*: operas *Not For Love Alone* (1961) and *Dead Souls* (after Gogol, 1977).

Vissarion SHEBALIN *Miaskovsky's top pupil made his mark with a *Lenin Symphony* (1931) that transcended agit-prop – notwithstanding narrated interludes and an ending in 'bright, positive attitudes'. He inscribed his 3rd symphony (1935) to Shostakovich, who responded with his 2nd string quartet; the two men had much in common. Shebalin avoided censure in *Stalin's first purge but was sacked in 1948 as director of the Moscow conservatory. Crippled by a stroke, he regained favour with a Shakespeare opera, *The Taming of the Shrew* (1957), a rare comic hit in Soviet rep. Of nine string quartets, the 3rd (1939) and 6th (1946) flirt with atonality.

    b. Omsk, Siberia, 11.vi.02; *d.* Moscow, 28.v. 63. *other works*: five symphonies, violin concerto (1940).

Shéhérazade Sensuous vocal triptych by *Ravel to poems by 'Tristan Klingsor'. fp: Paris, 17.i.04.

Noam SHERIFF Israeli composer of advanced proclivities who returned to his roots with a resurrection symphony, *Mechaye Hametim* (Amsterdam, 3.v.87), that traced Jewish life from diaspora, through holocaust to redemption in an impressive collage of traditional sounds. The materials range from cantorial Kaddish prayers to Mahlerian apotheosis. A pupil of *Blacher in Berlin, Sheriff followed *Ben Haim in seeking a fusion of European and Middle Eastern sounds. In 1989 he founded a high-calibre orchestra of Russian immigrants at Rishon-le-zion.

    b. Ramat Gan, Palestine, 7.i.35; founded Hebrew University SO 1955; *orch. works*: Song of Degrees (1959), Israel Suite (1965), Chaconne (1968), *La Folia* variations, violin concerto.

Nathaniel SHILKRET Media executive who lined up Schoenberg, Stravinsky, Milhaud, Toch, Castelnuovo-Tedesco, Tansman and himself at $300 a head to contribute movements to a biblical cantata, *Genesis* (Los Angeles, 18.xi.45). He single-handedly composed a trombone concerto for Tommy Dorsey (NY, 15.ii.45).

    b. NY, 1.i.1895; music dir. Victor Records 1915–35, then moved to Hollywood; *d.* Long Island, NY, 18.ii.82.

Vladislav SHOOT The Russian composer's dreamworld was outlined in three chamber symphonies (1973–78). His *Romantic Epistles* (1979) quotes a chunk of Mozart's G minor symphony as a means of self-extraction from musical impasse.

    b. Moscow, 3.iii.41;

Dmitri SHOSTAKOVICH The 15 symphonies of Dmitri Shostakovich amount to a secret history of Soviet Russia. His 15 string quartets are a private account of the torments of its greatest composer. Not since *Mahler was the public and the personal so literally related in music, nor was any music weighted with such irony to express and address social issues. Shostakovich chose these methods in order to preserve his inner freedom from the instruments of state terror. No composer has ever created under greater personal risk.

    Raised in the flush of revolution, his dream of a just society was shattered when Stalin began massacring the peasants, murdering his aides and manacling the arts. Fearing for his survival, Shostakovich devised a *code that the public understood and the commissars could not fault. He, above all artists, bore witness to the evils of totalitarianism.

    A youthful first symphony, his graduation exercise from the Leningrad Conservatoire (12.v.26), introduced him as the Great Red Hope; this fizzing firework with brash piano accompaniment was promptly performed in Berlin, where Weimar composers detected echoes of their own concerns. A choral, single-movement 2nd symphony marking the tenth anniversary of Bolshevism and riddled with dissonance was dedicated 'To October' (6.xii.27). His 3rd symphony was ardently titled 'First of May' (21.i.30) Somewhere between them was a Revolutionary Symphony that he destroyed. According to his son, he disavowed and disowned these dedicatory works.

    The 4th symphony signalled an end to optimism and the emergence of a sound that recalled *Mahler's bitter ironies and stark confrontations with immutable forces; it includes, at the end of the first movement, an allusion to the opening of Mahler's Ninth. Its potential political fallout was so frightening that Shostakovich withdrew the work from rehearsal and suppressed it for 25 years (fp: Moscow, 20.i.62). A bitter response to the cheery

tunes churned out by Stalin's symphonists, it is an unsettling piece, alternately noisy and nervy, its miniature *moderato* sandwiched between two huge outer movements. With the passage of years it has been recognized as one of the truest, least self-censored of Shostakovich's creations, flesh of the heaving flesh of his opera, *A Lady Macbeth of the Mtsensk District*.

It was opera that got him into touble with Stalin. A juvenile Gogol skit, *The Nose* (12.i.30) had the thrust and bustle of a student rag in three acts and an epilogue, lampooning the bourgeoisie with callous incision and an intuitive grasp of speech melodies. It was a testing ground for his major work, on which he embarked at the precocious age of 25. *Lady Macbeth (Len., 22.i.34) explored sexual greed and jealousy in a manner, musically and psychologically, midway between *Wozzeck and *Lulu. The heroine, whatever her carnal weaknesses, was the strongest and most likeable character – to an extent that parts of opera amount almost to a feminist manifesto. It was to have been the cornerstone of a tetralogy of operas on Russian women, a projected Soviet Ring cycle. But Stalin, who saw the opera in its second, Muscovite production, was outraged by the subject matter, by sexually explicit scenes and music, and by the rampant individualism of the composer and his heroine. He attacked the opera in a notorious *Pravda* article entitled 'Chaos instead of Music' which warned the composer that 'this could all end badly'. *Lady Macbeth* was withdrawn and not seen again until 1962, when a sanitized version was presented as *Katerina Ismailova*.

From the appearance of Stalin's article, Shostakovich did not know a day's peace.

Fellow-composers offered publicly to help 'straighten him out'. Attacked in the press and spat upon in the street, terrified that his family would be penalized, he made apparent amends in a 5th symphony (21.x.37) that, like defendants in Stalin's show-trials, confessed to imagined sins. Subtitled 'A Soviet Artist's Response to Just Criticism', the finale adopted a canonic classical motif that appeared innocuous until three As on the violins returned near the end to be shrieked out 252 times by the entire orchestra. Retrospective analysis and dissident conductors made his intentions abundantly clear. At the time, however, all that was heard was a hymn of praise to the Party and its Leader.

The opening of the 6th symphony (5.xi.39) quotes the bitter *Adagio* of Mahler's 10th; its funereal *Largo* is disrupted by hyper-activity and surface exuberance, a documentary report of daily life under the shadow of a tyranny that knocks at the door at the dead of night.

The *Leningrad* symphony (Kuibishev, 1.iii.42), named by the publisher for his besieged home town, buried the Stalinist trauma beneath a brilliant veneer of national solidarity. It scored propaganda points in the US, where *Toscanini gave the first performance, and earned a caustic parody from Bartók in his *Concerto for Orchestra* for its apparent simplemindedness. The first movement climax is brought about by 12 repetitions of the same short tune with steadily increased volume, rather like Ravel's *Boléro*; emphasis by repetition was a Shostakovich trademark. Russian musicians regard the wartime 8th (Moscow, 4.xi.43) as his deepest symphony; the terror is tangible in its half-hour opening movement and, though he tacked on a consolatory coda, the gloom is relieved only by fleeting vignettes – a 2nd movement piccolo solo representing a soldier walking off on furlough, a bassoon caricaturing puffed-up apparatchiks.

The 9th (3.xi.45) provoked Stalin's renewed wrath by failing to glorify his victory over Germany. The symphony is as insubstantial as a cabaret song and every bit as witty, although the humour is that of the graveyard. A *Poem for the Motherland* was rejected as insufficient for the 30th anniversary of revolution and Shostakovich was targeted as an Enemy of the People in the Stalin's second wave of artistic repression. The crime of *formalism was invented to describe his errors.

He was sacked from his teaching job for 'professional incompetence' and forced to write film music and agitprop songs, the musical equivalent of Siberia. He survived with dignity and integrity intact, hiding in his desk two furtive attacks on official anti-semitism in the shape of a first violin concerto for David *Oistrakh, rich in Jewish melodies, and a song cycle *From Jewish Folk Poetry*, neither of which could be released while the tyrant lived and breathed. His compassion for Jews was kindled by the Nazi holocaust and voiced in 1944 in an E minor piano trio that was banned after a single hearing. Listeners stumbled out of the concert hall in tears, shaken by the ferocity of its quadruple-*forte* ending. Shostakovich saw affinities between his fate and the survival of the Jewish people. 'Jews were tormented for so long, they learned to hide their despair,' he remarked to a biographer.

He celebrated Stalin's death with a 10th symphony (17.xii.53) its sombre opening burgeoning into a conclusive shout of triumph, a gripping resolution of the notes D S (E-flat) C H (B) that represented the initials of his name in German spelling (D SCHostakowitsch). Coherent and confident, its tone remained pessimistic. He was not fooled by the change of leaders, so long as dictatorship survived.

The next two symphonies, subtitled 'The Year 1905' (Moscow, 30.x.57) and 'The Year 1917' (1.x.61), were his weakest, wearily conformist, a payment of party dues. There are those who discern a political subtext – an 11th symphony protest against the crushing of the 1956 Hungarian uprising, some anti-Lenin allusions in the 12th – but these sentiments are not readily perceived, nor were the symphonies conceived with his usual coherence. Lulled by Khrushchev's tentative liberalization in 1962, he issued his only literal condemnation of the Kremilin, an attack on Soviet complicity in the Nazi genocide of Jews. His setting of Evgeny Yevtushenko's 'Babi-Yar' poem for bass solo and male

chorus in a 13th symphony (Moscow, 18.xii.62) proved too potent for officialdom and was swiftly suppressed. Yevtushenko was made to water down his text.

The last two symphonies meditate grimly on death. The 14th, set to poems by Lorca, Apollinaire, Rilke and Wilhelm Küchelbecker (29.ix.69), is dedicated to Benjamin *Britten (the two composers shared a mutual admiration), and modelled on *Das Lied von der Erde*. The 15th (Moscow, 8.i.72) is the most perplexing of all, trailing quotations from Rossini, Wagner, Tchaikovsky, Mahler and all of his own symphonies into an enigmatic abyss that veers from childish high spirits to the profoundest gloom. The finale swings twice from *adagio* to *allegretto* and back. In a lesser composer, this might be taken as a symptom of senile disorientation; in Shostakovich, who wrote in code, the meaning is glimpsed but still elusive – like the future of his troubled motherland.

He wrote copious and clever orch. scores for films, ballet, schools and public occasions, as well as concertos – two each for his friends Oistrakh and Rostropovich, one piano concerto for himself to play and another for his son, Maxim. The first concertos are generally superior to the second.

Just as the symphonies chronicle national traumas, the 15 string quartets relate Shostakovich's emotional history, his private reactions to external events. This odyssey started out experimentally with two contrasting quartet movements, the first adapted from Katerina's third act lament in *Lady Macbeth*, the other a polka from his ballet *The Golden Age*. The first full quartet (10.x.38) was realized in the dread period between the 4th and 5th symphonies; it conveys his quiet domestic happiness and his joy at the birth of a son and contains an unwitting echo of 'Run, rabbit, run'. The 2nd quartet (Moscow, 14.xi.44), written near the end of War as Stalin's fist descended again, has a theme-and-variations finale that submits a folk tune to extreme pressure but lets it emerge quietly triumphant from the ordeal. The moral was not lost on its Russian audience.

The 3rd quartet (Moscow, 16.xii.46) opened a triptych of private torture chamber works. The 4th and 5th quartets could not be performed until after Stalin's death. The 7th, written in 1954, mourns his first wife. The 8th publicly commemorates the victims of fascism and war; privately, Shostakovich said, 'I dedicated it to myself'. There is reason to believe that its anguish conveys his dismay at finally being forced to join the Party that destroyed his country. His final 12 years, a period spanned by the last two symphonies, yielded seven quartets of profound meditation on life and death.

The complete cycle is too intense to be experienced whole, its intimacy invoked insistently by the notes D S C H. The summits are the 8th and 10th quartets whose rich textures swing from morbidness to vivacity, betraying neither self-pity nor the false optimism of some of his symphonic finales. The 8th quotes with icy relevance a prison song familiar to many Russians; it also exists in a version for chamber orchestra by Rudolf Barshai. From the 12th quartet onwards he played ironically with 12-tone rows, never giving much credence to Schoenberg's method. The 15th, written in the year of his death, knits together six slow movements in a self-eulogy of unbroken intensity, the 20th century's equivalent to Beethoven's opus 131.

In contrast to the secretiveness of the quartets, other chamber works had a public purpose. The G-minor piano quintet (Moscow, 23.xi.40) was a bid to boost the people's morale at the end of the Great Terror, an emission of complex ideas in music so simple it was sung in the streets. He would weep at the sight of people sleeping nights on the Leningrad railway platform, waiting for trains that never came or friends they would never see again.

A visit to Leipzig in 1950 for the bicentenary of Bach's death prompted the idea of writing his own set of 24 preludes and fugues in the spirit of Bach's 48. It succeeded remarkably in evoking a classical keyboard manner without falling into pitfalls of pastiche. Covering every single key in disciplined succession, it began with self-effacing humility and ends in a massive triumph of the human spirit. The première was given by Tatiana Nikolayeva in Leningrad on 23 and 28.xii.52. While he rejected the various methods of modernism and was scorned by the western avant-garde, Shostakovich was almost without rival in his command of technique and structure. He was a master of every musical form and a teacher of wordless genius.

His health was broken by terror and poor diet and he died at an age when most composers enjoy their prime. Had he lived another 16 years to the not-unreasonable age of 85, he would have witness the collapse of the evil he so vividly documented. Every Soviet musician in his lifetime and beyond measured himself against Shostakovich. As a composer and a man, he was one of the great spirits of the century.
    b. St Petersburg, 25.ix.06; nourished at conservatory by *Glazunov, who sometimes procured food for his starving pupil; received Stalin Prize (1940) and Order of Lenin (1946, 56, 66) but did not join the Party until 1966; visited US in 1949 as Soviet stooge at World Peace Conference; thrice married, his only son, Maxim, fled West in 1981; *d.* Moscow, 9.viii.75. *other works:* ballets *The Golden Age* (26.x.30), *Bolt* (8.iv.31) and *The Limpid Brook* (4.iv.35); *Tahiti Trot* (orchestration of *Tea for Two*, 1928), suite for jazz orch. (28.xi.38), symphonic poem *October* (Moscow, 26.ix.67), *Overture on Russian and Kirghiz Folk themes* (Moscow, 10.x.65), *Death of Stepan Razin* for orch., chorus and bass soloist (Moscow, 28.xii.64), reorchestration of Mussorgsky's opera *Boris Godunov*; Suite for bass voice and piano to sonnets by Michelangelo (1970); violin sonata for Oistrakh (1968), viola sonata for Rudolf Barshai (1975), two piano sonatas, the first modelled friskily on Prokofiev's third.
    Bib: Solomon Volkov, *Testimony, the memoirs of Dmitri Shostakovich*, 1979. Ian Macdonald, *The New Shostakovich*, London (4th Estate), 1990.

Maximilian SHTAYNBERG (Steinberg)
*Rimsky-Korsakov's son-in law also rises, from time to distant time, on Russian concert schedules with four symphonies, the last of which celebrated the opening of the Turkestan-Siberian railroad. While in outlying republics, he composed folksong settings and a symphonic poem, *In Armenia* (Leningrad, 24.xii.40). He ran the Leningrad conservatory from 1934, though less independently than his predecessor,

*Glazunov. Shostakovich was among his pupils.

    b. Vilnius, Lithuania, 4.vii.1883; *d.* Leningrad, 6.xii.46.

Andrei SHTOGARENKO The Ukrainian symphonist played along with the Kremlin and kept his music folksy and hummable. He was one of *Khrennikov's deputies at the Union of Soviet Composers and ran the Kiev conservatory (1954–68).

    b. Noviye Kaidaki, nr. Ekaterinoslav, 15.x. 02; *works*: three symphonies, symphonic cantata *My Ukraine* (1943), violin concerto (1969).

Jean (Johan Julius Christian) SIBELIUS Between the two wars, Sibelius seemed to stand for the survival of the symphonic tradition against its rejection by Schoenberg and Stravinsky. This was subsequently exposed as an illusion, for Sibelius made no formal progress after 1918 and fell silent a decade later, living out the last third of his life in creative paralysis. There is a tendency among modernists to dismiss him as a kind of John Galsworthy or Somerset Maugham, a skilled narrator within a limited format. This is unjust, for Sibelius extended the intricacies of symphonic writing and, in an historic clash with *Mahler, defined its objectives. Where

Mahler insisted that the symphony must 'embrace everything', Sibelius sought to refine inner logic and textural clarity to discover fresh directions.

The orphaned son of an army surgeon, he made his mark as a national hero, earning stipends from a grateful nation for a series of patriotic tone-poems, capped by the thunderous rallying cry of *Finlandia* (Helsinki, 2.vii.1900). His symphonic odyssey began with the century in an E minor symphony (26.iv.1899) and acquired significance with the 2nd symphony in D major (8.iii.02), perceptibly warmed by a sojourn in Italy. Its universal appeal, cannot be ascribed to catchiness – it is short on big tunes, notwithstanding the finale's main theme and *Finlandia* fragments in the *Andante*. It derived instead from the composer's ability to create an atmosphere that seems to express something greater than himself. His next work, the *Valse triste*, a decadent piece of kitsch, swept the drawing-rooms like wildfire; he stupidly sold the copyright for a paltry 300 marks.

Sibelius was never an 'easy' composer and could not be accused of writing to please. The violin concerto (8.ii.04) required a sweeping revision, 30 years and Jascha *Heifetz to make its mark. More than half the work consists of a 14-minute allegro moderato that threatens to overbalance the tender but distant adagio and flashy, ice-cold finale. He liked to remark that while other composers manufactured multi-coloured cocktails, he served the public 'pure, cold water'. In incidental music to Maeterlinck's play *Pelléas et Mélisande* (17.iii.05), he drifted from an early reminiscence of *Finlandia* into passages sparer than anything in Debussy's opera. It ended in an erotic and moving elegy for the dead heroine, music that resembles the *Adagietto of Mahler's still-unheard 5th symphony.

His reaction against the heavy sauces of Strauss and Mahler was voiced in a 3rd symphony (25.ix.07) of ascetic and isolated classicality. He had married a general's daughter in 1892 and now moved his family to a cottage in the woods at Järvenpää, near Helsinki. He drank, smoked and ate to excess. The discovery of a throat tumour, life-threatening surgery and the enforced, though temporary, renunciation of addictive pleasures provoked another change of course. *In Memoriam* was provenly influenced by the funereal opening of Mahler's Fifth and its mortal introspections. He conducted it together with the 4th Symphony (3.iv.11), probably the most forbidding of all his major works, written while sunk in money worries and general depression. The Fourth is not quite as bleak as commonly painted. It has an arresting cello opening that uncannily presages the anguish of Elgar's concerto. Other clues to its meaning lie in Sibelius' only string quartet, *Voces Intimae* (Intimate voices, 25.iv.10), in which he trotted out passages from the symphony while trying to lighten its textures.

The Fifth, intended for his 50th birthday, underwent several public metamorphoses as he wrestled with diminishing musical resources. Its final version (24.xi.19) flourished a massive horn theme that is among the most famous and beloved in symphonic literature. He planned the 6th symphony (19.ii.23) as a violin concerto but, discouraged by his German publisher, plunged into polyphonic chorales of Reger-like complexity and brooding intensity – 'when shadows lengthen' was his working sub-title. The finale waves a friendly farewell. The 7th (Stockholm, 24.iii.24) was a single-movement condensation of ideas from his desk, darkly brooding for 20 minutes and unable to make an imposing structure from its interesting components. He struggled for a decade with an eighth symphony but burned its sketches before he died. From 1930 he subsided into alcoholic indolence, mortified at political and musical events. He fired the enthusiasm of Toscanini, Koussevitsky, Beecham and Karajan who performed his music with missionary fervour. Among British and American symphonists of the 1930s, he was the role model *par excellence*. No northern composer has equalled his achievement or influence and, whatever the state of his reputation, the popularity of his violin concerto and 1st, 2nd and 5th symphonies is permanently assured.

Such was his fixation with symphonic form that he never attempted an opera after

the early *Jungfrun i tornet* (Helsinki, 1896). His tone poems evoke Nordic landscape and folklore. He wrote around 100 songs to Swedish and Finnish texts, of which the opus 35 set of 1909–10 transcend language barriers, as does the concurrent *Luonnotar* for soprano and orch. (Gloucester, 10.ix.13), which blurs the borders between symphony and song as Mahler had done in *Das Lied von der Erde*.

b. Hämeenlinna (Tavastehus), Finland, 8.xii.1865; orphaned in cholera epidemic; befriended by *Busoni; st with *Fuchs and *Goldmark in Vienna; married Aino Järnefelt 1892; taught at Helsinki conservatory 1892–1900; visited US to conduct *Oceanides* commission (Norfolk, Connecticut, 4.vi.14); d. Järvenpää, 20.ix.57. *other tone poems*: En Saga (1892), *Karelia* suite (1893), *Wood Nymph*, *Spring Song* (1894), 4 *Lemminkäinen Legends* (1896), *Night Ride and Sunrise* (1905), *Pohjola's Daughter* (1906), *The Tempest* (1925), *Tapiola* (1926).

Elie SIEGMEISTER   Unusually for a US composer, he studied folk songs and blues with a view to building American music from the roots up. Yet his harmonic idiom was modern and the texts he set attacked inequities in American society. While his objectives mirrored *Copland's, his music was more forthright. A member of the brilliant post-war New York generation, *Toscanini conducted his Western Suite (NY 24.xi.45) and *Stokowski the first of six symphonies (NY, 30.x.47). He was persecuted in the McCarthy era and his career never recovered. The jazzy 1956 clarinet concerto is woefully underplayed.

b. NY, 15.i.09; st with *Riegger and *Boulanger (1927–32); formed American Ballad Singers 1939; taught at Hofstra U., Long Island, 1949–76; *d*. Manhasset, NY, 10.iii.91. *other works*: nine stage works and operas, flute concerto (Oklahoma City, 17.ii.61), *Sunday in Brooklyn* (NY, 21.vii.46), violin concerto (1985), *American* piano sonata (1944).

Roberto SIERRA   Sierra's string quartet *Memorias Tropicales* (*Tropical Memories*) for *Kronos (Los Angeles, 31.i.86) suggests the dense intimacy of Caribbean urban nights with whispered harmonics and *scat mutterings from the players. *Donna Rosita la Soltera* (*The Spinster*, NY, 7.xi.85) for soprano and wind quintet plays winsomely with a Lorca lyric.

b. Vega, Baja, Puerto Rica, 9.x.53; st London, Utrecht, Hamburg – with *Ligeti; chancellor of Puerto Rico music conservatory 1987– ; *other works*: *Salsa for winds (1983), *Mano a Mano* for two percussionists (1987) *Triptico* for guitar and string quartet (1989).

Kazimierz SIKORSKI Influential Polish teacher who despised asceticism and emulated the sensuality of *Szymanowski. He taught at the Warsaw Conservatory from 1927 and was its director from 1955–66; his pupils included *Panufnik and *Bacewicz. He composed four symphonies (1918–71), a bassoon concerto (1965) and three string quartets.
b. Zurich (of Polish parents), 28.vi.1895; *d.* Warsaw, 5.vii.85.

His son, **Tomasz SIKORSKI,** studied with his father and *Boulanger but turned to noisy modernisms in percussion-rich scores. In the 1980s he produced more sedate works for string orch., titled *Stings in the Earth* (1980) and *La Notte* (1984).
b. Warsaw, 19.v.39;

Der Silbersee (*The Silver Lake*) Opera by Weill. fp: Lepizig, 18.ii.33, cond. Brecher.

silence The value of silence was not precisely formulated, though many composers recognized it. Mahler and Boulez stipulated points of hush in various scores. Serialists from *Webern on measured precise durations of rest. Cage asked audience and performer to listen for silence in *4'33"* and Ligeti played similar games. The 'Sound of Silence' was a pop cliché (see *Simon).

Valentin SILVESTROV Stubborn Ukrainian who picked up serialism as a student and persisted with it against fierce official opposition. In the mid-1970s he adopted tonality and *collage techniques, although in truth his music was always tuneful. The 2nd symphony (1965) for piano, flute, strings and percussion reveals a taste for outlandish sonorities – massively agglomerated chords that anticipated Schnittke and Gubaidulina.
b. Kiev, 30.ix.37; st engineering and music; taught piano in Kiev from 1969; *other works*: 1st symphony (1963), piano quintet, string quartet, piano trio, much percussion music.

Paul SIMON After folk-ballad beginnings Simon blossomed with partner Art Garfunkel into America's foremost social songwriter after *Sondheim, with hits like 'Sounds of Silence' and 'Bridge over Troubled Water' (1970) that far transcended the thematic and melodic mundanity of pop songs. He sang of the world that Woody Allen depicted in his movies and acted in Allen's *Annie Hall* (1975). After breaking with Garfunkel in 1970, Simon explored other cultures for rhythmic innovation, initially Latin American and ultimately southern African, a trend that got him into trouble with apartheid-sanctionists but which won the region's indigenous black music a wider audience than ever before. His approach to these cultures was neither imitative nor plagiarist but absorptive, expressing their riches through the medium of urban north American popular song.
b. Newark, New Jersey, 5.xi.41.

Robert (Wilfred Levick) SIMPSON With a private pantheon consisting of Beethoven, *Nielsen, Bach and Bruckner, Simpson has written frowning tonal symphonies of vast structure. The 9th (Bournemouth, 8.iv.87), a 50-minute epic, is his pinnacle – an extended chorale-scherzo succedeed by a resounding fugal *Adagio*. His penchant for making an orchestra sound like a church organ, allied to a disinclination to dance, got some symphonies, especially the 10th and 11th (1988–91), bogged down under their own weight. The 3rd (Birmingham, 14.iii.63) was dedicated to Havergal *Brian, a forgotten symphonist whom Simpson as a BBC producer helped resuscitate. The 6th symphony is inscribed to a gynaecologist who showed him how a work of music could be germinated from a fertilized cell. The 8th string quartet has a movement that imitates the whining mosquito; the 10th recalls his experiences as an ambulance driver during the London blitz. All the quartets are modelled on Beethoven's, with the exception of the 9th which is a set of 32 variations and a fugue on the minuet of Haydn's 47th symphony.
b. Leamington, Warwickshire, 2.iii.21; st with *Howells; joined BBC as music producer 1951, resigning 1980 over the Corporation's abuse of music patronage;

published two monographs on Nielsen and an anti-BBC pamphlet, *The Proms and Natural Justice*; emigrated to Republic of Ireland.

Frank (Francis Albert) SINATRA Inimitable popular singer whose untrained, smoky baritone voice could express a wealth of sex and tenderness that women of several generations found irresistible. His songs were less memorable than the hooded manner of their delivery. His autumnal hit 'Strangers in the Night' (1966) and his crooning of *Weill's 'September Song' seemed deeply personal. He acted in many Hollywood films and founded his own Reprise record label, becoming a considerable showbiz powerbroker.
  b. Hoboken, New Jersey, 12.xii.15, of Italian parents.

Christian (August) SINDING The Leipzig-educated Norwegian composed in the anachronistic style of *Grieg until his death in 1941. An early suite for violin and orch. and a piano miniature, *Rustle of Spring (Frühlingsrauschen)*, are his passport to posterity.
  b. Kongsberg, Norway, 11.i.1856; *d.* Oslo, 3.xii.41. *works include*: four symphonies (1890, 1904, 1920, 1936), two violin concertos (1901, 17), opera *Der heilige Berg* (1914).

Sinfonia *Berio's mixed-media collage involving Brazilian myths, bits of Mahler's second symphony, a speech by Martin Luther King and other objets trouvés. fp: NY, 10.x.68.

Sinfonia antarctica *Vaughan Williams' 7th symphony, developed from a film score to *Scott of the Antarctic*. fp: Manchester, 14.i.53; cond. Barbirolli.

Sinfonia da requiem *Britten's orchestral epitaph to his parents, initially commissioned for a Japanese imperial anniversary but switched in wartime to America. fp: NY, 29.iii.41; cond. Barbirolli.

Sinfonia espansiva *Nielsen's lovely third symphony with wordless parts for soprano and baritone. fp: Copenhagen, 30.iv.12.

Sinfonia India 11-minute polyrhthmic 2nd symphony by the, Mexican cosmopolite Carlos *Chávez, his most indigenous piece. fp: NY, 23.i.36.

Sinfonia semplice Nielsen's 6th and last. fp: Copenhagen, 11.xii.25.

Sinfonietta 'Little symphony', a title used by Reger (1905), Prokofiev (1914), Hindemith (1916), Janáček (1926) Britten (op 1, 1933), Martinů (1942).

Leone SINIGAGLIA Late-romantic Italian whose Brahmsian music was introduced by *Mahler at the NY Philharmonic. Alone among his countrymen, he avoided opera.
  b. Turin, 14.viii.1868; *d.* there, 16.v.44. *orch. works*: *Danze piemontese* (Turin, 14.v.05, cond. Toscanini), symphonic suite *Piemonte* (1909), *Rapsodia piemontese* for violin and orch.; Variations on a Brahms theme for string quartet.

Giuseppe SINOPOLI Medically-trained musician, his fascination with creative psychology has moulded his idea of art. As a composer, Sinopoli enjoyed modest success with *Lou Salomé* (Munich, 10.v.81), an opera on the virginal love-object of Nietzsche, Rilke and, fleetingly, Freud. Musically, it is unprepossessing: *Berg without bite or *Lulu's plain daughter, held together by Mahlerian intermezzos that lack irony or menace. His mixed success as a conductor rests on a 'modern, probing' approach that can ignore the spirit or even the letter of a score in its quest for alternative meanings. In Mahler's 2nd symphony he diminished the resurrective climax; his Schumann performances took their cue from the composer's mental condition. His approach drew critical abuse, especially in London where he headed the Philharmonia Orch. It conformed with the interpretative licence claimed by contemporary opera *producers. When conducting opera, Sinopoli's approach was comparatively conventional.
  b. Venice, 2.xi.46; st medicine in Padua then conducting with *Swarowsky in Vienna; founded Maderna Ensemble in 1975 for performances of modern music; mus. dir. Philharmonia Orch. 1984– ; *other works*: *Sunyata* for string quartet (1970), *Symphonie imaginaire* (1983), piano concerto (1974), string quartet (1977).

Les Six Group invented by the French critic Henri Collet in 1920, comprising the disparate styles and personalities of *Auric, *Durey, *Honegger, *Milhaud, *Poulenc and *Tailleferre. They shared a taste for *Satie but, apart from friendship and 1920s *Zeitgeist*, had little artistically in common. Five of them wrote numbers for a 1921 ballet by Jean Cocteau, *Les mariés de la tour Eiffel*.

Nikos SKALKOTTAS   After seeing the future in Berlin as a pupil of Schoenberg and Weill, he returned to Athens with a gospel no-one wanted to hear, played violin for a pittance and died at 45 of a strangulated hernia. He planned an opera on the Odyssey but achieved only a 25-minute overture, *The Return of Odysseus* (London, 23.vi.69), of a remarkable tonality. Composed in pure sonata form, it uses rows of 18 notes to expand the composer's scope for *variation to almost Homeric dimensions. Uniquely, Skalkottas seemed able to set folk material, such as *36 Greek Dances* (1936), in 12-tone form without compromising either his source or his method. In a short life, he wrote 150 works.

b. Halkis, island of Euboea, Greece, 3.ii.04; *d*. Athens, 19.ix.49. *other works*: *The Unknown Soldier* (chorus and orch., 1929), three piano concertos, violin concerto (1938), double-bass concerto (1940), concerto for two violins (1945), Classical Symphony (1947), Sinfonietta (1948); Nine Greek dances for string quartet (1947), eight variations of a Greek folk tune for piano trio (1938), Bolero for cello and piano (1949).

Howard SKEMPTON   Relic of *Cardew's revolution, he has clung to the goal of music-for-all and composed simple, *Pärt-like mediations like *Lento* for orch. (London, 12.iii.91).

Skiffle   Impromptu kind of jazz played in 1920s Chicago on whatever household implements came to hand – washboard, jug, paper-and-comb – it had a second run in 1950s London with Lonnie Donegan and the Chris Barber band.

Alexander (Nikolayevich) SKRYABIN (Scriabin)   Skryabin wrote perfectly normal music while proclaiming himself the Messiah. Burying all kinds of cosmic secrets in his scores, he overdosed on Nietzsche, Wagner and theosophy and was rightly regarded as a crackpot. Like Stockhausen in a later age, the man has to be held at sensible distance from his best music.

A brilliant concert pianist, his 1896 piano concerto was modelled on Chopin's. His individuality increased around the turn of the century as he attained 'enlightenment'. The serene six-movement first symphony (Moscow, 29.iii.01) erupts in a choral finale whose melodic freshness overcomes the verbal banality of 'glory to art, forever glory!'. The sounds of Tchaikovsky and Rimsky-Korsakov shine through the less spectacular 2nd symphony (St Petersburg, 25.i.02). The 3rd (Paris, 29.v.05, cond. Nikisch), subtitled 'The Divine Poem', aspires to higher realms but occupies the tonal territory of Elgar, with many bells at the climax. He expanded the orchestra to Mahlerian size for the single-movement *Poem of Ecstasy* (Paris, 10.xii.08), applying frenetic rhythms and pre-Hollywood buildups of narrative tension.

The chorally-augmented *Prometheus* (Moscow, 15.iii.15), with a prominent piano part for his Saviour self, is based on an atonal 'mystical chord' of C F♯ B♭ E A and D, and was initially meant to exude smell and colours. He required a 'colour organ' to project hues that would match his keys (C major = red; F♯ major = ultramarine blue) but was laughed out of court whenever it was attempted – not that this stopped Sixties-minded musicians from trying. At his early death he was plotting a *happening under the title, *Mysterium*.

In addition to five symphonies he wrote ten piano sonatas on an ascending scale of atonal complexity. The first three are melodic and domesticated, the fourth (1903) is transitional; the 5th, composed in six days as soon as he finished the *Poem of Ecstasy* sets the single-movement, massively-chorded structure for all its successors. He described the 6th as 'nightmarish, murky, unclean, mischievous' and never played it, called the seventh his 'white Mass' and the eighth 'tragique'. The ninth is a tormented masterpiece, the tenth, in his own words, 'a sonata of insects'. None of the later works lasts longer than a dozen minutes. In addition, he wrote a multitude of Etudes, steadily extending Chopin's parameters.

His private life was a mess. After marrying a pianist in Moscow and fathering two children, he left with a stipend from a rich woman to live in Switzerland, where he set up home with Tatiana Schoelzer, a critic's sister. Their 1907 US tour was cut short by threat of bigamy prosecution. The outbreak of war confirmed his faith in an apocalypse from which he would emerge Almighty. Within months, he died suddenly at 43 from an infected pimple on his upper lip, apparently contracted in London. Posthumous tragedies pursued his family. An 11-year-old son, Julian, who showed musical promise, drowned in the Dnieper River; his daughter Ariadna joined the French Resistance and was murdered by the Nazis; a nephew changed his name to Molotov and became Stalin's henchman. Another daughter, Marina, became a Paris musicologist; a great-grandson has emerged in Israel as a child prodigy.

b. Moscow, 6.i.1872; st with Zverev, Taneyev, Safonov and Arensky; first European tour 1896, married Vera Isakovich 1897, taught at Moscow Conservatoire 1898–1903; visited the US in 1906–7 and the UK on several occasions; d. Moscow, 27.iv.15. other works: many piano miniatures, among them Satanic Poem and Towards the Flame.

Klement SLAVICKÝ A stream of religious music produced defiantly through the communist era was capped by a set of Latin Psalms for soloists, mixed chorus and organ (1970). Although he was a *Suk pupil, his music possesses a Janáček-like ruggedness and rhythmic thrust.

b. Tovacov, Moravia, 22.ix.10; other works: four sinfoniettas (1940–88); two string quartets.

His son, **Milan SLAVICKÝ**, is a radio producer who experimented with electronics and collated a composition out of news broadcasts of the 1989 'velvet revolution'. Other works include two symphonic triptychs, Terre des Hommes (1983) and The Well of Life (1986).

b. Prague, 7.v.47;

Nicolas SLONIMSKY Author of the concise, definitive study of Sex and the Music Librarian (1968), he chronicled the century's creativity in Music since 1900 (New York, 1937/86) and, as a conductor, pioneered the music of *Ives, *Cowell and *Varèse. To perform Three Places in New England (NY, 10.i.1931) he beat a different time with either arm. His Lexicon of Musical Invective (NY, 1952) collects many of the worst things ever written about composers.

b. St Petersburg, 27.iv.1894; emigrated 1920; amanuensis to *Koussevitsky in Paris and Boston; formed Chamber Orch. of Boston (1927); edited four editions of Thomson's International Cyclopedia of Music and Musicians (1946–58) and the 5th to 8th editions of Baker's Biographical Dictionary; on 13.iv.88 he became, at 94, the oldest musician ever to make a UK concert debut; Bib: N. Slonimsky, Perfect Pitch, NY (OUP), 1988.

His nephew, **Sergei SLONIMSKY**, is a Russian eclectic who imported advanced Western techniques and wrote a Mary Stuart opera (Kuibishev, 31.i.81) that used genuine Scots ballads and was staged to poor reviews at the 1986 Edinburgh Festival.

b. Leningrad, 12.viii.32; other works: nine symphonies, chamber opera on Bulgakov's novel The Master and Margarita (see Höller).

Slovakia Unlike Czech composers, the Slovaks were caught among too many alien cultures – German, Hungarian, Czech, Romanian – to establish an individual voice. Seven regimes and two world wars increased the creative confusion. The leading composer was *Suchon, a social realist.

Roger SMALLEY A sometime Stockhausen assistant, he preached an electronic and aleatory gospel until emigrating to a professorship at the U. of Western Australia, where his music has assumed the conventional dimensions of a symphony (1982) and piano concerto (1985).

b. Manchester, 26.vii.43; st with *Fricker; other works: music-theatre William Derrincourt (1978), Beat Music for four electronic instruments and orch. (1971).

Dmitri SMIRNOV Anglophile Russian who set to music 20 works by William Blake and applied for humanitarian asylum in the UK when the Russian economy crumbled in 1991. Blake's verse: 'To see a World in a Grain of Sand/And a Heaven in a Wild Flower/Hold Infinity in the palm of your hand/And Eternity in an Hour' defined for him the duties of a composer. His opus 2 for voice and 12 players was titled *A Handful of Sand* (1967) and his first symphony (Riga, 8.x.81) was named *The Seasons* and inscribed in Blake's memory. Both his operas, *Tiriel* (Freiburg, 28.i.89) and *The Lamentations of Thel* (London, 9.vi.89) have Blake texts. The music, however, is Russian and rich in *Shostakovich-like snatches of melodic reminiscence. Smirnov married Elena *Firsova, a subtler composer.

b. Minsk, Russia, 2.xi.48, the son of opera singers; spent his childhood in central Asia; st in Moscow; *other works*: 2nd symphony (1982), *Jacob's Ladder* for ensemble (1990, based on drawing by Blake), *Silent, Silent Night* for soprano and ensemble (1991).

Bessie SMITH The founder-empress of blues singing soaked her vocal chords in gin and delivered a jazzy punch that confounded purists. She made some 200 recordings, including 'St Louis Blues' with Louis Armstrong, starring in a 1929 movie of that name. She died in a bizarre double accident. While travelling between concerts in Mississippi, her car hit a truck and overturned. A doctor picked her up in his car, which was hit by another vehicle on its way to hospital, where she died after surgery.

b. Chattanooga, Tennessee, 15.iv.1894; *d.* Clarksdale, Mississippi, 26.ix.37.

(Dame) Ethel SMYTH The formidable female composer owed her fame partly to social connections and a flair for publicity. Daughter of a military family, she worked her way into the musical aristocracy with introductions to Brahms, Grieg, Mahler and other power figures. Her maiden opera, *Fantasio*, was staged at Weimar and *Nikisch in Lepizig premièred *The Wreckers* (11.xi.06), a Cornish remake of *The Flying Dutchman*; *Beecham took up her comic opera *The Bosun's Mate* (28.i. 16). None of the six operas made an indelible impression, nor did the Mass in D, performed at royal command (London 18.i.1893) but written in the throes of a lesbian infatuation for a devoutly catholic Irish girl. Other emotional attachments included the sewing-machine heiress, Princesse de Polignac, and the writer

Virginia Woolf. She joined the campaign for women's suffrage in 1911 and, as a token of her commitment, heaved a brick through the Home Secretary's window. This earned her two months with hard labour at Holloway Jail, reduced to four weeks on appeal. Beecham found her there conducting fellow-inmates with a toothbrush in a rousing chorus, *The March of Women* (20.i.11), that was her most celebrated composition.

b. London, 22.iv.1858; *d.* Woking, Surrey, 8.v.44. *other works*: horn-and-violin concerto (5.iii.27), oratorio *The Prison* (24.ii.31), a multi-part autobiography.

socialist realism *Stalin's command to visual artists to depict Soviet achievements in heroic dimensions was echoed by composers in hymns to the Party and upbeat symphonies. 'Positive' major chords and hummable melodies were the order of the day; all else was *formalist and forbidden. This official line persisted until the mid-1980s.

society Until the end of the 19th century, the role of music was to entertain and uplift. A chasm opened in the 20th century between composers and audiences. Mahler said he was writing for half a century hence. Schoenberg's priority was to discover new methods of composing rather than please the public. Cage declared that music had no purpose at all, and the European *avant-garde despised the expression of emotion. At the other extreme, *pop music was produced for instant consumption and rapid obsolescence.

Totalitarian societies obliged composers to write for the masses, an objective that rebounded when Shostakovich used symphonies to convey unspoken dissent. Marxism was confused about musical method. *Eisler had his workers sing in multi-part harmony, while *Adorno declared that only through a universal adoption of 12-note techniques would the social millennium be achieved. Most of the sociology of music has been written in the production-consumption terms of Marxist dialectic.

Socrate Symphonic drama for four sopranos and chamber orch. by *Satie. fp: Paris, 14.ii.20.

The Soldier's Tale *L'histoire du soldât*
First War parable of Russian soldier who
sells his fiddle to the devil, it was conceived
by *Stravinsky as a miniature union of all
the arts: dance, mime, narration, artistic
design and a pellucid score for seven instruments. There is no singing and the
musical episodes include a tango and *ragtime. fp: Lausanne, Switzerland, 28.ix.18,
cond. Ansermet.

The Soldiers *Die Soldaten* Powerful
opera by B.A.*Zimmermann after Jakob
Lenz's tale of an officer's rejected girlfriend who becomes the regimental whore.
Staged as 'total theatre', it is in many respects a sequel to *Wozzeck*. fp: Cologne,
15.ii.65.

sonata *Sonate, que me veux-tu?* – what
do you want of my life – demanded Boulez
in a trenchant 1960 essay on the genesis of
his 3rd piano sonata. The question had a
petulant poignancy for, as leader of a generation that rejected the past, Boulez was
unable to shake off the sonata either as a
form or tradition. Solo works were still
known as 'sonatas' because they were
arranged on a traditional musical basis of
statement, development and resolution.

Stephen (Joshua) SONDHEIM Sondheim is regarded as the saviour of the
American musical, though his shows have
usually lost money. *Follies* (4.iv.71), for
example, with two of his finest numbers –
'Losing my mind'; 'I'm still here' – left its
backers $800,000 lighter on Broadway and
£600,000 in London's West End. If the
musical was not there to make money, critics demanded, what was it doing in the
centre of town? And if Sondheim was its
foremost living exponent, why was he unable to produce a big hit?

His virtue or sin, depending on perspective, was a determination to apply high-art
values to a low-art form. The songs people
hum in the bath, he was wont to say derisi-
vely, are the same as all the songs they have
ever hummed before. He wrapped musicals
like *A Little Night Music* (NY, 25.ii.73)
around pure art-songs, 'Send in the
Clowns' and 'Liaisons', achieving effect by
colour and inflection rather than original
melody or clever words. He seemed so

intent on the quality of songwriting that
his shows lacked dramatic propulsion,
though their static nature may occasionally
have been intended.

Nor was he much concerned with boy-
meets-girl, boy-loses-girl. *A Little Night
Music*, with a classically allusive title, took
its story from a black-and-white 1955
Ingmar Bergman film of strained family
relations in Sweden. *Pacific Overtures*
(NY, 11.i.76) was a kabuki show relating
the history of modern Japan, hardly light
entertainment by any definition. *Sunday
in the Park with George* (NY, 2.v.84) was a
parable on the pointillist painter Georges
Seurat, with a heroine delicately named
Dot and scenery as bare as a canvas. Even
in relatively straight shows like *Company*
(NY, 24.iv.70) and *Follies*, redolent of the
theatre of Neil Simon and the movies of
Woody Allen, relationships were never
easy – 'you come out of *Company* whistling the Divorce Act' carped Broadway
wits – and the music was adventurous, epi-
sodically *12-note though centred eclectically in the worlds of *Ravel, *Copland,
*Rachmaninov and *Kern.

His overwhelming strength was the
asperity of his lyrics. 'The Little Things
You Do Together' in *Company* included
'Neighbours you annoy together/Children
you destroy together'. 'The Ladies who
Lunch' in the same show moan of 'Another
long exhausting day/Another thousand
dollars/A matinee, a Pinter play/Perhaps a
piece of *Mahler's.'

It was as a lyric writer that he made his
mark in Bernstein's *West Side Story*. The
child of a wealthy couple who divorced
when he was ten, he was nurtured by the
avuncular Oscar Hammerstein and studied
for two years with the *serial rigorist
Milton *Babbitt. He never married and
lived alone in Manhattan, writing shows
that Broadway did not want to know. Nor
did his musicals transfer readily to the
opera house, though *Pacific Overtures* had
a short run at English National Opera and
West End audiences were more sympathetic than Broadway's.

Adherents maintain he has written the
musicals of the future and even antagonists
concede that he has composed a corpus of
American art-songs superior to any in his

century. He may not be America's Franz Schubert, but he is not far short of its Hugo Wolf. In 1988 he was appointed to a chair of theatre at Oxford University.

b. New York, 22.iii.30; *other shows: A Funny Things Happened on the Way to the Forum* (1962), *Anyone Can Whistle* (1964), *Sweeney Todd* (1979), *Merrily we Roll Along* (1981), *Into the Woods* (1987).

Bib: S. Morley, *Song by Song by Sondheim*, London, 1979.

sonic imperialism Term coined by R. Murray *Schafer to describe the irrepressible need some people feel to disturb the peace with loud music.

Kaikhosru Shapurji SORABJI An English fire-worshipper of reclusive tendencies, he wrote weird and hypnotic piano music under the lifelong spell of *Busoni. He approached his hero after a three-day fast in November 1919 and was asked to play his first piano sonata, which Busoni found ugly but 'strange and voluptuous' like a primeval forest. He gave him a note of recommendation to publishers who were unmoved, so Sorabji issued his scores privately. Among them was the *Opus Clavicembalisticum* which he played in Glasgow on 1.xii.1930 as the longest non-repetitive solo piece ever written. It runs three hours, 45 minutes and 252 pages of closely printed score, including a passacaglia with no fewer than 81 variations. Critics as acute as *Brian and *Rubbra hailed it as a new pianistic dawn.

In 1936, dismayed by a poor concert, Sorabji removed himself and all his music from the public ear for almost 40 years, an act that recalled the self-incarceration of another of his icons, the quirky Parisian piano genius, Charles-Valentin Alkan. In a sense, he made the right decision, for his scores are like a house of cards in which a missing or misplaced note could bring the whole fragile futility crashing down. A cautious re-emergence in performances by such devotees as Ronald Stevenson and John Ogdon confirmed near the end of the century that Sorabji remained original and inimitable.

His work consists mainly of solo piano music and three Symphonies for Organ, the first of which (1923) he regarded as his threshold of maturity. At least 16 of his

pieces last longer than two hours. To describe his music as dense is an understatement. Its chords are overloaded like juggernauts and its cloudy textures thin out very rarely. It has to be heard many times before any sense can be made of structure or intent.

Sorabji delighted in mystification, issuing a public statement to declare that 'dates and places of birth relating to myself given in various works of reference are invariably false'. He was, in fact, born at Chingford in still-rural Essex of a Parsi civil engineer and a Spanish-Sicilian opera singer, who registered his baptismal names as Leon Dudley. He rejected these christian names, took the paternal Zoroastrian faith and denied any taint of Englishness – 'they are the stupidest race in Europe' – while living in a castle in Dorset. His critical essays, published in two collections in 1932 and 1947, show him to have been preternaturally aware of Mahler, Schoenberg and other progressive trends. He never married, and was said to enjoy puerile charms. In his extended life, he claimed never once to have set eyes on a television set.

b. Chingford, 14.viii.1892; *d.* Corfe Castle, Dorset, 15.x.88. *other works*: three pre-Busoni piano concertos, six symphonies for piano, six-hour Symphonic Variations for piano, Symphonic High Mass for chorus and orch., Pastiche on Chopin's Minute Waltz (1922), Fantasietta for poet Hugh McDiarmid's 70th birthday (1961).

soul music A *pop sector derived from gospel music and blues. Ray Charles and the Drifters were prime exponents before the *Tamla Motown sub-genre emerged with the Supremes and Marvin Gaye.

Sound of Music Rodgers and Hammerstein's tale of the Trapp family's flight from Nazis; in due course it became Salzburg's greatest musical attraction after Mozart. fp: NY, 16.xi.59.

John Philip SOUSA The composer of *Stars and Stripes Forever* toured the world with his military band and wrote a dozen operettas for Broadway.

b. Washington, D.C., 6.xi.1854; *d.* Reading, Pennsylvania, 6.iii.32.

Leo SOWERBY Chicago church musician of varied output, powerfully conceived in a neo-classical idiom. Stravinsky himself would not have disowned the opening of the cantata *Forsaken of Man* (Chicago 22.ii.40) and while *Hindemith quipped that the fourth B in the musical pantheon was Leo 'sour B' – this was not malevolently meant. Sowerby was organist and choirmaster at St James Episcopal Cathedral for 35 years (1927–62), earning the respect of Fritz Reiner and other conductors of the Chicago Symphony Orchestra, which commissioned his 3rd symphony (6.iii.41) for its jubilee. In addition to a vast amount of grandiose liturgical music, Sowerby wrote jazz for Paul *Whiteman, contrapuntal piano sonatas and more than 300 songs. He was the epitome of industry and, like Anthony *Burgess, might have won weightier consideration if he had restrained his busy pen.

> *b*. Grand Rapids, Michigan, 1.v.1895; moved to Chicago 1909; st with *Grainger; won Pulitzer Prize 1946 for *Canticle of the Sun*; founded College of Church Musicians at Washington Cathedral 1962; *d*. Port Clinton, Ohio, 7.vii.68. *other works*: two piano concertos, two organ concertos, two cello concertos, five symphonies, symphonic poems *From the Northland* (1924) and *Prairie* (1929).

Spain Music bloomed in Spain at the turn of the century with the rediscovery of a rich national heritage by French-trained composers Albeniz, Granados and de Falla. The sources were varied: from Arabian ululation to the precise discipline of Domenico Scarlatti's 555 sonatas. Civil war, followed by political isolation, returned the country to the dark ages; progressive composers emigrated or fell silent. Despite the mellifluous strains of Rodrigo, the fame of singers like Domingo and de Los Angeles and a thriving guitar cult, Spain lags behind most of Western Europe in musical creativity and institutions.

spatial music Beethoven and Wagner moved instrumental soloists out of the opera pit to deliver a dramatic message from an unexpected direction. *Mahler in his 2nd symphony placed an offstage band unseen at a celestial height to sound the apocalypse. Ives and Messiaen envisaged orchestras playing on mountain tops. Carter wrote a *Symphony of 3 orchestras* and Stockhausen in *Gruppen* deployed

three ensembles and conductors around the hall. The drama in *Birtwistle's two large-scale operas was heightened by external voices projected through loudspeakers. The consciousness of space was accentuated by the record industry's embrace of stereophonic sound in 1958, though consumers were unconvinced of the benefits of quadrophonic and surround-sound.

Leopold SPINNER A pupil of Webern and *serialist in all his works, he fled to England from the Nazis and lived there in total obscurity for 40 years. The 1936 sonata for violin and piano opus 1 is a classic of 12-note writing.

> *b*. Lvov, Austro-Hungary, 26.iv.06; *d*. London, 12.viii.80.

spirituals Religious songs of American blacks, a forerunner of gospel music and *soul. *Tippett borrowed some in *A Child of our Time*.

sponsorship The collapse of aristocratic wealth and the uncertainty of state patronage prompted musicians in many lands to seek the help of businessmen. In the United States, concert halls were named after private and corporate donors, the most famous being Carnegie in New York and Heinz in Pittsburgh. The Kodak photographic company founded the Eastman music school in Rochester. Concert series in Europe and Japan are sometimes named, like sporting leagues, after their sponsor. The Yamaha company had the neat idea of funding Morton *Subotnick to compose exclusively on their keyboards and sound systems.

sprechgesang (speech-song) A form of vocalizing that, in *Schoenberg's words, 'resembles neither natural speech nor true singing'. He invented it in *Pierrot lunaire*, calling it *Sprechstimme* (speaking voice), a term previously used by Humperdinck in his opera *Königskinder*. It combines an expressive intensity lacking in normal speech with a realism that is missing from drama. It prevails in *Gurrelieder, Die glückliche Hand, Jacob's Ladder* and *Ode to Napoleon*, and was adopted by *Berg in *Wozzeck* and *Boulez in *Le visage nuptial*.

Spring Symphony Choral-orchestral work by *Britten. fp: Amsterdam, 9.vii.49.

Bruce **SPRINGSTEEN** The hottest
singer-songwriter after Bob *Dylan, his
social criticism is less caustic, more melodic, and his private life apparently blameless. His style veers from *folk to *rock. Hit
albums include *The River* (1980), *Born in
the USA* (1984).
  b. Freehold, New Jersey, 23.ix.49;

squeaky-wheel music Pejorative term
used to decry serialist and electronic
works.

Joseph STALIN The first head of government since King Saul to voice formative
musical criticism, Stalin (1879–1953) made
two violent interventions that altered the
course of Russian art. In 1935, dismayed
by sexuality and dissonance in Shostakovich's opera *A Lady Macbeth of the
Mtsensk District*, he dictated, or caused to
be written, an article in the Party newspaper *Pravda* entitled 'Chaos instead of
Music'. This laid down the law that socialist music must have its roots in popular
culture and be approachable by workers
after their daily toil. Music, like everything
else, had to serve the revolution. In 1948,
angered by the absence of musical celebration of three decades of Bolshevism, he
appointed Andrei Zhdanov to whip composers pubilcly back into line. On both
occasions, the principal victim was
Shostakovich, joined in 1948 by Prokofiev,
Khatchaturian and Miaskovsky. These
composers had the creative resources and
guile to protect their art from state vanda-
lism. Others, less competent, were subdued into banality and generations of
musicians were forced to write and play
utter rubbish.
  Apologists have claimed that, given the
nature of the Soviet state, it was no more
than the leader's right and duty to impose
quotas and norms on musicians just as he
did on steelworkers. It showed the deep
concern that socialism felt for the arts, a
concern conspicuously lacking in capitalist
societies. This argument cannot, however,
begin to condone the ravages that were
unleashed under Stalin or the many artists
and musicians who were murdered at his
whim. No other dictator in a dictatorial
century sought such absolutism over art
(see *politics).

(Sir) Charles Villiers STANFORD
Explosive Irishman who, with *Parry, ran
English music education along Brahmsian
lines. Touchy as a grenade, he raised his
country's finest generation of composers –
*Bliss, *Bridge, *Goossens, *Gurney,
*Holst, *Howells and *Vaughan Williams –
with admonitions of 'It won't do, me boy,
it won't do'. His Shakespearean opera
Much Ado About Nothing folded after two
nights (30.v.01). The clarinet concerto was
spurned by Richard Mühlfeld who was
accustomed to the real thing from Brahms;
its jig of a rondo is sparkling fun. His cello
concerto, written at the same moment as
*Elgar's, bears no comparison in mood or
substance. The *Irish* Symphony of 1887 is
his finest; but the 7th (22.ii.12) has an
agreeable lilt, like middle-period Dvořák.
He brought freshness to Anglican church
ritual and left some rollicking *Songs of the
Sea* (1904).
  b. Dublin, 30.ix.1852; st at Leipzig with
*Reinecke; prof. at Royal College of Music,
London, 1883 and at Cambridge 1887, hold-
ing both posts till his death in London, 29.iii.
24. *other works*: seven symphonies, five Irish
rhapsodies (1901–14), six concertos, seven
operas, eight string quartets, more than 160
songs.
  Bib: C. V. Stanford, *Pages from an unwritten
diary*, London, 1914.

Robert STARER Composer of ballets
for Martha *Graham and two operas with
librettos by his novelist wife, Gail Godwin.
Born in Vienna, trained in Jerusalem, he
infused a violin concerto (Boston, 16.x.81)
with fiddler echoes of eastern Europe and
wavering melodies of the Middle East.
  b. Vienna, 8.i.24; fled to Palestine 1938; st
with *Tal, *Partos and *Copland; *works*:
three symphonies, three piano concertos,
Concerto a tre (1954), viola concerto
(Geneva) 3.vii.59), double concerto (Pittsburgh, 11.x.68), vocal settings of Bible texts.

Max(imilian Raoul Walter) STEINER
First among film composers, Steiner
moved from Mahler's Vienna to mercantile
Broadway and on to Hollywood where he
wrote 300 soundtracks including – you
must remember this – *Casablanca, King
Kong, The Big Sleep* and, most famous of
all, *Gone with the Wind*. His music was
soft-centred to the point of schmaltz, speckled with American syncopations.

b. Vienna, 10.v.1888; st with *Fuchs and Grädener; arrived NY 1914, Hollywood 1929; *d.* there, 28.xii.71.

Wilhelm (Karl Eugen) STENHAMMAR

On the strength of one song – 'Sverige' (1905), a quasi-national anthem from the cantata *Ett Folk* – Stenhammar became a patriarch of Swedish music, though most of his ideas came from abroad. Brahms was the model for his two piano concertos (1894 and 1907), Wagner for his music drama *Tirfing* (1898), Bruckner for his F major symphony (1903) and Sibelius for the G minor (1915). Later on, he became aware of Mahler and Nielsen. The 5th and 6th of his string quartets (1910–16) were neo-classical. The F major Serenade (1919), exquisitely crafted, sounds over-civilized.

b. Stockholm, 7.ii.1871, son of composer-architect Per-Ulrik Stenhammar; married artist Helga Westerberg, 1896; wrote Ibsen opera *The Feast at Solhaug* for Stuttgart, 1899; composed 1906–7 in Italy; dir. Gothenburg orch. society, 1907–22; cond. Royal Stockholm Opera, 1923–5; *d.* Stockholm, 20.xi.27. *other works*: incidental music to Strindberg and Shakespeare plays.

Rudi STEPHAN

Germany's greatest musical loss in the First War, Stephan's concert legacy consists of *Music for Violin and Orch.* (1914). The earlier *Music for 7 stringed instruments* (Danzig, 30.v.12) reveals an elegiac, almost Ravellian melancholy in which piano and harpsichord give sharp prods to a mushy string texture. An opera, *The First Men*, was posthumously staged (Frankfurt, 1.vii.20).

b. Worms, 29.vii.1887; *d.* Tarnopol, Galicia, 29.ix.15.

Isaac STERN

Key player in American music, he saved Carnegie Hall from becoming a parking lot and was behind-scenes fixer for all manner of good causes. Stern discovered and promoted a generation of Israeli and East Asian soloists, led by Perlman and Midori. A virtuoso violinist, he shunned technical rivalry with *Heifetz and Menuhin, staking his ground as a conviction-player. He premièred Bernstein's *Serenade* and concertos by Maxwell *Davies and *Dutilleux.

b. Kremenets, Russia, 21.vii.20; emigrated to US at one year old.

Edward STEUERMANN

He fell under *Schoenberg's spell at an impressionable age and devoted his pianistic career to his cause. He made piano reductions of the master's works and gave first performances of his post-tonal piano oeuvre, as well as music by Berg and Webern. His compositions deviated from orthodox dodecatonality by repeating notes within the row and admitting tonal episodes. 'The most important things in composing,' he wrote, 'are feeling and invention'. As a refugee in NY, he was a formative piano teacher at *Juilliard.

b. Sambor, eastern Galicia, 18.vi.1892; st with Vilem Kurz, Busoni and Schoenberg; emigrated to US 1936; *d.* New York, 11.xi.64. *works*: variations for orch. (1958), suite for chamber orch. (1964), orch. cantata *Auf der Galerie* (after Kafka, 1964); seven waltzes for string quartet (1946), 2nd string quartet entitled 'Diary' (1961).
Bib. Clara Steuermann (ed.), *The Not Quite Innocent Bystander*, U. of Nebraska Press, 1989.

Bernard STEVENS

In the spring of 1946, a shy music teacher shot to prominence when he won a contest for a Victory Symphony organized by the populist *Daily Express* newspaper. After a performance at the Royal Albert Hall, he was dropped like a hot potato. A committed communist, he was anathema to the capitalist press; a serious-minded man, he refused to write down to the masses. Even the award-winning *Symphony of Liberation* (London, 7.vi.46), in movements titled Enslavement, Resistance and Liberation, did not slavishly follow Stalinist realism and took a broad line that extended from Vaughan Williams to Bartók. Stevens quit the party in 1956 over the Soviet invasion of Hungary. His most attractive works are a concerto for violin (1946), which opens with an overt 12-note theme but avoids academicism, and another, almost equally appealing, for cello (13.v.52). The 2nd symphony (15.vi.77) is more austere but full of incident.

A quarter of his output was chamber music; the elegiac Theme and Variations for string quartet (1949) was favourably compared with *Britten. He wrote eloquent William Blake and John Donne songs and many agitprop chorales. Stevens taught at the Royal College of Music, numbering *Finnissy and *Lipkin among his pupils.

> *b*. London, 2.iii.16; st music and English literature at Cambridge; married Bertha, dedicatee of dreamy violin sonata (1943); *d*. Great Maplestead, Essex, 2.i.1983. *other works*: piano concerto (1955), Ricercar for string orch. (1944), Variations for Orch. (1964) Lyric Suite string trio (1958).

Halsey STEVENS US educator who was so devoted to tonality that he took 5 years to write a dissonant four-minute *Intrada* for piano solo (1949–54). He was generally prolific and tuneful, yearning for central Europe in three Hungarian folk songs for viola and piano (1950), 12 Slovakian folksongs for two violins (1962) and six Slovakian folksongs for harp (1966). These foreign interests derived from a fixation with *Bartók, on whom Stevens wrote an important study (1953). He taught composition at the U. of Southern California (1948–76) and wrote programme notes for the Los Angeles Philharmonic.

> *b*. Scott, NY, 3.xii.08, a farmer's son; st at Syracuse U. and with Ernest *Bloch, served US naval reserve 1943–46; *d*. Long Beach, California, 20.i.89. *other works*: three symphonies, concertos for clarinet (1969), viola (1976) and violin and cello (1973); three string quartets.

Ronald STEVENSON A compelling figure in Edinburgh salons, nationalist and leftist by conviction, Stevenson possessed the kind of character that arouses either passionate devotion or weary indifference. Much of his music was on Scots themes, not simplistically but informed with a knowledge of 20th-century progress. His *Scots Suite* for unaccompanied violin (21.viii.88) has distinct echoes of Bartók; *Dodecaphonic Bonfire* for solo piano (22.viii.88) is a commentary on Schoenberg. He was so transparent in his admiration for modern giants as to base major works on theirs. An 80-minute *Passacaglia on DSCH* (Capetown, 10.xii.62) pays homage to *Shostakovich in dimensions that recall *Sorabji. A piano concerto *Triptych* on themes from Busoni's *Doktor Faust* (Edinburgh, 6.i.66) and an evocative *Peter Grimes Fantasy* (1971) on Britten's opera were similar tributes. He has made interesting piano transcriptions of music by Purcell, Bach, Berlioz, Chopin, Alkan, Berg, Busoni, Delius, Paderewski, Pizzetti and Grainger.

> *b*. Blackburn, Lancashire, 6.iii.28;

William Grant STILL The first black American to win symphonic recognition, his role model was the Afro-British composer Samuel *Coleridge-Taylor. The *Afro-American Symphony*, his first (Rochester, 29.x.31; cond. *Hanson) depicted the life of black people in America with their indigenous sounds. The 2nd in G minor was premièred by *Stokowski (Philadelphia, 10.xii.37) but when New York City Opera staged *Troubled Island* in 1949, it insisted on a white-faced cast. Still lived in dangerous times for educated blacks and gave vent to powerful feelings in the cantata, *And they Lynched Him on a Tree* (NY, 25.vi.40). He saw the civil rights era and marked his 75th birthday with a 5th symphony, entitled *Western Hemisphere* (Oberlin College, Ohio, 9.xi.70). On top of nine operas and five symphonies, he wrote chamber music that transcends time and place; the violin and piano suite (Boston, 12.iii.44) has a moody rurality that might almost be Moravian.

> *b*. Woodville, Missouri, USA, 11.v.1895; worked for blues writer W. C. Handy; st with *Varèse and George Chadwick; married twice; moved to Hollywood 1934 to write film music; *d*. Los Angeles, 3.xii.78.

stochastic (Greek = goal) *Xenakis' method for calculating the outcome and structure of a work, using a theory of probability familiar to roulette-players.

Karlheinz STOCKHAUSEN There is an obvious contradiction between what Stockhausen says and the music he composes, between the richness of his ideas and the simplicity of his sound, between his universalism and his egocentricity, between his iconoclasm and his need to belong to tradition. The conflict is probably irresoluble. It may well be the wellspring of the extraordinary magnetism that Stockhausen has exerted on music in the second half of the century.

Ever since Messiaen singled him out with *Boulez in 1958 as harbingers of the future – just as Mahler once did with Schoenberg – Stockhausen has stood out as the one who achieved what others merely preached. While squeaks and howls emanated from most electronic studios, Stockhausen's sounds were civilized and entrancing. His *serialism appealed to uninformed audiences. His espousal of eastern creeds was ecstatic without being forcibly missionarist. Less agreeable was his aggressive and alienating self-belief, a case of my Stockhausen right or wrong. Several apprentices departed in disgust, with one long-serving aide joining a light-music orchestra to clear his mind. He assigned key roles to his wives and children in musical compositions, creating a *Bayreuth-like myth of a holy extended family. Latterly, he sought sole control of his output, becoming his own publisher and demanding to own every newspaper picture and taped interview that was taken of him. In no other composer would vanities of this kind be tolerated, but Stockhausen's early achievements were of such magnitude that progressive musicians prayed that, given his way, he might make another breakthrough.

His path to music was painful. His mother was hospitalized for depression when he was four years old and eventually murdered in the Nazi euthanasia programme. His father joined the Party, enlisted in the army and was killed in the final battles. Stockhausen played piano in *Cologne bars and assisted a travelling magician while studying for a music teacher's certificate. In 1951, his year of graduation and first marriage, he went to *Darmstadt to discover the serialism of *Webern and its refinement in *Messiaen's *Mode de valeurs et d'intensités*.

These ideas, allied to a two-piano sonata by *Goeyvaerts which he was unable to understand – 'this was terribly exciting, to discover that there was music which I could not make sense of' – led him to compose *Kreuzspiel* for oboe, bass clarinet, three percussion and piano. It was a crossover, hence the title, of extreme high and low sonorities with no emotional pretence or potential. What mattered most was the intrinsic value given to each separate note and their relation to one another. Stockhausen compared it to the architectural abstractions of Le Corbusier (1887–

1965). Performed at Darmstadt the following year, it prompted a phase of symphonic *pointillism with *Punkte* and *Kontrapunkte*, followed by the constructivist series of *Klavierstücke* for solo piano.

He spent 1952 with Messiaen in Paris, formed an uneasy coexistence with *Boulez and performed primitive electronic experiments in *musique concrète. On his return to *Cologne, he found a state-of-the-art studio on his doorstep and quickly outstripped its founder, *Eimert, with a work that brought electronic music before a general public. In *Gesang der Jünglinge (Young Boy's Song)* (broadcast 30.v.56), the voice of a boy chorister from Cologne Cathedral singing 'All ye works of the Lord, praise ye the Lord' was modulated and transformed against a parallel electronic track, so that electronics came to resemble the human voice and vice-versa. The text, from the Book of Daniel, reflected the composer's sense of being a young man in the burning fiery furnace. The 13'45" work was arranged on serial principles but sounded nothing like Webern's asceticisms. Its impact was instant and universal and it remains a stunning *tour de force*, the single greatest masterpiece of electronic music, much imitated, never equalled.

Searching for infinity, Stockhausen delegated details of composition to a string of assistants and refused to limit himself to any sector. In *Gruppen* (Cologne, 24.iii.59), he attacked the structure of the symphony orchestra by splitting it into three groups ranged in different parts of the house, each with its own conductor. This idea of *spatial dispersion went back to *Mahler's *Resurrection* Symphony but Stockhausen took it further than ever before, sensing that modern ears were ready for a surround-sound ambience. His next step was to form an ensemble to combine both ideas in concert works with live electronics, starting with *Mikrophonie 1* (1964) in which the microphone 'was played as a musical instrument' amid other instruments.

The tam-tam, a kind of gong, that he used with prodigious invention in *Mikorophonie*, presaged a fascination with exotic Asian sounds that he acquired on worldwide celebrity tours. *Mantra* for two pianists (1970) marked a return to simple melody. A 13-note tune is regrouped serially in 13 hypnotic cycles, each note carrying a particular emphasis – staccato, tremolo, accent at the end, and so on – the whole being transformed continuously by live electronics. Brimming with wit and exuberance, it marked the summit of Stockhausen's innovations. *Silence, *improvisation and political comment were assimilated into his work.

From the early 1970s he applied himself exclusively to a cycle of seven operas, *Licht*, each segment named after a day of the week and representing a man's progress through life. In future, he declared, 'composers will find it much more interesting to write one work during a whole lifetime and integrate everything they do'. The Wagnerian delusions were self-evident; there is even a 'yo-ho-to-ho' chorus in *Donnerstag (Thursday)*. But, despite a genuine dramatic gift and ingenious electronics and stagecraft, none of the sections so far has succeeded as opera. The stars of the performance were always Stockhausen himself at his mixing desk and various of his sons and lovers in central roles. Even committed admirers described *Licht* as 'an act of gigantic egomania' and it is impossible to forsee how Stockhausen can extricate his reputation from its arrant nonsensicality. His music has become virtually extinct on commercial records, as a result of personal disputes and public indifference, and his knack for original sound has long since been overtaken by Ligeti, who discovered his musical means on hearing *Gesang der Jünglinge*. Stockhausen, in the 1990s, seems like a sorry anachronism. His saving grace is the unmistakable pleasure he takes and communicates in making music, wherever he appears.

b. Burg Mödrath, nr. Cologne, 22.viii.28; *other key works* (of a total of almost 200): *Zeitmasze* (five woodwinds, 1956), *Carré* (four choirs and orch., Hamburg, 28.x.60), *Mikrophonie II* for 12 singers, Hammond organ and electronics (1965), *Telemusik* (electronic, 1966) *Hymnen* (electronic or orch., 1967/69), *Stimmung* for six voices (1968), *Aus den sieben Tagen*, '15 texts for intuitive music' (1968), *Trans* (orch., 1971), *Inori* (soloists and orch., 1973), *Licht*

(1977–), of which *Donnerstag*, *Samstag* and *Montag* have been staged and many fragments spun off into concert pieces.
Bib: Michael Kurtz, *Stockhausen: A Biography*, London (Faber), 1992.

Stockhausen Serves Imperialism Title of 1974 polemic by disaffected acolyte *Cardew.

Lozko STOIANOV The liturgy of the Orthodox Church in Bulgaria is audibly lighter than its Russian counterpart and continued to attract composers under the disapproving eye of communism. Stoyanov's *Liturgia Solemnis* (1977) is a fine example of religious renewal under external stress.
b. Sofia 1934, active there as conductor and choirmaster.

Petr (Lazar) STOJANOVIC Hungarian fiddler who became a key figure in Yugoslav music, he formed a violin school in Vienna before moving in 1925 to Belgrade, where he opened another school and composed late romantic scores, among them seven violin concertos.
b. Budapest, 6.ix.1877; *d.* Belgrade, Yugoslavia, 11.ix.57. *other works*: two Hungarian operas and three operettas, two ballets, two viola concertos, horn concerto.

Leopold (Boleslawowicz Stanislaw Antoni) STOKOWSKI The British-born conductor was a standard-bearer of 20th-century music, giving first performances of hundreds of scores. He headed the Philadelphia Orch. for quarter of a century and was the first maestro to exploit the outreach potential of film, radio and records. His Disney movie *Fantasia* (1939) introduced generations of children to Beethoven and Stravinsky. Although his accent was fake and his Bach transcriptions questionable, his populist ambition was above reproach. His world premières included: Ives 4th symphony, Varèse *Amériques*, Rachmaninov 4th piano concerto, Paganini Rhapsody and 3rd symphony; Schoenberg piano and violin concertos; Martinů 4th piano concerto, Panufnik *Universal Prayer*; Havergal Brian 28th symphony, Bruch two-piano concerto, Copland Dance Symphony, Cowell 6th and 12th symphonies and many others from Amfiteatrov to Zemachson. He gave

US premières of Berg's *Wozzeck*; Mahler's 8th and *Das Lied von der Erde*; four symphonies by Shostakovich, three by Sibelius, Elgar's 2nd; Stravinsky's *Rite of Spring*, Schoenberg's *Gurrelieder*, Strauss's Alpine Symphony, Webern's Passacaglia.

b. Marylebone, London, 18.iv.1882 of Irish and Polish parents; organist at St James's, Piccadilly, 1900–05, and St Bartholomew's, NY, 1905–08; cond. Cincinnati Symphony Orch. 1909–12, Philadelphia Orch. 1912–36, All-American Youth Orch. 1940–42, NBC Symphony Orch. 1942–3, NY Philharmonic 1949–50, Houston Symphony 1955–60, American Symphony Orch. 1962–72; married (1) Olga Samaroff, pianist, 1911–23, (2) Evangeline Brewster Johnson, drug heiress, 1926–37, (3) Gloria Vanderbilt, 'poor little rich girl', 1945–55; *d.* Nether Wallop, Hampshire, 13.ix.77, buried at Marylebone Cemetery, East Finchley.

Bib: O. Daniel, *Stokowski, a Counterpoint of View*, NY (Dodd Mead), 1982.

Oscar STRAUS Dropping the second S from his surname to distinguish himself from the waltz dynasty, Oscar made his name in operetta with *A Waltz Dream* (Vienna, 2.ii.07) and *The Chocolate Soldier* (Vienna, 14.xi.08) based (against G. B. Shaw's better judgement) on *Arms and the Man*. He was previously conductor at Berlin's Überbrettl theatre, where Schoenberg wrote cabaret songs. Exiled to the US in the Hitler years, he returned to Austria to write a memorable film score for Schnitzler's *La Ronde*.

b. Vienna, 6.iii.1870; st with Bruch in Berlin; *d.* Bad Ischl, 11.i.54. *other works*: Wagner parody *The Merry Nibelungen* (Vienna, 12.xi.04), a dozen operettas using American dances rather than the waltz; a serenade for strings and many piano pieces.

Richard (Georg) STRAUSS An uncomfortable inhabitant of modern times, Strauss combined the lyrical felicity of Mozart with the German craftsmanship of Bach, the bombast of Richard Wagner with a personal quality that resisted definition in his own time, or since. He was a testament to the essential amorality of music, composing for no purpose but personal satisfaction and financial gain, of which he was not a whit ashamed. He liked to boast that his Alpine house at Garmisch-Partenkirchen was built on profits from the steamy Dance of Seven Veils, extracted from his opera *Salome* and peddled like soft-porn. He built a post-imperial palace in central Vienna on royalties from the nearby opera house.

He was a man of firm loyalties to family, friends and, above all, himself. He accepted postions of honour from the Nazis, only to be sacked for continuing to correspond with a Jewish librettist, Stefan Zweig, on whose collaboration he depended. He is said to have marched up to the gates of a concentration camp, demanding to visit a relative by marriage who was incarcerated within. His worldly realism was tempered by rural, romantic naïvety. In a life that began before *Tristan* and ended in the year of *musique concrète*, he rarely revealed his feelings as man, or musician.

His serene professionalism was the antithesis of his friend *Mahler's symphonic self-immolation. He conceived a gargantuan *Alpine Symphony* on the day of Mahler's death but composed it 'as a cow gives milk' – as effortlessly as any natural process. It provides a literal description of a day out in the mountains, using wind and thunder machines (Berlin, 28.x.15). Strauss, in his symphonic vein, pushed literalism to the limits of decency. He depicted himself as the immodest hero in the tone poem *Ein Heldenleben* (1899) and as the paterfamilias of *Sinfonia Domestica* (NY, 21.iii.04), which describes a day in his home life, complete with bathing baby and conjugal intercourse. In *Intermezzo* (Dresden, 4.xi.24) he embarrassed everyone but himself with an opera about a mix-up that prompted his shrewish wife, Pauline, to accuse him of infidelity. In case anyone missed the point, the protagonists in the first production were made up as spitting images of Mr and Mrs Strauss.

The son of Wagner's rebel horn-player in the Munich orchestra, he began composing at six years old and had a symphony performed by Hermann Levi at 16. Hans von Bülow taught him to conduct, a function he performed elegantly and with the minimum of effort, rolling up his sleeves to play cards with the players in the interval. He was chief conductor at Weimar (1889–94) and co-director of the Vienna State Opera, 1918–24.

His symphonic utterances grew larger in scale and hollower in content. After *Taillefer* (Heidelberg, 26.x.03) – a Battle of Hastings ballad for soprano, tenor, baritone, 147-piece band and chorus, he virtually gave up composing concert works and concentrated on opera. In between the Wagner-imitative *Guntram* (1894) and the lighter, waltzier *Feuersnot* (Fire-Famine, Dresden, 21.xi.01), he wrote an unusual melodrama for speaking voice and piano on Tennyson's poem, *Enoch Arden*, a work that paralleled the cabaret music and tonal fissures of Arnold *Schoenberg. Strauss, at the dawn of the century, was at the forefront of modernism. A decade later, he had become a reactionary who encouraged Schoenberg to shovel snow for a living.

He saw Oscar Wilde's play *Salomé* in Max Reinhardt's Berlin production of 1901 and instantly saw that it would make an opera. Tautly stretched across a single act, its tensions are heightened by strained moments of 'schreckliche Stille' (terrible silence) and the persistent repetition of the

princess' demand for the head of John the Baptist. A clash of F# and F natural chords 16 bars from the end produces one of the most gruesome sounds ever composed. Wagner pervades the score's vain search for a *Tristan* chord, and Salome's vicious love-song to the severed head runs unsettlingly close to Isolde's *Liebestod*. Despite brilliant musical illumination of perverse psychologies, Strauss' exotic Palestine is as glibly touristic as his eroticism is voyeurist. The première (Dresden, 9.xii.05) produced a profitable scandal. Mahler was stopped from staging *Salome* at Vienna and Beecham had to bowdlerize the text before it could be seen in London, but the opera made Strauss's fame and fortune.

Having adapted his own text, he now entered a fruitful five-opera collaboration with the frustrated Viennese poet, Hugo von Hofmannsthal (1874–1929). *Elektra* (Dresden, 25.i.09) ended his flirtation with dissonance in some exquisitely refined ugliness – music in every way a match for its parricidal story but which ends in a resolving chord of C major. It failed to shock as much as he might have hoped and Strauss drew back from the cliff-edge of tonality into the cushioned warmth of the classical boudoir.

*Der *Rosenkavalier* (Dresden, 26.i.11) was genial in every sense. An anachronistic 18th-century farce with strong hints of *Figaro*, it flattered the middle classes without offending the nobility, endorsed both marriage and sexual libertinism, and glamourized young love while hinting at its brevity. Utterly devoid of moral or cerebral substance, it was a masterpiece studded with erotic allusions and ethereal, deceptive waltzes that sneered ever-so-lightly at Viennese corruption. There was a jewel-like perfection to every phrase and bar that composers ever after would study as a paragon of opera. Countless attempts to repeat its formula – including *Arabella* (Dresden, 1.vii.33) by Strauss and Hofmannsthal themselves – were stunted by comparison. *Arabella*'s swooping arias and seductive orchestration amount almost to self-parody.

Having exploited baroque atmospherics, they next attempted, in *Ariadne auf Naxos*, an opera about an opera set in the drawing-rooms of Mozart's Vienna. It was designed to follow Max Reinhardt's staging of Molière's *Le Bourgeois Gentilhomme* at Stuttgart (25.x.12), after which the partners recast it as a two-hour stage work (Vienna, 4.x.16), extracting Strauss's incidental music for Molière's play as a witty concert suite (Salzburg, 31.i.20). *Die Frau ohne Schatten (The Shadowless Woman*, Vienna, 10.x.19), Hofmannsthal's bid for a *Magic Flute*, is a grand perplexity. It is notable for an orchestra that includes wind machine, castanets and glass harmonica and a Cecil B. de Mille magniloquence. *Die ägyptische Helena (Helen of Egypt*, Dresden, 6.vi.28) was the nadir of their partnership, which recovered valedictory fluency in *Arabella* just before the poet's death. The best-selling biographer Stefan Zweig (1881–1942) raised the composer's hopes of a second coming with the half-baked *Die schweigsame Frau (The Silent Woman*, Dresden, 24.vi.35), set in Ben Jonson's 17th-century London where all was merry and bright.

Whether this was blithe indifference to social conditions or a camouflage of his feelings, reality brutally intervened when Zweig was banned from Germany by the Nazis. Apparently sympathetic to supremacism, to judge from his Nietzschean settings of the 1890s, and casually racist – listen to his caricature of the squabbling Temple priests in *Salome* – Strauss endorsed the Nazi regime and became founder-president of Goebbels' *Reichsmusikkammer* that regulated the racial purity of German music. *Das Bächlein (The Brook)*, a Schubertian song dedicated to the Nazi propaganda chief, lays triple emphasis on the climactic words, 'mein Führer'. He was disgraced two years later when his contacts were discovered with the outlawed Zweig and Strauss spent the rest of the Nazi era in official limbo. He offered triumphal marches for the Berlin Olympics (1936) and Festmusik (1940) for Hitler's Japanese allies but remained suspect to the authorities and needed protection from their occasional wrath. *Friedenstag (Day of Peace*, Munich, 24.vii.38), a one-act opera planned with Zweig, used Nuremberg-like forces of 14 soloists, several choruses and huge orchestra to utter an appeal for world peace.

The soprano vehicles *Daphne* and *Die Liebe der Danae* contain fine stretches of music but little dramatic propulsion. In *Capriccio*, with a text partly by its conductor, Clemens Krauss, (Munich, 28.x.42), Strauss turned tenderly to the timeless dilemma of whether music or words should come first, in the story of a Countess torn between two suitors, a poet and composer. It harked back to the world of *Ariadne* and revived Strauss's operatic inspiration.

His final works rediscovered the tonal world he shared with Mahler and Schoenberg in the 1890s. A 2nd horn concerto (Salzburg, 11.viii.43) and an oboe concerto (Zurich, 26.ii.46) greet the orchestra and its instruments as childhood friends. *Metamorphosen* for 23 string instruments (Zurich, 25.i.46), composed as Germany collapsed, recalls the stressed strings of **Verklärte Nacht*. A superb songwriter throughout his life, he distilled in *Four Last Songs* (London, 22.v.50, Flagstad, cond. Furtwängler) a sense of seasons passing and life drawing to a peaceful close. A refugee in his eighties, his fortune made and lost several times, he died as he had lived, without a show of emotion. 'Dying', he told a deathbed visitor, 'is just as I composed it 60 years ago in *Tod und Verklärung*.'

b. Munich, 11.vi.1864; married soprano Pauline de Ahna, a Bavarian general's daughter, 10.ix.1894; *d.* Garmisch-Partenkirchen, Bavaria, 8.ix.49. *other orch. works*: D-minor symphony (1881), violin concerto (1883), F-minor symphony (1884), 1st horn concerto (1885), tone poems *Don Juan, Aus Italien, Till Eulenspiegel, Also Sprach Zarathustra, Don Quixote* (1887–96), *Burleske* for piano and orch. (1890), *Macbeth* (1890), *Parergon* for left-hand piano and orch. (Dresden, 16.x.25), *Divertimento* on pieces by Couperin (Vienna, 31.i.43).
Bib: Kurt Wilhelm, *Richard Strauss, an intimate portrait*, London (Thames & Hudson), 1989.

Igor STRAVINSKY The life and works of Igor Stravinsky fell into three unequal phases. He lived in Russia until 1914 when war cut off from home and revolution prevented his return; he lived in Switzerland and France until 1939 when he emigrated

to the US. The transitions in his music were not contingent on his geographic movements – with the exception of the loss of his rhythmic first style, which was allied to loss of homeland.

If Schoenberg twice re-invented the rules of composition, Stravinsky twice rein-vented himself, each time opening a new window of musical discourse. The fiery Russian ballets that he brought to Paris gave rhythm an equal value with tone in the shaping of a musical work. His *neo-classical mode was mocked by modernists as reactionary but kindled a fresh aware-ness of history and its untapped resources. Finally, persuaded of Webern's ineluctable logic, he wrote wickedly accurate tone-rows which demonstrated that serialism was neither dusty nor dull. Each of his separate styles attracted significant fol-lowers. *Bartók and *Prokofiev picked up on his rhythmic innovations; neo-classicism set the tone in inter-War Paris for *Martinů and *Honegger; the late works were a shining light to *Boulez and *Birt-wistle. He lacked Schoenberg's messianic conviction but his influence extended further, looming larger than any composer in the entire century. With Stravinsky's death in 1971, music lost its last visible colossus.

The son of St Petersburg's finest operatic bass, he went to law school and took desul-tory music lessons until *Rimsky-Korsakov asked him home. There he wrote an F♯-minor piano sonata and learned the secrets of orchestration, writing an E-flat symphony that was played by the court

orchestra (4.ii.08). For the wedding of Rimsky's daughter he composed a *Fireworks* suite (17.vi.08) and for his funeral a wind-instrument *Chant funèbre*. The score was lost but he revived the form to eulogize Debussy in the morose *Symphonies of Wind Instruments* (London, 10.vi.21).

While Rimsky lit his fuse, it was the balletmaster Serge *Diaghilev who touched off the explosion that made him a world figure before he was 30. Three ballets in Paris won him instant acclaim and total self-assurance. The shimmering *Firebird* (Paris, 25.vi.10) bears many of *Rimsky's folkloristic hallmarks but is held together by rhythmic propulsion. *Petrushka* (13.vi.11) was a second stride down the same path, using the piano percussively as a spinal cord in the orchestra. He rescored both suites sparingly for concert use, but the stage versions are preferable. Diaghilev was busily transforming the lowly status of ballet music and commanding the attention of highbrow audiences. Stravinsky was the first great composer to believe in ballet as an art equal to opera. Caring little for its gyrations, he produced his liveliest inspi-rations in ballet form until he was past 80; his affinity to Diaghilev was such that he demanded to be buried beside him, in Venice.

Notoriety arrived with his third Diaghilev ballet, *The Rite of Spring*, subti-tled 'Scenes from Pagan Russia.' Its pre-mière (Théâtre des Champs Elysées, 29.v.13, cond. *Monteux) provoked riots among society balletomanes, ill-attuned to contemporary art. Any folksiness in Stravinsky's makeup had been rigorously eliminated in this portrait of village life red in tooth and claw, its violent discords linked by elemental rhythms that culmi-nated in a sacrificial virgin's fatal dance. It marked, even more than Schoenberg's *atonal leap, the birth of modernism – a music that did not need melody. It still sounds shockingly noisy, more 'advanced' than the concurrent *Pierrot Lunaire*, yet its structure is taut and its orchestra of 111 is smaller than Strauss's or Mahler's. It is music that young people will always re-spond to better than their elders and its opening theme is echoed unconsciously in dozens, perhaps hundreds, of other works.

The Rite presented Stravinsky as the angry young man of music, the first Russian to draw his ideas from the pre-civilized east, rather than the cultivated west. The score was anathema in Tsarist Russia and was banned by the communists until the 1960s. Stravinsky was startled enough by the hostility he provoked to tone down its brutalities in future works. *Zvezdoliki (King of Stars)*, an intriguingly dissonant male-chorus cantata written around the same time was not performed until 1939. In *Les Noces* (13.vi.23), a pulsating choral ballet describing a rural wedding, he cut back the orchestration to four pianos and 17 percussion instruments, and peppered the work with abstruse aphorisms. Others would now write more raucously while Stravinsky, appalled at his temerity, exercised self-restraint as a means of physical survival.

Stravinsky's neat handwriting

The outbreak of war found him in Switzerland, reduced to impotence, penury and playing piano rags. It was Diaghilev who once again set him on the road to invention, asking him to make a ballet out of unfinished manuscripts by Giovanni Battista Pergolesi (1710–36) and other pieces that he had picked up in Italy. 'Should my line of action with regard to Pergolesi be dominated by my love or my respect for his music?' Stravinsky asked himself. 'Is it love or respect that urges us to possess a woman? Is it not by love alone that we succeed in penetrating to the very essence of a being?' His solution in *Pulcinella* (15.v.20) came close to rape, as Stravinsky spiced music of an imaginary past with modern flavours and piquant rhythms. He patented and pursued this neo-classical course for the next 30 years,

revitalized by a new love that entered his life in February 1921, the wide-eyed Vera Sudeikina. There were always acolytes around Stravinsky to promote his every discovery, enabling him to avoid interviews and the taint of self-advertisement.

Ballet remained his most fertile outlet. *Apollo Musagète*, scored for a string ensemble small enough for the Library of Congress (Washington, 27.iv.28), is classically simple and texturally intricate – perhaps the most tuneful of all his works. *The Fairy's Kiss (Baiser de la fée*, 27.xi.28) was extrapolated from Tchaikovsky themes; *Jeu de cartes* (NY, 27.iv.37), a 'ballet in three deals', celebrated his favourite game of poker. In any other composer, such pieces would have been deemed plagiarist, trivial and opportunist. Stravinsky's genius, and to some extent his myth, set him above common critical criteria.

Although his ballets were descriptive, Stravinsky believed that 'music expresses nothing' and proved his point in abstract concert works. The faintly astringent violin concerto (Berlin, 23.x.31) defined its idiom in Baroque movements titled 'toccata, aria and capriccio' and an almost democratic equality between soloist and orch.; it did not convey the physical and emotional depths of the Brahms or Tchaikovsky concertos. A parallel Duo Concertant for violin and piano (Berlin, 28.x.32) stretches from a hillbilly Eclogue to an ethereal Dithyrambe – classical terms that Stravinsky used to mask his sources. The concerto for piano and wind instruments (22.v.24) slips jazz riffs mischievously into classical anachronisms, while the Capriccio for piano and orch. (6.xii.29) is a riotous travelogue of musical Europe.

He wrote two all-purpose concertos for string orchestra – *Dumbarton Oaks* (8.v.38), named after the Washington, D.C., estate of the family that commissioned it, and the Concerto in D (Basle, 27.i.47). Both can be played with total refinement, as *Karajan showed, or be transformed by an interpreter of *Bernstein's character into bubbling, unsettling concoctions. This ability to write chameleon music that changes colour with its interpreter was another of Stravinsky's attractions: you never know in advance quite what you are about to hear. The nearest he came to an instrumental showpiece was the nine-minute *Ebony Concerto* for Woody Herman's clarinet and swing band (NY, 25.iii.46) which, after a breezy beginning, settled into a mushy smooch. Its structure, though, was shaped by the disciplines that moulded the Symphony in Three Movements (NY, 24.i.46).

Stravinsky's approach to symphonic form was iconoclastic. The *Symphony in C* (Chicago, 7.xi.40) barely touched its nominated key before veering off into G and less certain regions. The Symphony in Three Movements could readily be said to have four. The summit of his symphonic mode was the tremendous Symphony of Psalms (Brussels, 13.xii.30), written for the jubilee of *Koussevitsky's Boston Symphony Orchestra and inscribed 'to the glory of God'. It combined echoes of Byzantine choral chant, Bach chorales and *Rite*-like rumblings to infer a profound faith. Russian Orthodox by adherence, Stravinsky wrote a marvellous male-chorus Mass (Milan, 27.x.48) for the Roman Catholic church in the hope of having it sung liturgically. It proved, unsurprisingly, too feral for the faithful and, along with the *Psalms*, found its place in the concert hall. His religious utterances are distinguished by a vigour that harks back to paganism rather than to the gloomy monodies of Byzantium.

They are also rich in humour, though not the ribald, giggly wit that surfaced in the *Circus Polka* (Boston, 13.i.44) and a *Greeting Prelude* for Monteux's 80th birthday (Boston, 4.iv.55). He nearly got arrested for tampering with the *Star-Spangled Banner* (14.i.44) – an expression of gratitude, he said, to the United States; his face would one day appear on US postage stamps.

Despite his balletic facility, his stage works are not brilliantly theatrical. He was strangely ambivalent about writing an opera (perhaps reflecting the relationship with his singer-father) and approached it through the halfway houses of *L'histoire du soldât* (Lausanne, 28.ix.19), which is acted but unsung, and *Renard* (Paris 18.v.22), which is danced rather than acted, with the four singers stationed in the orchestra

(Stravinsky composed it on the cimbalom, whose comically sour sonority permeates the 16-minute score). *Mavra* (1922), based on a Pushkin tale, is closer to the conventional genre but *Oedipus Rex* (Paris 30.v.27) is more oratorio than opera, not only because it is sung and narrated in the dead language of Latin. It is a static piece, no matter how imaginative the staging. Only *The Rake's Progress* (Venice, 11.ix.51) can be counted a real opera, with a text by *Auden and Chester Kallman after Hogarth's 18th-century etchings of London lowlife and sweet arias set among its wicked witticisms. With mock-Mozartian recitatives, it found a firm foothold in the operatic repertoire.

In 1957, after a decade's abstinence from ballet, Stravinsky wrote a seminal dance piece. *Agon* (Los Angeles, 17.vi.57), although modelled on 17th-century French dances, has a large orchestra, amazingly fast passages and *serial episodes of astonishing beauty that heralded his final phase. By this time, Stravinsky had crossed his final Rubicon. Around 1950 he began composing music in the *12-note style devised by his antipode, Schoenberg. Intermittently at first, in the *Canticum Sacrum (ad Honorem Sancti Marci Nominis)* (Venice, 13.ix.56), his confidence increased to the point where it dictated entire works from *Threni* (Venice, 23.ix.58) onwards. Purists claim the rapt and magnificent dirge *In memoriam Dylan Thomas* (1954) – 'do not go gentle into that good night' – as his first fully serial work, although it used a row of only five notes.

Stravinsky's conversion to serialism stunned the musical world in the same way as the Nazi-Soviet pact shook political Europe. Here were two radically opposed ideologies making common cause against the status quo ante. The twin poles of 20th-century music had drawn together, squeezing the middle ground and leaving it indefensible.

Stravinsky waited until after Schoenberg was dead before making his move, and attributed his change of mind largely to Webern. Yet his methods and subjects ran closer to the much-maligned originator than to his ascetic pupil. Stravinsky's serial music proceeded from a melodic and dramatic impulse, as did Schoenberg's, and his preoccupation with Biblical figures and the purpose of life had little in common with Webern's arid formulae. The ballad of *Abraham and Isaac* (Jerusalem, 23.viii.64) was hewn from the same source and prophetic certainty as *Moses und Aron*.

The reasons for Stravinsky's transformation were numerous. He was pushed towards it by an acolyte, Robert Craft, and sought the elixir of youth bestowed by *avant-garde approval. His inventiveness was flagging in the late 1940s and a fresh stimulus was needed. Always the most disciplined of artists – his desk, scores and dress were paragons of obsessive neatness – he was attracted by 12-note absolutism. His application of the technique was tuneful, rhythmic and unmistakably individual. With advancing age, beset by chronic ailments, he found strength in religion and produced his finest serial compositions in the Jeremiad *Threni* and the surprisingly, almost Mozartianly, light-hearted *Requiem Canticles* (Princeton, New Jersey, 8.x.66). His creative life closed with a smile in the 1966 vocal setting of Edward Lear's *The Owl and the Pussycat*.

In the course of three careers as a rhythm-man, neo-classicist and serialist, Stravinsky left infinite loose ends to motivate future composers. Like Picasso's, his was a 20th-century odyssey through a landscape of his own making, using rules that he improvised and changed at will. His music was rooted in tradition, and created its own tradition. In one of the longest creative lives, he left an inexhaustible legacy. All that is missing, and this may seem a small quibble, is a sense of the composer's blood-and-guts involvement in a score. A private and cautious man, as befits a triple exile, Stravinsky seemed to be writing at some distance from himself, describing the pain and passion of others but concealing his own. There is, at times, something voyeuristic about his music, although many cherish this quality as a mark of objectivity.

b. Oranienbaum (Lamonosov), near St Petersburg, 17.vi.1882; st U. of St Petersburg 1902–5; married cousin Catherine Nossenko 1906; settled in Switzerland 1915; cohabited with Vera Sudeikina in Paris from 1921; 1st

US visit 1925; French citizen 1934; months after wife's death of TB, married Vera 1940; suffered stroke in Munich 1956; *d.* New York, 6.iv.71 and buried by gondola in Venice. *other significant works*: melodrama *Perséphone* (Paris, 30.iv.34), TV opera *The Flood* (CBS, NY, 14.vi.62); opera-ballet *The Nightingale* (Paris, 26.v.14); ballet *Orpheus* (1948), *Aldous Huxley in memoriam* (Chicago, 17.iv.65), *Elegy for JFK* (words by Auden, NY, 6.xii.64); *Monumentum pro Gesualdo di Venosa* (Venice, 27.ix.60), double canon for string quartet (1959), *Pribaoutki* (peasant songs, Vienna, 6.vi.19); Bach-like piano sonata (1924) and serenade (1925), two-piano sonata (1944).

Morton SUBOTNICK Centre of electronic operations on the US West Coast, he has applied high technology to mixed-media shows with various performance artists. *Silver Apples of the Moon* (1967), reputedly the first electronic composition written for commercial record release, is squeaky and unsettling. *Return (a triumph of reason)* (1985), celebrating the reappearance of Halley's Comet, has a certain cosmic beauty.

b. Los Angeles, 14.iv.33; st with *Milhaud; dir. of electronic music at Calif. Institute of the Arts, 1969–; *other works*: *Before the Butterfly* for orch. (Los Angeles, 26.ii.76), *Angels* for string quartet and electronics (Los Angeles, 20.vi.84).

Eugen SUCHOŇ The doyen of Slovak composers arrived in 1938 with a massive *Psalm of the Lower Carpathians*, scored for tenor, huge orch. and chorus, vociferously bewailing the toughness of life in the local mountains. A scream of 'Zem!' (Land!) grimly set the scene and it was all struggle from then on. This prescient essay in *realism commended Suchoň to post-War communists; previously, his music was approved in Nazi Germany. He spent the 1940s writing a socio-emotional village drama, *Krútnava (The Whirlpool)* (Bratislava, 10.xii.49), that echoed Janáček's rhythms and subject matter but not his wit or subtlety. A 2nd opera, *Svätopluk* (1960), tinged uncomplicated nationalisms with a modicum of dissonance and missed its target. Thereafter he wrote mostly instrumental music.

b. Pezinok, Slovakia, 25.ix.08, st with *Novák; showered with CSSR honours and

1981 Herder Prize of Vienna University; *other works*: *Nox et solitudo* (song cycle for mezzo and small orch., 1933), *Metamorphoses* for large orch. (1953), symphonic fantasy on BACH (1971), concertino for clarinet and orch. (1977), *Kaleidoscope* (for varied instrumental combinations, 1968).

suite A baroque form revived in the late 19th century for potted concert highlights of a larger stage work, as in Tchaikovsky's *Nutcracker* and Stravinsky's *Firebird* suites. Debussy and Schoenberg used the term to describe abstract piano compositions in several sections.

Josef SUK Dvořák's star pupil proved himself at 18 with a heartwarming Serenade for Strings and in 1898 married his master's daughter, Otylka. A nuptially brash E minor symphony (Prague, 25.xi.1899) was followed by a mournful Elegy for piano trio (1900) echoing in a poignant phrase recalling the dying kiss of Verdi's *Otello*. In the symphonic poem, *Prague* (18.xii.04), he was starting to break out of folk-based late romanticism when his world fell apart with Dvořák's death, followed 14 months later by the demise of his beloved Otylka, aged 31. To a tripartite epitaph he was writing for Dvořák – the second movement based on direct quotations from his own Requiem – Suk added a 4th movement eulogizing Otylka and a finale promising ultimate consolation. Named *Asrael* after the Angel of Death, the symphony (Prague, 3.ii.07) sways between hope and despair in the manner of *Mahler's 9th, though less agitatedly. It stands out as the Czech symphonic masterpiece of the century, a monument of national art whose themes were cited hauntingly in music composed in the Theresienstadt concentration camp.

Suk never attained the same concentrated intensity in subsequent symphonic poems, *A Summer's Tale* (26.i.09) and *Ripening* (30.x.18). Mahler planned to conduct his works and *Novák's in New York but died before the concert and such fame as Suk enjoyed abroad was as violinist in the celebrated Bohemian (later Czech) Quartet, with whom he gave 4,000 concerts. He wrote two string quartets (1896, 1911) and a trenchant *Meditation on the Saint Wenceslas Chorale* (1914) for string quartet or orch. When independence

dawned in 1918, he was honoured as a national figurehead and a living link with Dvořák. His grandson, the violinist Josef Suk (*b*.Prague, 8.viii.29), is founder of the Suk Trio and a leading exponent of Czech music.
   b. Krecovice, 4.i.1874, st with *Foerster, Hans Wihan and Dvořák, founded Bohemian Quartet 1892, *d*. Benesov, 29.v.35. *other works*: *Pohadka* suite (7.ii.01), Fantasia for violin and orch. (9.i.04), *Epilogue* for soloists chorus and orch. (1932).

Lepo SUMERA Estonian *minimalist with two symphonies made of tiny cells.
   b. Tallinn, 5.v.50;

Summer Night on the River Pastoral suite by *Delius. fp: Leipzig, 23.x.13, cond. Nikisch.

Sun Treader Tough orchestral cookie by Ruggles. fp: Paris, 25.ii.32, cond. Slonimsky.

Sunday in the Park with George Musical invasion by *Sondheim of the mind of impressionist painter Georges Seurat (1859–91) as he portrayed his mistress and friends on the island of La Grande Jatte in 1884. fp: NY (Booth Theater), 2.v.84.

the SUPREMES The Motown quartet hit the US top ten 16 times between 1964 and 1969, becoming the hottest girl group in pop history. 'Baby Love' and 'You Can't Hurry Love' were folksongs of their era. The lead vocalist Diana Ross (*b*. Detroit, 26.iii.44) went on to solo success.

A Survivor from Warsaw Schoenberg's eight-minute evocation for narrator, male chorus and orch. of the Nazi massacre of Polish Jews. It climaxes in the Hebrew prayer, 'Hear, O Israel, the Lord thy God, the Lord is One'. fp: Albequerque, New Mexico, 4.xi.48.

Viktor SUSLIN Russian composer involved, with *Gubaidulina, in seeking a dialogue between ethnic musics and western experimentalism. His 13-minute sonata for cello and percussion (1983) combines Azerbaijani intonations, 12-tone techniques and artificial noises.
   b. Miass, Urals, 1942; emigrated to West Germany 1981.

Hermann SUTER His devotional oratorio *Le Laudi di San Francesco d'Assisi* (1925), based on a sickbed meditation by the animal-loving saint, proclaimed the family ties between all of God's creations – man, beasts, Brother Moon and Mother Earth. It was admired by *Furtwängler and late romantics.

b. Kaiserstuhl am Rhein, Switzerland, 28.iv.1870; st with the great renaissance historian Jacob Burkhardt; head of Basle conservatory 1918–21; *d.* Basle, 22.vi.26. *other works*: symphony, string sextet and three quartets.

Heinrich SUTERMEISTER Straitlaced Swiss who espoused natural rhythms based on the human heartbeat. He wrote ten operas with Verdi as his model, and much melodic music for string orch, of which the *First Divertimento* (Basle, 1937) has a moody charm. His anti-modernism delighted German conservatives and he won several commissions for TV operas.

b. Feuerthalen, Switzerland, 12.viii.10; st at the Sorbonne and in Munich with *Pfitzner and *Orff; prof. at Hamburg U. 1963–75; *operas include: Die schwarze Spinne*, about a woman who gives birth to spiders (Berne Radio, 15.x.36), two Shakespearian hits in Dresden – *Romeo und Julia* (13.iv.40) and *Die Zauberinsel* (*The Tempest*, 31.x.42); *Raskolnikoff* (after Dostoyevsky's *Crime and Punishment*, Stockholm, 14.x.48), Wilde's *Canterville Ghost* (TV, 6.ix.64) *Le Roi Berenger* (Munich, 1985); *other works*: Three piano concertos, two cello concertos, clarinet concerto (Berne, 12.viii.75), eight cantatas and a quasi-requiem.

Shin'ichi SUZUKI The method of teaching children to play violin by manual exercises and peer-group pressure produced competence at the expense of pleasure and interpretative insight. Suzuki's method has been taught internationally for half a century without producing a single important virtuoso.

b. Nagoya, Japan, 18.x.1898, son of violinmaker.

Georgi SVIRIDOV Russian traditionalist respected by modernists, he wrote timelessly morose songs in the manner of Tchaikovsky and Mussorgsky. His soprano songs to lyrics by Alexander Blok and Sergei Esenin are particularly poignant; his *Oratorio Pathétique* (1959) enjoyed wide circulation.

b. Fatezh, nr. Kursk, Russia, 16.xii.1915; st with Shostakovich; *other works*: symphony for string orch. (1940), Music for Chamber Orch. (1964); piano quintet (1945).

Howard SWANSON A black clerk with the Inland Revenue Service, his songs reached the soprano Marian Anderson and his tuneful *Short Symphony* was premièred by *Mitropoulos at the NY Philharmonic (23.xi.50). It won Swanson a music critics' prize and a Guggenheim fellowship which enabled him to jack in his job and go to live in Paris.

b. Atlanta, Georgia, 18.,vii.07; st with *Boulanger 1938–40; *d.* NY, 12.xi.78. *other works*: Concerto for Orch. (1956), 3rd symphony (NY, 1.iii.70).

Giles SWAYNE A visit to West Africa transformed Swayne's music from traditional to exciting, involving Gambian rhythms and lashings of percussion.

b. Stevenage, Herts, UK, 30.vi.46; *works*: *Cry* for 28 amplified voices (1980), Pentecost Music for orch. (1981), symphony (1982), *Songs of Hadi* for drums and instruments (1983); opera *Le nozze di Cherubino* (1985).

swing The big-band era of the 1935–47 was characterized by rhythms that were slightly stretched across the bars, encouraging easy dancing and plentiful improvisation. Less daring than *jazz, its audience was middle-class and largely middle-aged. Glenn *Miller's band was tops. The fad was crushed by the post-1945 fecundity of New York jazz.

Switzerland The butt of many musical jokes produced more good composers in the 20th century than ever before, from Honegger and Martin to Holliger and Huber, exercising a disproportionate influence on German academies.

Symphonia domestica Tone poem by Strauss describing his domestic routine, fp: NY, 21.iii.04.

Symphonic Dances Orchestral works by Hindemith (1937) and Rachmaninov (1940).

Symphonie liturgique Honegger's 3rd symphony, a rejection of tyranny and bureaucracy. fp: Zurich, 17.viii.46.

Symphony of a Thousand Impresario's slogan for Mahler's 8th, which required eight soloists, two mixed choruses, a boys' choir and augmented orch. – a total of almost 1,000 performers. fp: Munich, 12.ix.10.

Symphony of Psalms Stravinsky's masterpiece for chorus and orch., sung in Latin and dedicated 'to the glory of God on the occasion of the 50th anniversary of the Boston Symphony Orchestra.' fp: Brussels, 13.xii.30.

symphony Almost every non-Italian 19th-century composer of consequence, Wagner included, wrote a symphony. It was the test of a composer's technique and his chance to make a mark on concert repertoire. Twentieth-century masters eschewed the symphony as an antiquity. None of the *Second Vienna School nor Bartók, Debussy or Janáček composed a full-blown symphony. In midcentury it was customary to dismiss the symphony as dead.

Its survival and latter-day revival are the product of a dichotomy that emerged in the first years of the century when orchestras had been expanded to their limits. In November 1907, an historic confrontation took place in Helsinki between *Sibelius and *Mahler. Sibelius, who had three symphonies to his name, expressed the view that the symphony needed to be purified further by the rules of its own severe logic. Mahler, who had completed his massive 8th symphony and was contemplating *Das *Lied von der Erde*, rejected any form of contraction. The symphony, he said, 'must be like the world – it must embrace everything'. The Sibelian line prevailed among north European conservationists like Vaughan Williams, and in the United States where the first flowering of American music was expressed in 'pure' symphonies by Hanson, Harris, Barber and Piston.

Mahler, having demolished the four-movement instrumental format by writing five or six movements and adding choral and vocal finales, was poised to extend the symphony into psychological, philosophical and theological realms in his concluding trilogy. His legacy was carried into the major symphonic edifice of Shostakovich, who codified his resistance to Stalin in symphonic form, creating a language that common people understood and the authorities could not suppress. His 15 symphonies amounted to a clandestine history of Soviet Russia; they are also the major symphonic utterance of the totalitarian century. Schnittke, his successor in many ways, applied Mahlerian irony and outrageous *collage to lampoon the authorities. Prokofiev and Martinů used symphonies to comment on the progress of the Second World War. Copland and Bernstein collated icons from their political and religious environments. Stravinsky wrote his first mature symphony when he was pushing 50, and his triptych is characteristically iconoclastic. Ives and Messaien flirted with unusual dimensions and instruments.

Until 1945, German composers were ambivalent. Schoenberg wrote *chamber symphonies, avoiding anything larger. Reger and Hindemith were deterred by the excesses of Strauss and Mahler. Webern's 'Symphony' was almost a deliberate travesty. The post-Hitler era generated cycles from Hartmann and Henze as the symphony regained the high ground of musical argument. Stockhausen and Boulez stood aloof but by the end of the century mainstream composers were writing symphonies again and some, like Lutosławski, were producing modest masterpieces.

syncopation Misplaced beats and notes that give jazz its *swing.

synthesizer A machine that simulated sounds by electronic synthesis was invented in America around 1954. It was adapted by Robert Moog in 1966 into a domestic keyboard that anyone could play. Walter (Wendy) Carlos started a vogue with synthesized Bach and the instrument became indispensable to rock bands and *computer musicians.

Boleslaw SZABELSKI Like many Polish artists, Szabelski underwent a sea change when the 1956 liberalization admitted currents of Western modernism. In his case, it marked a shift from the neo-classical

Concerto Grosso (1954) to a set of *Webernian *Aphorisms* '9' for chamber ensemble leading to a stylistically integrated, angry 5th symphony (1968) with chorus and organ.

   b. Radoryz, nr Lublin, 3.xii.1896; st with *Szymanowski; *d.* Katowice, 27.viii.79. *other works*: Sinfonietta for string orch. and percussion (1946), flute concerto (1964), oratorio *Nicolaus Copernicus* (1976).

Endre SZÉKELY Conductor of workers' choruses, he shocked the Communist Party by turning serialist and experimental in his sixties.

   b. Budapest, 6.iv.1912; *d.* there, 14.iv.89. *works*: operetta *The Golden Star* (1951), sinfonia concertante (1961), *Humanisation* for chamber ensemble and tape (1974).

Sándor SZOKOLAY Composer of Hungarian operas on *Samson* (1973), Lorca's *Blood Wedding* (1964), *Hamlet* (1968) and *Szávitri* (1989).

   b. Kunagota, Hungary, 30.ii.31;

András SZÖLLŐSY *Petrassi's most refined Hungarian pupil, he made up *Sonorità* (1974) for orch. from a fragment of the Italian's *Concerto per archi* and paid further tributes in five concertos for string orch.

   b. Szaszvaros, Transylvania, 27.ii.21; prof. at Budapest 1950– ; other works: *Transfigurazioni* (1972) for symphony orch.; string quartet (1988).

Pavel SZYMANSKI Collector of objets trouvés that he scatters in disruptive conjunctions in works like *Appendix* for piccolo and ensemble (1983) and *quasi una sinfonietta* (1990). He experimented extensively in *electronics, providing *Crux Fidelis* (1983) as sound background for an exhibition of crucifixes at the Church of Divine Mercy in Warsaw. *Sixty-odd Pages* (1991) signalled a conversion to minimalism.

   b. Warsaw, 28.iii.54; st with *Baird, *Haubenstock-Ramati.

Karel SZYMANOWSKI Polish music was inseparable from nationalism until Szymanowski asserted the right of transcendence. His early piano preludes (1900) echoed Chopin's romantic yearnings and his involvement in the *Young Poland group with *Karlowicz and Fitelberg merely reinforced nationalism with Wagnerism and Germanic indigestibles. He withdrew a two-movement first symphony (Warsaw, 26.iii.09) immediately after the première.

   His formative experiences were gained in seven pre-war years that he spent in Berlin, Paris and Vienna, summering in Italy, Algeria and Morocco. He acquired tastes for Debussy, Mahler and orientalia and would happily have spent his life in the sun but the outbreak of hostilities caught him in Russia and he spent the next three productive years in isolation in a woodland hut on his country estate. The individualism he cultivated there belonged to no single culture or sphere of influence. It amounted to a declaration of artistic independence from the national and social objectives that had hamstrung his forbears.

   Any comparison of works from before and after his transition reveals the enormity of his wartime leap. The 2nd symphony (Warsaw, 7.iv.11; cond. Fitelberg) can readily be mistaken for Reger with its heavy textures and contrapuntal patterns. The 3rd, titled *Song of the Night* (comp. 1916, fp London, 26.xi.21, cond. *Coates), is allusive only in its Tristanesque connotations of love and death. The rest is flagrantly, decadently exotic, a weave of Persian texts and ecstatic sonorities, written for tenor, chorus and orchestra in music that blurs and shines alternately like an autumnal sun. *Sorabji, himself a product of east and west, considered it the most gorgeous and authentic occidental evocation of oriental colours.

   The smaller pre-war works for violin and piano are similarly eclipsed by the sinuously impressionistic richness of *Mythes* (1916) and the exuberance of the 1st violin concerto (comp. 1916, fp Warsaw, 1.xi.22). Until the day a Bolshevik mob set fire to his estate, Szymanowski was oblivious to world events, immersed in the furnace of creation.

   He moved to Kiev and Elisavetgrad, where he composed a string quartet and started writing a homosexual novel. It told in two volumes of a prince who is seduced at school and emerges into gay Parisian society. It took Szymanowski two years to write and he left it to a cousin to publish after his mother's death; it perished in the next German invasion of Warsaw. Family sensitivities apart, Szymanowski made no secret of his sexual orientation. His sets of love songs were homoerotic in gesture if not in name and the relationship in his great opera between *King Roger*, his Arab adviser and the mysterious shepherd who entices the queen away with talk of a 'new god' is charged with emotion and sensuality. He worked seven years on the opera, extending its finale beyond dramatic tolerance to incorporate music of outstanding beauty and power. The atmosphere throughout is stiflingly rich, broken by frightening episodes of mass hysteria – an uncanny commentary on crowds and power – and Queen Roxana's lovely arias, one of which was extracted as a violin and piano piece. The opera, premièred in Warsaw on 12.vi.1926, was a landmark in Polish history (its US première waited until 3.iv.92).

Stripped of his estates, Szymanowski lived from hand to mouth. Poland honoured him with laurels, not cash, but he declined an invitation from his publisher, *Universal Edition, to live in Vienna and moved to Warsaw to enjoy the rebirth of national autonomy. In the winter of 1922–23, while in the mountain resort of Zakopane, he broached a third and final style that reintroduced selective national elements to his now-unimpeachable cosmopolitanism. The fruits of this fusion were the ballet *Harnasie* (Prague, 11.v.32) on the life of Tatra peasants and the 4th and liveliest of his symphonies, actually a symphonie concertante for piano and orch. in which the composer played the solo part

(Poznan, 9.x.32). He was appointed principal of the Warsaw Conservatory in 1927 but was forced to resign three years later in poor health, which also curtailed his international concert career. He was often lovelorn, occasionally suicidal and usually penniless. Friends like the conductor Fitelberg and the pianists Arthur Rubinstein and Jan Smeterlin helped with money and warmth but tuberculosis set in and the Swiss mountains failed to work their reputed magic. He was brought home to Warsaw for burial and Paderewski, representing the oldest tradition in Polish music, was the first to lay a wreath on his bier.

An exact contemporary of *Bartók and *Stravinsky, Szymanowski was just 54 at his death. He has been depicted by some adherents as 'the last romantic', but his outlook was as modern and questing as Bartók's and his music as individual. It is insufficiently known outside Poland, where the generation of *Panufnik and *Lutosławski was infinitely grateful for the rich and subtle flavours he imparted to their music.

b. Tymoszowska, Ukraine, 24.ix.1882; *d.* Lausanne, Switzerland, 27.iii.37. *other works*: opera *Hagith* (Warsaw, 13.v.22), 2nd violin concerto (Warsaw, 6.x.33), *Stabat Mater* for three soloists, chorus and orch. (Warsaw, 11.i.29), 2nd string quartet (1927), three piano sonatas (1904–17), 20 Mazurkas (1924–26), around 100 songs to various poets, including *Tagore, Mohammed Hafiz and Szymanowski's librettist and flatmate, Jaroslaw Iwaskiewicz.

Bib: B. M. Maciejewski, *Karol Szymanowski, his life and music*, London (Poets and Painters Press), 1967. J. Samson, *The Music of Szymanowski*, London, 1980.

Rabindranath TAGORE The poet-philosopher, whose influence on modern India was as great in its way as Gandhi's, composed more than 2000 songs including the future national *anthems of India and Bangladesh. His verse and short stories won him the 1913 Nobel Prize for literature, along with the admiration of W. B. Yeats and many European artists, among them *Zemlinsky, who set seven of his poems in the seminal *Lyric Symphony.

b. Bengal, 1861; *d.* there, 1941.

Germaine TAILLEFERRE The lady in Les *Six, Tailleferre flourished in 1920s Paris but could not match the panache of Poulenc or the mischief of Milhaud. She composed steadily through a long life, converting to *serialism at a late stage without losing delicacy or charm. Neither feminist nor militant, her Ballade for piano and orch. (1923) and concertino for harp and orch. (Cambridge, Massachusetts, 3.iii.27) are pleasant pastoral pieces conducted at a gentle pace without serious dissonance or upset. Her 1957 harp sonata for Nicanor Zabaleta is a classic of that instrument.

b. Parc-St.-Maur, near Paris, 19.iv.1892; st at Conservatoire and with *Ravel; married American author Ralph Barton and French lawyer Jean Lageat; lived in New York during Second World War and for some years thereafter; *d.* Paris, 7.xi.83. *other works*: three comic operas and a musical comedy *Parfums* (1951), *Pastorales* for chamber orch. and individual instruments, string quartet (1918), two violin sonatas (1921, 1951).

Jenö TAKÁCS Hungarian composer who travelled to the near and far east, inflecting his music with heavy exoticism.

b. Siegendorf, 25.ix.02; st with *Marx, *Gal; taught at Cairo and Manila in the 1930s, ran Pecs conservatory 1942–48, taught piano in Cincinnati 1951–71; *d.* Siegendorf. *works include*: ballet *The Nile Legend* (1940), two piano concertos, *Homage to Pan* for four pianos.

Toru TAKEMITSU The perception of Japan as a relentless industrial society is refuted by the gentle pastorality of its art. Takemitsu penetrated western consciousness, the first Japanese composer to do so, with a slowly moving, fragrant confection called *November Steps* for the New York Philharmonic and such unusual guest instruments as the lute-like biwa and shakuhachi flute (NY, 9.xi.67).

Eclectic and meditative, he drew techniques and textures from Webern, Cage and Messiaen and likened his music to a garden in which the listener might stroll, pausing to smell a flower or walking back to catch a second whiff. His works are conventionally scored, often with one or more instruments in a quasi-concerto role. Most have evocative titles – *A Flock Descends into the Pentagonal Garden* (San Francisco, 30.xi.77), or the *Waterscape series (Rain Coming, Rain Spell)* begun in 1974. He has also composed electronically.

His music is tranquil to the point of somnolence; there is a sameness about each new piece that allows listeners to identify the composer but shows no recognizable sign of artistic growth. Some of his finest music has been written for masterpieces of Japanese cinema – Hiroshi Teshigara's *Woman of the Dunes* (1964), Akira Kurosawa's *Ran* (1985) and Shohei

Imamura's *Black Rain* (1989). As an accompanist and modulator of visual imagery, Takemitsu has few equals, east or west.

b. Tokyo, 8.x.30; largely self-taught; founded Tokyo 'Experimental Laboratory', 1951, designed Space Theatre at Expo 70 in Osaka; *other orch. works*: *Requiem for Strings* (1957), *Music for Trees* (1961), *Green (November Steps II*, Tokyo, 3.xi.67), *Cassiopeia* (percussion solo, Ravinia Festival, 8.vii.71), *To the Edge of Dream* (guitar solo, Liège, 12.iii.83), *riverrun* (piano solo, Los Angeles, 14.i.85, cond. Rattle), *Tree Line* (London, 20.v.88); chamber works include *Quatrain* (1975), *Ring* (1961), *Sacrifice* (1962).

Josef TAL   Israeli composer favoured by German modernists, he wrote seven operas on biblical themes and many blends of instrumental and electronic music as his country's first explorer of that genre. His four symphonies and 11 concertos have occasional national themes.

b. Pinne, nr Poznan, Poland, 18.ix.10; st with *Trapp in Berlin; migrated to Palestine 1934; dir. Israel Centre for Electronic Music 1961– ; *operas include*: *Saul at En-dor* (1961), *Ashmedai* (part-electronic, Hamburg State Opera, 9.xi.71), *Die Versuchung (The Temptation*, Munich, 26.vii.76), *Der Garten (The Garden of Eden*, Hamburg, 1990).

Václav TALICH   Conductor who won the Czech Philharmonic international status, he promoted *Janáček's operas in Prague and premièred music by *Suk and *Novak.

b. Kormeriz, 28.v.1883; st with *Nikisch; chief cond. Czech Philharmonic 1919–41, Prague National Theatre 1935–44, founded Slovak Philharmonic 1949–52; *d.* Beroun, Czechoslovakia, 16.iii.61.

Karen TANAKA   Japanese composer with a persuasive line in gentle east-west dialogue.

b. Tokyo 1961; st in Paris with *Murail; *orch. works*: *Prismes* (1986), *Anamorphose* (1986) and *Hommage au cristal* (1991) for piano and string orch.

Sergei TANEIEV   A refusenik in pre-revolutionary Russia, he quit the Moscow Conservatory faculty in 1906 to form a People's Conservatory with other democrats. His inner feelings were funnelled into chamber music, of which the G minor piano quintet of 1910 was his most personal utterance.

b. Vladimir district, Russia, 25.xi.1856; *d.* Dyudkovo, Zvenigorodsk district, 19.vi.16. *works include*: *Oresteia* operatic trilogy, four symphonies, three string quintets, nine quartets.

Tanglewood   Estate in Massachusetts where *Koussevitsky in 1937 founded a summer music festival with an emphasis on bringing young musicians, especially budding conductors, together with established professionals. It provided a career springboard for *Bernstein, *Foss, Lorin Maazel, Zubin Mehta and many others. Bernstein taught there to the year of his death and co-founded festivals on similar lines at Schleswig Holstein in Germany and Sapporo in Japan. *Copland, *Schuller and *Messiaen were significant composition teachers there.

tango   Ferociously sensual 2/4 Latin American dance, taking its name from the Latin *tangere* = to touch.

Alexandre TANSMAN   Polish-Jewish composer who flourished in 1920s Paris with an eclectic mix of atonality, jazz, exoticism and anything goes. His *Witches Dance* suite from an aborted ballet made his name in a wind quintet version at the *ISCM (Zurich, 22.vi.26); its lively rhythms are offset by harmonies outlandish enough to intrigue academe. Fleeing to Hollywood when Paris fell, Tansman found work in movie scores but returned home in 1946 to write the rest of his music in French neo-classical style.

b. Lodz, Poland, 12.vi.1897; *d.* Paris, 15.xi. 86. *works include*: operas *The Kurdish Night* (1927) and *Shabbetai Zevi, the False Messiah* (1961); five ballets; oratorio, *Isaiah the Prophet*; eight symphonies; two piano concertos, *Rapsodie polonaise* (St Louis, 14.xi.41), eight string quartets.

Tapiola   *Sibelius' last orch. poem. fp: NY, 26.xii.26.

Taras Bulba   Orch. rhapsody by *Janáček on Gogol tale. fp: Brno, 9.x.24.

Vladimir TARNOPOLSKY   Raised in the monumental Soviet style, to which he contributed a precocious cello concerto, Tarnopolsky withdrew into religious contemplations. His *Chorale-Prelude* (1987) has a string trio on side of the stage playing a Lutheran hymn, mocked by a wind ensemble on the opposite side and physically challenged by an advancing pair of percussionists.

b. Dniepropetrovsk, 1955; *other works: Brooklyn Bridge* for soprano, tenor and orch. (1989), concerto for two violins (1990); *Cassandra* for chamber orch. (1991).

Francisco TARREGA (y Eixa) Pioneer of modern guitar playing, he favoured a more robust instrument and expanded its repertoire with short Hispanic pieces and a gamut of transcriptions from Bach to Wagner. *Recuerdos de la Alhambra* and *Capricho Arabe* are his most affecting melodies.

b. Villareal, Castellón, Spain, 21.xi.1852; *d.* Barcelona, 15.xii.09.

John (Kenneth) TAVENER The curious case of an English modernist who adopted the archaic, unreformed faith of Orthodoxy and applied himself entirely to decorating its rituals. Christian music, he announced, had been ruined in the renaissance by excess sophistication; all it needed was simple monody. He became a composer on hearing *Stravinsky's *Canticum Sacrum* in 1956 and was converted by its ethos to join the native church of its creator 20 years later. He dissociated himself from early works, including an impressive cantata, *The Whale* (London, 24.i.68), that used electronics and *Messiaenist soundblocks to heighten narrative tension.

b. London, 28.i.44; st with *Berkeley, *Lumsdaine; *other works:* one-act Christian opera *Thérèse* (London, Covent Garden, 1.x.79), chamber operas *A Gentle Spirit* (Bath, 6.i.77) and *Mary of Egypt* (1992); chamber concerto (London, 12.vi.68), *The Protecting Veil* for cello and strings (1989), *The Repentant Thief* for clarinet and orch. (London, 19.ix.91); *Akhmatova: Requiem* (Edinburgh, 20.viii.81), *Lament of the Mother of God* (Norwich Cathedral, 28.vi.89), *Resurrection* (Glasgow, 17.iv.90) and many other large-scale choral works; orch. *Variations on 'Three Blind Mice'* (BBC, 1.ii.73, cond. Maazel), *In memoriam Igor Stravinsky* for two alto flutes, organ, handbells (1971).

Taverner Maxwell *Davies' opera on apocryphal torments of Reformation-era English composer. fp: Covent Garden, 12.vii.72.

(Joseph) Deems TAYLOR The only man to write two operas for the Met,

Taylor became a famous radio commentator when his creative powers waned. *The King's Henchman* (NY, 17.ii.27), to a script by popular novelist Edna St Vincent Millay, survived three years; *Peter Ibbetson* (7.ii.31) was staged in four successive seasons. Taylor's late-romanticism was alleviated by gentle wit and his music worked well with English speech rhythms – though not quite well enough to last. He appeared with *Stokowski in Walt Disney's music movie, *Fantasia*.

b. NY, 22.xii.1885; wrote show with Jerome Kern, 1906; war correspondent in France 1916–7; editor of *Musical America* 1927–9; president of *ASCAP 1942–8; *d.* NY, 3.vii.66. *other works:* orch. suite *Through the Looking Glass* (after Lewis Carroll, 1923), two cantatas, *The Chambered Nautilus* and *The Highwayman* (1914).

Alexander TCHEREPNIN Centre of a dynasty of Russian émigrés, he wrote melodies on a nine-tone scale, married Chinese pianist Lee Hsieng-Ming and encouraged their sons, Serge (b.1941) and Ivan (b.1943) to compose *electronically. His father Nikolas (1873–1945) wrote an early ballet for Diaghilev and many Russian songs but was best known for completing Mussorgsky's opera *The Fair at Sorochinsk* (Monte Carlo, 17.iii.23). Alexander Tcherepnin completed Mussorgsky's *The Marriage* (Essen 14.ix.37).

b. St Petersburg, 20.i.1899; *d.* Paris, 29.ix.77. *works include:* three operas, 12 ballets, four symphonies, six piano concertos.

Telemusik Mixed tape and live piece by *Stockhausen. fp: Warsaw, 23.ix.69.

The Telephone Comic one-acter by *Menotti. fp: NY, 18.ii.47 together with *The *Medium*.

television In contrast to radio, visual broadcasting has scarcely affected musical style and appreciation. Its sound was poor until stereo and HDTV arrived in the 1990s and, as a medium of mass communication, TV was inherently unsuited to specialized arts. It took a rare charisma like *Bernstein's to seduce the camera as a means of public enlightenment. Attempts by *Karajan and others to make orchestras look interesting were laughable.

Television commissioned little music of any quality. *Menotti's opera *Amahl and the Night Visitors* was an early exception. In opera relays, television failed to invent a visual language that could replace the lost dimensions of intimacy, immediacy and stage depth.

tenth symphonies Beethoven's, Schubert's and Mahler's were realized by British musicologists Barry Cooper, Brian Newbould and Deryck Cooke.

Mikis THEODORAKIS Greece's best-known musician made his name with a 1963 film score for *Zorba* and became a *cause célèbre* four years later when the colonels' regime tortured and imprisoned him. He was released and exiled as a result of international pressure and returned home when democracy was restored to serve for a decade as a communist MP, before emigrating again in despair at political conditions. As a youth, Theodorakis fought the Nazi occupation and was imprisoned after liberation by the monarchist regime. Broader political involvement led him to write a national anthem for the Palestine Liberation Organization.

Theodorakis's work was reviled by the Greek musical establishment as *rebetiko* – urban pop, or uncultured agitprop, that flew in the face of officially sponsored romantic nationalism. Closer listening reveals subtle strains. While aiming for instant appeal, his songs apply variations of tempo and colouring, using classical Arabic sonorities on the bouzouki (lute) to achieve an integral perfection. From his teacher *Messiaen and his friend *Xenakis, he absorbed structural principles.

The Ballad of Mathhausen (1966), trenchant material for a popular song-writer, is delicately though unsparingly treated for soprano and pop orchestra. He coined the term 'song-river' to describe linked cycles and was drawn to poems by living masters, notably George Seferis. Altogether, he has written more than 500 songs, many immortalized on record by the earth-motherly Maria Farandouri, others memorably incanted by the operatic mezzo-soprano, Agnes Baltsa.

As a student in Paris, and an Athenian rebel of the 1960s, Theodorakis wrote a number of indigenously-flavoured concert works. His orchestral music includes a symphony (1950), three vocal suites, the strings suite *Oedipus Tyrannus* (1955) and highly-coloured ballet suites *Greek Carnival* (1954) and *Antigone*, which was premièred at Covent Garden (19.x.59). Among 30 film scores, he wrote an award-winning soundtrack while in prison for Costa-Gavras's unabashedly political, Z.

> *b*. Hios island 29.vii.25; st in Athens 1943–50 and in Paris with *Messiaen and *Leibowitz 1953–59; won Copley Prize (US) for best European Composer, 1959; returned to Athens with a Manifesto for the Reorganization of Greek Music (1960); imprisoned 1967–70; exiled to Paris 1970–76; member of Greek Parliament 1976–86; returned to Paris 1986– ; returned to Paris, 1986–90; Minister without portfolio in Greek government, 1990–92.
> *Bib*: George Giannaris, *Mikis Theodorakis*, NY (Prager), 1972.

Leon THEREMIN Russian inventor of a remarkable device that emitted music without manual interference (1923). The 'theremin' or 'thereminovox' consisted of two antennae attached to an electric device. When hands were waved nearby, it produced a wavering musical pitch, whose tone and volume was readily adjustable. The invention was personally approved by Lenin and excited a number of composers, especially *Schillinger, *Cowell and Varèse, who composed for it. Theremin enjoyed celebrity and concupiscence in 1930s New York but mistakenly returned home in 1938 and was sent to the gold mines. He eventually transferred to a KGB centre to work on surveillance and espionage equipment. His instrument was refined in America by Robert Moog and revived in the Beach Boys' 1966 hit 'Good Vibrations' which started a fad for synthesized music. Theremin was, by any measure, one of the fathers of *electroacoustic music.

> *b*. St Petersburg, 15.viii.1896;

Third Stream Union between jazz and concert music proposed in 1957 by *Schuller.

Third Viennese School Ironic name for 1960s group of Austrian iconoclasts and chansonniers led by *Schwertsik and *Gruber.

Randall THOMPSON A member of the band of pioneers who put the American symphony on the world map, his first two symphonic works were premiered by Howard *Hanson at Rochester (1930–2). Thomson became a respected teacher at the Curtis Institute (1939–48) and Harvard (1949–65), numbering Bernstein and Foss among his pupils. In the fullness of time it became apparent that his principal gift was choral writing in the fine old English style. *Alleluia* (Tanglewood, 8.vii.40), commissioned by *Koussevitsky, is a magnificent *a cappella* throat-opener. He was damned by modernists as 'E.C. Schirmer's house composer'.

b. NY, 21.iv. 1899; d.Boston, 9.vii.84. *other works: The Testament of Freedom* for narrator and orchestra, words by Thomas Jefferson (Boston, 6.iv.45); *Requiem* (1958).

Virgil THOMSON A midwestern American in Paris, Thomson sat at *Boulanger's feet imbibing neo-classical style. He returned home as America's most pungent music critic ('sassy but classy', he called himself). His compositions were sometimes played by conductors hopeful of receiving favourable reviews. On its own merits, his music was too understated to produce high excitement. In 1954 he became a full-time composer, writing with grace and good humour. His orchestral works are generally impersonal. Several are mere embellishments of juvenilia – the 3rd symphony (1972) made out of his second quartet (1932), the harp concertino (1964) out of his 2nd piano sonata (1929).

Thomson's finest achievement was to set Gertrude Stein's gnomic epigrams in two mildly-notorious, plotless operas, *Four Saints in Three Acts* (Hartford, Connecticut, 8.ii.34) and *The Mother of Us All* (NY, 7.iii.47). Neither is a masterpiece, but they shifted American opera off a plain narrative course; his third opera, *Lord Byron* (NY, 13.iv.72), failed.

Three vivid movie scores – *The Plow that Broke the Plains* (1936), *The River* (1937) and the award-winning *Louisiana Story* (1948) – provided imaginative instrumentation for tunes of the Old West. He wrote fluent blues, jazz and tangos but his ambitions were coloured by Boulanger's ultra-serious criteria and his character expressed itself more sharply in words than in chords. His close friends were composers, sculptors and writers, many of them gay; he made no permanent enemies.

b. Kansas City, Missouri, 25.xi.1896; critic of NY *Herald Tribune* 1940–54; d. New York, 30.ix.89; *other works*: concertos for cello (Philadelphia, 24.iii.50) and flute (Venice, 18.ix.54), ballet *The Filling Station* (1938), and many songs and piano pieces.

Three-Cornered Hat (*El sombrero de tres picos*) Ballet suite by de *Falla for *Diaghilev. fp: London, 22.vii.19.

Threepenny Opera (*Die Dreigroschenoper*) Brecht and Weill's Weimar adaptation of John Gay's *The Beggar's Opera*, a leftist commentary on the roots of crime. fp: Berlin, 31.viii.28.

Three Places in New England Orchestral suite by *Ives depicting his native locale in a completely unique way – not as a set of fixed snapshots but as a film of passing and criss-crossing activity, present and historic. The places are: The 'St-Gaudens' at Boston Common (Colonel Shaw and his Colored Regiment); Putnam's Camp, Redding, Connecticut; and The Housatonic at Stockbridge. fp: NY, 10.i.31; cond. Slonimsky.

Three virgins and a devil Ballet by *Respighi for Agnes de Mille. fp NY, 11.ii.41.

Threni Threnodies, or Lamentations of the Prophet Jeremiah, was *Stravinsky's final turning point, his first comprehensive *12-tone composition. It set biblical texts, for six solo voices, chorus and orchestra. fp: Venice, 23.ix.58, cond. Stravinsky.

Threnody for the victims of Hiroshima *Penderecki's breakthrough work for 52 stringed instruments. fp: Warsaw, 31.v.61.

Tiefland D'Albert's opera of Catalan passions. fp: Prague, 15.xi.03.

Tin Pan Alley Area around 28th Street, NY, where most music publishers set up office from the 1890s. A columnist wrote that the noise in that vicinity was like the banging of tin pans, and the name has stuck ever since to the popular music industry.

Dimitri   TIOMKIN   Contrapuntal Russian who wrote the ultra-simple anthem of the American Midwest in the Oscar-winning theme song of the movie *High Noon* (1952), allegedly based on a Ukrainian folktune. In addition to 'Do Not Forsake Me', Tiomkin wrote a further slice of American folklore, 'The green leaves of summer', for John Wayne in *The Alamo*. Other highpoints of more than 100 movies were *Rawhide*, *The Guns of Navarone*, *Lost Horizon* and *The Old Man and the Sea*.

 b. St Petersburg 10.v.1894; st with Isabella Vengerova; moved to Berlin 1921, then Paris, New York, Hollywood and London, where he *d.* 11.xi.79. *other works: Rhapsody of Steel* (1959) for city of Pittsburgh.

(Sir) Michael (Kemp) TIPPETT Adulation came late to Tippett after a lifetime of hard knocks that included a prison spell and savage criticism. Neither was wholly deserved. His music was innocently eclectic, reflecting whatever took his fancy from Beethoven to television soap opera. Some works plummet from a genuine spiritual sensation to utter banality and his librettos are, *King Priam* apart, almost beyond redemption. Told to write his own texts by T. S. Eliot, he mixed pop culture, colloquial chat and Jungian psycho-drama. He was the polar opposite of the severely disciplined Benjamin *Britten.

 Unable to make a living as a composer until he was past 50, he scratched around through the 1930s, living in a farm hovel, organizing unemployed men into ad hoc orchestras and teaching at workers' associations. Most of what he composed went back into the drawer, apart from two strong pieces – a piano sonata built around a Scottish folksong but modelled on Beethoven, and the Concerto for Double String Orchestra (London, 17.vii.43) with captivating cross-rhythms and a *bluesy central melody – not to mention echoes of Orlando Gibbons and Northumbrian bagpipes.

 A conscientious objector in wartime, he refused to do mandatory farm-work or teaching on the grounds that as a composer he was serving a lofty moral cause. His principles landed him in the West London prison of Wormwood Scrubs, where Britten and Peter Pears employed him as a page-turner at a recital for inmates.

 Soon after his release, the oratorio *A Child of Our Time* (London, 19.iii.44, cond. Walter Goehr) won him national fame and the gratitude of thinly-served choral societies. Drawing on the dilemma of a Jewish child in Nazi Germany, it blazed with hope in a revitalized humanity.

 His music increasingly outraged an uptight establishment. Sir Malcolm Sargent, his sometime teacher, talked of purging the concert halls of 'all this intellectualism'; the pianist Julius Katchen pronounced his concerto unplayable; the BBC published a letter in *The Times*, blaming him for its orchestra's breakdown two bars into Sir Adrian Boult's performance of his 2nd symphony (5.ii.58). Tippett was a homosexual, intellectual and internationalist in an insular, conservative society.

 Critics deemed him 'too eccentric a figure to be taken seriously' and had a field day with his mystical first opera. *The Midsummer Marriage* (27.i.55), featuring Joan Sutherland as Jenifer. A revised production 13 years later was widely acclaimed; it was said that his notes took time to settle on the page. His Greek tragedy *King Priam* (Coventry, 29.v.62) was, by his own admission, 'harder to take' though stronger in substance and structure.

 A first visit to America in 1965 taught him a populist lesson. Aaron Copland played him music by Charles *Ives and he realized that the old iconoclast's collagism mirrored his own magpie tendency. He adopted *Gershwin, whom he heard play Rhapsody in Blue back in 1924, as a new role model, inserting a cool jazz aria in his next opera, *The Knot Garden* (Covent Garden, 2.xii.70). It was a jumble of confused relationships and ambi-sexual frustrations strung together with blues rhythms, an incongruously placed Schubert *Lied*, a snatch of 'We Shall Overcome', a psychiatrist and inter-racial rape. The shrink sang of 'whistling to keep my pecker up'; hip Sixties people loved it. The best music was extracted in Songs for Dov and a 3rd symphony (22.vi. 72). His next opera, *The Ice Break* (Covent Garden, 7.vii.77) experimented with laser beams; the last, *New Year* (Houston, 27.x.89), seeks refuge from social mayhem in a spaceship rescue.

Oddly for so operatic a spirit, it is orch. music that shows him at his best. The *Fantasia concertante on a theme of Corelli*, (Edinburgh, 29.viii.53) is typically deceptive. Taken off the page, it looks like a straight neo-classical reworking of the main theme in Arcangelo Corelli's Concerto Grosso op 6 no 2. Tippett discovered, however, that by shifting the bass from F minor to Ab major he produced a sound world remarkably like Puccini's. This fantasy enabled him to knit baroque instrumentalism with late-romantic lyricism in an inimitable, jagged-ended style.

The Concerto for Orchestra (Edinburgh, 28.viii.63) took its cue from Alban *Berg, opening with an echo of Marie's lullaby from *Wozzeck* and proceeding through shades of *Lulu* in a form patented by *Bartók. The finale is self-admittedly botched: cobbled together from bits of *King Priam* to meet a Festival deadline. Yet its colours are strangely original and surprisingly soft.

The Triple Concerto (London, 22.viii.80), planned on Beethoven lines, revealed a sentimentalist who resorts to smooch in the 'very slow' section to exude rich amatory odours. While Berg and the Javanese gamelan were audible influences, Tippett named Elgar's cello concerto as his formal archetype, writing a central passage of serene and sensuous yearning. The Ritual Dances from *The Midsummer Marriage* form a taut, sensuous orch. suite (Basle, 2.ii.1953; cond. *Sacher); the 1955 piano concerto and 2nd symphony both had roots in that opera. Of five string quartets and four piano sonatas, the first of each appeared at his mid-1930s turning point, representing his art, in many respects, at its purest. Despite the support of a German publisher, Schott, his music has never caught on in continental Europe.

b. London, 2.i.05; *other major works*: 4th symphony (Chicago, 6.x.77, cond Solti), oratorio *The Mask of Time* (Boston 5.iv.84, cond. Davis); 5th string quartet (Sheffield, 9.v.92).
Bib: Michael Tippett, *Those Twentieth Century Blues*, London (Hutchinson), 1991.

Boris TISHCHENKO A *Shostakovich pupil though not a slavish follower, he eulogized the master in 1974 in a turbulent 5th symphony, the finest of the late Soviet era. He shared with Shostakovich a love for the poetry of Anna Akhmatova and in 1966 wrote a 3rd symphony and a Requiem on her eulogy for a husband murdered by the Bolsheviks. He refined Shostakovich's irony and ribald mockery in a devilishly satirical 2nd violin concerto (1982). Although conversant with *serial and *aleatory techniques, Tishchenko was overwhelmingly attached in his music to Russian traditions.

b. Leningrad, 23.iii.39; st with *Ustvolskaya and Shostakovich; *other works*: two cello concertos, five string quartets, *Hard Frost* for mezzo-soprano and orch. (1975).

Ernst TOCH Viennese refugee in Hollywood, he lived out his days teaching movie composers, among them André *Previn. His early work was romantic – a 6th quartet (1905) was played by the distinguished Rosé Quartet; the mature output was *neo-classical; his last quartet, the 13th (1953) was composed on a row of *12 notes. In early 1920s Berlin, Toch enjoyed equal status with *Hindemith.

b. Vienna, 7.xii.1887; *d.* Los Angeles, 1.x.64. *works*: four operas, seven symphonies, two piano concertos, two sinfoniettas, *Big Ben*, variations on Westminster chimes (1955), *Pinocchio* overture (1936), film scores for *The Cat and the Canary*, *First Comes Courage*, etc.

Le tombeau de Couperin Ravel's *neo-classical advent – a six part piano suite, later partly orchestrated, that took its theme from the French Baroque composer François Couperin (1668–1733). fp: Paris, 11.iv.19.

tone clusters Several piano notes struck together by the fist or forearm, a device noticed in *Bartók's piano sonata (1926) but invented a dozen years earlier by the teenaged American Henry *Cowell in such misnamed works as *Amiable Conversations*. Stockhausen used clusters in *Klavierstück X* and applied the idea to orchestral music. Something of the kind was foreshadowed in the nine-note chords that Mahler massed in his 10th symphony's *Adagio*.

Michael TORKE First of a US generation who viewed *minimalism as an ingredient rather than a style, Torke used a repetitive, rhythmic motif as a grid on which he was free to impose his own collage of *Stravinsky, Debussy, jazz and whatever. *The Yellow Pages* (Yale U., 8.iv.85) for five instruments, his breakthrough work, imitated the process of flicking through a telephone directory in search of a plumber. *Rust* (Huddersfield, 21.xi.89), a small-scale piano concerto that proclaimed *pop synergies, came out anachronistically Glenn-Millerish. Torke appealed directly to his own age-group and a string of his works were danced at NY City Ballet.

> *b*. Milwaukee, Wisconsin, 22.ix.61; st with *Schwantner, *Schuller. *other orch. works: Vanada* (Amsterdam, 11.x.85), *Ecstatic Orange* (NY, 10.v.85), *Bright Blue Music* (NY, 23.xi.85), *Verdant Music* (Milwaukee, 20.xi.86), *Purple* (NY, 11.vi.87), *Black & White* (NY, 7.v.88).

Federico Moreno TORROBA Spanish zarzuela composer who produced volumes of virtuosic guitar pieces for Segovia, based essentially on folk tunes. A sonatina of 1953 is among his more ambitious inventions; he also expanded a *Concierto de Malaga* for guitar and orchestra, from Celedonio Romero's Andalusian suite of flamenco dances.

> *b*. Madrid, 1891; *d*. there, 1982.

Paul TORTELIER The great French cellist was devoted, like *Casals, to the causes of world peace and liberty; he composed a concerted set of variations on his own theme 'May Music Save Peace' (1983).

> *b*. Paris, 21.iii.14; *d*. nr. Paris, 18.xii.90. *other works: Israel Symphony* (written on a kibbutz, 1955–6), two cello concertos, piano concerto (1976).

Tosca Puccini's tabloid opera of sex and sadism, derided as a 'shabby little shocker,' contains some of his cleverest musical ideas – e.g. the use of a background Te Deum to heighten the tyrant's muttered threats at the end of Act One. It was the first of a triptych writen by *Ricordi's 'Holy Trinity' of Puccini, Giacosa and Illica. fp: Rome, 14.i.1900.

Arturo TOSCANINI Well into his 70s, the 'dictator of the baton' looked for new music to perform. He made his name in Italy with the premières of *Pagliacci* (La Scala, 1.ii.1896) and *La *Bohème* (Turin, 1.ii.1896) and at the Metropolitan Opera raised the curtain on *Puccini's *Girl of the Golden West* (10.xii.10). At La Scala in the 1920s, he introduced Boito's posthumous *Nerone* (1.v.24) and Puccini's *Turandot* (25.v.26). With his NBC orchestra in New York, he discovered Samuel *Barber's *Adagio for Strings* and made it the most performed piece of American music. The music he espoused was invariably melodic. He abhorred dissonance, modernism and all Austro-Germans after Brahms, Strauss alone excepted.

> *b*. Parma, Italy, 25.iii.1867; debut aged 19 conducting *Aïda* in Rio; as music director at La Scala 1898–1908 he conducted 'Va, pensiero' at Verdi's funeral; artistic director at NY Metropolitan Opera 1908–15, displacing *Mahler; artistic director at La Scala, 1921–29; conducted at Bayreuth and Salzburg until the Nazis took over; conducted New York Philharmonic and Symphony orchestras 1920–26, NBC Symphony Orch. 1937–54; *d*. NY, 16.i.57 and buried in Milan.
> *Bib*: Harvey Sachs, *Toscanini*, London (Weidenfeld), 1978.

total serialism The application of *12-note rules to all aspects of a composition, arranging its rhythms, tempi, instrumentation and dynamics according to the four methods prescribed by Schoenberg. *Boulez in *Structures Ia* provided a textbook example.

Die tote Stadt (*The Dead Town*) Korngold's decadent opera. fp: Hamburg/Cologne, 4.xii.20.

Charles (Arnould) TOURNEMIRE Organ composer in the César Franck line – he succeeded *Pierné, who was Franck's heir, at the organ of Ste-Clothilde (1898–38). His church music was traditional and melodic; *L'orgue mystique* (1932) covers the entire liturgical year. He also had an opera staged in 1924 called *Les Dieux sont Morts* (The Gods are Dead).

> *b*. Bordeaux, 22.i.1870; st with Franck and d'*Indy; *d*. Archachon, nr. Bordeaux, 3.xi.39. *other works include*: three unplayed operas, eight symphonies, several cantatas and much chamber music.

Donald Francis TOVEY 'The cleverest man in music' convinced his countrymen of the supremacy of German symphonists and dazzled Pablo Casals with his concerto. Half a century on, he is still read with pleasure, but no longer performed.

b. Eton, UK, 17.vii.1875; privately educated; gave chamber music series in London 1900–14; professor of music at Edinburgh U., 1914–40; organized and conducted Reid Symphony Orchestra there, 1917–40; toured US as pianist 1925 and 1927–8; knighted 1935 *d.* Edinburgh, 10.vii.40 *works include*: six volumes of *Essays in Musical Analysis*, one opera, *The Bride of Dionysus* (1932), a symphony in D major (1913), a piano concerto that he played at the 1903 Proms, a cello concerto that Casals premièred in Edinburgh (22.xi.1934), two string quartets and a proposed completion of Bach's *Art of the Fugue*.

Joan (Peabody) TOWER The first woman to win the biggest prize in contemporary music, the $150,000 *Grawemeyer Award granted in 1990 for her orchestral work *Silver Ladders* (St Louis, 9.i.87), Tower emerged from a *serialist training to reject the static pointillism of 12-note orthodoxy. Her orchestral works were painted on a large canvas with ambitious scope and a typically American energy. *Sequoia* (NY, 18.v.81), intended to represent a native tree, caught the national imagination; the *Noon Dance* sextet (1982) used folk motifs; 3 *Fanfares for the Uncommon Woman* (1986–91) offered a sexual-political slant to *Copland's universalist blast. Tower spent her childhood in South America, where her father was a mining engineer and she acquired a taste for local rhythms reflected in her first orchestral work, *Amazon II* (Hudson Valley, 10.xi.79).

b. New Rochelle, NY, 6.ix.38; st with *Luening at *Columbia; founded Da Capo Chamber Players 1969; taught Bard College 1972-; composer in residence at St Louis 1985–88; *other works*: concertos for cello (NY, 29.ix.84), clarinet (NY, 10.iv.88), flute (NY, 28.i.90) and orch. (St Louis, 16.v.91); *Petroushkates* for five instruments (1980), *Island Prelude* for oboe and strings (St Louis, 9.iv.89).

(Hermann Emil Alfred) Max TRAPP *Reger-like composer, avid Nazi.

b. Berlin, 1.xi.1887; *d.* there, 31.v.71. *works include*: seven symphonies, three concertos for orch.

Gilles TREMBLAY Canadian pupil of *Messiaen and *Boulez, he learned in Paris to play the *ondes Martenot and manipulate electronics, composing instrumental works of dreamy texture and poetically allusive titles. He uses medieval hymns in *Kékoba* (1965) for ondes, percussion and voices, and drone-like Eskimo mouthmusic in *Katadrone (contrecri)* (1988).

b. Arvida, Quebec, 6.ix.32; professor at Montreal Conservatoire 1962-; *other works*: three pieces called *Champs* for different ensembles, *Envoi* piano concerto.

Triumph of Time Birtwistle's orchestral breakthrough. fp: London, 1.vi.72.

Manfred TROJAHN Under pressure of the most invasive totalitarian regime, Trojahn preserved his privacy by writing symphonies of Mahlerian irony. His settings of texts by Georg Heym and Georg Trakl had a bleakness reminiscent of *Pettersson. The authorities had only to listen to this music to know they had a potential dissident on their hands.

b. Cremlingen, nr. Braunschweig, Germany, 22.x.49; *works*: three symphonies (1974–84), Five *See-Bilder* (Lake pictures) for mezzo and orch. (1983), Requiem (1985), three string quartets.

Vaclav TROJAN Czech composer whose early jazz inclinations gave way to a folk style acceptable to all political regimes. His children's opera *Merry-go-round* (1939) held the stage for half a century.

b. Plzen, 24.iv.07; *d.* Prague, 5.vii.83.

tropes Medieval name for musical notes, used by *Hauer in his 12-note law.

trumpet Was co-equal soloist in *Shostakovich's 1st piano concerto and acquired important new concerted works from *Zimmermann and *Birtwistle.

Richard TRUNK Prominent Nazi composer whose works included a setting of the Horst Wessel Lied in a cantata, *Feier der neuen Front*, with words by the Hitler-Youth chief Baldur von Schirach. He was head of the Munich Akademie der Tonkunst 1934–45, retiring thereafter from public life. The published list of his works omits all mention of political pieces.

b. Tauberbischofsheim, Baden, Germany, 10.ii.1879; *d.* Herrsching-am-Ammersee, 2.vi.68. *works include: Walpurgisnacht*, rhapsody for orch. (1905), String serenade

(1925), string quartet (1943), numerous Lieder and choral works.

tuba Gained a short concerto by Vaughan Williams and F minor sonata by Hindemith.

Eduard TUBIN Concurrent with *Shostakovich, Tubin lived on the front-lines of 20th-century totalitarianism and documented its impact in ten symphonies. He started writing the Third shortly after Stalin marched into his native Estonia and gave its first performance under Nazi occupation (22.ii.43). The audience needed no prompt cards to read the coded defiance in its pounding fortissimi and the swelling hope of its finale. After one further hearing, it was banned for the next four decades.

Tubin fled the USSR for Sweden two years later and no longer needed to cryptify his symphonies. Cut off from his roots, however, he endured prolonged obscurity until a compatriot, Neeme Järvi, led a late revival on record. The 8th Symphony (Talinn, 5.iv.66) still resembles the wartime idiom of Shostakovich, replacing its ironic undercurrent and vicious counter-blasts with a mournful chorale for a blighted country; it is the most hauntingly personal of his symphonies, bleakly nordic but stiffened by a sense of national resistance.
b. Kallaste, Estonia, 18.vi.05; *d.* Stockholm, 17.xi.82. *other major works: Requiem for fallen soldiers* (1979), two violin concertos (1942, 45), balalaika concerto (1964); also two Swedish operas and two ballets.

David TUDOR *Avant-garde US pianist who served *Cage, *Feldman and *Boulez in various capacities. In Cage's *Water Music* (NY, 2.v.52) he shuffled cards, blew a whistle and turned on the radio; in *4'33"* (Woodstock, 29.viii.52), he sat on the piano stool doing nothing. In the US première of Boulez's 2nd sonata (NY 17.xii.50), he showed a technique and sensitivity that prompted *Bussotti and *Stockhausen to write difficult pieces for him. He learned to play the Argentine bandonéon and composed an eponymous piece for it.
b. Philadelphia, 20.i.26; st with *Wolpe; played organ at St Mark's Church, Philadelphia, and Swarthmore College 1938–48; *other works: Fluorescent Sound* (1964), *Talk 1* (with Cage, 1965).

Turandot Chinese love-or-death riddle turned into opera by *Busoni, *Puccini-Alfano, Jensen-*Kienzl and Neumeister after various 19th-century failures. Only Puccini's is outstanding. fp: Milan, 25.iv.26.

Turangalîla-symphonie *Messiaen's erotic contemplation of the act of creation, written in ten movements that interleave 'love' themes with universal issues. fp: Boston, 2.xii.49, cond. *Bernstein.

Joaquin TURINA Purveyor of Spanish orchestral postcard scenes and pieces for guitar and lute. The *Oracion del torero (Bullfighter's prayer*, 1925) was intended for a lute quartet but became popular as a smoochy chamber orchestra piece. *The Gardens of Andalucia* (1924), *Song of Seville* (1927), *Memories of Old Spain* (1931) constitute his touristic legacy; his piano music is less sentimental.
b. Seville, 9.xii.1882; *d.* Madrid, 14.i.49.

Turn of the Screw Chamber opera by *Britten, after Henry James story. fp: Venice, 14.ix.54.

Mark-Anthony TURNAGE Angry young Brit whose disquiet erupted in *Greek* (Munich, vi.88), a polemic against social inequalities – bravely, an opera attacking the opera public. Turnage's music was more *bluesy than violent and he conveyed affection between characters with considerable warmth.
b. Grays, Essex, 10.vi.60; st with *Knussen and *Henze, whose protégé he became; *other works*: orch. *Ekaya*, (*Elegy in memory of Marvyn Gaye*) (Greenwich, 29.iii.85), *On All Fours* for chamber ensemble (Lon, 4.ii.86), *Lament for a Hanging Man* for soprano and ensemble (texts from Hebrew Bible and Sylvia Plath, Durham, 4.ii.84), *Three Screaming Popes* for orch. (1989).

Zbigniew TURSKI A competition for an art-work to commemorate the 1948 Olympics in London was won by the 2nd symphony by this cosmopolitan Pole, henceforth known as his Olympian symphony. Written before Stalin's clampdown it was growlingly stark in a *Wozzeck-like atonality and classically structured in three movements that continually cross-refer to one another. Turski's violin concerto three years later was similarly *Bergian, pushing him beyond the pale of officially sanctioned composers.

b. Konstancin, nr. Warsaw, 28.vii.08; formed Baltic Philharmonic in Gdansk 1945–6; chairman Polish Composers' Union 1959–60; *d.* Warsaw, 7.i. 79. *other works*: 3rd symphony (1954), 2nd violin concerto (1963).

twelve-note music Also known as twelve-tone, dodecaphonic and serial music – the method by which *Schoenberg in 1921 proclaimed that he had 'assured the supremacy of German music for the next 1,000 years'. Instead of writing music in known keys, the composer invented his own key by setting all 12 white and black notes of the piano keyboard in the order of his choice. Once this *note row (or *series) was drawn up, it stayed fixed for an entire movement, just as C major or A flat minor would have done in a traditional work. The composer then used the row of notes in four specified ways: forwards, backwards (retrograde), upside down (*inversion) and upside down backwards (retrograde inversion).

It was, in Schoenberg's definition, a 'method of composition with 12 tones related only to one another'. The relations thus formed between the notes were free of all past constraints, though many composers found the method unbearably restrictive and many listeners called it arid. For Schoenberg it supplanted the unsatisfactory anarchy of *atonality.

While he remained open to modifications, his apostles split in opposite directions according to personal temperament. *Berg adopted the rule in principle but never held to it for the duration of a movement. Rather, he used it as a framework into which he worked folk-song, Bach chorales and whatever else he fancied. His violin concerto and *Lulu* represent 12-note music at its most liberal and easy-listenable.

*Webern, on the other hand, felt the method was far too lax. It should be applied not only to the notes in a piece of music but also to rhythms, dynamics and the choice of instruments. He wrote perfect 12-note counterpoints, wondrous in their precision, and his strictures gave rise to the *total serialism of the post-1945 *avant-garde.

Another Austrian, J. M. *Hauer, claimed to have discovered the method at least a year ahead of Schoenberg. His method, however, was circuitous and mystical, working in units of six notes that he called 'tropes' within a cosmic '12 note law'. Outside Schoenberg's circle, early converts to 12-tone music were *Krenek, *Babbitt and *Dallapiccola. The conversion of *Stravinsky early in the 1950s brought the major tributaries of modernism together in a serialist orthodoxy that outsiders attacked as *fascist in its methods and authoritarianism.

twist Dance craze of 1960 involving sharp and unnatural pelvic swivels; the dance was conceived by Hank Ballard and the theme song was belted out by Chubby Checker.

Tzigane Gypsy rhapsody for violin and piano by Ravel. fp: London, 26.iv.24.

Alfred UHL A pupil of Franz *Schmidt, he extended the Viennese oratorio tradition with a Babylonian epic, *Gilgamesh* (1956/68), and a curiously titled cantata, *Wer einsam ist, der hat es gut (Only the lonely are happy)* 1960. His instrumental music is intellectually undemanding.

b. Vienna, 5.vi.09; *d.* there 8.vi.92.

Victor ULLMANN After a feckless musical career, Ullmann was rounded up by the Nazis with Prague's Jews in 1942 and crammed into barracks at Terezin, pending deportation to death camps. There, he began composing in earnest: songs, sonatas, choral music, cadenzas to four Beethoven concertos, operas. 'Let no-one say we sat by the waters of Babylon and wept,' he wrote.

*The *Emperor of Atlantis*, his operatic fantasy of Death going on strike, is riddled with images and sounds grimly familiar to fellow-inmates – a narrator named Loudspeaker, the opening fanfare of *Suk's *Asrael* symphony and the Lutheran hymn *Ein feste Burg*; the climax is a tune resembling 'That's Why the Lady is a Tramp'. Smuggled out, the opera eventually found an audience (Amsterdam, 16.xii.75). Detached from its grim setting, it is an affecting creation with strong hints of self-parody.

Like Mahler, Ullmann liked to unsettle listeners by using familiar tunes out of context. The piano sonata, subsequently orchestrated as a symphony (Stuttgart, 18.x.89), ends in a disturbing Variations and Fugue on a Hebrew Folksong, punctuated by ironic blasts of the notes B A C H.

A pupil of *Schoenberg and *Hába, Ullmann vacillated between their contradictory styles. His piano variations on a Schoenberg theme (1925) and an autobiographical string quartet (1936, lost) were performed, though unpublished; a concerto for orchestra (1928) was programmed alongside Mahler's ninth symphony. Schoenberg sent him to Zemlinsky, who engaged him (1920–7) at the German Opera in Prague. He worked for a season at Aussig, failed to find another conducting post, composed sporadically and earned his living in a bookshop.

From *Hába, he developed a form of polytonality in an Op 10 piano sonata (1936) whose second movement is inscribed 'in memorial Gustav Mahler' but owes more to Busoni. In Terezin, he wrote Hebrew and Yiddish songs, as well as German settings of Persian, Chinese and English poems. A Trakl poem, *Verklärte Herbst (Transfigured Autumn,* 24.i.1943) for bass singer and string trio is nostalgically turn-of-century. On 16 October 1944, along with his family, librettist Peter Kien and countless fellow-martyrs, he was transported to his death at Auschwitz.

b. Teschen, Polish-Czech border, 1.i.1898, son of an Austrian Army officer; murdered at Auschwitz, German-occupied Poland, 17 or 18.x.44. *surviving mss include*: theosophist opera, *Der Sturz des Antichrist* (1935, unperformed), two-act opera to Kleist play, *The Broken Jar* (1941), sonata for quarter-tone clarinet and piano (1937), Slavonic rhapsody for saxophone and orch. (1940), seven piano sonatas.

The Unanswered Question Five-minute orch. riddle on the meaning of life by Charles Ives, written in 1908 but unperformed for half a century. The question is posed atonally by a trumpet against a lush string background, which is disrupted as strings and woodwind flutter around for a solution.

Chinary UNG An expert player of the Cambodian roneat-ek, a kind of xylophone, Ung moved to the US in 1964 to study composition with George *Crumb and *Chou Wen-Chung. His compelling 14-minute trio, *Spiral*, enfolds the plangent timelessness of Buddhist ritual with a dreamy aureola of the psychedelic era. *Inner Voices* (1986), the longest of his half-dozen published pieces at 25 minutes, is a hypnotic orch. portrait of an old Cambodian woman slowly patching together a quilt. In 1989, Ung was plucked from total obscurity to receive the $150,000 *Grawemeyer award, the largest prize given to a living composer.

b. Prey Lovea, Cambodia, 24.xi.42; professor at Arizona State U.; *other works*: *Mahori* for mezzo and ensemble; *Khse Buon* for solo cello or viola, *Tall Wind* for soprano and four instruments.

Universal Edition Publishing house formed in Vienna in 1901 to promote new music. Mahler and Bartók were its top names, followed by the entire *Second Viennese School and Janáček. UE founded the important bi-monthly *Musikblätter des Anbruch* (1919–31) and scored commercial success with operas by Weill and Weinberger. Suppressed in the Nazi era, the imprint became an organ of the Darmstadt avant-garde, headed by Boulez, Berio and Stockhausen.

Vladimir (Alexis) USSACHEVSKY Russo-American electronics pioneer who used the gift of a newfangled tape-recorder to Columbia U. to form (with Otto *Luening) the first US studio. Their experiments and concerts led to the formation of the *Columbia-Princeton Electronic Music Center in 1959. Much of Ussachevsky's music was written in collaboration with Luening. His own inventions are tinged with reverberations of the Russian Orthodox liturgy in which he was raised. In 1968 he started working with synthesizers and computers.

b. Hailar, Manchuria, China, 3.xi.11, son of a Russian army officer; moved to US 1930; st with *Hanson; taught Columbia U. 1947–80; d. NY, 2.i.90. *orch. works*: *Jubilee Cantata* (1938); *electronic works*: *Transposition, Reverberation, Underwater Valse, Sonic Contours* (all 1952), *Piece for Tape Recorder* (1956), *No Exit* (tape soundtrack for George Tabori's movie of Jean-Paul Sartre's play, 1962), *An Incredible Voyage* (track for CBS TV documentary, 1968).

Galina USTVOLSKAYA Hidden muse of Russian music, she was the composer closest to *Shostakovich in sound, spirit and introspection. Although she was his pupil and 13 years his junior, their relationship was bilateral. Shostakovich took a theme from the finale of her clarinet trio (1949, fp: 11.i.68) as the leitmotiv for his 5th string quartet which, like her works, could not be played while Stalin lived. He sent his manuscripts to her for comment and defended her against attacks in the Composers Union. The music she wrote during the terror and later was indomitable and individual, lacking barlines and sometimes adopting a repetitive rhythmicism akin to *minimalism. But the scale of her scores was monumental – 'my music is never chamber music, even when it is a solo sonata,' she proclaimed. It contained the suffering and endurance of her native city, as characteristic of St Petersburg as Dostoyevsky's epics. Religious in essence, unfeminine in gesture, her music defied classification. She wrote symphonies for huge forces, or just four instruments, in a spidery, tiny handwriting that resembled Charles Ives transcribed by Pierre Boulez.

b. Petrograd, 17.vi.19; st with *Shostakovich 1937–47; *major works*: 1st symphony for large orch. and two boys' voices (1955/66), 2nd symphony – *True and Eternal Bliss* – for orch. and solo voice (Leningrad, 8.x.80), 3rd symphony – *Jesus Messiah, Save Us!* – for orch. and soloist (Leningrad, 1.x.87), 4th symphony, *Prayer*, for trumpet, tamtam, piano and contralto (Heidelberg, 24.vi.88), 5th symphony for five instruments (1992); *Compositions 1–3* for various instruments (1970–75); four piano sonatas (1947–57), 5th and 6th sonatas (1986–88), 12 preludes for piano (1953, fp: 20.iii.68).

Moisei VAINBERG Soviet symphonist of mild modernist inclinations, he recanted during the *Zhdanov purge and centred his music on Jewish, Armenian and Polish folk melodies. Whether there is a secret agenda in his 16 symphonies and 12 string quartets remains to be discovered.

b. Warsaw, 8.xii.19; lived in Moscow 1943– ; *other work*: cantata, *Hiroshima Haiku* (1966).

Fartein VALEN The music librarian at Oslo U. became a symphonist at the age of 50 on hearing Bruckner's 1st played on the radio in 1937. Expecting the world to end at any moment, he expanded an existing atonal piano sonata into his grim 1st symphony which, performed 20 years later (Bergen, 2.ii.56), broke the nationalist stranglehold on Norwegian art. Valen had been composing non-tonally since 1924, during nine years of solitude on the family farm. He was impressed by *Schoenberg but devised a personal scheme of working simultaneously on several *note-rows of varying lengths.

He wrote two more symphonies during the Nazi occupation; in the 2nd symphony he recorded the shock of seeing two ships bombed in the fjord outside his window, and hearing the cries of the wounded seamen. The 4th symphony emerged in the second half of the 1940s. He won recognition with a violin concerto at the 1947 Copenhagen *ISCM festival, but could not get the symphonies performed and died lonely and embittered. His art, like Strindberg's, lacks any hint of joy but the structures are impressive and the variations he winds around folk and hymn tunes in his symphonies are surreptitiously hypnotic. The Bach chorale in his violin concerto is uncannily like *Berg's.

b. Stavanger, Norway, 25.viii.1887; *d.* Valevaag, 14.xii.52. *other works: Pastorale* (Oslo, 9.iii.31); Michelangelo Sonnets (15.i.34); keynote piano trio (1924), contemporary with Schoenberg's seminal Serenade.

La Valse Ghostly orch. parody of Habsburg Vienna by *Ravel. fp: Paris, 12.xii.20.

Valses nobles et sentimentales Piano waltzes by Ravel (1911), later orchestrated for ballet. fp (as ballet): Paris, 22.iv.12.

Valse triste Sibelius' bestseller, a piece of incidental music that left him seething because he had sold all rights for a pittance. fp: Helsingfors, 2.xii.03.

Nancy VAN DE VATE US composer living in Indonesia and central Europe. She reacted to the 1986 Soviet nuclear disaster with *Chernobyl*, a 12-minute orch. lament for the victims that recalls the slow atonality of Penderecki's famous *Threnody for the victims of Hiroshima*. In the second part, anger is resolved by ringing bells and harmonies that could have been written by Pärt. Her 1986 violin concerto is folksily late-romantic with just enough modernity to avoid anachronism.

b. Plainfield, New Jersey, 30.xii.30; *other works: Dark Nebulae* (1981), *Distant Worlds* for violin/orch. (1985), *A Night in the Royal Ontario Museum* for soprano/tape.

Bernard VAN DIEREN Strong-minded Dutchman who moulded British music from his Hampstead sickbed, plagued by kidney disease. Inspired by *Busoni, he preached an aggressive, cosmopolitan individualism, aware of history but opposed to Stravinskian *neo-classicism. His complex, *pointillist scores enthused *Warlock, Bliss, Gray and *Sorabji but many failed to find a publisher. His 1914 Chinese symphony for five soloists, chorus and orch. set the same Li Tai Po poems that Mahler used in Das *Lied von der Erde. *Six Sketches* for piano were published by *Universal Edition in 1921. The fifth of six string quartets is said to be his masterpiece. Never an atonalist, he used familiar chords in startling juxtapositions. He was the live model for Jacob Epstein's statue of Christ.

b. Rotterdam, Holland, 27.xii.1887; moved to London 1909, married (1910) Busoni pupil Frida Kindler (sister of Washington conductor Hans Kindler); *d.* London, 24.iv.36. *other works*: opera *The Tailor* (1917), *Belsazar* for baritone/orch. (1911), Elegy for cello/orch. (1908), *Spenser Sonnet*, incandescent book of essays *Down among the Dead Men*.

Vanessa Samuel *Barber's first opera, an attempted *Rosenkavalier to *Menotti's libretto. fp: NY Met, 15.i.58, cond *Mitropoulos.

Edgar(d) VARÈSE At the dawn of the century Varèse envisaged a music that was free of manual intervention and instrumental constraints. In the middle of the century he achieved it. Modernism has no greater parable of vision and fulfilment.

*Busoni urged him to seek a new music, *Debussy offered encouragement, Romain *Rolland transferred his obsessive quest onto his fictional hero, *Jean-Christophe*: 'The difficulty began when he tried to cast his idea in the ordinary musical forms: he made the discovery that none of the ancient moulds were suited to them; if he wished to fix this vision with fidelity he had to begin by forgetting all the music he had heard, all that he had written. . . .'

After a short spell in the First War, Varèse migrated to New York in 1916, got a walk-on part in a John Barrymore silent movie and conducted inspirational concerts of modern works. He founded the International Composers Guild and Pan-American Association of Composers to foster new-world creativity, but remained stringently economical in his own output. He dreamed of a sound that was 'set free' and flowed 'like a river,' anticipating *electronic music and working with the inventor *Theremin and Western Electric Company on primitive devices. These experiments crystallized his idea of an 'organized sound' in which the progress of a piece was determined purely by its constituent elements. In the meantime he composed for large and unconventional orchestras, scoring *Amériques* (Philadelphia, 9.iv.26, cond. *Stokowski), an impression of his adoptive land, for Heckelphone, heavy brass and woodwind and 21 percussion instruments. The 22-minute monstrosity conveys something of the noisy energy of a new society, but the work developed in static blocks of sound rather than offering a programmatic sound-picture. Motor and other noises are imitated by instrumental combinations in preference to the household objects prescribed by the *futurists. Varèse had no time for anyone else's theories; he scorned Stravinsky and Schoenberg in equal measure.

He composed *Arcana* for Stokowski and an orchestra of 120, including eight percussionists playing 40 instruments (Philadelphia, 8.iv.27) and various smaller works for percussive combinations – *Hyperprism* (NY, 4.iii.23), *Intégrales* (NY, 1.iii.25) and *Ionisations* (NY, 6.iii.33). He returned to Paris at the end of the 1920s but was back in New York by 1933 to stimulate composers, especially *Cowell, with his mission. The extraordinary *Ecuatorial* (NY, 15.iv.34, cond. *Slonimsky) was composed for bass voices, four trumpets, four trombones, piano, organ, 15 percussion and thereminovox; a revised version substituted the newly-invented *ondes Martenot. In both instances, the intention was the same: to provide an ethereal shimmer by non-physical means. The music has a consistency similar to end-of-century *IRCAM compositions.

It was still not clear what Varèse was after. *Density 21.5* (1936) for solo platinum flute – 21.5 is the density of platinum – was his only composition for a decade. After the war he was invited to lecture at *Darmstadt and around the time of his 70th birthday, he finally declared 'Eureka'. Electronic sound had caught up with his imagination and he was able to compose *Déserts* for wind instruments, percussion and tapes manufactured in Philadelphia and processed at Radio France. Its première (Paris, 2.xii.54) was the first public concert work to interpolate electronic sound, cruder than his instrumental inventions but awesomely effective at the time. He composed a *poème electronique* for the Philips pavillion designed by *Xenakis at the 1958 Brussels World Exposition, where it was played over 400 speakers, spatially distributed according to the composer's prescription. These landmarks in modernism were formative to *Boulez, who made a cult of conducting Varèse when he headed the NY Philharmonic. This did not make his music popular, nor is it ever likely to be so, for Varèse was searching for a soundworld rather than an assimilable message and his achievement was intended for fellow-creators more than for passive consumers.

b. Paris, 22.xii.1883; *d.* New York, 6.xi.65. *other works:* Offrandes (voice, chamber orch; NY, 23.iv.22); *Études pour Espace* (chorus, two pianos, percussion; NY, 23.ii.47); *Nocturnal* (unfinished, for soprano, bass, 12 wind, strings, piano, percussion; NY, 1.v.61).
Bib: Louise Varèse, *Varèse, a looking-glass diary*, NY (Norton), 1972.

variable metre Method of composing proposed by Boris *Blacher in which rhythms are used in a predetermined order – much as notes and intervals are governed in Webern's 12-note rows. Starting with two beats in a bar, the composer selects his own combinations and order of time signatures – 2/8, 8/8, 3/8, 9/8 and so on. Variable metre became part of *total serialism.

variations Method of elaborating and altering a musical theme used by the late-romantics *Elgar and *Strauss in *Enigma* and *Don Quixote* and an important device for *serialists after *Schoenberg's demon-strative *Variations for orchestra* op 31 and Webern's *Variations for piano*, op 27.

Variations on a theme by Frank Bridge Suite for string orch. by Benjamin Britten, honouring his teacher by quoting *Bridge's 2nd Idyll for string quartet and naming each variation after a trait in his personality. fp: Hilversum Radio, 25.vii.37.

Mario VARVOGLIS French-trained Greek composer and painter who gave a Gallic flavour to local tunes; *Caprice grecque* (1914) for cello and orch. was much played.
b. Athens, 22.xii.1885; *d.* there, 31.vii.67. *other work:* symphonic poem, *Behind the Wire Fence* (1945).

Sergei VASILENKO Eastern-oriented Russian composer, his cantata/opera on *The Legend of the Great City of Kitezh* (Moscow, 1.iii.02) anticipated *Rimsky's opera. His fascination with Asian music resulted in a 1938 mission to Tashkent, Uzbekistan, where he founded a conservatory and composed three operas.
b. Moscow, 30.iii.1872; *d.* there, 11.iii.56. *other works:* operas *Christopher Columbus* (1933), *The Grand Canal* (1941), five symphonies.

Sarah VAUGHAN Jazz and scat singer, she formed a trinity of immortals with Ella *Fitzgerald and Billie Holiday, venturing boldly into both pop and symphonic concerts. Her greatest hit was 'Passing Strangers'.
b. Newark, New Jersey, 27.iii.24; *d.* Los Angeles, 3.iv.90.

Ralph VAUGHAN WILLIAMS There is an irresoluble dichotomy at the heart of Vaughan Williams' music. To foreign listeners in his own time and since, he represented the very acme of pastoral Englishness, stubbornly isolated from continental turmoil. Yet, apart from youthful outings collecting folktunes with *Holst, his creative ground was staked between *Ravel and *Sibelius and his outlook was determinedly internationalist. Nor was his music at all homogenous. Each of the nine symphonies had a distinctive language and agenda. *A Sea Symphony* (Leeds, 12.x.10), with texts by Walt Whitman, was a Mendelssohnian oratorio in all but name. *A*

London Symphony (London, 27.iii.14; rev. 4.v.20) made allusions to indigenous noise, notably the chimes of Big Ben, but was in the main an abstract impression of urban life – 'a symphony by a Londoner', as vivid as the soundtracks of a yet-unborn British cinema. *A Pastoral Symphony* (London, 26.i.22), his 3rd, is the most beautiful and the only one to answer a strict definition of Englishness, with its folkish sources and wordless soprano finale. The composer intended it not as a celebration of his green and pleasant land but as a requiem for a rural society racked by war and unstoppable progress. The 4th symphony in F minor (London, 10.iv.35) was, like *Shostakovich's contemporaneous 4th, a furiously dissonant commentary on political events. Radicalism raged throughout and it withheld his customary solace of a pianissimo finale. Consolation was reserved for the opening of the Blitz-time 5th symphony (London, 24.vi.43), dedicated to Sibelius and Sibelian in sound and grandeur. The 6th symphony (London, 21.iv.48) reverted to anger and discord, apart from a hushed finale which seemed sunk in despair. The 7th (Manchester, 14.i.53) depicts a geographic wasteland, drawn from a score he had written for the film *Scott of the Antarctic* and prefaced by a doughty verse of Shelley's. The 8th (Manchester, 2.v.56) suggests an awareness of *Bartók's *Concerto for Orchestra and the elderly 9th (London, 2.iv.58) was resigned to the verdict of fate.

His typecasting was prompted by two works that were played the world around as nostalgic images of unspoilt England: the Elizabethan-era ballad 'Greensleeves', rearranged as a suite for strings from his Falstaffian opera *Sir John in Love* (London, 21.iii.29) and *The Lark Ascending* (1914, fp: London, 14.vi.21) for violin and orch.

Neither was significant among his historical excavations, crowned by the *Fantasia on a theme by Thomas Tallis* for double string orch. and string quartet (Gloucester Cathedral, 6.ix.10), which milked an amber flow of riches from defunct and unprepossessing material, well before Stravinsky's *neo-classical awakening. Bar for bar, it was his most direct approach to raw emotion until, in his final

year, he composed ten William Blake songs for tenor and oboe (1957), a cycle that demonstrated to a newly affluent age the sincerity of simplicity. 'The Lamb,' a poem he hated, provoked a tune as appealing as anything of *Wolf's. Vaughan Williams habitually deprecated his own originality and talked of 'cribbing' kleptomanically from folk sources and other composers. In stating the obvious, however, he deliberately concealed his innovatory gifts. *Ravel's sinewy manner is audible in his orchestrations but applied to specific purposes. The works that can be termed Ravellian were those he wrote on his return from Paris in 1908 – incidental music for Aristophanes' *The Wasps*, rich in harp and flute foundations; the string quartet; and in the controlled lushness of *On Wenlock Edge*, a cycle of Housman poems for tenor and piano quintet.

A great-nephew of the scientist and explorer Charles Darwin, Vaughan Williams was bred comfortably among the English middle-classes but preserved a healthy scepticism. A socialist and egalitarian, he refused royal honours and lived simply in London and the Surrey village of Dorking, extending help to many less fortunate than himself. He was blessed with intuitive interpreters in Adrian Boult and John Barbirolli; his music, like Delius's, seemed to require an extra degree of conviction from its performers.

b. Down Ampney, Gloucestershire, 12.x. 1872; st with *Bruch, 1897, and *Ravel, 1908; served First War in France and Greece; prof. at RCM London 1919–55; married 1897 Adeline Fisher, 1953 Ursula Wood; US lecture tour 1954 aged 82; *d*. London, 26.viii.58. *other works*: concertos for violin (1925), *Flos Campi* for viola, chorus and orch. (1933, arr. for two pianos, 1946), oboe (1944), harmonica (1953), tuba (1954); concerto grosso (1950); Norfolk Rhapsody (1905); six operas of limited consequence, including *Hugh the Drover* (1924), *The Poisoned Kiss* (1937), *Riders to the Sea* (1937), *The Pilgrim's Progress* (1951); a huge amount of choral and vocal music and many folksong arrangements. *Five Tudor Portraits*, choral suite on poems by Skelton (1936).

Aurelio de la VEGA   Cuban modernist, livened up his string quartets by getting players to shuffle their feet to the music.

b. Havana, 28.xi.25, moved to California 1959; *works include*: Quartet in memoriam Alban *Berg (1957).

Venetian Games *Aleatory composition by Lutosławski. fp: Venice, 24.iv.61.

Veni Creator Spiritus (Latin = Come, creative spirit) Opening cry of Mahler's 8th symphony.

Sándor VERESS He learned rhythm from *Bartók, instrumentation from *Kodály and the folktune-collecting habit from both. The three qualities continued to enrich his music after his 1948 emigration to Switzerland and adoption of *serialism. His most attractive works are a tremulous violin concerto (1939) and tributes to his teachers: a Threnody for Bartók (1945) and Variations on a Kodály theme (1962).
    b. Koloszvár, Austro-Hungary (now Cluj, Romania), 1.ii.07; taught at Budapest academies 1937–48, Berne conservatoire 1950–77; *d*. Berne, 6.iii.92. *other works*: ballet *The Miraculous Pipe* (1937), two symphonies (1940, 1952), Hommage à Paul Klee for two pianos and string orch. (1951), clarinet concerto (1982), two string quartets (1931–7).

verismo Realistic, slice-of-life opera developed in the 1890s by Mascagni and Leoncavallo, elevated by Puccini and ultimately closing down Italian opera. Charpentier gave a French imitation in *Louise*. Verisimilitude penetrated modernism through the tragedies of Janáček, Berg and Britten.

Verklärte Nacht German: *Transfigured Night* String sextet by Schoenberg moodily relating an adulterous tale by Richard Dehmel. Once described as *Tristan played while the ink was wet and smeared across the page, it captivated *Mahler at a private audition and he arranged its première by the augmented Rosé Quartet. fp: Vienna, 18.ii.02. In 1917 Schoenberg issued a string orch. version that became his most popular concert work.

Matthijs VERMEULEN After savaging the Concertgebouw orchestra and its conductors in his concert reviews, Vermeulen was amazed to find them unwilling to perform his music. Seven single-movement symphonies are wild and often woolly-headed works that offended the Dutch sense of order. Their alienness stemmed from self-exile in Paris (1921–46) and from a *Skryabin-like mysticism. The 4th and 5th, his most impressive, were written during the War while penniless and mourning the death of his first wife and son. He returned home after *Mengelberg's expulsion, and became the son-in-law of the respected *Diepenbrock but remained a marginal figure.
    b. Helmond, Netherlands, 8.ii.1888; *d*. Laren, 26.vii.67; *works include*: *Les lendemains chantant* (5th symphony, Amsterdam, 2.x.49, cond. Van Beinum), *Dithyrambes pour les temps à venir* (7th symphony, Amsterdam, 2.iv.67, cond. Haitink).

vibraphone Percussive jazz keyboard with a capacity for vibrato, it was introduced by Berg in *Lulu* and thence into the bloodstream of modern music.

Laszlo VIDOVSKY Co-founder of Budapest's new music studio in 1970, he started out with Double (1969–72) for two Cageian *prepared pianos. *Schroeder's Death* (1979) for solo piano depicts a character in the Peanuts cartoon playing scales on an instrument whose sonority is being altered all the time. *Narcissus and Echo* (1981) for soloists, girls' choir and five instruments, a voyage through late romanticism, inaugurated a series that continued with *Narcissus and the Harpies* (1987) for percussion ensemble.
    b. Békécsaba, Hungary, 25.ii.44.

Vienna Despite giving birth to the *Second Vienna School of Schoenberg and his apostles, the Austrian capital remained a hotbed of reaction and personal intrigue. Attempts to reform its opera house by *Mahler (1897–1907) and *Karajan (1956–64) were cut short by political cabals and press intrigues. Modernist concerts provoked uproar. The Philharmonic Orchestra (founded 1842) played the safest of symphonies under the most distinguished conductors. The musical establishment disgraced itself during the Nazi era.

Louis VIERNE   Blind organist of Notre Dame (1900–37), composer of six organ symphonies.
  b. Poitiers, France, 8.x.1870; st with Cesar Franck and *Widor; *d*. Paris, 2.vi.37.

Anatol VIERU   Quietly subversive Rumanian, converting folk-music into five technically sophisticated symphonies (1966–85).
  b. Iasi, Romania, 8.vi.26; st with *Khatchaturian; taught Bucharest Conservatoire, 1954-, Jerusalem 1982–83; *other works*: cello concerto (1962), double concerto (1979), five string quartets, three operas on local themes.

Heitor VILLA-LOBOS   The musical voice of Brazil was blessed with an inexhaustible invention and a temperamental inability to read a score after he had finished writing it. The outcome was an uncatalogueable profusion of more than 2,000 works, few of which are consistently interesting from start to finish. Villa-Lobos added to the confusion by slipping entire movements from one piece into another that was waiting to be premièred, and falsifying dates on his manuscripts to give them novelty or antiquity as the situation required. Such was his carelessness that, after the first performance of his most famous work, *Bachianas Brasilieras* ♯5 (Rio de Janeiro, 25.iii.39), deciding that the introductory bar needed lengthening, he inserted a repeat mark in the manuscript. Asked why he didn't write an extra bar of music, he replied: 'To tell the truth, I felt lazy'. He liked playing practical jokes on a gullible public, attaching a fictitious Barbadian shipwreck to the genesis of one work and luridly describing his deep jungle forages in pursuit of native folklore, excursions that probably never took place. Nowhere among his possessions was there documentary evidence of tunes he collected. The music he wrote was, for better or worse, his own.

At best, it was rhythmically irresistible and aurally stimulating in the 1920s piano works *Rudepoema* and *Parole do Bebe*, in the guitar preludes, intermittently in the erotically scored light opera *Magdalena* (Los Angeles, 26.vii.48) and, needless to say, in *Bachianas Brasilieras* ♯5.

He was discovered accompanying silent films in a Rio fleapit in 1922 by the pianist Arthur Rubinstein who borrowed some of his manuscripts and played them around the world. The heated complexities of Rudepoema (1923) were intended to portray the benevolent pianist's hedonistic personality. With Rubinstein's help and a grant from the Brazilian government he reached Paris and stayed there for seven years, feted as the hero of an 'art sauvage' that stemmed supposedly from the source of the Amazon. He returned home in 1930 as director of musical education for Rio and proposed a pedagogic system based on choral singing.

Over the next 15 years he composed a sequence of nine Bachianas Brasilieras for different combinations, intending to combine the spirit of Bach with that of his native land. The first (Rio, 12.ix.32), for an ensemble of at least eight cellos, sound like prehistoric *minimalism, a repetitive groundbass sustaining small fragments of melody. The 5th, also for cellos, unleashes a soprano voice to soar wordlessly over the strings with a melody that was coveted and *covered by female pop singers. Its second, worded, section was a late and unnecessary afterthought. The rest of the series is orchestral, except for ♯4 which is for piano solo and ♯6 for flute and bassoon. Each movement had twin titles, one Bachian, the other Brazilian. The 8th and 9th are abstract impressionisms. There is neither coherence nor development in the series, unlike the set of 15 Choros (1920–28) in which the composer was audibly progressing; the 11th Choros for piano and orchestra lasts longer than an hour.

The sum of his orchestral works contains 12 symphonies and five piano concertos; the best known are a guitar concerto (1951) that holds its own against *Rodrigo's, a harp concerto (1955) of comparable felicity and a nasal concerto for harmonica and orch. (Jerusalem, 27.x.59) which doubled the instrument's concert repertory, after *Vaughan Williams' contribution. Among the voluminous piano music is a 1940 piece called *New York Skyline* in which he traced a photograph of New York onto graph paper and converted its lines into musical notes and durations, thereby anticipating *Cage and *Feldman techniques by a decade or more. After 1949 he spent most of his time pleasurably in Europe, without severing connections with his homeland.

> *b.* Rio de Janeiro, 5.iii.1887; *d.* there 17.xi.59. *other works*: opera *Yerma* (after Lorca, 1955), four orch. suites *Descobrimento do Brasil* (1937–39), two sinfoniettas, *The Origin of the Amazon River* (Louisville, Ky., 7.xi.51), *Dawn in a Tropical Forest* (Louisville, 23..i.54), 17 string quartets (1915–58).

Vingt regards sur l'enfant Jésus 20 watches over the child Jesus – devout piano album by *Messiaen. fp: Paris, 26.iii.45.

Claude VIVIER Hell-raising French-Canadian, Vivier made his name with a 1969 *happening called *Proliferation*, in which the performers drowned out what they were meant to be playing with increasingly animated conversation. Studying with *Stockhausen in Cologne (1971–4), he rebelled by writing music that was melodic, exotic and listenable. His personality, by contrast, was abrasive and lonely. 'It is my own death that I will celebrate,' he wrote, in January 1983. Weeks later, he picked up a young man at a Paris bar and was found the next morning strangled and stabbed. His music possesses a simplified cosmopolitanism. The key work is *Lonely Child* (1980) for soprano and orchestra, a self-portrait of his deprived infancy.

> *b.* Montreal, Canada, 14.iv.48; *d.* Paris, 6.iii.83. *other work*: opera *Kopernikus* (1980).

Roman VLAD Rumanian composer, settled in Rome after studying with *Casella and gradually turned from *neoclassicism to full-scale serialism. The tension inherent in his conversion is heard in the ballet *La strada sul caffè* (Rome, 9.vi.45). He became a world authority on *Stravinsky.

> *b.* Cernauti, Romania, 29.xii.19; moved to Rome 1938; Italian citizen 1951; *other works*: *Sinfonia* (Venice, 8.ix.48), Concert variations on a supposed 12-note series in Mozart's *Don Giovanni* (Venice, 18.ix.55), *Studi dodecafonici* for piano (1957), TV opera *La fontana* (1967).

Pantcho VLADIGEROV Leading Bulgarian composer of five piano concertos and an opera, *Tsar Kaloyan* (Sofia, 20.iv.36), based on folk melodies.

> *b.* Zurich, 13.iii.1899; *d.* Sofia, Bulgaria, 8.ix. 79. *orch. works*: *7 Bulgarian symphonic dances* (1951), *Jewish Poem* (1951). His son, Alexander VLADIGEROV (*b.* 1933), wrote children's operas.

Jan van VLIJMEN 1968 Student rebel appointed head of The Hague conservatory in 1971, he exerted a progressive pull on Dutch music. His operas, *Reconstructie* and *Axel*, were written in collaboration with other composers.

> *b.* Rotterdam, 11.x.35;

Wladimir VOGEL A mixture of European opposites, he was Russian and German by parentage, Skryabinist by inclination, until he heard *Busoni's neoclassical ideas in Berlin while absorbing the *12-tone notions of Schoenberg. In a 1937 violin concerto, he wrote two classical movements and two serial, although the dodecatonality of the finale is somewhat fancifully modelled on the imagined noterow in Mozart's *Magic Flute* overture. A moral opponent of Nazism, Vogel left Germany in 1933 for Belgium, where he composed the national epic of *Thyl Ulenspiegel* as an oratorio, *Thyl Claes*, for soprano, two speakers and speaking chorus, split high and low. He finally settled in Switzerland.

> *b.* Moscow, 29.ii.1896; *d.* Zurich, 19.vi.84. *other works*: *4 etudes for orchestra* (1930), Epitaph for Alban Berg (piano, 1936), *Spiegelungen* for orch. (1952), cello concerto (1954).

voice Until the 20th century, the musical voice was used exclusively for speech and singing. *Schoenberg combined the two in *sprechgesang. The post-1945 *avant-garde added laughter, humming, throat sounds and bodily noises to their range of effects. *Ligeti designed *Aventures* on a completely new palette of vocal timbres; *Berio wrote adventurously for his versatile wife. Their ideas filtered into *popular music, but the art-music audience overwhelmingly preferred large, mellifluous voices.

La voix humaine (*The human voice*) Telephone monologue masquerading as opera, by *Poulenc. fp: Paris, 6.ii.59.

Kevin VOLANS A South African who spent eight years in the citadel of *avant-gardism, studying with *Stockhausen and *Kagel in Cologne, he emerged with a disdain for complexity and an awakening curiosity in the native music of his homeland. Recording trips in the veldt for German radio set Volans on course to write two hit quartets for *Kronos – *White Man Sleeps* (1986) and *Hunting:Gathering* (1987) – rooted in African cries and songs. Although sounding *minimalist to the ear owing to fragmentary repetitions, they contained constantly changing melodic material in a taut framework. A friendship with the writer Bruce Chatwin yielded a 3rd quartet, *The Songlines* (1988), based on his aboriginal study and a chamber opera, *The Man with the Soles of Wind* (1992), on the voyages and death of the poet Arthur Rimbaud.

b. Pietermaritsburg, 26.vii.49; st Cologne 1973–81; taught at Durban 1982–4 and Belfast 1986–9; *other works*: *Chevron* for small ensemble (1987), 4th quartet *The Ramanujan Notebooks* (London, 16.xii.90), *She Who Sleeps with a Small Blanket* for solo percussion (1986), *Kneeling Dance* for two pianos (1985).

Andrei VOLKONSKY Rare instance of a Western-born composer who opted to live in the USSR, Volkonsky was active in underground art but returned to Switzerland in 1973 when Brezhnev imposed a clampdown. A pupil of Nadia *Boulanger's, he emigrated to Moscow in 1947 and co-founded a chamber orchestra with Rudolf Barshai. In 1964 he set up the first Soviet early music ensemble, Meridian. His compositions were essentially *serial but took in ethnic sounds from Soviet central Asia.

b. Geneva, 14.ii.33; *works include*: concerto for orch. (1953), string quartet (1955), *Mirrors Suite* for soprano, organ, flute, violin, guitar, percussion (1960), *Lamentations of Schchaza* (1962), *Itinerant Concerto*, after Rubaiyyat of Omar Khayyam (1968), *Replica* (1970).

Von heute auf morgen *From today till tomorrow* Domestic opera by Mr and Mrs *Schoenberg. fp: Frankfurt, 1.ii.30.

Vojislav VUCKOVIC Yugoslav nationalist composer murdered by Gestapo on Christmas Day.

b. Pirot, Serbia, 18.x.1910; st in Prague with *Suk and *Hába; cond. Belgrade Philharmonic and professor at music academy 1936–42; killed Belgrade, 25.xii.42. *works*: three symphonies, four symphonic poems, with some *microtonalities.

Alexander VUSTIN Gritty Russian composer, working with large forces and unflinching sonorities, rather like *Birtwistle.

b. Moscow, 1943; *works include*: percussion concerto dedicated to Beethoven (1984), *White Music* for organ (1990).

Ladislav VYCPALEK *Novak pupil, wrote a *Czech Requiem* (1940) when the Germans took over.

b. Prague, 23.ii.1882; *d*. there 9.i.69.

Johan WAGENAAR Dutch composer of Straussian tone poems for special occasions. *Saul and David*, with harp obbligato, was turned out for the Rembrandt tercentenary in 1906; *Amphitrion* showed off the Concertgebouw orch. on its 1938 jubilee. He wrote incidental music for Shakespeare plays, *Taming of the Shrew* and *Twelfth Night*, and contributed, like Ravel, a sardonic commentary on the Viennese *waltz in *Wiener Dreiviertelakt* (1929). He headed the Utrecht conservatory from 1896 and the Royal Conservatory in The Hague from 1919 to 1937.
  b. Utrecht, 1.xi.1862; *d.* The Hague, 17.vi.71.

His son, **Bernard WAGENAAR,** moved to the US in 1920, played violin in the New York Philharmonic and was an important teacher at *Juilliard (1927–68). He composed four symphonies, four string quartets and a wartime *Fantasietta* on British-American ballads for chamber orchestra (1940).
  b. Arnhem, Netherlands, 18.vii.1894; *d.* York, Maine, US, 19.v.71.

Siegfried WAGNER Richard Wagner's only son wrote light comedies that opera houses staged at the behest of his formidable mother. *Der Bärenhäuter (The Bearskinner* 1899) lasted longest. He took over Bayreuth in 1908 and ran it sensibly. He married an English orphan, Winifred Williams (1897–1980), who on his death turned the festival into a Nazi temple; she was succeeded by their sons, Wieland (1917–66) and Wolfgang (1919–).

b. Triebschen, nr. Lucerne, Switzerland, 6.vi.1869; st with *Humperdinck; *d.* Bayreuth, 4.viii.30. *other operas: Herzog Wildfang* (1901), *Der Kobold* (1904), *Bruder Lustig* (1905), *Sterngebot* (1908), *Banadietrich* (1910), *Schwarzschwanenreich* (1918), *Der Schmied von Marienburg* (1923), *Der Friedensengel* (1926). Orch. works include a 1915 violin concerto.

Rudolf WAGNER-RÉGENY *Schreker pupil of Transylvanian stock who was active under both Nazism and Communism. He survived by writing apparently innocuous works with mildly subversive music. After recomposing Mendelssohn's music to *A Midsummer Night's Dream* for the Nazis, he gave the regime an exportable romantic hit, *Der Günstling (The Favourite*, Dresden, 20.ii.35, cond. Böhm). His next opera, *Die Bürger von Calais* (Berlin, 28.i.39), was pulled off after three nights. Its message was unmistakably pacifist and the rhythms were reminiscent of *Weill. *Johanna Balk* (Vienna, 4.iv.41), to a text by Weill's partner Caspar Neher, was subtly anti-totalitarian and Wagner-Régeny was made to atone for it with hymns for party occasions. Under communism, he confined himself mainly to ballets and orch. suites, some of which show wistful modernist and 12-tone tendencies. His watchwords were: clarity, simplicity, truth, discipline and the avoidance of any superfluity.
  b. Régen, Austro-Hungary, 28.viii.03; *d.* East Berlin, 18.ix.69. *works include*: 13 operas, symphonic poems, *Schir haschirim* (song of songs, for two soloists, women's choir and orch., 1964), 8 *commentaries in the manner of Guillaume de Machaut* (1967).

Walkman Akio Morita, co-founder of the Japanese electronics giant Sony, wanted to have music wherever he went. He ordered a miniature TC-50 tape recorder, built for the Apollo 10 space mission, to be commercially adapted and on 23.vii.1979 unveiled a personal stereo cassette player under the generic name of Walkman. Sony and its imitators sold more than 120 million of these machines in a decade, making music as *portable as the paperback book.

William WALLACE Scots eye-surgeon, composed a 1905 symphonic poem, *William Wallace*, commemorating 14th-century national hero and namesake.
    b. Greenock, nr Glasgow, 3.vii.1860; *d.* Malmesbury, Wilts., 16.xii.40.

Fats (Thomas Wright) WALLER Jazz entertainer, he wrote 'Ain't Misbehavin'' and 'Honeysuckle Rose'.
    b. Waverley, NY, 21.v.04; *d.* Kansas City, 25.xii.43.

Bruno WALTER Mahler's 2nd conductor at Vienna posthumous premières of *Das *Lied von der Erde* and the 9th Symphony, as well as Pfitzner's powerful opera, *Palestrina*. Anti-modernist, he composed ingratiating late-romantic chamber music and songs.
    b. Berlin, 15.xi.1876 (as B. W. Schlesinger); cond. Riga, 1898–1900, Vienna Court Opera, 1901–12; dir. Munich Opera 1912–22, Städtische Oper, Berlin, 1923–29, Leipzig Gewandhaus concerts 1929–33, Vienna State Opera 1936–38; *d.* Beverly Hills, California, 17.ii.62.

(Sir) William (Turner) WALTON The pre-War darling of English music awoke in 1945 to find himself eclipsed by Benjamin *Britten. His music never recovered from the shock.
    A streak of insecurity was evident from the outset in Walton's failure to establish a consistent personal style. A northern chorister adopted at Oxford by the literary Sitwells and their fashionable crowd, he played court musician and gigolo to the London leisured classes in the 1920s. Exporting a serious string quartet (Salzburg, 4.viii.23; later withdrawn), he startled polite society with *Façade* (London, 12.vi.23), a *Satie-like pastiche with echoes of Edward Lear to verses written and

recited by Edith Sitwell. It amounted to a milk-and-water *Pierrot Lunaire*, lacking *Schoenberg's piercing sound. *Stravinsky imbued his breezy overture *Portsmouth Point* (Zurich, 22.vi.26), and Prokofiev his viola concerto, rejected by Lionel Tertis and premièred by Paul *Hindemith (London, 3.x.29; revised for small orch. 1962).
    Acceptability was achieved with *Belshazzar's Feast* (Leeds, 8.x.31), a middle-of-the-road English oratorio in the Handel-to-Elgar tradition with dashes of modernism; easier to sing than to sit through. He struggled over a symphony in B flat minor (London, 6.xi.35) that came out rather like *Sibelius' Fifth turned sour – the Presto movement is marked 'con malizia' and the finale reflects a change of mistresses from Baroness Imma Doernberg to Lady Alice Wimborne. Walton lived in considerable comfort and cropped up in Anthony Powell's sequence of London society novels, *A Dance to the Music of Time*.
    He was the white hope of English music through the Thirties and when Jascha Heifetz commissioned a concerto, Walton feared he was 'just about ripe for critical damnation'. He tailored the work to the violinist's acidulous sweetness, with a dreamy opening that burst into pyrotechnic virtuosity (Cleveland, Ohio, 7.xii.39). It was Walton's finest hour and Heifetz's single contribution to regular modern repertoire.
    During the war he wrote a propagandist movie score for *Went the Day Well?* (1942) and magnificent string sequences for Laurence Olivier's *Henry V* (1944), a Shakespearean trilogy continued with *Hamlet* (1948) and *Richard III* (1955). His string technique was perfected in a serene 2nd quartet (1947), reworked as a Sonata for String orch. (1972). But the triumph of *Peter Grimes* pushed Walton into the shade and he felt unable to compete. He left England in 1948, married a girl he met at a party in Argentina and settled on the Neapolitan island of Ischia. His attempted comebacks yielded diminishing returns. The Chaucerian opera *Troilus and Cressida* flopped at Covent Garden (3.xii.54) for more that just creative reasons – Walton mainly blamed the conductor, Malcolm Sargent – and the long-postponed 2nd

symphony (Edinburgh, 2.ix.60) proved antediluvian and second-rate Sibelian. Embittered at newspaper critics, though not losing his humour, he lived a languid Mediterranean existence among friends who included W. H. Auden and Hans Werner Henze. He was even reconciled to Britten and sent a Chekhovian chamber opera, *The Bear*, for performance at Aldeburgh (3.vi.67).

> *b.* Oldham, Lancashire, 29.iii.02, of singing parents; chorister at Christ Church Cathedral, Oxford, 1912–18; lived with Sitwells 1919–34; knighted 1951; *d.* Ischia, 8.iii.83. *other works*: *Crown Imperial*, coronation march for King George VI (12.v.37), *Orb and Sceptre*, coronation march for his daughter Elizabeth II (2.vi.53); Johannesburg Festival Overture (Johannesburg, South Africa, 25.ix.56); Sinfonia concertante for piano and orch. (London, 5.i.28); Cello concerto (for Gregor Piatigorsky, Boston, 25.i.57); Variations on a theme by Hindemith (London, 8.iii.63); Improvisations on an Impromptu by Britten (San Francisco, 14.i.70), 5 Bagatelles for solo guitar (for Julian Bream, 1972; orch. as *Varii Capricci*).
> *Bib*: Susana Walton, *William Walton: Behind the Façade*, Oxford, 1988.

waltz The three-four Viennese dance founded on local speech rhythms – mir ist so *wunderbar* – came to symbolize decadence. Richard *Strauss's waltzes in *Rosenkavalier* and *Ravel's *Valses nobles et sentimentales*, both dated 1911, mocked social stratification and emotional falsity. Sibelius's *Valse triste* was heavy with forebodings. Ravel buried old Vienna in *La Valse* (1920), while Strauss mourned his home town in *Munich* (1945). Gavin Bryars' *Three Viennnese Dancers* (1970s) mock the genre.

War and Peace (Voyna i mir) Prokofiev's mammoth wartime opera on Tolstoy's epic novel. The original 13 scenes were cut to 11 in a 1953 revision. fp: Moscow, 17.x.44 (8 scenes only); fp revision: Florence, 26.v.53.

War Requiem Pacifist oratorio by Britten for the opening of the new Coventry Cathedral, replacing the one flattened by German bombs. Musically indebted to Verdi, it combines the Latin Mass with First War poems by Wilfred Owen. fp: Coventry, 30.v.62.

Robert (Eugene) WARD His operatic setting of Arthur Miller's witchhunt play *The Crucible* (NY, City Opera, 26.x.61) was one of America's most workable operas, though rarely seen abroad. Miller originally envisaged the play with musical accompaniment and Ward's score is melodic but rough-hewn, suggesting the rugged ways of the early settlers. It won him a Pulitzer Prize, but four further operas and many orch. works won him no greater fame.

> *b.* Cleveland, Ohio, 13.ix.17; st with *Hanson; *other operas*: *The Lady from Colorado* (1964), *Abelard and Heloise* (1980); five symphonies, piano concerto.

Peter WARLOCK Satanic pseudonym of sharp-toothed London critic, Philip Heseltine, who took a false name to protect the music he composed from the vengeance of musicians he had wronged. A Twenties trend-setter, depicted in novels by D. H. Lawrence and Antony Powell, he failed to win serious recognition and, one night when his girlfriend was away, put his cat outside the door and turned on the gas.

His depressive side is heard in *The Curlew* (1920–1), a mustard-dressing of lovelorn W.B. Yeats poems for tenor, string quartet, flute and cor anglais. His many other songs veer between melancholia and madcap Delian modernity and a penchant for Tudor japes. The *Capriol Suite* (1926) is an insipid remake of an Elizabethan dancing treatise. A *Serenade for Delius* on his 60th birthday (1922) was followed by a friendly biography. He also co-authored a study of Gesualdo, murderer and madrigalist, and founded a music journal, *The Sackbut*.

> *b.* London, 30.x.1894, *d.* there, 17.xii.30. *other works*: *Sociable Songs* (1925), *The Five Lesser Joys of Mary* (1929), *Mr Belloc's Fancy* (1921–30), *Peter Warlock's Fancy* (1924), *The Cricketers of Hambledon* (1928), *The Fox* (1930); edition of 300 old English songs.

Warsaw Autumn The tide of Stalinism turned in eastern Europe at the 1956 festival in Warsaw, which coincided with Khrushchev's secret denunciation to the Soviet Politburo. Bartók swept back into favour, serialism became permissible and the first strains of avant-garde ideas filtered through. Liberated from total censorship, *Lutosławski and *Penderecki emerged onto the world stage. *Nono, Carter and other Westerners were invited to subsequent festivals which became the central meeting point of new ideas from east and west.

The Wasps Orch. suite by *Vaughan Williams, extracted from incidental music to Aristophanes' comedy. fp: London, 23.vii.12.

Michael Blake WATKINS His assertive 1988 trumpet concerto for the Swedish virtuoso Håkan Hardenberger ends in the disconcerting pessimism of his teacher, *Lutyens.
b Ilford, Essex, 4.v.48; *other works*: double concerto for oboe and guitar; oboe quartet.

Wat Tyler Peasants' revolution opera staged in the East German workers' state by the British Stalinist, Alan Bush. fp: Berlin, 3.iv.52.

Franz WAXMAN A Berlin café musician, he got a job orchestrating and conducting Friedrich Holländer's score for *The Blue Angel* at the Babelsberg studios. Beaten up by Hitler thugs, he skipped to Hollywood where he scored some 140 movies, winning successive Oscars for *Sunset Boulevard* and *A Place in the Sun* (1950–1). Waxman was a clever, cultured composer who avoided cheap thrills and wrote jagged themes rather like *Shostakovich; *A Place in the Sun* uncannily anticipates a passage in the Russian's 11th symphony, 'the year 1905'.

He recycled some of his music into concert works. A symphonic fantasy on the Lutheran hymn *Ein Feste Burg* was extracted from *Edge of Drakness* (1943); the brilliant *Carmen Fantasy* for *Heifetz and orch. from *Humoresque* (1947). His oratorio *Joshua* (1959) contains the theme from Billy Wilder's *Spirit of St Louis*. His most serious music was *The Song of Terezin* (1965) to children's poems from a Nazi concentration camp. A keen conductor, Waxman founded the Los Angeles Music Festival in 1947, giving West Coast premières of Britten's *War Requiem*,

Debussy's *Martyre de Saint Sébastien* and symphonies by Shostakovich, Prokofiev and Walton.
b. Chorzow, Poland, 24.xii.06; *d*. Los Angeles 24.ii.67. *other concert works*: Sinfonietta (1955), *Taras Bulba* (1962) – neither resembling Janáček – and a piano story for his ten-year-old son, *The Charm Bracelet* (1949), in the style of Shostakovich.

waveform The notational representation of an *electronic sound wave.

Andrew Lloyd WEBBER – See LLOYD WEBBER

Ben (William Jennings Bryan) WEBER One of the first *12-note Americans, he adapted the technique in such a way that a melodic base was preserved in a *Symphony on Poems of William Blake* (NY, 28.x.52) for baritone and orch.
b. St Louis, Missouri, 23.vii.16; *d*. NY, 9.v. 79. *other works*: violin and piano concertos, *Prelude and Passacaglia* for orch. (Louisville, 1.i.55), two string quartets.

Anton (Friedrich Wilhelm) von WEBERN History has thrown up some strange leaders of men and ideas but few so

unlikely as Anton von Webern. A middle-class Austrian of provincial outlook and uneven temperament, grovelling to his teacher *Schoenberg, violently intolerant of sceptics, he alternated between maudlin self-pity and unprovoked bursts of fury. He suffered several nervous breakdowns and was unable to hold a job for more than a few months. Very little in his character was attractive; 'he was a pedant,' said one of his daughters. He had a few friends and fewer adherents. Apart from two published lectures, he issued no theoretical writings. Most musicians of his time abominated his punctilious *pointillism. 'This is not music at all, but mathematics,' announced a London cellist, pulling out of a 1938 performance of his string trio.

No sooner was Webern killed in September 1945, by an American soldier in a bizarre policing accident, than he was resurrected as god of the nascent *avant-garde. Composers alighted upon the totality of his *serialism as the bible of a new music, discarding Schoenberg's messianic moralism for Webern's precise order. Where Schoenberg merely reorganized the relations of notes in his 12-note technique, Webern applied the idea meticulously to every filament of musical fabric. Durations, intervals, tempi, intrumentation and dynamics (sound levels) could be sorted in rows and shapes that resembled natural phenomena and thus took their form from heaven, regardless of how they sounded. To this divine authority, he added the precedent of structures borrowed from Bach's hallowed canons and the polyphony of medieval masters.

Scholars admired his perfect symmetries; listeners were perplexed by the absence of any conventionally pleasing features in his music. Webern had effectively invented composing-by-numbers. Once a composer laid out his *row, the system did the rest. For the generation of 1945, appalled by romantic traditions that had precipitated two holocausts, Webern promised a route to progress, the more so since his scheme could govern the unfolding options of electronic and computerized composition, reorganizing sinewaves and mysterious forces of time and space.

Webern never saw himself as a great innovator and deferred habitually to Schoenberg's genius. From his personal correspondence one can deduce that, beyond the satisfaction he derived from making art, he had no burning desire to change the world. He was a private man of narrow ambitions and character. Yet posthumous followers perceived him as a superior alternative to Schoenberg. *Boulez entitled his momentous pro-Webern polemic 'Schoenberg is Dead' and *Stravinsky announced his conversion to Webernism with undimmed derision for his mentor.

There were cogent reasons why the post-war world found it convenient to worship Webern at Schoenberg's expense. Schoenberg demanded spiritual qualities in a composer, more than technical aptitude. His highmindedness was alien to the times and, to some denizens of Hitler's fallen dominions, alien by race, faith and the distance of exile. Webern, on the other hand, was a pure Austro-German, a son of Bach and Haydn who demanded nothing but craftsmanship. His martyrdom at the hands of the US military was a suggestive focus of Euro-revivalism. He was 'one of us' and his doctrines were so sparse they could be adapted to various extreme ends without risk of heresy. In the specific case of Stravinsky, Webern did not represent a rival – as Schoenberg, even dead, so disturbingly did. Thus Webern was deified by default.

He had come to Schoenberg as a private pupil in 1903 after *Pfitzner turned him down. As his tuition came to an end he shared the excitement, though not the conviction, of the leap into atonality. His graduation piece was a 12-minute Passacaglia for orchestra (Vienna, 4.xi.08) which, while preserving tonal restraints, set the tone for his life's work.

Its title and form were taken from Bach, the indicated tempo was 'very moderate' and the piece, though barely long enough for a concert overture, was in fact the very longest of his works. Its theme consisted of eight quarter-notes, separated from one another by a rest of equivalent duration. There were 23 variations – a magic number for his friend *Berg – and, notwithstanding a certain aphoristic inscrutability, the Passacaglia made an impression at first hearing with the weight of its portentous emotions. His tonal ambience remained

Mahlerian-to-morose in *5 Pieces* for string quartet or string orch., opus 5 (1909), and his sound did not alter appreciably in the *6 Pieces for Orchestra*, op 6 (Vienna, 31.iii. 13), his principal contribution to the atonal era, except that its episodes are shorter, slower and more clearly defined. It was his last composition for large orchestra, and he subsequently slimmed it down for a reduced ensemble.

The lack of a tonal framework left him unhappier than ever and he sought consolation and constraints in words, setting verses by Stefan George, Rainer Maria Rilke and, in opus 13, a Chinese poem, from the set that the much-admired *Mahler used in *Das Lied von der Erde*. He married his cousin, Minna, and had four children but could not settle. When Schoenberg moved to Berlin, Webern followed like a stray pup. *Zemlinsky offered him a post on the conducting staff at Prague but he dithered and finally went to Stettin, where he collapsed and was sent back to Vienna. His *5 Orchestral Pieces* opus 10 (1911–13) had one movement that was just seven bars and 19 seconds long. He was locked into ever-smaller cells.

During the War he was briefly in the army then, on Schoenberg's return to Vienna, moved to a house nearby in the outer suburb of Mödling, where he spent the rest of his life. He conducted the local male chorus and Schubert society and from 1923 headed the workers' orchestra run by the Social Democratic Party until its dissolution in a 1934 wave of gunfire. He was a capable conductor of late romantic and modern scores and in the 1930s was engaged several times by Edward Clark, an ex-Schoenberg pupil at the BBC. None of this sufficed to provide a reasonable livelihood for his family. His greatest pleasure was tending his garden and taking long country walks.

Webern was saved, perhaps from madness, by Schoenberg's discovery of a method of composing of 12 notes with equal value. Here, at last, was absolute order – though Webern, as usual, lagged three or four years behind Schoenberg in assimilating the technique. After quiet experiments with morbid texts by Georg Trakl his baptism arrived with the nine-minute string trio opus 20, slow, squeaky and disjointed yet possessed of an overpowering inner logic. Its 12-note row is repeated 36 times in fluctuating combinations. He followed it with a Symphony, opus 21 (NY, 18.xii.9), which was nothing of the sort. Scored for clarinet, bass-clarinet, two horns, harp and string quartet, it was an unsubtle parody of romantic excesses, a ten-minute funereal procession of shifting textures. Here, Webern split the row of 12 notes in two, using the second half as a mirror image of the first. Canon, sonata form and variations provided a rigid structure. Webern envisaged the second movement as a musical image of a Pompeiian magic formula which reads the same forwards, backwards and upside down:

SATOR
AREPO
TENET
OPERA
ROTAS.

He started sketching a 3rd movement but soon gave up. He may have been frightened of attempting anything larger. He constructed the concerto for nine instruments, op. 24 (Prague, 4.ix.35), from a *cell of three notes that he manipulated every which way. He became progressively terser and more miniaturist in the Variations for piano, op 27 (Vienna, 26.x.7) and the string quartet, opus 28 (Pittsfield, Massachusetts, 22.ix.38), densely riddled with patterns and codes and demanding the utmost listening concentration in order to drain a drop of beauty.

A final friend entered his life in 1926 in the person of Hildegard Jone, poetess wife of the sculptor Josef Humplik. Her nature-verses provided texts for a succession of choral and vocal works that closed his output. The rise of the Nazis affected him less than Schoenberg and Berg. He mourned his master's exile to America and was inconsolable at his friend's death, throwing a fit at a Barcelona rehearsal and almost sabotaging the world première of Berg's violin concerto by refusing to yield the baton to another conductor.

His attitude to the Nazis was, however, ambivalent. On the day the Germans marched into Vienna he wrote to

Hildegard Jone: 'I am totally in my work, and must not be disturbed.' According to Alma Mahler, he had joined the Party in secret in 1934, along with various members of his family, in the absurd hope of persuading the Gauleiters of the merits of modernism. His son, Peter, was an active Hitlerite and one his daughters married an SS officer. Webern was left alone by the Nazis and survived the war by performing menial copying tasks for the purified *Universal Edition. He was allowed to visit Switzerland in 1943 for the première of *Variations for Orchestra*, opus 30 (Winterthur, 3.iii.43, cond. *Scherchen).

When Vienna came within range of Russian guns and news arrived of his son's death, he took his family to Mittersill, near Salzburg, to see out the war in rural poverty. After months of hunger and illness, his daughter invited him to dinner with the promise of a fat cigar from his son-in-law, the former SS man now turned black-marketeer. Walking out into the night to smoke his gift, he lit up just as soldiers arrived to arrest his host. Seeing a sudden flare, a nervous sentry shot and killed the composer. The soldier was haunted by the tragic error and ten years later took his own life. Webern was buried at Mittersill beneath a simple cross that Humplik carved. Anna Mahler sculpted a permanent tombstone. Webern had just begun to live.

> *b*. Vienna, 3.xii.1883; spent adolescence in Klagenfurt; wrote doctoral thesis on 15th century composer Heinrich Isaac; married Wilhelmine Mörtl in Danzig, 1911; *d*. Mittersill, Austria, 15.ix.45. *other works*: early orch. idyll *Im-Sommerwind* (1904; fp: Seattle, 25.v.62); choral works – *Das Augenlicht* for chorus and orch. (London, ISCM, 17.vi.38), *First Cantata* for soprano, chorus and orch. (London, 12.vii.46), *Second Cantata* (Brussels, 23.vi.50).
>
> *Bib*: H. Moldenhauer, *Webern*, London (Gollancz), 1978.

Karl WEIGL Perplexed by *Schoenberg's ideas, Weigl composed in Vienna as if the 1890s had never ended. Three romantic songs for contralto and string quartet (1936) encapsulate his musical Jugendstil, amiably listenable, elegantly safe. He learned style from *Zemlinsky and dedication from *Mahler, who employed him as a repetiteur. Forced to escape the Nazis, his emigré compositions voiced nostalgia, not anger.

> *b*. Vienna, 6.ii.1881; won Beethoven Prize for 3rd quartet, played by Rosé Quartet, 1910; emigrated 1938 to US teaching at Hartford, Brooklyn College and Boston Conservatory; *d*. New York, 9.viii.49. *other works*: children's opera, *The Pied Piper of Hamelin* (1932), six symphonies (the 5th, 'Apocalyptic', in memory of F. D. Roosevelt, fp: Carnegie Hall, NY, 27.x.68, cond. Stokowski), eight string quartets, hundreds of songs and choruses.

Kurt (Julian) WEILL Weill was not one composer but three. An intensely serious

Brecht (l.) and Weill at Baden Baden (1927)

pupil of the intellectual *Busoni, he produced a stiffly competent, sinuous 1st symphony (1921, fp Cologne, 20.ii.57) and string quartet. At 24, he wrote a concerto for violin and wind orch. (Paris, 11.vi.25), astringent in the manner of *Berg or *Hindemith, yet riddled with fidgety rhythms and a finale that portended the swinging choruses of his American musicals. Weill was a barometer of 1920s *Berlin, searching for an identity amid the social and moral anarchy of military defeat and, all the while, suggesting a utopian idealism in which music would heal a wounded society. Alongside Hindemith, with whom he wrote a radio opera on *Lindberg's Flight* (Frankfurt, 27.vii.29), he pondered long and hard on ways to make music useful to mankind.

He decided 'that my special field of activity would be the theatre' and made his debut with a children's pantomime

Zaubernacht (Magic Night) (Berlin, 18.xi.22). Reworked as an orch. suite, *Quodlibet (As you please,* Dessau, 15.vi.23), it echoed Busoni's fixation with Bachian counterpoint and Mahler's with maudlin marches. The piece, rarely played, betrays his antecedents with informative clarity.

Before he met the struggling *Brecht in 1927, Weill established a solid reputation with two one-act operas that he staged with the *expressionist playwright Georg Kaiser – *The Protagonist* (Dresden, 27.iii.26, cond. Busch) and *The Tsar has his Photograph Taken* (Leipzig, 18.ii.28). He worked on a third opera, *Royal Palace* (Berlin, 2.iii.27), with the Dadaist Iwan Goll. These pieces contained elements of the spiky rhythms and waspish tunes that hallmarked his work with Brecht, though the revolutionary ardour and dramatic finesse is still lacking. At Kaiser's home he met and married an unemployed Viennese actress, Lotte Lenya, whose cracked voice and chirpy character figured centrally in his life and work. He would rejoin Kaiser in a German valediction, *Der Silbersee (The Silver Lake: A Winter's Tale,* Leipzig, 18.ii.33) that failed to blend a taxing score with an overlong mystical drama but left a residue of two brittle ballads, 'Fennimore's Lied' and 'Caesar's Death'.

Brecht and Weill started out with a 25-minute *Mahagonny Songspiel* about a 'paradise city' consumed by the urge for economic consumption. Staged in a boxing ring, its radical politics, acidulous harmonies and idealization of an imaginary America in the moony 'Alabama Song' caught the ears of the avant-garde (Baden-Baden Festival, 18.vii.27). Not until it was expanded into a fullblown opera did *The Rise and Fall of the City of Mahagonny* (Leipzig, 9.iii.30) acquire notoriety. By then, the pair were internationally famed for *The Threepenny Opera* (Berlin, 31.viii.28), a bawdy, brutal update of John Gay's 18th-century *Beggar's Opera* that became a film by G. W. Pabst. Its spell was cast by the revolving tune of the introductory 'Ballad of Mack the Knife,' though this was not Weill at his most hypnotic. 'Salomon's Song', a morbid afterthought, was all the more compelling for the singer

leaving its refrain hanging in mid-air to be finished by the accordion. Weill's music for agit-prop numbers like 'The Ballad of Sexual Dependency' sharpened and lightened the thrust of Brecht's polemic. In America, he resisted moves by Brecht and others to update his opera, and history proved him resoundingly right.

In the *Berlin Requiem* (Radio Frankfurt, 22.v.29) he again showed genius for bringing out the human colours and grim humour in Brecht's strident manifestos; 'To Potsdam under the Oaks', resembling an early Mahler song, ends in an ironic jibe from Mozart's *Magic Flute.*

The rest of their collaboration was beset by dissension. *Happy End* (Berlin, 2.ix.29) was anything but. Written mostly by Brecht's discarded mistress Elisabeth Hauptmann, it yielded two of Lenya's greatest hits, the bouncy 'Bilbao Song' and shameless 'Surabaya-Johnny'. Some further music was recycled in Weill's 1934 Parisian fiasco *Marie Galante,* whose songs have a distinct cabaret tang. *Der Jasager (The Yes-sayer,* Radio Berlin, 23.vi.30) was a crude political exercise for schoolchildren. Their final reunion came in *The Seven Deadly Sins* (Paris, 7.vi.33), a 35-minute *Songspiel* for dancers that returned to the Mahagonny format but lacked its shocking novelty.

The widows of Weill and Brecht would fight like wildcats over which husband had contributed most to a body of art that sang a requiem for the Weimar Rebublic. Brecht was vain enough for his acolytes to claim that he had written most of Weill's music. This fallacy is easily refuted. After Weill, Brecht added nothing of musical significance, whereas Weill remained theatrically fertile. Their relationship was in any case non-exclusive. Brecht worked at the same time with *Eisler and Weill wrote incidental music for other dramatists as well as a full opera, *Die Bürgschaft (The Pledge,* Berlin, 10.iii.32) with his designer, Caspar Neher, whose wife Erika comforted him when Lenya ran off with a handsome tenor. Fleeing Germany with the Nehers after Hitler came to power, Weill struggled in Paris and London. He briefly reverted to early ideals in a 2nd symphony (Amsterdam, 11.x.34, cond. Walter) that fixed fizzy rhythms and bluesy tunes in a classic frame. He divorced Lenya, then remarried her before they sailed together for the America they had sung of but not seen. Broadway started him on a third musical career. His hit musicals, many sounding naïve and sentimental to modern tastes, are immortalized by isolated numbers that Lenya recorded. The ridiculously-titled *Knicker-bocker Holiday* (1938) contained two gems: 'It Never Was You' and the ballad of middle-aged regret, 'September Song'. *One Touch of Venus* (1943) had the moodily seductive 'Speak Low'; *Lost in the Stars* produced 'Trouble Man'. His writers included Maxwell Anderson, Ira Gershwin and Ogden Nash.

Determined to contribute to American culture, Weill dreamed of creating a form of opera that was genuinely American. He toyed with Western folk heritage in a college opera, *Down in the Valley* (1945), then brought to Broadway a real-life tragedy of New York street life, comparable in many respects to *Porgy and Bess*. Weill's score for *Street Scene* (NY, 16.xii.46), an intriguing symbiosis of bittersweet *Mahagonny* and brassy Glenn Millerisms, is richer than Gershwin's and, while his tunes are less catchy than 'Summertime', the aria 'Lonely House' is unforgettable and the Ice Cream Septet provides a dazzling display of synchronized vocalism. *Street Scene* took a dozen years to be accepted by an opera house and still awaits full recognition.

At his premature death of heart disease, brought on by stress, Weill was contemplating nine ideas for an American opera, including *Moby Dick* and John Steinbeck's *Grapes of Wrath*. His social and moral outrage carried over into his last musical, *Lost in the Stars* (30.x.49), based on Alan Paton's novel of South African oppression, *Cry the Beloved Country*.

Weill's changes of direction were attacked by highbrows and lowbrows alike as opportunistic, but they were impelled by a strong personal ideology and only their timing was dictated by circumstance. Weill was, above all, a communicator who needed to feel audience response to what he composed and aimed to work slightly ahead of public taste. He brought jazz into European opera houses and added panache to the American stage, with profound implications for the musicals of Bernstein and Sondheim. Detested by *Webern as a 'traitor' to central European tradition, he followed other principles and wrote music that is instantly recognizable as his own, the mark of a great composer.

b. Dessau, 2.iii.1900, son of a synagogue cantor; st philosophy at Berlin U. and music with Busoni and *Jarnach, earning his living as synagogue organist and cabaret pianist; met Lenya 1924; fled Germany 21.iii.33; US citizen 27.viii.43; suffered massive coronary 15.iii.50; *d*. New York, 3.vi.50.
Bib: David Drew, *Kurt Weill: A Handbook*, London (Faber & Faber), 1987.

Der Wein Concert aria by *Berg, inscribed to his mistress's oenophile husband. fp: Königsberg, 4.vi.30, cond. Scherchen.

Jaromir WEINBERGER The Czech composer enjoyed inter-War acclaim with a folk-opera, *Schwanda the Bagpiper* (Prague, 27.iv.27), whose Polka and Fugue became a concert encore. Exiled to the US, he wrote a set of variations on the children's song *Under the Spreading Chestnut Tree* (1940) and a grandiose *Lincoln Symphony* (1941) but committed suicide in depression at his obscurity.
b. Prague, 8.i.1896; *d*. St Petersburg, Florida, 8.viii.67. *other work*: epic opera *Wallenstein* (Vienna, 18.xi.37).

Leo WEINER Bachelor musician who taught Hungary's finest talent at the Budapest Academy for almost half a century (1908–49) and composed chamber music of endearing unsolemnity. His 2nd string quartet won the *Coolidge prize in 1922. He dined every day of his life at the same restaurant.
b. Budapest, 16.iv.1885; *d*. there, 13.ix.60.

(Paul) Felix von WEINGARTNER The Austrian conductor believed himself to be at least as important a composer as *Mahler. His seven operas and seven symphonies received scattered performances during his prodigious lifespan. He was an avid polemicist on the art of conducting, particularly on Beethoven interpretation.
b. Zara, Austria, 3.vi.1863; cond. Königsberg 1884, Danzig 1885–87, Hamburg Opera

1887–89, Mannheim 1889–91, Berlin 1891–1907; dir. Vienna Court Opera 1907–11, Hamburg (again) 1912–14, Darmstadt 1914–18, Vienna Volksoper 1919–24, Basel Conservatoire 1927, cond. Vienna State Opera 1934–38; *d.* Winthertur, Switzerland, 7.v.42.

Judith WEIR   The folkmusic and themes in this Scots composer's small opera, *The Vanishing Bridegroom* (Glasgow, 17.x.90) had an integrality that recalled Janáček – and none could aspire higher. Her characters were gritty and her instrumentation interesting. All she lacked was Janáček's emotional thunderbolt, but that may come with time. A scholar of medieval music and Haydn, she exploited native Scots sonorities as no-one before in such evocative pieces as The Bagpiper's String Trio (1985). Her debut opera, *Night at the Chinese Opera* (Cheltenham, 8.vii.87), is a compendium of theatrical puzzles with no emotional engagement.
   b. Aberdeen, 11.v.54; st with *Tavener; *other works*: The Consolations of Scholarship (soprano and nine players; London, 15.x.85), *The Black Spider* (three-act opera, Canterbury, 6.iii.85).

Hugo WEISGALL   Prolific Baltimore composer of audience-acceptable modernisms.
   b. Ivancice, Moravia, 13.x.12; arrived US 1920; *works*: nine operas including *The Stronger* (after Strindberg, 1952) and six *Characters in Search of an Author* (NY, 26.iv.59).

Julius WEISSMAN   German opera composer; *Leonce und Lena* (1925) was main hit.
   b. Freiburg-im-Breisgau, 26.xii.1879; *d.* Singen, 22.xii.50.

Egon WELLESZ   As an exiled Viennese medievalist in Oxford, Wellesz assisted the *early music revival and quickened local interest in Mahler and Bruckner. Involved equally in modernism, he incurred Schoenberg's wrath with an unofficial biography in 1921. He made a pre-Anschluss mark as a composer with a Shakespearian concert suite, *Prosperos Beschwörungen* (Vienna, 19.ii.38, cond. Walter) and after the war composed nine symphonies that started out in Mahlerian vein and wound up partly *serialist. His music received reparatory performances in Vienna.

b. Vienna, 21.x.1885; st with Guido Adler; taught at U. of Vienna 1911–38; lecturer in music at Oxford 1938–48, Reader in Byzantine music 1948–56; *d.* Oxford, 9.xi.74. *other works*: six operas including *Die Bacchantinnen* (Vienna, 20.vi.31).

Lars Johan WERLE   His first full-length opera, *Resan (The Voyage*, Hamburg, 2.ii.69), contained live film-projection and created a storm in Sweden by challenging the value of the welfare state and underlining the loneliness of individuals within it. A pop group expressed violent protest from the opera stage amid a score of otherwise inoffensive modernities. The piece was a storm in the Scandinavian teacup and its composer has not ruffled the waters since.
   b. Gävle, Sweden, 23.vi.26;

Richard WERNICK   Pulitzer-winner of 1977 with *Visions of Terror and Wonder*, he has composed numerous middle-of-the-road concert works.
   b. Boston, 16.i.34; st with *Fine, Kirchner, *Blacher, *Copland and others; taught U. of Pennsylvania 1968– .

Westdeutscher Rundfunk (WDR – West German Radio) Cologne broadcasting station that set up early electronics studio run by *Eimert and *Stockhausen.

Peter WESTERGAARD   American modernist, *Webern follower, teaching at Princeton from 1968.
   b. Champaign, Illinois, 28.v.31; st with *Piston, *Milhaud, *Sessions and *Fortner; *works include*: chamber opera *Mr and Mrs Discobbolos* (1966), three act Shakespearian opera, *The Tempest* (1988).

West Side Story   *Bernstein's Broadway and movie hit, transplanting Romeo and Juliet among Hispanic immigrants in New York. The weightiest concept ever seen on the Great White Way, replete with a 12-tone 'Cool' fugue, it gained the status of high art but never quite transferred to the opera house. fp: New York (Winter Gardens), 26.ix.57.

white noise   A stream of sound like escaping steam, it contains all audible frequencies. It is the electronic equivalent to a C-major chord.

Paul WHITEMAN   NY bandleader who commissioned Gershwin's *Rhapsody in

Blue for a formal concert of jazz, a cute gimmick that won him accolades as the originator of symphonic jazz or, simply 'King of Jazz'. Whiteman was a former viola player in San Francisco and US Navy bandsman with an eye for the main chance and a link to Hollywood, where his outfit appeared in *Strike up the Band* (1940) and other hits. His orchestrations were the work of Grofé and his particular sound was fashioned by such employees as Bix *Beiderbecke and Benny *Goodman. Whiteman's fame was sustained by a brilliant publicity machine and, along with Glenn *Miller, by a public inclination to prefer white figureheads to genuine black jazzmen.

> *b.* Denver, Colorado, 28.iii.1890; *d.* Doylestown, Pennsylvania, 29.xii.67.

the WHO British 1960s group that voiced the tide of teenaged rebellion in 'My Generation' and invented 'rock opera' in the movies *Tommy* (1969) and *Quadrophenia* (1979). The group broke up in 1982 after the death of drummer Keith Moon. Its energizers, Pete Townsend and Roger Daltrey, remain active on the philosophical fringes of popular music.

Charles-Marie(-Jean-Albert) WIDOR Towering French organist and pedagogue, he inherited César Franck's chair at the Paris Conservatoire in 1890 and taught the grandeurs of Bach to generations of pupils from *Schweitzer and *Boulanger to *Honegger and *Milhaud. He invented a 'symphony' for organ solo. The march from his 5th symphony (1880) attained wedding-day ubiquity. He also composed three orchestral symphonies, two piano concertos and an opera, *Les Pêcheurs de Saint Jean* (Paris, 26.xii.05).

> *b.* Lyons, 21.ii.1844; organist at Ste-Sulpice, 1870–1934; *d.* Paris, 21.iii.37.

Jean WIENER *Satie-an pianist who captured 1920s Paris in fervently jazzy, never too serious, works like *Concerto franco-américain* for clarinet and strings and *Sonatine syncopée* for solo piano (both 1923). He moved into movie writing but left his mark on Milhaud, Poulenc and possibly Stravinsky.

> *b.* Paris, 19.iii.1896; *d.* there, 8.vi.82.

Alec WILDER Songwriter and musical arranger for Frank Sinatra and Judy Garland – *Who Can I Turn To?* – Wilder composed charming chamber operas and concert pieces. *Miss Chicken Little* was premièred on CBS TV (27.xii.53) and a 1950 concerto for oboe and strings is delightful. He wrote further concertos for euphonium and saxophone, four *Entertainments* for wind ensemble and a vast amount of chamber music.

> *b.* Rochester, NY, 16.ii.07; *d.* Gainesville, Florida, 22.xii.80.

Friedrich WILDGANS A clarinettist at the Vienna State Opera until the Nazis kicked him out, he composed in various styles, including the *serialism of his friend *Webern. Most was for his own instrument, for which he left two concertos. He married the soprano Ilona Steingruber (the first recorded Lulu), and headed the *ISCM's Austrian section from 1949.

> *b.* Vienna, 5.vi.13; st with *Marx; *d.* Mödling, 7.xi.65.

(James) Healey WILLAN Anglo-Canadian composer of two late-romantic symphonies (1936, 48) and much neo-Baroque choral and organ music for the Anglican rite.

> *b.* London, 12.x.1880; emigrated 1913; *d.* Toronto, 16.ii.68. *other works*: opera *Deidre* 1946), C-minor piano concerto (1944), *Coronation Suite* (1953) for chorus and orch.

Herbert WILLI The colours and shapes of Austrian landscapes enrich Willi's scores in geometric form, a trend started by *Webern and continued by *Cerha. His music has been particularly championed by Claudio *Abbado.

> *b.* Voralberg, Austria, 1956; st with *Eder, B. *Schaeffer; *orch. works*: *Aurora-giove* (1989), *Il combattimento di Cecco e la sua compagnia* (1989), Mass (1991).

Alberto WILLIAMS The 'father of Argentine music' wrote nine symphonies (1907–39) in early-modern international style, speckled with local rhythms. He founded a conservatory in Buenos Aires in 1893 and ran it until 1940; he headed the national commission of fine arts and the Argentine concerts association.

> *b.* Buenos Aires, 23.xi.1862; *d.* there, 17.vi.52.

Grace (Mary) WILLIAMS Welsh friend envied by *Britten for reaching Vienna to study with *Wellesz, she spent 15 years as a London school-mistress trying to get performed, but could not overcome metropolitan male prejudice and went home defeated in 1946. Her sole contributions to national repertory were the *Fantasy on Welsh Nursery Tunes* (1940) and *Sea Sketches* (1944). Welsh National Opera has staged her domestic opera, *The Parlour* (1961).
   b. Barry, Wales, 19.ii.06; *d.* there 10.ii.77.

John WILLIAMS The most vivid of movie composers, he specialized in brassy spectaculars – *Jaws, Star Wars, Close Encounters of the Third Kind, E.T.* and *Return of the Jedi*. The scale of his scores permits few intimacies, although his earliest Oscar was won for setting the sour-sweet Yiddish melodies of *Fiddler on the Roof* (1971). He conducted the Boston Pops Orchestra (succeeding its founder, Arthur Fiedler, in 1980) and composed two symphonies, a violin concerto, flute concerto and an Essay for Strings.
   b. Flushing, NY, 8.ii.32; st with *Castelnuovo-Tedesco.

Malcolm (Benjamin Graham Christopher) WILLIAMSON A puzzling case of composer's block. Williamson was fluent enough until they named him Master of the Queen's Music in 1975 – the first Australian in the role. Thereafter he found it increasingly difficult to complete a work, leaving royal weddings bereft of an obligatory fanfare. After astringently modern – almost *Boulezian – beginnings, he had shifted under Britten's influence to simple tunefulness in the early 1960s, going over the top to reach a public in *Three Cassations* for audience and orchestra (or piano) (Brighton, 22.iv.67).
   His opera *Our Man in Havana* (London, 2.vii.63), after Graham Greene's novel, pleased the author and was seen in seven countries; *The Violins of Saint Jacques* (29.xi.66) held its place at the English National Opera for four seasons; *Menuhin commissioned and recorded his violin concerto (Bath, 15.vi.65). He may have done too much too soon, however, writing seven symphonies and as many

operas by the age of 53, and his middle-age was lamentably fallow.
   b. Sydney, 21.xi.31; st with *Goossens and *Lutyens; emigrated to UK 1953; *other works*: two children's operas, *The Happy Prince* and *Julius Caesar Jones*; three piano concertos, and an organ concerto (1961).

Thomas (Brendan) WILSON A solemn Celtic voice with religious predilections, Wilson's music is grimly atmospheric. The St Kentigern Suite (1986) is a memento of the bleakness that Christian missionaries encountered in Scotland. He has composed three symphonies (1956–82), a piano concerto (1985) and an opera, *Confessions of a Justified Sinner* (1976).
   b. Trinidad, Colorado, 10.x.27; taught Glasgow U. 1957– .

Gerhard WINKLER Austrian experimentalist, conquered the 1991 Zurich ISCM with an 11-minute *Chronogramm* (13.x.91) for large orch.
   b. Salzburg, 1959; *other works*: *Heimwärts (homewards,* 1989–), for instruments and live electronics in memory of the writer Thomas Bernhard; *Cassandra-Fragment* for dramatic mezzo and ensemble (1988).

Winter Words Britten's equivalent to Schubert's *Winterreise*, using texts by Thomas Hardy. fp: Harewood House, Leeds, 8.x.53.

Dag (Ivar) WIRÉN His unprepossessing *Serenade for Strings* (1938) contained the ideal jingle for television newsreels in its *alla marcia* movement and made Wirén the most played of all Swedish composers. 'I believe in God, Mozart and Carl *Nielsen,' was his credo. The 3rd (1944) of his five symphonies is strongest; he also wrote five string quartets.
   b. Striberg, Sweden, 15.x.05; vice-president Swedish Composers Society 1947–63; *d.* Danderyd, Stockholm, 19.iv.86.

Trevor WISHART Electronic experimenter from the north of England, achieved some renown with vocally simulated bathroom noises in his Vox series (1980–88).
   b. Leeds, 11.x.46;

Ermanno WOLF-FERRARI The Italian's operas are popular only in Germany; elsewhere his string serenades are sometimes heard.

b. Venice, 12.i.1876; *d.* there, 21.i.48. *operas include*: *Cenerentola* (1900), *Le donne curiose* (1903), *Il segreto di Susanna* (1909), *Il gioielli della madonna* (1911), *Sly* (1927), *Gli dei a Tebe* (1943).

Christian WOLFF Crowned by *Cage 'the most important composer of his generation' – the *avant-garde delighted in bestowing such accolades – this naturalized Frenchman taught classics at Dartmouth College while pondering the beauties of *silence and chance. He composed sparingly and with careful computation of the mathematical possibilities of every sound he notated. Wolff resolved around 1957 that music existed only in performance and that 'the freedom and dignity of the performers' was paramount. He wanted to surprise listeners, performer and the composer himself with the variety in each performance. He offered musicians numerous choices and developed striking works for Merce Cunningham's ballet troupe including *Chance* (1952), *Rune* (1959) and *Tread* (1970). In the 1970s his music embraced political activism; in the 1980s he fell silent.
b. Nice, 8.iii.34; arrived US 1941; *works include*: *Summer* for string quartet (1961), *For 5 or 10 Players* (1962), septet for any instruments (1964), *Snowdrop* for harpsichord (1967), *You Blew It* for chorus (1970).

Stefan WOLPE German refugee of great intellectual influence in New York, where his pupils included *Feldman, *Shapey and *Wuorinen. Leaving Berlin on Hitler's ascent, he studied with *Webern on his way to Palestine, where he absorbed semitic sonorities and arrived at a mature style. This amounted to a *serialism that was not afraid to make romantic gestures and resisted enervating pointillisms.
Wolpe held the unfashionable Weimar Republic view that music must be useful to society. Although atonal, it could be experienced painlessly and should contain enough activity to intrigue the uninformed ear. His compositions were often called simply *Piece* or *Chamber Piece* for so-and-so many instruments. *Enactments* (1950–53) for three pianos is considered his masterpiece, proving that spiritual depth could surmount the most ascetic of structures. For sheer technique Webern himself could not have bettered the Passacaglia in *Four*

Studies on Basic Rows (1936–72), yet the work communicates incisively and even entertains.
b. Berlin, 25.viii.02; st with *Busoni, *Juon and *Schreker; arrived US 1938, taught privately in NY 1938–52, Black Mountain College, North Carolina, 1952–56, Long Island U. 1957–68; thrice married; *d.* NY, 4.iv.72. *other works*: ballet *Man from Midian* (1942), incidental music to three Brecht plays, *Cantata about Sport* (1952), symphony (1964), string quartet (1969), violin sonata (1949), two Palestinian Songs (1936).

women Although women's rights advanced, their status barely altered in music. There were star singers and soloists as ever before and a rising number of orchestral players from 1920 on, but no woman joined the front rank of conductors and none was counted among top composers. Social expectations unquestionably retarded the progress of women in music. Many, like Elizabeth *Maconchy, put family before career. Those, like Elisabeth *Lutyens, who did not were condemned for mannish callousness. Amy Beach, Cécile Chaminade, Rebecca Clarke, Ethel Smyth, Germaine Tailleferre and Thea Musgrave won a modicum of recognition. In the century's closing decade two Russians, Sofia Gubaidulina and Elena Firsova, won universal respect and the American Joan Tower won the prestigious Grawemeyer award. The century's most influential teacher of composers was the Frenchwoman, Nadia Boulanger.

Henry J(oseph) WOOD Founder of London's summer Promenade Concerts in 1895, he composed an ever-popular *Fantasia on Sea Songs* for the Trafalgar centenary in 1905 and assumed a Russian pseudonym, Paul Klenovsky, to write potboilers. He premièred hundreds of pieces by British composers and gave the first British performance of symphonies by Mahler, Sibelius and Skryabin.
b. London, 3.iii.1869; *d.* Hitchin, Herts., 19.viii.44.

Hugh WOOD Good intentions, general knowledge and genuine feelings should create a listenable composer, but Hugh Wood was inhibited in much of his music by Anglo-academic constraints. His harmonic language draws from both *Vaughan

Williams and *Schoenberg. In his 3rd quartet (Bath, 31.v.78), dealing with death and rebirth, a dullish texture drains the blood from any passions. After the murder of his adult daughter, Wood wrote a piano concerto (London, 10.ix.91) which applied Latin rhythms and a trace of Rachmaninov into a bold structure that threatened to shake off serialism, but held on by the skin of its score.

> *b.* Parbold, Lancashire, 27.vi.32; taught London (1956–67), Glasgow (1966–70), Liverpool (1971–5) and Cambridge (1976–); *other works*: cello and violin concertos, symphony (BBC, 23.vii.82).

The Wooden Prince Ballet by *Bartók. fp: Budapest, 12.v.17.

Woodstock Festival Gathering of folk and rock singers and 450,000 fans on a farm site 100 miles up-river from Manhattan for a three-day festival (21–24.viii.69) in Bob Dylan's backyard. He had prudently escaped to Europe but most other top names turned out. Many in the audience shed their clothes and inhibitions, hallucinogenic drugs were openly traded and the event, never repeated, was seen as a ceremony of innocence, the apotheosis of flower power, a generation's rejection of commerce and violence.

John WOOLRICH *Birtwistle's obsessions passed to a new generation in Woolrich's *Figures in a Landscape* (1986), a complex piece for chorus and orchestra which describes life's passing parade. His other works are mainly vocal and less than ten minutes long.

> *b.* 1954;

William WORDSWORTH The poet's namesake and near-descendant wrote eight symphonies and six string quartets. He excelled at pastel songs, brought to fame by the contralto Kathleen Ferrier. 'Red Skies' and 'Clouds' are exquisite miniatures.

> *b.* London, 17.xii.08; *d.* Kingussie, Scotland, 10.iii.88.

world music Also known as world beat and 'sono mondiale', this loose term attempts to define art music that exists outside the Western concert tradition. It can apply to anything from Argentine tango to the Congolese *Missa Luba*, from Caribbean calypso to Arab ballads, from Javanese gamelan to Andean troubadours. Interaction of these cultures with western recording techniques and marketing, and with one another, produced transient phenomena that enthralled ears jaded by an excess of musical sophistication. *Kronos popularized unknown African musicians and the tangos of Astor *Piazzola.

Wozzeck Conscripted into the Austrian Army during the First War, Alban Berg

Poster for the first performance of Wozzeck

empathized with Georg Büchner's tragedy of a tormented soldier who kills his wife. Wozzeck is destroyed by military and medical brutality, Marie by his helplessness and her own carnality. *Atonally wrought, the opera is overwhelmingly lyrical, using folksong and Mahler-like quotations in an astonishing structure that governs every note of music, word of text and visual prop. Not a single sound or action is irrelevant to Berg's overall design. The opera, in 15 scenes, lasts just 90 minutes. fp: Berlin, 14.xii.25, cond. Erich Kleiber.

Charles WUORINEN Academic composer of unregenerate complexity, he was the bane of US audiences until the mid-1980s when, in a 3rd piano concerto, he seemed to recognize the importance of tradition. Until then, he had composed Varèse-like blocks on serial principles and occasional electronic excursions, dedicated to an ideal of intellectual progress in music. His role models were *Babbitt, *Carter and *Wolpe, though he became as productive as Hovhaness, turning out some 170 scores by his 50th birthday, despite the handicap of poor eyesight. Fiercely nationalist, he proclaimed that US music had nothing to learn from Europe. He won the 1970 Pulitzer prize for electronic *Time's Encounter*.

b. NY, 9.vi.38, of Finnish descent; st with *Ussachevsky; taught Columbia U. 1964–71; *other works:* 'intellectual porn' opera *The W(hore) of Babylon* (1975), three symphonies (1958–59), concerto for amplified violin and orch. (Tanglewood, 4.viii.72), *Percussion Symphony* (1978), *The Golden Dance* (1986), horn trio (1981).

Ivan WYSHNEGRADSKY Independent explorer of *microtonal options, he went to Paris in 1919 to persuade Pleyel to make him a quarter-tone piano. Thereafter, he composed for two or four pianos, played simultaneously and tuned a quarter-tone apart. He abhorred *serialism and preached a mystic kind of Skryabinist pantonality in his handful of orchestral works.

b. St Petersburg, 4.v.1893; *d.* Paris, 29.ix.79. *works:* *The Day of Existence* for narrator, chorus and orch. (1917/40), *Thus Spake Zarathustra* for orch., (1930), *7 variations on the note C* for two pianos (1918/45), *Cosmos* for four pianos (Paris, 10.xi.45), *transparences* for ondes Martenot and two pianos (1956/63), two string quartets.

X Anthony *Davis opera on the turbulent life of Malcolm X. fp: NY (City Opera) 28.1x.86.

Iannis XENAKIS It is tempting to indict Xenakis for musical ravages of the kind that his architect friends inflicted on inner city housing. The Paris-based Greek composer was a close associate of Le Corbusier (1887–1966) who, more than any other planner, reduced houses to 'machines for living', accommodation modules lacking formal or ornamental beauty, a box within a tower block that became a breeding ground for discontent and crime.

Xenakis worked 13 years (1947–60) for Le Corbusier, took over his Philips pavilion at the 1958 Brussels Expo, and applied construction principles to an ethereal art. He declared that music which was made through 'geometry' was less perishable than works generated by a passing impulse. Structure was paramount, mathematics must rule music. Borrowing an idea from probability theory he invented *stochastic music, a process by which the outcome of a work is predetermined by a formula based on its contents and structure. Where *Cage gave performers the right to choose in *aleatory music, Xenakis maintained there was no random chance in real art.

The severity of his outlook, however, was modified by a passionate Mediterranean nature and a modest personality that, in contrast to *Boulez and *Stockhausen, made little propaganda and sought no power.

An anti-Nazi resistance fighter in Greece, he lost an eye in battle and fled the country under sentence of death during the civil war. He learned his music from *Messiaen and *Scherchen but did not make it a full-time occupation until 1959. Almost all his works have Greek titles.

Rejecting *serialism, he erupted with *Metastaseis* for 61 instruments (*Donaueschingen, 15.x.55), modelled on the floor-plan of his Brussels pavilion. It redefined the balance of orchestral power by splitting and manipulating the string sounds. Like many advanced works, it reached a popular audience through Balanchine's ballet version.

His play with numbers struck chords with *Lutosławski, *Penderecki and the veteran *Varèse, who wrote a *Poème électronique* for his Brussels construction. Xenakis was drawn to *musique concrète and *electronics – *Hibiki-Hana-Ma* (1970) requires 800 loudspeakers – but was more concerned with live instruments. Probably his most enchanting sounds are made by massed voices in *Oresteia* (1966) and mixed percussion in *Pleiades*, a rippling gamelan-like ensemble subjected to rigid stochastic disciplines.

b. Braïla, Romania, 29.v.22; migrated to Athens 1932; st engineering; emigrated 1947; French citizen 1965; founder-director CEMAMu (Centre d'études de mathématique et d'automatique musicales); *other works*; *Pithoprakta* for 50 players (Munich, 8.iii.57, also Balanchine ballet), *Kraanerg* for 23 players (Ottawa ballet, 2.vi.69); *Naama* for solo harpsichord (Luxembourg, 20.v.84).

Kosaku YAMADA The founder of Japan's first symphony orchestra was a Berlin pupil of Max *Bruch who organized the Tokyo Philharmonic in 1915 and toured it to Europe and the US, programming delicate works of his own – *Festival of Autumn, Flower of Madras* and *Oriental Suite*. He composed five operas, several symphonic poems and hundreds of songs, many of them destroyed in manuscript when his Tokyo home was bombed in May 1945. Some were reconstructed from parts with painstaking ancestral reverence.
  b. Tokyo, 9.vi.1886; *d.* there, 29.xii.65. *other works*: cantata *Dawn of the Orient* (Tokyo, 7.vii.41), *Red Dragonfly, Rain falls on Jogashima* for chamber ensemble.

Richard YARDUMIAN US composer of Armenian parentage, he was local to the Philadelphia Orchestra, married its conductor's secretary and raised a family of 13.
  b. Philadelphia, 5.iv.17; married *Stokowski's assistant Ruth Seckleman; *d.* Bryn Athan, Pennsylvania, 15.viii.85. *works include*: *Desolate City* (6.iv.45), *Armenian Suite* (5.ii.54), piano and violin concertos and two symphonies.

Yesterday Seminal *Beatles ballad quoting a Tchaikovsky theme.

Pietro YON Organist of St Peter's in Rome (1905–7) and St Patrick's Cathedral in New York (1926–43), his organ piece *Gesù Bambino* (1917) was arranged for voice and became a seasonal favourite of divas. He composed several masses and devotional works.
  b. Settimo Vittone, Italy, 8.viii.1886; *d.* Huntington, NY, 22.xi.43.

Vincent (Miller) YOUMANS Songwriter whose tune 'Tea for Two' from the Broadway show *No, No, Nanette* (1925) caught the spirit of the age and was reset by *Shostakovich.
  b. NY, 27.ix.1898; *d.* Detroit, 5.vi.46. other hits include: 'Bambalina' (1923).

Young Composers' Group Talent that banded in 1930s New York around *Copland and *Sessions.

Young France Jeune France – Anti-*neoclassical composers in 1930s Paris who fought for a national, progressive ethos in music. The leaders were *Messiaen, *Jolivet and *Daniel-Lesur.

Young Poland Turn-of-century nationalist movement headed by the post-Wagnerian Mieczyslaw *Karlowicz and later by the more austere *Szymanowski.

Young Person's Guide to the Orchestra Hand-held round-the-band tour by *Britten. fp: Liverpool, 15.x.46.

Douglas YOUNG British electicist whose tastes extend from Wagner to electronics and are combined to maximum effect in *Ludwig, fragments from a mystery* (Munich, 14.vi.86), a ballet about the tragic Bavarian king. It contains electronically altered excerpts from *Lohengrin, Meistersinger* and the *Wesendonk Lieder*, which set the scene for dreamy meanderings through the monarch's befuddled mind.
  He shared a Lewis Carroll fixation with *Del Tredici, writing an unfinished

chamber opera on *Alice in Wonderland* (1968–84) and a dramatic cantata, *The Hunting of the Snark* (1982), which uses mathematical formulae to parody the precisional preoccupations of contemporary music. Within its stern framework, snatches of *Siegfried*, christmas carols and English composers ancient and recent are amusingly interpolated.

b. London, 18.vi.47; st RCM; formed Dreamtiger ensemble 1974; *other works*: three *Night Journeys under the Sea* (two for chamber orchestra, the 3rd for large ensemble), *Virages* – cello concerto (1978), *Rain, Steam and Speed* (after a Turner painting, 1981), various orchestrations of *Satie and *Ives.

La Monte (Thornton) YOUNG

Natural father of *minimalism, Young belonged to the Cageian circle who shattered the historic definition of music. Returning from *Darmstadt in 1959, he presented himself to New York with a *Piano Piece for David *Tudor* which read:

Bring a bale of hay and a bucket of water onto the stage for the piano to eat and drink. The performer may then feed the piano or

leave it to eat by itself . . .

His *Composition #2* that year consisted of building a fire; *Composition #7* consisted of a two-note chord, a perfect fifth, 'to be held for a long time'. In one performance, stones were placed on the pedals of an organ and left there for a week. Another score amounted to the command, 'Urinate'. To the spaced-out denizens of Haight Ashbury and newly-enlightened cult-seekers, all this seemed uncommonly profound. He organized a seminal series of loft concerts in Yoko Ono's apartment.

Young's claim to minimalist precedence rests on his string trio of 1958, comprising long, drawn-out notes and silences. It was the first work, but not the catalyst of the new phenomenon: that honour belonged in 1964 to *Riley's *In C*. Young devoted the prime of his composing years to the *Well-Tuned Piano*, started in 1964 and continuing to develop as it changed and grew with each performance. It lasts over six hours. Another running project was *Dream House*, 'a permanent space with sound and light environments [created by his wife, Marian Zazeela] in which a work would be played continuously'. In 1970 he discovered a guru, Pandith Pran Nath, grew his beard and wore a topknot and Indian garb.

b. Bern, Idaho, US, 14.x.35; founded Kirana Center for Indian Classical Music, 1971; *other works*: *Orchestral Dreams* (1985).

Eugène YSAŸE

A legend among violinists, romantically intense yet technically serene, Ysaÿe was also a formidable conductor and fluent composer. His playing inspired César Franck's much-loved sonata; the string quartet he led nudged *Debussy to write his only quartet. He founded a concert society in Brussels, declined an approach to head the New York Philharmonic in 1898 but directed the Cincinnati Symphony Orchestra (1918–22) with great flair.

His compositions include the first opera in Walloon dialect – *Peter the Miner* (Liège 4.iii.31) – and a *poème élégiaque* (1895) that prompted Chausson to write his celebrated work for violin and orchestra. He wrote a number of concerted works for violin and cello and eight violin concertos but his lasting monument is a series of six sonatas for solo violin, opus 27, written in 1923 and each designated for a master of the instrument. The first, inscribed to Joseph Szigeti, is fearsomely virtuosic and inconsolably moody. The second, for Jacques Thibaud, performs variations on the *Dies Irae* theme beloved of Rachmaninov and works in snatches of Bach that Thibaud used in daily practice. The third and shortest, for *Enesco, is a ballade with Transylvanian undertones. The 4th, for *Kreisler, is in a classical format that imitates the Viennese fiddler's own pastiches. The 5th is relaxedly dedicated to his quartet partner, Mathieu Crickboom, while the 6th revels in the Spanish fire of the short-lived Manuel Quiroga. Too rich to be absorbed at a single hearing, the six sonatas demand to be heard individually in virtuoso recitals.

Gregarious and life-loving, Ysaÿe enjoyed a long and happy marriage and, on his wife's death, was united at 70 with a 24 year-old American pupil, Ginette Dincin. In his last years, diabetes took its toll with a leg amputation and he was carried, dying, to hear his only opera. Queen Elisabeth of the Belgians founded an international violin contest in his memory in 1937. The first winner was David Oistrakh.

> *b.* Liège, Belgium, 16.vii.1858; st with Wieniawski and Vieuxtemps; UK debut 1891, US debut 1894; *d.* Brussels, 12.v.31. *other orch.* works: *Exil* for strings (NY, 1917), *Amitié* for two violins and orchestra (1922).

Théophile YSAŸE Eugène's younger brother was a pianist who wrote a concerto, a symphony in F major and a symphonic poem, *Le Cygne*.

> *b.* Verviers, Belgium, 22.iii.1865; *d.* Nice, 24.iii.18.

Isang YUN The Korean composer became a cause célèbre when, in June 1967, he and his wife were snatched from their West Berlin home and flown to Seoul, where he was tried for sedition and sentenced to life imprisonment. Mrs Yun was given three years as his accomplice. Western outcry, led by Igor Stravinsky, achieved their release two years later in broken health. They flew home to Berlin, where Yun was appointed professor at the Musikhochschule. In 1976, the Seoul regime tried again to abduct him from Japan but were beaten off by his bodyguards. North Korea retaliated with an annual Isang Yun festival.

Yun's music strives for east–west dialogue. *Reak* for large orchestra (Donaueschingen, 23.x.66) applies symphonic style to ancient Korean court ceremonies; a 1984 clarinet quintet, plaintive and slow, winds its way sinuously towards diatonic harmony.

> *b.* Tongyong, Korea, 17.ix.17, son of a poet; jailed by Japanese in 1943 for resistance work; married Sooja Lee 1950; moved to Berlin 1956; *other works*: Four operas *Liu Tung's Dream* (Berlin, 25.ix.65), *Butterfly Widow* (Bonn, 9.xii.67), *Geisterliebe* (Kiel, 20.vi.71), *Sim Tjong* (Munich, 1.viii.72); *Om mani padme hum* for soloists, chorus and orch. (Hanover, 30.i.65); five symphonies; 1976 cello concerto representing his prison experiences; 1977 flute and harp concerto recounting a Korean fairy-tale; oboe concerto (Bonn, 16.ix.91); much chamber music.

Riccardo ZANDONAI Last of the Italian late-romantics, he scored three quick hits with *Il grillo del focolare* (*The Cricket on the Hearth*, after Dickens, Turin 28.xi.08), *Conchita* (after Pierre Louÿs, Milan 14.x.11) and *Francesca da Rimini* (after d'Annunzio, Turin, 19.ii.14). Then he became an anachronism. In the First War he was a nationalist agitator and in 1932 he fronted a Fascist manifesto calling for the restitution of 19th-century artistic values.

    b. Sacco, Trentino, Italy, 30.v.1883; *d*. Pesaro, 5.vi.44. *other works*: *Guilietta e Romeo* (Rome 14.ii.22); patriotic tone poems.

Frank (Vincent) ZAPPA Rock iconoclast, father of the mid-60s Mothers of Invention band, he veered from extreme bad taste and cheap satire – *Why Does It Hurt When I Pee/Broken Hearts are Assholes* – to advanced computer-music technology. He experimented at *IRCAM, where *Boulez conducted his 1984 album, *The Perfect Stranger*. A protagonist of live music and free expression, he testified to a congressional committee on censorship, arguing against restraints on violent rock music proposed by educators and born-again Christians. 'Composers are supposed to provide some reflection of the environment in which they write,' he averred.

    b. Baltimore, Maryland, 21.xii.1940;

Zdravitsa Prokofiev's fawning ode for Stalin's 60th birthday. fp: Moscow, 21.xii.39.

Ruth ZECHLIN Eminent Berlin teacher and wife of pianist Dieter Zechlin, she composed three symphonies, *Emotions* for large orchestra, a Lidice-cantata and *Reflections on a Piano Piece by Prokofiev* for piano and 10 instruments.

    b. Grosshartmannsdorf bei Freiberg, Saxony, 22.vi.26; professor of composition at Berlin Musikhochschule 1950– .

Eric ZEISL Viennese refugee in California, writing diatonic chamber music – with Judeo-cantorial inflections.

    b. Vienna, 18.v.05; *d*. Los Angeles, 18.i.59. *works include*: two string quartets, *Arrowhead* trio (Los Angeles, 25.i.57) for flute, viola and harp.

Zeitoper *Weimar-era operas dealing with burning issues, among them Hindemith's *Neues vom Tage*, Brand's *Maschinist Hopkins*, Schoenberg's *Von Heute auf Morgen* and Weill's *Dreigroschenoper*. The concept has revived to some extent in the news-oriented operas of *Adams and *Tippett.

Alexander ZEMLINSKY Brahms' last protégé, he became *Mahler's acolyte and *Schoenberg's brother-in-law, yet preserved a creative independence that was recognised long after his death. His double-bill of Oscar Wilde's *A Florentine Tragedy* (Stuttgart, 30.i.17) and *Der Zwerg* (*The Dwarf*) (Cologne, 28.vi.22) form a neat contrast of late-romantic lushness and neo-classical wit. His symphonic output was slim. After two Brahmsian symphonies in the 1890s, he produced a brightly-coloured fantasy, *The Mermaid* (Vienna, 29.i.05), but was dismayed by its reception at the concert where Schoenberg premièred his *Pelleas* suite and gave up the genre for life.

His only reversion was the *Lyric Symphony* (Prague, 4.vi.24), modelled on Mahler's *Das *Lied von der Erde* and itself the coded source of Alban Berg's *Lyric Suite*. Its seven stanzas by *Tagore, alternately sung by baritone and soprano, conjure up a sensations of insatiable yearning and regret.

An outstanding opera conductor in Prague, where he ran the German Theatre for 16 years, Zemlinsky was a remote individual who revealed his personality in chamber music. A Viennese of mixed Catholic, Jewish and Moslem blood, his first quartet (1896) recalls Schubert's *Death and the Maiden*. His romantic early songs, opus 7 (1901), are inscribed to a voluptuous pupil, Alma Schindler, who became Mahler's wife. Mahler's death and his own departure from Vienna in 1911 marked an abandonment of romanticism. Six impressionistic Maeterlinck Songs of 1910–13 are imbued with foreboding, while the 40-minute, single-movement second quartet (1915) sums up all his previous connections from Schubert to Schoenberg, whose *Verklärte Nacht* it initially resembles. It is, however, a distinctly forward-looking masterpiece whose emotional density steadily lightens into something like the nervous energy of 1920s Berlin.

His third quartet of 1924 is discordant but tonal, avoiding Schoenberg's *12-tone methods (he nevertheless premièred *Erwartung*). *Klemperer brought him to Berlin to conduct at the Kroll Opera but he left with the Nazi rise. His 1934 Lieder are remorseful and bemused; the fourth quartet of 1936 opens with a mournful chorale for Berg, before dancing the burlesque of a world gone mad. His final songs flicker between gloom, nostalgia and glimpses of America, where he fled in 1939. They include a moody blues number called 'Misery'. Reluctant to promote himself, he once said, 'It's not enough to have elbows in this throng, you need to know how to use them.' 'Zemlinsky can wait,' wrote Schoenberg with unintended callousness. He was dead 40 years before his excellence was acknowledged.

b. Vienna, 14.x.1871, as Alexander von Zemlinszky – he dropped the z early on and the 'von' when Austria became a republic; met Brahms and taught Schoenberg 1895; cond. Vienna Volksoper 1904–7, Court Opera 1907–11, Prague, German Theatre, 1911–27, Berlin, Kroll Opera, 1927–31; married (1) Ida Guttmann 1906, (2) Luise Sachsel 1930; paralysed by stroke 1939; *d*. Larchmont, NY, 15.iii.42. *other operas*: *Sarema* (Munich, 1897), *Once Upon a Time* (after Hans Christian Andersen, Vienna, 22.i.1900, cond. Mahler), *Kleider machen Leute* (*Clothes Maketh Man*, Vienna 2.xii.10), *Der Kreidekreis* (*The Chalk Circle*, Zurich, 14.x.33), *Der Traumgorge* (1906; posthumously premièred, Nuremberg, 11.x.80); three Psalms for chorus and orchestra, Nos 83 (1900), 23 (10.xii.10) and 13 (1935/perf. 8.vi.71).

Hans ZENDER Hamburg Opera's chief conductor achieved creative recognition with *Stephen Climax* (1984), an opera splicing the life of Saint Simon with stretches of James *Joyce. Staged in Germany and recorded commercially, it has not yet been rendered back into English.

b. Wiesbaden, Germany, 22.xi.36; st with *Fortner; mus. dir. in Kiel 1971–84, Hamburg 1984–87, Hilversum Radio 1987- ; *other work*: flute concerto (1987).

Zhdanovschina Russian name for the second wave of terror that Stalin unleashed against artists in 1948, prosecuted by Andrei Zhdanov.

(Count) Géza ZICHY One-armed piano pupil of Liszt and opponent of *Mahler, he ran the conservatory (1875–1918) and musical politics in Budapest and composed a trilogy of operas on the life of the national hero, Rakoczi (1905–12).

   b. Sztára Castle, Hungary, 22.vii.1849; *d* Budapest 14.i.24. *other work*: piano concerto for the left-hand (1902).

Winfried ZILLIG German composer of seven operas, he studied with *Schoenberg but stuck with romanticism; he was assigned the task of orchestrating the posthumous première of *Jakobsleiter* (1961).

   b. Würzburg, Germany, 1.iv.05; *d*. Hamburg, 18.xii.63. *operas include*: *Die Windsbraut* (Leipzig, 12.v.41), *Troilus und Cressida* (Düsseldorf, 3.ii.51).

Bernd Alois ZIMMERMANN Two sudden deaths 35 years apart wrecked the prospects for *atonal opera. *Berg's demise in

1935 with *Lulu* unfinished left modernism without a populist moderator. The suicide in 1970 of Bernd Alois Zimmermann, the

only man since Berg to write an effective non-tonal opera, sealed the fate of their genre. Soon after, Bruno *Maderna sounded the retreat from asceticism in his riotous *Satyricon*.

Zimmermann's masterpiece *Die Soldaten* (*The Soldiers*, Cologne, 15.ii.65) is a younger brother of *Wozzeck*. Its tale of a respectable towngirl who, betrayed by her officer lover, becomes a regimental whore, draws ineluctable connections between militarism and sexual oppression. Both operas are based on early romantic German literature – Lenz's play was written in 1771 – but proclaim an up-to-the-minute message. Both speckle an atonal score with shards of melody and identifiable Bach quotations, although Zimmermann dispensed with Berg's consolatory music. Berg aimed to create 'total theatre' by running a movie film in Lulu; Zimmermann used jazz, dance, film, pantomime and pre-recorded tape in *Die Soldaten*. He intended the action to run concurrently on 12 stages, with the audience swivelling from one to the next. Although he simplified the final version, *Die Soldaten* gained a reputation of being unperformable.

It requires a cast of 26, including six high tenors, and an orchestra of 100 with more percussion than can fit into any opera pit. One production had 377 vocal rehearsals and 33 orchestral sessions. The music is hard to sing accurately and is consistently tough on the ear. Yet the impact of the unfolding drama vindicates its textural complexity and the character of Marie, namesake of Wozzeck's heroine, is unforgettable. The last German opera to win a foothold in world repertoire, *Die Soldaten* closed a chapter in music history.

Despite modernist appearances, Zimmermann was out of tune with the *avant-garde. He rejected *serialist orthodoxy and wrote music that came from the heart. Immediately before the opera he produced a cello concerto, *Canto di Speranza* (*Song of Hope*, Baden-Baden, 28.vii.58), that freewheeled through a spectrum of sonorities and subtly mocked *Webern's arid concept of the cantata. It was an uncommonly optimistic work for Zimmermann, who spent most of his life veering between elation and depression. He described himself as part-monk, part-Bacchus.

Born at the end of the First World War, he was invalided out of the Second with a skin disease that enabled him to resume studies with *Jarnach, Busoni's assistant. His vision was affected by *photopsis*, flashing sparks, a condition that he composed vividly in a 1968 orchestral piece of that name. As his eyesight worsened, he became terrified of incipient blindness. *Requiem for a Young Poet* (Düsseldorf, 11.xii.69) set verses from Mayakovsky, Bayer and Esenin, all of whom took their own lives. One weekend in August 1970, he sent his family to the country, finished his Ecclesiastian cantata *I Turned and Saw all the Injustices that are Committed under the Sun* and shot himself.

b. Bliesheim, nr. Cologne, 20.iii.18; worked for WDR radio 1950–6, head of German section of *ISCM 1957–70; *d*. Grosskönigsdorf, nr. Cologne, 10.viii.70. *other orch. works*: violin concerto (Baden-Baden, 10.xii.50), Symphony in one movement (Brussels, 20.xi.53), oboe concerto (1952), *Nobody Knows de Trouble I See* – trumpet concerto (Hamburg, 11.x.55); *Dialogue* (WDR Radio, 5.xii.60), two-piano concerto in memory of Debussy but quoting extensively from Bach, Beethoven and Messiaen; ballet noir *Le Roi Ubu* (1968), *Stille und Umkehr* (*Stillness and return*, Nuremberg, 19.iii.71).

Udo ZIMMERMANN Haunted by an event in the year of his birth – the 1943 beheading of two Munich students, Hans and Sophie Scholl, for distributing anti-Nazi pamphlets – Zimmermann wrote two chamber operas about their resistance group, known as *The White Rose*. The first (Dresden music academy, 19.vi.67) flicked through their brave, brief lives in flashbacks. A rewrite (Hamburg, 27.ii.86), set inside their prison cells, examined broader themes of hope, resistance and resignation. It struck a global chord, achieving more than 70 productions in four years. Too static to survive as staged opera, it amounts to a darkly lyrical 80-minute song-cycle for soprano, tenor (or baritone) and 15 instruments, woven around recurrent four-note motifs and percussive dissonances reminiscent of *Berg and early *Shostakovich.

Zimmermann founded a New Music Studio in Dresden in 1974, introducing to East Germany music by Ives, Xenakis, Schnittke and Varèse. A Christian and pan-European, he moved to Bonn but returned east when the Berlin Wall came down and took charge of the moribund Leipzig state opera. His vigorous renovations precluded much composition. His most striking concert work to date is *L'homme* (1970), four violinless meditations on a humanist text with plenty of scope for aleatoric variation.

b. Dresden, 6.x.43; intendant Leipzig Opera, 1990– ; *other works*: four operas including *The Shoemaker's Prodigious Wife* (after Lorca; Dresden, 2.i.77) and *Die Sündflut* (Cologne, 1992); dramatic impression of the death of John F. Kennedy, for cello and orchestra (1963); concertos for violin (1964), viola (1982) and timpani (1983); song cycle on Hiroshima (1982).

Walter ZIMMERMANN Morton *Feldman's German disciple shrugged off prevailing orthodoxies and opened his mind to Zen Buddhism and *new simplicity. His struggles are conveyed in a 1974 work for 21 instruments entitled, in English, *In Understanding Music, the Sound Dies*. He travelled widely in North Africa and among the Amerindians, returning with nine folk-based cycles called *Lokale Musik* (1977–81). His largest work is the 100-minute simple-themed *Vom Nutzen des Lassens* (1975–85) and he has won a place as Germany's least predictable composer.

b. Schwabach, Franconia, 15.iv.1949; *other work*: *Sternwanderung* cycle (1985).

John ZORN Active in both rock and art music, Zorn's technique has been likened to Jackson Pollock's (1912–56) random scrawling on a floor-sized canvas, later cut up into marketable rectangles. Noisy by nature, he has worked with *Kronos and other new-music missionaries.

b. NY, 1953;

Rob ZUIDAM Crossover Dutchman, writing much the same aggressive *minimalism for concerts as for rock gigs. In *Dinamismo di cane al guinzaglio* (*Dynamism* of a *Dog on a Leash*) (1990), he took an idea of motion and restraint from a 1912 painting by the *futurist, Giacomo Balla.

b. Gouda, Netherlands, 1964; st with *Boesmans, *Foss, *Knussen;

Zvezdoliki (*King of Stars*) Remarkably dissonant choral work by Stravinsky, composed 1912, fp: Brussels Radio, 19.iv.39.

Der Zwerg (*The Dwarf*) One-acter by Zemlinsky on Oscar Wilde's sadistic story, *The Birthday of the Infanta*. fp: Cologne 28.v.22, cond. *Klemperer.

Ellen Taaffe ZWILICH The first woman composer to win a Pulitzer Prize, she played violin in Stokowski's American Symphony Orchestra (1965–73) while studying with *Sessions and *Carter at Juilliard. *Boulez conducted her *Premier Symposium* (31.i.75) and eight years later she won the prize for her first symphony (NY, 5.v.82). Her music is flowing, melodic and subtly coloured.
  b. Miami, Florida, 30.iv.39; married Joseph Zwilich 1969–79; *other orch. works*: Concerto Grosso (1985), *Symbolon* (1988).

Zwölftonspiel Games for 12 tones – *Hauer's title for compositions.

zydeco The only kind of *blues coloured by white men, this Louisiana music echoed the singing of French trappers, its name being a corruption of a one-step dance entitled 'Les haricots sont pas salés' (the beans ain't salted). Clifton Chenier (1925–87) was the leading exponent. Traces of zydeco can be heard in Leadbelly and Lightnin' Hopkins recordings.

Otto M. ZYKAN Viennese rebel against *12-tone supremacy, he accused the serialists of *fascism and composed satirical songs on *Schoenberg theoretical texts – *Polemical Arias* (1968) on the statement: 'I have discovered something that will assure the supremacy of German music for the next 1000 years.'
  b. Vienna, 1935; involved in 1968 student revolt; friend of *Gruber; *other works*: *Singer's sewing machine is the best* (1966), *Staatsoperette* (1977).

NEW MUSIC PERFORMED	THE ARTS	WORLD EVENTS
1901 Mahler, 4th symphony Rachmaninov, 2nd piano concerto	Chekhov, *Three Sisters* Verdi *d.*	Queen Victoria *d.* US President McKinley assassinated First Nobel prizes awarded Marconi sends wireless message across Atlantic
1902 Debussy, *Pelléas et Mélisande* Scott Joplin, *Ragtime Dance* Nielsen, *Saul and David* Schmidt, 1st symphony Schoenberg, *Verklärte Nacht* Sibelius, 2nd symphony	Gustav Klimt depicts Mahler as knight in Beethoven- frieze. Picasso, Blue Period. Hugo von Hofmannsthal abandons poetry. Caruso cuts his first records.	Boer War ends in South Africa Pierre and Marie Curie discover radium.
1903 Bruckner, 9th symphony Glazunov, 7th symphony Enesco, Rumanian Rhapsodies	Franz Wedekind, *Pandora's Box.* Gauguin *d.*	Wright brothers make first aeroplane flight. Henry Ford forms motor company.
1904 Busoni, piano concerto Janáček, *Jenůfa* Mahler, 5th symphony Puccini, *Madama Butterfly* Ravel, *Shéhérezade;* string quartet Sibelius, violin concerto Strauss, *Domestic Symphony*	Chekhov, *The Cherry Orchard.* Dvořák *d.*	War between Russia and Japan.
1905 Debussy, *La Mer* Glazunov, violin concerto Lehár, *Merry Widow* Mahler, *Kindertotenlieder* Schoenberg, *Pelleas und Melisande* Skryabin, *Divine Poem* Strauss, *Salome*	Picasso, Pink Period. G. B. Shaw, *Man and Superman*	Revolution quelled in Russia. Albert Einstein publishes theory of relativity.
1906 Mahler, 6th symphony Glazunov, 8th symphony Vaughan Williams, Norfolk Rhapsody	Ibsen *d.* Cézanne *d.*	San Francisco earthquake.
1907 Berg, piano sonata Ravel, Introduction and Allegro Schoenberg, 1st Chamber Symphony Sibelius, 3rd symphony Suk, Asrael Symphony	Rainer-Maria Rilke, *New Poems.* Grieg *d.*	Bakelite invented. Suffragettes attack homes of 6 British cabinet ministers.
1908 Debussy, Children's Corner Elgar, 1st symphony Mahler, 7th symphony Rachmaninov, 2nd symphony Schoenberg, 2nd string quartet Skryabin, *Poem of Ecstasy*	Arthur Schnitzler's *Der Weg ins Freie* exposes Viennese racialism. Rimsky-Korsakov *d.*	Sicilian town of Messina wiped out by quake and tidal wave.
1909 Delius, *Mass of Life* Rachmaninov, 3rd piano concerto; *Isle of the Dead* Rimsky-Korsakov, *Le coq d'or* Strauss, *Elektra*	Diaghilev brings Ballets Russes to Paris. Braque and Picasso embark on Cubist period. Futurists issue first manifesto in Italy.	Bleriot flies English channel by monoplane. Japan annexes Korea.
1910 Bartók, 1st string quartet Debussy, *Ibéria* Elgar, violin concerto Mahler, 8th symphony Schoenberg, *Book of Hanging Gardens* Stravinsky, *Firebird*	Tolstoy *d.*	

NEW MUSIC PERFORMED	THE ARTS	WORLD EVENTS
1910 Vaughan Williams, *Tallis Fantasia*		
1911 Irving Berlin, 'Alexander's Ragtime Band'	Thomas Mann writes *Death in Venice*	Amundsen reaches South Pole.
Busoni, Berceuse élégiaque	Blaue Reiter group formed in Munich by Kandinsky and Marc.	Russian premier Stolypin murdered at opera.
Elgar, 2nd symphony		Sun Yat-Sen is president of China.
Granados, *Goyescas*	Franz Werfel publishes first collection of poems.	
Mahler, *Das Lied von der Erde*	Mahler *d.*	Madame Curie wins 2nd Nobel prize.
Ravel, *L'Heure espagnole*		
Sibelius, 4th symphony		
Strauss, *Der Rosenkavalier*		
Stravinsky, *Petrushka*		
Szymanowski, 2nd symphony		
1912 Janáček, *In the Mists*	George Bernard Shaw, *Pygmalion*	*Titanic* sinks with loss of 1500 lives.
Mahler, 9th symphony		
Nielsen, 3rd symphony; violin concerto	Kandinsky publishes, *The Art of Spiritual Harmony*.	Woodrow Wilson elected US president.
Prokofiev, 1st piano concerto	First sheet publication of blues	
Ravel, *Daphnis et Chloe*		
Schoenberg, *Pierrot Lunaire*		
Schreker, *Der ferne Klang*		
Strauss, *Ariadne auf Naxos*		
1913 Berg, Altenberg-lieder	The word 'jazz' appears in a San Francisco newspaper.	Vitamin A isolated.
Debussy, *Jeux*	D. H. Lawrence, *Sons and Lovers*	Ford inaugurates assembly line manufacture.
Fauré, *Pénélope*		
Rachmaninov, *The Bells*	Marcel Proust quietly issues *Du Côté de Chez Swann*, first part of *A la recherche du temps perdu*.	
Schoenberg, *Gurrelieder*		
Stravinsky, *Rite of Spring*	Piet Mondrian titles his cubist canvases 'Composition'.	
1914 Busoni, Indian Fantasy for piano and orch.	Oskar Kokoschka paints himself with Alma Mahler in *Die Windsbraut*	Austrian Crown Prince shot in Sarajevo.
Reger, Mozart variations	Paul Klee develops abstract art.	Germany invades Belgium to start First World War.
Schmidt, *Notre Dame*		
Suk, Meditations on St Wenceslas Chorale		
Strauss, Josephslegende		
Stravinsky, *The Nightingale*		
1915 Falla, *El Amor brujo*	D. W. Griffiths' *Birth of a Nation*, first epic film.	Armenians massacred by Turks.
Skryabin, *Prometheus*	Scryabin *d.*	
Strauss, Alpine Symphony		
1916 Falla, *Nights in the Gardens of Spain*	Dadaist movement forms in Zurich.	Easter Rebellion in Ireland.
Granados, *Goyescas*	James Joyce, *A Portrait of the Artist as a Young Man*	Tanks first used in war.
Nielsen, 4th symphony		Emperor Franz-Josef of Austria *d.*
Szymanowski, *Mythes*	Max Reinhardt, Hofmannsthal and Strauss conceive the Salzburg summer festival of music and drama.	
1917 Bartók, *The Wooden Prince*		February and October revolutions in Russia.
Bloch, Schelomo		
Busoni, *Turandot*		Lenin seizes power to establish communist state.
Debussy, violin sonata	Rodin *d.*	
Pfitzner, *Palestrina*		USA joins War against Germany.
Satie, *Parade*		
Schreker, Chamber symphony		
Zemlinsky, *A Florentine Tragedy*		
1918 Bartók, *Duke Bluebeard's Castle*	Viennese artists Klimt and Schiele *d.*	End of War. Germany and Austria become republics.
Irving Berlin, 'God Bless America'	Debussy *d.*	Czechoslovakia, Poland and Hungary gain independence.
Grainger, Country Gardens		

NEW MUSIC PERFORMED	THE ARTS	WORLD EVENTS
1918 Holst, *The Planets* Prokofiev, Classical Symphony Stravinsky, *A Soldier's Tale* Suk, *Ripening*		Russian Tsar and family executed.
1919 Elgar, cello concerto Enesco, 3rd symphony Fall, *Three Cornered Hat* Hauer, *Nomos* (1st 12-note work) Ravel, *Le Tombeau de Couperin* Sibelius, 5th symphony Strauss, *Die Frau ohne Schatten*	Walter Gropius founds Bauhaus movement in architecture. Auguste Renoir *d.*	First transatlantic non-stop flight. Communists attacked in Berlin; Rosa Luxemburg killed. Treaty of Versailles humiliates Germany.
1920 Holst, Hymn of Jesus Korngold, *Die tote Stadt* Milhaud, *Le boeuf sur le toit* Ravel, *La Valse* Satie, *Socrate* Stravinsky, *Pulcinella*	Les Six coalesce in Paris. Picasso paints portrait of Stravinsky. Modigliani *d.* Lawrence, *Women in Love* Edith Wharton, *The Age of Innocence* Charlie Chaplin stars as *The Kid* Picasso, '3 Musicians'.	League of Nations formed. Britain accepts mandate for Palestine, France for Syria.
1921 Hindemith, Kammermusik no. 1 Honegger, *King David* Janáček, *Katya Kabanova*; *Diary of one who disappeared* Prokofiev, *Love for 3 Oranges* Stravinsky, *Symphonies of wind instruments* Szymanowski, 3rd symphony, *Song of the Night* Vaughan Williams, *The Lark Ascending*		Regular radio broadcasting begins. Lenin announces New Economic Plan
1922 Hába, microtonal 2nd string quartet Janáček, violin sonata Nielsen, 5th symphony; wind quintet Szymanowski, 1st violin concerto; *Hagith* Vaughan Williams, *A Pastoral Symphony*	Foundation of International Society for Contemporary Music James Joyce, *Ulysses*. T. S. Eliot, *The Waste Land* Proust *d.*	Mussolini marches on Rome to found fascist state. Ireland partitioned. Mahatma Gandhi imprisoned in India for sedition.
1923 Milhaud, *La création du monde* Sibelius, 6th symphony Stravinsky, *Les Noces* Walton, *Façade* Ysaÿe, 6 sonatas for solo violin	André Gide, *Four Socratic dialogues on homosexuality* Jaroslav Hasek, *The Good Soldier Schweik* G. B. Shaw, *St Joan*	Rampant inflation in Germany. Adolf Hitler arrested after Munich putsch attempt 300,000 die in Tokyo quake.
1924 Fauré, string quartet Gershwin, Rhapsody in Blue Honegger, *Pacific 231* Janáček, *Cunning Little Vixen* Kreutzer sonata, 1st string quartet Poulenc, *Les Biches* Respighi, Pines of Rome Schoenberg, *Erwartung*, Serenade, op 24 Sibelius, 7th symphony Zemlinsky, Lyric Symphony	First Surrealist manifesto, followed by Paris exhibition. E. M. Forster, *A Passage to India* Franz Kafka *d.* Busoni, Fauré, Puccini *d.*	On Lenin's death, Stalin takes control in USSR. First Labour government in Britain.

NEW MUSIC PERFORMED	THE ARTS	WORLD EVENTS
1925 Berg, *Wozzeck* Busoni, *Doktor Faust* Gershwin, Concerto in F Lehár, *Paganini* Prokofiev, 2nd symphony	Kafka, *The Trial* appears posthumously. F. Scott Fitzgerald, *The Great Gatsby* Sergei Eisenstein launches Soviet cinema with *Battleship Potemkin*.	Hitler issues *Mein Kampf*.
1926 Antheil, *Ballet mécanique* Bartók, *The Miraculous Mandarin*; piano sonata Hindemith, *Cardillac* Janáček, *Makropoulos Case*; Sinfonietta Puccini, *Turandot* Shostakovich, 1st symphony Szymanowski, *King Roger* Varèse, *Amériques*	Monet, Rilke d. Lawrence, *Lady Chatterley's Lover* Fritz Lang's formative film, *Metropolis*	General Strike in Britain. John Logie Baird demonstrates television.
1927 Bartók, 1st piano concerto Berg, Chamber concerto; Lyric Suite Gliere, *The Red Poppy* Janáček, Glagolitic Mass Jerome Kern, *Show Boat* Kodály, *Háry János* Krenek, *Jonny Spielt Auf* Rachmaninov, 4th piano concerto Schoenberg, 3rd string quartet Stravinsky, *Oedipus Rex*	BBC incorporated. Virginia Woolf, *To the Lighthouse* First talking film, *The Jazz Singer* Anna Akhmatova, *47 Love Poems*	Lindbergh makes solo Atlantic flight. Trotsky expelled from Soviet Communist Party.
1928 Gershwin, *An American in Paris* Honegger, *Rugby* Janáček, *Intimate Letters*, 2nd string quartet Nielsen, clarinet concerto Ravel, *Boléro* Roussel, 'Jazz dans la nuit' Schoenberg, Variations for Orch. Stravinsky, *Apollon Musagète* Weill, *Threepenny Opera*	Janáček d. Magritte, 'The False Mirror'	Alexander Fleming discovers penicillin. Hirohito crowned king of Japan.
1929 Bartók, 3rd string quartet Noël Coward, *Bitter Sweet* Prokofiev, *The Gambler*; 3rd symphony Webern, Symphony Weill, *Berlin Requiem*	Robert Graves, *Goodbye to All That* Ernest Hemingway, *A Farewell to Arms* Jean Cocteau, *Les Enfants terribles* First Academy Awards ceremony in Hollywood Diaghilev d. in Venice.	Wall Street Crash; worldwide depression St Valentine's Day mob massacre in Chicago.
1930 Janáček, *From the House of the Dead* Milhaud, *Christophe Colombe* Roussel, 3rd symphony Shostakovich, *The Nose*; 3rd symphony, 'First of May' Sorabji, *Opus Clavicemballisticum* Stravinsky, Symphony of Psalms Weill, *Rise and Fall of the City of Mahagonny*	Marlene Dietrich stars in *The Blue Angel* Joseph Roth, *Job* D. H. Lawrence d.	Stalin forcibly collectivizes Soviet farming.

NEW MUSIC PERFORMED	THE ARTS	WORLD EVENTS
1931 Brant, *Music for a five-and-dime store* Hába, *Matka* (microtonal opera) Ives, *Three places in New England* Ravel, Left-hand piano concerto Stravinsky, violin concerto Walton, *Belshazzar's Feast*	Robert Musil issues the first part of his *fin-de-siècle* social trilogy, *The Man without Qualities* Fritz Lang's film, *M* Nielson *d.*	Japan invades China.
1932 Gershwin, Cuban overture Prokofiev, 5th piano concerto Ravel, G-major piano concerto Ruggles, *Sun-treader* Szymanowski, *Harnasie*; Symphonie concertante	Hermann Broch, *The Sleepwalker*. Aldous Huxley, *Brave New World* Roth, *Radetzky March*	F. D. Roosevelt elected in landslide victory.
1933 Bartók, 2nd piano concerto Shostakovich, 1st piano concerto Strauss, *Arabella* Varèse, *Ionisations* Weill, *Seven Deadly Sins*	Federico Garcia Lorca, *Blood Wedding* Mass cultural emigration from Germany.	Hitler seizes power in Germany; books burned; Jews banned. Polythene invented. Roosevelt announces New Deal.
1934 Gershwin, 'I Got Rhythm' variations Glazunov, saxophone concerto Rachmaninov, Rhapsody on a theme of Paganini Schmidt, 4th symphony Shostakovich, *Lady Macbeth of Mtsensk* Thomson, *Four Saints in Three Acts* Vaughan Williams, Fantasia on 'Greensleeves' Weill, 2nd symphony	Matisse 'Pink Nude' points to new simplicity. Elgar, Delius, Holst *d.*	Nazis assassinate Austrian Chancellor Dolfüss.
1935 Bartók, 5th string quartet Gershwin, *Porgy and Bess* Hindemith, *Der Schwanendreher* Strauss, *Die schweigsame Frau* Walton, 1st symphony Webern, Concerto for 9 instruments	Berg *d.*	Italy invades Abyssinia.
1936 Berg, violin concerto Bridge, *Oration* for cello and orch. Chávez, *Sinfonia India* Enesco, *Oedipe* Gershwin, preludes for solo piano Goldschmidt, 2nd string quartet Prokofiev, *Peter and the Wolf* Rachmaninov, 3rd symphony	Lorca shot	Civil War in Spain. First executions in Stalin's show-trials. Edward VIII abdicates English throne. Nazis stage-manage Olympics in Berlin.
1937 Bartók, Music for percussion, strings and celesta Berg, *Lulu* Britten, *Variations on a theme of Frank Bridge* Copland, *El Salón México* Eisler, Lenin Requiem	Picasso, 'Guernica' 'Degenerate Art' exhibitions toured in Nazi Germany André Malraux, *Days of Hope* John Steinbeck, *Of Mice and Men* Gershwin, Ravel, Roussel *d.*	

NEW MUSIC PERFORMED	THE ARTS	WORLD EVENTS
1937 Messiaen, *Poèmes pour Mi* Orff, *Carmina Burana* Prokofiev, *Lieutenant Kijé* suite Schoenberg, 4th string quartet Shostakovich, 5th symphony Webern, Variations for piano		
1938 Barber, Adagio for Strings Bartók, sonata for 2 pianos and percussion Copland, *Billy the Kid* Diamond, *Elegy for Maurice Ravel* Hanson, 3rd symphony Hindemith, *Mathis der Maler* Honegger, *Joan of Arc at the stake* Martinů, *Julietta* Prokofiev, *Romeo and Juliet; Alexander Nevsky* Schmidt, *Book of Seven Seals* Stravinsky, *Dumbarton Oaks* Wiren, Serenade for Strings	Jean Renoir's film *La bête humaine* Leni Riefenstahl, *Olympia* Jean-Paul Sartre's novel *Nausea*	Germany annexes Austria and part of Czechoslovakia. Freud exiled Nylon invented.
1939 Bartók, (2nd) violin concerto Cage, *Imaginary Landscapes 1* Eisler, *German Symphony* Harris, 3rd symphony Ives, Concord Sonata Martinů, Field Mass Poulenc, organ concerto Shostakovich, 6th symphony Schuman, *American festival Overture* Villa-Lobos, *Bachianas Brasilieras #5* Walton, violin concerto	Freud, *Moses and Monotheism* Mann, *Lotte in Weimar* Steinbeck, *The Grapes of Wrath* Christopher Isherwood, *Goodbye to Berlin*	Germany invades Poland to start Second World War (to 1945). Soviet Union attacks Finland.
1940 Dallapiccola, *Volo di Notte* Hartmann, Concerto funèbre Martinů, 1st cello sonata Rodrigo, Concierto de Aranjuez Schoenberg, violin concerto Stravinsky, Symphony in C	Hemingway, *For Whom the Bell Tolls* Chaplin in *The Great Dictator*	France falls; Luftwaffe wages aerial Battle of Britain. Churchill becomes UK premier. Stalin murders 4,000 Polish officers at Katyn.
1941 Bartók, 6th string quartet Britten *Sinfonia da Requiem* Dallapiccola, *Canti di prigionia* Eisler, Variations on American nursery songs Gerhard, Symphony: homage to Pedrell Lutosławski/Panufnik, Paganini variations Messiaen, *Quatuor pour la fin du temps* Schuman, 3rd symphony	Brecht, *Mother Courage* Orson Welles presents *Citizen Kane*	Germany invades USSR; Leningrad besieged. Japan bombs Pearl Harbour; US enters War.
1942 Irving Berlin, 'White Christmas' Casella, *Paganiniana* Khatchaturian, *Gayaneh* Martin, *Le vin herbé* Shostakovich, 7th symphony 'Leningrad' Strauss, *Capriccio*	Albert Camus in *L'Étranger* invents literature of alienation. Zweig commits suicide in Brazil	Genocide waged against Jews. German advance halted in North Africa

NEW MUSIC PERFORMED	THE ARTS	WORLD EVENTS
1943 Britten, Serenade for tenor, horn and strings Copland, Fanfare for the Common Man Martinů, Memorial to Lidice Orff, *Catulli Carmina* Shostakovich, 8th symphony Vaughan Williams, 5th symphony	Jean Genet publishes *Notre dame des fleurs* Rachmaninov *d.*	Mussolini toppled and reinstated.
1944 Bartók, Concerto for Orchestra Bernstein, 1st symphony 'Jeremiah' *Fancy Free/On the Town* Copland, *Appalachian Spring* Hindemith, Symphonic metamorphoses on themes of Weber Prokofiev, *War and Peace* Schoenberg, piano concerto Stravinsky, Circus Polka Tippett, *A Child of our Time*	Artists Mondrian, Munch *d.* T. S. Eliot, *The Four Quartets* Sartre stages *Huis-clos (No exit)* Jean Genet's play, *Our Lady of the Flowers*	Allies storm France and Italy. V-1 rocket attacks on London. Roosevelt re-elected for 4th term.
1945 Britten, *Peter Grimes*, John Donne songs Martinů, 3rd symphony Prokofiev, 5th symphony Shostakovich, 9th symphony	Broch, *Death of Virgil* George Orwell, *Animal Farm* Webern, Bartók *d.*	Germany defeated; Hitler commits suicide. Roosevelt *d.*; Churchill ousted in Labour election victory. Atom bombs dropped on Hiroshima and Nagasaki. Europe partitioned behind Iron Curtain. Cold War begins.
1946 Bartók, 3rd piano concerto Boulez, 1st piano sonata Britten, *Rape of Lucretia* Carter, piano sonata Copland, 3rd symphony Hindemith, *When Lilacs Last in the Dooryard Bloom'd* Honegger, Symphonie liturgique Ives, 3rd symphony Messiaen, *Harawi* Schoenberg, string trio Strauss, Metamorphosen Stravinsky, Ebony Concerto	Picasso, 'La Joie de vivre'	United Nations formed. Juan Peron becomes Argentine president.
1947 Blacher, Variations on a theme by Paganini von Einem, *Dantons Tod* Martinů, 5th symphony Prokofiev, 6th symphony; 9th piano sonata Weill, *Street Scene*	Jackson Pollock abandons brushes, pouring paint straight on to canvas. Hollywood Ten summoned before Un-american Activities Committee in Washington.	India independent; war and partition with Pakistan. US offers Marshall Aid to Europe.
1948 Henze, 1st symphony; violin concerto Milhaud, 4th symphony '1848' Schoenberg, *A Survivor from Warsaw* Stravinsky, *Mass* Vaughan Williams, 6th symphony Villa-Lobos, *Magdalena* Weill, *Down in the Valley*	Zhdanov hounds composers at Stalin's behest. Brecht stages *The Caucasian Chalk Circle* Norman Mailer, *The Naked and the Dead* Long-playing record introduced.	State of Israel founded; war with 7 Arab states. Communist coup in Czechoslovakia. Allied airlift to blockaded Berlin Transistor invented. Gandhi assassinated. Apartheid enforced in South Africa

NEW MUSIC PERFORMED	THE ARTS	WORLD EVENTS

1949 Barber, piano sonata;
  Knoxville: Summer of 1915
Bernstein, Age of Anxiety
Britten, Spring Symphony
Finzi, clarinet concerto
Messiaen, Turangalîla
  Symphony
Panufnik, Homage to Chopin
Seiber, Ulysses
	Mann, Doctor Faustus
	Orwell, 1984.
	Simone de Beauvoir, The
	  Second Sex
	R. Strauss d.
		Mao leads communist
		  revolution in China.
		US Congress intensifies anti-
		  red hearings.
		NATO formed

1950 Cage, string quartet
Copland, clarinet concerto
Dallapiccola, Il prigioniero
Hartmann, 2nd symphony
Strauss, Four Last Songs
	Graham Greene, The Third
	  Man
	Eugene Ionesco inaugurates
	  theatre of the absurd.
	George Bernard Shaw d.
		North Korea invades South
		  (war to 1954)

1951 Britten, Billy Budd
Feldman, Structures
Irving Fine, Notturno
Menotti, Amahl and the
  Night Visitors
Stravinsky, The Rake's
  Progress
	Schoenberg d.
	South Bank concert hall built
	  for Festival of Britain
		Aging Churchill re-elected.

1952 Cage, 4′33″; Music of
  Changes
Henze, Boulevard Solitude
Martin, harpsichord concerto
		US explodes hydrogen bomb.
		Dwight D. Eisenhower
		  elected US president.

1953 Carter, 1st string quartet
Martinů, rhapsody –
  concerto for viola and
  orch.
Shostakovich, 10th
  symphony
	Francis Bacon, 'Pope
	  Innocent X'
	Samuel Beckett, Waiting for
	  Godot in Paris.
	Ingmar Bergman directs
	  Summer with Monika
	Arthur Miller stages The
	  Crucible
	Prokofiev d.
	Dylan Thomas d.
	Domaine Musical founded in
	  Paris
		Stalin d.
		Elizabeth II crowned Queen
		  of England.
		East German uprising
		  crushed by Soviet tanks.

1954 Arnold, flute concerto
Bernstein, Serenade (after
  Plato's Symposium)
Britten, The Turn of the
  Screw
Lutoslawski, Concerto for
  Orch.
Prokofiev, The Fiery Angel
Schoenberg Moses und Aron
Varèse, Deserts
	Nikos Kazantkzakis, The
	  Greek Passion
	Dylan Thomas, Under Milk
	  Wood
	Akira Kurosawa's film, The
	  Seven Samurai
	Vladimir Nabokov, Lolita
	Tennessee Williams, Cat on a
	  Hot Tin Roof
	Mann d.
		Gamal Abdul Nasser takes
		  power in Egypt.
		France defeated in Indo-
		  China.
		
		Warsaw Pact formed by
		  USSR and its allies.

1955 Boulez, Le marteau sans
  Maître
Shostakovich, 1st violin
  concerto
Xenakis, Metastaseis
Tippett, The Midsummer
  Marriage		

1956 Bernstein, Candide
Henze, König Hirsch
Krenek, Sanctus
Loewe/Lerner, My Fair Lady
Maderna/Berio, Notte in città
Martinů, Frescoes of Piero
  della Francesca
Nono, Il canto sospeso
Stockhausen, Gesang der
  Jünglinge
	Allen Ginsberg defines Beat
	  Generation in Howl
	John Osborne shakes up
	  British theatre with Look
	  Back in Anger
	Brecht d.
		Nikita Khruschev, new
		  Soviet leader, denounces
		  Stalin.
		Hungarian uprising crushed
		  by Soviet forces.
		Nasser claims Suez Canal;
		  Anglo-French and Israeli
		  forces attack Egypt.
		Civil rights campaign begins
		  in southern US states.

NEW MUSIC PERFORMED	THE ARTS	WORLD EVENTS
1957 Bernstein, *West Side Story* Hindemith, *Die Harmonie der Welt* Vaughan Williams, William Blake songs	Boris Pasternak, *Doctor Zhivago* published abroad. Bergman's film masterpiece *Wild Strawberries* Harold Pinter, *The Birthday Party* Sibelius *d.*	Soviet launch space satellite. European Community formed by Treaty of Rome. After Algerian upheavals, General de Gaulle becomes French president (to 1968).
1958 Barber, *Vanessa* Berio, *Omaggio a Joyce* Cage, Concert for Piano and Orch. Ligeti, *Metamorphoses; nocturnes;* 1st string quartet Lutoslawski, *Funeral Music,* in memoriam Bartók Messiaen, *Catalogue d'oiseaux* Stravinsky, *Threni* Varèse, *Poème electronique* Zimmermann, *Canto di speranza*	Beckett, *Krapp's Last Tape* Stereo recordings introduced.	
1959 Blomdahl, *Aniara* (space opera) Hartmann, 7th symphony Martinů, nonet Rodgers/Hammerstein, *The Sound of Music* Stockhausen, *Gruppen* Villa-Lobos, harmonica concerto	Günter Grass, *The Tin Drum* J Guggenheim Museum opens in NY; its architect Frank Lloyd Wright *d.*	Fidel Castro rises to power in Cuba.
1960 Barraqué, . . . *au delà du hazard* Lionel Bart, *Oliver!* Miles Davis, 'Sketches of Spain' Shostakovich, 8th string quartet	D. H. Lawrence, *Lady Chatterley's Lover* acquitted of obscenity in UK trial. Isaac Bashevis Singer, *The Slave*	Laser developed. John F. Kennedy elected US president. Sharpeville massacre in South Africa.
1961 Havergal Brian, *Gothic Symphony* Carter, double concerto Henze, *Elegy for Young Lovers* Lustoslawski, *Venetian Games* Martinů, *The Greek Passion* Penderecki, *Threnody for the victims of Hiroshima* Poulenc, *Gloria*	Marc Chagall paints 12 tribes of Israel in glass windows for Jerusalem hospital. Beckett, *Happy Days*	Berlin Wall erected. Soviets put man into space. Nuclear brinkmanship in Cuba missile crisis.
1962 Arnold, Concerto for 2 violins Boulez, *Pli selon pli* Britten, War Requiem Ligeti, *Aventures; Poème symphonique for 100 metronomes* Shostakovich, Babi Yar Symphony	Jacob Epstein sculpts Archangel Michael for Coventry Cathedral. Beatles shoot to stardom. Andy Warhol, 'Marilyn Diptych'; '100 Soup Cans' Marilyn Monroe *d.*	US launch telecommunications satellite. Nelson Mandela jailed in South Africa.
1963 Bernstein, *Kaddish* symphony (dedicated to JFK) Britten, Cello Symphony Theodorakis, *Zorba the Greek*	Yukio Mishima, *The Sailor Who Fell from Grace with the Sea* Federico Fellini, *8½* Roy Lichtenstein, 'Whaam!'	Kennedy assassinated. British government rocked by Profumo sex scandal.
1964 Jerry Bock, *Fiddler on the Roof* Britten, *Curlew River* Copland, *Music for a Great City* Stravinsky, *Elegy for JFK*	Peter Weiss' play, *Marat . . . Sade*	Khruschev deposed; Leonid Brezhnev is new Soviet strongman. Cassius Clay (Mohammed Ali) is heavyweight boxing champion.

NEW MUSIC PERFORMED	THE ARTS	WORLD EVENTS
1965 Bernstein, *Chichester Psalms* Ginastera, harp concerto Ives, 4th symphony Ligeti, *Requiem* Lutosławski, string quartet B. A. Zimmermann, *The Soldiers*	Le Corbusier *d.*	US marines sent to Vietnam. Indo-Pakistan War.
1966 Barber, *Antony and Cleopatra* Tubin, 8th symphony Xenakis, *Oresteia*	NY Metropolitan Opera moves to Lincoln Center	Indira Gandhi becomes Indian PM. England defeat W. Germany to win soccer World Cup.
1967 Feldman, *In Search of an Orchestration* Françaix, flute concerto Goehr, *Arden must die* Stockhausen, *Hymnen*	Philip Roth, *Portnoy's Complaint* Milan Kundera, *The Joke*	Israel inflicts six-day defeat on Arabs, conquers West Bank, East Jerusalem and other territories. Human heart transplanted in South Africa.
1968 Beatles, *Abbey Road* Berio, *Sinfonia* Birtwistle, *Punch and Judy* Panufnik, *Katyn Epitaph* Pettersson, 7th symphony	Alexander Solzhenitsyn, *Cancer Ward* Mikhail Bulgakov, *The Master and Margarita*	Soviet forces crush Czech liberalization. Richard Nixon elected US President.
1969 Cage, *HPSCHD* Henze, *Essay on Pigs* Ligeti, 2nd string quartet Maxwell Davies, *Eight Songs for a Mad King* Penderecki, *The Devils of Loudun* Sculthorpe, 8th string quartet Shostakovich 14th symphony	Mark Rothko, 'Orange Yellow Orange'	Man steps on the moon. Concorde makes first supersonic passenger flight Troubles resume in Northern Ireland.
1970 Boulez, *cummings ist der dichter* Crumb, *Black Angels* Feldman, *Madame Press Died Last Week at 90* Reich, *Drumming* Sondheim, *Company* Stockhausen, *Mantra* Tippett, *The Knot Garden*	Beatles disband	First jumbo passenger jets enter service.
1971 Argento, *Postcard from Morocco* von Einem, *The Old Lady's Visit* Kagel, *Staatstheater* Lloyd Webber, *Jesus Christ Superstar*	Luchino Visconti films *Death in Venice* David Hockney paints self-portait beside pool. Stravinsky *d.* and buried in Venice. Ingmar Bergman, *Cries and Whispers*	Wave of terrorist skyjackings. Bangladesh independent; Indo-Pakistan war.
1972 Birtwistle, *The Triumph of Time* Cardew, *The Great Learning* Copland, *Night Thoughts* Crumb, *Vox balance* Maderna, *Aura* Maxwell Davies, *Taverner* Nono, *Como una ola del fuerza y luz* Shostakovich, 15th symphony	Louis Buñuel's surreal film, *The Discreet Charm of the Bourgeoisie.*	Nixon visits China; reelected in landslide vote. Palestinians kill Israel sportsmen at Munich Olympics. Britain joins European Community.
1973 Britten, *Death in Venice* Kancheli, 3rd symphony Ligeti, *Clocks and Clouds* Maderna, *Satyricon* Sondheim, *A Little Night Music*	Sydney Opera House opens Picasso *d.* Peter Shaffer, *Equus*	Yom Kippur War between Israel, Egypt and Syria. 3-day working week temporarily enforced in UK.

NEW MUSIC PERFORMED	THE ARTS	WORLD EVENTS
1974 Arnold, 7th symphony Henze, *Tristan* Messiaen, *Des canyons aux étoiles* Shostakovich, 15th string quartet	Alexander Solzhenitsyn expelled from USSR. Duke Ellington *d.*	Nixon forced to abdicate in Watergate scandal. Turkey invades Cyprus.
1975 Boulez, Rituel in memoriam Bruno Maderna Ferneyhough, Sonatas for string quartet Ligeti, *San Francisco Polyphony* McCabe, *Chagall Windows*	Shostakovich, Dallapiccola, Blacher *d.* Primo Levi, *The Periodic Table*	Lebanon civil war, followed by Israel invasion. South Vietnam falls to northern forces. On Franco's death, Spain becomes democratic monarchy.
1976 Andriessen, *De Staat* Britten, 3rd string quartet Dutilleux, *Ainsi la nuit*, string quartet Glass, *Einstein on the Beach* Gorecki, 3rd symphony Sondheim, *Pacific Overtures*	Britten *d.*	Mao *d.*
1977 Carter, Symphony of 3 Orchestras Corigliano, clarinet concerto	Chagall stained glass window in Chichester Cathedral. Elvis Presley *d.*	Egyptian president Sadat flies for talks in Israel.
1978 Ligeti, *Le grand macabre* Penderecki, violin concerto Reimann, *Lear* Pärt, Cantus in memoriam Benjamin Britten		Polish cardinal becomes Pope John Paul II.
1979 Birtwistle, . . . *agm* . . . Knussen, 3rd symphony Kubelik, Mass Rochberg, string quartets 4–6	Peter Shaffer, *Amadeus*	Shah of Iran toppled in Islamic revolution. Margaret Thatcher elected UK premier. USSR invades Afghanistan.
1980 George Benjamin, *Ringed by the Flat Horizon* von Einem, *Jesus' Wedding* Glass, *Satyagraha* Lutoslawski, harp and oboe concerto Tippett, triple concerto	John Lennon shot on his NY doorstep. Umberto Eco, *The Name of the Rose*	Solidarity union formed in Poland during shipyard strikes. Ronald Reagan elected US President.
1981 Boulez, Répons Cerha, *Baal* Gubaidulina, *Offertorium* for violin and orch. Kancheli, 6th symphony Knussen, *Where the Wild Things are* Lloyd Webber, *Cats* Reich, Tehillim Rihm, 3rd string quartet Stockhausen, *Donnerstag* – start of Licht cycle		Martial law in Poland. Assassination attempt on Pope. François Mitterrand elected president of France. First reports of AIDS
1982 Denisov, *Death is a Long Sleep*, for cello/orch. Panufnik, Sinfonia Votiva Pärt, St John Passion Tishchenko, 2nd violin concerto	Orff *d.*	Falklands War between England and Argentina. Israel invades Lebanon. Iraq attacks Iran. Brezhnev *d.* Reagan announces Star Wars programme.
1983 Lutoslawski, 3rd symphony Messiaen, *St François d'Assise* Reich, *Desert Music* Schnittke, 3rd string quartet	First recordings issued on compact disc. Jean Miró *d.*	US invades Grenada. Argentina returns to democracy. Indira Gandhi murdered.
1984 Berio, *Un re in ascolto*; *Voci*; *Requies*	Kundera, *The Unbearable Lightness of Being*	UK miners' strike.

NEW MUSIC PERFORMED	THE ARTS	WORLD EVENTS
1984 Glass, *Akhnaten*; string quartet 'Company' Henze, 7th symphony Penderecki, *Polish Requiem* Reimann, *Ghost Sonata* Sondheim, *Sunday in the Park with George*		
1985 Albert, *Riverrun* Del Tredici, *March to Tonality* Dutilleux, *L'Arbre des songes*, violin concerto Scelsi, *Avion* Schnittke, *(K)ein Sommernachtstraum*	Live Aid rock concert raises £40m ($70m) for famine relief.	Mikhail Gorbachev becomes Soviet communist leader, starting process of reform and détente.
1986 Birtwistle, *Mask of Orpheus* Anthony Davis, *X* Kagel, *Opus posthumum* Lutoslawski, *Chaine 2* Panufnik, bassoon concerto Penderecki, *The Black Mask* Udo Zimmermann, *Die Weisse Rose*		Nuclear disaster at Chernobyl. Swedish PM Olof Palme shot as he leaves cinema.
1987 Adams, *Nixon in China* Birtwistle, *Endless Parade* Cage, *Europera Nos 1 and 2* Feldman, *For Samuel Beckett* Firsova, *Earthly Life*	Tom Wolfe, *Bonfire of the Vanities* Andy Warhol *d.*	Margaret Thatcher re-elected for 3rd term. Stock market crash on Black Monday.
1988 Aho, 7th symphony Carter, oboe concerto Goldschmidt, 3rd string quartet Gorecki, 1st string quartet Reich, *Different Trains*	Gabriel Garcia Marquez, *Love in the Time of Cholera*	
1989 Höller, *Der Meister und Margarita* Lindberg, *Kinetics* Maw, *Odyssey* Meredith Monk, *Book of Days*	Iran orders death of author Salman Rushdie over his novel, *Satanic Verses*. John Updike, *Rabbit at Rest* describes decrepitude of US economy and family values. Bastille Opera opens in Paris. Bernstein, Copland *d.*	Collapse of communism in eastern Europe Berlin Wall opened Havel enters Prague Castle Ceaucescu overthrown and killed in Romania.
1990 Bernstein, Arias and Barcarolles Corigliano, 1st symphony Ferneyhough, 4th string quartet Henze, *Das verratene Meer* Weir, *The Vanishing Bridegroom*		Iraq invades neighbouring Kuwait. Start of world economic recession. Germany reunited. Thatcher deposed.
1991 Adams, *Death of Klinghoffer* Birtwistle, *Gawain* Corigliano, *Ghosts of Versailles*	Deaths of authors Graham Greene and Isaac Bashevis Singer. Panufnik, Miles Davis *d.* Composers emigrate as USSR collapses.	Iraqis evicted in Gulf War. Failed coup in Moscow Soviet Union dissolves, replaced by Russian-led commonwealth Boris Yeltsin succeeds Gorbachev. Rajiv Gandhi assassinated.
1992 Gerhard, *The Duenna* (stage fp) Panufnik, cello concerto	Messiaen, Cage *d.* Painter Francis Bacon *d.*	Civil war in Yugoslavia. Czech and Slovaks vote to split up.

DISCOGRAPHY

The following recordings are seminal documents of the 20th century, the kind of discs that can be put into a time capsule to reveal to a future generation, from an authoritative source, what the epoch was all about.

Béla Bartók plays *Contrasts*, with Benny Goodman and Joseph Szigeti, (Sony)

Cathy Berberian, *MagnifiCathy* (Wergo)

Leonard Bernstein conducts *West Side Story* and *Candide* (DG)

Pierre Boulez conducts *Rituel in memoriam Bruno Maderna* (Sony)

Adrian Boult conducts Holst's *Planets* (EMI)

Benjamin Britten conducts *Peter Grimes* (Decca)

John Cage, Works for piano and prepared piano (Wergo)

Aaron Copland conducts *Appalachian Spring* (Sony)

Dietrich Fisher-Dieskau in Pfitzner's *Palestrina* (DG)

George Gershwin plays *Rhapsody in Blue*

Jascha Heifetz plays Sibelius and Walton concertos (EMI)

Paul Hindemith conducts the *Mathis* symphony (DG)

Jascha Horenstein conducts Mahler's 9th symphony (Music & Arts)

Vladimir Horowitz plays Barber Sonata (RCA), Bach-Busoni transcriptions (DG)

Erich Kleiber conducts *Der Rosenkavalier* (Decca)

Otto Klemperer conducts *Das Lied von der Erde* (EMI)

Kronos Quartet play Reich's *Different Trains* and Crumb's *Black Angels* (Nonesuch)

Lotte Lenya sings Kurt Weill (Sony)

Yehudi Menuhin plays Elgar's violin concerto with the composer conducting (EMI).

Olivier Messiaen plays his organ music (EMI)

David Oistrakh plays the Shostakovich violin concertos (EMI)

Sergei Rachmaninov plays his piano music and transcriptions (BMG)

Ravel conducts *Boléro* (Philips)

Fritz Reiner conducts Bartók Concerto for Orch. (BMG)

Sviatoslav Richter plays Prokofiev and Skryabin sonatas (DG)

Gennady Rozhdestvensky conducts Shostakovich and Schnittke (Melodiya)

Arthur Rubinstein plays Ravel, Szymanowski, Stravinsky (BMG)

Arnold Schoenberg directs *Pierrot Lunaire* (Sony)

Karlheinz Stockhausen performs *Gesang der Jünglinge* (Chrysalis)

Richard Strauss conducts tone poems (DG)

Igor Stravinsky conducts *The Rite*

of Spring (Sony)

Václav Talich conducts Janáček and Suk (Supraphon)

Arturo Toscanini conducts Barber's *Adagio* (BMG) and Debussy's *La Mer* (EMI)

Anton Webern conducts the Berg violin concerto (Continuum)

Eugene Ysaÿe plays Debussy and Fauré.

BIBLIOGRAPHY

Since 20th century music is a living art, much of its information is contained in periodicals rather than books. I have found *Tempo* (London), *Le Monde de la Musique* (Paris), *Neue Zeitschrift für Musik* (Mainz), *Österreichische Musikzeitschrift* (Vienna), *Perspectives of New Music* (Seattle), *Hungarian Music News* (Budapest) and the Darmstadt annual reports particularly helpful, as well as defunct magazines like *Die Musik* (Berlin) and *Music Survey* (London). Record sleeve notes and concert programmes are invaluable sources, as are publishers' leaflets. In addition, the following books were useful in many ways:

Alfred Baumgartner, *Musik des 20. Jahrhunderts*, (Kiesel Verlag), 1985.

Reginald Smith Brindle, *The New Music*, Oxford (OUP), 1987.

Donald Clark (ed.), *The Penguin Encyclopedia of Popular Music*, London, 1989.

Hermann Danuser, *Die Musik des 20. Jahrhunderts*, (Laaber), 1984.

Ulrich Dibelius, *Moderne Musik 1 & 2*, Munich (Piper), 1968, 1988.

Richard Dufallo, *Trackings: Composers speak with RD*, Oxford (OUP), 1989.

Robert Fink and Robert Ricci, *The Language of 20th-Century Music*, NY (Macmillan), 1975.

Frederick Goldbeck, *20th-Century Composers: France, Italy and Spain*, London (Weidenfeld), 1974.

Paul Griffiths, *Electronic Music*, London (Thames and Hudson), 1979.

Howard Hartog, *European Music in the 20th century*, London (Routledge), 1957.

Wim Mertens, *American Minimal Music*, London (Kahn and Averill), 1983.

Donald Mitchell, *The Language of Modern Music*, London (Faber), 1963.

John Newline Rockwell, *All-American Music*, London (Kahr and Averill), 1985.

Fred K. Prieberg, *Musik im dritten Reich*, Frankfurt (Fischer), 1982.

John Schaeffer, *New Sounds*, NY (Harper & Row), 1987.

Boris Schwartz, *Musical Life in Soviet Russia*, London (Barrie & Jenkins), 1972.

Nicolas Slonimsky, *Music since 1900*, NY (Scribner), 1973 et. seq.

H. H. Stuckenschmidt, *20th-Century Music*, London (Weidenfeld), 1970.

Swedish Institute, *Musical Life in Sweden*, Stockholm, 1987.

John Vinton, *Dictionary of 20th Century Music*, London (Thames and Hudson), 1974.

John Vinton, *Essays after a Dictionary*, Lewisburg (Bucknell UP), 1977.

Kevin Volans, *Summer Gardeners: Conversations with Composers*, Durban, 1984.

Arnold Whittall, *Music since the First World War*, London (Dent), 1988.

Justin Wintle, *Makers of Modern Culture*, London (Routledge), 1981.

ACKNOWLEDGEMENTS

I have been particularly influenced in sampling and critical techniques by Martin Seymour-Smith's incomparable *Guide to Modern World Literature* (Macmillan Press, 1985) and wish to record my admiration and gratitude for his world-embracing efforts. No researcher of 20th-century music would know where to begin without Nicolas Slonimsky's *Music Since 1900* (Scribner's, 1973, 1986), a primary source of dates and wisdom.

A great many musicians in various countries have helped me with materials, advice and hospitality. To list them all would steal space from the *Companion* but a number of individuals at record companies and music publishers have been especially kind. My thanks to Isabella de Sabata at DG, Christopher Raeburn at Decca, Marius Carboni at EMI, Peter Andry at Warner, Katharine Howard at Sony, Bernard Coutaz at Harmonia Mundi, David Drew and Janice Susskind at Boosey and Hawkes, Robin Anderson formerly at UE, Jane Williams at Chester Music, Dr Donald Mitchell and Sally Cavender at Faber Music, Dr Pekka Hako at the Finnish Music Information Centre, Dr Jitka Slavíková of Hudebni Rozhledy, Dr Viera Polavicova at the Slovak Music Fund, Jim Potts at the British Council.

In the course of my researches I have enjoyed convivial, at times heated, discussions with composers whom I need to thank for their time. They include: Luciano Berio, the late Leonard Bernstein, Harrison Birtwistle, Pierre Boulez, Elena Firsova, Berthold Goldschmidt, Hans Werner Henze, the late Andrzej Panufnik, Krzysztof Penderecki, Steve Reich, Robert Saxton, Dmitri Smirnov, Michael Tippett, Udo Zimmermann.

My valiant editors at Simon & Schuster were Richard Wigmore and Bob Bender. David Cummings has been through the manuscript with a fine toothcomb to eliminate errors of date and fact. The remaining mistakes, and the opinions within, are entirely my own.

NOTE ON ILLUSTRATIONS